THE ORGANIZATIONAL FRONTIERS SERIES

The Organizational Frontiers Series is sponsored by the Society for Industrial and Organizational Psychology (SIOP). Launched in 1983 to make scientific contributions to the field, the series has attempted to publish books that are on the cutting edge of theory, research, and theory-driven practice in industrial/organizational psychology and related organizational science disciplines.

Our overall objective is to inform and to stimulate research for SIOP members (students, practitioners, and researchers) and people in related disciplines, including the other subdisciplines of psychology, organizational behavior, human resource management, and labor and industrial relations. The volumes in the Organizational Frontiers Series have the following goals:

1. Focus on research and theory in organizational science, and the implications for practice
2. Inform readers of significant advances in theory and research in psychology and related disciplines that are relevant to our research and practice
3. Challenge the research and practice community to develop and adapt new ideas and to conduct research on these developments
4. Promote the use of scientific knowledge in the solution of public policy issues and increased organizational effectiveness

The volumes originated in the hope that they would facilitate continuous learning and a continuing research curiosity about organizational phenomena on the part of both scientists and practitioners.

Measuring and Analyzing Behavior in Organizations

Measuring and Analyzing Behavior in Organizations

Advances in Measurement and Data Analysis

Fritz Drasgow

Neal Schmitt

Editors

Foreword by Neal Schmitt

JOSSEY-BASS
A Wiley Company
www.josseybass.com

Published by

JOSSEY-BASS
A Wiley Company
989 Market Street
San Francisco, CA 94103-1741

www.josseybass.com

Jossey-Bass books and products are available through most bookstores. To contact Jossey-Bass directly, call (888) 378-2537, fax to (800) 605-2665, or visit our website at www.josseybass.com.

Substantial discounts on bulk quantities of Jossey-Bass books are available to corporations, professional associations, and other organizations. For details and discount information, contact the special sales department at Jossey-Bass.

We at Jossey-Bass strive to use the most environmentally sensitive paper stocks available to us. Our publications are printed on acid-free recycled stock whenever possible, and our paper always meets or exceeds minimum GPO and EPA requirements.

Library of Congress Cataloging-in-Publication Data

Measuring and analyzing behavior in organizations : advances in measurement and data analysis / Fritz Drasgow, Neal Schmitt,
editors ; foreword by Neal Schmitt.
     p. cm.—(The Jossey-Bass business & management series)
    Includes bibliographical references and index.
    ISBN 0-7879-5301-6 (alk. paper)
    1. Organizational behavior—Evaluation. 2. Organizational
change—Evaluation. I. Drasgow, Fritz. II. Schmitt, Neal. III.
Series.
HD58.8 .M43 2002
158.7—dc21

2001001763

FIRST EDITION
HB Printing 10 9 8 7 6 5 4 3 2 1

The Jossey-Bass
Business & Management Series

The Organizational Frontiers Series

Contents

Part Three: Examining the Interrelationships Among Variables and Testing Substantive Hypotheses

Foreword

This is the fifteenth book in a series of books published by Jossey-Bass and initiated by the Society for Industrial and Organizational Psychology (SIOP) in 1983. Originally published as the Frontiers Series, the SIOP Executive Committee voted in 2000 to change the name of the series to Organizational Frontiers Series to enhance the identity and heighten the visibility of the series. The purpose of the series in a general sense is to promote the scientific status of the field.

Ray Katzell first edited the series. He was followed by Irwin Goldstein and Sheldon Zedeck. This volume is the first proposed and developed under my editorship. As usual, topics and the volume editors are chosen by the editorial board. The series editor and the editorial board then work with the volume editor in planning the volume and, occasionally, in suggesting and selecting chapter authors and content. During the writing of the volume, the series editor works with the editor and the publisher to bring the manuscript to completion.

The success of the series is evident in the high number of sales (now over forty thousand). Volumes have received excellent reviews, and individual chapters as well as volumes have been cited frequently. A recent symposium at the SIOP annual meeting examined the impact of the series on research and theory in industrial/organizational (I/O) psychology. Although such influence is difficult to track and volumes have varied in intent and perceived centrality to the discipline, the conclusion of most participants was that the volumes have exerted a significant impact on research and theory in the field and are regarded as being representative of the best the field has to offer.

This volume, edited by Fritz Drasgow and myself, considers the manner in which I/O psychologists collect and analyze data and use these data to develop and evaluate theories of work behavior. Most doctoral programs in I/O psychology, organizational behavior, and human resources provide a good foundation in statistics, measurement, and research methods. However, as in many other disciplines, the innovations of statisticians, psychometricians, and methodologists and advances in the technology required to use these innovations cause these fields to be highly dynamic. Most of the topics addressed in this volume would not have been part of a doctoral-level sequence in methods and data analyses twenty years ago.

The purpose of this volume is to provide up-to-date discussions of many of the most important areas of measurement, applied statistics, research methods, and data analysis. Each chapter author was asked to develop a chapter with five major parts. The chapters all include a description of the method and assumptions about data that must be satisfied to use the analysis appropriately. Second, authors were asked to describe the types of problems researchers should or could address with the approach being discussed and what advantages this approach provides in terms of better understanding data. Third, authors were asked to describe the limitations of the method and discuss the extent to which the method is robust to violations of its assumptions. Each author was also asked to present an example that highlights the manner in which the method should be used. Finally, chapter authors provided information on computer software and instructional materials. To the degree appropriate, we believe that the chapter authors have met these specifications.

Our target audiences are graduate students in I/O psychology and organizational behavior, as well as doctoral-level researchers and practitioners who want to update themselves on analyses and measurement methods about which they have scant information. We believe that this book will make recent developments in psychometrics and statistics accessible to professionals who do not necessarily read or understand the basic literature in these areas. To the degree it does so, this volume will meet the primary goal of the Organizational Frontiers series.

The chapters address two major issues (see Chapter One), though there is certainly overlap in several instances. In seven of the chapters, the authors primarily address issues concerning the way in which researchers collect data and evaluate the quality of those data. In the other seven chapters, the authors' primary interests are in the assessment of the interrelationships among different types of variables and the degree to which the data provide support for the substantive hypotheses and questions that motivated the research. We believe that this book will stimulate and promote more intelligent reading of the basic research literature in our field and will advance and improve the investigation of various questions in the organizational sciences. The chapter authors deserve our gratitude for pursuing the goal of clearly communicating the nature, use, and advantages and limitations of the methods addressed in this volume.

Publication of a volume such as this involves the hard work and cooperative effort of many individuals. The chapter authors and the editorial board played important roles in this endeavor. Because all royalties from the series volumes are used to help support SIOP financially, none of them received any remuneration. They deserve our appreciation for engaging a difficult task for the sole purpose of furthering our understanding of organizational science.

We also express our sincere gratitude to Cedric Crocker, Julianna Gustafson, and the entire staff at Jossey-Bass. Over many years and several volumes, they have provided support during the planning, development, and production of the series.

September 2001   NEAL SCHMITT
                                                        Michigan State University
                                                        Series Editor, 1998–2003

Preface

Our motivation for developing this volume lies in the rapid advances in measurement theory and methods for data analysis. These innovations have occurred over such a broad front that it is virtually impossible to keep up by reading original journal articles. Imagine trying to track important developments published in *Psychometrika, Applied Psychological Measurement, Journal of Educational Measurement, Psychological Methods, Multivariate Behavioral Research, Educational and Psychological Measurement,* and *Journal of Behavioral Statistics,* methodological papers in *Journal of Applied Psychology* and *Personnel Psychology,* and the many books describing advances in measurement and data analysis.

The purpose of this Organizational Frontiers volume is to provide readable, up-to-date discussions of many of the most important areas of measurement, applied statistics, research methods, and data analysis. The authors of the chapters have invested many hours in keeping up with the voluminous technical research in their area, and their chapters provide clear, carefully written summaries of each topic. Thus, this book allows substantive researchers to learn about recent developments without having to spend countless hours reading highly technical articles and books.

We appreciate the efforts of the authors of the chapters of this book. As the book progressed, we made numerous requests to add explanations and clarifications, explain difficult concepts in ways more easily understood, and provide examples to illustrate methods of analysis. The authors were invariably responsive; throughout, they have been highly committed to crafting a book that readers will find useful.

Despite these efforts, this book is not light reading. The methods described in the chapters address important questions with sophisticated analyses that can extract more information from the data than simpler methods do. Of course, when simple methods suffice, they should be used. But we often ask questions that require measuring change, studying person-environment fit, understanding the effects of error, and so forth; simple methods are unable to provide satisfactory means of analysis to answer such questions. The methods described in this book provide elegant solutions to many heretofore intractable problems.

We believe that individuals who have a good foundation in statistics, measurement, and research methods from a doctoral program in industrial/organizational psychology, human resources, organizational behavior, or related fields will find value in this book. Despite good training, the innovations of statisticians, psychometricians, and methodologists cause methods for measurement and data analysis to be dynamic and constantly changing; the material we learned in graduate school quickly becomes dated. The wide variety of topics described here alerts readers to new developments and provides illustrations of their use.

September 2001

FRITZ DRASGOW
Champaign, Illinois

NEAL SCHMITT
East Lansing, Michigan

The Contributors

Fritz Drasgow is director of the University of Illinois Center for Human Resources Management. His research focuses on psychological measurement and the application of quantitative methods to important practical problems. He has also used multimedia computer technology to assess social and interpersonal skills not easily measured by paper-and-pencil tests. Drasgow is a former chairperson of the American Psychological Association's Committee on Psychological Tests and Assessments, the U.S. Department of Defense's Advisory Committee on Military Personnel Testing, and the Department of Defense and Department of Labor's Armed Services Vocational Aptitude Battery Norming Advisory Group. Drasgow is a member of the editorial review board of nine journals, including *Applied Psychological Measurement, Journal of Applied Psychology, Multivariate Behavioral Research,* and *Personnel Psychology.* He received his Ph.D. in quantitative psychology from the University of Illinois at Urbana-Champaign in 1978.

Neal Schmitt is University Distinguished Professor of Psychology and Management at Michigan State University. He has also been a Fulbright Scholar at the University of Manchester Institute of Science and Technology and received the Society for Industrial/Organizational Psychology's Distinguished Scientific Contributions Award (1999) and Distinguished Service Contributions Award (1998). He served as the society's president in 1989–1990. He was editor of *Journal of Applied Psychology* from 1988 to 1994, has served on ten editorial boards, and has coauthored three textbooks (*Staffing Organizations* with Ben Schneider, *Research Methods in Human Resource Management* with Richard Klimoski, and *Personnel Selection* with David Chan), coedited *Personnel Selection in Organizations* with Walter Borman, and published approximately 130 articles. His current research centers on the effectiveness of organizations' selection procedures and the outcomes of these procedures, particularly as they relate to subgroup employment and applicant reactions and behavior. He obtained his Ph.D. from Purdue University in 1972 in industrial/organizational psychology.

Paul D. Bliese is chief of the Department of Operational Stress Research at Walter Reed Army Institute of Research (WRAIR), an affiliate of the Industrial/Organizational Department at the University of Maryland. His research interests center on theoretical and statistical issues associated with modeling multilevel data. He has published articles in *Journal of Applied Psychology, Journal of Management, Journal of Organizational Behavior,* and *Organizational Research Methods.* In addition, he is the author of the multilevel package for the open-source language R. He received his Ph.D. in organizational psychology from Texas Tech University in 1991.

Michael Borenstein is director of biostatistics at Hillside Hospital/Long Island Jewish Medical Center, associate professor at Albert Einstein College of Medicine, and director of Biostatistical Programming Associates, which develops software for power analysis and meta-analysis. Borenstein has lectured and published widely on issues related to significance testing, power analysis, effect size estimation, and meta-analysis. He is a member of the statistical methods group of the Cochrane Collaboration and of the Campbell Collaboration. He received his Ph.D. from New York University in 1982.

David Chan is associate professor in the Department of Social Work and Psychology, National University of Singapore. His research includes areas in personnel selection, longitudinal modeling, and adaptation to changes at work. He has published over thirty articles, authored several chapters in the fields of measurement, data analysis, and organizational psychology, and coauthored a textbook in personnel selection. He has received several awards, including the Williams Owens Scholarly Achievement Award and the Edwin Ghiselli Award for Innovative Research Design presented by the Society for Industrial and Organizational Psychology. He is on the editorial boards of *Human Performance, Journal of Organizational Behavior, International Journal of Selection and Assessment,* and *Asia Pacific*

Journal of Management. Chan is currently consultant to the Public Service Division of the Prime Minister's Office in Singapore and scientific adviser to the Centre for Testing and Assessment, also in Singapore. He received his Ph.D. in industrial/organizational psychology from Michigan State University.

Richard P. DeShon is an associate professor in the industrial/ organizational psychology program at Michigan State University. His substantive research interests address the assessment of individual differences responsible for workplace performance. His methodological research interests focus on the use of statistical models to represent data structures and the theory of measurement error. His research has been published in the *Journal of Applied Psychology, Organizational Behavior and Human Decision Processes, Personnel Psychology, Psychological Bulletin,* and *Psychological Methods.* He currently serves on the editorial board of *Psychological Methods* and *Organizational Behavior and Human Decision Processes.* He won the 1999 McCormick Early Career Award (APA, Division 14) for the scholar who has had the greatest impact in industrial/organizational psychology within seven years of earning a Ph.D. He received his Ph.D. in industrial/organizational psychology from the University of Akron in 1993.

Jeffrey R. Edwards is the Belk Distinguished Professor of Management at the Kenan-Flagler Business School, University of North Carolina. His research examines person-environment fit, stress and coping, and research methods. His methodological work has examined difference scores, polynomial regression, and issues regarding measurement and construct validation using structural equation modeling. He is editor of *Organizational Behavior and Human Decision Processes* and associate editor of *Organizational Research Methods,* and serves on the editorial boards of the *Journal of Applied Psychology* and *Personnel Psychology.* He has been elected to the Society of Organizational Behavior, is past chair of the Research Methods Division of the Academy of Management, and is founder and coordinator of RMNET, the electronic question-and-answer network of the Research Methods Division. He received his Ph.D. from Carnegie Mellon University.

Barbara B. Ellis is associate professor in the Department of Psychology at the University of Houston. Her primary research interests are in psychometrics and test development, including the application of item response theory in developing translations and adaptations of tests that are administered cross-culturally. She received her Ph.D. in industrial/organizational psychology from the University of South Florida.

David A. Harrison is a professor of management at Penn State University. His research on work role adjustment (especially absenteeism and turnover), time, executive decision making, and organizational methodology has appeared in *Academy of Management Journal, Information Systems Research, Journal of Applied Psychology, Personnel Psychology,* and elsewhere. He is associate editor at *Organizational Behavior & Human Decision Processes,* serves on the editorial boards of several other journals, and has been chair of the Research Methods Division of the Academy of Management. He received his Ph.D. in industrial/organizational psychology from the University of Illinois at Urbana-Champaign.

Charles Hulin is professor emeritus at the University of Illinois. The coauthor of five books, he has published in the areas of job attitudes and job behaviors, organizational withdrawal, evaluations of translations of scales into foreign languages, sexual harassment in work organizations, temporary workers, and computational modeling. He is a codeveloper of a software package designed to simulate organizational withdrawal behaviors that employees enact in response to job attitudes and environmental constraints and characteristics. He received the Ghiselli Award for Excellence in Research Design in 1989 and 1997 and the Career Scientific Contributions Award from the Society for Industrial and Organizational Psychology in 1997. He received his Ph.D. in industrial/organizational psychology from Cornell University in 1963.

Charles E. Lance is professor and chair of the applied psychology program at the University of Georgia. He is the former president of the Atlanta Society of Applied Psychology and a fellow of the Society for Industrial and Organizational Psychology and the American Psychological Association. He serves on the editorial boards of *Organizational Research Methods, Personnel Psychology, Group and Organization Management,* and *Human Resource Management Review.* His research interests include research methods and statistics, structural equation modeling, performance measurement, and personnel psychology. He received his Ph.D. in industrial/organizational psychology from the Georgia Institute of Technology in 1985.

Karen Locke is associate professor of business administration at the College of William and Mary's School of Business. She joined the faculty there in 1989 after earning her Ph.D. in organizational behavior from Case Western Reserve University. Locke's work focuses on developing a sociology of knowledge in organizational studies and on the use of qualitative research for the investigation of organizational phenomena. Her work appears in journals such as *Academy of Management Journal, Organization Science, Journal of Management Inquiry,* and *Studies in Organization, Culture and Society.* She is the author of *Grounded Theory in Management Research* and coauthor of *Composing Qualitative Research.*

Michael A. McDaniel is a faculty member at Virginia Commonwealth University in the School of Business and president of Work Skills First, a human resources consulting firm. McDaniel is nationally recognized for his research and practice in personnel selection system development and validation. In 1996, he received the Academy of Management Best Paper Award in human resources and in 2000 was made a fellow of the Society for Industrial and Organizational Psychology, the American Psychological Society, and the American Psychological Association. McDaniel has published in several major journals, including *the Academy of Management Journal,* the *Journal of Applied Psychology,* and *Personnel Psychology.* He received his Ph.D. in industrial/organizational psychology from George Washington University in 1986.

Roger E. Millsap is a professor of psychology in the Department of Psychology at Arizona State University. Millsap's research interests include multivariate statistics and psychometric theory, especially methods for the detection of measurement bias in multiple populations and the relationship between bias in measurement and predictive bias. He is the editor of *Multivariate Behavioral Research,* the journal of the Society of Multivariate Experimental Psychology. He is the president-elect of that society and is also on the board of trustees of the Psychometric Society. He earned his Ph.D. in quantitative psychology at the University of California-Berkeley in 1983.

Andrew G. Miner is an assistant professor in the Department of Human Resources and Industrial Relations at the University of Minnesota. His interests lie in the use of alternative methods to address theoretical issues not fully accessible with traditional designs. He has applied this focus to the study of job attitudes, job affect, and individual differences in work organizations. Specifically, he has used experience sampling and computational modeling techniques to investigate theoretical propositions that require multilevel and time-series data to be tested. He received his Ph.D. in industrial/ organizational psychology from the University of Illinois.

Julie B. Olson-Buchanan is a professor of human resource management at the Craig School of Business, California State University, Fresno. Her research interests focus on the development of nontraditional assessments (particularly technology based), the antecedents and consequences of voicing discontent in the workplace, and work stress. Her work has been published in such journals as the *Journal of Applied Psychology, Personnel Psychology, Journal of Vocational Behavior,* and *International Journal of Conflict Management.* She has published several chapters relating to computerized assessment and recently coedited *Innovations in Computerized Assessment.* She is a recipient of the Edwin E. Ghiselli Award for Research Design. She received her Ph.D. in industrial/organizational psychology from the University of Illinois, Urbana-Champaign, in 1992.

Nambury S. Raju is Distinguished Professor in the Institute of Psychology at the Illinois Institute of Technology. His research interests include psychometric theory and industrial/organizational psychology, especially in the areas of reliability, personnel selection, and differential item functioning or item bias. He also has research interests in validity generalization and meta-analysis and the utility of organizational interventions. He serves on seven editorial boards and is a fellow of the American Psychological Association (APA) and the Society for Industrial and Organizational Psychology (SIOP).

He received his Ph.D. in mathematics in 1974 from the Illinois Institute of Technology.

Steven Paul Reise is an associate professor and chair in measurement at the University of California in Los Angeles. His primary specialty areas are in measurement and data modeling, with particular specializations in item response theory and multilevel models. Reise's research has mostly focused on the application of item response theory measurement models to typical performance assessment data. He received his Ph.D. in psychometrics from the University of Minnesota in 1990.

Hannah R. Rothstein is professor of management at Baruch College of the City University of New York. Rothstein has published numerous articles concerning methodological issues in meta-analysis, and, with Michael Borenstein and others, she has developed computer software for meta-analysis and for power and confidence interval analysis. Rothstein is a member of the methods group of the Campbell Collaboration. She received her Ph.D. in industrial/ organizational psychology from the University of Maryland in 1980.

Steven T. Seitz is an associate professor at the University of Illinois. His current work focuses on the logic of computational modeling in social research and its application to policy analysis. He is the developer or codeveloper of several software simulation packages. His recent computational modeling publications have been in the areas of HIV/AIDS and worker withdrawal behaviors. He served as book review editor for the *American Political Science Review* from 1981 to 1985 and has been director of the Computational Modeling Laboratory since 1994. He received his Ph.D. from the University of Minnesota in 1972.

Robert J. Vandenberg is professor and coordinator of the organizational behavior program for the Department of Management, Terry College of Business at the University of Georgia. A member of the Academy of Management and the American Psychological Association, he serves on the editorial boards of *Organizational Research Methods, Journal of Applied Psychology,* and *Organizational Behavior and Human Decision Processes.* His research interests include research methods and statistics, structural equation modeling, and high-performance work systems. He received his Ph.D. in social psychology from the University of Georgia in 1982.

Niels G. Waller is a professor of psychology in the Department of Psychology and Human Development at Vanderbilt University. Among the numerous awards he has won for his work in individual differences and psychometrics are the 1998/1999 American Psychological Association Distinguished Scientific Award for Early Career Contribution to Psychology in the area of Individual Differences, the 1997 Raymond B. Cattell Award for Multivariate Experimental Research from the Society for Multivariate Experimental Psychology, the 1997 Morton Prince Award from the International Society for the Study of Dissociation, and the 1989 Thomas Small Prize from Harvard University. He received his Ph.D. in clinical and quantitative psychology from the University of Minnesota in 1990.

Michael J. Zickar is an assistant professor of psychology at Bowling Green State University. His research interests center on applying item response theory to solve theoretical and practical problems. Much of his current research has focused on the issue of measurement distortion on personality tests. His research has been published in various journals, including *Journal of Applied Psychology, Personnel Psychology,* and *Organizational Behavior and Human Decision Processes.* He received his Ph.D. in industrial/organizational psychology from the University of Illinois at Urbana-Champaign in 1997.

Measuring and Analyzing Behavior in Organizations

PART 1

Introduction

CHAPTER 1

Applied Problems and Methods of Analysis
A Road Map
Neal Schmitt
Fritz Drasgow

Researchers in the organizational sciences and in the social and be-havioral sciences in general encounter a host of problems as they seek to describe, predict, and understand behavior. The procedures we use to measure and analyze behavior are constantly improving as a result of the efforts of psychometricians and applied statisti-cians, among others. Many of the techniques discussed in this book were not available to researchers even a decade or two ago. More-over, the sheer number of methods has grown tremendously in the past few decades. Maintaining currency in these areas is a constant challenge for substantive researchers in all areas.

Our goal in assembling the chapters in this book was to provide readable and up-to-date discussions of some of the most important advances in measurement, applied statistics, research methods, and data analysis. Each chapter describes a particular research method or data analysis technique, sets out an illustration of its use, and summarizes the advantages and disadvantages of the method. Many of the methods are quite complex, and the authors have made con-certed efforts to present key ideas in ways that are as accessible as possible.

In this chapter, we discuss the various types of problems ap-plied researchers face in describing and understanding the data they collect and what specific chapters and techniques might be used to understand a set of observations best. At the outset, it is important to note several points. First, readers with introductory graduate-level expertise in data analysis should understand the chapters in this book; however, there is variability in the degree to which they can expect to use the techniques immediately. Some require additional study, but we hope that each chapter provides enough detail so that readers can make a judgment as to whether to invest additional learning time so as to use the technique to resolve a specific question. Second, our bias is that more sophisticated tools should never be used when a simple mean, standard deviation, frequency table, correlation, regression analysis, or plot of the data is sufficient to answer a research question. Having made this statement, we are equally certain that these simple techniques must often be supplemented with more complex multivariate, nonlinear procedures and that these procedures contribute in important ways to our understanding of the complexities of human behavior.

Our sense is that in very general terms, the chapters in this book address two issues. The first concern is for the accurate description of some behavioral phenomenon. The second set of questions relates to the interrelationships among different behaviors. Each of these major questions has different components, and some of the chapters address questions related to both of these research objectives. To help in organizing the set of questions addressed in this book and by organizational scientists, we pose a set of questions or research objectives that address these two major objectives and indicate which chapters may help provide techniques or ideas about how to analyze and present research results.

Description and Measurement of Variables

The chapters in Part Two address issues related to variables and how they are measured.

From Observations to Variables

At a very basic level, researchers begin by observing some behavior that is interesting to them for some practical or theoretical reason. After multiple observations, the researcher attempts to organize these observations in some parsimonious manner or in a way that attempts to provide an explanatory framework. The basic questions at this point are, What are the variables we are studying? and How can we organize our observations and systematize our measurement? We believe that these questions are addressed most directly in Chapter Two by Karen Locke, which describes one form of qualitative research. She begins with comprehensive verbal descriptions of behavior and describes the development of a sophisticated and detailed measurement system. That system can then be used to develop more systematic and easy-to-administer measurement methods that allow for the collection of many more observations. The procedures she describes represent a way to gain insight into data that many organizational scientists have been unable to describe systematically and have ignored or dismissed as situational vagaries.

Issues related to variables are also considered in the penultimate chapter of this book. Charles Hulin, Andrew Miner, and Steven Seitz describe a method of combining empirical research and theoretical notions and considering the full implications of these observations for situations that have not yet been encountered or observed. Their technique also involves the organization of studies and theoretical statements to describe some behavioral phenomenon better.

Both of these chapters are oriented toward the development of additional theoretical questions about which we can and should collect data. If the objective in analyzing a set of observations is the development of new theory and research questions based on a set of seemingly disjointed or not clearly understood observations, these two chapters may be helpful.

Data Collection

Questionnaires, tests, interviews, observational techniques, and ratings of behavior represent some of the more frequent ways in which organizational scientists collect data; less often used in our discipline are the qualitative techniques that Locke describes. The repertoire of data collection procedures has been radically expanded with the use of the computer technology described in Chapter Three by Julie Olson-Buchanan. The author explores useful ways

to standardize data collection, facilitate data coding and processing, and, perhaps most important, measure variables that we have
not previously been able to assess efficiently.

Item Quality

In constructing measures, we usually recognize that any single item
is a highly fallible measure of the underlying construct we wish to
assess. Consequently, we use multiple items to increase the reliability of our measures and ensure content coverage. An important research question then relates to the manner in which each item
constitutes an acceptable indicator of the construct measured. In
classical test theory, item difficulty (the percentage getting an item
right or the mean of the item) and the correlation of the item with
the remainder of the items measuring a construct are the two major
indexes examined. In most test or scale construction exercises
today, we use item response theory to calibrate items. Items are described in terms of their relationship with an underlying trait continuum using difficulty, discrimination, and guessing parameters.
Once items are calibrated (that is, these three parameters have
been estimated), they are selected so as to maximize the information available about respondents at a given trait level. Hence, item
quality and person trait level are jointly considered in determining
the utility or quality of an item. Item response theory formulations
for dichotomously scored items are described in Chapter Four by
Steven Reise and Niels Waller; in Chapter Five, Michael Zickar describes similar formulations for items with three or more response
alternatives.

Test and Scale Quality

An important conclusion from item response theory is that measures
are more or less reliable at different points on the ability continuum.
Note that this conclusion contrasts with the usual interpretation of
classical test theory's standard error of measurement as a single
value. The conclusion based on item response theory results from
explicitly modeling responses to individual items, and it is an in-
eluctable result that the precision of measurement varies as a function of the person's trait level (and, of course, the set of items used

to measure the person). These questions are more fully addressed in Chapter Four for dichotomously scored items and Chapter Five for polytomously scored items.

Bias in Measurement

Organizational scientists have long been interested in the degree to which scores on their instruments are affected by variables that are conceptually unrelated to the construct in which they are interested. The outside contaminants are usually demographic in nature and often include gender, race, age, and so forth, but they can also be psychological, such as social desirability. These issues have been examined at both the item level and the test level. An item is usually considered biased when there are group differences on the item after controlling for an individual's standing on the underlying construct. Similarly, tests are considered biased when there are group differences in the expected total test score (the true score in the terminology of classical test theory) after controlling for the trait presumably assessed by the measure. In Chapter Six, Nambury Raju and Barbara Ellis describe methods to study both item and test bias using methods based on item response theory. In this literature, bias is referred to as differential item functioning (DIF) and differential test functioning (DTF).

Item quality issues can also be examined using generalizability theory (see Chapter Seven by Richard DeShon) and confirmatory factor analysis (see Chapter Eight by Charles Lance and Robert Vandenberg). In Chapters Seven and Eight, researchers can examine or model various influences on item types so the research question often shifts to understanding the nature of bias as well as its presence.

Reliability and Error in Measurement

A fundamental concern of measurement for the past century has been the reliability of the data collected. The question addressed here concerns the replicability of observations. Perhaps the first and most frequently mentioned concern is for replicability of measurement or observation across time. However, researchers are often also concerned with other sources of error in measurement as well—for example, the items used to measure a construct, the people who record observations, and the situation that is the basis for the observation. Interactions among these different sources of error are also possible. A system to evaluate these multiple sources of error has been available for a relatively long time (Cronbach, Gleser, Nanda, & Rajaratnam, 1971), but we have not frequently used generalizability theory to evaluate the multiple potential sources of error that might be present in a set of observations. The power and uses of generalizability theory to inform us about the quality of our measurement efforts are described in Chapter Seven.

Dimensionality

Finally, we include concerns about the dimensionality of measures as a component of measurement and description. Because of the complexity of human behavior, we are almost never interested in a single behavioral index. Organizational scientists are interested in multiple dimensions of ability and personality. At a lower level, we ask questions about the dimensionality of job satisfaction, organizational commitment, mood, and nearly every other construct of interest in the workplace. Conceptually, we can identify multiple aspects of constructs such as commitment and job satisfaction. However, a major research question involves the degree to which we can empirically distinguish among these aspects. Traditionally, we used exploratory factor analyses to examine the dimensionality of measures. Although there were certainly exceptions, the usual approach was to use some arbitrary quantitative criterion (such as a set of eigenvalues or a scree plot) to determine how many dimensions were represented in a set of item responses. We then interpreted these factors by examining the correlations or loadings of each variable on the derived factors. Using confirmatory factor analysis as described in Chapter Eight, we begin with a priori hypotheses about the number and nature of the dimensionality represented in response to a set of items. These hypotheses are then systematically evaluated using tests of significance and indexes of the degree to which a specific factor model fits the covariances between measures.

Dimensionality issues are also considered by Reise and Waller in Chapter Four in the context of item response theory. The assumption that a set of items measures a single underlying latent trait is critical for item response theory; failure to satisfy the unidimensionality assumption adequately renders conclusions based on this method invalid.

Examining the Interrelationships Among Variables and Testing Substantive Hypotheses

The remaining chapters in this book are devoted primarily to methods for examining hypotheses about the interrelationships among the variables measured to test substantive hypotheses. It is certainly true that the chapters and analytic methods already described can be and are used to examine substantive questions and that the techniques described in Part Three often yield important information about the quality of measures.

Evaluations of Theoretical Models

Organizational and behavioral scientists have long used regression and analysis of variance to test models of the relationships between a set of independent or predictor variables and one or more outcome variables. In the past several decades, the literature often suggests models that include multiple predictor-outcome relationships and regression equations. The ability to model and simultaneously evaluate several regression equations, as well as complex mediator and reciprocal relationships, is provided by structural equation modeling. Available since the 1960s, the use of structural equation modeling has become widespread in the organizational sciences only in the past fifteen years. In Chapter Nine, Roger Millsap provides a useful descriptive summary and an example of the use of structural equation modeling. This analytic technique can be used to examine simultaneously the relative importance of multiple theoretical explanations of behavioral phenomena. For example, one can compute the size of various direct and indirect effects on some outcome variable given a particular theoretical model.

Modeling Change

When studying time-related phenomena, we are often tempted to compute respondents' change scores. A researcher who has observations across at least three points in time can examine a whole series of interesting questions about growth or change. A methodology that has evolved from structural equations modeling, latent growth models allow researchers to examine change while avoiding the unreliability of difference scores. As described by David Chan in Chapter Ten, latent growth modeling involves the computation of regression parameters (that is, slopes and intercepts) for the individuals in a study. One then can use latent growth modeling to ask whether there are significant individual differences in slopes and intercepts and whether slopes and intercepts correlate. In addition, one can examine hypotheses about the correlates of the regression parameters and the shape of the change curve, and examine the similarity of the change process and its correlates across multiple groups. Latent growth modeling, which became available only in the 1990s, represents a highly useful way to examine important research questions that cannot be addressed using more familiar data analytic techniques. Since the method involves the analysis of parameters for latent growth constructs and can explicitly model the measurement process, relationships among latent variables are corrected for unreliability in change indexes.

Concern with time and when or if some discrete event occurs are addressed in the set of analytic techniques discussed in Chapter Thirteen by David Harrison.

Differences as Constructs

Change involves a difference between a single variable at two points in time; *fit* is ordinarily assessed as a difference between two variables at a single point in time. Fit (for example, the match between an individual's ability and the requirements of a job) has long been a concern of psychologists interested in individual differences. This concern has been extended to questions of common values or interests and the degree of fit between a person and the organization (Kristof, 1996). The level of congruence is thought to have important implications for a variety of outcome variables, including performance, organizational commitment, satisfaction, and stress.

Psychometricians have long pointed to the fact that, similar to change scores, measures of fit that are computed by subtracting one measure from another often have very low reliability, which makes these measures less than useful in examining substantive questions. In Chapter Eleven, Jeffrey Edwards examines the assumptions underlying the computation of various measures of fit and reformulates data analyses questions about fit in terms of polynomial regression. He also uses graphical displays and response surfaces methods to explain the nature of fit hypotheses.

Levels of Analyses

In the past decade or so, psychologists who usually focus on individual determinants of behavior have come to realize that individual behavior is embedded in teams or groups, which are parts of an organization. These organizations, in turn, are units in a larger society or culture. This embeddedness makes multiple theoretical and analytical demands on the organizational scientist (Klein & Kozlowski, 2000). One popular analytic method by which these multilevel hypotheses or concerns can be addressed is hierarchical linear modeling. In Chapter Twelve, Paul Bliese provides a very readable exposition of the reasons that levels of analysis issues are important analytically. He then proceeds to use examples to show how to evaluate hypotheses about relationships among variables at a single level (including the appropriateness of doing so) as well as cross levels of analysis.

Discrete Outcome Variables

Occasionally, organizational researchers are interested in the occurrence or nonoccurrence of some variable, such as employees' leaving an organization or accidents or job acceptance. Occasionally, also, several potential outcomes that are not ordered are considered a variable, such as job choices. A whole family of techniques has been developed to handle these special data analytic problems, and some organizational researchers are beginning to use these methods to help them understand data. Harrison in Chapter Thirteen begins by showing why and when these alternative methods should be used. He also provides a variety of examples of their use in addressing various questions. Some of these situations involve individuals whose data are censored, that is, observations of these cases begins and ends at different times. In these situations, the question that is addressed is when or if some event occurs. Harrison describes nonlinear methods (for example, Cox regression) that are applicable in these instances.

Computational Modeling

When empirical data are lacking or difficult to obtain, researchers may test various theoretical propositions using computational modeling. In Chapter Fourteen, Hulin, Miner, and Seitz describe situations in which traditional correlational and experimental research designs cannot be implemented or will not be helpful. In those instances, researchers who are willing to use existing data and various theoretical propositions can go well beyond currently available data to develop new knowledge about the potential interrelationships of variables. Interestingly, Hulin, Miner, and Seitz note that most theories are incomplete and underspecified; attempts to write computer programs to simulate the behavior described by the theories reveal many ambiguities and uncertainties about what should take place. Researchers can also use computational modeling to develop new hypotheses about these interrelationships, which can then be tested in subsequent empirical studies. Chapter Fourteen contains several examples in which the use of this novel technique provided information unavailable using any more traditional method of research.

Cumulating Data Across Studies

On some organizational questions, researchers have conducted dozens or even hundreds of studies, and very often, if not always, the results of these studies appear to differ. In the past twenty-five years, researchers have developed several different methods of meta-analysis that involve the analysis of data collected in different studies by different researchers. These methods are designed to estimate an overall effect size across studies to quantify the magnitude of a relationship between two or more variables. In addition to the effect size itself, many meta-analysis methods estimate the variance of the effect size in order to quantify the variability of the relationship due to moderators. The most common and least interesting reason that a measure of effect size may vary across studies is sampling error; often other methodological artifacts, such as variability in range restriction, also affect the magnitude of relation. When variance in effect size remains after sampling error and methodological artifacts have been accounted for, researchers turn to the consideration of substantively interesting moderator variables.

In the final chapter of this volume, Hannah Rothstein, Michael McDaniel, and Michael Borenstein provide a guide to different methods of meta-analyses and examples of the use of meta-analyses to represent the cumulative results of large bodies of data. The burgeoning use of meta-analysis in literature reviews demonstrates that it provides a significant advance over the more qualitative summaries previously used, in which reviewers often mistakenly concluded that a body of literature produced conflicting results, when in fact the variability in results could be easily explained on the basis of limitations of individual studies.

Conclusion

We believe that the methods described in this book help address questions that either cannot be addressed using simpler and more familiar techniques or that represent significant advances over the more traditional methods. We hope that this book will help researchers recognize the value of the methods described, educate themselves concerning the applicability and use of these techniques in their own research, and begin to use the methods to address important research questions. When this happens, we believe that we will have advanced the frontiers of organizational science.

References

Cronbach, L. J., Gleser, G. C., Nanda, H., & Rajaratnam, N. (1972). *The dependability of behavioral measurements: Theory of generalizability for scores and profiles.* New York: John Wiley & Sons.

Klein, K. J., & Kozlowski, S.W.J. (Eds.). (2000). *Multilevel theory, research, and methods in organizations.* San Francisco: Jossey-Bass.

Kristof, A. L. (1996). Person-organization fit: An integrative review of its conceptualizations, measurement, and implications. *Personnel Psychology, 49,* 1–49.

PART 2

Description and Measurement of Variables

CHAPTER 2

The Grounded Theory Approach to Qualitative Research

Karen Locke

Grounded theory is a general research approach designed to support the inductive development of theory about a phenomenon through a set of systematic procedures for the collection and analysis of qualitative data. It was first articulated over thirty years ago by two sociologists, Barney Glaser and Anselm Strauss, in *The Discovery of Grounded Theory* (1967). Since that time, this style of qualitative research has traveled extensively from its originating domain of sociology to other disciplines, including psychology, information science, education, health care and management, and organization studies. Norman Denzin, one of the editors of the highly regarded *Handbook of Qualitative Research,* highlights the status of the grounded theory approach by characterizing it as "the most widely used interpretive framework in the social sciences today" (Denzin, 1994, p. 513).

Although the grounded theory approach enjoys such status, it is important to recognize that qualitative research as a professionally established field-oriented practice for knowledge generation has enjoyed almost a century of development across the social science disciplines. Accordingly, the term *qualitative research* describes a broad and pluralistic universe (Locke & Golden-Biddle, 2001). One way to understand this variety is as stemming from different traditions. (The notion of tradition here is consistent with Kuhn's [1970] use of the term to describe scientific activity as prosecuted through different groups of scholars who agree on the nature of the world they are studying, its important questions, and the means for investigating them.) Qualitative research is best understood as comprising a range of disciplinary and subdisciplinary traditions or schools of thought (Jacob, 1988). Besides the grounded theory approach described here, other schools of qualitative research practice include ethnography (Agar, 1980; Hammersley & Atkinson, 1983), ethnomethodology (Garfinkle, 1967; Heritage, 1984), conversation analysis (Sacks, Schegloff, & Jefferson, 1974), case studies (Stake, 1995; Yin, 1994), and semiotics (Eco, 1976; Manning, 1987), to name but a few. In academia, younger professional schools such as management, education, and nursing science have drawn variously from the analytic perspectives and techniques associated with these and other schools of thought to pursue their research interests. Readers interested in surveying some of the breadth of qualitative research approaches are referred to Denzin and Lincoln (1998a, 1998b) and Bryman and Burgess (1999a, 1999b). In addition, Feldman (1995) offers an illuminating explication of some of the variety in qualitative approaches through her application of four styles of qualitative analysis to aspects of the same body of data collected from an extended field study of a large university housing office.

This chapter outlines and introduces the grounded theory building approach to qualitative data analysis. It begins by outlining the particular disciplinary and historical contexts in which the approach was articulated, noting how these informed grounded theory. Following this, the basic procedures composing the approach are presented and illustrated. As part of the presentation of procedures, the opportunities afforded by computer-assisted software packages to support many of the mechanical aspects of data storage and retrieval are considered. Finally, the opportunities afforded by the grounded theory approach are noted.

A Historical Perspective

The grounded theory approach grew from the Chicago School of Sociology. Specifically, it is associated with the school's rich tradition of field research and with symbolic interactionism ideas about the social world.

Sociology in the Mid-1960s

Sociology in the mid-1960s had an established research tradition of field-based participant-observation studies with their associated data-gathering practices of conducting extended observations, carrying out informal semistructured interviews, and examining documentary materials. The Chicago school had by then sponsored the first hand-detailed empirical investigation of focused social situations for over half a century. By the 1960s, that tradition had waned, and in its stead, sociology was pursuing the development of grand theoretical schemes generated by sociologists of eminence such as Talcott Parsons. This was an era in which high general theory was favored, and it was to a great extent separated from detailed empirical research (Collins & Makowsky, 1978).

The originators of the grounded theory approach were among a group of sociologists who were interested in reviving the Chicago school tradition of sociological inquiry and who shared a commitment to dirtying their hands in direct observation and to developing theory that conformed closely to those observations (Woods, 1992). In the Preface to *The Discovery of Grounded Theory* (1967), Glaser and Strauss accordingly claimed that sociology was struggling with a divide between elaborated theories and empirical research. They directly critiqued Parsons's and other grand theoretical schemes as having little to do with people's everyday lives. They challenged this form of empirically dissociated theorizing in which theory is developed by thinking things through in a logical manner and sought to replace it with theory developed from rich observational data. In many ways, it is appropriate to think of the grounded theory approach to qualitative research as a further elaboration and extension of the Chicago school's established fieldwork research practices. Its originators worked out an approach to data collection, analysis, and theory generation that introduced a set of systematic procedures extending and significantly supplementing the practices long associated with participant observation in order to achieve their purpose of developing grounded theories of action in context.

The grounded theory approach reflects its originators' commitment to research and theory building through direct contact with the social world, coupled with a rejection of a priori theoretical categories and propositions. This does not mean that grounded theorists should embark on research without the guidance of some disciplinary school of thought that provides an orienting theoretical perspective. An orienting theoretical perspective informs researchers' understanding of complex social realities. It guides researchers in what they should pay attention to but does not focus the research so narrowly as to exclude data whose importance may not be recognized at the outset of a research project (Foote Whyte, 1984). Indeed, many researchers would argue that qualitative theory-building research without the benefit of a broad orientating framework for understanding social reality would be impossible because researchers would not otherwise be able to orient themselves in the stream of actions, events, and words that are the indicators of the phenomena that qualitative researchers investigate. For the grounded theory approach, that orienting framework is traditionally symbolic interactionism.

It is worth noting that a number of researchers have drawn on grounded theory procedures to support their qualitative data analysis while they have drawn on other broad schools of thought for their orienting theoretical perspective. Pettigrew (1990), for example, identifies contextualism as the broad theoretical perspective that informs his qualitative research on organizational change. Similarly, Harris and Sutton (1986) have drawn on structural functionalism as their orienting theoretical perspective in a study of parting ceremonies in organizations.

Symbolic Interactionism

Grounded theory is informed by the symbolic interactionist school of sociology. The set of ideas associated with symbolic interactionism developed from the work of early twentieth-century American pragmatist philosophers such as William James, George H. Mead, Charles Peirce, Charles Horton Cooley, and John Dewey. These philosophers were committed to developing a way of understanding human behavior that attended to people's everyday practices and their lived realities and that conceived of social reality in dynamic terms, that is, "in the making" (Prus, 1996). Mead, who is generally associated with the set of ideas that are at the core of the symbolic interactionist perspective, focused on articulating the role that subjective experience plays in everyday interaction and behavior. Mead perceived that individuals act in a social context in which they ascribe meaning to objects and actions and base their own actions on those construed meanings (Layder, 1994). This notion that meaning is central to social behavior is the cornerstone idea in the symbolic interactionist perspective. It was one of Mead's pupils at the University of Chicago, Herbert Blumer, who coined the term *symbolic interactionism,* thereby underscoring the relationship between meaning and action central to this school of thought. And it was Blumer who extended these ideas and elaborated their methodological implications.

Blumer (1969) articulated three premises that undergird the symbolic interactionist school of thought. First, people interpret the meaning of objects (conceived broadly) in the world and then take action based on those interpretations. Consequently, if as researchers we are to understand the actions of recruiters, for example, we need to learn the meanings that relevant physical, social, and verbal objects have to them. This means being aware of what composes their world of recruiting: their experiences, recruits' varied educational backgrounds, categories of recruits, particular organizational policies, and being aware of the particular language terms that they use to define these objects. The second tenet of symbolic interactionism is that meaning arises out of social interaction, not from the object itself. Thus, the meaning that recruiters may make of a new organizational mission statement or of various types of recruit is not given in these objects themselves. They arise out of recruiters' experience of these objects in the context of communication and interaction with relevant others, whether they be recruits, recruiters, or any other actors. And, finally, meaning is not fixed or stable; it is always modifiable. These recruiters can alter the meaning of any one of the objects relevant to them in the light of changing events and circumstances.

Given this overriding concern with the meaning that subjects make of their world, it is not surprising that the most important premise of symbolic interactionism is that all social inquiry must be grounded in the particular empirical world studied. Such grounding is necessary in order to learn about the meanings that relevant objects hold and the day-to-day patterns of behavior that both shape and follow from those meanings (Woods, 1992). Firsthand, detailed participant observation is the research ideal. To continue with the recruiting illustration, researchers must enter the worlds of recruiters in order to understand recruiting from the subjects' point of view and to observe firsthand what recruiters find meaningful and how they make meaning.

The association of grounded theory with symbolic interactionism has been repeatedly underscored by its originators and their students (Charmaz, 1990; Chenitz & Swanson, 1986; Glaser, 1978; Strauss, 1987). As a set of research practices, grounded theory reflects the assumptions of symbolic interactionism that the social world should be studied in a way that keeps faith with it. This is certainly expressed in the conviction that researchers should pursue data gathering through practices that afford familiarity—for example, through firsthand observation and face-to-face interviews. However, the notion of keeping faith with the empirical world studied is also reflected in other tenets. Grounded theory researchers believe that the kinds of issues appropriate for study are those that are problematic to the people in the setting studied. What is problematic for recruiters? They believe that researchers should approach inquiry as a learning rather than a testing task, bringing to it as few advanced concepts and propositions as possible. And they believe that the conceptual framework resulting from grounded theory research should fit and closely conform to the situation studied.

The Grounded Theory Model of Qualitative Research

The grounded theory approach is designed to support the development of theory. In hypothetico-deductive models of research, investigation begins with the specification of concepts and their proposed relationships and then moves out into the empirical world where, according to the posed theory, they should be observed. Such research, of course, is oriented toward theory testing. In contrast, in the grounded theory approach, research begins with empirical observation and moves from there to the definition of concepts. The set of research procedures that compose grounded theory are designed to help researchers make this move from empirical observation to composing conceptual categories and identifying the ways in which they relate to each other.

Given its concern with theory building, grounded theory researchers work to be able to make plausible claims about the theoretical elements they compose from their empirical observations. The naturalistic empirical observations are generalized in the developed conceptual framework. Yin (1994) distinguishes this "analytic generalization" from statistical generalization, which addresses the extent to which inferences can be made about proposed theoretical elements in a population on the basis of empirical information collected from an appropriate sample. The end products of the grounded theory process, by comparison, have little to say about the extent of their expression in a population. Rather, the framework is considered to have analytic generalizability when it can plausibly account for a large number and range of empirical observations. That is when the researchers have "generalized findings to 'theory'" (Yin, 1994, p. 37).

Written accounts of the grounded theory approach (Glaser & Strauss, 1967; Glaser, 1978; Strauss, 1987; Strauss and Corbin, 1990, 1998) assume an audience that has been trained in a particular disciplinary tradition and in the procedures for collecting naturalistic data. The discussion of grounded theory procedures therefore is oriented toward the analytic act in the qualitative research process. As such, this approach assumes that researchers have clarified their purposes and identified the issues they hope to understand in conducting the study (Maxwell, 1998). Although sampling issues as they attend data gathering are addressed in detail and are integral to its analytic logic, grounded theory has little to offer researchers unschooled in basic qualitative data-gathering techniques. The presumption is made that researchers understand how to observe and develop field notes and how to conduct interviews and such that the raw materials for analysis (such as field notes, interview transcripts, and documentary data) have been accurately and systematically collected.

For researchers interested in pursuing qualitative research but who have yet to develop those skills, a number of resources are available. There are useful guides to conducting field-based observations (Agar, 1980; Burgess, 1984; Lofland & Lofland, 1984; Schatzman & Strauss, 1973; Spradley, 1980) and for conducting indepth interviews (Chenitz, 1986; McCracken, 1988; Rubin & Rubin, 1995; Spradley, 1979). Observation and interviewing are two core qualitative data-gathering procedures. Qualitative data can, of course, come from other sources, including any kind of documentary information such as letters, memos, and reports. For example, grounded theories have been developed from the records of formal inquiry proceedings (Turner, 1976), newspaper articles (Ross & Staw, 1993), and academic journal articles (Locke & Golden-Biddle, 1997). In short, anything that may shed light on the phenomenon being studied is appropriate as data and can be analyzed in the same way as interview transcripts or field notes developed from observations. Although little specific advice has been given about data gathering, Glaser and Strauss (1967) do suggest that researchers gather several "slices" of data relating to the phenomenon; by this, they mean that researchers should gather various types of data pertaining to the issue investigated.

General Contours of the Analytic Process

These procedures for developing conceptual categories follow a concept-indicator model of theory development (Glaser, 1978); that is, conceptual categories are developed that account for perceived patterns in sets of data observations that cross the collected data set. In their writings, Glaser and Strauss variously speak of these conceptualized elements as both codes and categories. For the sake of clarity, I use only the term *conceptual category* or *category* (Locke, 2001; Rennie, Phillips, & Quartaro, 1988). Each conceptual category is indicated by a set of empirical observations. For example, the conceptual category of social loss (Glaser & Strauss, 1967) was conceived by the approach's originators to account for the behavior and comments of hospital professional staff that indicated a differential significance to the death of various patients. Reduction of the data observations therefore occurs by researchers' conceptualizing what they have in common. Ultimately, the quality of a grounded theory rests on the goodness of fit between the empirical observations and the conceptual categories they purport to indicate.

As Figure 2.1 indicates, the constant comparative method and theoretically driven sampling provide the procedural foundation for the development of theoretical elements. The constant comparative method is a procedure in which two activities, naming data

**Figure 2.1. Model of the Analytical Procedures Comprised
in the Grounded Theory Approach.**

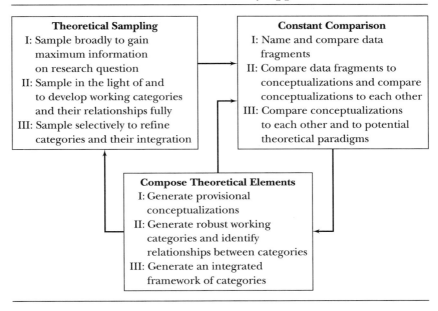

fragments and comparing data incidents and names, occur in tandem (Locke, 2001). The process of building conceptual categories is discussed in terms of three phases that span various levels of development in the conceptual categories. In each of these phases, analytic activity takes a slightly different form as conceptualization moves from an initial phase in which potential categories are provisionally identified through to later stages of analysis, when they are developed fully and integrated into an organizing theoretical framework. Although this description suggests a certain linear progression in the analytic task as each phase is transformed into the next, analysis does not progress in a linear pattern. Rather, it is highly recursive and iterative as new conceptual categories may be identified and old categories revisited and renamed at any stage of the analytic process. Consequently, researchers are typically working simultaneously with categories at various levels of development.

Sampling in the grounded theory approach always proceeds on theoretical grounds. That is, the logic for sampling derives from researchers' commitment to developing theory about a phenomenon or an issue. This commitment drives sampling decisions throughout the study as researchers are always actively thinking about and searching for sampling data that will support development of the theoretical framework. This means that data collection is an open and flexible process that will undergo modification over the course of the research as conceptual categories and the overall framework are developed and refined.

Early Phase of Category Development

As researchers begin a study, they select settings, particular individuals, groups, or documents to sample because they believe that those choices will yield rich and varied information on the topic of interest. Initial sampling therefore is purposive (Patton, 1990). Furthermore, it is helpful if researchers build comparative settings, individuals, groups, or documentary information into their data gathering. For example, in a study of an organization's adoption and use of a policy on paid time off, initial sampling decisions about who to interview focused on capturing demographic variety among organizational members that might be relevant to use of the policy—for example, whether they lived with a chronic disease or had a role in elder care.

The beginning point for analysis, then, are those data texts (for example, field notes, interview transcripts, and documents) that have been purposefully collected with the view to understanding a particular problem. Once researchers have an initial data set in hand, they move to fracture its text into discrete data fragments for analysis and to open up those fragments to interpretation by assigning meanings to them. Glaser and Strauss (Glaser, 1978; Strauss, 1987; Strauss & Corbin 1990, 1998) use the term *open coding* to describe this initial phase of category development. Exhibit 2.1 offers an illustration of this process. It depicts a verbatim excerpt from an interview with a manager about the implementation of paid time off (PTO). In this excerpt, the manager is responding to a question about the advantages and disadvantages of the policy. The hash marks on the interviewee's responses in the center column

Exhibit 2.1. Illustration of the Process of Fracturing a Data Document and Assigning Provisional Category Names.

Line	Excerpt from Transcript	Provisional Category Names
1	A: The good is, again, it gives people flexibility	People can take care of
2	to do what they need to do //, and use their	needs/flexibility
3	time in the way they see best for their family,	Needs are family related
4	especially with families //, I'm not going to say	Family responsibility not
5	just mothers, but mothers and fathers // that	gendered
6	have that emergency, need to take care of their	Needs are children's
7	children, // that they don't have to call in	emergencies
8	and lie and say "I don't feel good today (fake	Removes need to lie—
9	coughs), I can't come in", but really something	encourages honesty
10	happened // and they can't use child care, or	Needs are children's
11	the baby's sick, or whatever. // So, it gives	emergencies
12	them that ability to be honest, and I like that—	Encourages honesty
13	I think that's really positive. // I think that's	Honesty is positive
14	really the big positive with that, // and then	
15	also that they can call in and say "I need a	Needs are for mental health
16	mental health day, I just got to go to the beach	
17	today" or whatever. // And, you know, as long	Be up front—honest/ mgrs.
18	as you know everything's OK, you know,	monitor personal life
19	please be upfront and free with me with that. //	
20	Again, the negative is that they can take more	PTO breaks non-work time
21	of this time in small pieces, instead of most	into smaller pieces with
22	people take vacation chunks, and they only	the result that there are
23	get say two weeks or something, and those	more (now smaller) units
24	two chunks of vacation, and I find people take	of time off time taken
25	more single days here, // so I'm constantly	PTO creates more work
26	trying to balance PTO, and departments, and	coordinating more
27	who wants to take what, and a day here and a	individual absences
28	day there, and unscheduled PTO, // and you	Travelling exacerbates
29	know, so and being away a lot it's very	coordination
30	difficult, // and I've found that sometimes I get	More units of time off
31	3 out of 4 people in a department have decided	means maintaining work
32	to call in on a PTO day, and I'm like sitting	coverage on a daily basis is
33	there going "OK, nobody wants to work for me	problematic
34	today" you know.//	

break this response into individual observations or data fragments to which researchers assign meaning. (The line numbering in the left column provides a means to track the location of fragments.)

Fracturing the data into fragments in this way helps researchers to examine the disaggregated elements and conceptualize them in a way that transcends the particular interview, field observation, or document in which they were embedded. In terms of guidance regarding the size of data fragments, a good rule of thumb is that researchers should break the data into fragments on a sentence-by-sentence basis to create working units of meaning (Glaser, 1978; Turner, 1981). As the fragments created in Exhibit 2.1 indicate, however, sometimes the fragment is only part of a sentence and occasionally more than a single sentence. Researchers have to use some judgment as to what is a meaningful unit while maintaining the discipline to fracture, name, and compare small discrete units of data. This process facilitates the microscopic analysis of the data, and it precludes any tendency to assign meaning in a general way, for example, by reading through the data documents and creating impressionistic themes as opposed to data-specified, grounded categories.

Researchers initiate conceptualization through the two processes of naming and comparing. In the process of naming, a data fragment is studied; it is then named such that its name or label represents researchers' interpretation of what is happening in that data fragment, and the name is noted in the margins. In Exhibit 2.1, the provisional meanings assigned to the data fragments are expressed in the naming phrases recorded in the right-hand column. Furthermore, during the early phase of analysis, a fragment of data is named in as many ways as can be reasonably extrapolated from it in order to open the data up to a broad possible set of interpretations. (The final name for the data fragment will be settled through comparison with other fragments as the analysis develops.)

In this activity, it is important from the outset that researchers not assign a name to the words that compose the data fragments. When researchers stay too close to the denotative meaning of the data fragment, they run the risk of creating categories that do little more than repeat the text (Rennie, 1998). As Corbin and Strauss (1990) note, meaningful conceptual categories cannot be created by naming raw data. Rather, the fragments have to be examined and named as potential indicators of phenomena, which are given conceptual labels through naming. During analytic activity, researchers are always working to apprehend their data in terms of conceptual possibilities. To assist in this process of conceptually naming data, Glaser (1978) offers a number of neutral generative questions that researchers can pose to the data: What is happening? What is the basic problem faced by the people here? What category or what aspect of a category does this fragment suggest? What does this fragment suggest this is a theory of? We might take these questions and pose them to this data fragment from Exhibit 2.1: "Again, the negative is that they can take more of this time in small pieces, instead of most people take vacation chunks, and they only get say two weeks or something, and those two chunks of vacation, and I find people take more single days here." The questions certainly help to open up implications of the PTO policy for the patterning of time away from work.

Turner (1981) offers some additional advice on the creation of category names. When researchers initially are creating provisional categories in the margins, he suggests that names can take any form; they can be short, metaphorical, or ungainly and long-winded. The only important thing is that the name is a good fit for the data fragment—that it provides a recognizable description of it.

In order to stay close to the situation studied and to allow examination of the data to inform conceptualizing fully, researchers should hold in abeyance any preconceived ideas and any previous theorizing related to the issue being studied so as to prevent their prematurely influencing conceptualizing. As the discussion of the context in which grounded theory was articulated indicates, the originators of the approach wanted to ensure that researchers did not enter their research task with ready-to-hand conceptual elements or specific propositions that had not been developed through detailed empirical observations.

Naming in and of itself is insufficient to create conceptual categories. Comparing has to occur in tandem with naming. Comparing fragments of data with each other and with the category name achieves two important aims. First, it helps to develop a common name and category for multiple fragments of data, thereby facilitating reduction of the data set through the development of more general categories. Second, it supports the naming act by helping to sharpen and refine what the data fragments potentially indicate. Each fragment is compared with every other fragment, and data fragments are compared to the names for the in-process categories. The process of looking at what is similar and different in the data fragments and of examining the conceptual category that researchers created in the light of them helps to clarify what is perceived as uniform and stable in the data fragments. To push researchers to work for greater conceptual clarity, Turner (1981) suggests another step in the naming activity once comparison has resulted in several data fragments as indicating a category. When a conceptual category contains more than six and fewer than twelve data fragments, researchers should push themselves to write a formal definition of the working category label that is self-explanatory to someone unacquainted with the research.

In addition to working to develop category names, researchers should also write memos on their analytic process. For example, during the early stages of creating provisional labels after an initial period of reading interview transcripts, writing a free-flowing memo on an idea sparked by a particular data fragment captures that idea and at the same time notes an illustration of it. Once categories begin to be indicated by multiple data fragments, the various ideas that the process of comparing triggers can be explored in memo form. This free-form writing, through which thoughts are allowed to flow and ideas can be tried out, is very helpful in clarifying and working through what is perceived in the data.

As this early phase of analytic activity unfolds, then, researchers will have created and be working with three forms of analytic documents to help organize their sense-making process: the transcribed data document with its fractured data units and their noted provisional category names, the analytic memos with their record and exploration of ideas occurring to the researchers, and category cards or files. The category file creates a record of the in-process conceptual categories that facilitates the process of comparing data incidents. The process of physically adding each data fragment to the category file helps to force the comparison of each new data fragment with those already recorded and the comparison of the data fragments with the category name.

Computer-assisted qualitative data analysis packages, such as QSR NVIVO, ATLAS.TI, and ETHNOGRAPH, greatly facilitate the making of such documents, and as data documents, memos, and category files are generated, these packages help to keep them organized and accessible for flexible retrieval. Such packages enable researchers to work with data documents such as transcribed interviews, field notes, or documentary text and to code on-screen—that is, to create named categories and link them to their indicating data fragments. NVIVO, for example, can store these created categories and their data fragments in category nodes, an indexing system that allows creation of an unlimited number of categories and allows researchers to retrieve flexibly and search their data through the created categories.

In this early phase of analytic activity, then, researchers engage and become immersed in their data. Through the processes of naming and comparing and the supportive writing of memos, they will have several conceptual categories under development. Some of these early provisional categories may be more heavily indicated by data fragments than others. In addition, provisional categories may fall into natural groupings dealing with common issues. The presence of some heavily indicated conceptual categories and the apparent clustering of categories naturally usher in a new form of analytic activity as researcher attention shifts to their focused development. (This does not mean that the development of provisional categories halts; it continues as researchers work through their data documents.)

As the interview excerpt in Exhibit 2.1 indicates, the issue of lying and honesty is a salient advantage of the policy for this manager. Exhibit 2.2 illustrates a working category (captured in a category file) for this issue. As it indicates, that perspective on the policy is shared by others too. Furthermore, it indicates how categories are continually under revision during the analytic process. For example, most of the data fragments concern a reduction in the lying of employees, but the subject of the last fragment is the manager. Although the behavior he is describing—looking the other way—is not technically lying, it does overlap with lying. Accordingly, a larger category can be created by combining the data fragments under a new category name whose working label underscores pretense. Keeping track of previous category names assigned to data fragments allows researchers to keep track of revisions, thereby recording the direction of their thinking over the analytic process.

Exhibit 2.2. Illustration of Category Development.

File Number 5:	Working Label: "Reduces Pretense Between Manager and Employees"
Data Source and Location	*Data Fragments*
Interview 4 Mgr. DB (7–9)*	That they don't have to call in and lie and say "I don't feel good today" (fake coughs), I can't come in, but really something happened
Interview 4 Mgr. DB (11–13)	So, it gives them that ability to be honest, and I like that—I think that's really positive.
Interview 4 Mgr. DB (18–20)	And, you know, as long as you know everything's OK, you know, please be upfront and free with me with that
Interview 10 Mgr. WD (112–117)	I appreciated the fact that if someone needed the day off, or some number of hours off, to take care of some personal business, that they didn't call here and tell me they were sick, knowing full well they weren't sick
Interview 10 Mgr. WD (120–121)	They no longer have to call in here and lie
Interview 3: Mgr. JM (54–60)	So, the concept of PTO, all encompassing, is calling a spade a spade. It's saying, OK you got this time off, we're not going to call it sick pay, and you're not going to call in and say I'm sick when you're not really because you want to take the day off
Interview 3: Mgr. JM (89–93)	The way it [my attitude] has changed is that the other way, basically, looking the other way because I knew that if the person called in, they weren't necessarily sick, or felt that they weren't. This way I don't have that.
Links with: ?	Earlier category names: Encourages honesty/No more looking the other way

Note: Numbers refer to line numbers in transcript.

Occasionally, researchers fall into the trap of creating too many thinly indicated provisional categories because they have not worked through constant comparison to create categories that are sufficiently general to account for a number of data fragments across the set of data documents. Indeed, one potential problem associated with the use of computer-assisted software programs for the analysis of qualitative data is that it is easy to have proliferating hundreds or even thousands of provisional categories, each with only a few indicating data fragments because researchers feel sure that the computer will be able to keep track of them all. However, the computer programs do not do the work of fully developing each of the hundreds of categories, nor do they work out how to organize and integrate them so that they tell a coherent story about the subject studied. Doing so requires much in the way of both researchers' analytic resources and data resources.

When researchers run into the problem of generating too many thin provisional categories, they may profitably follow this strategy. They make laundry lists of all the provisional category names and, following the comparative logic that is central to these analytic procedures, examine them and try to cluster them on the basis of similarities and differences. Then they inspect the clusters and see if they can develop a more general name and definition for them. These will become working categories that can be developed further (Swanson, 1986).

Given this revision in the working conceptual categories, which is a feature of grounded theory's recursive analytic process, it is important that researchers working with the support of computer-assisted programs be able to accommodate such changes easily. For example, in the older NUDIST software programs, merging and reformulating theoretical categories was cumbersome and highly problematic. That is not the case with the most recent version, NVIVO; it easily accommodates such revisions.

Intermediate Phase of Category Development

In the intermediate phase of category development, researchers aim to advance articulation of the in-process conceptual categories to the point that they can account for both similarity and variation in the indicating data incidents. They also aim to integrate those conceptual categories into a broader organizing theoretical framework. Working toward this, researchers move the focus of their attention away from the naming and comparing of individual data fragments toward the task of developing the individual conceptual categories and integrating them into a broader theoretical framework. They spend comparatively less time comparing data fragments to each other in favor of more analytic resources devoted to comparing incidents to the composed conceptual category and comparing categories with each other. Specifically, researchers are now concerned with developing fully—that is, identifying all the elements that might constitute—the theoretical category. Data fragments are compared to the in-process categories to determine if they suggest a dimension that has not yet been articulated. Also, categories are compared to each other as researchers begin thinking about how they may be related. As is the case in the first phase of analytic activity, this thinking is greatly facilitated by the writing of theoretical memos, which is directed toward exploring thoughts about the implications of the conceptual categories.

Armed with a set of in-process categories, researchers turn to further sampling and data collection in order to advance their development. They use those in-process categories to direct further data collection in order to describe the categories, their properties or subcategories, and relationships better. Inevitably, the developed categories will suggest questions and issues that researchers would like to have more information on to understand better the phenomenon their conceptualizing is pointing to. Furthermore, Strauss and Corbin (1990, 1998) suggest that researchers can pose the following simple questions: Who? When? Why? How? With what consequences? When these are posed to the in-process theoretical categories, they will likely suggest additional information that is important to gather in order to understand more fully what is involved with the theoretical categories.

For example, with regard to the working category noted above, "PTO breaks non-work time into smaller pieces with the result that there are more (now smaller) units of non-work time taken," the posing of these questions would help researchers consider for whom (what individuals, roles, or groups) in the organization this patterning of time off occurs and is an issue. Being able to answer comprehensively this Who? question would result in a category that was able to account conceptually for the patterning of and concerns regarding time off across individuals and groups in the organization. The When? question suggests being able to understand what occasions particular patterns—the conditions under which one or another patterning is likely to occur, and so on. Until a category has some such dimension to it, it offers little in the way of understanding a phenomenon.

As researchers start thinking about their categories in this way, they will doubtless have other categories under development that relate to these questions. However, they will also feel that they need to engage in more data gathering to understand further the relevant dimensions of the category. Researchers will thus alter their data gathering based on their in-process categories. This is theoretical sampling.

Theoretical sampling can progress along a number of different avenues. First, researchers may make sampling decisions about who or what else should be sampled to shed more light on the categories. For example, whereas initial sampling decisions were made on the basis of demographic characteristics, subsequent decisions about sampling will be based on considerations of what groups, individuals, or roles would have more information to offer on the issue of the patterning of time off. For example, researchers will look to interview individuals who have just taken time off in various patterns—one day in the past month, a week in the past month, one day in two weeks of the past month, and so on. Researchers will also want to access organizational records regarding the use of PTO.

Second, researchers will very likely reshape data gathering so that new questions will be added to interviews, specific kinds of events sought out for observation, and particular kinds of documents gleaned. This restructuring of data gathering will permit researchers to gather more information pertinent to the categories and the issues that they raise. They might engage in more focused questioning with employees about decisions to take time off in the configuration they did and with their supervisors about the consequence of that configuration of time off.

Finally, researchers can double-back over their already analyzed data documents to make sure that they have captured in their categories all the information that the documents have to offer on concerns and phenomena now expressed in the in-process categories. It is not unusual for researchers to find such information; for example, they might notice that a phrase that was part of a larger data fragment might indeed be separately interpreted (Hawks, 1991; Locke, 2001).

As new data come in, they are subject to those same analytic procedures comprised in the initial phase of analysis. In this way, researchers are simultaneously working with categories at various levels of development.

Accordingly, a collection of conceptual categories will not necessarily add up to a coherent theoretical framework. This requires researchers to think about what all of the categories might add up to: What kind of a theory do all their categories suggest that they are working toward? This is facilitated by two overlapping analytic moves. First, researchers examine and actively consider whether their categories can be subsumed under a few more general core categories, which account for a preponderance of their data. Second, researchers consider and look for possibilities to relate their conceptual categories in terms of those core conceptualizations. These developmental and organizing analytic moves are facilitated by the use of coding paradigms. These are conceptual templates that heuristically support thinking about the categories and clarify and organize the relationship that each category has to other working categories. They allow researchers to consider various theoretical schemes flexibly as they work to compose one that fits with their data. Thus, entertaining various theoretical paradigms is a helpful analytic move in thinking about how the in-process conceptual categories might be tied together.

Glaser (1978) offers some eighteen families of what he calls theoretical codes or coding paradigms that help researchers to think analytically about the possible organization for their categories. Strauss (1987) and Strauss and Corbin (1990, 1998) similarly suggest that a theoretical paradigm is a useful heuristic to help researchers think through what kind of theory their developing categories are adding up to. For example, researchers' subsequent analytic and data-gathering efforts may indicate that their conceptual categories could be integrated into a conditions and consequences theoretical framework that explains the patterning of time off in the organization under the PTO policy. In much the same way as the Who? When? Why? and other questions were used as a template, researchers can use a theoretical paradigm to explore potential relationships in their categories and identify further sampling needs. For example, researchers would examine and compare their existing categories and ask the following: Does this pretense category provide the context for another category? Does it occasion another category? Are these pretenses action or interaction strategies that address another category? Is this pretense category a consequence of another category?

It is imperative that researchers look for multiple instances of these relationships so that they earn their way into the framework through persistence and consistency in the data. For example, two data fragments that suggest that manager travel occasions a single-day absence from work does not suggest an adequately developed category regarding what occasions this behavior.

The theoretical paradigms offer many possibilities for researchers to explore their thinking. For example, the preponderance of data may suggest a strategy paradigm that has researchers thinking about a theory of strategies or a stage model that demonstrates changes in behavior over time and identifies possible triggers for the movement from one stage to another. The heuristic exploration of various theoretical paradigms helps researchers to approach flexibly the analytic task of thinking about what kind of theoretical framework their categories might add up to (Glaser, 1978). Their categories may fit one or part of a theoretical paradigm, or they may not. Nevertheless, exploring such paradigms constrains researchers to think about the integration possibilities inherent in their in-process categories.

Final Phase of Category Development

In the final phase of category development and integration, researchers bound and bring to a close their analysis by engaging in a more selective and limited phase of naming and comparing. This phase presumes that the forms of naming and comparing activity that have come before have enabled them to settle on their core conceptual categories and the theoretical framework that expresses them. That is, researchers will have developed their response to the last of Glaser's (1978) neutral analytic questions: What is this a theory of? This delimiting occurs at the levels of individual conceptual categories and the organizing theoretical framework. At the level of individual conceptual categories, categories achieve a level of development at which incoming data provide no new information about that category, its dimensions, or its relationships. In the grounded theory vernacular, this is the point of *theoretical saturation.* Similarly, at the level of the broader theoretical framework, a particular organization of the data stabilizes, and researchers make a commitment to telling a particular kind of story from their data.

In this final phase of category development, researchers engage in mopping-up analytic activity—that is, activity designed to ensure that the core conceptual categories, their constituent subcategories, and their relationships are adequately specified and developed. (The term *selective coding* is frequently used to denote this phase of analytic activity.) Thus, researchers engage in either a highly selective sampling of additional new data or a reexamination of their existing data resources to make sure that they have fully described the theoretical categories on which their analytic focus settles.

This is also the stage in the analytic process at which it is appropriate to introduce into researchers' thinking existing theorizing that is relevant to the theoretical categories. Thus, researchers look for ways in which their theoretical framework confirms, challenges, or extends existing ways of conceptualizing the phenomena of interest.

As the process of analysis draws to resolution, researchers' commitment to the story their data allow them to tell through the developed theoretical framework will invariably leave remaining some categories and their expressing data fragments that are of no relevance. Those categories will be dropped from the theoretical framework. However, to make sure that they do not prematurely eliminate from analytic consideration data and categories that are material to their developed framework, researchers can go through the following checking procedures (Corbin, 1986). First, they can examine the category to see if its indicating data fragments can be incorporated under another broader existing category. Second, they can examine the categories and their data fragments with an eye toward collapsing the outlying category with another into a renamed and reworked more general category. If these checks cannot identify any materiality to the outlying category, it may be dropped at the conclusion of the analysis. In the final stage of analysis, researchers do not have to force their framework to account for all the variation in their data.

In bringing this discussion of the development of conceptual categories to a close, it is important to recognize that although the conceptual categories and their proposed integrating framework certainly do stabilize in the light of the collected data, the theoretical framework will never be finished in any ultimate sense. Rather, the research will reach a point where the theoretical frame is sufficiently robust to have something substantive to say about the research topic. In this light, the theoretical framework is perhaps better thought of more as a kind of theoretical place marker (Weick, 1995) in the development of thinking about a phenomenon and less as a completed formal theory.

Advantages to a Grounded Theory Building Approach

This theory-building approach to inquiry has much to recommend it in the study of phenomena in complex social systems such as work organizations. Five features in particular stand out (Locke, 2001). First, the grounded theory approach is well suited to capture the complexity that may be involved in the issue being researched. Grounded theory is able to produce a generalized account of organizational action that is multifaceted (Martin & Turner, 1986), explaining that action, for example, in terms of the context in which it occurs, the actions of key players, and the processes through which action unfolds.

Second, grounded theory links well to practice. Because it conforms closely to the situations studied, its theoretical outcomes are likely to be understandable and useful to those who live and work in those situations (Turner, 1983). Kahn's (1993) study of a social service agency draws on a grounded theory approach to conceptualize behaviors and patterns of caregiving among agency members. The conceptualization of agency members' own communications and behaviors results in theory through which members can readily apprehend and gain perspective on themselves and their work experiences.

Third, the approach's theory-building orientation grounded in naturalistic data permit the investigation and theoretical development of new phenomena and issues as they arrive on the organizational scene. For example, when plant closings and downsizing became a feature of managerial life in the 1980s, Harris and Sutton (1986) drew on grounded theory to conceptualize those processes associated with organizational death. Fourth, the grounded theory building approach is useful in bringing new perspectives to already mature theoretical areas, thereby enlivening them. For example, Parry (1998) has described how a grounded theory building approach might be used to refresh the mature area of leadership. Indeed, Strauss (1970) himself noted that grounded theory's analytic procedures could be used to extend and enrich existing theory that has been empirically developed. Vaughan (1983, 1992) has applied the procedural logic of grounded theory to elaborate Robert Merton's theory on social structure and anomie into a broad theory of organizational misconduct.

Finally, the grounded theory building approach is useful in the development of dynamic process-oriented theories that explain how outcomes come about. For example, Eisenhardt (1989) developed a model that explained how and why senior executives are able to make fast strategic decisions in turbulent environments. Similarly, Turner (1976) drew on the grounded theory approach to explain how large-scale industrial disasters occur.

References

Agar, M. H. (1980). *The professional stranger: An informal introduction to ethnography.* Orlando, FL: Academic Press.

Blumer, H. (1969). *Symbolic interactionism: Perspective and method.* Upper Saddle River, NJ: Prentice Hall.

Bryman, A., & Burgess, R. (Eds.). (1999a). *Methods of qualitative research.* Thousand Oaks, CA: Sage.

Bryman, A., & Burgess, R. (Eds.). (1999b). *Analysis and interpretation of qualitative data.* Thousand Oaks, CA: Sage.

Burgess, R. (1984). *In the field: An introduction to field research.* London: Allen & Unwin.

Charmaz, K. (1990). "Discovering" chronic illness: Using grounded theory. *Sociology of Science and Medicine, 30*(11), 1161–1172.

Chenitz, W. C. (1986). The informal interview. In W. C. Chenitz & J. M. Swanson (Eds.), *From practice to grounded theory: Qualitative research in nursing* (pp. 79–90). Reading, MA: Addison-Wesley.

Chenitz W. C., & Swanson, J. M. (1986). Qualitative research using grounded theory. In W. C. Chenitz & J. M. Swanson (Eds.), *From practice to grounded theory: Qualitative research in nursing* (pp. 3–15). Reading, MA: Addison-Wesley.

Collins, R., & Makowsky, M. (1978). *The discovery of society.* New York: Random House.

Corbin, J. (1986). Qualitative data analysis for grounded theory. In W. C. Chenitz & J. M. Swanson (Eds.), *From practice to grounded theory: Qualitative research in nursing* (pp. 91–101). Reading, MA: Addison-Wesley.

Corbin, J., & Strauss, A. L. (1990). Grounded theory research: Procedures, canons and evaluative criteria. *Qualitative Sociology, 13,* 3–21.

Denzin, N. (1994). The art and politics of interpretation. In N. K. Denzin & Y. S. Lincoln (Eds.), *Handbook of qualitative research* (pp. 500–515). Thousand Oaks, CA: Sage.

Denzin, N., & Lincoln, Y. (Eds.). (1998a). *Strategies of qualitative inquiry.* Thousand Oaks, CA: Sage.

Denzin, N., & Lincoln, Y. (Eds.). (1998b). *Collecting and interpreting qualitative materials.* Thousand Oaks, CA: Sage.

Eco, U. (1976). *A theory of semiotics.* Bloomington: University of Indiana Press.

Eisenhardt, K. M. (1989). Making fast strategic decisions in high-velocity environments. *Academy of Management Journal, 32,* 543–576.

Feldman, M. S. (1995). *Strategies for interpreting qualitative data.* Thousand Oaks, CA: Sage.

Foote Whyte, W. (1984). *Learning from the field: A guide from experience.* Thousand Oaks, CA: Sage.

Garfinkle, H. (1967). *Studies in ethnomethodology.* Cambridge: Polity Press.

Glaser, B. G. (1978). *Theoretical sensitivity.* Mill Valley, CA: Sociology Press.

Glaser, B. G., & Strauss, A. L. (1967). *The discovery of grounded theory.* Hawthorne, NY: Aldine de Gruyter.

Hammersley, M., & Atkinson, P. (1983). *Ethnography: Principles in practice.* New York: Tavistock.

Harris, S. G., & Sutton, R. I. (1986). Functions of parting ceremonies in dying organizations. *Academy of Management Journal, 29,* 5–30.

Hawk, T. F. (1991). *Collateral/parallel organizing for strategic change.* Unpublished doctoral dissertation, University of Pittsburgh.

Heritage, J. (1984). *Garfinkel and ethnomethodology.* Cambridge: Polity Press.

Jacob, E. (1988). Clarifying qualitative research: A focus on traditions. *Educational Researcher, 17*(1), 16–24.

Kahn, W. A. (1993). Caring for the caregivers: Patterns of organizational caregiving. *Administrative Science Quarterly, 38,* 539–563.

Kuhn, T. (1970). *The structure of scientific revolutions* (2nd ed.). Chicago: University of Chicago Press.

Layder, D. (1994). *Understanding social theory*. Thousand Oaks, CA: Sage.

Locke, K. (2001). *Grounded theory in management research*. Thousand Oaks, CA: Sage.

Locke, K., & Golden-Biddle, K. (1997). Constructing opportunities for contribution: Structuring intertextual coherence and problematizing in organization studies. *Academy of Management Journal, 40*(5), 1023–1062.

Locke, K., & Golden-Biddle, K. (2001). An introduction to qualitative research: Its potential for industrial/organizational psychology. In S. Rogelberger (Ed.), *Handbook of research methods in industrial and organizational psychology*. Cambridge, MA: Blackwell.

Lofland, J., & Lofland, L. (1984). *Analyzing social settings: A guide to qualitative observation and analysis* (2nd ed.). Belmont, CA: Wadsworth.

Manning, P. K. (1987). *Semiotics and fieldwork*. Thousand Oaks, CA: Sage.

Martin, P., & Turner, B. (1986). Grounded theory and organizational research. *Journal of Applied Behavioral Science, 22*, 141–157.

Maxwell, J. A. (1998). Designing a qualitative study. In L. Bickman & D. J. Rog (Eds.), *Handbook of applied social research methods* (pp. 69-100). Thousand Oaks, CA: Sage.

McCracken, G. (1988). The long interview. *Qualitative research methods, 13*. Thousand Oaks, CA: Sage.

Parry, K. W. (1998). Grounded theory and social process: A new direction for leadership research. *Leadership Quarterly, 9*, 85–106.

Patton, M. Q. (1990). *Qualitative evaluation and research methods* (2nd ed.). Thousand Oaks, CA: Sage.

Pettigrew, A. M. (1990). Longitudinal field research on change: Theory and practice. *Organization Science, 1*, 267–292.

Prus, R. (1996). *Symbolic interaction and ethnographic research: Intersubjectivity and the study of human lived experience*. Albany: State University of New York Press.

Rennie, D. L. (1998). Grounded theory methodology: The pressing need for a coherent logic of justification. *Theory and Psychology, 8*, 101–120.

Rennie, D. L., Phillips, J. R., & Quartaro, G. K. (1988). Grounded theory: A promising approach to conceptualization in psychology? *Canadian Psychology, 29*, 139–150.

Ross, J., & Staw, B. M. (1993). Organizational escalation and exit: Lessons from the Shoreham nuclear power plant. *Academy of Management Journal, 36*, 701–732.

Rubin, H., & Rubin, I. (1995). *Qualitative interviewing: The art of hearing data*. Thousand Oaks, CA: Sage.

Sacks, H., Schegloff, E., & Jefferson, G. (1974). A symplist systematics for the organization of turn-taking in conversation. *Language, 50*, 696–735.

Schatzman, L., & Strauss, A. L. (1973). *Field research: Strategies for a natural sociology*. Upper Saddle River, NJ: Prentice Hall.

Spradley, J. P. (1979). *The ethnographic interview*. New York: Holt.

Spradley, J. P. (1980). *Participant observation*. New York: Holt.

Stake, R. E. (1995). *The art of case study research*. Thousand Oaks, CA: Sage.

Strauss, A. L. (1970). Discovering new theory from previous theory. In T. Shibutani (Ed.), *Human nature and collective theory*. Upper Saddle River, NJ: Prentice Hall.

Strauss, A. L. (1987). *Qualitative analysis for social scientists*. Cambridge: Cambridge University Press.

Strauss, A. L., & Corbin, J. (1990). *Basics of qualitative research: Grounded theory procedures and techniques*. Thousand Oaks, CA: Sage.

Strauss, A. L., & Corbin, J. (1998). *Basics of qualitative research: Techniques and procedures for developing grounded theory* (2nd ed.). Thousand Oaks, CA: Sage.

Swanson, J. M. (1986). The formal qualitative interview for grounded theory. In W. C. Chenitz & J. M. Swanson (Eds.), *From practice to grounded theory: Qualitative research in nursing* (pp. 65–78). Reading, MA: Addison-Wesley.

Turner, B. A. (1976). The organizational and interorganizational development of disasters. *Administrative Science Quarterly, 21,* 378–397.

Turner, B. A. (1981). Some practical aspects of qualitative data analysis: One way of organising the cognitive processes associated with the generation of grounded theory. *Quality and Quantity, 15,* 225–247.

Turner, B. A. (1983). The use of grounded theory for the qualitative analysis of organizational behavior. *Journal of Management Studies, 20,* 333–347.

Vaughan, D. (1983). *Controlling unlawful organizational behavior: Social structure and corporate misconduct*. Chicago: University of Chicago Press.

Vaughan, D. (1992). Theory elaboration: The heuristics of case analysis. In C. C. Ragin & H. S. Becker (Eds.), *What is a case? Exploring the foundations of social inquiry* (pp. 173–202). Cambridge University Press.

Weick, K. E. (1995). What theory is not, theorizing is. *Administrative Science Quarterly, 40,* 385–390.

Woods, P. (1992). Symbolic interactionism: Theory and method. In M. D. LeCompte, W. L. Millroy, & J. Preissle (Eds.), *The handbook of qualitative research in education* (pp. 337–404). Orlando, FL: Academic Press.

Yin, R. K. (1994). *Case study research: Design and methods* (2nd ed.). Thousand Oaks, CA: Sage.

CHAPTER 3

Computer-Based Advances in Assessment

Julie B. Olson-Buchanan

Recent changes in computer technology have been revolutionary. Computers are now relatively inexpensive and accessible, and they can incorporate multiple types of media, including sound, video, and animation. These technological changes have important implications for how individual differences can be measured. We are no longer limited to the traditional assessments on which most of our practice and research was founded. Advances in computer technology allow us more easily to develop such innovative assessments as those that adapt to an assessee's ability (for example, Segall & Moreno, 1999), use full-motion video and sound (for example, McHenry & Schmitt, 1994), or simulate a complex job (for example, Hanson, Borman, Mogilka, Manning, & Hedge, 1999).

Several researchers have examined issues related to computer-based assessment (CBA) and have developed innovative CBAs for selection or training purposes. However, in general, the innovations in CBA have not kept pace with the progress in computer technol-

I thank Ellen M. Day for her help with the literature review, Timothy J. Buchanan and Constance Jones for their editing assistance, and Alan D. Mead for his very helpful suggestions and comments on a draft of this chapter.

ogy. This disparity can be attributed to at least three major factors: (1) the earlier prohibitive costs of CBA development (Drasgow, Olson, Keenan, Moberg, & Mead, 1993), (2) the lag in scientific guidance for addressing the psychometric and methodological issues raised by CBAs (Desmarais et al., 1992; Olson-Buchanan & Drasgow, 1999), and (3) the concern about whether the financial investment in CBAs will result in commensurate improvements (such as increased reliability and validity).

This chapter discusses the innovative ways in which computers can be and have been used to measure individual differences. It begins by briefly describing some of the earlier uses of computers to measure individual differences and then explores assessments that use unique characteristics of computers to display stimuli or measure responses. In the second section, some of the reasons for using CBA are presented. The third section focuses on problems that might be encountered in developing and using CBAs. Finally, it describes the typical development process, provides an illustrative example, discusses available platforms, and then presents possible directions for future research.

Types of Computer-Based Assessment

The research on types of CBAs has been varied. Some research focuses on the type of stimuli presented, and other research emphasizes the adaptivity of the assessment or the mode by which it is delivered. The three-dimensional taxonomy of CBAs in Figure 3.1 (A. D. Mead, personal communication, June 1, 2000) provides a useful structure for discussing this research. Three simplified dimensions of CBAs, selected because of their theoretical or practical significance, are presented in the taxonomy. The Interactivity dimension is the extent to which the presented stimuli vary by the examinees' responses. The Stimuli Presentation dimension reflects the variety and to some extent the realism of the items (or stimuli) presented to examinees. The third dimension, Delivery Mode, is the means by which the assessment is delivered. Some of the cells are fairly sparse (primarily for technical reasons). For example, delivering a multimedia CBA over the Internet is still a technical challenge.

Figure 3.1. A Three-Dimensional Taxonomy of CBAs.

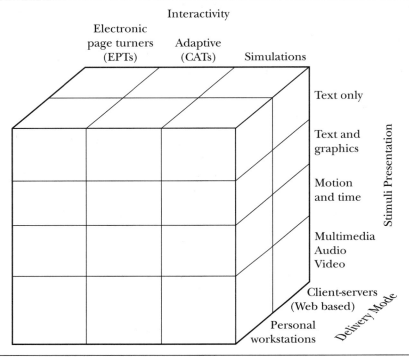

Source: A. D. Mead, personal communication, June 1, 2000.

Interactivity

Most of the earliest research relates to the Interactivity dimension. This dimension ranges from CBAs that are in no way affected by examinees' responses (electronic page turners) to assessments tailored to the examinees' responses.

Electronic Page Turners

Some of the earliest CBAs simply used the technology as a means of administering tests that had traditionally been presented on paper (Fleishman, 1988). These tests are low in interactivity because all examinees receive the same items regardless of their responses. The items in electronic page turners (EPTs) are static in that they do not take advantage of some of the dynamic capabilities of computers (to display motion and so forth). However, the computers of this era were considerably less capable than modern computers.

Although EPTs do not exploit the unique capabilities of modern computers, they do offer several potential advantages over their paper-and-pencil counterparts. First, they can help make the test administration process easier and more standardized. That is, the computer can perform several duties traditionally performed by test administrators: control the amount of time a test taker has to complete a section, distribute and collect different sections of the test, and give consistent directions. Also, computers can minimize scoring errors and ease data management and analysis. In addition, with proper programming safeguards, EPTs can be used to protect the content of a test to some extent. Given the amount of money spent on developing and validating tests, the security of test content is of great concern to organizations.

When EPTs were introduced, it was not clear if the change of medium would affect their validity (see for example Fleishman, 1988). Specifically, would the test taker's familiarity and facility with computers affect performance on such tests, and would computerized tests measure a different construct? Mead and Drasgow's meta-analysis (1993) included a comparison of computerized assessments (which varied in Interactivity) and their paper-and-pencil counterparts. They found strong evidence for the equivalence of paper-and-pencil and computerized power tests. This is an especially encouraging finding because of the heavy use of power tests for selection.

Mead and Drasgow (1993) also indicated that there was a medium effect of computerized administration for speeded tests. Given that the meta-analysis was based on studies primarily conducted in the 1980s, when most people were less familiar with computers, it would not be surprising to see this effect lessened (or eliminated) in a follow-up meta-analysis of more recent studies. Perhaps today test takers are more computer savvy and are becoming equally adept at striking a key on a keyboard as they are filling in a bubble on a sheet.

Computer-Adaptive Tests

A substantial amount of research has focused on the development and use of computer-adaptive tests (CATs). CATs are an excellent example of using the advancements in technology as a vehicle to support innovation in measurement theory (Chapters Four through Six, this volume). With conventional tests, all examinees are given the same set of items to answer. As a result, high performers typically answer a number of questions that are far too easy, and low performers attempt to answer a number of questions that are far too difficult. Items that are considerably too easy or too difficult provide relatively little, if any, useful information and are not the most efficient use of time. In contrast, CATs use item response theory (IRT) as a foundation (see for example, Drasgow & Hulin, 1990). Instead of estimating an examinee's underlying trait by summing the number of correctly answered items, as is done for true score with classical test theory, IRT gives an estimate of an examinee's underlying trait (usually called theta) based on the difficulty of the items correctly or incorrectly answered. The difficulty of the items is determined by fitting item models to a substantial amount of pretest data for a large pool of potential items. The test taker's ability can then be inferred from item responses even if different test takers respond to different sets of items.

For a given CAT, examinees are often first presented with a set of test items of average difficulty. If the examinee answers these questions well, then a set of more difficult items is presented. Conversely, if an examinee answers this first set poorly, then he or she would be presented with a set of easier items. This process continues until the examinee's ability can be estimated at a certain, predetermined level of accuracy. (For additional details of IRT as it relates to CATs, see Lord, 1980.)

Consequently, items in an IRT-based assessment will vary between test takers because the test adapts to their performance. This type of assessment would be very labor intensive (and tedious) to administer by paper or face-to-face. However, the proliferation of computers has enabled the practical application of IRT to the development of CATs.

Although it can be expensive to develop and calibrate the requisite item pool for CATs, these assessments do offer several advantages. First, because it is unlikely that examinees will be presented with identical items (even those who are performing similarly), the integrity of the test is less likely to be threatened (Mead & Drasgow, 1993; Zickar, Overton, Taylor, & Harms, 1999). Second, items in a CAT are carefully selected to provide the maximum amount of information. Consequently, examinees (and organizations) do not need to spend unnecessary time and effort with items that are too difficult or too easy. This may result in less fatigue for the examinees and less time needed for test administration.

A wide range of organizations have already developed and implemented CATs for a variety of purposes and benefits. For example, Zickar et al. (1999) developed a CAT for computer programmers that helped to improve test security. The CAT version of the Armed Services Vocational Aptitude Battery enjoys significantly better parallel-forms reliability for many of its subtests relative to its paper-and-pencil counterpart (Segall & Moreno, 1999). A CAT version of the Graduate Record Examination (Mills, 1999) and CAT versions of certification exams (Bergstrom & Lunz, 1999) have also been developed and successfully implemented.

Other Adaptive Tests

Other adaptive tests have been developed that branch to different items (or scenarios) based on the test taker's responses to earlier items. For example, Olson-Buchanan et al. (1998) developed the Conflict Resolution Skills Assessment (CRSA) using full-motion video. Each assessee views the same main scene that depicts a manager as he or she learns about a conflict (either directly or indirectly) from others in the organization. At a critical decision point in the scenario, the video freezes, and the assessee is presented with four options for responding to the situation. After the assessee selects one of the options, the computer branches to another scene that corresponds with a possible consequence of the option the assessee selected. Thus, the CRSA adapts to the test taker's responses to the assessment.

This type of branching or adaptive assessment raises several psychometric issues. Unlike CATs, there is no underlying measurement theory (like IRT) to drive the scoring or determine how to measure the reliability. However, researchers have developed solutions that work for these and similar tests. For example, Olson-Buchanan et al. (1998) used a combination of conflict theory and empirical scoring to determine test takers' scores (and these scores were significantly related to performance on the job). Such psychometric issues are discussed in more detail below.

Simulations

Given the capabilities of modern computers, CBAs could be developed in the form of partial or full simulations. This would be especially useful for jobs in which the organization expects applicants to already have the requisite knowledge, skills, and abilities to perform the job. In the CBA taxonomy (see Figure 3.1), a simulation would be a highly fluid assessment, with the content of the rich stimuli continually changing based on the test taker's responses. For example, consider products created in the video game industry. Some "assessments" are highly fluid in that the game player's responses (for example, throwing a water balloon by hitting a button; the water balloon misses the target and splatters on the floor) and affect what is displayed (the player's image slips on the water on the floor and is dropped to a lower level). These responses and consequences ultimately affect the player's score. Although we do not have examples of such fluid simulations in our field, it is conceivable that they could be developed for appropriate jobs. Simulations may be especially useful for jobs that require continuous motion and coordination.

Stimuli Presentation

Even before technological advances and increased computer manufacturing competition made color monitors and CD-ROM drives commonplace, several test developers were exploring the ways in which computers could present different stimuli. That is, how could these slick features be used to measure different knowledge, skills, and abilities or measure the old standbys better? The ways in which the computer has been used to present assessment stimuli to examinees will be discussed here.

Text Only

One of the simplest forms of presentation, text, has often been used in EPTs as well as many CATs (see Mead & Drasgow, 1993, for examples). Given the popularity (and history) of using text as stimuli in conventional paper-and-pencil tests, the practice of computerizing text has not generated much interest as a research topic. However, when presenting text in CBAs, developers often pay close attention to the readability of the text (on a monitor) and whether one or more questions can be shown on a page. Many of the assessments discussed here have at least some text in the stimuli or item presentation.

Text and Graphics

Historically, illustrative graphics and pictures have also been used as test stimuli for a number of selection measures. For example, the Bennett Mechanical Comprehension test presents black-and-white drawings of everyday objects and simple tools, and the Differential Aptitude Tests (DAT) Space Relations subtest presents drawings of unfolded and folded boxes. Tests like these have certainly been useful and valid for organizations over the years (for example, Muchinsky, 1993). The simple black-and-white drawings are fairly inexpensive to reproduce yet convey enough information to make important distinctions among examinees.

Certainly, high-resolution color graphs or photographs have been used as stimuli without the assistance of computers. For example, photographs and color graphics can be printed in test booklets or presented to examinees on slides. However, printing in color can be prohibitively expensive, and presenting test stimuli using a slide projector creates problems with respect to whether examinees have equal proximity to the projected image, whether the amount of time allowed to view the slide is accurately controlled, and whether group administration is the most efficient use of time.

In contrast, it has become fairly easy to display and modify high-resolution color graphs and photos on a computer. Ackerman, Evans, Park, Tamassia, and Turner (1999) took advantage of this technology advancement by developing a computerized assessment for diagnosing skin disorders that served to replace an existing slide-based test. Each examinee is given a description of the patient's history and symptoms and is shown a high-resolution image of the afflicted skin. Examinees are then able to zoom in or out on the picture before selecting a diagnosis.

The use of computer-based color graphics and photographs as test stimuli offers several potential benefits. This technology could be used for a variety of employment tests. For example, work simulations of occupations that rely heavily on graphical input (such as architects and graphic artists) or pictorial input (such as medical slide examiner or those in law enforcement) could be developed.

Computers can allow all test takers an unobstructed, equal view of the test stimuli and can standardize the amount of time examinees view the stimuli. The items can be richer, realistic, and presumably more interesting to the examinees than simple black-and-white drawings or low-resolution photographs. This increased interest may translate into higher motivation to perform well on the test. Whether these potential advantages result in higher validity remains to be seen, but they may serve to improve perceptions of face validity. However, the high-resolution color images may be expensive in terms of memory required, and color blindness may affect test takers' performance.

Motion

The benefits of CBAs go beyond convenience and clarity: computers can provide the means to measure abilities that cannot be measured as well as or at all with traditional testing methods. In particular, the computer's capability of displaying motion is useful for creating dynamic stimuli that arguably better reflect the moving world in which we learn and work.

The multidimensionality of visual-spatial ability (for example, Lohman, 1979) and its importance in predicting job performance for certain occupations has been well established. However, Hunt, Pellegrino, and colleagues have argued (for example, Hunt & Pellegrino, 1985) that conventional measures of visual-spatial ability are too narrow because they have primarily been limited to static paper-and-pencil tests. For example, in the DAT's Spatial subtest (Bennett, Seashore, & Wesman, 1974), a sample item consists of a black-and-white drawing of an unfolded box on the left and several folded boxes on the right. The test takers are asked to fold the box mentally and identify which box on the right it matches. However, items like these do not require a test taker to visualize how these objects might move in space. Suppose these same boxes were thrown into the air at a certain trajectory. At what point would the box's path intercept with another target object, like a wall? Hunt, Pellegrino, and colleagues suggest that the ability to visually manipulate static displays (such as an unfolded box) may or may not predict the ability to reason about objects in motion.

Computers provide the means to present visual-spatial ability test items with a motion component. Hunt, Pellegrino, Frick, Farr, and Alderton (1988) developed six computer-based visual-spatial ability tests that included a motion component and compared performance on these dynamic displays to performance on traditional static tests (both paper and pencil and computer based). Their results indicated that the ability to reason from dynamic visual-spatial items was "correlated with, but distinct from" (p. 98) the ability to reason from traditional static visual-spatial ability items. In addition, the researchers reported reasonably high reliabilities for most of these dynamic display computer-based tests.

The Project A test battery (Peterson, 1987; Peterson et al., 1990) includes a computer-based dynamic visual-spatial ability test. The Cannon Shoot Test requires test takers to release a cannon shell so it will intersect a moving target. Thus, to perform well on this test, examinees must be able to extrapolate the paths (or motion) of the shell and moving target. The researchers reported moderate (test-retest) to high (split-half) reliabilities with this assessment, and it is included in a battery of tests demonstrated to be strongly related to job performance criteria.

As we continue to think outside of the box, we will likely identify other ways in which definitions of constructs may be limited by the staticity of conventional measurement tools. For example, are there other dimensions of g that have a motion component? The computer's ability to display motion has already been used to develop tracking tests that display a moving target and measure how well examinees anticipate the moving target. These applications will be discussed more fully later in this chapter.

Time

Often test administrators control the amount of time a test taker has to attempt to complete a conventional paper-and-pencil test. Time limits are usually imposed on EPTs as well. However, rarely has conventional test administration limited the amount of time that test takers can spend on individual test items. CBA provides a relatively easy means for controlling the amount of time a test item is presented or the amount of time an examinee can use to respond to an item; assessing response latency is discussed later in this chapter.

There are several ways in which the time-control features of computers can be and have been used to create useful assessments.

One of the most popular applications is the computer-based memory and cognition assessment. Researchers (Barrett, Alexander, Doverspike, Cellar, & Thomas, 1982; Chiang & Atkinson, 1976) have used Sternberg's paradigm (1966) to create reliable CBAs of short-term memory in which the test taker has a limited time to view the stimuli. The cognitive revolution of the 1980s brought increased attention to how these "content-free" measures of intelligence could be applied to a selection context (Drasgow et al., 1993). For example, a short-term memory assessment was developed for Project A and was included in the final battery (Peterson, 1987; Peterson et al., 1990). Similar computer-based measures are included in selection test batteries for helicopter pilots (Myers, Schemmer, & Fleishman, 1983) and airplane pilots (Caretta, 1987).

The time-control feature of computers can also be used to help create computer-based test batteries for jobs that require speed and accuracy, especially those that involve extensive computer usage. For example, Schmitt, Gilliland, Landis, and Devine (1993) developed a CBA for selecting secretaries consisting of eight secretarial tasks typically done by computer, such as using e-mail and word processing. Both the word processing test and correction test were time controlled. Specifically, the time feature was used to help determine typing speed and accuracy, as well as to control the amount of time applicants could attempt to identify errors within a body of text. In addition, the computer controlled the timing of another interruption. The battery has many desirable features, including job relevance, favorable examinee reactions, and ease of administration.

The time-control feature of CBAs should prove to be of continuing value in the future. Perhaps a new generation of perceptual speed and accuracy CBAs can be developed. In addition, there are a number of jobs (among them, bank tellers, inspectors, and assembly-line workers) in which workers have very little time to identify and categorize stimuli. A simulation that relies on the time-control feature of computers would be well suited for these types of jobs.

Audio Multimedia

Audio stimuli have long been used for measuring skills such as foreign language or musical abilities (see for example Seashore, 1919). In the past, such tests typically required dedicated equipment and a great deal of administrative effort. Audio-based tests have evolved with the changes in computer technology. Earlier assessments used specialized audio equipment with a mainframe computer (for example, Kuhn & Allvin, 1967), and then personal computers equipped with videodiscs (for example, Vispoel & Coffman, 1992) were used. Today, cheap, high-capability hard drives or CD-ROM drives can be efficient means to store high-quality audio stimuli, and virtually all PCs are equipped with sound cards and speakers or headphones.

Vispoel (1999) developed a CAT for measuring tonal memory. Assessees listen to two sets of notes and are asked whether the two sets are the same or different. Items include tonal and atonal strings of notes played on a piano or synthesizer. The CAT has been developed or modified for three platforms: the PLATO mainframe with a synthesizer box, a PC-video disk version, and a Power Macintosh-HyperCARD version (Vispoel, 1999). Several studies have demonstrated that the CAT achieves the same reliability as other tonal memory tests with anywhere from 72 to 93 percent fewer items than non-CAT versions (Vispoel, 1999). In addition, the CAT matched the nonadaptive versions' concurrent validity with significantly fewer items (50 to 87 percent).

The audio capabilities of computers are well suited for other types of listening skills as well. Several jobs, such as customer service operators and computer help-desk technicians, require a great deal of auditory input. Audio-based computer-administered items of customers describing various complaints, clients describing software problems, or callers leaving messages could be used to measure an applicant's ability to attend to the key information needed to perform well on the job.

Hanson et al. (1999) used the audio capabilities of computers to develop the Computer-Based Performance Measure (CBPM) to serve as a criterion measure for validating a computer-based test battery for air traffic controllers. Given the complexities and importance of measuring job performance accurately, the researchers decided to develop a work sample assessment that would allow an even playing field for participants in the concurrent validation study.

The air sector that the job incumbents are required to control in the CBPM is generic to prevent advantage derived from experience with a particular sector yet simple enough for the incumbent to learn easily for the assessment. The graphical image shown on the computer screen represents the display that is seen on an air traffic controller's radar screen. In conjunction with visual stimuli, voices of pilots and other controllers are presented with the use of a CD-ROM. Interestingly, audio is also used in the presentation of the questions. The items (with multiple-choice options) are read aloud as they are presented in written format on the screen to prevent the possible influence of reading ability on performance scores. Hanson et al. (1999) present strong construct validity evidence for the CBPM. In particular, performance on the CBPM correlates highly with performance on a very expensive air traffic control simulator. Thus, the Hanson et al. assessment takes full advantage of standard computer features (such as CD-ROM) to measure job performance efficiently and innovatively.

The use of sound as stimuli has several benefits, including possible increased realism and increased accessibility for the blind or for individuals with limited reading ability. However, there are several practical issues to consider. Specifically, how should the sound be projected (speakers or headphones)? Also, test developers need to pay close attention to distortion problems. Some technologies may result in more distortion than others or may distort under varying conditions.

Multimedia: Full-Motion Video and Audio

The introduction of disc players—laser, CD-ROM, and now digital video display (DVD)—has provided the technological means to present full-motion video and stereo audio using a personal computer. Certainly, video stimuli can be presented in noncomputer-based assessments (such as videocassette recorders). However, CBAs that present video stimuli offer several potential benefits. First, these assessments are easier to administer in a standardized manner because the computer performs all necessary cueing, and discs do not degrade even after repeated use. Stimuli can be edited postproduction using the computer if necessary. In addition, the programming capabilities of a computer can be used to create adaptive or interactive assessments that, like CATs, will branch to new items (or scenes) depending on the test takers' responses.

Several pioneers developed computer-based video assessments soon after the technology became available but before it became widely accessible, as it is today. One early effort was the Workplace Situations Test developed by IBM to select manufacturing employees (see for example Desmarais et al., 1992). The assessment was constructed to measure situational judgment skills. Test takers view scenes of Quintronics (a fictional organization) employees dealing with such job-related issues as poor performance and demanding workloads. At the end of each scene, the test takers are given five multiple-choice options and are asked to select the one that best reflects how they would respond to the situation depicted in the scene.

In Allstate's Multimedia In-Basket (Ashworth & Joyce, 1994; Ashworth & McHenry, 1993), test takers take on the role of customer service agent for a fictional airline. In that role, the assessees must consult flight schedules, regulations, and policies to set up and revise travel plans for clients. In addition, the assessees must communicate with the customers on these arrangements.

Given the proprietary nature of IBM's and Allstate's assessments, most information about the psychometric properties (specifically validity) is unavailable. However, the developers were able to share their experiences in developing (Ashworth & McHenry, 1992; Desmarais et al., 1992) and scoring the assessments (Ashworth & Joyce, 1994; Desmarais, Masi, Olson, Barbera, & Dyer, 1994).

Haak (1993) developed a computer-assisted interactive video simulation to measure clinical nursing judgment performance. The video stimulus begins with a patient complaining of chest pain. The test taker is asked to identify the most urgent problems and courses of action, if any. If the test taker recommends a particular action, the assessment branches to a video that provides feedback about that action (such as the patient's response or test results). Haak used a set of experts to develop and score the test takers' responses to the simulation. She found the video simulation was useful for differentiating among levels of nurse performance and found evidence for moderate to high content validity, as well as some evidence for construct validity.

Olson-Buchanan et al. (1998) developed the adaptive CRSA that was discussed earlier. The content for the conflict scenarios was derived from critical-incidents collected from a variety of managers representing a number of industries. After several development steps (see Drasgow et al., 1999), the final assessment included full-motion video and stereo sound to present the instructions, main conflict scenes, and branch scenes. The CRSA's validity results (from a diverse set of managers) are very encouraging.

Most video-based assessments were presented in various stages at academic conferences in the early 1990s. Topics included developing the stimuli, managing the logistics of the project, scoring issues, and validity results, among others. Although the demonstrations were crowd pleasers, relatively few researchers have pursued this research. This can be explained, at least in part, by the relatively high barriers to entry in terms of both development and equipment cost in the early 1990s. In addition, these types of assessments introduced a number of unique psychometric issues, which will be highlighted and explained later in this chapter.

Delivery Mode

The means by which CBAs are administered have changed considerably since their inception. Many of the first CBAs were created for large, cumbersome mainframe computers. Options are considerably more flexible today. This section discusses two modes that are primarily used today: personal workstations and the Web.

Personal Workstations

The majority of CBAs discussed in this chapter were developed for use with personal workstations. A typical workstation consists of the CPU, monitor, keyboard, and whatever additional apparatus is needed (such as a CD-ROM drive, mouse, or headphones). If the organization decides to conduct all assessments on-site, a considerable amount of money must be spent to purchase and maintain the necessary equipment. Unfortunately, this equipment is likely to become out-of-date fairly quickly, and the assessment program may need to be changed accordingly (for example, Segall & Moreno, 1999; Vispoel, 1999). In addition, a large organization may have to acquire and maintain the requisite equipment at a number of sites. Researchers at IBM took a creative approach: they created a portable testing station by outfitting a full-size bus with multiple state-of-the-art workstations (Midkiff, Dyer, Desmarais, Rogg, & McCusker, 1992).

Web-Based Assessments

The widespread accessibility of the Internet has enabled computerized assessments to be administered over the World Wide Web. This advancement allows organizations to administer a variety of measurement tools outside the walls of the organization. Applicants can submit applications and resumés or even complete selection assessments from their homes or public Internet access locations.

This technique may provide organizations with a variety of benefits. First, fewer (if any) personal workstations are needed for administering assessments to applicants. This not only saves money but may also free up valuable space. Second, assessments can easily be customized for different purposes and placed on different sites (Donovan, 2000). Third, this method may help break down physical barriers to recruiting and selecting the best people for the job. Applicants or respondents can submit selection information from halfway around the world. In addition, physically disabled applicants can submit information from the comfort of their homes and, possibly, through the use of their computers that have been modified for their needs. However, the additional cost of the server(s) and administrators must be considered.

Several researchers have already developed and successfully administered Internet-based computerized assessment tools. Reynolds, Sinar, Scott, and McClough (2000) designed an electronic version of a biodata instrument and administered it over the Internet to nearly fifteen hundred applicants for a sales position with a large pharmaceuticals firm. They compared the factor structure of the Internet version to a paper-and-pencil version and found sufficiently high-congruence coefficients to conclude that the structures were in fact the same. They did, however, find some demographic differences between Web users and those who elected a paper-and-pencil alternative. The Web-based version resulted in lower effect sizes on the overall score favoring Caucasians over African Americans or Hispanics. However, there was a higher gender effect size (favoring males) in the Web-based version as opposed to the paper-and-pencil version. Stanton (1998) found supportive evidence for the equivalence between Internet-administered and paper-and-pencil versions of a survey.

PricewaterhouseCoopers (Vlug, Furcon, Mondragon, & Mergen, 2000) developed the on-line career link (OCL) to recruit and screen entry-level accountants (and, later, other service lines). The OCL consists of an application form, a biodata and fit questionnaire, and two open-ended questions. Completion of the OCL results in eight competency measures. The concurrent validation revealed significant validities for the eight competencies, with an overall multiple R of .49. Applicants who were recruited on-line did better in the subsequent in-depth interview and assessment center. In addition, the OCL served to reduce the application and screening process by two to three weeks, which is especially important given the high demand and low supply of qualified candidates for these positions.

Web-based assessments can be used for other purposes as well. Donovan (2000) used the Internet as an effective way to collect responses to an attitude survey. One particularly encouraging result from her research was a very high response rate (76 percent). Thus, the convenience of the Internet may serve to improve one of the more frustrating aspects of the research process: getting people to participate. Additional research is needed to determine if this high response rate is consistent after repeated requests and whether it is a robust finding in a variety of samples. Internet companies might use the Internet to collect data for a work sample. For example, Internet search engines must constantly update their databases with information from new or changed sites. Consequently, some companies give applicants for "surfer" positions a period of time to conduct searches on the Internet to determine whether they would be qualified for these jobs.

The use of Web-based assessments is exciting, but there are some potential hurdles. One of the best advantages, convenience, is related to a major drawback, security. Individuals can access the Internet from virtually anywhere. Thus, there is nothing to prevent them from writing down questions or consulting sources before responding (Stanton, 1999). Similarly, there is no way to know if the individual thought to be responding is in fact the individual who is responding (as many chatroom anecdotes will attest). Also, some individuals may be concerned about confidentiality if asked to answer personal questions. Donovan (2000) addressed the confidentiality concern by issuing identification numbers for her survey. Other suggestions, like requiring verifiable personal data or collecting information that can be double-checked in a face-to-face interview, have also been offered (N. J. Mondragon, cited in Stanton, 1999). The accessibility and convenience of the Internet may also lead to less than ideal testing sessions. That is, sources of error (such as distractions) could potentially affect the integrity of the scores. Issues raised by the convenience of Web-based assessments will certainly be hot topics for future research.

Another concern is the variance in transfer time across servers and connections and the variance in legal requirements across countries. The speed variance may have implications for varying reactions to the on-line assessment process (Mead, 2000), in that slower connections may be related to a more frustrating experience for on-line users. International legal issues need to be carefully considered before implementing Web-based assessments globally.

It is interesting to note that the development of Web-based assessments is paralleling the development process of CBAs in general. This is a fairly early stage for Web-based assessment, although its client-server predecessors (mainframes) have been around for a long time. Like early CBTs in general, the Web-based assessments are primarily EPTs, with research emphasis on measurement equivalence. As on-line assessments mature, we will probably see even more innovative uses of the Web for assessing individual differences.

Response Measurement

Another important area of assessment research relates to the development of innovative ways to measure examinee responses to computer-based stimuli. Several of the assessments described present test stimuli in an innovative way but still rely on conventional response measures, such as standard multiple choice (for example, Desmarais et al., 1992; Olson-Buchanan et al., 1998). Other researchers have concentrated on computerizing other types of assessee responses or developing new ways to measure assessee's responses to test stimuli. This section could be added as a fourth dimension of the taxonomy presented in Figure 3.1.

Pen-Based Computer

Although Mead and Drasgow's (1993) meta-analysis demonstrated construct equivalence between paper-and-pencil and computer-based versions of power tests, it did not find a similar pattern for speeded tests. Perhaps the physical differences between entering a key on a keyboard and circling an answer on an answer sheet are especially apparent when time is of the essence. For example, test takers who are more facile with a computer keyboard than a pencil may improve their relative ranking on a computer-based speeded test.

Overton, Taylor, Zickar, and Harms (1996) argue that a pen-based computer that allows a test taker to enter a response by touching a stylus to the monitor may be a closer representation of the motor activities associated with responding to paper-and-pencil tests. In support of this argument, they found strong evidence of construct equivalence between pen-based computer and paper-and-pencil versions for two of three speeded tests examined. This technological innovation and others warrant further investigation as a way to mitigate physical response differences between CBAs and traditional assessments. Regardless of the technology used, when computerizing paper-and-pencil speeded tests, the time limits of the computerized version should be carefully selected and monitored to maximize comparability.

Open-Ended Responses

Researchers have demonstrated ways in which computers can be used to measure more complex responses to computers than simple multiple choice responses. For example, Haak's (1993) interactive video assessment of clinical nursing judgment uses a verbal protocol technique in which respondents type in the questions they would ask the patient, as well as the diagnoses and tests they would request. The computer scans these open-ended responses to determine the next branch scene and stores them for experts to judge and score.

A push in the field of education to develop ways in which computers can be used to score open-ended answers (Bennett, 1998) has already resulted in some successful developments. For example, Page and Peterson (1995) reported that the Project Essay Grade program rated essays nearly as accurately as the combined judgments of three human judges. Bennett, Steffen, Singley, Morley, and Jacquemin (1997) found that the accuracy of their automated program for scoring open-ended responses to mathematical items was largely comparable to the accuracy of scanned multiple-choice responses. Other Educational Testing Service researchers have developed the e-rater automatic scoring system, which "uses natural language processing techniques to model the performance of human evaluators" (Powers, Burstein, Chodorow, Fowles, & Kukich, 2000, p. 4). Powers et al. reported that in a study of two thousand prospective graduate students who wrote two essays, e-rater scores were either exact or within one point of human judges' scores 94 percent of the time. Researchers are continuing to examine ways in which the e-rater system can be improved.

Bejar and colleagues (for example, Bejar, 1991; Williamson, Bejar, & Hone, 1999) have developed and refined a mental-model-based automated method for scoring responses to graphic simulation divisions of the architectural licensing exam. The mental-model was derived from several comprehensive empirical studies designed to capture and identify the bases (criteria, relative weighting, and so forth) that expert raters use to score the items holistically. Not only does this mental-model approach demonstrate a high agreement with independent experts' scores, the validation process is designed to identify and explain why agreements do not occur, thereby allowing further improvement and standardization of the scoring process. Although the amount of effort required to develop mental-models is daunting, the potential to improve validity may make the work worthwhile.

Time

Before the advent of computerization, we had crude ways to measure response latencies. Researchers could measure the amount of time to complete the entire test (and divide by the number of items) or measure the number of items completed during a fixed time interval. Although this provides an overall measure of average time per item, it does not give specific information about, for example, the amount of time needed to respond to simple versus complex items.

A computer can easily and accurately measure response latencies, which can be a useful tool for measuring a test taker's perceptual speed or speed of cognition. Indeed, several organizations have successfully incorporated reaction time measures into their assessment batteries. For example, some of Project A's computerized assessments included response latency measures, all of which had acceptable (or higher) reliability and were shown to be strong predictors of job performance (McHenry, Hough, Toquam, Hanson, & Ashworth, 1990). To illustrate, the Choice Reaction Test gives two target words. The participant must watch the computer screen for these target words and tap the appropriate computer key as quickly as possible after seeing the target. Given all the time in the world, most participants would probably be 100 percent accurate on this type of test. However, military personnel do not have all the time in the world to distinguish accurately between targets and nontargets. Thus, measuring both reaction time and accuracy is critical to the utility of these types of assessments. Other researchers have similarly employed reaction time measures (for example, Carretta, 1987; Myers & Schemmer, 1990).

Motion

Not only can computers present motion in the test stimuli, they can measure the test taker's motions. This capability can be especially useful for measuring a psychomotor skill that requires continuous tracking and motion. Certainly, such skills can be assessed through a performance test or a simulation. For example, bus drivers may have to demonstrate the ability to maneuver a bus between cones in a parking lot, and pilots' skills may be assessed using a flight simulator. However, the financial costs of some simulators may be prohibitive, and organizations may want to prescreen with a computerized assessment. In addition, some organizations (such as the military) are interested in identifying which applicants are most likely to learn well in an expensive training program (such as flight training). Thus, a computerized assessment may provide a less risky or less expensive way to measure a previously developed psychomotor skill or a way to identify who is likely to do well at learning that skill.

Assessments that measure test taker motion have ranged from simple tracking tests (track a moving stimulus with one limb) to complex tracking tests (track a moving stimulus with more than one limb). Simple tracking tests have successfully been used to predict helicopter pilot performance in basic training (Bartram, 1987), nuclear power plant operator performance (Myers &

Schemmer, 1990), and U.S. Army personnel performance (McHenry et al., 1990). Similarly, complex tracking tests have been successfully used to predict success in pilot training (Cox, 1988) and U.S. Army personnel performance (McHenry et al., 1990).

Audio and More?

The innovations to date in computer-based response measurement will appear rudimentary when audio- and even visual-based responses can be easily measured. Vispoel (1999) discussed the possibility of using Musical Instrument Digital Interface (MIDI) devices to record a test taker's musical performance. Similar advances with voice recognition systems might be used to measure verbal fluency, presentation skills, or foreign language skills. High-quality computer cameras could record visual input from applicants and measure such qualities as nonverbal skills. Furthermore, advancements could enable the automatic scoring of this recorded audio input. For example, a voice recognition system could record (and decode) the content of an individual's oral presentation. These data could then be scored with a system similar to what is used for scoring open-ended essays.

When or Why Would CBAs Be Used?

Given the host of assessments that are not computer based, a rational question to ask is, Under what conditions would an organization or researcher benefit from developing or using a CBA?

Ease of Administration

CBAs were originally touted for their improvements in test administration. First, there is less reliance on proctors. Computers can deliver the instructions consistently and, if desired, at the test taker's individual pace or in the test taker's preferred language. This should help to minimize, if not eliminate, potential sources of test administrator error that can threaten an assessment's reliability. Second, assessments can be administered just as easily to individuals or groups because the computer controls the presentation of stimuli, the measurement of responses, and the amount of time allowed. Third, the computer can record and score the response data automatically.

This can help minimize data recording and transfer errors. Overall, the increased ease of administration may result in fewer threats to reliability. Finally, computer-based administration may reduce overall testing and administration time. CATs require fewer items to achieve an acceptable level of reliability (see for example Vispoel, 1999), and CBAs may require less response time to hit a key than fill in a bubble on a test form (Olsen, Maynes, Slawson, & Ho, 1989). Burroughs et al. (1999) demonstrated how a computer-based system could be used to reduce substantially the amount of time needed to make evaluation decisions.

Increased Test Security

Computers can also enhance the integrity of individual test items or entire tests. CATs draw questions from a large item pool and adapt to the examinee's ability. Even test takers with the same ability are unlikely to see the same set of items (Mead & Drasgow, 1993). Non-CATs can enjoy increased test security as well. Personal workstations can be programmed to prevent individuals from saving text information on a disk or to prevent the computer from recognizing unauthorized disks. If an organization is aware that certain items have been leaked, those items can be modified quickly (assuming psychometric equivalence) without additional printing expense. However, the software should be programmed to handle these contingencies, and the costs of incorporating such security safeguards can be high.

Increased Accessibility

Access to computers has increased dramatically in the past decade. In 1998, over 40 percent of American families owned their own computers, a 15 percent increase from 1997 and nearly a 40 percent increase from 1994 (U.S. Department of Commerce, 1999). Access to the Internet has increased considerably as well. By 1999, roughly one-third of all Americans had Internet access (U.S. Department of Commerce, 1999). Globally, it is estimated that 400 million people will have Internet access by 2002 (U.S. Department of Commerce, 1999).

The increased accessibility of personal computers (and the Internet) translates into a wider variety of ways in which an assessment can be delivered. Certainly, organizations can dedicate on-site computers for assessment purposes, but with proper programming, nondedicated on-site computers can be used when applicant volume is unusually high or when it is not financially efficient to dedicate computers for assessment purposes. Assessments can be portable as well. That is, organizations could give applicants a diskette with the assessment on it (or send it as an attachment by e-mail). Organizations have also successfully used the Internet to locate hard-to-find job candidates (Vlug et al., 2000).

Feedback

Some organizations are interested in providing detailed information about why an examinee's overall score is high or low. This information might be desired for a number of different reasons: to diagnose training needs, for personal development, or for heightened fairness perceptions. For example, Schmitt et al.'s (1993) CBA was designed to provide immediate feedback to applicants about their performance on the eight components of the assessment. The organization wanted to continue its practice of providing performance feedback information to applicants so they could pinpoint the skills they need to sharpen and reapply later. Although there is very little published information in the selection literature about how CBAs can be used to provide detailed feedback to examinees, researchers have successfully used the feedback feature for training purposes (Cooper, Phillips, & Ford, 1994).

Accommodation of Disabled Individuals

Computers can better accommodate disabled individuals in a number of ways during the assessment process. For example, instructions and test items can be presented in audio to assessees who are vision impaired or have reading disabilities (see for example Johnson, 1983). Audio-based items can be captioned for hearing-impaired assessees. Applicants with limited hand movements can complete an assessment on a modified computer. Internet-based assessments are particularly accessible to physically disabled individuals in that applicants can complete the assessment in the convenience of their own homes and on their own (possibly modified) computers. Not only can these types of accommodations enable organizations to attract and measure the skills of a rich labor pool better, but they could also help to meet the requirements of the Americans with Disabilities Act of 1990. The extent to which these types of modifications are appropriate is an important area for future research (Campbell & Reilly, 2000).

Improving Examinee Reactions

Several studies have demonstrated that examinees react favorably to CBAs. Schmitt et al. (1993) reported that examinees who completed the new CBA had significantly (and "substantially") better perceptions of the assessment's relevance and fairness compared to examinees who completed the non-computer-based selection battery.

Most recently, researchers have examined assessees' reactions to multimedia assessments and on-line assessments. Richman, Olson-Buchanan, and Drasgow (2000) compared examinee reactions to three versions of the same interactive assessment: paper and pencil, EPT, and multimedia. They found that examinees who completed the multimedia assessment had the highest perceptions of face validity, were more satisfied with the assessment, and found it to be more enjoyable than examinees in the other two conditions. Interestingly, the EPT was not perceived more favorably than the paper-and-pencil counterpart.

Reactions to on-line assessments have been similarly positive. Vlug et al. (2000) reported that 84 percent of those who used the on-line procedure reported a positive experience. Reynolds et al. (2000) found that applicants who completed the Web-based instrument rated it as significantly more fair and more satisfying than did applicants who completed the paper-and-pencil version.

It would be interesting to track examinees' reactions to technology-driven assessments over the next few years. Perhaps as computers become even more commonplace, assessees will expect even more bells and whistles. EPTs have been around for a long time, and this may explain why Richman et al. (2000) did not find enhanced reactions to EPTs relative to a paper-and-pencil version. We may see similar findings for multimedia and on-line assessments a few years from now.

Adverse Impact

Some researchers have found that computerized assessments result in smaller performance differences between various demographic groups. For example, Segall (1997) and Wolfe, Alderton, Larson, Bloxom, and Wise (1997) found smaller differences between African Americans and whites on cognitive computerized assessments than what is typically found on their paper-and-pencil counterparts. Reynolds et al. (2000) found smaller effect sizes for whites over African Americans or Hispanics on the Web-based assessment. Olson-Buchanan et al. (1998) found that African Americans scored significantly higher than whites on their multimedia assessment of conflict resolution skills. However, given the demographic differences in computer ownership and access to the Internet (U.S. Department of Commerce, 1999), researchers should be cautious when designing a computerized assessment to minimize adverse impact.

Incremental Validity

One major factor to consider before investing time and money in developing a new assessment is whether it can provide incremental validity above other measures. There is at least some evidence that CBAs can meet this important criterion. For example, conflict resolution skills would be fairly difficult to measure using traditional assessment methods. However, Olson-Buchanan et al. (1998) found that their CBA of conflict skills provided incremental validity beyond what was provided by a CBA of cognitive ability. Thus, a CBA of a construct that is otherwise difficult to measure can provide additional useful information that may not be provided by the measurement of more pedestrian constructs such as cognitive ability.

Alternative Desiderata

Organizations might consider developing a CBA because it can offer different features from conventional paper-and-pencil assessments or stimulus-rich predictors like assessment centers. First, multimedia CBAs offer increased standardization of the stimuli relative to role-playing exercises and increased administration ease relative to VCR-driven assessments. Second, multimedia CBAs can offer increased fidelity of the stimuli relative to conventional paper-and-pencil assessments. Interactive assessments can provide additional fidelity. Third, CBAs can provide cost-effectiveness relative to such alternatives as assessment centers. CBAs can reduce testing time relative to conventional paper-and-pencil assessment. Fourth, CBAs may project a technologically advanced appearance to candidates.

Challenges in Developing CBAs

CBAs offer many desirable and some unique features. However, researchers are likely to encounter some stumbling blocks in developing or implementing them.

Scoring

Some of the most innovative types of CBAs present the most challenging issues with respect to scoring. For example, consider an adaptive video assessment in which all assessees are shown the same main scene and are directed to select one of four alternatives. Then the video branches to the consequence of the selected option, and the assessee is given a second set of options. How should points be assigned to the options of a follow-up scene that is derived from a "correct" response to the main scene versus those from an "incorrect" response to the main scene? That is, should the assessees be given a clean slate after an incorrect response, or should the scoring algorithm follow the lines of a CAT? In response to this dilemma, one set of test developers elected not to use a branching approach (Desmarais et al., 1994), and another group chose the clean slate approach (Olson-Buchanan et al., 1998).

Fortunately, there is some research that addresses scoring issues. Researchers have described the complex scoring methods they used for multimedia assessments (see for example Ashworth & Joyce, 1994; Drasgow et al., 1999). McHenry and Schmitt (1994) present possible ways to develop scoring keys for multimedia assessments that use either fixed-choice or free-response alternatives. Several groups of researchers have developed innovative ways to evaluate open-ended responses (for example, Bejar, 1991). In addition, a number of articles and chapters describe scoring dilemmas and solutions for CATs (see Drasgow & Olson-Buchanan, 1999, for a review).

Reliability

The reliability of most CBAs poses few, if any, unique challenges. For example, reliability estimates of EPTs can take the form of their paper-and-pencil counterparts (such as coefficient alphas). With more innovative assessments, like tracking tests, researchers can assess test-retest reliability, although there may be some concern about practice effects. A CAT's reliability can be approximated by calculating the posterior variance of the ability estimates or the estimated standard error of measurement (Olson-Buchanan et al., 1998). Many of the audio- or video-based assessments can assess reliability through standard internal consistency measures (for example, Hanson et al., 1999).

However, assessing the reliability of interactive assessments is problematic (Drasgow et al., 1999). Not everyone sees the same branches, which limits the usefulness of internal consistency measures. Unfortunately, test-retest measures are not desirable because assessees are likely to change their answers in a second session because they saw the "consequences" of their actions in the first session. One possible solution is to attempt to make the items as homogeneous as possible to allow item-total correlations to be used instead. However, this may be impractical, and alternative methods need to be developed.

Rapid Changes and Computer Jargon

It is difficult to keep up with the changes in computer technology. Everyone who uses a personal computer knows that a state-of-the-art system becomes outdated all too quickly. Before investing in the development of a CBA, researchers need to understand the capabilities of current technology, as well as anticipate the progression of technology over the expected life of the assessment. These rapid changes in technology can make earlier work obsolete. Pioneers in CBA have commented on the difficulties in maintaining the technology needed to operate an assessment (for example, Midkiff et al., 1992), and others have described how assessments have been updated with new platforms (for example, Vispoel, 1999).

The computer technology field has its own lexicon, even for concepts similar to constructs used by industrial/organizational psychologists. As test developers, we need to have some basic understanding of computers to interact intelligently with computer programmers. It may be especially useful to include a computer analyst or researcher who has special knowledge of computers or programming on the development team. This inclusion of a technology translator may help the developers to ask the right questions and exploit the technology fully.

Expense

Developing a CBA can be extremely expensive. In addition to the typical costs of developing an assessment (such as collecting data), researchers also need to budget for equipment, development, and maintenance. If the assessment is going to present or measure video or audio, there are additional costs for equipment, performers, professional recording, editing, and reproduction. Sometimes computers that are already available for assessment purposes may need to be modified (or replaced) in order to maintain consistency in assessment administration.

The Development Process

Until recently, little information had been published about how researchers tackled the task of creating innovative CBAs. However, one point about this development process is abundantly clear in most, if not all, of the research that has been published: the process of CBA development is fluid and dynamic. This section outlines the major steps that appear to be common or consistent across various research projects that have successfully resulted in valid tests, focusing on the process of developing assessments that use video or audio input. The process described can be modified for assessments that make greater use of graphics or text, and there are already detailed accounts that describe CAT development (for example, Sands, Waters, & McBride, 1997). In addition, the process will be illustrated with an example of how each step could be applied to the development of an interactive audio assessment of listening skills.

Step One: Job Analysis

The development process typically starts with a careful job analysis. Several test developers used the critical-incident approach (for example, Desmarais et al., 1992; Hanson et al., 1999) because it results in a job-relevant, detailed set of dimensions of job performance. The critical-incident technique may be especially appropriate for developing assessments that present (or measure) video and audio because the resulting data can be easily used to create realistic (and perhaps colorful) items.

Although the critical-incident technique may be a popular choice, it does not preclude the use of other job analysis techniques, such as structured interviews or task analysis inventories (see for example Schmitt et al., 1993), to identify important tasks and knowledge, skills, and abilities. Indeed, these techniques may be crucial for identifying which constructs to focus on in critical-incident interviews. Regardless of which approach is used, by the end of this step, test developers should identify the constructs to be measured and demonstrate how the constructs are linked to important aspects of the job.

Example: For the purpose of illustration, assume that Learn English! is a fairly large company that develops audiotapes and interactive video training materials for improving individuals' English writing and speaking skills. The company offers a twenty-four-hour toll-free "English-learner" hot line and employs 220 "tutors" to answer calls. Learn English! is interested in developing a computer-based selection device for its tutors.

In the first step, the test developers conduct a task-analysis inventory on the tutor job and identify several tasks that appear to be the most important: (1) diagnosing the software problems the customers (with limited English-speaking skills) are having, (2) identifying the proper solutions to the problems, and (3) successfully communicating the steps necessary to correct the problems. Next, the developers conduct critical-incident interviews with job incumbents to identify examples of very good performance, average performance, and low performance on these tasks. Let us assume that the company initially decides to focus on the ability to listen and understand nonnative speakers.

Step Two: Determining Test Specifications

In the second step, test developers should identify the specifications of the proposed CBA. In that regard, many projects have used a team of researchers (see for example Dyer, Desmarais, Midkiff, Colihan, & Olson, 1992) to generate and evaluate possible alternatives for how an assessment could be developed. At this point, it may be especially helpful to involve a computer expert who can explain the limits and horizons of computer capabilities (McHenry & Schmitt, 1994).

A host of issues need to be addressed in identifying the specifications of a CBA. First there are the specifications associated with traditional assessment techniques such as the length of the assessment and the number and type of items. A CBA requires additional focus on some specifications in particular. For example, test developers should give careful thought to measurement issues. That is, how will the assessment be scored, and how can the reliability of the assessment be measured or maximized? This is especially a concern if the assessment is going to be interactive (Drasgow et al., 1999; McHenry & Schmitt, 1994). In addition, test developers should carefully consider how the format of the CBA might affect test takers' responses. Richman, Kiesler, Weisband, and Drasgow (1999) found, for example, that allowing test takers to backtrack on computer-administered questionnaires helped to minimize social desirability effects.

The proposed computer platform should be fully explored. Specifically, how likely is it that a given platform will be able to deliver the assessment consistently (with few breakdowns) and will continue to be available in the expected lifespan of the assessment? For example, IBM test developers (Midkiff et al., 1992) noted the difficulty in acquiring and maintaining the necessary video hardware for the validation phase of their assessment battery. In addition, test developers should discuss how likely it is that the proposed platform will be perceived positively and be accepted by applicants and administrators. In particular, test developers should consider whether prior computer experience would (or should) give an examinee an advantage.

Before arriving at a final set of specifications, test developers should conduct literature reviews on the target constructs, as well as the proposed method of assessment (such as audio or video input). Given the relative newness of this field and the lag in publications, it would be wise to contact other test developers who may be developing similar types of assessments.

Example: Next, the developers add an analyst with a degree in computer science and an M.B.A. to the development team. The team decides to develop a modified work sample of the tutor job, which it calls TUTOR. In Phase I (twenty minutes), the test taker will complete a brief self-guided training session on an easy-to-learn software package. In Phase II (thirty minutes), the assessee will be given a headset (similar to a telephone headset) connected to the computer. The assessee will receive various calls from clients (derived from critical-incidents) asking how to use the software (which the assessee can access directly on the computer). At critical points in the "conversation," the audio will stop, and the computer will display several options for how the assessee could respond to the client (for example, ask the assessee to repeat the question or verify the client's problem). The team decides to develop an empirically based scoring key and to keep the construct measured using homogeneous items so that item-total correlations might be used to approximate reliability. Finally, the team decides on the computer platform: an original program will be written in Delphi to run on Windows 95/98/NT/2000 computers with voice data stored on a CD-ROM. To safeguard the integrity of the test, CD-ROM content will be encrypted.

Step Three: Developing the Prototype and Revising

Given the expense of developing computerized assessments, several test developers have chosen to develop an inexpensive mock-up of the proposed assessment in a different medium before developing the computerized assessment. For example, Hanson et al. (1999) developed a paper-and-pencil version of their technical skills assessment, and Olson-Buchanan et al. (1998) developed a paper-and-pencil version and hand-held camcorder version of their interactive video before making the computerized versions. These prototypes allow test developers the opportunity to conduct preliminary analyses on the appropriateness of the items, the scoring key, and so forth. Hanson et al. used their mock-up to determine which information was missing, which items should be eliminated, and whether there were one or more correct answers. Prototypes could also be used to determine (1) if the test will meet the time requirement, (2) if the test reflects the content of the job, (3) if the directions are clear, (4) if the users and administrators have a positive reaction to the test, and (5) if the options have one (or more) clearly socially desirable answers. At this step, test developers may determine that additional critical-incident job interviews need to be conducted to improve the realism or variety of items or that the test specifications need to be modified. Prototypes can be an effective way to minimize the number of costly revisions that need to be made later.

Example: Because Learn English! decided to develop an interactive assessment, there are several possible sequences of client dialogue that an assessee could hear. For example, suppose everyone hears the same initial thirty seconds of a telephone call from a caller named Bjorn. Bjorn indicates that he is having trouble getting the software started. Assessees would be presented with four options for how they could respond to Bjorn's initial message. If an assessee selects option A, he or she would hear a different response from Bjorn than if he or she selected option B. Accordingly, the team uses in-house staff to record all possible iterations of the items on tape. The developers have ten participants listen to and evaluate the same sequence of dialogue. They then use these evaluations to refine the items. Additional studies on scoring and other components could also be conducted at this time.

Step Four: Developing a Pilot Version, Pilot-Testing, and Revising

Now, the assessment is produced, evaluated, and refined for the final version. One important part of producing the assessment is recording the test items. There is a wide range of ways that items can be taped for production, from professional studios to community or university studios to the test developer's personal camcorder (see Drasgow et al., 1999, for a review). Obviously, these possibilities also vary in quality, expense, and the amount of test developer expertise required. After the items are videotaped, they need to be edited and then digitized for use on the computer (using DVD, CD-ROM, or digital files).

Another crucial part of developing the assessment is the required programming. Several test developers have written their own code (see for example Ashworth & Joyce, 1994). However, there are several multimedia authoring and test delivery systems available (for example, C++ and Visual Basic).

Once the assessment has been developed, it is ready for pilot testing. Pilot testing a CBA is very much like pilot testing any other assessment, with a few additional concerns. Test developers must pay particular attention to user acceptance of the test and difficulties noted with hardware and software. In particular, the test developer should identify aspects of the test that need to be "dummy-proofed." For example, can the examinee cause the program to crash by accidentally (or purposely) hitting a wrong key? If so, these keys may need to be disabled. Upon identifying areas that need to be revised, the developers may choose first to create a prototype of the modified assessment before creating the computerized version.

Example: The test developers create a full version of TUTOR. First, a professional production company produces the audiotape. Then a CD-ROM is made from the audiotape. A programmer is hired to write the code for TUTOR, including the easy-to-learn software package that the examinees are supposed to learn in Phase I and use for the assessment in Phase II. After conducting some pilot studies, they learn that several users were frustrated that the dialogue could not be replayed. As a result, the test developers add the replay as an option, and incorporate it into the scoring scheme. Problems with the hardware and software are noted and corrected.

Step Five: Developing and Validating the Final Assessment

Reviewing the results from the pilot tests can enable test developers to make finishing touches on the final assessment. For example, Hanson et al. (1999) identified one item that needed to be dropped and determined that several examinees had timed out of some of the items. As a result, the developers made such revisions as adding a clock to the screen and providing a five-second warning bell. After revising the assessment based on pilot studies, it is ready for final production and validation. Fortunately, CBAs do not introduce too many unique challenges in the validation phase. However, it is especially important to train all administrators on how to start and stop the assessment properly, as well as restart it in the event of a crash.

Example: After making the final modifications to the assessment, the test developers prepare TUTOR for final production. After the test administrators are trained, the developers conduct a concurrent validation study. The incumbents complete the assessment, and their job performance measures are collected through client telephone surveys, supervisor ratings, and random recordings of telephone calls.

Software and Hardware

By the time this chapter is read, the software and hardware presented in this section as new might seem as antiquated as eight-track cassettes. Thus, this section presents generalities.

Software has improved considerably since computerized assessments were introduced. For maximum flexibility, several test developers have elected to write their own code in such languages as Turbo Pascal (for example, Olson-Buchanan et al., 1999; Vispoel, 1999). Today such developers might choose to use Delphi instead. However, multimedia authoring software packages are fairly easy to learn and are designed specifically for interactive video assessments. There are an increasing number of alternatives in hardware and accessories as well. Accessories such as digital cameras, MIDI, voice synthesizers, earphones, pen-based computers, and touch-screens open up the possibilities of how computers can present stimuli or measure examinees' responses. Given the speed with which computer technology is progressing, it is best to contact an expert, or several experts, before deciding how to create the necessary software or purchase the hardware.

Future Directions

The field of CBA has made some important advancements. Concern over equivalence for power tests has lessened (Mead & Drasgow, 1993), CATs are being used in a number of domains (such as military and private business), and information about the development and validation of interactive video and multimedia assessments is starting to be published. Nevertheless, much about CBAs still needs to be examined and explored.

One of the most important areas for future research concerns the scoring and measurement of reliability in interactive video assessments. Several researchers have noted the measurement difficulties inherent in these dynamic assessments. Perhaps the best way to advance in this field is to develop detailed, a priori models of the target construct. The model should serve to outline the content of the assessment and drive its scoring (Mead, 2000), much like how items were developed from specifications in Bejar and colleagues' model-based automated scoring method (Williamson et al., 1999). Progress in this regard would help to stimulate further development of such tests.

The possibilities for presenting different stimuli and measuring different responses warrant additional attention. We can already present such stimuli as video, audio, graphics, time-sequenced stimuli, and text and measure responses (reaction time, sound, motion) in a variety of ways. Soon we may be able to combine these into virtual worlds where examinees could receive high-fidelity stimuli and respond in an open format. However, regardless of the features available, it is of paramount importance to examine whether these additions can improve assessments or measure something important that we could not otherwise measure. Future researchers should be careful not to use technology for technology's sake.

One theme throughout this chapter is the time and expense involved in developing CBAs. Accordingly, this may limit an organization's ability to develop CBAs for all critical knowledge, skills, and abilities or, in the case of a work sample, all important job tasks for a given job. However, CBAs may be especially appropriate for measuring competencies that span several jobs or the entire organization. Although research on competency-based modeling and measurement is still in its infancy (Heneman, Judge, & Heneman, 2000), it appears that several practitioners are concerned with identifying general knowledge, skills, and abilities that expand beyond a particular job (Harris, 1998). For example, an organization in the rapidly changing technology industry might define a construct of ability to learn as a competency for several job families. The dynamic nature of CBAs could be used to develop a measure of this construct by making information available to assessees through a variety of means (text, audio, tactile, or some other possibility) for a number of fictitious products or processes. The examinees could be given twenty minutes to learn about each product or process (using any of the means available by computer) before being asked to apply the learned material in a subsequent testing session.

Findings from research on CBAs and adverse-impact issues have been mixed. Some researchers have found mean differences favoring majority groups to be lessened (Reynolds et al., 2000) or even nonexistent (e.g., Olson-Buchanan et al., 1998) with CBAs. However, other findings suggest the existence of a racial digital divide. For example, a recent report by the U.S. Department of Commerce (1999) indicated that access to the Internet and a computer at home differs considerably by race, even when income is held constant. In fact, the "gap between White and Black households *grew* 39% . . . between 1994 and 1998" (p. 8). Thus, the digital divide is widening at the same time that more organizations are considering implementing Internet-based assessments and application procedures. To the extent that this divide creates or heightens adverse-impact problems, the progress of the use of CBAs in organizations will be hampered. Further research is needed to investigate possible explanations and solutions to this divide.

A number of studies discussed in this chapter have produced evidence that CBAs offer advantages over traditional testing methods. Certainly, a number of studies have demonstrated equivalent validity with traditional methods, but can CBAs offer improved or enhanced validity? Future research should focus on developing ways to design CBAs to maximize validity. For example, Bejar's mental-model-based method shows promise for enhancing validity by improving the reliability of scoring open-ended responses to carefully constructed test items. Future efforts could also focus on harnessing the power of computers to measure skills that are not redundant with cognitive ability (see for example Olson-Buchanan et al., 1998) or minimize redundancy with reading comprehension (for example, Hanson et al., 1999).

Several researchers have presented evidence that CBAs are associated with more positive examinee reactions. Additional research should focus on how technology can be used to improve the assessment experience further by providing detailed developmental feedback to examinees about their performance. That is, instead of merely providing examinees information about their scores on various sections of an assessment, imagine being able to provide an explanation for why they received the scores they did. For the purpose of illustration only, consider a reading comprehension assessment. A CBA could be equipped with an optical attachment to measure eye movement and be programmed to measure reaction time as well. The eye movement measure might be used to measure the amount of time spent reading (and rereading) a given passage, and the reaction time measure could indicate the amount of time spent selecting an answer. As a result, the assessment could provide information about the relative amount of time spent reading and deciding on answers to items answered correctly versus those answered incorrectly. Perhaps advancements in IRT or model-based scoring could be used to identify common patterns in items that were correctly or incorrectly answered.

All signs indicate that computerized assessment will continue to increase in popularity. The assessments discussed in this chapter are the first in what promises to be a long stream of research. As more and more jobs require a substantial amount of computer interaction, CBAs will likely take the form of work samples and simulations. In addition, as the Internet gains additional acceptance and standardization, more innovative assessments (including multimedia) and application processes will be designed for the Web. Perhaps in the not-too-distant future, there will be a number of tests that represent the full range of possible combinations indicated in the CBA taxonomy: Interactivity, Stimulus Presentation, Delivery Mode, and Response Measurement.

References

Ackerman, T. A., Evans, J., Park, K. S., Tamassia, C., & Turner, R. (1999). Computer assessment using visual stimuli: A test of dermatological skin disorders. In F. Drasgow & J. B. Olson-Buchanan (Eds.), *Innovations in computerized assessment* (pp. 137–150). Hillsdale, NJ: Erlbaum.

Ashworth, S. D., & Joyce, T. M. (1994, Apr.). Developing scoring protocols for a computerized multimedia in-basket exercise. In F. Drasgow (Chair), *Scoring interactive video assessments: Trials and tribulations.* Symposium conducted at the Ninth Annual Conference of the Society for Industrial and Organizational Psychology, Nashville, TN.

Ashworth, S. D., & McHenry, J. J. (1993, Apr.). *Developing a multimedia in-basket: Lessons learned.* Paper presented at the Eighth Annual Conference of the Society for Industrial and Organizational Psychology, San Francisco.

Barrett, G. V., Alexander, R. A., Doverspike, D., Cellar, D., & Thomas, J. C. (1982). The development and application of a computerized information-processing test battery. *Applied Psychological Measurement, 6,* 13–29.

Bartram, D. (1987). The development of an automated testing system for pilot selection: The MICROPAT project. *Applied Psychology: An International Review, 36,* 279–298.

Bejar, I. I. (1991). A methodology for scoring open-ended architectural design problems. *Journal of Applied Psychology, 76,* 522–532.

Bennett, G. K., Seashore, H. G., & Wesman, A. G. (1974). *Differential aptitude tests.* New York: Psychological Corporation.

Bennett, R. E. (1998). *Reinventing assessment: Speculations on the future of large-scale educational testing.* Princeton, NJ: Educational Testing Service.

Bennett, R. E., Steffen, M., Singley, M. K., Morley, M., & Jacquemin, D. (1997). Evaluating an automatically scorable, open-ended response type for measuring mathematical reasoning in computer-adaptive tests. *Journal of Educational Measurement, 34,* 163–177.

Bergstrom, B. A., & Lunz, M. E. (1999). CAT for certification and licensure. In F. Drasgow & J. B. Olson-Buchanan (Eds.), *Innovations in computerized assessment* (pp. 67–92). Hillsdale, NJ: Erlbaum.

Burroughs, W. A., Murray, J., Wesley, S. S., Medina, D. R., Penn, S. L., Gordon, S. R., & Catello, M. (1999). Easing the implementation of behavioral testing through computerization. In F. Drasgow & J. B. Olson-Buchanan (Eds.), *Innovations in computerized assessment* (pp. 197–220). Hillsdale, NJ: Erlbaum.

Campbell, W. J., & Reilley, M. E. (2000). Accommodations for persons with disabilities. In J. F. Kehoe (Ed.), *Managing selection in organizations* (pp. 319–370). San Francisco: Jossey-Bass.

Carretta, T. R. (1987). *Basic attributes tests (BAT) system: Development of an automated test battery for pilot selection* (Rep. No. 87–9). Brooks Air Force Base, TX: Air Force Human Resources Laboratory.

Chiang, A., & Atkinson, R. (1976). Individual differences and interrelationships among a select set of cognitive skills. *Memory and Cognition, 4,* 661–672.

Cooper, D., Phillips, R., & Ford, D. (1994). Improving safety attitudes with computer based training. *Safety and Health Practitioner, 12,* 38–40.

Cox, R. H. (1988, July). Utilization of psychomotor screening for USAF pilot candidates: Enhancing predictive validity. *Aviation, Space, and Environmental Medicine,* 640–645.

Desmarais, L. B., Dyer, P. J., Midkiff, K. R., Barbera, K. M., Curtis, J. R., Esrig, F. H., & Masi, D. L. (1992, May). *Scientific uncertainties in the development of a multimedia test: Trade-offs and decisions.* Paper presented at the Seventh Annual Conference of the Society for Industrial and Organizational Psychology, Montreal, Quebec.

Desmarais, L. B., Masi, D. L., Olson, M. J., Barbera, K. M., & Dyer, P. J. (1994, Apr.). Scoring a multimedia situational judgment test: IBM's experience. In F. Drasgow (Chair), *Scoring interactive video assessments: Trials and tribulations.* Symposium conducted at the Ninth Annual Conference of the Society for Industrial and Organizational Psychology, Nashville, TN.

Donovan, M. A. (2000). Web-based attitude surveys: Data and lessons learned. In N. Mondragon (Chair), *Beyond the demo: The empirical nature of technology-based assessments.* Symposium conducted at the Fifteenth Annual Society for Industrial and Organizational Psychology Conference, New Orleans, LA.

Drasgow, F., & Hulin, C. L. (1990). Item response theory. In M. Dunnette & L. M. Hough (Eds.), *Handbook of industrial and organizational psychology* (Vol. 1, pp. 577–636). Palo Alto, Calif.: Consulting Psychologists Press.

Drasgow, F., & Olson-Buchanan, J. B. (Eds.). (1999). *Innovations in computerized assessment.* Hillsdale, NJ: Erlbaum.

Drasgow, F., Olson, J. B., Keenan, P. A., Moberg, P. J., & Mead, A. D. (1993). Computerized assessment. In G. R. Ferris & K. M. Rowland (Eds.), *Research in personnel and human resources management* (Vol. 11, pp. 163–206). Greenwich, CT: JAI Press.

Drasgow, F., Olson-Buchanan, J. B., & Moberg, P. J. (1999). Development of an interactive video assessment: Trials and tribulations. In F. Drasgow & J. B. Olson-Buchanan (Eds.), *Innovations in computerized assessment* (pp. 177–196). Hillsdale, NJ: Erlbaum.

Dyer, P. J., Desmarais, L. B., Midkiff, K. R., Colihan, J. P., & Olson, J. B. (1992, Apr.). Designing a multimedia test: Understanding the organizational charge, building the team and making the basic research commitments. In P. J. Dyer (Chair), *Computer-based multimedia testing: Merging technology, reality and scientific uncertainty*. Symposium conducted at the 1992 Society for Industrial and Organizational Psychology Conference, Montreal, Quebec.

Fleishman, E. A. (1988). Some new frontiers in personnel selection research. *Personnel Psychology, 41*, 679–701.

Haak, S. W. (1993). *Development of a computer tool including interactive video simulation for eliciting and describing clinical nursing judgment performance*. Unpublished doctoral dissertation, University of Utah, College of Nursing.

Hanson, M. A., Borman, W. C., Mogilka, H. J., Manning, C., & Hedge, J. W. (1999). Computerized assessment of skill for a highly technical job. In F. Drasgow & J. B. Olson-Buchanan (Eds.), *Innovations in computerized assessment* (pp. 197–220). Hillsdale, NJ: Erlbaum.

Harris, M. (1998). Competency modeling: Viagraized job analysis or impotent imposter? *Industrial-Organizational Psychologist, 36*, 37–41.

Heneman, H. G., Judge, T. A., & Heneman, R. L. (2000). *Staffing organizations*. Middleton, WI: Irwin McGraw-Hill.

Hunt, E., & Pellegrino, J. (1985). Using interactive computing to expand intelligence testing: A critique and prospectus. *Intelligence, 9*, 207–236.

Hunt, E., Pellegrino, J. W., Frick, R. W., Farr, S. A., & Alderton, D. (1988). The ability to reason about movement in the visual field. *Intelligence, 12*, 77–100.

Johnson, J. W. (1983). Things we can measure through technology that we could not measure before. In R. B. Ekstrom (Ed.), *New directions for testing and measurement: Measurement, technology, and individuality in education: Proceedings of the 1982 Educational Testing Services Invitational Conference* (pp. 13–18). Princeton, N.J.: Educational Testing Service.

Kuhn, W. E., & Allvin, R. L. (1967). Computer-assisted teaching: A new approach to research in music. *Journal of Research in Music Education, 15*, 305–315.

Lohman, D. F. (1979). *Spatial ability: A review and reanalysis of the correlational literature* (Tech. Rep. No. 8). Stanford, CA: Stanford University.

Lord, F. M. (1980). *Application of item response theory to practical testing problems*. Hillsdale, NJ: Erlbaum.

McHenry, J. J., Hough, L. M., Toquam, J. L., Hanson, M. A., & Ashworth, S. (1990). Project A validity results: The relationship between predictor and criterion domains. *Personnel Psychology, 43*, 335–353.

McHenry, J. J., & Schmitt, N. (1994). Multimedia testing. In M. G. Rumsey & C. B. Walker (Eds.), *Personnel selection and classification* (pp. 193–232). Hillsdale, NJ: Erlbaum.

Mead, A. D. (2000, Apr.). Discussant. In N. J. Mondragon (Chair), *Beyond the demo: The empirical nature of technology-based assessments.* Society for Industrial and Organizational Psychology Conference, New Orleans, LA.

Mead, A. D., & Drasgow, F. (1993). Equivalence of computerized and paper-and-pencil cognitive ability tests: A meta-analysis. *Psychological Bulletin, 114,* 449–445.

Midkiff, K. R., Dyer, P. J., Desmarais, L. B., Rogg, K., & McCusker, C. R. (1992, May). The multimedia test: Friend or foe? In P. J. Dyer (Chair), *Computer-based multimedia testing: Merging technology, reality and scientific uncertainty.* Symposium conducted at the 1992 Society for Industrial and Organizational Psychology Conference, Montreal, Quebec.

Mills, C. N. (1999). Development and introduction of a computer adaptive Graduate Record Examinations general test. In F. Drasgow & J. B. Olson-Buchanan (Eds.), *Innovations in computerized assessment* (pp. 117–136). Hillsdale, NJ: Erlbaum.

Muchinsky, P. M. (1993). Validation of intelligence and mechanical aptitude tests in selecting employees for manufacturing jobs [Special issue]. *Journal of Business and Psychology, 7*(4), 373–382.

Myers, D. C., & Schemmer, F. M. (1990). *Development of a valid computer-based test of time sharing ability for operators in nuclear power plants.* Charlotte, NC: Duke Power Co.

Myers, D. C., Schemmer, F. M., & Fleishman, E.A. (1983). *Analysis of computer interactive tests for assigning helicopter pilots to different missions* (Rep. No. R83–8). Bethesda, MD: Advanced Research Resources Organization.

Olsen, J. B., Maynes, D. D., Slawson, D., & Ho, K. (1989). Comparisons of paper-administered, computer-administered and computerized adaptive achievement tests. *Journal of Educational Computing Research, 5,* 311–326.

Olson-Buchanan, J. B., & Drasgow, F. (1999). Beyond bells and whistles: An introduction to computerized assessment. In F. Drasgow & J. B. Olson-Buchanan (Eds.), *Innovations in computerized assessment* (pp. 1–6). Hillsdale, NJ: Erlbaum.

Olson-Buchanan, J. B., Drasgow, F., Moberg, P. J., Mead, A. D., Keenan, P. A., & Donovan, M. (1998). The Conflict Resolution Skills Assessment: Model-based, multi-media measurement. *Personnel Psychology, 51,* 1–24.

Overton, R. C., Taylor, L. R., Zickar, M. J., & Harms, H. J. (1996), The pen-based computer as an alternative platform for test administration. *Personnel Psychology, 49,* 455–464.

Page, E. B., & Peterson, N. S. (1995, Mar.). The computer moves in essay grading: Updating the ancient test. *Phi Delta Kappan,* 561–565.

Peterson, N. G. (1987). *Development and field test of the Trial Battery for Project A* (ARI Tech. Rep. No. 739). Alexandria, VA: U.S. Army Research Institute for the Behavioral and Social Sciences.

Peterson, N. G., Hough, L. M., Dunnette, M. D., Rosse, R. L., Houston, J. S., Toquam, J. L., & Wing, H. (1990). Project A: Specification of the predictor domain and development of new selection/classification tests. *Personnel Psychology, 43,* 247–276.

Powers, D. E., Burstein, J. C., Chodorow, M., Fowles, M. E., & Kukich, K. (2000). *Comparing the validity of automated and human essay scoring.* Princeton, NJ: Educational Testing Service.

Reynolds, D. H., Sinar, E. F., Scott, D. R., & McClough, A. C. (2000). Evaluation of a Web-based selection procedure. In N. Mondragon (Chair), *Beyond the demo: The empirical nature of technology-based assessments.* Symposium conducted at the Fifteenth Annual Society for Industrial and Organizational Psychology Conference, New Orleans, LA.

Richman, W. L., Kiesler, S., Weisband, S., & Drasgow, F. (1999). A meta-analytic study of social desirability distortion in computer-administered questionnaires, traditional questionnaires, and interviews. *Journal of Applied Psychology, 84,* 754–775.

Richman, W. L., Olson-Buchanan, J. B., & Drasgow, F. (2000, Dec.). Examining the impact of administration medium on examinee perceptions and attitudes. *Journal of Applied Psychology, 85*(6), 880–887.

Sands, W. A., Waters, B. K., & McBride, J. R. (1997). *Computerized adaptive testing: From inquiry to operation.* Washington, DC: American Psychological Association.

Seashore, C. E. (1919). *Manual of instructions and interpretations of measures of musical talent.* Chicago: C. F. Stoelting.

Schmitt, N., Gilliland, S. W., Landis, R. S., & Devine, D. (1993). Computer-based testing applied to selection of secretarial applicants. *Personnel Psychology, 46,* 149–165.

Segall, D. O. (1997). Equating the CAT-ASVAB. In W. A. Sands, B. K. Waters, & J. R. McBride (Eds.), *Computerized adaptive testing: From inquiry to operation* (pp. 181–198). Washington, DC: American Psychological Association.

Segall, D. O., & Moreno, K. E. (1999). Development of the computerized adaptive testing version of the Armed Services Vocational Aptitude Battery. In F. Drasgow & J. B. Olson-Buchanan (Eds.), *Innovations in computerized assessment* (pp. 35–66). Hillsdale, NJ: Erlbaum.

Stanton, J. M. (1998). An empirical assessment of data collection using the Internet. *Personnel Psychology, 51,* 709–726.

Stanton, J. M. (1999). Validity and related issues in Web-based hiring. *Industrial and Organizational Psychologist, 36,* 69–77.

Sternberg, S. (1966). High-speed scanning in human memory. *Science, 153,* 652–654.

U.S. Department of Commerce. (1999). *Falling through the net: Defining the digital divide.* Washington, DC: National Telecommunications and Information Administration.

Vispoel, W. P. (1999). Creating computerized adaptive tests of music aptitude: Problems, solutions, and future directions. In F. Drasgow & J. B. Olson-Buchanan (Eds.), *Innovations in computerized assessment* (pp. 151–176). Hillsdale, NJ: Erlbaum.

Vispoel, W. P., & Coffman, D. D. (1992). Computerized adaptive testing of music-related skills. *Bulletin of the Council for Research in Music Education, 112,* 29–49.

Vlug, T., Furcon, J. E., Mondragon, N., & Mergen, C. Q. (2000, Apr.). Validation and implementation of a Web-based screening system in the Netherlands. In N. Mondragon (Chair), *Beyond the demo: The empirical nature of technology-based assessments.* Symposium conducted at the Fifteenth Annual Society for Industrial and Organizational Psychology Conference, New Orleans, LA.

Williamson, D. M., Bejar, I. I., & Hone, A. S. (1999). Mental model comparison of automated and human scoring. *Journal of Educational Measurement, 36,* 158–184.

Wolfe, J. H., Alderton, D. L., Larson, G. E., Bloxom, B. M., & Wise, L. L. (1997). Expanding the content of CAT-ASVAB: New tests and their validity. In W. A. Sands, B. K. Waters, & J. R. McBride (Eds.), *Computerized adaptive testing: From inquiry to operation* (pp. 329–250). Washington, DC: American Psychological Association.

Zickar, M. J., Overton, R. C., Taylor, L. R., & Harms, H. J. (1999). The development of a computerized selection system for computer programmers in a financial services company. In F. Drasgow & J. B. Olson-Buchanan (Eds.), *Innovations in computerized assessment* (pp. 7–34). Hillsdale, NJ: Erlbaum.

CHAPTER 4

Item Response Theory for Dichotomous Assessment Data

Steven Paul Reise
Niels G. Waller

Item response theory (IRT) is a rubric for a family of measurement models that describe the relationship between an individual's performance on a test item and his or her standing on a continuous latent trait. IRT models have generated considerable interest in recent years because they resolve longstanding problems with classical test theory (CTT) in the areas of test construction, evaluation, administration, and scoring (Embretson & Reise, 2000). In this chapter, we describe several IRT models for dichotomously scored items (for example, true-false, agree-disagree, correct-incorrect, like-dislike).

Our chief objective is to provide a nontechnical review of IRT modeling for binary items. Where appropriate, we provide citations for more detailed treatment of technical topics. Advanced topics, such as multidimensional IRT models (Reckase, 1997), are not reviewed. We first describe basic features and properties of three IRT models for binary items and illustrate these models with real data. We then discuss the process of statistically evaluating IRT model

---

We would like to thank Beverly Kaemmer for providing the data used in this study.

assumptions and the topic of assessing model-to-data fit, including the assessment of item and person fit. In the final section, we describe important advantages of IRT over CTT and illustrate these advantages in several major applications.

Minnesota Multiphasic Personality Inventory for Adolescents Depression Factor Scale

Our working examples use data from 19,326 adolescent males who completed the Minnesota Multiphasic Personality Inventory for Adolescents (MMPI-A; Butcher et al., 1992). All analyses will be conducted on the thirty items of the MMPI-A Depression Factor scale (DEP_F; Waller, 1999a). These data were drawn from a larger data set supplied by the University of Minnesota Press for the purpose of developing factorially homogeneous scales for the MMPI-A that can be administered by computerized adaptive testing (Waller & Reise, 2001).

The DEP_F scale was developed from an item tetrachoric factor analysis of the 478 dichotomously scored items of the MMPI-A (a thorough description of these analyses is provided in Waller & Reise, 2001). The items of the factor scales were chosen so that each scale would be factorially homogeneous, would have high internal consistency, and would be well modeled by one of the IRT models described in this chapter. In the sample of 19,326 adolescent boys, the item responses on DEP_F had a coefficient alpha (Cronbach, 1951) of .91. Raw scores on the scale spanned the scale range (min = 0, max = 30) and had median and mean values of 10.00 and 11.35, respectively, with a standard deviation of 7.31. The adolescent boys in this diverse sample were administered the MMPI-A in inpatient, outpatient, and school settings. At the time of the assessments, the average age of the boys was 15.2 years (median age, 15 years) with a standard deviation of 1.39 years.

Table 4.1 presents a listing of the DEP_F items with some classical test theory item statistics. A perusal of the items in the table reveals that many symptoms believed to be pathagnomonic of adolescent depression are represented in the scale, including feelings of guilt, hopelessness, sadness, and worry.

**Table 4.1. Abbreviated Item Content and Classical Item
Statistics for the MMPI-A Depression Factor Scale.**

MMPI-A Item Number	Abbreviated Items	Item Difficulty	Item-Total Biserial Correlation
62	I feel blue.	.27	.82
53	I wish I could be happy.	.53	.68
91	Most of time happy. (F)	.33	.79
177	Think about killing myself.	.26	.73
185	Often worry.	.53	.64
90	Feel like I did something evil.	.31	.61
255	Life is a strain.	.42	.77
20	No one understands me.	.40	.65
124	I feel useless.	.48	.75
85	Hardest battles with myself.	.50	.46
283	I often wish I were dead.	.15	.71
404	About to go to pieces.	.36	.72
14	Work under tension.	.41	.50
70	Lacking in self confidence.	.33	.72
1	Life is worthwhile. (F)	.23	.66
27	Shrink from facing difficulty.	.27	.47
15	Think of things too bad to say.	.53	.50
360	Seldom have the blues. (F)	.44	.54
259	Feel lonely often.	.31	.72
134	Restful sleep. (F)	.48	.48
163	Afraid of losing my mind.	.27	.48
424	Feeling little stress. (F)	.57	.50
253	Feel more intensely than others.	.46	.46
142	Never felt better than now. (F)	.64	.41
9	Interested in life. (F)	.40	.53
399	Future seems hopeless.	.21	.68
379	Think I'm no good.	.38	.78
88	Don't care what happens.	.25	.59
372	Don't care about anything.	.43	.56
242	No one cares about you.	.21	.56

Note: An *F* indicates a reversed scored item.

Unidimensional IRT Models for Binary Data

The basic unit of IRT modeling is the item response curve (IRC). An IRC mathematically represents the relationship between examinee level on a dimensional latent variable (denoted by θ) and the probability of a correct (or keyed) item endorsement. The three major dichotomous IRT models differ in the functional form used to specify an IRC. Specifically, the three models differ in the number of item parameters used to define the relationship between θ and the item endorsement probability.

We begin by describing the model with the greatest number of parameters, the so-called three-parameter logistic model (3-PLM), shown in equation 4.1:

$$P(X_{ij}=1|\theta) = c_j + \frac{1-c_j}{1+\exp[-1.7a_j(\theta_i-\beta_j)]},\qquad(4.1)$$

where θ represents an examinee's trait level, $P(X_{ij} = 1|\theta)$ is the probability of endorsing item j as a function of examinee trait level, c_j denotes a pseudo-guessing parameter, β_j is an item difficulty parameter, a_j is an item discrimination parameter, and 1.7 is a constant that scales the logistic item parameters to the metric of a normal ogive model.

Equation 4.1 contains a single-person parameter. This person parameter, denoted by a Greek theta, represents individual differences on a single latent trait that is assumed to cause—probabilistically—item response behavior. In IRT applications the θ scale is arbitrary. Technically, without additional constraints, the scale of the latent trait scores is unidentified. To identify the scale, latent trait scores are typically defined to have a mean of zero and a variance of one, that is, to have a z-score metric in the population. Given this stipulation, the metric for the item parameters is identified.

The 3-PLM IRC defined by equation 4.1 contains three item parameters. The a_j parameter is called item discrimination. Item discrimination values typically range from 0.5 to 1.5, with higher values indicating a more discriminating item. The a_j parameter determines the steepness of the IRC. Higher a_j values indicate that the IRC increases rapidly as a function of the latent trait; therefore, small changes on the latent trait lead to large changes in item endorsement probabilities. A completely nondiscriminating item has an a_j of 0.0. Under this condition, the IRC is flat because item endorsement probabilities are the same for all trait levels (the item cannot discriminate between different trait levels). Item discrimination values are similar to factor loadings. When factor scores are distributed normally and other conditions hold, an a_j of 1.0 is equivalent to a factor loading of 0.707 (Takane & de Leeuw, 1987).

The β_j parameter characterizes item difficulty and is on the same scale as examinee θ. Typically, β_j values range from −2.0 to 2.0. Difficult (unpopular) items have large, positive β_j values and have IRCs that are relatively shifted to the right on the trait continuum. Consequently, even examinees with high θ values will be unlikely to endorse or respond correctly to the item. Easy (popular) items have large, negative β_j values and IRCs that are shifted to the left. When β_j is low, even examinees with low θ values will have a high probability of endorsing or responding correctly to the item.

Finally, the c_j parameter represents the lower asymptote of the IRC in the 3-PLM. This so-called guessing parameter typically ranges from 0.0 to 0.20 and indicates the probability that individuals with extremely low trait values will endorse the item in the keyed direction. The need for this parameter is most apparent in multiple-choice aptitude tests where examinees can obtain correct answers by chance. For example, on a five-option multiple-choice problem, guessing should result in around 20 percent correct answers even for the least knowledgeable examinees. The relevance of the c_j parameter in personality data remains unclear.

To illustrate the 3-PLM, the item parameter estimates for the thirty items of the MMPI-A Depression Factor scale (see Table 4.1) are shown in columns 1 to 3 of Table 4.2. These marginal maximum likelihood parameter estimates were generated from BILOG (Mislevy & Bock, 1990). (Annotated BILOG code is provided in the chapter appendix.) The items have mean discrimination and difficulty values of 1.01 and 0.60, respectively, with standard deviations of 0.33 and 0.41. Note that only four items—85, 424, 142, and 9—have c_j parameters of 0.10 or higher. Twenty-two of the thirty items have c_j estimates less than or equal to 0.05. To illustrate this model further, the IRCs for items 283, 360, and 142 are shown in Figure 4.1. These items provide good examples of the types of items that can be characterized by this model because

**Table 4.2. IRT Item Parameters
for the MMPI-A Depression Factor Scale: Males.**

Item	Three-Parameter Model			Two-Parameter Model	
	α	β	c	α	β
62	1.59	.75	.00	1.41	0.75
53	1.14	.00	.03	1.04	−0.10
91	1.67	.62	.03	1.30	0.58
177	1.23	.88	.01	1.09	0.90
185	0.93	−.07	.00	0.90	−0.11
90	0.84	.79	.00	0.79	0.80
255	1.43	.33	.02	1.26	0.26
20	1.08	.49	.06	0.87	0.37
124	1.46	.18	.04	1.25	0.07
85	0.65	.28	.11	0.53	−0.01
283	1.21	1.33	.00	1.09	1.41
404	1.14	.50	.00	1.07	0.49
14	0.61	.50	.01	0.58	0.47
70	1.20	.64	.01	1.07	0.63
71	1.44	1.09	.05	0.92	1.12
27	0.60	1.26	.01	0.55	1.29
15	0.63	−.04	.02	0.60	−0.12
360	0.84	.49	.09	0.65	0.27
259	1.15	.67	.00	1.07	0.67
134	0.62	.24	.05	0.55	0.09
163	0.61	1.21	.01	0.56	1.23
424	0.76	.10	.16	0.59	−0.33
253	0.59	.37	.05	0.52	0.22
142	1.02	.42	.41	0.48	−0.82
9	0.87	.65	.10	0.64	0.45
399	1.09	1.11	.00	0.98	1.16
379	1.50	0.44	.01	1.33	0.39
88	0.90	1.06	.02	0.77	1.08
372	0.76	0.32	.01	0.72	0.29
242	0.81	1.32	.01	0.73	1.38

Figure 4.1. Three-Item Response Curves from the 3-PLM.

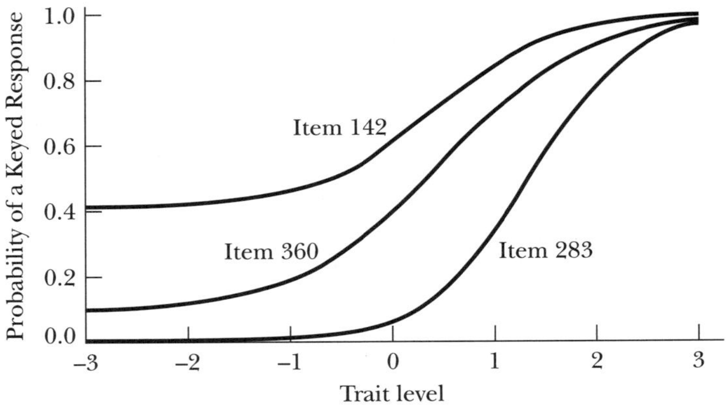

Note: Item 42: $a = 1.02$; $\beta = 0.42$; $c = 0.41$. Item 360: $a = 0.84$; $\beta = 0.49$; $c = 0.09$. Item 283: $a = 1.21$; $\beta = 1.33$; $c = 0.00$.

they differ in difficulty, discrimination, and pseudo-guessing (lower asymptote).

Notice in Figure 4.1 that in the range where $\theta_i = \beta_j$, the slope of the IRC is steepest. Also notice that the IRC is shifted to the right—relative to the center of the trait scale—for items with positive item difficulty values and shifted to the left for items with negative difficulty values. As will be clearer after the subsequent section on item information, the desired range of item difficulty parameters depends on the goals of assessment. If the researcher is interested in scaling individuals precisely along the entire range of the latent trait, such as in computerized adaptive testing, then a wide range of item difficulty values is most desirable. If the objective of a scale is to make a dichotomous decision, as in criterion-referenced testing, then it may be advantageous to have many items with difficulties that cluster around an informative cut-point.

The second IRT model for binary items that we consider is the two-parameter logistic model (2-PLM). The function for the 2-PLM is shown in equation 4.2:

$$P(X_{ij}=1|\theta) = \frac{1}{1+\exp[-1.7a_j(\theta_i-\beta_j)]} \quad (4.2)$$

Note that we can derive the 2-PLM from the 3-PLM (equation 4.1) by setting the c_j parameter to zero. Items in the 2-PLM vary in difficulty (β_j) and in the strength of their relationship with the underlying latent trait (θ). Item parameters in the 2-PLM have simple interpretations. The β_j parameter indicates the θ level necessary to have a 50 percent chance of endorsing the item in the keyed direction. As in the 3-PLM, the a_j parameter in the 2-PLM determines the steepness of the IRC at its inflection point. The inflection point occurs when the $\theta_i = \beta_j$ in both the 2- and 3-PLM.

Our own research indicates that the 2-PLM appears reasonable for many dichotomously scored personality items (Reise & Waller, 1990) and for most items of the MMPI-A (Waller & Reise, 2001). A number of other researchers have demonstrated the utility of the 2-PLM in personality assessment (see Embretson & Reise, 2000). Perhaps a lesson to be learned from this literature is that the 2-PLM is most applicable to personality scales that have been carefully constructed using factor-analytic methods.

To continue our running example, 2-PLM item parameter estimates for the MMPI-A DEP$_F$ scale are shown in the second set of columns in Table 4.2. To illustrate this model, Figure 4.2 displays IRCs for Items 62, 90, and 185.

Figure 4.2. Three-Item Response Curves from the 2-PLM.

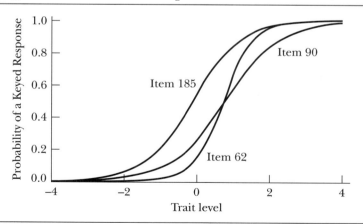

Note: Item 185: $a = 0.90$; $\beta = -0.11$. Item 90: $a = 0.79$; $\beta = 0.80$. Item 62: $a = 1.41$; $\beta = 0.75$.

Finally, the least complex IRT model for binary items is the so-called Rasch or one-parameter logistic model (1-PLM). Equation 4.3 gives the formula for the IRC in this model:

$$P(X_{ij}=1|\theta) = \frac{1}{1+\exp[-1.7(\theta_i-\beta_j)]} \qquad (4.3)$$

Notice in this equation that the probability of an item endorsement is a simple function of the difference between an examinee's trait level and an item's difficulty value. Importantly, in the 1-PLM, items are presumed to vary in difficulty level only. In other words, all items are assumed to have the same relationship with the latent trait (that is, all $a_j = 1.0$) and thus the discrimination parameter is unnecessary.

Although at first blush, the 1-PLM appears unrealistic because it inherently assumes that all items have equal factor loadings, it is an extremely popular model, especially in countries outside the United States (in our data, the item discrimination estimates in Table 4.2 ranged from 0.48 to 1.41; thus, we did not estimate Rasch item parameters). There are several reasons for the popularity of the 1-PLM. First, it is often arguable whether the added complexity of the two-and three-parameter models results in tangible improvements in the estimation of trait values. Simply stated, some researchers question whether the validity of test scores (that is, estimated θ values) increases when moving from the least complex 1-PLM to the increasingly complex 2- and 3-PLM. Moreover, due to their greater number, parameters in the 2- and 3-PLM are more difficult to estimate and require larger calibration sample sizes.

Some researchers also argue that a "good" unidimensional measurement scale requires nonoverlapping IRCs. This can occur only when item discriminations are constant—that is, when the items fit a Rasch model (Lumsden, 1976). In the 2- or 3-PLM models, two items with different discrimination values can cross, a possibility that is philosophically undesirable for some researchers. For instance, in lower trait ranges, item A may be more difficult than item B, whereas in higher trait ranges, the opposite ordering of item difficulty may occur (see items 62 and 90 in Figure 4.2).

Perhaps the best way to summarize these complex issues is to point out that the Rasch, or 1-PLM, is more than just a relatively parsimonious model that is useful when sample sizes are small. Rather, this model represents a philosophy of measurement called *objective measurement* (Rasch, 1966; Wilson & Engelhard, 2000). Scales that meet the assumptions of the Rasch model ostensibly have desirable properties. For instance, raw scores are sufficient estimates of examinee trait level, person and item parameters can be estimated separately during calibration, and interval-level measurement is achieved. (For an interesting discussion of this latter issue, see McDonald, 1999, on modern test theory.)

Item and Test Information

An important concept in all IRT models is the information function (Birnbaum, 1968). Both items and scales have information functions. At the item level, the estimated parameters of the IRC can be converted into an item information curve (IIC). The formula for this curve in the 2-PLM is shown in equation 4.4:

$$I_j(\theta_i) = 1.7^2 a_j^2 P_{ij}(\theta_i)\,(1 - P_{ij}(\theta_i)) \qquad (4.4)$$

An IIC indicates the relative ability of an item to discriminate among contiguous trait scores at various locations along the trait continuum. Items with relatively high discrimination values provide more information than items with lower discrimination values. Information is greatest at the point along the trait continuum where $\theta_i = \beta_j$. In other words, we learn most about an examinee's trait level (we obtain the greatest amount of information) when we administer items that are perfectly matched to the trait level. Not surprisingly, because the c_j parameter is a pseudo-guessing parameter—in that it represents the probability that an individual with a low trait value will endorse the item in the keyed direction by chance—items with large c_j parameters provide relatively less item information.

For illustrative purposes, Figure 4.3 displays item information curves for MMPI-A items 62, 185, and 90. These curves were generated using equation 4.4. A useful property of item information curves is that they are additive. Summing the curves across test items produces a test information curve (TIC). Figure 4.4 displays the TIC for the MMPI-A Depression Factor scale (using the parameters from

Figure 4.3. Three Item Information Functions.

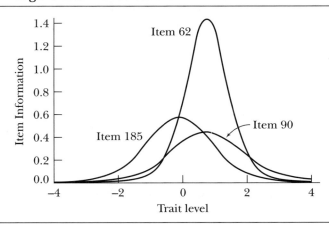

Figure 4.4. Test Characteristic Curve for MMPI-A Depression Factor Scale.

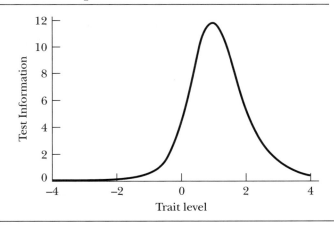

the 3-PLM). The TIC figures prominently in IRT applications because test information is inversely related to the conditional standard error of measurement, as shown in equation 4.5:

$$SEM(\theta) = \frac{1}{\sqrt{Info(\theta)}} \qquad (4.5)$$

The test information curve provides a visual depiction of where along the trait continuum a test is most discriminating (informative). In other words, in contrast to classical test theory, where test reliability is assumed to be constant for all trait scores, the TIC shows that measurement precision can differ along various ranges of the latent trait.

Notice in Figure 4.4 that the MMPI-A Depression Factor scale provides relatively precise measurement for individuals with high trait values (between 0.00 and 2.00). Test information is considerably lower in lower trait regions where depressive symptoms are absent or not extreme. Thus, we might conclude that the depression measure provides a good distinction between very depressed and modestly depressed adolescents, but does a poor job of discriminating among adolescents low in depressive symptoms. This picture is common in measures of psychopathology. Other tests have relatively flat TICs and thus can provide equally precise measurement for all examinees. To achieve a scale with this property, a test must contain items with difficulty parameters spread out over the trait range.

The key message here is that item and test information curves are useful tools for identifying items that provide the greatest degree of measurement precision along specific trait regions. Item and test information curves play key roles in the following:

Scale construction. Tests can be designed to target measurement precision in specific areas of the latent trait.

Item analysis. Researchers can study the precise impact on measurement errors of adding and subtracting items to a scale.

Computerized adaptive testing. Given an examinee's current trait estimate, the most informative item can be administered in a dynamically tailored test.

Binary Item Factor Analysis of the MMPI-A Depression Factor Scale

The models reviewed in the previous sections assume that a single dimension accurately characterizes a set of scale items. Prior to an IRT analysis, this unidimensionality assumption is typically assessed by factor analysis. Statistically rigorous methods for the factor analysis of continuous data (Jöreskog, 1969; for a review, see Waller, 1993) are well known. However, the MMPI-A items do not have a continuous item response format; thus, traditional factor-analytic methods cannot be used legitimately with the MMPI-A or with other inventories composed of binary items. As pointed out many decades ago (Carroll, 1945; Guilford, 1941; Wherry & Gaylord, 1944; for a review of this issue in the context of MMPI research, see Waller, 1999b), the maximum phi correlation of two binary items is a direct function of the item distributions (Lord & Novick, 1968). Accordingly, a classical factor analysis of binary items reflects differences in both item distributions and commonalities of item content. The obfuscating effects of distribution differences can be avoided by avoiding phi coefficients. Alternatively, researchers can use factor-analytic methods, such as full information methods, that do not rely on correlations. We discuss both of these alternatives in the following sections and demonstrate how they can be used to assess the dimensionality of the MMPI-A Depression Factor scale.

Factor Analyses of Tetrachoric Correlations

Many psychometricians have advocated using tetrachoric correlations when factor-analyzing binary items. Surprisingly, although this suggestion was made more than fifty years ago (Wherry & Gaylord, 1944), the number of published factor analyses of tetrachoric correlations is still relatively small. Two reasons for the small number is that until relatively recently, tetrachoric correlations were expensive to calculate, and few software programs were capable of computing tetrachorics accurately (approximation formula were used often). With advances in computer technology, both of these hindrances have been removed, and maximum likelihood estimates of tetrachoric correlations among hundreds of items can now be computed efficiently with widely available software (Jöreskog & Sörbom, 1996; Muthén & Muthén, 1998; Waller, 2000; Wilson, Wood, & Gibbons, 1991). In the analyses reported below, we used MicroFACT 2.0 (Waller, 2000) because it includes a number of features for testing model assumptions that are not widely available in other programs.

A Brief Tutorial on Tetrachoric Correlations

Pearson (1900) derived the tetrachoric correlation at the turn of the last century. He wanted an index that would estimate the Pearson product moment correlation that would have been observed had two dichotomously scored variables been measured on continuous scales. In other words, a tetrachoric correlation is a correlation among latent variables that have been measured with binary variables. An important assumption of Pearson's equations is that the joint distribution of the latent variables is bivariate normal. This point is illustrated in Figure 4.5a, where we have plotted a bivariate normal frequency surface for a latent correlation of .73. We chose this value because it equals the tetrachoric correlation between items 62 and 91 on the MMPI-A Depression Factor scale in our sample.

MMPI-A items are scored either true or false; thus, the observed joint distribution contains four points only. In our example, the four points correspond to the four cells of the 2×2 table that results when items 62 and 91 are cross classified. The tetrachoric correlation for these items was calculated by tabulating the proportion of individuals who responded true to both items—$P(v62=1, v91=1)$—converting this proportion into a probability value, and then iteratively estimating the correlation (r_{tet}) that provides a similar probability value for the corresponding cell of the table.

For instance, let $P(v62=1, v91=1)$ denote the observed probability of responding true to items 62 and 91 on the Depression scale. When the assumptions of the tetrachoric are tenable (that is, the latent joint density is bivariate normal), we can estimate this proportion by performing a double integration of the bivariate distribution function:

$$\hat{P}(v62=1, v91=1) = \int_{\tau_{62}}^{\infty} \int_{\tau_{91}}^{\infty} \varphi(z_{62}, z_{91}; r_{tet}) \, dz_{62} dz_{91} \qquad (4.6)$$

**Figure 4.5. Bivariate Normal Density Surface
and Contour Map of Bivariate Normal Surface.**

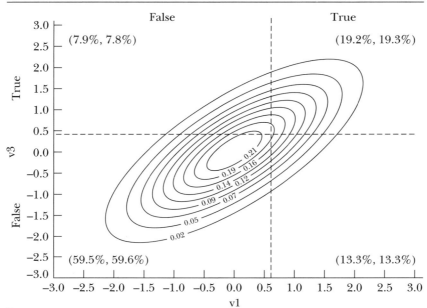

a.

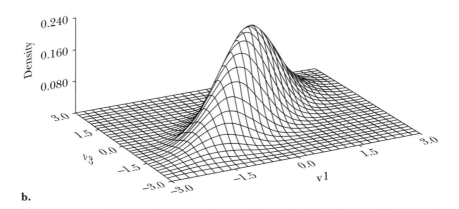

b.

where $\varphi(z_{62}z_{91};r_{tet})$ denotes the density of the standard bivariate normal density with tetrachoric correlation r_{tet}, and item thresholds z_{62} and z_{91}. The item thresholds are simply the z-scores corresponding to the proportions of subjects who endorsed items 62 and 91. With fixed threshold values, the tetrachoric correlation is estimated iteratively using maximum likelihood procedures until the observed and estimated cell proportions are as close as possible given the fixed model parameters. Fast and accurate equations for calculating equation 4.6 are given by Divgi (1979).

Figure 4.5b reports the observed and model-implied cell proportions for the two Depression items. Each quadrant of the figure reports two numbers: the observed cell proportion and the model-implied proportion from equation 4.6. Notice that the figure also displays a contour map that reports the height of the bivariate normal surface for different regions of the joint latent distribution. Importantly, although the observed and model-implied proportions are reassuringly close, this finding does not provide sufficient justification for adopting the tetrachoric model. The verisimilitude of this model rests on the validity of its underlying assumptions. Therefore, before adopting the tetrachoric model, we should assess the model assumptions.

The tetrachoric model presumes that the joint distribution of the underlying (latent) variables is well approximated by a bivariate normal density (see Figure 4.5a). Although this assumption cannot be tested with a single pair of variables, it can be tested with three or more variables. To do so, we use a procedure developed by Muthén and Hofacker (1988), who demonstrated how the hypothesis of trivariate normality could be assessed for triplets of binary items.

Using MicroFACT, we ran Muthén and Hofacker's (1988) triplet test on all triples from the items of the MMPI-A Depression Factor scale. With thirty items, our analysis had 4,060 triplet tests. The results of these tests are summarized in Figure 4.6. This figure can be interpreted as follows. The Depression Factor scale contains thirty items. Each item is included in 406 triplets. Using the results from the triplet tests, we calculated median chi-square values for each item and plotted these values in the figure. The null hypothesis of Muthén and Hofacker's procedure states that the eight cells

Figure 4.6. Triplet Test of Trivariate Normality.

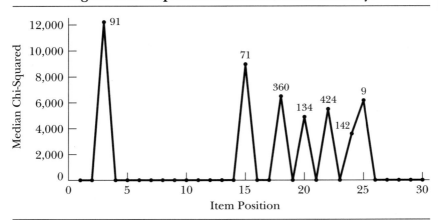

of the $2 \times 2 \times 2$ table that result from the cross-classification of three binary items can be reproduced from the parameters of a single common factor model (thus avoiding the necessity of a triple integration). When the null hypothesis is correct, the model test statistic is distributed as a chi-square variate with a single degree of freedom.

Inspection of Figure 4.6 reveals that for most items, the hypothesis of trivariate normality cannot be rejected (that is, the median chi-square values are appropriately low). Note, however, that the chi-square values are exceedingly large for seven items (items 91, 71, 360, 134, 424, 142, and 9). These discrepant results raise an important question: Can tetrachoric correlations be legitimately used to describe the pattern of covariation among the seven identified items? Stated differently, does violation of the underlying distribution assumptions vitiate the tetrachoric's usefulness? We return to these questions later. First, we will set them aside and conduct an exploratory factor analysis on the tetrachoric correlations from the Depression items. The findings from the one-factor model are reported in Table 4.3.

For the moment, focus attention on the first column of Table 4.3. These factor loadings were calculated from an iterated principal axis factor analysis of a (smoothed) tetrachoric correlation matrix. The

Table 4.3. Factor Loadings from Item Factor Analysis of MMPI-A Depression Factor Scale.

Item	Abbreviated Items	Tetrachoric PFA Loading	Full Information Loading	Corrected for Guessing	
				Tetrachoric PFA Loading	Full Information Loading
62	I feel blue.	.81	.77	.81	.78
53	I wish I could be happy.	.71	.69	.74	.70
91	Most of time happy.	−.79	−.75	−.83	−.79
177	Think about killing myself.	.73	.69	.74	.71
185	Often worry.	.66	.64	.66	.64
90	Feel like I did something evil.	.62	.59	.61	.59
255	Life is a strain.	.78	.75	.80	.76
20	No one understands me.	.67	.63	.72	.68
124	I feel useless.	.77	.75	.80	.77
85	Hardest battles with myself.	.48	.46	.54	.51
283	I often wish I were dead.	.71	.68	.70	.68
404	About to go to pieces.	.73	.69	.72	.69
14	Work under tension.	.51	.48	.52	.49
70	Lacking in self confidence.	.72	.69	.74	.70
71	Life is worthwhile.	−.67	−.62	−.77	−.75
27	Shrink from facing difficulty.	.48	.45	.49	.46
15	Think of things too bad to talk about.	.53	.50	.54	.51
360	Seldom have the blues.	.56	.53	.63	.59
259	Feel lonely often.	.73	.69	.72	.69
134	Restful sleep.	.50	.47	.53	.49
163	Afraid of losing my mind.	.49	.46	.50	.47
424	Feeling little stress.	.52	.50	.61	.57
253	Feel more intensely than others.	.48	.45	.50	.47
142	Never felt better than now.	−.45	−.42	−.70	−.65
9	Interested in life.	−.56	−.52	−.65	−.60
399	Future seems hopeless.	.69	.65	.68	.66
379	Think I'm no good.	.79	.76	.80	.77
88	Don't care what happens.	.61	.57	.63	.60
372	Don't care about anything.	.59	.56	.60	.56
242	No one cares about you.	.58	.54	.59	.56

Note: Technically, there is no such thing as guessing on a personality item. However, we used the term *corrected for guessing* to maintain consistency with the IRT literature. Perhaps a more appropriate term in our context is *correction for nonzero lower asymptote*.

first ten eigenvalues of this matrix are 12.83, 1.70, 1.38, 1.00, 0.89, 0.81, 0.74, 0.73, 0.70, and 0.67. The ratio of the first to second eigenvalues is 7.55, and the ratio of the second to third eigenvalues is substantially smaller, at 1.23. These values provide convincing evidence that a strong first dimension dominates the correlation matrix (see Hattie, 1985, for a justification of this claim). The large absolute values for all of the factor loadings on the first dimension provide further support for the model. Moreover, a detailed analysis of the model residuals, defined as the computed tetrachoric correlations minus the reproduced correlations, demonstrated that a single dimension accounts for the brunt of the matrix common variance. After extracting a single factor, the mean squared residual was 0.003, the root mean squared residual was 0.054, the mean residual was -0.0001, and the standard deviation of residuals was only 0.05.

Notice in Table 4.3 that seven items have negative factor loadings. Because these items are keyed false, their negative loadings are to be expected. Nevertheless, Figure 4.6 indicated that these seven items, and only these items, are rejected by the triplet test. The signs of the correlations do not affect the triplet test, and thus we cannot ascribe these results to item keying. What, then, do these results imply?

Returning to Table 4.2, we find that the seven false-keyed items on the MMPI-A Depression Factor scale have the largest estimates of the pseudo-guessing parameter, c_j, when the items are parameterized with the 3-PLM. Specifically, the median estimated c_j parameter for the seven false-keyed items is .09, whereas the median estimated c_j parameter for the remaining items is only .01 (see Schmitt & Stults, 1985, for a discussion of factor-analytic problems caused by examinees carelessly misreading negatively worded questions). Regardless of the origin of the positive c_j parameter in these seven false-keyed items, this finding is important because tetrachoric correlations are biased in the presence of guessing (or in this personality context, in the presence of a positive lower asymptote of the IRC). In an important series of papers, Carroll (1945, 1961, 1983) demonstrated how the magnitude of this bias could be estimated, and he provided correction equations for calculating unbiased tetrachoric correlations. Carroll's estimation methods are also available in MicroFACT 2.0, and thus we were able to compare factor results when using corrected versus uncorrected tetrachorics.

The factor loadings that resulted from the corrected tetrachoric correlations are reported in the third column of Table 4.3. Notice that without exception, the loadings for the false-keyed items are larger than their previous estimates. This demonstrates that the presence of guessing (a positive lower asymptote) tends to bias tetrachoric correlations negatively unless they are calculated using Carroll's method. The first ten eigenvalues of the corrected correlation matrix are 13.98, 1.75, 1.46, 0.99, 0.87, 0.79, 0.72, 0.70, 0.65, and 0.65. The ratio of the first to the second eigenvalue is 7.87, whereas the ratio of the second to the third eigenvalue is only 1.20. Notice that these values provide even stronger support for a single-dimension model. Carroll (1945, 1983) has demonstrated that failure to correct tetrachoric correlations in the presence of guessing (positive lower asymptote) distorts factor-analytic results by incorrectly suggesting the presence of an additional factor. This point is important to keep in mind when testing the unidimensionality assumption of the IRT models that we review.

A principal axes (or unweighted least squares) factor analysis of tetrachoric correlation matrices is a so-called limited information model because it does not use all of the information in the item response vectors. When variables are scored dichotomously, 2^p distinct response vectors are possible in a p-item test. The tetrachoric factor analysis model considers the joint distribution of only two variables at a time when calculating the tetrachoric correlations. Moreover, during the estimation phase (equation 4.6), item thresholds and correlations are typically computed in separate stages for computational efficiency. Factor-analytic models that consider three- and four-way item cross-classifications were developed by Christoffersson (1975) and extended by Muthén (1978). Muthén simplified Christoffersson's approach by demonstrating how higher-order information could be used with tetrachorics by weighting the correlations by their sampling variances and covariances. He also showed how model parameters (such as factor loadings, factor correlations) could be consistently estimated by generalized least squares (GLS) and how to derive chi-square measures of model fit. Unfortunately, estimating the GLS weight matrix for tetrachorics is computationally burdensome and is impractical for models with more than twenty-five or thirty items.

Full Information Factor Analysis

Bock and Lieberman (1970) described the first factor-analytic model to use all of the information in a binary item data matrix. Their so-called full information model works directly on item response patterns rather than correlations and provides true maximum likelihood parameter estimates. Although their model was an important statistical advance, it was too limited from a practical standpoint due to its computational demands. The initial approach handled single-dimensional models only. Later work by Bock and Aitkin (1981) demonstrated how full information parameters could be estimated more easily using marginal maximum likelihood and the expectation-maximization algorithm of Dempster, Laird, and Rubin (1977). Technical details of this approach are beyond the scope of this chapter (readers may consult Mislevy, 1986, or Bock, Gibbons, & Muraki, 1988, for computational details). For our purposes, full information item factor analysis can be defined as a multidimensional extension of the normal ogive model that is used in item response theory. Currently, TESTFACT (Wilson et al., 1991) is the only program capable of estimating full information parameters in the multiple factor analysis model.

Full information factor loadings for the MMPI-A Depression items are displayed in Table 4.3. Although TESTFACT provides a chi-square measure of model fit, for reasons discussed shortly, this index is unreliable. Moreover, with nearly 20,000 subjects in our sample, any model with a small number of factors is rejected. For instance, the chi-square for the one-factor model (no guessing) was a whopping 237,641.64 with 17,712 degrees of freedom. The chi-square for the two-factor model was almost as large, at 233,877.42 with 17,683 degrees of freedom. Clearly, model selection should not rely on statistical significance alone. Moreover, in smaller-sized samples, chi-square test statistics may not even have chi-square distributions.

As implied by its name, full information factor analysis considers all of the information in the 2^p distinct-response patterns of a p-item test. Consequently, models with more than a handful of items can have an extremely large number of response patterns.

For instance, a scale with ten items can have $2^{10} = 1,024$ unique response patterns; a scale with twenty items can have $2^{20} = 1,048,576$ response patterns! Furthermore, many of these response patterns occur with low probability, and a complete set of response patterns is unlikely to be observed unless samples are composed of millions of subjects. An important consequence is that the so-called chi-square test of model fit in full information item factor analysis often does not follow a chi-square distribution (Reiser & VandenBerg, 1994).

For these and other reasons, we believe that investigators will often do well to assess dimensionality in binary item data matrices using principal axes factor analysis on (unweighted) tetrachoric correlations. Our view also finds support in the simulation results of Knol and Berger (1988, 1991), who performed an extensive Monte Carlo study to compare parameter recovery in limited and full information factor analysis models of binary items. A noteworthy conclusion of their study was that principal axes factor analysis of tetrachoric correlations frequently outperforms the statistically more complicated approaches. Having considered methods for assessing the unidimensionality assumption of IRT models, we now turn our attention to the assessment of model fit.

Evaluating Model Fit

The purported advantages of IRT models depend entirely on how well a particular model fits a data set. Before detailing some specific approaches to IRT fit assessment, we make several observations regarding the assessment of fit in covariance structure analysis (CSA) versus IRT. First, in CSA, there are many well-researched fit indices to evaluate model accuracy. In IRT, on the other hand, no such set of indices with clearly superior properties has emerged. Second, in CSA, one goal of a model is to estimate parameters that recapture an observed covariance matrix. Thus, CSA fit indices are often based on quantifying differences between observed and model reproduced covariances. Contrast this with IRT, where one desires a set of item and person parameters that recapture an observed response pattern and where fit statistics are based on differences between observed and predicted response patterns.

In IRT, overall model fit and model comparisons are rarely studied. Instead, researchers focus their attention on the fit of the estimated model (an IRC) on an item-by-item basis. This process is called the study of item fit. There are two basic approaches to studying item fit: one based on graphical analyses and the other on statistical analyses. In the graphical approach, an estimated IRC is compared with the observed item endorsement probabilities (conditioning on $\hat{\theta}$) for different points along the trait scale. Large discrepancies between the IRC and observed proportions (that is, large residuals) indicate lack of fit. Item misfit can result from a multitude of factors, including multidimensionality of the latent space, poor item writing, and improper model specification.

The graphical approach is implemented as follows. An empirical IRC is formed by grouping examinees on the basis of their estimated trait level ($\hat{\theta}$). For instance, in a calibration sample of 1,000 individuals, a researcher might divide the $\hat{\theta}$ scale into ten groups of equal size. Within each group, she would compute the observed item endorsement proportion for a particular item. Taking the individual group mean or median $\hat{\theta}$ values, she then would plot the observed endorsement proportions next to the item's IRC (estimated from the item parameters). Large differences (that is, residuals) between the empirically derived response proportions and the model implied (IRC values) proportions indicate model-data misfit.

Item fit also can be assessed statistically. Typically, this involves the computation of a chi-square fit statistic that quantifies the differences between the observed and estimated response proportions (McKinley & Mills, 1985; Rogers & Hattie, 1987). These statistics follow the same procedure as the graphical approach described above. (Orlando & Thissen, 2000, can be consulted for a recent review of the item-fit literature.) In the following section, we review the chi-square item-fit statistic that is implemented in BILOG (Mislevy & Bock, 1990).

Prior to studying item fit, item parameters must first be estimated. The estimated item parameters are then used to generate person parameters (trait levels). Examinees are sorted into contiguous groups based on their estimated trait level, and for each group the item endorsement frequency is tabulated. A chi-square fit statistic is then calculated by comparing the observed endorsement frequencies with those predicted from the IRC:

$$\chi^2 = 2\sum \left[R_g \ln\left(\frac{R_g}{N_g P(\theta_M)}\right) + (N_g - R_g) \ln\left(\frac{N_g - R_g}{N_g (1 - P(\theta_M))}\right) \right] \quad (4.7)$$

In equation 4.7, R_g represents the item endorsement frequency within group g, N_g is the number of examinees in group g, and $P(\theta_M)$ is the model-implied endorsement probability that corresponds to the estimated IRC value at the mean trait level within each group. The chi-square degrees of freedom is equal to the number of groups.

Although most IRT fit research is concerned with item fit, a fair amount of research has focused on the complementary topic of person fit (Meijer & Sijtsma, 1995). Whereas item-fit statistics consider the correspondence between observed and expected item responses for a single item, person-fit statistics examine the degree to which item parameters reproduce item response patterns. Specifically, person-fit statistics attempt to assess the consistency between an individual's item response pattern and the expected response pattern from the item parameters.

Person-fit statistics are known by various names—for example, *test-score appropriateness measures* (Drasgow, Levine, & Williams, 1985; Levine & Rubin, 1979), *caution indices* (Tatsuoka, 1984, 1996), and *scalability indices* (Reise & Waller, 1993; Waller & Reise, 1992). All of these statistics are based on similar logic: they assume that item responses are predictable. When an examinee's trait level is higher than an item's difficulty value, the examinee is predicted to endorse the item. When the trait level is lower than the item's difficulty value, the examinee is predicted not to endorse the item. Violations of this simple rule result in person misfit.

Most person-fit research has examined deviant test-taking behavior, such as cheating, fumbling, response carelessness, or response dissimulation (Birenbaum, 1986; Harnisch, 1983; Wright & Stone, 1979). Some research also has been concerned with the diagnosis of specific skill deficits (Tatsuoka & Tatsuoka, 1983). More recently, researchers have explored the application of person-fit statistics in personality assessment. For example, Reise and Waller (1993) used person-fit statistics to identify individual differences in personality trait structure (see also Waller & Reise, 1992, for a behavior genetics application), and Zickar and Drasgow (1996) explored the use of person-fit measurement in the detection of faking. We expect more work in this area to appear in upcoming years.

Application of IRT and Advantages

In this final section, we consider several major applications of IRT models. Each application speaks to a central question: Why use IRT over classical test theory? To answer this question, we focus our discussion around two topics: computerized adaptive testing (CAT) and the assessment of differential item functioning (DIF). Before describing these applications, we review several foundational issues that highlight major ways in which IRT differs from traditional psychometrics.

An often-touted difference between IRT and CTT concerns the so-called invariance property of IRT item and person parameters. In this context, invariance is defined as equivalence across (possibly) nonrandom samples from a given population. In traditional psychometrics, item and person parameters are sample dependent. Item difficulty, being defined as the item endorsement proportion, must change across samples when the samples have different mean trait levels. Moreover, item discrimination, which is defined as the item-test correlation, must also vary as a function of sample trait-level variances.

Classical test theory trait estimates are also sample dependent because they depend on a particular set of items. In CTT, an individual's raw score (the number correct) is the best estimate of his or her true score. However, for reasons cited above, this estimate must be test specific. Consequently, a well-known limitation of CTT is that examinees can be compared only when they receive the same or parallel tests. Obviously, if one examinee receives a twenty-item test and another a five-item test, their scores are not comparable, even when the tests measure the same construct. When two tests have items with different difficulty values (say, when one test includes five challenging questions and the other includes five easy questions), raw scores from those tests are also not comparable.

This discussion is not meant to dismiss the utility of CTT. Clearly, traditional psychometrics has served many fields well. We bring up these limitations of CTT to set a foundation for describing two important properties of IRT: item-parameter and person-parameter invariance. We describe these invariance properties in the context of the 2-PLM.

A calibration sample is needed to estimate item parameters in the 2-PLM or any other IRT model. It is customary to solve the item identification problem by standardizing the calibration trait scores to have a mean of zero and a variance to 1.0. Because of this standardization, the estimated item parameters are influenced by the characteristics (trait level and dispersion) of the calibration sample in much the same way they are in CTT. For example, on an achievement test, all items will look easy (have negative difficulty parameters) if the calibration sample is composed of very bright individuals.

In IRT, however, if the model holds for the data (that is, the model assumptions are justifiable), then the obtained item-parameter estimates are linearly transformable—within sampling error—from one sample to the next *even when the samples are not matched on trait level*. This situation is analogous to that of ordinary simple regression where the estimates of the (unstandardized) slope and intercept parameters do not depend on the sample variances of the two variables. This invariance property allows researchers to use IRT to study item and test bias (called *differential item and test functioning* in the IRT literature).

IRT person statistics (that is, trait estimates) are said to be item free. In IRT, an individual's item response pattern is used to estimate his or her trait score. Because item properties are explicitly accounted for in the model, a person's location on the latent trait can be estimated using any subset of items with known item parameters. Thus, scores from different tests—even tests that are not parallel—can be compared on the same metric. This is the basis of computerized adaptive testing.

Computerized Adaptive Testing

Computerized adaptive testing is one of the most important and the most successful applications of IRT to date. Its underlying logic is straightforward. A computer is programmed to administer to each examinee an individually tailored test that best matches his or her ability or trait level. In many applications, this is accomplished by administering, from a large item pool, items that have the highest information function conditional on the current trait-level estimate. This results in extremely efficient testing. For instance, on a CAT-administered achievement test, bright examinees would receive the more difficult items, whereas less bright examinees would receive the easier items. Everyone's time is wasted when bright examinees are given extremely easy items that they are certain to pass. CAT avoids this by administering dynamically tailored tests. By matching test item difficulty with an examinee's trait score, CAT typically reduces the number of items administered (compared with paper-and-pencil exams) by 50 percent or more, with no loss in measurement precision.

Recently, CAT has moved beyond the research stage and has been implemented by large testing programs. For example, examinees can now take computerized adaptive math, reading, and writing exams (American College Testing, 1993); the CAT version of the Armed Services Vocational Aptitude Battery (Curran & Wise, 1994; McBride, 1997; Moreno & Segall, 1992; Moreno, Wetzel, McBride, & Weiss, 1984), and a CAT-adaptive version of the Graduate Record Examination (Educational Testing Service, 1993). It is only a matter of time before CAT becomes a mainstay of personnel assessment in business settings.

The literature on CAT is large and complex and cannot be covered adequately in a short chapter. Readers wishing further information are advised to read more extended treatments in recent IRT books (Embretson & Reise, 2000), special topic books (Drasgow & Olson-Buchanan, 1999; Wainer, 2000), and numerous review articles (Weiss, 1982, 1985).

Differential Item Functioning

When tests are used in decision making, such as in hiring decisions, examiners must be confident that the test provides invariant and unbiased measurement for all examinees. By *invariant,* we mean that the test items should measure the same trait in the same way across different examinee groups (that is, have equal item response curves). We are not referring to whether test scores predict criterion variables in the same way across groups. (For further discussion of this distinction between measurement invariance—our topic—and predictive invariance, see Drasgow, 1982, 1987.)

It is difficult to measure item and test invariance with CTT methods because CTT item statistics are sample dependent. Consider the following example. An item has a 0.40 difficulty (proportion endorsed) in a sample of men and a 0.20 difficulty (proportion endorsed) in a sample of women. Is the item biased, or do the endorsement differences reflect true group differences on the latent trait? This question can be addressed effectively with IRT (Millsap & Everson, 1993; Reise, Widaman, & Pugh, 1993).

In IRT, a test item is considered measurement invariant when it has the same relationship with a latent variable across two or more groups. This will occur when the item has the same item-response curves across two or more groups. Under this condition, and only under this condition, group differences in raw scores are meaningful. Differential item functioning is said to occur when the IRCs (for the same item) are not the same across groups. Because of the invariance property of IRT item parameters, it is relatively easy to compare IRCs computed within different groups (after the item parameters have been equated), even if the groups differ in mean trait level.

If an item displays DIF, then examinees from the reference and focal groups who have equal latent trait scores do not have equal item endorsement probabilities. Using the same item-parameter estimates to score examinees in the presence of DIF will produces scores that are relatively too high or too low for members of one group. Several procedures are available for detecting DIF and the consequences of DIF for trait scores estimates (Raju, 1988, 1990, see Waller, Thompson, & Wenk, 2000, for an application with the MMPI). Holland and Wainer (1993) present a thorough treatment of this important topic. See also Chapter Six in this volume.

Conclusion

In large-scale aptitude testing, item response theory has essentially replaced classical test theory. It is only a matter of time before IRT methods dominate the entire field of applied testing. In this chapter, we provided a basic overview of IRT models for dichotomous items. We introduced the important concepts of item and test information and briefly reviewed the basic approaches to item- and person-fit assessment. Finally, we discussed the related concepts of item and person invariance and provided examples of how IRT can be used in the applied testing world (that is, CAT and DIF assessment). Although this chapter necessarily left out many complexities, illustrations, and details of IRT modeling, we hope that we have piqued readers' curiosity about binary item IRT models. If we have, then we encourage exploration of these models in more detail by consulting book-length treatments by Lord (1980), Hambleton and Swaminathan (1985), Hambleton, Swaminathan, and Rogers (1991), or Embretson and Reise (2000).

Appendix: Annotated BILOG Code for Three-Parameter Logistic Model

MALE ADOLESCENT DEPRESSION ALL 3PL
>COMMENT

MALE ADOLESCENT DEPRESSION ALL 3PL, N = 19,326

>GLOBAL   DFN='MAADEP.DAT',NPA=3,
KFN='MAADEP.DAT',SAVE;
Names the data file and specifies the 3-PLM be estimated and that the metric for the item parameters is the normal ogive ($D = 1.7$ by default). The answer key is in the first line of the data file, and SAVE instructs the program to save relevant information to a file.

>SAVE   PARM='MAADEP3.PAR',SCORE='MAADEP3.SCO';
Save files to disk for later use, in particular, the estimated item parameters (PARM) and examinee scores (SCORE).

>LENGTH   NITEMS=30;
Test contains thirty items.

>INPUT   NTOT=30,SAMPLE=19326,NIDC=20;
There are thirty item responses total, and we will sample all cases. The number of identification characters (NIDC) is twenty.

>TEST TNAME=MAADEP3, ITE(1(1)30), INAMES= ('62','53', '91','177','185', '90','255','20','124','85','283','404', '14','70','71', '27','15', '360','259','134','163','424','253','142','9','399','379','88', '372','242');
Defines test name (TNAME) and item names (INAMES) for items 1 to 30.

(20A1,30A1)
Fortran code for reading subject ID and item responses. Note that the key is in the first line of the data file with the same format.

>CALIB CYCLES=100,NEWTON=50,FRE,PLOT=1,FLOAT;
Estimate item parameters; use a maximum of one hundred expectation-maximization cycles and fifty Newton-Raphson iterations. Use an empirically derived prior distribution for the latent trait (FRE), plot the estimated item response functions, and allow the prior means used in item parameter estimation to float (change) between estimation cycles.

>SCORE METHOD=2,IDIST=3, NOPRINT;
Score examinees using the expected a posteriori (method = 2) method. Use the estimated empirical prior (IDIST = 3), and do not print the scores to the screen (NOPRINT).

References
American College Testing (1993). *COMPASS user's guide.* Iowa City: Author.
Birenbaum, M. (1986). Effect of dissimulation motivation and anxiety on response pattern appropriateness measures. *Applied Psychological Measurement, 10,* 167–174.
Birnbaum, A. (1968). Some latent trait models and their use in inferring an examinee's ability. In F. M. Lord & M. R. Novick (Eds.), *Statistical theories of mental test scores.* Reading, MA: Addison-Wesley.
Bock, R. D., & Aitkin, M. (1981). Marginal maximum likelihood estimation of item parameters: Application of an EM algorithm. *Psychometrika, 46,* 443–459.
Bock, R. D., Gibbons, R., & Muraki, E. (1988). Full information item factor analysis. *Applied Psychological Measurement, 12,* 261–280.
Bock, R. D., & Lieberman, M. (1970). Fitting a response model for N dichotomously scored items. *Psychometrika, 35,* 179–197.
Brown, M. B., & Beneditti, J. (1977). On the mean and variance of the tetrachoric correlation coefficient. *Psychometrika, 42,* 347–355.

Butcher, J. N., Williams, C. L., Graham, J. R., Archer, R. P., Tellegen, A., & Ben-Porath, Y. (1992). *MMPI-A (Minnesota Multiphasic Personality Inventory-Adolescent): Manual for administration, scoring, and interpretation.* Minneapolis: University of Minnesota Press.

Carroll, J. B. (1945). The effect of difficulty and chance success on correlations between items and between tests. *Psychometrika, 26,* 347–372.

Carroll, J. B. (1961). The nature of the data, or how to choose a correlation coefficient. *Psychometrika, 26,* 347–372.

Carroll, J. B. (1983). The difficulty of a test and its factor composition revisited. In H. Wainer & S. Messick (Eds.), *Principals of modern psychological measurement.* Hillsdale, NJ: Erlbaum.

Christoffersson, A. (1975). Factor analysis of dichotomized variables. *Psychometrika, 40,* 5–32.

Cronbach, L. J. (1951). Coefficient alpha and the internal structure of tests. *Psychometrika, 16,* 297–334.

Curran, L. T., & Wise, L. L. (1994). *Evaluation and implementation of CAT-ASVAB.* Paper presented at the annual meeting of the American Psychological Association, Los Angeles.

Dempster, A. P., Laird, N. M., & Rubin, D. B. (1977). Maximum likelihood from incomplete data via the EM algorithm. *Journal of the Royal Statistical Society, Series B, 39,* 1–38.

Divgi, D. R. (1979). Calculation of the tetrachoric correlation coefficient. *Psychometrika, 44,* 169–172.

Drasgow, F. (1982). Biased test items and differential validity. *Psychological Bulletin, 92,* 526–531.

Drasgow, F. (1987). Study of the measurement bias of two standardized psychological tests. *Journal of Applied Psychology, 72,* 19–29.

Drasgow, F., Levine, M. V., & Williams, E. A. (1985). Appropriateness measurement with polychotomous item response models and standardized indices. *British Journal of Mathematical and Statistical Psychology, 38,* 67–86.

Drasgow, F., & Olson-Buchanan, J. B. (1999). *Innovations in computerized assessment.* Hillsdale, NJ: Erlbaum.

Educational Testing Service. (1993). *GRE 1993–94 guide to the use of the Graduate Record Examinations Program.* Princeton, NJ: Author.

Embretson, S. E., & Reise, S. P. (2000). *Item response theory for psychologists.* Hillsdale, NJ: Erlbaum.

Guilford, J. P. (1941). The difficulty of a test and its factor composition. *Psychometrika, 6,* 67–77.

Hamdan, M. A. (1970). The equivalence of tetrachoric and maximum likelihood estimates of *r* in 2 × 2 tables. *Biometrika, 57,* 212–215.

Hambleton, R. K., & Swaminathan, H. (1985). *Item response theory: Principles and applications.* Norwell, MA: Kluwer.

Hambleton, R. K., Swaminathan, H., & Rogers, H. J. (1991). *Fundamentals of item response theory*. Thousand Oaks, CA: Sage.

Harnisch, D. L. (1983). Item response patterns: Applications for educational practice. *Journal of Educational Measurement, 20,* 191–206.

Hattie, J. (1985). Methodology review: Assessing the unidimensionality of tests and items. *Applied Psychological Measurement, 9,* 139–164.

Holland, P. W., & Wainer, H. (1993). *Differential item functioning*. Hillsdale, NJ: Erlbaum.

Jöreskog, K. G. (1969). A general approach to confirmatory maximum likelihood factor analysis. *Psychometrika, 34,* 183–202.

Jöreskog, K. G., & Sörbom, D. (1996). *PRELIS 2: User's reference*. Chicago: Scientific Software International.

Kim, S. (1997). BILOG 3 for windows: Item analysis and test scoring with binary logistic models. *Applied Psychological Measurement, 21,* 371–376.

Knol, D. L., & Berger, M.P.F. (1988). *Empirical comparison between factor analysis and item response models* (Research Rep. No. 88–11). Twente, The Netherlands: Department of Education, Division of Educational Measurement and Data Analysis, University of Twente.

Knol, D. L., & Berger, M.P.F. (1991). Empirical comparison between factor analysis and multidimensional item response models. *Multivariate Behavioral Research, 26,* 457–477.

Levine, M. V., & Rubin, D. B. (1979). Measuring appropriateness of multiple-choice test scores. *Journal of Educational Statistics, 4,* 269–290.

Lord, F. (1980). *Applications of item response theory to practical testing problems*. Hillsdale, NJ: Erlbaum.

Lord, F. M., & Novick, M. R. (1968). *Statistical theories of mental test scores*. Reading, MA: Addison-Wesley.

Lumsden, J. (1976). Test theory. In M. R. Rosenzweig & L. W. Porter (Eds.), *Annual review of psychology*. Palo Alto, CA: Annual Reviews.

McBride, J. R. (1997). Technical perspectives. In W. A. Sands, B. K. Waters, & J. R. McBride (Eds.), *Computer adaptive testing*. Washington, DC: American Psychological Association.

McDonald, R. P. (1999). *Test theory: A unified approach*. Hillsdale, NJ: Erlbaum.

McDonald, R. P., & Ahlawat, K. S. (1974). Difficulty factors in binary data. *British Journal of Mathematical and Statistical Psychology, 27,* 82–99.

McKinley, R., & Mills, C. (1985). A comparison of several goodness-of-fit statistics. *Applied Psychological Measurement, 9,* 49–57.

Meijer, R. R., & Sijtsma, K. (1995). Detection of aberrant item score patterns: A review of recent developments. *Applied Measurement in Education, 8,* 261–272.

Millsap, R. E., & Everson, H. T. (1993). Methodology review: Statistical approaches for assessing measurement bias. *Applied Psychological Measurement, 17,* 297–334.

Mislevy, R. J. (1986). Recent developments in the factor analysis of categorical variables. *Journal of Educational Statistics, 11,* 3–31.

Mislevy, R. J., & Bock, R. D. (1990). *BILOG-3; Item analysis and test scoring with binary logistic models* [Computer software]. Mooresville, IN: Scientific Software.

Moreno, K. E., & Segall, D. O. (1992). CAT-ASVAB precision. *Proceedings of the Thirty-Fourth Annual Conference of the Military Testing Association, 1,* 22–26.

Moreno, K. E., Wetzel, D. C., McBride, J. R., & Weiss, D. J. (1984). Relationship between corresponding Armed Services Vocational Aptitude Battery (ASVAB) and computerized adaptive testing (CAT) subtests. *Applied Psychological Measurement, 8,* 155–163.

Muraki, E., & Engelhard, G. (1985). Full information item factor analysis: Application of EAP scores. *Applied Psychological Measurement, 9,* 417–430.

Muthén, B. (1978). Contributions to factor analysis of dichotomous variables. *Psychometrika, 43,* 551–560.

Muthén, B. (1987). *LISCOMP: Analysis of linear structural equations with a comprehensive measurement model.* Chicago: Scientific Software International.

Muthén, B. (1989). Dichotomous factor analysis of symptom data. *Sociological Methods and Research, 18,* 19–65.

Muthén, B., & Hofacker, C. (1988). Testing the assumptions underlying tetrachoric correlations. *Psychometrika, 53,* 563–578.

Muthén, L. K., & Muthén B. O. (1998). *Mplus user's guide.* Los Angeles: Muthén and Muthén.

Orlando, M., & Thissen, D. (2000). Likelihood-based item-fit indices for dichotomous item response theory models. *Applied Psychological Measurement, 24,* 50–64.

Pearson, K. (1900). On the correlation of characters not quantitatively measurable. *Royal Society Philosophical Transactions, Series A, 195,* 1–47.

Raju, N. S. (1988). The area between two item characteristic curves. *Psychometrika, 53,* 495–502.

Raju, N. S. (1990). Determining the significance of estimated signed and unsigned areas between two item response functions. *Applied Psychological Measurement, 14,* 197–207.

Rasch, G. (1966). *Probabilistic models for some intelligence and attainment tests.* Copenhagen: Denmarks Paedagogiske Institute.

Reckase, M. D. (1997). The past and future of multidimensional item response theory. *Applied Psychological Methods, 21,* 25–36.

Reise, S. P., & Waller, N. G. (1990). Fitting the two-parameter model to personality data: The parameterization of the Multidimensional Personality Questionnaire. *Applied Psychological Measurement, 14,* 45–58.

Reise, S. P., & Waller, N. G. (1993). Traitedness and the assessment of response pattern scalability. *Journal of Personality and Social Psychology, 65,* 143–151.

Reise, S. P., Widaman, K. F., & Pugh, R. H. (1993). Confirmatory factor analysis and item response theory: Two approaches for exploring measurement invariance. *Psychological Bulletin, 114,* 352–566.

Reiser, M., & VandenBerg, M. (1994). Validity of the chi-square test in dichotomous variable factor analysis when expected frequencies are small. *British Journal of Mathematical and Statistical Psychology, 47,* 85–107.

Rogers, H., & Hattie, J. (1987). A Monte Carlo investigation of several person and item fit statistics for item response models. *Applied Psychological Measurement, 11,* 47–57.

Rouse, S. V., Finger, M. S., & Butcher, J. N. (1999). Advances in clinical personality measurement: An item response theory analysis of the MMPI-2 PSY-5 scales. *Journal of Personality Assessment, 72,* 282–307.

Schmitt, N., & Stults, D. M. (1985). Factors defined by negatively keyed items: The result of careless respondents? *Applied Psychological Measurement, 9,* 367–373.

Smith, L. L., & Reise, S. P. (1998). Gender differences on negative affectivity: An IRT study of differential item functioning on the Multidimensional Personality Questionnaire Stress Reaction scale. *Journal of Personality and Social Psychology, 75,* 1350–1362.

Steinberg, L., & Jorgensen, R. (1996). Assessing the MMPI-based Cook-Medley Hostility scale: The implications of dimensionality. *Journal of Personality and Social Psychology, 70,* 1281–1287.

Takane, Y., & de Leeuw, J. (1987). On the relationship between item response theory and factor analysis of discretized variables. *Psychometrika, 52,* 393–408.

Tatsuoka, K. K. (1984). Caution indices based on item response theory. *Psychometrika, 49,* 95–110.

Tatsuoka, K. (1996). Use of generalized person-fit indices, zetas for statistical pattern classification. *Applied Measurement in Education, 9,* 65–75.

Tatsuoka, K. K., & Tatsuoka, M. M. (1983). Spotting erroneous rules of operation by the individual consistency index. *Journal of Educational Measurement, 20,* 221–230.

Wainer, H. (2000). *Computerized adaptive testing: A primer* (2nd ed.). Hillsdale, NJ: Erlbaum.

Waller, N. G. (1993). Seven confirmatory factor analysis programs: EQS, EzPATH, LINCS, LISCOMP, LISREL 7, SIMPLIS, and CALIS. *Applied Psychological Measurement, 17,* 73–100.

Waller, N. G. (1999a). *Searching for structure in the MMPI-A*. Talk delivered at the 1999 Annual Meeting of the American Psychological Association, Boston.

Waller, N. G. (1999b). Searching for structure in the MMPI. In S. E. Embretson & S. L. Hershberger (Eds.), *The new rules of measurement: What every psychologist and educator should know* (pp. 185–217). Hillsdale, NJ: Erlbaum.

Waller, N. G. (2000). *MicroFACT 2.0 user's manual.* St. Paul, MN: Assessment Systems Corporation.

Waller, N. G., & Reise, S. P. (1992). Genetic and environmental influences on item response pattern scalability. *Behavior Genetics, 22*(2), 135–152.

Waller, N. G., & Reise, S. P. (2001). *Development and interpretation of the MMPI-2 and MMPI-A factor scales.* Minneapolis: University of Minnesota Press.

Waller, N. G., Tellegen, A., McDonald, R. P., & Lykken, D. T. (1996). Exploring nonlinear models in personality assessment: Development and preliminary validation of a Negative Emotionality scale. *Journal of Personality, 64,* 545–576.

Waller, N. G., Thompson, J. S., & Wenk, E. (2000). Using IRT to separate measurement bias from true group differences on homogeneous and heterogeneous scales: An illustration with the MMPI. *Psychological Methods, 5,* 125–146.

Weiss, D. J. (1982). Improving measurement quality and efficiency with adaptive testing. *Applied Psychological Measurement, 6,* 473–492.

Weiss, D. J. (1985). Adaptive testing by computer. *Journal of Consulting and Clinical Psychology, 53,* 774–789.

Wherry, R. I., & Gaylord, R. H. (1944). Factor pattern of test items and tests as a function of the correlation coefficient. *Psychometrika, 9,* 237–244.

Wilson, D. T., Wood, R., & Gibbons, R. (1991). *TESTFACT: Test scoring, item statistics, and item factor analysis.* Mooresville, IN: Scientific Software.

Wilson, M., & Engelhard, G. Jr. (2000). *Objective measurement: Theory into practice* (Vol. 5). Norwood, NJ: Ablex.

Wright, B. D., & Stone, M. H. (1979). *Best test design: Rasch measurement.* Chicago: Mesa Press.

Zickar, M. J., & Drasgow, F. (1996). Detecting faking on a personality instrument using appropriateness measurement. *Applied Psychological Measurement, 20,* 71–88.

Zimowski, M. F., Muraki, E., Mislevy, R. J., & Bock, R. D. (1996). *BILOG-MG: Multiple-group IRT analysis and test maintenance for binary items.* Chicago: Scientific Software.

CHAPTER 5

Modeling Data with Polytomous Item Response Theory

Michael J. Zickar

There are two primary reasons to use item response theory (IRT) for modeling psychological test data. The first is that IRT can be used to generate precise predictions about test behavior; these predictions are essential for many applications, such as adaptive testing in which items are chosen that are predicted to be challenging to individuals. Another domain in which test behavior predictions are necessary is computer simulation work, in which it is important to be able to determine predicted response behavior to generate realistic data responses. The second reason for modeling data with IRT is to understand better the functioning of respondents, items, and, most important, the process that respondents use to respond to those items. Polytomous IRT, which can be used to model items with more than two options, can provide better prediction and insight than dichotomous IRT, which is limited to items with two options.

There are few true dichotomies among the item types that psychologists encounter. Occasionally, items have only two options: right versus wrong, true versus false, like me versus unlike me, or forced-choice personality tests (Edwards, 1957); however, those cases are the exception. Most item types that psychologists encounter have multiple options. Polytomous formats, such as multiple-choice ability exams, Likert scales that range from Strongly Disagree to Strongly Agree or behaviorally anchored rating scales (Smith & Kendall,

1963) are more prevalent than dichotomous formats. To understand or predict responses to items with polytomous response formats, it is important to use IRT models that can accommodate all of the information present in the response data.

Polytomous IRT relies on the same concepts that were presented in Chapter Four. Therefore, central concepts of IRT, such as theta and information, will be skipped in this chapter. Instead, this chapter focuses on differences between polytomous and dichotomous IRT and highlights situations in which polytomous models have high utility.

One difference between polytomous and dichotomous IRT is that instead of a single response function that is used to characterize an item as in dichotomous IRT, each item has as many response functions as there are options for that item. Figure 5.1 presents a set of option response functions (ORFs) for a three-option personality item presented under instructions to respond honestly or to fake good. The probability on the y-axis is the probability of endorsing a particular option instead of the probability of endorsing the correct answer, as in dichotomous IRT. With dichotomous IRT, there are really two ORFs; however, because the ORF for the wrong option is inversely related to the ORF for the correct option, there is no need to present the ORF for the incorrect option. With polytomous IRT, the sum of all option probabilities for a respondent with a particular value for theta must sum to 1.0. For the first set of ORFs (the honest condition) in Figure 5.1, respondents with thetas equal to -1.0 would be expected to endorse option 1 (Unlike Me) about 5 percent of the time, whereas option 2 (Neutral) would be endorsed 60 percent of the time, and option 3 (Like Me) would be expected to be endorsed by 35 percent of those with theta equal to -1.0. As can be seen in this example, the probabilities of choosing the various options depend on the particular theta value of the respondent. Using a dichotomous model for this item would force the researcher to collapse two of these options into a single category; this reduction would result in a loss of information.

This chapter discusses the benefits of using polytomous IRT models, describes various types of polytomous IRT models that are available, and discusses several issues that are necessary to consider when using polytomous IRT. In addition, a description of a research study (Zickar & Robie, 1999) that used polytomous model-

**Figure 5.1. Personality Item Modeled by
GRM Under Faking and Honest Conditions.**

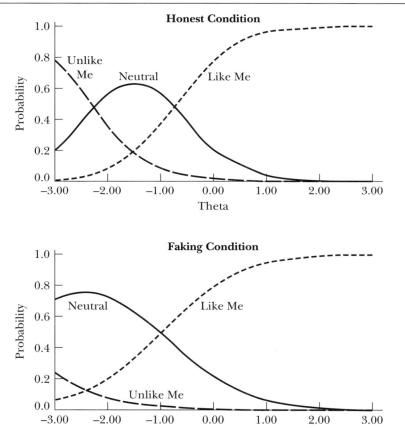

ing with Samejima's (1969) graded response model (GRM) is used to illustrate the practical benefits of this type of modeling and to outline the steps in the modeling process.

Benefits of Using Polytomous Models

It is possible to uncover more psychometric information from a given data set using polytomous data. De Ayala (1992) found that a computer adaptive test (CAT) could be made 23.4 percent shorter by using a polytomous model compared to a dichotomous model; the polytomous-based CAT could maintain the same measurement precision at a length shorter than the dichotomous-based CAT. This occurred because the polytomous model extracted more information from the data set than the dichotomous model did. This additional information results in reduced standard errors in theta estimation. Everything else equal, test designers could reduce test lengths by using polytomous models. This would minimize the time needed to administer and complete tests, which may be important in this era of overassessment and oversurveying.

Besides the practical reduction in scale length, the additional information brought about by using polytomous modeling could result in improved accuracy in detecting aberrant responses with appropriateness measurement techniques, improved accuracy of IRT-based equating, and increased sensitivity of differential item function analyses. The exact improvement brought about by polytomous models has yet to be quantified for most of these applications (and would differ depending on specific features of the test and data set), though it is likely to be considerable in many situations.

In addition to increasing the power of IRT applications, polytomous models are necessary if a researcher wants to understand the response process to items that have polytomous response formats. A mismatch between item format and analysis format might obscure important findings. For example, with the Zickar and Robie (1999) analysis, presented in greater detail later in the chapter, a polytomous analysis of three-option personality items determined that faking most affected whether respondents chose options 1 and 2; faking had little impact on the probability of choosing the most positive option (option 3). If a dichotomous model that collapsed options 1 and 2 had been used for this analysis, Zickar and Robie (1999) might have concluded falsely that faking did not influence the response process.

Types of Polytomous Models

There are several types of polytomous IRT models, each with special features that make that model suited for a particular type of data. The choice of which model to apply to a particular data set is crucial because if appropriate restrictive assumptions are made, the number of parameters to be estimated can be reduced. By reducing unnecessary parameters, it is possible to minimize the sample size needed to have a reasonable amount of precision in parameter estimates. With polytomous IRT models, several types of assumptions can be made about the data to reduce the number of item parameters to estimate. These include psychometric distance between response options, ordering of options, and the shape of response option functions. More restrictive models will be presented first, with less restrictive models following.

Rating Scale Models

One of the first assumptions that an analyst may want to make with Likert-scale items is that the way that the response format is used by respondents is similar to all other items in the scale that have that same format. For example, it might be plausible to assume that the response scale for an attitude survey that ranges from 1 (Strongly Disagree) to 5 (Strongly Disagree) will be interpreted similarly across all items on a scale. If so, the psychological distance between the response options will be identical across items. The difference between 1 (Strongly Disagree) and 2 (Disagree) will be identical for different items in the attitude scale.

If this is the case, the generalized partial credit model (GPCM) created by Muraki (1990) can be used. There are three types of parameters estimated under this model. The first parameters, category response parameters, specify the boundaries between options for all items. This model assumes that the width between response categories is identical for all items. A useful way of thinking about the width of response categories would be to examine the mean thetas of individuals choosing each option for a particular item. For a hypothetical three-option item, the mean theta for option 1 might be -2.0, for option 2 the mean might be 0.0, and for option 3 the mean might be 2.0. The distance between options 1 and 2 would be two theta units and the difference between options 2 and 3 would also be two theta units. For another item, the mean for option 1 might be -1.0, for option 2 the mean might be 1.0, and the mean for option 3 might be 3.0. For both of these items, the width between categories would be identical even though the mean thetas for categories were not identical. In essence, the first item would be considered easier because the mean theta of endorsement of the higher categories is lower than the mean theta for corresponding options of item 2. One set of category parameters, which corresponds to the distance between options, is estimated for all items on the test. The number of category parameters to be estimated is one fewer than the number of response options. It should be noted that this model can be applied only to scales that have items with the same response format throughout all items.

The GPCM model has one discrimination parameter as well as one general threshold parameter for each item. The item discrimination parameter determines the slope of the option response functions. Items with large discrimination parameters will produce option response functions that have rapidly increasing or decreasing slopes throughout the region of theta that the option is most discriminating. As a consequence, assuming all other parameters are equal, items with large discrimination parameters will have little overlap in response probabilities of the option response functions, whereas items with low discriminations will have much overlap between the option response functions. Because there is one discrimination parameter for each item, the number of discrimination parameters to be estimated equals the number of items in the scale.

In addition to the discrimination parameters, the item threshold parameters allow differences among items in terms of overall endorsement rates. The item threshold parameter is used in conjunction with the category response parameters to determine the location of the option response functions along the x-axis (the theta axis). This parameter allows for some items to be easier than others but still requires the spacing between options to be similar to other items. In the previous example using two hypothetical items that had equal widths between categories, the item threshold parameter would model the differences in mean endorsement across the two items. The number of item threshold parameters to be estimated equals the number of items in the scale.

Figure 5.2 presents option response functions for two items modeled with Muraki's (1990) GPCM. For both items, the category parameters and the item threshold parameters were identical across the two items, with only the item discriminations differing. For the more discriminating item $(a = 2.0)$, there is little overlap among the option probabilities. At any given point in the theta continuum, re-

**Figure 5.2. High- and Low-Discrimination
Items Modeled by GPCM.**

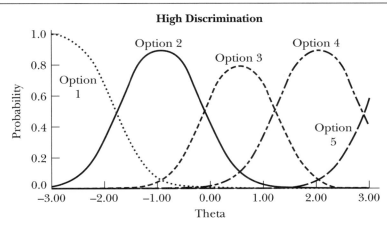

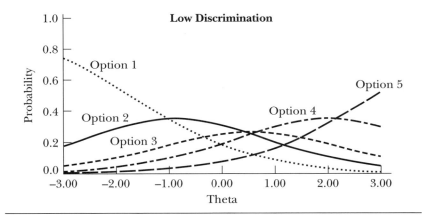

spondents have a high probability of choosing one option and little probability of choosing other options. For the less discriminating item ($a = .50$), there is considerable overlap among option probabilities, and, as a consequence, at any given area of the continuum, respondents will have large probabilities for several options.

This type of model requires relatively few parameters and so would be attractive to modelers who have small data sets from which to estimate those parameters. This model would be especially important when analyzing data with well-defined response options. For example, an item that asked, "During the typical week, how often do you think about quitting your job?" that is accompanied with the following response options, "0. not at all, 1. one day a week, 2. two days a week, . . . 7. each day of the week," could be assumed to fit this assumption. The meaning of the scale is unambiguous and unlikely to be interpreted differently across items. Unfortunately, many psychological test items might fail to fit this restrictive model; hence, this model is used less frequently than other polytomous models. An interesting research question is whether items with Likert scale formats, such as Strongly Disagree to Strongly Agree, fit the GPCM assumptions. The next class of models relaxes the assumption of identical distance between options and only requires that options be ordered in terms of valence.

Ordinal Response Options

Graded models assume that there is some a priori ordering of response options so that respondents who choose option 1 will tend to have less of the trait being measured by the item than respondents who choose option 2. This assumption of ordinal levels of response options is plausible for many personality and attitudinal items, especially those that rely on a Likert format. For example, items from Goldberg's Adjective Checklist (1992) require people to respond to personality traits (for example, "calm") with a nine-point response scale that ranges from Extremely Inaccurate to Extremely Accurate. It can be assumed that people who choose Extremely Inaccurate tend to be more neurotic (the trait being measured by that item) than those who choose the Somewhat Inaccurate response option. A polytomous IRT model that can model graded-response data is Samejima's Graded Response Model (GRM; Samejima, 1969). Unlike the GPCM, the GRM does not assume that the distance between options is equivalent across all items within a scale.

This model differs from Muraki's (1990) GPCM in that there is no overall category threshold parameter. Each item has a discrimination parameter that determines the slope of ORFs. Like the GPCM, items with high-discrimination parameters, all else equal, will have relatively more distinct ORFs compared to items with smaller-discrimination parameters. Because of this, items with high discriminations are better at differentiating among individuals of varying thetas compared to items with low discriminations. The other set of GRM parameters are the threshold parameters of which there are one fewer than the number of options. Therefore, a three-option item will have two threshold parameters. These threshold parameters incorporate both the width between categories and the overall difficulty of items. The item threshold parameters, because they are estimated for each item (unlike the GPCM), allow items to differ in both width between categories *and* overall difficulty of the item. This results in a more flexible model than the GPCM. The GRM, however, is still restricted in that an assumption of the model is that options must be ordered in difficulty. This assumption may be implausible for some types of data encountered by industrial/organizational (I/O) psychologists.

Nominal Response Options

One of the potential strengths of polytomous IRT is its capability to handle items with nominal response options. An example of this type of item might include ability test items that have correct options but also have three distractors of unknown difficulty level. Without pretesting, test designers may have no sound basis for determining which options indicate low ability and which indicate relatively higher ability. By fitting a polytomous model to nominal data, it would be possible to understand the response options better.

Hanisch (1992) provided a nice demonstration of the utility of nominal models. The Job Diagnostic Inventory (JDI; Smith, Kendall, & Hulin, 1969), a commonly used measure of job satisfaction, has items that ask respondents to consider if an adjective or phrase is descriptive of their jobs. An example item stem is, "Is your job challenging?" The response format of all JDI scales is Yes, No, and ??? There is some ambiguity over whether the ??? response is indicative of a middle response that is chosen by people with attitudes that lay in between those who chose Yes and those who chose No. Alternatively, it may be that people choose ??? because they do not understand the item or do not think that phrase is relevant to understanding their job. If the latter were true, the ??? response would need to be treated differently. To resolve this dilemma, Hanisch (1992) fit Bock's Nominal Model (1972) to the

JDI. ORFs for the ??? option lay in between the ORFs of the Yes option and the ORFs of the No option, although Hanisch did not specify the ordering of response options. Thus, the data determined that the majority of people who chose the ??? option interpreted it as lying between Yes and No.

Bock's (1972) Nominal Model does not explicitly model guessing by lower asymptote parameters (see the description of the three-parameter logistic model in Chapter Four, this volume). Thissen and Steinberg's (1984) Multiple-Choice Model, Samejima's (1979) left-sided modification of Bock's Nominal Model, and Levine's (1984) nonparametric model, Multilinear Formula Scoring, incorporate additional parameters to model guessing. These models would be good for cognitive ability tests in which even low-ability respondents should have a $1/k$ probability of guessing the correct answer, where k is the number of options.

Nominal models must estimate more parameters for each option than the previously mentioned models. For example, Bock's Nominal Model (1972) uses separate discrimination and threshold parameters for all but one option for every item. Because of these extra parameters, nominal models require larger calibration samples compared to those needed for ordinal and interval models. These types of models are used frequently in ability test item analysis when there is often little way to rank-order the attractiveness of options without collecting data. Nominal models are used less frequently with data that are more ordered, such as personality.

If you can make valid assumptions about your data, it is possible to rely on fewer data to estimate the model accurately. For example, if it were clear that response options were ordered in difficulty, an ordinal model, such as the GRM, would be preferred to a nominal model. Estimating a model that has assumptions that are invalid for a particular data set will result in a model that misfit the data. Alternatively, by refusing to make reasonable assumptions about a data set and, hence, estimating more parameters than are needed, it is likely that the accuracy of parameter estimates will be lower than if a more appropriate and parsimonious model was chosen. At times, however, a very unrestrictive model might be necessary.

Nonparametric Polytomous Models

All of the previous models assume that the shapes of ORFs are smooth. Accordingly, with these models, small differences in theta will produce small changes in response probability. There may be times, however, when researchers would be unwilling to make any assumptions about the nature of response ordering or even the shapes of ORFs. In these cases, there is a polytomous model that is extremely flexible in fitting all kinds of data. Levine's Multilinear Formula Scoring (MFS; Levine, 1984) relaxes nearly all assumptions about data; the approach taken by MFS modelers is to fit the data as much as possible; considerations about interpreting ORFs and interpreting item parameter estimates are secondary in this type of modeling. MFS works by fitting a series of complex, orthogonal polynomials to a set of items; resulting MFS ORFs can be extremely nonmonotonic and jagged. This is in contrast to all previously discussed models, which produce ORFs that are smooth throughout the range of the latent trait dimension.

The flexibility of MFS allows ORFs to assume different shapes that can be used to fit multidimensional data structures. Drasgow, Levine, Tsien, Williams, and Mead (1995) demonstrated the effectiveness of MFS in modeling responses to ability-test data. They fit several polytomous models to responses from the Scholastic Aptitude Test (SAT), the Armed Services Vocational Aptitude Test (ASVAB), and the American College Test (ACT). For the ASVAB and ACT, MFS fit the data as well as best-fitting parametric models. For the SAT, however, MFS had a superior fit compared to the other models. Drasgow et al. (1995) attributed this superiority for the SAT (but not on the other tests) to the instructions for guessing on the SAT. For the SAT, there is a correction for guessing so that excessive guessing will not result in an improved score. Therefore, respondents are encouraged to guess only if they can eliminate some of the options before guessing. On the ACT and ASVAB, there is no correction for guessing. Drasgow et al. (1995) concluded that on the SAT, the ability to use intelligently omitting influenced test scores in addition to the cognitive ability measured by the test, whereas for the ACT and ASVAB, omitting strategy was not an important influence. Because of this added dimensionality for the SAT, the additional flexibility of MFS was necessary to obtain good model-data fit.

Discussion of Model Choice

Table 5.1 presents a summary of the models that I have discussed, as well as ballpark estimates of the necessary sample sizes to fit these models accurately. These estimates were derived from consideration of several simulation and real data studies that considered various influences on model fit (see De Ayala & Sava-Bolesta, 1999; Drasgow et al., 1995; Maydeu-Olivares, Drasgow, & Mead, 1994). These ballpark estimates should be used only for general purposes. Besides sample size, other relevant factors influence the accuracy of parameter estimates: the number of items, distributional properties of the latent trait (the flatter the distribution, the smaller n necessary), dimensionality of the test, and the frequency of aberrant responses. Besides these conditions, different levels of accuracy may be demanded for different types of tasks. For example, if the goal is theta estimation, a relatively small sample size can be tolerated if there is a large number of items. Alternatively, for differential item functioning analyses, more precise item parameter estimates may be necessary. In short, all good IRT modeling efforts should include a rigorous evaluation of model fit to data and judicial use of common sense.

Computer Programs

Several commercially available programs estimate polytomous models. Table 5.1 lists the programs that can fit each model. MULTILOG (Thissen, 1991) estimates Bock's Nominal Model and Samejima's GRM, in addition to other models. It is flexible in that these two models can be constrained in various ways. PARSCALE (Muraki & Bock, 1996) is able to estimate Samejima's GRM, Master's Partial Credit Model, and Muraki's version of the GPCM. Both MULTILOG and PARSCALE are DOS based and cannot be considered user friendly. FORSCORE (Williams & Levine, 1993) is a UNIX-based software package that estimates Levine's Multilinear Formula Scoring model. At this time, there are no Windows-based software packages that estimate polytomous models.

Table 5.1. Several Polytomous Models.

Model:	Generalized Partial Credit Model
Source:	Muraki (1990)
Assumptions:	Equal discrimination across options
	Ordinal patterning of options
	Smooth option response functions
	Intervals between options same for all items
Sample Size:	Low
Program:	PARSCALE
Application:	Muraki (1990)

Model:	Graded Response Model
Source:	Samejima (1969)
Assumptions:	Equal discrimination across options
	Ordinal patterning of options
	Smooth option response functions
Sample Size:	Low
Programs:	MULTILOG, PARSCALE
Applications:	Flannery, Reise, and Widaman (1995)
	De Ayala, Dodd, and Koch (1992)

Model:	Nominal Model
Source:	Bock (1972)
Assumption:	Smooth option response functions
Sample Size:	Medium
Program:	MULTILOG
Application:	De Ayala (1992)

Model:	Multilinear Formula Scoring
Source:	Levine (1984)
Assumptions:	No significant assumptions
Sample Size:	High
Program:	FORSCORE
Application:	Drasgow et al. (1995)

Note: Sample size heuristics: low, 500; medium, 1,000; and high, 3,000.

Faking on Personality Tests

This illustration walks readers through the modeling process using MULTILOG by presenting a behind-the-scenes look at previously published research. The following modeling example (Zickar & Robie, 1999) demonstrates the utility of polytomous modeling and guides modeling novices through the polytomous modeling process as implemented in MULTILOG.

One of the primary benefits of polytomous modeling is a better understanding of the response process that respondents use when answering items. This potential for understanding is important in the personality domain in which there is such great confusion about the nature of respondent behavior. Using a multitude of research strategies, researchers have concluded that some people distort their responses when answering personality items in high-stakes settings, such as the job application process (Rosse, Stecher, Miller, & Levin, 1998; Viswesvaran & Ones, 1999). The nature of faking applicants' strategies, the prevalence of faking, and the consequences of faking are questions that are still unresolved.

Previous studies that have investigated faking have used scale-level statistics (Hough, Eaton, Dunnette, Kamp, & McCloy, 1990) or factor-analytic strategies (Schmit & Ryan, 1993) to understand faking behavior. Both are useful in providing information about faking. For example, with scale-level statistics, it is possible to determine that there are mean differences among fakers and nonfakers. With factor-analytic methodologies, Schmit and Ryan (1993) determined that the factor structure of personality inventories differed between fakers and nonfakers. Even given these advances, Zickar and Robie (1999) believed that modeling personality data using a polytomous IRT model would provide a finer level of analysis, which might lead to insights about faking that were not possible with the other strategies.

Zickar and Robie (1999) analyzed data from an experiment conducted by the U.S. Army in which some recruits were instructed to respond honestly to a personality inventory called the Assessment of Background and Life Events (ABLE) (White, Nord, Mael, & Young, 1993), whereas other recruits were instructed to fake the

ABLE (Young, White, & Oppler, 1991). Because the ABLE has three response options that are ordered (Inaccurate, Neither Accurate nor Inaccurate, and Accurate), Zickar and Robie fit a graded polytomous IRT model, Samejima's GRM, to the data (Samejima, 1969). Separate IRT analyses were conducted for the fakers and the honest responders, and the differences between the samples were analyzed using Raju's (1995) differential item and test functioning software.

Running MULTILOG

This analysis was conducted using MULTILOG on an IBM-compatible computer. To run MULTILOG, an input file is used that contains all of the commands that MULTILOG uses to determine, among other things, which type of model to estimate, the estimation routines, and how many data cases to read. This input file is created by another program, INFORLOG, which is part of the MULTILOG software package. Exhibit 5.1 presents the input commands that were created using INFORLOG. Exhibit 5.2 presents excerpts from the MULTILOG output file.

The input file used to run the GRM analysis has several key statements. The PROGRAM command line dictates what type of data are

Exhibit 5.1. MULTILOG Input Commands for Zickar and Robie (1999) Data.

Analysis of Work Orientation Data: Coached Faking Condition
>PROGRAM RA IN NI=19 NG=1 NE=527;
>TEST ALL GR NC=(3(0)19);
>SAVE;
>END;
          3
123
1111111111111111111
2222222222222222222
3333333333333333333
(5X,19A1)

Exhibit 5.2. Excerpts of MULTILOG Output
for Zickar and Robie (1999).

Analysis of Work Orientation data—Coached Faking Condition
  DATA PARAMETERS:
  NUMBER OF LINES IN THE DATA FILE: 527
  NUMBER OF CATEGORICAL-RESPONSE ITEMS: 19
  NUMBER OF CONTINUOUS-RESPONSE ITEMS, AND/OR GROUPS: 1
  TOTAL NUMBER OF "ITEMS" (INCLUDING GROUPS): 20
  THE M-STEP CONVERGENCE CRITERION IS: 0.000100
  THE EM-CYCLE CONVERGENCE CRITERION IS: 0.001000
  THE RK CONTROL PARAMETER (FOR THE M-STEPS) IS: 0.9000
  THE RM CONTROL PARAMETER (FOR THE M-STEPS) IS: 1.0000
  THE MAXIMUM ACCELERATION PERMITTED IS: 0.0000
  THETA-GROUP LOCATIONS WILL REMAIN UNCHANGED

Analysis of Work Orientation data—Coached Faking Condition
READING DATA.
KEY-
CODE CATEGORY

1	1111111111111111111
2	2222222222222222222
3	3333333333333333333

FORMAT FOR DATA-

  (5X,19A1)
FIRST OBSERVATION AS READ-

  ITEMS 2121133212233112311

ITEM SUMMARY
Analysis of Work Orientation data—Coached Faking Condition

ITEM   1:   3 GRADED CATEGORIES

	P(#)	ESTIMATE	(S.E.)
A	1	1.78	(0.35)
B(1)	2	−3.09	(0.51)
B(2)	3	−1.57	(0.18)

@THETA:	−2.0	−1.5	−1.0	−0.5	0.0	0.5	1.0	1.5	2.0
I (THETA):	0.84	0.83	0.62	0.36	0.17	0.08	0.03	0.01	0.01

Exhibit 5.2. Excerpts of MULTILOG Output
for Zickar and Robie (1999), Cont'd.

OBSERVED AND EXPECTED COUNTS/PROPORTIONS IN

CATEGORY(K):	1	2	3
OBS. FREQ.	6	53	468
OBS. PROP.	0.01	0.10	0.89
EXP. PROP.	0.02	0.11	0.87

ITEM 2:   3   GRADED CATEGORIES

	P(#)	ESTIMATE	(S.E.)
A	4	1.79	(0.22)
B(1)	5	−1.74	(0.17)
B(2)	6	−0.72	(0.10)

@THETA:	−2.0	−1.5	−1.0	−0.5	0.0	0.5	1.0	1.5	2.0
I (THETA):	0.79	0.92	0.93	0.81	0.55	0.29	0.14	0.06	0.02

OBSERVED AND EXPECTED COUNTS/PROPORTIONS IN

CATEGORY(K):	1	2	3
OBS. FREQ.	47	93	387
OBS. PROP.	0.09	0.18	0.73
EXP. PROP.	0.11	0.20	0.70

TOTAL TEST INFORMATION

@THETA:	−2.0	−1.5	−1.0	−0.5	0.0	0.5	1.0	1.5	2.0
I (THETA):	19.4	20.7	19.2	14.7	9.1	5.1	2.9	1.8	1.4
SE (THETA):	0.23	0.22	0.23	0.26	0.33	0.44	0.59	0.74	0.85

MARGINAL RELIABILITY: 0.82
NEGATIVE TWICE THE LOGLIKELIHOOD=   3818.3
(CHI-SQUARE FOR SEVERAL TIMES MORE EXAMINEES THAN CELLS)

being analyzed and what types of parameters are to be estimated. The IN command dictates that individual responses are read in from the data file (grouped data can also be read in). The RA command dictates that item parameters will be estimated (other commands, such as SC, are used if other types of parameters, such as person parameters, are to be estimated). Other commands dictate that the number of items (NI = 19) to be analyzed is 19, that there is one group (NG = 1), and that the number of respondents and examinees equals 527 (NE = 527). Although previous versions of MULTILOG had limitations on the number of items that could be analyzed, the current version, MULTILOG 6.3, has no set limits on number of items or respondents.

The second command line, TEST, dictates that the graded response model (GR) be estimated (other models could have been specified) and that each of the nineteen items has three categories or options. The command (NC = (3(0)19) is a programming shortcut; alternatively, I could have typed (NC = 3, 3,. . ., 3) with nineteen 3s entered. One of the strengths of MULTILOG is that it can be used to analyze scales with items that differ in number of options. If that were the case for this scale, the NC command would be changed accordingly (for example, NC = 3,4,3,4,. . .,3). This flexibility in analyzing items with differing numbers of options without making special corrections (for example, standardizing all items to put them on the same scale) has been noted elsewhere as a special benefit of IRT compared to traditional test theory (Thissen, 1993; Zickar, Russell, Smith, Bohle, & Tilley, 2000).

The SAVE command line dictates that item parameter estimates will be saved in a separate file. This file can be used to do a statistical analysis of item parameter estimates and to generate plots. The subsequent lines detail the number of options per item, the values for each response option or category, and the answers that specify the value for each option for each item. The streams of nineteen 1s, nineteen 2s, and nineteen 3s are all of the same value because all items were keyed in the same direction for this scale. It would be possible to analyze reverse-scored items using MULTILOG; however, I usually manipulate the data file (using SPSS) so that all items are keyed in the same direction before doing the IRT analysis. The final command line (5X,19A1) is a FORTRAN format statement that dictates that the data file has five columns at the beginning of each line that should not be analyzed (in this case, these five spaces were experimental condition and ID codes) and then nineteen columns that correspond to the nineteen items in the scale. Other commands could have been specified in this input file (for example, estimation convergence criteria or Bayesian priors), but because they were not specified, program default options were used.

MULTILOG Output

Exhibit 5.2 presents excerpts from the output file for this analysis. The first part of the output prints out the commands that were read in from the input file. For example, the output file lists that nineteen categorical-response items were analyzed and that 527 lines were in the data file. It is important to check these statements to determine if the input file was read correctly. Another important check is the first data observation, which is also printed in the output file. This is important to check to see if it corresponds with the actual data file; it is possible (and, indeed, a common problem) that the data were read incorrectly due to a misspecification of format.

In the Item Summary section of the output, parameter estimates along with standard errors are printed. Because the GRM was estimated, for each item there is a discrimination parameter estimate and two threshold parameter estimates. Comparing item 1 and item 2, the discriminations are nearly identical (1.78 versus 1.79), whereas the threshold estimates are more negative for the first item than the second (-3.09 versus -1.74, -1.57 versus -0.72). Because the thresholds are more negative for the first item, the first item should have fewer respondents who chose the smaller options compared to the second. The observed frequency of respondents who chose each option is also provided, so it is possible to check this. As can be seen in the output, only 1 percent of the respondents chose option 1 for item 1, whereas 9 percent of the respondents chose option 1 for item 2. These observed proportions can be compared to theoretical proportions to get a rough sense of model fit. The theoretical proportions are computed based on the model; if all of the assumptions about the model are correct, the theoretical proportions specify what proportion of the sample would be expected to choose each option. If there are large discrepancies between the theoretical and observed proportions, that would be prima facie evidence of model misfit. As will be discussed later, further steps should be taken to evaluate model fit.

A few other sections of the output file should be noted. For each item, information values are given for nine intervals of the theta scale in the row labeled I(theta). At the end of the output, the total test (scale) information values for these nine intervals are also given. The last value of the output is a negative twice the log-likelihood function. Lower values indicate better fit of the model to the data. The likelihood value by itself, however, has little practical value, because the level of this index that constitutes good fit varies across testing situations. The value in this output, 3,818.3, may indicate excellent fit or gross misfit depending on the number of cases and the number of items. The value can be interpreted only if nested models are tested. For example, using MULTILOG, it is possible to constrain all item discrimination parameters to be equal and to test whether those constraints result in poorer model fit (Thissen, Steinberg, & Wainer, 1993). A limitation of the test of relative model fit is that even the best-fitting model of several nested models may still not fit the data.

Testing Model-Data Fit

To test absolute model fit, further analyses need to be conducted beyond those available through MULTILOG. Goodness-of-fit analyses described by Drasgow et al. (1995) allow the test evaluator to compute chi-square statistics that can be used to evaluate absolute fit. These procedures have been implemented into an EXCEL-based program, Multiple Model Data Fit (MMDF; Stark, 2000). With these procedures, the proportion of individuals expected to choose an item is computed based on probabilities computed from the item response model and estimated parameters, as well as the expected theta distribution. This expected proportion is then compared to the observed proportion of respondents who chose that option. A chi-square statistic is computed from both these theoretical and observed probabilities; a high value for this chi-square statistic would indicate that the estimated item response model does not represent the real data.

Because it may be possible that an item response model fits the data at the item level but fails to fit at a higher level of analysis, it is important to compute chi-squares for the fit of combinations of two items (item doubles) and three items (item triples). These chi-squares are computed by using two-way and three-way contingency tables. For example, a two-way contingency table compares expected and observed probabilities for answering 0 on item 1 and 0 on item 2, and the other three possible combinations: 0 1, 1 0, and 1 1. It is important to evaluate the fit of these item doubles and item triples because scales that have high levels of multidimensionality may still have low item single chi-squares that indicate model fit; it may be only at the item-double and item-triple level where misfit is evidenced. MMDF can compute chi-squares at the item-single, item-double, and item-triple level. For the Zickar and Robie (1999) analysis, none of the item-single, item-double, or item-triple chi-square statistics were significant. It could be concluded that the GRM fit all nineteen items of the WO scale.

As an additional method of investigating fit, MMDF can generate fit plots that display empirical proportions of respondents selecting each option at various theta values as well as the estimated ORFs. These plots can be useful because they can provide suggestions on why misfit is occurring. For example, if ORFs misfit at the extremely negative range of the theta continuum, it could suggest that guessing is a factor and a left-sided model should be used (Samejima, 1979).

Substantive Conclusions from Faking Analyses

Once it has been concluded that the model fits the data, it is legitimate to evaluate the IRT results to generate substantive conclusions. The Zickar and Robie (1999) GRM analysis of personality faking data clarified how faking affects the ABLE personality instrument.

As expected, Zickar and Robie (1999) found that across all constructs, there was a mean scale score difference, usually about 0.5 to 1.0 standard deviations higher for fakers, that was consistent with meta-analytic research on faking (Viswesvaran & Ones, 1999). With IRT, though, it is possible to get beyond simply examining mean differences and instead focus on the nature and shape of differences between groups. Differential item functioning (DIF; Raju, 1995) procedures test whether estimated ORFs differ across distinct samples and populations. In this study, we examined differences in ORFs across faking and honest conditions. By scrutinizing the nature and extent of the differences, it was possible to make inferences about the nature of faking.

For many of the ABLE items, there were no differences, besides a simple mean difference in that fakers received consistently higher scores on the items compared to honest responders. These consistent mean differences are eliminated by an equating procedure that is part of DIF procedure. When there were differences in ORFs, there was a tendency that responses to the least desirable and neutral options were most affected (see Figure 5.1 for an example of this). For this item, the ORF for the least desirable option is shifted to the right for honest responders. That shift means that for respondents with identical standings on the latent trait, honest responders will have a higher probability of choosing the least desirable option compared to those who were faking. This is not surprising; however, there is no substantial shift in the ORFs for the most positive option. Therefore, it appears that faking, at least for this item, affects the probabilities of choosing the negative and neutral options but does not affect the probability of choosing the positive option. Given these results, it might be inferred that people who fake have the lowest trait scores to begin with; other respondents who have a reasonably high level of the trait do not change their response behavior.

Another lesson we learned from this analysis was that the item discriminations remained relatively equivalent between the faking and honest conditions. It might be hypothesized that faking would lower the discrimination of items because scores of people who are faking would be related to some other trait (for example, faking ability) in addition to their true standings on the personality trait being assessed. Our analysis did not demonstrate that. This suggests that most fakers augment their standing on personality traits by exaggerating already existing characteristics instead of completely fabricating personality characteristics. Regardless, the finding that items maintained discrimination despite the presence of faking suggests that faking may not have as deleterious effects as previously thought.

This type of analysis is a good example of how a polytomous model can reveal insights that are not possible with a dichotomous IRT model or non-IRT methods. The IRT model can be used to generate insights about faking behavior (Zickar & Robie, 1999), to model faking (Zickar, 2000), and to detect faking (Zickar & Drasgow, 1996).

Further Issues with Polytomous Models

Although I have discussed several reasons that researchers might want to apply polytomous IRT models to polytomously scored data, there may be some instances in which dichotomous models would be preferred. All things equal, it is best to use models that can use all of the information present in the data. There are several situations, however, in which applying polytomous IRT models may not be feasible. In these situations, a mismatch between the data format and the model format could be tolerated in lieu of other considerations.

With limited sample sizes, parsimonious models might be preferred. Because polytomous models have more parameters to estimate than dichotomous models, it may be better with small data sets to use the simpler models. Some of the polytomous models (such as MFS) require calibration sample size requirements that are so large that they preclude use except by extremely large organizations, such as the military, or testing companies, such as the Educational Testing Service. With small sample sizes, researchers may be forced to use dichotomous models to obtain accurate parameter estimates.

In addition to overall sample size, it is often the case that many of the options on tests will be infrequently chosen. On personality items, very few people choose items that are low in social desirability. In a data set I collected using Goldberg's Adjective Checklist (1992), no one in a sample of 120 students selected the two most socially undesirable options on a nine-point Likert scale for the item Kind. Only one student out of 120 selected an option that indicated that he or she was even moderately unkind. Given these endorsement rates, it would be impossible to estimate parameters for these options without exorbitantly large sample sizes. In these cases, it is likely that researchers would collapse nearby options for the IRT analysis, thereby reducing the nine-point scale to a smaller number of options. Although overall sample size is important for parameter estimation, it is also important to have each option endorsed by a minimum number of individuals. Unfortunately, there has not been enough research to come up with well-reasoned guidelines for these minimum numbers.

Another reason for using dichotomous models for polytomous data is that if there is no pattern among the distractors, a dichotomous model would be preferred. For example, with a knowledge item, all of the wrong answers might be equally plausible (or implausible). Therefore, there would be no pattern among the wrong answers and polytomous models would not be able to extract additional information. Figure 5.3 presents two different hypothetical items fit with a nominal model. For the first ORF (the low payoff item), there would be little payoff in using a more complex polytomous model instead of a simpler dichotomous model. For this item, option 1 is scored correct; respondents with low ability have little expectation of answering the item correctly, whereas high-ability respondents answer correctly a large percentage of the time. All of the other options have roughly equal chances of being chosen. For this item, it is likely that people who do not know the answer choose randomly among the other options. All of the wrong options could be combined with little loss of information.

The second item (the high payoff item) in Figure 5.3 presents the ORFs for an item in which a polytomous model would provide more information compared to a dichotomous model. In this case, the highest-ability respondents still choose option 1 at the highest level. However, there also is a tendency for low-ability respondents to choose option 4 and for average-ability respondents to choose option 5. Option 5 might be closer to being correct than option 1; respondents who chose this option should be given more credit than those who chose the other wrong options. Also, notice that option 2 is chosen very infrequently at all levels of ability. This option should be revised because as is, it is little more than a space filler. For items such as presented in Figure 5.3, using the correct polytomous model (in this case a nominal model) will result in more psychometric information than would a dichotomous model.

A final reason for using dichotomous models is that the complexity of the polytomous model might not be offset by better results compared to the simpler dichotomous models. For example, Zickar and Drasgow (1996) found that a dichotomous IRT model (the two-parameter logistic model; 2-PLM) provided equivalent results in an appropriateness measurement study compared to a polytomous model (GRM). Accuracy of detecting people who were faking using IRT models did not increase when using polytomous

**Figure 5.3. Low- and High-Payoff Items
for Using a Nominal Model.**

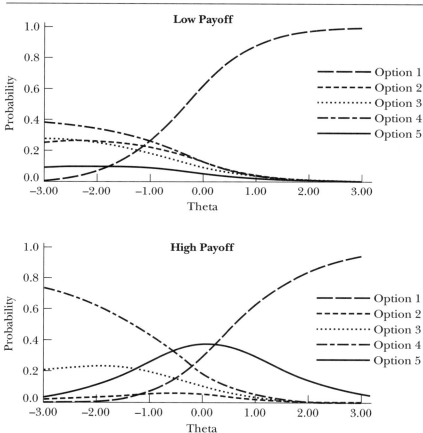

models. If possible, it would be desirable to compare results for dichotomous and polytomous models to see if there is an advantage. Future research should also be directed to identifying applications in which polytomous models provide much better results than dichotomous models.

To dichotomize polytomous data, it is necessary to collapse data across different response categories. For example, if there is a seven-option Likert scale ranging from Strongly Disagree to Strongly

Agree, a decision needs to be made as to how to group the seven categories into two distinct categories. Essentially, there are six plausible ways that the options can be combined. For example, option 1 could be coded 0, whereas options 2 through 7 could be coded 1. A more plausible coding would be to combine all of the options that indicate disagreement into category 0 and all of the agreement options into category 1. The neutral category (option 4) could be combined into either category 0 or category 1. Options that are combined should be chosen by respondents who share similar levels of the trait being measured by the test. This process is subjective, and therefore it may be prudent to use several different dichotomizations to determine which leads to the best fit.

Potential Applications of Polytomous Models

There are several untapped areas where polytomous IRT modeling can provide unique advantages not possible with traditional dichotomous IRT modeling.

Personality Measurement

I believe that the biggest area for contributions of polytomous IRT modeling is in the personality domain. Almost all personality scales, excluding the Hogan Personality Inventory (Hogan & Hogan, 1992), have polytomous response formats. As has been noted elsewhere (Steinberg & Thissen, 1995; Zickar, 2001), IRT has been developed primarily in the cognitive ability domain and only recently has been applied to the personality domain with increasing frequency. With ability items, it is likely that many of the items have patterns similar to the low-payoff item in Figure 5.3. For personality items with the graded format, however, it is more likely that different options will be chosen by systematically different respondents.

Polytomous IRT should be able to provide advances in both practical measurement areas and personality theory development. With respect to practical issues, polytomous IRT should be able to inform researchers about the best response option formats. Currently, there is little consensus among personality instruments with respect to the number of options and the labels associated with those options. By conducting experiments in which response format is varied, it would be possible to determine which format leads to items with more psychometric information and discrimination among individuals. Another practical problem is that it is difficult to write personality items that are discriminating at high, positive ranges of the personality trait continuum. For example, items that discriminate among people who are extremely low in conscientiousness from those who are only moderately low are relatively easy to write. Items that discriminate between people high in conscientiousness and those extremely high, however, are extremely difficult to write. It may be possible to develop response formats that help increase discrimination in the desired ranges. Polytomous IRT models would be necessary for this type of research.

With respect to personality theory development, polytomous IRT has been found to be useful in answering important theoretical questions. Personality theorists have theorized that some individuals may exist who cannot be correctly placed on personality dimensions that are assumed to be necessary for summarizing individual behavior (Bem & Allen, 1974). Tellegen (1988) suggested that individuals who cannot be characterized by common personality trait dimension be labeled "untraited." Reise and Waller (1993) used a dichotomous 2-PLM to identify untraited individuals on the Multidimensional Personality Questionnaire. They had limited success, though, because of the low reliability of the untraitedness index. Zickar (1997), using the MFS model on HPI and ABLE data, had more success in measuring untraitedness reliably; he determined that extreme forms of untraitedness were extremely rare. In this case, polytomous IRT seemed to be an essential tool for determining the nature and prevalence of untraitedness.

As noted in the extended illustration in this chapter, polytomous IRT has also been useful in understanding how respondents respond to personality items when faking (Zickar & Robie, 1999). What is clear from this research is that to really understand how people respond to items, it is important that the model be consistent with the response format being used by respondents. Polytomously scored items require polytomous models to advance understanding.

Verifying Interval Measurement

Many statistical methods, especially those based on Pearson product-moment correlations, require data to be interval level. However, it is difficult to demonstrate that psychological scales have the properties of an interval scale. For example, the psychological distance between Strongly Disagree and Disagree is assumed to be equal to the psychological distance between Disagree and Slightly Disagree. It is true that the quantitative values assigned to those options possess interval properties, but the assignment of numbers to options is arbitrary (except for the ordering). Using polytomous IRT, it is possible to determine whether a particular set of items possess interval properties. It would be possible to use a model that assumes only ordinal-level measurement to test whether data fit the interval level. The GRM could be fit to a personality scale with a traditional Likert format and used to determine whether the ORFs are equally spaced through the theta continuum. As shown by the ORF presented in Figure 5.1, it is likely that many items would fail to satisfy the interval-level requirements. It would also be possible to determine the consequences of violating interval assumptions using Monte Carlo simulation methods.

Scaling Nominal Options

Another untapped potential of polytomous models is to use nominal, polytomous models to scale items for nominal response formats. There are several areas where this might be relevant for organizational researchers. Situational judgment tests present a scenario to respondents and then a set of options that the respondent can choose. A good example of such a test is the video-based assessment of conflict resolution skills developed by Olson-Buchanan et al. (1998). Respondents watch a scenario unfold (for example, a recalcitrant employee refuses to adapt to a new policy) and then choose one of four possible responses to how they would deal with this employee (for example, to be conciliatory or aggressive). Olson-Buchanan et al. (1998) used a theory-based approach to determine the scoring weights for each option. Another approach would have been to use scoring weights estimated by a nominal response model. Using this approach, it would be possible to determine that people who choose the conciliatory option tend to have higher conflict skills than those who choose the more aggressive approach (or vice versa). Therefore, nominal models would provide a good inductive approach to item scoring and theory development. It should be noted, though, that the nominal scaling would take a relatively larger sample size than theory-based methods. Biographical data forms might provide another arena where nominal models would provide help in scoring, though these data are often not sufficiently unidimensional to allow the use of IRT models.

Conclusion

Polytomous IRT modeling is an excellent tool in the I/O psychologist's toolbox. By better matching method of analysis with method of responding, psychologists can improve prediction of responses and increase understanding. When I was interviewing for my current position, one of my future colleagues commented that IRT was limited as a data-analytic technique for applied psychologists because it was restricted to items with right or wrong answers. Dichotomous IRT models were developed first, and applications of these methods became well known in the 1980s. Roznowski (1989), in analyzing the three-option items of the Job Diagnostic Inventory (Smith et al., 1969), used a dichotomous model because programs to estimate polytomous models were unavailable. She predicted that "algorithms that allow multistep data and analysis of [polytomous] JDI data using such methods likely will be forthcoming" (p. 813). As she forecasted, polytomous IRT is alive and well. My colleague was wrong.

Like other complex data-analytic techniques (such as structural equation modeling), there is a danger in having the methodology used in inappropriate situations. This can occur when the technique used for analysis does not correspond to the data. For example, using the polytomous IRT modeling techniques discussed in this chapter to model highly multidimensional data would be inappropriate. The computer estimation program may estimate ORFs for the data, and those ORFs might be used for interpretation even though they would grossly misfit the data. This type of inappropriate use of polytomous modeling, though, is easy to detect by the goodness-of-fit techniques discussed in this chapter.

The other type of inappropriate use of IRT modeling is perhaps even more prevalent. This occurs when a complex methodology, like polytomous IRT modeling, is used for a task in which a simpler technique would provide the same answer. Many psychometric questions can be answered through simpler techniques, like classical test theory item analysis. Poor items can usually be identified in an analysis of item-total correlations, which is much easier to conduct than polytomous IRT modeling. Because I/O psychologists are fascinated with complex data-analytic techniques, they often choose the more complex, circuitous route over the simpler, more direct approach. We should save polytomous modeling for the tasks that require its complexity. As described throughout the chapter, there are many psychometric problems that require its use.

Polytomous IRT modeling advances the state of psychometric modeling and should be an important tool to help I/O psychologists develop practical techniques and advance theory. In short, judicious and creative use of polytomous IRT will advance both science and practice.

References

Bem, D. J., & Allen, A. (1974). On predicting some of the people some of the time: The search for cross-situational consistencies in behavior. *Psychological Review, 81,* 506–520.

Bock, R. D. (1972). Estimating item parameters and latent ability when responses are scored in two or more nominal categories. *Psychometrika, 37,* 29–51.

De Ayala, R. J. (1992). The nominal response model in computerized adaptive testing. *Applied Psychological Measurement, 16,* 327–343.

De Ayala, R. J., Dodd, B. G., & Koch, W. R. (1992). A comparison of the partial credit and graded response models in computerized adaptive testing. *Applied Measurement in Education, 5,* 17–34.

De Ayala, R. J., & Sava-Bolesta, M. (1999). Item parameter recovery for the nominal response model. *Applied Psychological Measurement, 23,* 3–19.

Drasgow, F., Levine, M. V., Tsien, S., Williams, B., & Mead, A. D. (1995). Fitting polytomous item response theory models to multiple-choice tests. *Applied Psychological Measurement, 19,* 143–165.

Edwards, A. L. (1957). *The social desirability variable in personality assessment and research.* Orlando, FL: Dryden Press.

Goldberg, L. R. (1992). The development of markers for the big-five factor structure. *Psychological Assessment, 4,* 26–42.

Hanisch, K. A. (1992). The Job Descriptive Index revisited: Questions about the question mark. *Journal of Applied Psychology, 77,* 377–382.

Hogan, R., & Hogan, J. (1992). *Hogan personality inventory manual.* Tulsa, OK: Hogan Assessment Systems.

Hough, L. M., Eaton, N. K., Dunnette, M. D., Kamp, J. D., & McCloy, R. A. (1990). Criterion-related validities of personality constructs and the effects of response distortion on those validities. *Journal of Applied Psychology, 75,* 581–595.

Levine, M. V. (1984). *An introduction to multilinear formula score theory.* Champaign: University of Illinois, Department of Educational Psychology.

Maydeu-Olivares, A., Drasgow, F., & Mead, A. D. (1994). Distinguishing among parametric item response models for polychotomous ordered data. *Applied Psychological Measurement, 18,* 245–256.

Muraki, E. (1990). Fitting a polytomous item response model to Likert-type data. *Applied Psychological Measurement, 14,* 59–71.

Muraki, E., & Bock, R. D. (1996). *PARSCALE 3.0* [Computer software]. Chicago: Scientific Software International.

Olson-Buchanan, J. B., Drasgow, F., Moberg, P. J., Mead, A. D., Keenan, P. A., & Donovan, M. A. (1998). Interactive video assessment of conflict resolution skills. *Personnel Psychology, 51,* 1–24.

Raju, N. (1995). *DFITPU: A Fortran program for calculating DIF/DTF* [Computer program]. Atlanta: Georgia Institute of Technology.

Reise, S. P., & Waller, N. G. (1993). Traitedness and the assessment of response pattern scalability. *Journal of Personality and Social Psychology, 54,* 143–151.

Rosse J. G., Stecher, M. D., Miller, J. L., & Levin, R. A. (1998). The impact of response distortion on preemployment personality testing and hiring decisions. *Journal of Applied Psychology, 83,* 634–644.

Roznowski, M. (1989). An examination of the measurement properties of the Job Descriptive Index with experimental items. *Journal of Applied Psychology, 74,* 805–814.

Samejima, F. (1969). Estimation of latent ability using a response pattern of graded response scores. *Psychometrika, 34*(4, pt.2).

Samejima, F. (1979). *A new family of models for the multiple choice item* (Res. Rep. No. 79-4). Nashville: University of Tennessee, Department of Psychology.

Schmit, M. J., & Ryan, A. M. (1993). The big five in personnel selection: Factor structure in applicant and nonapplicant populations. *Journal of Applied Psychology, 78,* 966–974.

Smith, P. C., & Kendall, L. M. (1963). Retranslation of expectations: An approach to the construction of unambiguous anchors for rating scales. *Journal of Applied Psychology, 47,* 149–155.

Smith, P. C., Kendall, L. M., & Hulin, C. L. (1969). *The measurement of satisfaction in work and retirement.* Skokie, IL: Rand McNally.

Stark, S. (2000). *Multiple model data fit* [Computer program]. Champaign, IL: Author.

Steinberg, L., & Thissen, D. (1995). Item response theory in personality research. In P. Shrout & S. Fiske (Eds.), *Personality research, methods and theory: A festschrift honoring Donald W. Fiske* (pp. 161–181). Hillsdale, NJ: Erlbaum.

Tellegen, A. (1988). The analysis of consistency in personality assessment. *Journal of Personality, 56,* 621–663.

Thissen, D. (1991). *MULTILOG: Multiple, categorical item analysis and test scoring using item response theory (Version 6.0).* Chicago: Scientific Software International.

Thissen, D. (1993). Repealing rules that no longer apply to psychological measurement. In N. Fredricksen, R. J. Mislevy, & I. I. Bejar (Eds.), *Test theory for a new generation of tests.* Hillsdale, NJ: Erlbaum.

Thissen, D., & Steinberg, L. (1984). A response model for multiple choice items. *Psychometrika, 49,* 501–519.

Thissen, D., Steinberg, L., & Wainer, H. (1993). Detection of differential item functioning using the parameters of item response models. In P. W. Holland & H. Wainer (Eds.), *Differential item functioning* (pp. 67–113). Hillsdale, NJ: Erlbaum.

Viswesvaran, C., & Ones, D. S. (1999). Meta-analysis of fakability estimates: Implications for personality measurement. *Educational and Psychological Measurement, 59,* 197–210.

White, L. A., Nord, R. D., Mael, F. A., & Young, M. C. (1993). The Assessment of Background and Life Experiences (ABLE). In T. Trent & J. H. Laurence (Eds.), *Adaptability screening for the armed forces* (pp. 101–162). Washington, DC: Office of Assistant Secretary of Defense.

Williams, B., & Levine, M. V. (1993). *Introduction to FORSCORE.* Paper presented at the annual meeting of the Psychometric Society, Urbana, IL.

Young, M. C., White, L. A., & Oppler, S. H. (1991). *Coaching effects on the Assessment of Background and Life Experiences (ABLE).* Paper presented at the meeting of the Military Testing Association, San Antonio, TX.

Zickar, M. J. (1997). *Identifying untraited individuals using model-based measurement.* Unpublished doctoral dissertation, University of Illinois, Urbana-Champaign.

Zickar, M. J. (2000). Modeling faking on personality tests. In D. Ilgen & C. L. Hulin (Eds.), *Computational modeling of behavior in organizations* (pp. 95–108). Washington, DC: American Psychological Association.

Zickar, M. J. (2001). Conquering the next frontier: Modeling personality data with item response theory. In B. Roberts & R. Hogan (Eds.), *Personality psychology in the workplace* (pp. 141–158). Washington, DC: American Psychological Association.

Zickar, M. J., & Drasgow, F. (1996). Detecting faking on a personality instrument using appropriateness measurement. *Applied Psychological Measurement, 20,* 71–87.

Zickar, M. J., & Robie, C. (1999). Modeling faking at the item-level. *Journal of Applied Psychology, 84,* 551–563.

Zickar, M. J., Russell, S. S., Smith, C. S., Bohle, P., & Tilley, A. J. (2000). *Evaluating two morningness scales with item response theory.* Unpublished manuscript.

CHAPTER 6

Differential Item and Test Functioning

Nambury S. Raju
Barbara B. Ellis

Differential item functioning (DIF) refers to a property of a test item. An item displays DIF when individuals from different groups who have the same standing on the attribute assessed by the item have different probabilities of answering the item correctly or have different expected raw scores on the item (Hambleton & Swaminathan, 1985; Hambleton, Swaminathan, & Rogers, 1991; Hulin, Drasgow, & Parsons, 1983; Lord, 1980). Performance differences among individuals from different groups who are equal with respect to the attribute measured are presumably a function of unexpected differences between examinee groups.

Early studies of DIF, formerly referred to as item bias, began in the 1960s. As a result of civil rights legislation, American psychometricians undertook a comprehensive effort to identify test items that were responded to differently by minority groups compared to the majority group (Angoff, 1993; Cole, 1993). Angoff (1993) wrote, "These studies were designed to develop methods for studying cultural differences and for investigating the assertion that the principal, if not the sole, reason for the great disparity in test performance between Black and Hispanic students and White students on tests of cognitive ability is that the tests contain items that are outside the realms of the minority cultures" (p. 3). In other words, it was assumed that "biased items" were biased "against" the minority in comparison with the majority group. If such items could be identified and eliminated from the test, group differences at the test level presumably would vanish or be reduced.

The shift in terminology from item bias to DIF came about in the late 1980s for reasons that were more political-linguistic than psychometric. Cole (1993) presents an in-depth discussion of the conflict between the social and technical connotations of *bias* and *fairness.* To laypersons, *item bias* understandably has a negative con- notation; common synonyms for *bias* include *prejudice, unfairness,* and *partiality.* The technical definition of DIF, or item bias, was only poorly understood outside the testing community.

Ultimately, it was recognized that it was necessary to differen- tiate the social and technical terminologies more clearly. Psycho- metricians are now careful to define DIF, bias, and the relationship between these terms. Hambleton et al. (1991) wrote:

> Investigations of bias involve gathering *empirical* evidence concern- ing the relative performances on the test item of members of the minority group of interest and members of the group that repre- sents the majority. Empirical evidence of differential performance is necessary, but not sufficient, to draw the conclusion that bias is present; this conclusion involves an inference that goes beyond the data. To distinguish the empirical evidence from the conclusion, the term *differential item functioning* (DIF) rather than bias is used commonly to describe the empirical evidence obtained in investiga- tions of bias [p. 109].

Item response theory (IRT; Lord, 1980; Lord & Novick, 1968), as opposed to classical test theory (CTT; Gulliksen, 1950), provides a context for a psychometrically sound operational definition of DIF. It is well known that CTT indices of item difficulty (p values) and discrimination (item-total correlations) depend on group dif- ferences in the trait. For example, an item's p value from a popu- lation low in cognitive ability will be lower than the p value for the same item from a population high in cognitive ability. IRT models (discussed in depth in other chapters in this volume), in contrast, control for individual differences in ability when item parameters are estimated, so that item difficulty and discrimination indices are not confounded with group differences.

The use of the term *DIF* rather than *item bias* fortuitously creates other advantages, because applications of these methods go beyond minority-majority comparisons. DIF methods are used to examine the equivalence of test items administered to a multitude of examinee groups, for example, groups differing in culture, language, age, gender, disability status, and so forth. DIF methods can even be used to understand the psychological processes involved in testing and "the subtle differences in content of a stimulus to which individuals react differently" (Cole, 1981, p. 1076).

Our discussion of differential functioning (DF) has so far focused at the item level, but Drasgow and Hulin (1990) have noted that the effects of DF should be examined at the level at which decisions are made—"at the level of total scale or test scores, not at the level of individual items" (p. 623). In this chapter, we examine DF at the item level (DIF) as well as at the test level (differential test functioning; DTF).

Differential Functioning

DF examines the degree to which two individuals with identical ability or identical standing on a construct (such as job satisfaction) but each representing a different group (for example, male-female, or African American–Caucasian) have the same expected raw score (true score or probability of success) on an item or a test. If an individual's probability of success on a dichotomously scored (right-wrong) item depends not only on his or her ability but also on the person's group membership, the item is said to function differently across groups (typically two groups, which are commonly referred to as the *focal group* and the *reference group*). In the case of nondichotomous items, examination of DIF centers on the expected item raw score or item true score. At the test or scale level, DTF is designed to assess the degree to which the expected raw score or true score at the scale level is the same for two examinees with identical standing on the construct being measured, regardless of group membership. There are several procedures for assessing DIF and DTF. Some are grounded in IRT, and others rely on the classical test theory framework (see Clauser & Mazor, 1998, and Millsap & Everson, 1993, for overviews).

DF does not imply or require that the two groups under consideration are of equal ability or are equal on the construct being assessed; the definition of non-DF requires only that examinees with equal ability have the same expected raw score on the item, regardless of their group membership. It is not uncommon to find the focal group and reference group means to be significantly different on the construct assessed by the test or scale. Such a difference in means is referred to as the *impact* (Drasgow & Hulin, 1990). Impact and DIF or DTF are different concepts; one does not necessarily imply the other. This chapter deals only with DIF and DTF in unidimensional tests and scales. (Readers interested in multidimensional DIF may want to refer to Mazor, Hambleton, & Clauser, 1998; Oshima, Raju, & Flowers, 1997; and Stout, Li, Nandakumar, & Bolt, 1997.)

Following Millsap and Everson (1993), a definition of non-DF at the item level for a dichotomously scored item may be expressed as

$$P_i(+|\theta_s, g_s) = P_i(+|\theta_s). \tag{6.1}$$

In equation 6.1, the left-hand side refers to the probability of answering an item (i) correctly ($+$) given a person's ability (θ_s) and his or her group membership (g_s), whereas the right-hand side refers to the probability of answering the item correctly ($+$) given a person's ability level regardless of group membership. The equality in this 6.1 means that the probability of answering an item correctly depends on the person's ability, not on his or her group membership. If equation 6.1 holds true for item i at all ability levels, then the item is said to be functioning equally across groups and hence is said to have no DIF; that is, such an item is said to be invariant across groups under consideration. On the other hand, if

$$P_i(+|\theta_s, g_s) \neq P_i(+|\theta_s), \tag{6.2}$$

meaning that group membership influences the probability of success, such an item is said to function differentially across groups and hence is designated as a DIF item.

In equations 6.1 and 6.2, theta (θ) denotes a latent construct such as ability, personality, or job satisfaction. For the sake of brevity, we will often refer to θ as ability, but it can also denote other uni-dimensional constructs. It is treated as an underlying or unobserved construct and therefore needs to be estimated in practice. As Reise and Waller explain in Chapter Four and Zickar in Chapter Five, the theta for a given person is related to his or her observed scale or test score, but the two measures are not identical. In the IRT context, the relationship between the observed test score and the underlying construct (θ) is not linear but monotonically increasing. According to Millsap and Everson (1993), DIF definitions based on underlying constructs fall under the category of unobserved conditional invariance models. On the other hand, observed conditional invariance models make use of observed test or scale scores in formulating DIF definitions. Because θ plays a central role in IRT, the θ-based DIF or DTF definitions or procedures are commonly referred to as the IRT-based DIF-DTF procedures. Similarly, the observed-score-based DIF definitions are referred to as the non-IRT-based or nonparametric DIF-DTF definitions. We adopt this terminology in describing several currently popular DIF-DTF procedures. (See Millsap & Everson, 1993, for additional information about the unobserved and observed conditional invariance models.)

The definitions of non-DIF and DIF for dichotomous items can easily be generalized to polytomous items. In the polytomous case, a definition of DIF is couched in terms of the nonequality of item-level true scores or expected raw scores across groups. In the dichotomous case, the item true score (or the expected item raw score) and the probability of answering an item correctly are identical. At the test level, the true test score or the expected test score is simply the sum of item-level true scores or expected raw scores. The lack of DF at the item or scale level is sometimes referred to as measurement equivalence (MEQ) or invariance, especially in the context of confirmatory factor analysis (Jöreskog & Sörbom, 1996). MEQ refers to the equality of true scores or expected raw scores when the value of the underlying construct is held constant across groups. A brief description of the relationship between MEQ and DF will be offered later.

An analysis of DF at the item or scale level is typically confined to two generally well-accepted definitions of groups or subpopulations, typically based on gender or race (such as males versus females or blacks versus whites). Two important features about this practice should be noted. First, a DF analysis need not be confined to just two groups. Recent work by Kim, Cohen, and Park (1995) makes it possible to carry out DIF analyses (within the IRT context) across several groups simultaneously. Second, the definition of groups or subpopulations does not have to be confined to demographic characteristics. For example, two groups for a DF analysis could be employees and their immediate supervisors or peers, where ratings of employees by themselves and their supervisors (or peers) may be evaluated for DF (Maurer, Raju, & Collins, 1998). In the context of establishing the fidelity of translated tests or scales, groups could be defined as clusters of individuals taking different versions of a translated scale (Ellis, 1989, 1991; Ellis & Kimmel, 1992; Hulin et al., 1983). For example, in the case of an English attitude scale translated into Chinese, French, German, and Japanese, there are potentially five different groups or subpopulations for a DF analysis. The important point is that the number and types of groups considered relevant for a DF analysis should depend on the measuring device and its use.

Some Techniques for Assessing DIF-DTF

In this section, two sets of DIF-DTF procedures for tests or scales with dichotomously scored items will be described. The first set of procedures uses IRT (or an underlying construct), and the second set relies on CTT (or observed scores).

Some IRT-Based DIF-DTF Methods for Dichotomous Items

Within the IRT context, the probability of answering an item correctly depends on a person's ability and one or more item parameters. For a dichotomous item with three parameters, the probability of answering the item correctly, given θ, may be expressed as

$$_3P_i(+|\theta) = c_i + (1-c_i)\frac{1}{\{1+\exp[-Da_i(\theta-b_i)]\}}, \qquad (6.3)$$

where a_i, b_i, and c_i are the three parameters reflecting the properties of item i, and equation 6.3 is commonly referred to as the three-parameter logistic model (3-PLM). D in equation 6.3 is a scaling factor, usually set to 1.7 to make the logistic ogive approximately equivalent to the normal ogive (Lord, 1980). A graph of this equation as a function of θ is referred to as the item response function (IRF) for item i. If $c_i = 0$, equation 6.3 reduces to

$$_2P_i(+|\theta) = \frac{1}{\{1+\exp[-Da_i(\theta - b_i)]\}}, \tag{6.4}$$

which is called the two-parameter logistic model (2-PLM). If, in addition, $a_i = 1$, equation 6.3 can be written as

$$_1P_i(+|\theta) = \frac{1}{\{1+\exp[-(\theta - b_i)]\}}, \tag{6.5}$$

which is well known in the literature as the one-parameter, or Rasch, model (1-PLM; Hambleton et al., 1991). The three item parameters (a_i, b_i, and c_i) are referred to as the discrimination parameter, difficulty parameter, and pseudo-guessing parameter or the lower asymptote, respectively. (See Chapter Four, this volume, for additional information about the item parameters, these three IRT models, and their underlying assumptions.)

When the IRT assumptions are satisfied, it is expected that the item parameters are invariant across subpopulations; that is, when the underlying assumptions are met, the item parameters for the focal and reference groups should be identical, after appropriate rescaling. When the IRFs are not equal, the probability of responding correctly to an item depends on not only a person's ability (θ) but also other factors, such as group membership. An example of nonequivalent IRFs for the focal and reference groups is shown in Figure 6.1 for the 2-PLM. In this figure, $a_F = .8$ and $b_F = 0.0$ for the focal group, $a_R = 1.7$ and $b_R = 0.0$ for the reference group, and the two IRFs cross at $\theta = 0.0$. Above and below this theta level, two persons with identical abilities will have different probabilities of success on the item. At $\theta = 1.00$, the probability of success on this item is 0.69 for a member of the focal group and 0.85 for a member of the reference group. Although these two individuals have the same abil-

**Figure 6.1. 2-PLM Response Functions
for Focal and Reference Groups.**

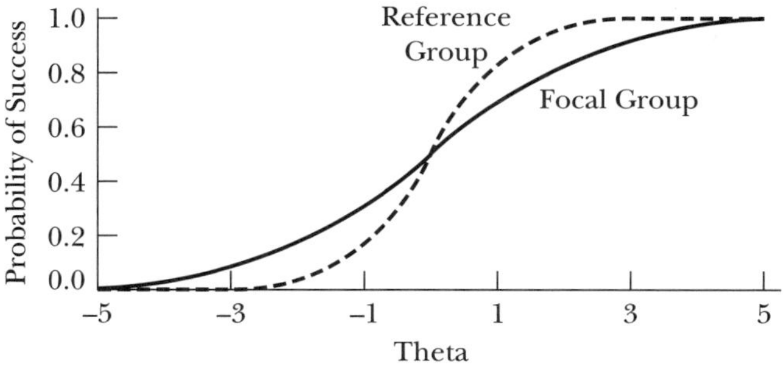

ity, the individual from the focal group has a lower probability of success than the individual from the reference group; that is, the item under consideration favors the reference group at this level of theta. At $\theta = -1.00$, the probability of success on the item also varies as a function of group membership, but this time, the reference group member has a lower probability of success than the focal group member, thus favoring the focal group. An item of this type is said to have significant DIF, and the kind of DIF displayed in Figure 6.1 is called nonuniform DIF; that is, the type of DIF does not favor the same group across all levels of theta. According to Raju (1988), the 3-PLM and 2-PLM will always exhibit nonuniform DIF when the a parameters for the focal and reference groups are unequal. Conversely, by definition, a is equal to 1 for both groups in the 1-PLM (or Rasch model), and therefore the focal and reference group IRFs never cross in the Rasch model; such DIF, if it exists, is referred to as uniform DIF. There can be both uniform and nonuniform DIF in the 2-PLM and 3-PLM, but only uniform DIF in the 1-PLM.

In summary, when the focal group's and reference group's IRFs are different, the item under examination is said to have DIF. Given comparable metrics, the focal and reference groups' IRFs are equal if and only if the item parameters for the focal and reference groups are equal. Therefore, an assessment of DIF can be made in terms of either IRFs or item parameters. Almost all operational definitions of DIF use one of these criteria. Some of the currently known DIF techniques are described below.

Lord's Chi-Square

In practice, only estimated item parameters are ever known. Even when the item parameters are equal in the focal and reference populations, it is extremely unlikely that, due to sampling error, the estimated item parameters will be identical for these groups. Lord (1980) proposed a chi-square statistic for testing the null hypothesis that the item parameters are equal in the two (focal and reference) populations, given the sample-based item parameter estimates. Kim et al. (1995) extended Lord's chi-square statistic for two groups to multiple groups.

In view of the known problems associated with obtaining stable estimates of the lower asymptote (c parameter), Lord (1980) recommended that all item parameters be estimated first using the combined sample of focal group and reference group examinees. Subsequently, the a and b parameters are reestimated separately for the focal group and reference group, with the c parameters fixed at values obtained from the combined sample analysis. If this recommendation is followed, one needs to test only for the equality of the a and b parameters across the focal and reference groups. In view of the extra calibration (IRT analysis based on the combined sample) involved in Lord's recommendation and if the sample sizes are really small, one may opt to set the c parameter for an item at a prespecified value for both (focal and reference) groups. Regardless of which option an investigator chooses, one must make sure that the specific IRT model employed is consistent with the data at hand.

Prior to using Lord's chi-square test of significance, one must make sure that item parameters from the focal group are on the same metric as the item parameters from the reference group. (Consult Chapters Four and Five in this volume for information about the arbitrariness of metrics in IRT calibrations and the need for establishing a common metric prior to comparing item and ability parameters from different calibrations.) An additive constant and a multiplicative constant (linking constants) are needed to transform the focal group metric to the reference group metric. Two computer programs that can provide the necessary linking or equating constants are Baker's EQUATE (1995) and Lee and Oshima's IPLINK (1996). Iterative equating is recommended for optimizing DIF detection (Candell & Drasgow, 1988); additional information about iterative linking is provided later as part of the DIF example.

Area Measures

The area between the focal group's and reference group's IRFs for a given item is recommended as a measure of DIF (Rudner, Geston, & Knight, 1980). Because of the potential for nonuniform DIF in the 2-PLM and 3-PLM, one must be careful in computing the area between two IRFs. In Figure 6.1, for example, if the sign of the area between the two IRFs is positive for θ below 0.00, then the sign of the area above $\theta = 0.00$ will be negative. Therefore, the total area between the two IRFs, in absolute terms, could be less than either the positive or negative area. That is, the positive and negative areas could cancel each other out, at least partially if not totally; the cancellation is complete if the a parameters are different for the focal and reference groups and the b parameters are identical and equal to 0.00 in the 2-PLM. In view of this, two different measures of area are defined and used in DIF research: signed area (SA) and unsigned area (UA). In the 1-PLM (or Rasch model), where the IRFs never cross, the distinction between the SA and UA measures is not relevant because the SA and UA measures will be identical except for the sign.

Raju (1988) offered formulas for computing the exact SA and UA measures. Raju (1990) also proposed statistical significance tests for the estimated SA and UA measures. As in the case of Lord's (1980) chi-square test, the item parameters from the focal and reference groups must be on a common metric prior to estimating the area measures and computing Raju's significance tests. Programs by Baker (1995) and Lee and Oshima (1996) may be used to put the item parameters on a common metric. When the item parameters for the focal and reference groups are identical, the focal and reference group IRFs will also be identical, thus resulting in zero SA and UA measures. That is, both Lord's chi-square and Raju's area measures try to get at the same information, with Lord's procedure examining the differences in the focal and reference groups' item parameters and Raju's procedure assessing the area between the focal and reference groups' IRFs. A meaning-ful practical difference between these two methods is that Raju's pro-cedure offers an index (an area measure) and a significance test for DIF analysis, whereas Lord's procedure provides only a significance test. (Additional information about the area measures may be found in Kim & Cohen, 1991; Raju, 1988, 1990; and Rudner et al., 1980.)

Likelihood Ratio Test

Thissen, Steinberg, and Wainer (1988, 1993) proposed the likeli-hood ratio (LR) test for evaluating the item responses from two groups. In the LR test, the likelihood from a compact model is compared to the likelihood from an augmented model. The com-pact model is one in which no items are said to have significant DIF, whereas in the augmented model, one or more items are treated as having significant DIF. According to Thissen et al. (1993), the LR test may be expressed as

$$G^2(df) = 2\log\left[\frac{Likelihood[A]}{Likelihood[C]}\right], \tag{6.6}$$

where A and C stand for the augmented and compact models, re-spectively, and df is the difference between the number of parame-ters in the augmented model and the number of parameters in the compact model. G^2 is assumed to have a chi-square distribution with degrees of freedom equal to df. The LR-DIF test is quite general and allows for testing of many different hypotheses concerning the focal and reference group item parameters. But it requires two separate calibrations for each comparison: one for the compact model and the other for the augmented model. The number of comparisons in a DIF analysis can be quite substantial, and therefore an LR-DIF analysis can be very time-consuming (Kim & Cohen, 1995). An ad-vantage of the LR test is that it does not require the equating of focal and reference group item parameters prior to a DIF analysis; an anchor set of non-DIF items is used to define the common met-ric. Like Lord's chi-square, the LR test does not offer an index of DIF, only a significance test. Thissen's MULTILOG computer pro-gram (1991) may be used to carry out the needed LR tests. (Addi-tional information about the LR-DIF test can be found in Thissen et al., 1988, 1993; and Kim & Cohen, 1995.)

DFIT Framework

Raju, van der Linden, and Fleer (1995) recently proposed a general IRT-based framework for assessing differential functioning of items and tests (DFIT). According to Raju et al. (1995), the central theme of the DFIT framework is as follows. Given a person's score on the underlying construct (θ), what is that person's true score on item i when the individual (s) is viewed as a member of the focal group (t_{is_F})? Also, what is the same person's true score on the same item when he or she is viewed as a member of the reference group (t_{is_R})? In IRT, the item true score is simply the probability of getting the item right; equations 6.3, 6.4, and 6.5 represent such probabilities for the 3-PLM, 2-PLM, and 1-PLM, respectively. Given the focal group's and reference group's item parameters for an item, two true scores can be computed for each person: one true score using the focal group's item parameters and the other using the reference group's item parameters. In view of equations 6.3 through 6.5, the two true scores are identical whenever the focal group's and reference group's item parameters are identical, that is,

$$d_{is}=t_{is_F}-t_{is_R}=0 \tag{6.7}$$

for all values of θ. This also means that the focal and reference groups' IRFs are identical for item i. Similarly, the difference in true scores at the test level for person s may be defined as

$$D_s=(T_{s_F}-T_{s_R})=d_{1s}+\ldots+d_{ns}, \tag{6.8}$$

where

$$T_{s_F}=t_{1s_F}+\ldots+t_{ns_F}, \tag{6.9}$$

$$T_{s_R}=t_{1s_R}+\ldots+t_{ns_R}. \tag{6.10}$$

Equation 6.9 represents the true score on the test for person s from the focal group, and equation 6.10 represents the true score if the same person (s) were a member of the reference group. In each case, the true score on the test is simply the sum of true scores on each of the n items in the test. Equations 6.9 and 6.10 are also referred to as the test response functions.

Using equations 6.7 and 6.8, Raju et al. (1995) defined two indices:

$$NCDIF = \varepsilon(d^2) = \mu_{d^2} = \sigma_d^2 + \mu_d^2 \tag{6.11}$$

and

$$DTF = \varepsilon(D^2) = \mu_{D^2} = \sigma_D^2 + \mu_D^2, \tag{6.12}$$

where ε denotes the expected value. The NCDIF (noncompensatory DIF) index is defined at the item level, whereas the DTF index is defined at the test score level. According to equation 6.11, the NCDIF index reflects the average squared difference between the focal group's and reference group's item-level true scores; that is, it is the weighted squared area between the two IRFs. Similarly, according to equation 6.12, the DTF index is the average squared difference in true scores at the test level. The IRFs or the focal and reference groups' item parameters must be identical if the NCDIF index is zero. The extent to which the two IRFs differ from each other reflects the degree of DIF at the item level. Similar interpretations are valid for the DTF index. It should be noted that $\sqrt{NCDIF}$ and $\sqrt{DTF}$ approximate the average absolute true score difference at the item level and at the test or scale level, respectively. Raju et al. proposed chi-square significance tests for assessing if the estimated DIF and DTF indices are significantly different from zero. It should be noted that of the four IRT-based DF procedures described here, only the DFIT framework offers a mechanism for assessing DF at the test level. As Raju et al. noted, it is quite possible for a test to have nonsignificant DTF while containing items with significant DIF. This can happen because of cancellation effects; that is, one item may have significant DIF favoring the focal group, and another item may have significant DIF favoring the reference group. This information can be very useful for practitioners when decisions about examinees are made at the test score level and not at the item level. It should also be noted that the DFIT framework is equally valid for polytomous and multidimensional items and scales (Flowers, Oshima, & Raju, 1999; Oshima et al., 1997).

In addition to the NCDIF index, Raju et al. (1995) defined a compensatory DIF (CDIF) index at the item level. The sum of CDIF indices equals the DTF index, so the information from CDIF may be used to decide which items to delete in order to render a significant DTF index nonsignificant. Raju et al. showed that if all items in the test except the one item under consideration have zero NCDIF, then the NCDIF and CDIF indices are equal for that item; that is, the CDIF index reflects DIF in other items in the test, whereas the NCDIF index reflects the DIF only in the item under consideration. Raju's (1999) DFIT5D computer program may be used for analyzing dichotomous items for DIF-DTF within the DFIT framework.

Assessment of IRT-Based Methods

The four IRT-based DIF methods were investigated by several researchers, especially with respect to the extent to which similar DIF results would be obtained across methods. Unfortunately, no single investigation to date has included all four methods. For example, Cohen and Kim (1993) and Kim and Cohen (1995) included Lord's chi-square, Raju's area measures, and the LR test in their studies; Raju, Drasgow, and Slinde (1993) evaluated Lord's chi-square and the area measure; Raju et al. (1995) compared Lord's chi-square, Raju's area measures, and the DFIT framework; and Donoghue and Isham (1998) offered a comparison of Lord's chi-square and Raju's area measures. The general conclusion appears to be that these four methods typically yield comparable results, with some methods yielding slightly more accurate results than other methods in some studies. For a more detailed assessment of the accuracy and the ease of use of the DIF methods just described, readers may want to consult the original sources.

Some Non-IRT-Based or Nonparametric DIF-DTF Methods for Dichotomous Items

There are several other DIF methods that are non-IRT based or have a nonparametric orientation. A few of these will be described below. One of the most popular of these methods is the Mantel-Haenszel technique.

Mantel-Haenszel Technique

The Mantel-Haenszel (MH) technique, originally developed by Mantel and Haenszel (1959), compares the item performance of focal and reference group examinees across score groups. The definition of a score group may vary from one investigation to the next, but it typically consists of all examinees with the same raw score. For example, in a thirty-item dichotomously scored test, there could potentially be thirty different score groups, one for each nonzero raw score. A score group may also consist of all examinees with raw scores in a prespecified score interval.

At each score group level, the focal group of examinees is assumed to be comparable to the reference group of examinees on the trait being measured by the item under consideration, and if the item has no DIF, the focal and reference group examinees are expected to function equally well on it. At score group level j, the number of examinees from the focal and reference groups passing the item may be shown in a 2×2 table (Table 6.1). In this table, A_j is the number of examinees in reference score group j who answered the item correctly, B_j is the number of examinees in reference score group j who answered the item incorrectly, and $N_{jR} = A_j + B_j$. The C_j, D_j, and N_{jF} are similarly defined for focal score group j. N_{j1} and N_{j0} are the number of examinees in score group j who passed and failed the studied item, respectively. Finally, $T_j = N_{jR} + N_{jF} + N_{j1} + N_{j0}$. The MH estimate of a, the common odds ratio across the 2×2 tables, can be expressed as

$$\hat{a}_{MH} = \frac{\Sigma (A_j D_j)/T_j}{\Sigma (B_j C_j)/T_j},$$

(6.13)

where the summation is taken over all score groups. According to Holland and Thayer (1988), $\hat{a}_{MH}$ varies between 0 and ∞ with $a_{MH} = 1$ representing the null hypothesis of no difference or non-DIF. Mantel and Haenszel (1959) proposed a chi-square statistic (with one degree of freedom) to test whether an observed a is significantly different from 1. When $\hat{a}_{MH}$ is not significantly different from 1, one may conclude that the studied item is unbiased or has no DIF or that the focal and reference groups perform equally well on the item when their abilities are controlled. According to Holland and Thayer (1988), the MH technique offers

Table 6.1. Performance of Focal and Reference Examinees in Score Group j on an Item.

	1 (Pass)	0 (Fail)	Total
Reference group	A_j	B_j	N_{jR}
Focal group	C_j	D_j	N_{jF}
Total	N_{j1}	N_{j0}	T_j

a chi-square test that is powerful against realistic alternatives to the null hypothesis of $a_{\text{MH}} = 1$.

Unlike the IRT-based DIF procedures, the MH technique is easy to use and may not require large sample sizes. It is recommended that the number of score groups correspond to the number of possible raw scores based on all the items in the test. Holland and Thayer (1988) point out some important relationships between the MH technique and the Rasch model. Swaminathan and Rogers (1990) note that the MH technique may not be sensitive to nonuniform DIF. (Additional information about the MH technique may be found in Holland & Wainer, 1993.)

Logistic Regression Procedure

Swaminathan and Rogers (1990) proposed a DIF procedure using the well-known logistic regression function, in which the probability of answering an item correctly (+) may be expressed as

$$P(+\mid z) = \frac{e^z}{1+e^z}, \quad z = b_0 + b_1 x + b_2 g + b_3(xg), \tag{6.14}$$

where x refers to the observed ability measure (for example, raw score on the test), $g = 1$ if the examinee belongs to the reference group and $g = 0$ if the examinee belongs to the focal group, and xg represents the interaction between group membership and examinee ability. Of the four regression coefficients in equation 6.14, b_2 and b_3 have special significance in terms of DIF. According to

Swaminathan and Rogers, the condition that $b_2 \neq 0$ and $b_3 = 0$ represents uniform DIF, whereas the condition $b_3 \neq 0$ (whether or not $b_2 = 0$) represents nonuniform DIF. The four logistic regression coefficients in equation 6.14 are estimated for each item in the test and then tested to determine which coefficients are significantly different from zero. This information forms the basis for assessing the type and extent of DIF in a given item. Like the IRT-based DIF procedures, the logistic regression approach is also model based, but unlike the IRT-based procedures, it can be used with the observed raw score as an estimate of an examinee's ability. Like the MH technique, the logistic regression procedure is easy to use and may not require large samples. Unlike the MH technique, the logistic regression approach is sensitive to nonuniform DIF. A strength of the logistic approach is its greater flexibility in constructing and evaluating more elaborate models (Camilli & Shepard, 1994).

SIBTEST

Shealy and Stout (1993a, 1993b) proposed a simultaneous item bias test (SIBTEST) for assessing DIF. The basic rationale underlying SIBTEST is that a test designed to measure a trait or construct of interest may also measure other traits, often referred to as the nuisance traits. Given this situation, DIF is a function of how much the nuisance traits affect the focal and reference group performance. The SIBTEST procedure starts with a subset of DIF-free or valid items. This subset of items is referred to as the valid subtest. The remaining items in the test under consideration are denoted as the studied subtest. As in the MH technique, each possible raw score on the valid subset may be used to form score groups such that the focal and reference examinees belonging to a given score group have the same raw score on the valid subset. The average performance of focal and reference examinees belonging to a score group is then examined on each item or a subset of items from the studied subtest.

The SIBTEST procedure, like the DFIT framework, is designed for assessing both DIF and DTF. The MH and SIBTEST techniques typically provide similar results in detecting uniform DIF, with a slight edge for the SIBTEST. A modified version of SIBTEST (Li & Stout, 1996) is also sensitive to nonuniform DIF, and its accuracy is comparable to the accuracy of nonuniform DIF detection with the logistic regression procedure (Narayanan & Swaminathan, 1996).

Other DIF-DTF Methods

The descriptions of DIF-DTF methods just provided do not cover all known DIF methods. Readers are referred to the References at the end of this chapter for information about methods not explicitly discussed here. Recommended books on differential item functioning include those by Holland and Wainer (1993) and Camilli and Shepard (1994). Details about a non-IRT-based DIF method, called *standardization* (Dorans & Kulick, 1986), can be found in Dorans and Holland (1993). Many of the DIF-DTF techniques described for the dichotomously scored items have been extended for assessing DIF-DTF in polytomous items. Interested readers are encouraged to consult the following sources for information: Cohen, Kim, and Baker (1993) for Lord's chi-square and Raju's SA and UA measures; Thissen et al. (1988, 1993) and Kim and Cohen (1998) for LR; Chang, Mazzeo, and Roussos (1996) for SIBTEST; Zwick, Thayer, and Mazzeo (1997) for MH; and Flowers et al. (1999) and Raju et al. (1995) for DFIT.

Measurement Equivalence Versus Differential Functioning

According to Drasgow and Kanfer (1985), a test or item is said to have measurement equivalence (MEQ) across groups if persons with identical scores on the underlying or latent construct have the same expected raw score or true score at the test or item level. When MEQ is present, the relationship between the latent variable and the observed variable remains invariant across groups. It is often difficult to interpret observed group mean differences meaningfully without MEQ.

A careful examination of the definition of MEQ reveals that MEQ and DF, as psychometric concepts, are quite similar; both look at the relationship between the underlying construct and the true score or the expected raw score. The concept of MEQ is grounded in confirmatory factor analysis (CFA), and therefore the relationship between the latent construct and the observed variable is assumed to be linear. As a methodological tool, CFA is well known and quite advanced (Jöreskog & Sörbom, 1996). Given the current state of affairs, it is rather straightforward to assess MEQ across multiple groups and multiple variables simultaneously. On the other hand, given the important role IRT plays in DF, the relationship between the underlying construct and the observed variable is assumed to be nonlinear in DF. Also, the DF methodology is relatively new. Thus far, only a few studies have examined the relationship between the MEQ and DF methodologies (Maurer et al., 1998; Reise & Widaman, 1999; Reise, Widaman, & Pugh, 1993; Raju, Laffitte, & Byrne, 2000), and there is a need for more analytical and empirical investigations. For additional information about MEQ, readers are referred to Chan (2000), Cheung and Rensvold (1999), Vandenberg and Lance (2000), and Lance and Vandenberg (Chapter Eight, this volume).

Illustration of DF Techniques

In this section, examples of several DF statistics are illustrated for a set of dichotomously scored items. These examples are intended for illustrative purposes only.

Ellis and Mead (2000) recently used the DFIT framework (Raju et al., 1995) to examine DIF and DTF in a pilot version of a Spanish translation of the Sixteen Personality Factor (16PF) Questionnaire (Cattell, Cattell, & Cattell, 1993). The 16PF, a measure of adult, normal-range personality, was administered in English to 309 English-speaking Anglo Americans and in Spanish to 244 Spanish-speaking Mexican nationals. The questionnaire consists of seventeen scales: fifteen personality scales, one reasoning scale, and one impression management scale. In the example, we report only the results of a DIF analysis for the fifteen-item reasoning scale. The analysis uses five indices of DIF: four IRT-based indices (Lord's chi-square, Raju's exact signed and unsigned area measures, and Raju's NCDIF indices) and one non-IRT- based index (the Mantel-Haenszel). In addition, we present the DTF results for this scale. Readers are referred to Ellis and Mead (2000) for a complete description of the samples, DFIT results for other 16PF scales, and the translation procedures used in this study.

Phase 1 in a DIF analysis involves the selection of an appropriate model: the 1-PLM, 2-PLM, or 3-PLM for dichotomous versus polytomous responses and for a unidimensional versus multidimensional scale. In the example, all items have three response alternatives and are dichotomously scored right or wrong. Classical test statistics indicate that reasoning items differ in item discrimination and item difficulty. Furthermore, the multiple-choice format enables examinees to guess the correct answer. In the light of these considerations, the 3-PLM (Lord, 1980) was assumed to be the more appropriate model. Finally, previous research (Chan, Chernyshenko, & Stark, 1997; Conn & Rieke, 1994) has suggested that the 16PF scales are unidimensional, and an examination of the factor structure of the scales using the modified parallel analysis procedure outlined by Drasgow and Lissak (1983) also supported the conclusion that the scales were relatively unidimensional. Thus, the 3-PLM for a unidimensional scale composed of dichotomous responses was selected as the appropriate model.

Phase 2 in a DIF analysis (within the IRT context) involves selecting a computer program for item calibration. Among the several commercially available computer programs that could have been selected for this analysis, we used the computer program BILOG 3.08 (Mislevy & Bock, 1990) because it is relatively user friendly, is available in a Windows version, and can be used to calibrate relatively unidimensional scales composed of dichotomously scored items.

Phase 3 of a DIF analysis requires multiple steps. In the example, after raw data were dichotomously scored for each examinee, BILOG was used to estimate item and person parameters. In the light of the fact that the 3-PLM (Lord, 1980) was selected as the appropriate model, phase 3 of this DIF analysis involved several additional steps to estimate the c parameter that are not required if the 1-PLM or 2-PLM are used. First, the c parameters for the fifteen items were estimated by combining the reference and focal groups as recommended by Lord (1980). Next, the a and b parameters were estimated separately for the reference group examinees and the focal group examinees, with the c parameter constrained (or fixed) at the estimates based on the combined sample analysis. In addition to assessing item parameters, every DIF analysis requires that careful attention be paid to assess model-data fit at this phase of the analysis. Most computer programs for item calibration include output that can be used in assessing model fit. However, the range and usefulness of available fit indices for IRT analyses are limited and not as well developed as those available for confirmatory factor analysis. In this example, model-data fit was assessed using output provided by BILOG. (Readers are referred to Ellis & Mead, 2000, for a detailed description of the procedures used to assess model fit for these data.)

Phase 4 of any DIF analysis is an iterative process, recommended by Candell and Drasgow (1988), that requires the following steps: (1) equating item parameters, (2) identifying DIF items, (3) removing the DIF items identified in step 2 and recalculating equating constants, and (4) conducting a new DIF analysis for all items using the equating constants determined in step 3. The DIF researcher continues to apply steps 2 and 3 until the same set of DIF items is identified on two successive iterations. The items identified as having significant DIF in the last iteration are considered the final results of the DIF analysis. In the example, after the estimation of item parameters, the initial DIF analysis was conducted using indices described in Raju et al.'s (1995) DFIT framework. Item parameters were placed on the same metric using Baker's (1995) EQUATE 2.1 program. In the example, item parameters for the reference group (the English speakers) were put on the same scale as that of the focal group (the Spanish speakers). Once the initial equating constants (A = the slope and K = the intercept) were determined, these values were used as input to the DFIT5 computer program along with output from BILOG (for example, the score and covariance files). Next, items with statistically significant NCDIF indices were identified. For dichotomous items, an NCDIF index is considered statistically significant when it is more than .006 *and* the associated chi-square is statistically significant at the .01 level. Following this initial identification of DIF items, the linking procedure using EQUATE 2.1 was applied. In this instance, DIF items identified in the previous step were removed from the linking process, and item parameters were reequated using only non-DIF items. The new linking constants (A and K from EQUATE 2.1) were used in second application of DFIT5 to identify DIF in all reasoning items. The iterative process of applying EQUATE to non-DIF items to determine equating constants and subsequently using these constants to assess DIF in all fifteen items was continued until two successive iterations of the output from DFIT5 revealed the same set of items identified as DIF items using the NCDIF index. In the example, four iterations were required before the same set of items with significant DIF appeared on two successive iterations. The final linking constants were $A = .878$ and $K = 1.358$.

DIF and DTF results from the DFIT analysis presented in Table 6.2 are based on the output from the final application of DFIT5. Twelve of fifteen items (numbers 1, 2, 4, 5, 6, 7, 8, 9, 10, 11, 13, and 14), shown in boldface in the table, were flagged as having significant DIF using the NCDIF index. In addition, DTF is considered statistically significant when the index is more than .090 (the number of items times the NCDIF cutoff) *and* the associated chi-square is statistically significant at the .01 level. The "importance" of each item's CDIF was assessed indirectly by removing those items with the largest removal index (2CDIF-NCDIF) until DTF was no longer statistically significant. Only one item, number 9, was classified as being flagged using the CDIF-DTF index of importance; that is, the DTF was no longer significant when item 9 was removed.

Additional IRT-based indices of DIF (Lord's chi-square and the exact signed and unsigned area measures), along with one non-IRT-based index (the Mantel-Haenszel index), were calculated using a computer program developed by Raju. The BILOG item parameters and covariance output described in phase 3, along with the final equating constants described in phase 4, were used as input to this program. Results of the additional DIF analyses are also shown (in boldface type) in Table 6.2. For Lord's index, a chi-square of 9.2 (alpha = .01, $df = 2$) was used to identify items with statistically significant DIF. Thus, Lord's chi-square index revealed that seven items (numbers 2, 5, 8, 9, 10, 13, and 14) displayed significant DIF. For the signed and unsigned area measures, critical z-values (alpha = .01, two-tailed test) of less than -2.58 and greater than $+2.58$ were used to identify statistically significant DIF items. The exact signed and unsigned area indices identified the same seven of fifteen items as DIF (numbers 2, 5, 8, 9, 10, 13, and 14). Finally, the critical value for identifying items displaying

Table 6.2. Estimated Item Parameters and Associated DIF Indices.

Item	Focal Group Parameters			Reference Group Parameters			Lord's Chi-Square	SA	Z-SA	UA	Z-UA	NCDIF	M-H
	a	b	c	a	b	c							
1	1.334	−0.261	0.249	1.225	0.220	0.249	7.337	0.362	2.064	0.362	−2.064	**0.017**	0.82
2	0.582	2.789	0.230	0.638	0.254	0.230	**9.617**	−1.952	−2.835	1.952	2.835	**0.091**	52.11
3	0.495	0.980	0.310	0.568	1.051	0.310	0.209	0.049	0.184	0.152	0.419	0.001	0.10
4	0.818	1.714	0.254	0.998	2.335	0.254	4.945	0.464	1.453	0.465	1.545	**0.006**	8.37
5	0.816	1.287	0.199	0.745	2.359	0.199	**13.609**	**0.859**	3.026	**0.859**	−3.026	**0.015**	12.83
6	0.832	4.139	0.202	1.057	0.238	0.202	3.851	−3.111	−1.859	3.111	1.859	**0.161**	132.77
7	1.032	3.505	0.219	1.121	0.981	0.219	3.696	−1.971	−1.662	1.971	1.662	**0.054**	58.34
8	1.030	0.430	0.163	1.326	0.994	0.163	**10.035**	0.472	3.124	0.474	3.174	0.027	6.44
9	1.356	−0.430	0.266	0.636	1.445	0.266	**93.985**	1.376	8.270	1.392	−8.906	**0.121***	**58.65**
10	1.108	0.676	0.119	1.080	1.451	0.119	**19.442**	0.683	4.357	0.683	−4.357	**0.032**	15.59
11	1.309	0.004	0.168	0.870	−0.267	0.168	1.419	−0.225	−0.822	0.325	−1.081	**0.008**	3.01
12	1.302	0.578	0.134	0.877	0.853	0.134	3.341	0.238	1.448	0.334	−1.917	0.005	0.05
13	1.242	0.568	0.128	0.905	1.045	0.128	**7.779**	0.416	2.641	0.436	−2.904	**0.012**	2.65
14	1.036	0.560	0.192	1.178	1.243	0.192	**13.225**	0.552	3.613	0.552	3.614	**0.028**	10.16
15	1.416	1.190	0.138	1.539	1.397	0.138	1.315	0.179	0.958	0.179	0.971	0.003	0.05

Note: Focal group: Spanish speakers; Reference group: English speakers. The reference group's parameters were transformed to the focal groups. SA: signed area index; Z-SA: z-value associated with SA index; UA: unsigned area index; Z-UA: z-value associated with UA index; NCDIF: noncompensatory DIF index; M-H: Mantel-Haenszel index. The boldface entries are significant at the .01 level. An asterisk indicates that the item was identified as DF using CDIF-DTF importance index.

Critical values for DIF indices (alpha = .01): Lord's chi-square ($df = 2$) = 9.2; z-value for signed and unsigned area indices (two-tailed test) ± 2.58; NCDIF > .006 and the associated chi-square is significant at the .01 level; Mantel-Haenzsel ($df = 1$) = 6.6.

statistically significant DIF using the non-IRT-based Mantel-Haenszel chi-square index was 6.6 (alpha =.01, $df = 1$). Using the Mantel-Haenszel index, eight of fifteen items (number 2, 4, 5, 6, 7, 9, 10, and 14) were identified as items with significant DIF.

Examination of the results across all DIF indices indicates that five of fifteen reasoning items were identified as having significant DIF by all five indices (items 2, 5, 9, 10, and 14), and two additional items (number 8 and 13) were identified by the four IRT-based indices. Overall, more items were identified as having significant DIF by the NCDIF than by any other index of DIF. An examination of the b parameters across all items with significant NCDIF indicates that for reference and focal group examinees with equal theta (equal reasoning ability), Spanish speakers had a lower probability of answering four items correctly (items 2, 6, 7, and 11), and English speakers had a lower probability of answering eight items correctly (items 1, 4, 5, 8, 9, 10, 13, and 14). However, there was no significant DTF after item 9 was removed. These results point out the benefits of examining DF at both the item and scale levels. In this case, although there was significant DTF at the scale level (DTF = .246), there were considerably fewer DIF items to be concerned about when the compensatory nature of DF was taken into account at the scale level. Finally, IRFs for item 2 (lower probability of answering correctly for Spanish speakers) and item 10 (lower probability of answering correctly for English speakers) are shown in Figures 6.2 and 6.3, respectively.

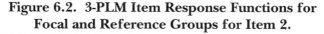

Figure 6.2. 3-PLM Item Response Functions for Focal and Reference Groups for Item 2.

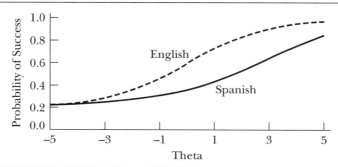

**Figure 6.3. 3-PLM Item Response Functions for
Focal and Reference Groups for Item 10.**

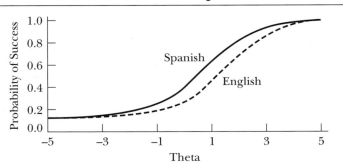

Conclusion

The methods described in this chapter are relatively new and, therefore, we urge that before applying one or another of them, researchers become thoroughly familiar with all DIF-DTF detection procedures and their underlying assumptions. We also offer our recommendations for making choices among the methods we have described. Finally, it is important that researchers move beyond simply *identifying* DIF-DTF. In the last section of this chapter, we discuss the next frontier for DF researchers, solving the problem of identifying and resolving the sources of DF.

Choice Among DIF-DTF Procedures

Because most of the currently known DIF-DTF procedures are relatively new, it is difficult to recommend a single procedure for practitioners. Several factors must be carefully considered in choosing a procedure: IRT versus non-IRT, dichotomous versus polytomous, unidimensional versus multidimensional, and uniform versus nonuniform. With respect to the first factor, some researchers believe that IRT-based methods are preferable to non-IRT-based methods on theoretical grounds (Drasgow & Hulin, 1990; Hulin et al., 1983). The remaining factors depend largely on the data in question (dichotomous versus polytomous responses and unidimensional versus multidimensional scales) and whether

DIFFERENTIAL ITEM AND TEST FUNCTIONING **181**

one suspects or is interested in assessing uniform versus nonuniform DIF. In addition, one should consider the sample sizes and scale lengths involved, availability of computer programs, and the ease with which DIF results can be communicated to nontechnical administrators and educators.

IRT Context

Lord's chi-square is probably one of the more popular IRT-based DIF procedures. Because it does not provide an index of DIF, Millsap and Everson (1993) suggest that Lord's chi-square with an area measure such as Raju's may prove beneficial to practitioners. Thissen et al. (1989, 1993) contend that because Lord's chi-square procedure requires accurate estimates of standard errors of item parameters, which may be difficult to obtain, their LR test may be preferable. Unlike Lord's chi-square and Raju's tests for area measures, the LR test does not require prior equating of item parameters, but the DIF analysis itself can be quite time-consuming.

Among the four IRT-based procedures described in this chapter, only the DFIT framework offers a definition of DTF. It also offers indices for DIF and DTF and a comprehensive framework for assessing DF in dichotomous, polytomous, and multidimensional items and tests or scales. Because the DFIT-based DIF-DTF indices are couched in IRFs, it is easier to explain DF to nontechnical administrators and educators. In addition, if decisions are to be made at the test level, it seems appropriate to consider DF at the same level. Furthermore, a DFIT analysis may also provide justification for not stripping a test of DF items, especially those that display compensatory DIF at the scale level. As Drasgow and Hulin (1990) noted, eliminating all DIF items is "not necessarily a good idea" (p. 623), because it may have the unwanted effect of reducing the test's predictive validity (Roznowski, 1987). However, because it is relatively new compared with the other DIF procedures, additional empirical investigations of the DFIT framework are recommended.

Non-IRT Context

Within the non-IRT realm, the MH technique appears to be quite popular, despite the fact that it is known to be insensitive to nonuniform DIF. The MH technique is easy to use and may not require large sample sizes. The SIBTEST and MH procedures appear to provide comparable results in identifying nonuniform DIF; of the two, only SIBTEST provides a measure of DTF. Both MH and SIBTEST procedures have been generalized for assessing DIF in polytomous items. If one is concerned about nonuniform DIF, the logistic regression approach has a lot to recommend. The implementation of this procedure is straightforward and can be used with moderate-size samples. The crossing SIBTEST procedure is also appropriate for nonuniform DIF.

Understanding and Resolving DF

When some items are identified as having significant DIF, what is a practitioner to do? One typical reaction is to replace such items with new items, evaluate the new items for DIF, and repeat this process until all items are DIF free, an expensive and time-consuming process. Another typical reaction is to revise such items so that they no longer exhibit significant DIF and use them in the final test or scale. These two approaches implicitly or explicitly assume that the test or scale developer knows the reasons for DIF. Unfortunately, the reasons for DF are mostly unknown. In fact, it is one of the biggest challenges facing DF researchers.

When items with significant and substantial DIF are identified, a researcher or practitioner may assemble a committee of subject matter and editorial experts from both the focal and reference groups to review all items, including those with no significant DIF. This exercise may help identify reasons for DIF in some instances, but it may not always result in plausible or defensible explanations for DIF. According to Engelhard, Hansche, and Gabrielson (1990), it is very unlikely that experts will flag the same items that are statistically identified as having significant DIF, but they may be able to provide post hoc explanations for DIF that can be evaluated in future studies.

An exploration of the reasons for DIF in specific items may follow several avenues. Along one avenue, panels of experts may be called on to examine individual items for potential sources of DIF. This panel may include "sensitivity experts" but in most test development situations, a "sensitivity review" will have taken place prior to a DIF analysis. In a sensitivity review, items are examined for content that may be offensive or demeaning to members of a focal group. Most commercial test publishers have well-documented guidelines in place for use by their editorial staffs. These guidelines are designed to eliminate sexist and racist language and to avoid stereotypes about women and minorities. But as Clauser and Mazor (1998) noted, "Sensitivity reviews are separate and distinct from DIF analyses—both are important, and neither can substitute for the other" (p. 32). Following a DIF analysis, a committee of experts may have to concentrate on things other than a sensitivity review to come up with plausible explanations for DIF that would need to be tested in subsequent DIF studies.

Another avenue for exploration is the question of multidimensionality. DIF results from multidimensionality; that is, in addition to the intended construct, an item with significant DIF may tap one or more constructs that the focal and reference groups differ on. Unfortunately, the task of identifying the extra construct in items with significant DIF is not an easy one. More work is needed to articulate reasons for DIF in different content areas. Interested readers are referred to Camilli and Shepard (1994) and Holland and Wainer (1993) for further discussions on this topic.

References

Angoff, W. H. (1993). Perspectives on differential item functioning methodology. In P. W. Holland & H. Wainer (Eds.), *Differential item functioning* (pp. 3–23). Hillsdale, NJ: Erlbaum.

Baker, F. B. (1995). *EQUATE 2.1: Computer program for equating two metrics in item response theory* [Computer program]. Madison: University of Wisconsin, Laboratory of Experimental Design.

Camilli, G., & Shepard, L. A. (1994). *Methods for identifying biased test items.* Thousand Oaks, CA: Sage.

Candell, G. L., & Drasgow, F. (1988). An iterative procedure for linking metrics and assessing item bias in item response theory. *Applied Psychological Measurement, 12,* 253–260.

Cattell, R. B., Cattell, A. K., & Cattell, H.E.P. (1993). *Sixteen Personality Factor Questionnaire* (5th ed.). Champaign, IL: Institute for Personality and Ability Testing.

Chan, D. (2000). Detection of differential item functioning on the Kirton adaptation-innovation inventory using multiple-group mean and covariance structures. *Multivariate Behavioral Research, 35,* 169–199.

Chan, K., Chernyshenko, O. S., & Stark, S. (1997). *Factor analysis of the Fifth Edition of 16PF.* Champaign, IL: Institute of Personality and Ability Testing.

Chang, H. H., Mazzeo, J., & Roussos, L. (1996). Detecting DIF and polytomously scored items: An application of the SIBTEST procedure. *Journal of Educational Measurement, 33,* 333–353.

Cheung, G. W., & Rensvold, R. B. (1999). Testing factorial invariance across groups: A reconceptualization and proposed new method. *Journal of Management, 25,* 1-27.

Clauser, B. E., & Mazor, K. M. (1998). Using statistical procedures to identify differentially functioning test items. *Educational Measurement: Issues and Practice, 17,* 31–44.

Cohen, A. S., & Kim, S.-H. (1993). A comparison of Lord's χ^2 and Raju's area measures in detection of DIF. *Applied Psychological Measurement, 17,* 39–52.

Cohen, A. S., Kim, S.-H., & Baker, F. B. (1993). Detection of differential item functioning in the graded response model. *Applied Psychological Measurement, 17,* 335–350.

Cole, N. S. (1981). Bias in testing. *American Psychologist, 36,* 1067–1077.

Cole, N. S. (1993). History and development of DIF. In P. W. Holland & H. Wainer (Eds.), *Differential item functioning* (pp. 25–33). Hillsdale, NJ: Erlbaum.

Conn, S. R., & Rieke, M. L. (1994). *The 16PF Fifth Edition technical manual.* Champaign, IL: Institute for Personality and Ability Testing.

Donoghue, J. R., & Isham, S. P. (1998). A comparison of procedures to detect item parameter drift. *Applied Psychological Measurement, 22,* 33–51.

Dorans, N. J., & Holland, P. W. (1993). DIF detection and description: Mantel-Haenszel and standardization. In P. W. Holland & H. Wainer (Eds.), *Differential item functioning* (pp. 35–66). Hillsdale, NJ: Erlbaum.

Dorans, N. J., & Kulick, E. (1986). Demonstrating the utility of the standardization approach to assessing unexpected differential item performance on the Scholastic Aptitude Test. *Journal of Educational Measurement, 23,* 355–368.

Drasgow, F., & Hulin, C. L. (1990). Item response theory. In M. D. Dunnette & L. M. Hough (Eds.), *Handbook of industrial and organizational psychology* (2nd ed., Vol. 1, pp. 577–636). Palo Alto, CA: Consulting Psychologists Press.

Drasgow, F., & Kanfer, R. (1985). Equivalence of psychological measurement in heterogeneous populations. *Journal of Applied Psychology, 70,* 662–680.

Drasgow, F., & Lissak, R. I. (1983). Modified parallel analysis: A procedure for examining the latent dimensionality of dichotomously scored item responses. *Journal of Applied Psychology, 68,* 363–373.

Ellis, B. B. (1989). Differential item functioning: Implications for test translation. *Journal of Applied Psychology, 74,* 912–921.

Ellis, B. B. (1991). Item response theory: A tool for assessing the equivalence of translated tests. *Bulletin of the International Test Commission, 18,* 33–51.

Ellis, B. B., & Kimmel, H. D. (1992). Identification of unique cultural response patterns by means of item response theory. *Journal of Applied Psychology, 77,* 177–184.

Ellis, B. B., & Mead, A. D. (2000). Assessment of the measurement equivalence of a Spanish translation of the 16PF Questionnaire. *Educational and Psychological Measurement, 60,* 787–807.

Engelhard, G., Hansche, D., & Gabrielson, S. (1990). Accuracy of bias review judges in identifying differential item functioning on teacher certification tests. *Applied Measurement in Education, 3,* 347–360.

Flowers, C. P., Oshima, T. C., & Raju, N. S. (1999). A description and demonstration of the polytomous-DFIT framework. *Applied Psychological Measurement, 23,* 309–326.

Gulliksen, H. (1950). *Theory of mental tests.* New York: McGraw-Hill.

Hambleton, R. K., & Swaminathan, H. (1985). *Item response theory: Principles and applications.* Norwell, MA: Kluwer.

Hambleton, R. K., Swaminathan, H., & Rogers, H. J. (1991). *Fundamentals of item response theory.* Thousand Oaks, CA: Sage.

Holland, P. W., & Thayer, D. T. (1988). Differential item performance and the Mantel-Haenszel procedure. In H. Wainer & H. Braun (Eds.), *Test validity* (pp. 129–145). Hillsdale, NJ: Erlbaum.

Holland, P. W., & Wainer, H. (Eds.) (1993). *Differential item functioning.* Hillsdale, NJ: Erlbaum.

Hulin, C. L., Drasgow, F., & Parsons, C. K. (1983). *Item response theory: Applications of psychological measurement.* Homewood, IL: Dow Jones-Irwin.

Jöreskog, K. J., & Sörbom, D. (1996). *LISREL 8: User's reference guide.* Chicago: Scientific Software.

Kim, S.-H., & Cohen, A. S. (1991). A comparison of two area measures for detecting differential item functioning. *Applied Psychological Measurement, 15,* 269–278.

Kim, S.-H., & Cohen, A. S. (1995). A comparison of Lord's chi-square, Raju's area measures, and the likelihood ratio tests on detection of differential item functioning. *Applied Measurement in Education, 8,* 291–312.

Kim, S.-H., & Cohen, A. S. (1998). Detection of differential item functioning under the graded response model with the likelihood ratio test. *Applied Psychological Measurement, 22,* 345–355.

Kim, S.-H., Cohen, A. S., & Park, T.-H. (1995). Detection of differential item functioning in multiple groups. *Journal of Educational Measurement, 32,* 261–276.

Lee, K., & Oshima, T. C. (1996). IPLINK: Multidimensional and unidimensional item parameter linking in item response theory. *Applied Psychological Measurement, 20,* 230.

Li, H.-H., & Stout, W. (1996). A new procedure for detection of crossing DIF. *Psychometrika, 61,* 647–677.

Lord, F. M. (1980). *Applications of item response theory to practical testing problems.* Hillsdale, NJ: Erlbaum.

Lord, F. M., & Novick, M. R. (1968). *Statistical theories of mental test scores.* Reading, MA: Addison-Wesley.

Mantel, N., & Haenszel, W. (1959). Statistical aspects of the analysis of data from retrospective studies of disease. *Journal of the National Cancer Institute, 22,* 719–748.

Maurer, T. J., Raju, N. S., & Collins, W. C. (1998). Peer and subordinate performance appraisal measurement equivalence. *Journal of Applied Psychology, 83,* 693–702.

Mazor, K. M., Hambleton, R. K., & Clauser, B. E. (1998). Multidimensional DIF analyses: The effects of matching on unidimensional subtest scores. *Applied Psychological Measurement, 22,* 357–367.

Millsap, R. E., & Everson, H. T. (1993). Methodology review: Statistical approaches for assessing measurement bias. *Applied Psychological Measurement, 17,* 297–334.

Mislevy, R. J., & Bock, R. D. (1990). *BILOG3: Item analysis and test scoring with binary logistic models* [Computer program]. Chicago: Scientific Software International.

Narayanan, P., & Swaminathan, H. (1996). Identification of items that show non-uniform DIF. *Applied Psychological Measurement, 20,* 257–274.

Oshima, T. C., Raju, N. S., & Flowers, C. (1997). Development and demonstration of multidimensional IRT-based internal measures of differential functioning of items and tests. *Journal of Educational Measurement, 34,* 253–272.

Raju, N. S. (1988). The area between two item characteristic curves. *Psychometrika, 53,* 495–502.

Raju, N. S. (1990). Determining the significance of estimated signed and unsigned areas between two item response functions. *Applied Psychological Measurement, 14,* 197–207.

Raju, N. S. (1999). *DFIT5D: A Fortran program for calculating dichotomous DIF/DTF* [Computer program]. Chicago: Illinois Institute of Technology.

Raju, N. S., Drasgow, F., & Slinde, J. A. (1993). An empirical comparison of the area methods, Lord's chi-square, and the Mantel-Haenszel technique for assessing differential item functioning. *Educational and Psychological Measurement, 53,* 301–314.

Raju, N. S., Laffitte, L. J., & Byrne, B. M. (2000, Apr.). *Measurement equivalence: A comparison of methods based on confirmatory analysis and item response theory.* Paper presented at the annual meeting of the Society for Industrial/Organizational Psychology, New Orleans, LA.

Raju, N. S., van der Linden, W., & Fleer, P. (1995). An IRT-based internal measure of test bias with applications for differential item functioning. *Applied Psychological Measurement, 19,* 353–368.

Reise, S. P., & Widaman, K. F. (1999). Assessing the fit of measurement models at the individual level: A comparison of item response theory and covariance structure approaches. *Psychological Methods, 4,* 3–21.

Reise, S. P., Widaman, K. F., & Pugh, R. H. (1993). Confirmatory factor analysis and item response theory: Two approaches for exploring measurement equivalence. *Psychological Bulletin, 114,* 552–566.

Roznowski, M. (1987). Use of tests manifesting sex differences as measures of intelligence: Implications for measurement bias. *Journal of Applied Psychology, 72,* 480–483.

Rudner, L. M., Geston, P. R., & Knight, D. L. (1980). Biased item detection techniques. *Journal of Educational Statistics, 5,* 213–233.

Samejima, F. (1969). Estimation of latent ability using a response pattern of graded scores. *Psychometrika Monograph,* no. 7.

Shealy, R., & Stout, W. (1993a). A model-based standardization approach that separates true bias/DIF from group ability differences and detects test bias/DTF as well as item bias/DIF. *Psychometrika, 58,* 159–194.

Shealy, R., & Stout, W. (1993b). An item response theory model for test bias and differential item functioning. In P. W. Holland & H. Wainer (Eds.), *Differential item functioning* (pp. 197–239). Hillsdale, NJ: Erlbaum.

Stout, W., Li, H.-H., Nandakumar, R., & Bolt, D. (1997). MULTISIB: A procedure to investigate DIF when a test is intentionally two-dimensional. *Applied Psychological Measurement, 21,* 195–213.

Swaminathan, H., & Rogers, H. J. (1990). Detecting differential item functioning using logistic regression procedures. *Journal of Educational Measurement, 27,* 361–370.

Thissen, D. (1991). *MULTILOG: Multiple, categorical item analysis and test scoring using item response theory (Version 6.0)* [Computer program]. Chicago: Scientific Software International.

Thissen, D., Steinberg, L., & Wainer, H. (1988). Use of item response theory in the study of group differences in trace lines. In H. Wainer & H. I. Braun (Eds.), *Test validity* (pp. 147–169). Hillsdale, NJ: Erlbaum.

Thissen, D., Steinberg, L., & Wainer, H. (1993). Detection of differential item functioning using the parameters of item response models. In

P. W. Holland & H. Wainer (Eds.), *Differential item functioning* (pp. 67–113). Hillsdale, NJ: Erlbaum.

Vandenberg, R. J., & Lance, C. E. (2000). A review and synthesis of the measurement invariance literature: Suggestions, practices, and recommendations for organizational research. *Organizational Research Methods, 3,* 4–69.

Zwick, R., Thayer, D. T., & Mazzeo, J. (1997). Descriptive and inferential procedures for assessing DIF in polytomous items. *Applied Measurement in Education, 10,* 321–344.

CHAPTER 7

Generalizability Theory
Richard P. DeShon

Is psychology a field of cumulative inquiry, or do we continually reinvent the wheel? Or, stated in a less extreme manner, why does it often seem that the rate of theoretical and empirical progress in our field is agonizingly slow? Many recent authors have argued that the widespread reliance on null-hypothesis testing is responsible for the observed lack of progress (Cohen, 1994; Loftus, 1994) and some have even suggested that null-hypothesis testing should be abandoned entirely (Schmidt, 1996). There is little doubt that null-hypothesis testing can be applied inappropriately and result in inaccurate inferences. However, is this the best target of our scrutiny? There are many good arguments supporting the judicious use of null-hypothesis testing (Cortina & Dunlap, 1997; Frick, 1996). Furthermore, before concluding that null-hypothesis testing is the culprit, it would be wise to eliminate alternative explanations that are precursors to the hypothesis testing process, such as the quality of the data and the selection of models used to represent the relations among the data (DeShon & Morris, in press).

The primary message of this chapter is that the measures used to represent critical constructs in our field often yield data that are incapable of supporting the broad inferences researchers desire. If the data were of higher quality, many of the problems associated with null-hypothesis testing would be minimized. To understand this perspective better, consider how inferences are commonly supported using psychological data. A prototypical research strategy is to obtain self-report assessments on multiple Likert-scaled items.

Coefficient alpha is then computed and reported as the estimate of reliability. Relationships between the scale and other measures of interest are corrected for unreliability using the traditional disattenuation formula or structural equation modeling software. Finally, significance tests (typically having low statistical power) are used to evaluate the research hypotheses. A procedure less likely to result in scientific progress can hardly be imagined.

To understand why this research strategy inhibits progress, it is important to understand the fundamentals of generalizability theory (henceforth referred to as G-theory). For now, I will simply state that examining the internal consistency of a measure provides information only on the extent to which research inferences may be generalized across items in the domain of items that might possibly be used to assess the construct. The internal consistency of the measure provides absolutely no information on whether inferences may be safely generalized across time, research settings, contexts, time of day, raters, or methods of administration, to mention just a few inferential hazards. Unless we are incredibly lucky, making progress without examining the extent to which our inferences generalize across factors other than item content is nearly impossible. Once the fundamentals of G-theory have been reviewed, the logic behind these statements should be clear.

My goals for this chapter are ambitious. I hope to first convince you that the dominant method of scientific inquiry in industrial/organizational (I/O) psychology does not promote progress. Second, I hope to demonstrate the need for improving the measurement of psychological constructs in I/O psychology and to encourage researchers to focus critically on measurement when conducting research. Third, I provide an overview of methods that may be used to improve the psychometric quality of measures and change the simplistic way we think about error in psychological research. The fundamental theme throughout this presentation is that scientific progress in I/O psychology could be greatly enhanced by a switch in focus from correcting relationships for measurement error (such as LISREL) to a focus on understanding the causes for measurement error in our data structures (such as G-theory).

The hazards of our current methodology can be demonstrated in part by considering the effects of measurement error corrections that occur using either structural equation model (SEM) procedures or the traditional disattenuation formula. I have previously (DeShon, 1998) discussed the limitations of the corrections for measurement error that occur when using SEM. I demonstrated that estimating measurement models without considering the substantive variables affecting the observed responses results in biased assessments of reliability and biased corrections of parameter estimates. To be concrete, consider the simple scenario where we obtain supervisor ratings of subordinate performance and assess the "reliability" of the resulting data. Assume that a researcher uses only a single supervisor to get ratings on multiple items assessing performance for each person. A result of this research design is that the only source of error that can be assessed in a measurement model is the internal consistency of the items. This design implicitly treats supervisors as perfectly interchangeable. If the researcher believes that different supervisors would provide different ratings of the individuals, then the researcher has not adequately captured the error structure of the measurement process, and the resulting measurement model used to estimate reliability is inaccurate (DeShon, 1998).

If the indicators used in a measurement model do not reflect the sources of variability known (or suspected) to influence the observed responses, then the resulting error structure will be incomplete and the reliability estimates inaccurate. This argument holds equally for SEM and traditional corrections using the disattenuation formula. Feldt and Brennan (1988) summarized this perspective perfectly when they stated, "In many situations, there can be little opportunity and only crude methodology to document the potential seriousness of error. But lack of knowledge about measurement error does not remove it from any set of scores" (p. 105).

The issue just discussed highlights some limitations of the correction for measurement error that occur using either classical test theory or SEM. However, a deeper issue has to do with whether measurement error corrections should be used at all. Consider one of the most important dependent variables in I/O psychology: supervisory ratings of job performance. Visweswaran, Ones, and Schmidt (1996) performed a meta-analysis of the literature and concluded that the average reliability of supervisory ratings across raters was a paltry .52. This means that nearly half of the variance in supervisory ratings is due to some form of measurement error. How can we base a science on a dependent variable that has just as much noise as signal (from a signal detection perspective)? Can reasonable inferences be made by correcting observed relationships with supervisory ratings of performance for measurement error? To answer this question, we need to understand what is being corrected for when the measurement error corrections are applied.

So, just what are we correcting for when we correct for unreliability in measures? Reliability is an assessment of the amount of error variance (or, conversely, true score variance) present in the observed scores. This is a reasonable statement, but exactly what are the errors? In classical true score theory, errors (E) are anything that cause the observed scores (O) to differ from the true scores (T), that is, $E = O - T$. Some of this variance is likely due to truly random processes that affect measurement. However, a substantial portion of the observed variance is due to the systematic effects of nonfocal variables on the measurement process. Murphy and DeShon (2000a) highlighted many variables—for example, rater biases, rater idiosyncrasies, and rater goals—that systematically lead raters to disagree when providing ratings of the same target. Hoyt (2000) recently made a similar point. The sources of systematic variance not due to the focal construct are sources of criterion contamination. In other words, they are sources of systematic variance in the observed scores that are due to variables other than the focal construct.

This means that any source of criterion contamination is a source of invalidity and results in errors: observed scores are different from true scores. If the errors are due in part to the systematic effects of variables other than the target construct, then part of the error variance is due to sources of invalidity. Stated more succinctly, the error variance, indexed by the reliability coefficient, is an assessment of the combined magnitude of the sources of invalidity in the observed scores. This means that the reliability coefficient is in part an assessment of the validity (or invalidity) of the measure rather than just an assessment of random error. Given this, corrections for measurement error are corrections for a lack of knowledge (or ignorance!) about the variables that influence the assessment process. The reader must determine whether it makes sense to correct observed relations for ignorance. From my perspective, the corrections answer the question, "What would the relationship look like if I understood all of the variables that influence the assessment process?" that is, the cognitive processes affecting ratings. From a more cynical perspective, the answered question might be, "What would my data look like if they did not look like they do?"

These issues are discussed in more detail in DeShon (1998) and Murphy and DeShon (2000a, 2000b). The basic message in these articles is that we have a very poor understanding of the measurement properties of assessment techniques and that this lack of knowledge severely inhibits inference. Moreover, these articles question the utility of the corrections for measurement error that occur using classical test methods or SEM. Instead of correcting for measurement error, we need to understand the causes for measurement error and do everything possible to eliminate them from our assessment methods. This is exactly the domain of G-theory.

What Is G-Theory?

The foundations of G-theory, an elegant and insightful extension of classical test theory, were presented by Cronbach, Glaser, Nanda, and Rajaratnam (1972). According to Spearman (1907), an individual's observed score (O) on a particular variable comprises the individual's true score (T) on the variable and random error (E), which implies the well known relation, $O = T + E$. The reliability of a measure is then defined as the ratio of true score variance over the sum of the true score variance and the error variance: $\sigma_t^2/\sigma_t^2+\sigma_{t'}^2$ The reliability of a measure can then be estimated as an intraclass correlation by estimating these variance sources through the analysis of variance (Hoyt, 1941).

The critical insight that led to the development of G-theory was that the random error term (E) in classical test theory was really composed of a multitude of unmeasured, and perhaps interacting, variables. Moreover, since a simple two-way ANOVA could be used to estimate the variance components for the intraclass correlation, more complicated designs could be used to decompose the error structure into its constituents. G-theory represents a major advance in the conceptualization and assessment of error structures over classical test theory. Given the fundamental nature of measurement in the development and validation of theoretical models in the social sciences, the fact that applications of G-theory are the exception rather than the norm is surprising.

Another difference between G-theory and classical methods is the role of parallel measures. Classical methods assume that alternate forms, such as items, scales, raters, and time periods, are parallel measures of the construct. This is a remarkably restrictive assumption and is almost never met in practice. As a result of this assumption, intraclass correlations may be interpreted as reliability coefficients. G-theory, on the other hand, views parallelism as too restrictive a condition. Instead, it uses a domain sampling approach to the measurement process. In G-theory, the forms used to obtain measurements are viewed as being sampled from a distribution (assumed to be normally distributed). The fundamental question asked of the measures is the extent to which they are exchangeable, or, alternatively, how generalizable inferences are across different forms in the population of possible forms. If there is a great deal of variance in measures obtained from different forms in the population, then the forms are not very exchangeable. In other words, the use of different forms would likely lead to substantially different obtained measurements. As a result, inferences based on the measures used in an actual experiment would not generalize across alternate forms.

The focus of G-theory is on understanding the error structure of the measures used in psychological research. Instead of correcting for the effects of measurement error, G-theory focuses attention on identifying the sources of measurement error, thereby helping researchers reduce errors in their measurements. Stated another way, G-theory represents an attempt to reduce ignorance instead of correcting for it when examining relationships among variables.

Why Did G-Theory Fail to Flourish?

G-theory has had less scientific impact than it deserves for a number of reasons. First, the development of SEM likely overshadowed the development of G-theory. Second, the presentation of G-theory is laden with measurement theory jargon. As others have stated (Goldstein & McDonald, 1988; Rubin, 1974), terms such as *facet of generalization, universe score, universe of admissible observations,* and *G versus D studies* serve only to make the literature on G-theory inaccessible to the uninitiated. Third, the theory was developed and presented in the psychometric tradition with a focus on individual differences. This presentation may have obscured the applicability of the theory to virtually all research domains and focuses other than individuals (Cardinet & Allal, 1983). Fourth, the utility of G-theory is dependent on the precision of the variance component estimates and the flexibility with which the procedure may be applied to various "messy data" situations. Unfortunately, the current method of estimating variance components in G-theory has numerous limitations, including the common occurrence of negative variance estimates and balanced data requirements. Finally, the lack of a modern computer program for carrying out the analyses has limited the use of the methodology. It is likely that these limitations have resulted in researchers' choosing other methods to conduct research.

Boiling G-Theory Down to Its Basics

The primary advantage of G-theory is that it focuses attention on the dimensionality or breadth of a population (termed an *inference space*) to which the results of a study are applicable. The number of variables that influence system behavior, and the variance of these variables in the population, determine the confidence one should have in generalizing sample-based study results to a larger population. G-theory allows the researcher to examine flexibly the degree to which results may be generalized to various inference spaces. The broadest inference space consists of all the variables that simultaneously, and perhaps interactively, influence the system's behavior. These variables are considered to be random, in the sense that the particular levels of the variable represent samples from a larger population of potential values that are assumed to be normally distributed with a mean of zero and an unknown variance. For instance, the raters included in an interrater reliability study may be considered to be a random sample from a larger population of potential raters who might have been selected and the researcher wishes to generalize the inferences across the population of potential raters.

The confidence that a researcher has in generalizing the results of a particular study to a larger population may be increased by placing conceptual constraints on the population of interest. For instance, the inference space in a supervisory rating study may be narrowed by restricting inference to the particular raters included in the study. The same raters will be used in future decisions, and the variance in the population of raters is not relevant to the conclusions drawn from the study. The narrowest inference space occurs when none of the variables is considered to be random samples from a population, and inference is restricted to the particular levels included in the analysis. In this trivial case, the issue of generalizability is irrelevant.

The conceptual issue of inference space restrictions leads to the statistical distinction between fixed- and random-effect linear models, on which G-theory is founded. The primary difference between fixed- and random-effect models is the way in which the levels of the variables being studied are conceptualized and selected for inclusion in an experiment. The traditional approach to linear models (regression or ANOVA) corresponds to the narrow inference space and models the levels of a factor as fixed effects. Here, the factor levels included in the linear model are selected on the basis of design optimality criteria, response surface coverage, or simply a rational choice based on the preferences of the researcher. No assumptions are made with respect to an underlying distribution of possible values for the independent variables, and if the experiment were replicated or cross-validated on a new sample of units (for example, people, animals, or products), the same factor levels would be used again and again. In this case, inference is—or should be—restricted to the levels of the factors included in the model, and the issue of generalizability to larger populations is irrelevant. The analysis simply focuses on differences among the fixed effects (say, treatments or groups).

Random-effects models correspond to the broadest inference space. The focus of this analysis is on estimating the magnitude of the unknown population variances, and the particular levels of the independent variables included in the analysis are interesting only to the extent that they represent the population. Placing restrictions on the inference space is modeled statistically by treating the levels of the restricted factor as fixed effects. This process results in a mixed-effects model that contains both random and fixed effects and corresponds to an intermediate inference space. This presentation will focus on the random-effects model, and then the procedure will be generalized to include mixed-effects models (where some of the factors are treated as fixed effects).

G-Theory for Random-Effect Models

Consider a situation in which a researcher is interested in examining the generalizability of inferences concerning supervisory ratings of employee performance across job tasks. Assume that ten employees (a_i; $i = 1, \ldots, I$) are randomly selected to be rated on four randomly selected job tasks (β_j; $j = 1, \ldots, J$) by ten randomly selected observers (γ_k; $k = 1, \ldots, K$). If all ten employees are rated by each observer across the four tasks, we have an EMPLOYEES (a $\times$ TASKS (β) $\times$ RATERS (γ) fully crossed design (in G-theory terms it is a two-facet crossed design). In this scenario, all the factors are considered to be random, and there are seven sources of variance that must be considered to understand the generalizability of inferences concerning employee performance ratings. The sources of variance can be represented by the following linear model,

$$Y_{ijk} = \mu + a_i + \beta_j + \gamma_k + (a\beta)_{ij} + (a\gamma)_{ik} + (\beta\gamma)_{jk} + (a\beta\gamma)_{ijk} + e_{ijk}, \quad (7.1)$$

where μ is a constant representing the grand mean, a, β, γ, $a\beta$, $a\gamma$, $\beta\gamma$, $a\beta\gamma$ and e are independent, normal random variables with a mean of zero and respective variances σ_a^2, σ_β^2, σ_γ^2, $\sigma_{a\beta}^2$, $\sigma_{a\gamma}^2$, $\sigma_{\beta\gamma}^2$, $\sigma_{a\beta\gamma}^2$, σ_e^2. Because employees are treated as a factor in this design, there is only one observation in each cell of the design and the variances associated with $\sigma_{a\beta\gamma}^2$ and are σ_e^2 confounded. Following convention, this combined source of variance will be referred to as $\sigma_{a\beta\gamma,e}^2$. In contrast to fixed-effect models, the focus in random-effect models is estimating the variances (such as σ_a^2) associated with the random-effect terms in equation 7.1. The total observed variance in the ratings could be decomposed into the respective variance components associated with each random effect in equation 7.1. The estimation of these variance components is the central issue in G-theory.

In the example, there are seven variance components. The variance in the performance ratings across employees is captured by σ_a^2. This is the focal variable in the study (termed the *facet of differentiation* in G-theory). We want to understand how differences in employee performance ratings generalize across task dimensions and raters. All other sources of variance are considered to be error that limits our ability to generalize inferences concerning employee performance. For instance, σ_γ^2 captures the variance in ratings across the raters. Ideally, we want disagreements between raters to be as small as possible. The larger the variance component associated with raters is, the less able we are to generalize inferences about employee performance across raters. The variance in performance ratings across tasks, σ_β^2, indicates the extent to which inferences concerning employee performance can be generalized across tasks. Again, to generalize inferences across tasks, it is important that the variance in performance ratings across the tasks is small.

The interpretation of the variance components associated with the interactions is a bit more complex. The variance component representing the interaction between employees and tasks, $\sigma_{\alpha\beta}^2$, indicates the extent to which the variance in employee performance ratings varies across task dimensions. In other words, are the employees more or less differentiable when performing particular tasks? If this variance component is large, then the generalizability of employee performance across task dimensions is questionable. Similarly, the extent to which the variance in employee performance ratings varies across raters is indexed by $\sigma_{\alpha\gamma}^2$. In other words, certain raters are providing ratings of employee performance that are more or less variable than other raters. The variance of the interactions between raters and tasks, $\sigma_{\beta\gamma}^2$, captures the extent to which the variance in ratings of employee performance across tasks varies depending on the rater. Certain raters are providing ratings of employee performance that make larger or smaller distinctions depending on the task. The highest-order interaction, $\sigma_{\alpha\beta\gamma,e}^2$, is best interpreted as an estimate of the error present in the ratings of employee performance that cannot be explained by tasks, raters, or the interactions of these sources with employees.

Variance Component Estimation

The seven sources of variance in equation 7.1 are generally unknown quantities and must be estimated in some fashion. The monographs on G-theory (Brennan, 1992; Cronbach et al., 1972; Shavelson &

Webb, 1991) recommend calculating the mean square for each effect through the analysis of variance and then equating each source to its expectation. The limitations of this method are substantial. The expected mean squares (EMS) method is complex, requires balanced data structures, and often results in negative values for the variance components (Searle, Casella, & McCulloch, 1992). The most troubling limitation of the EMS method is the requirement of no missing data (a balanced design).

The data structures used to estimate variance components in G-theory are classified as nonreplicated designs where only a single unit, such as a rating, is observed under each combination of the factors being studied. Therefore, missing data are more serious than simply having unequal sample sizes because the entire cell representing the specific combination of factors is empty. Unfortunately, unbalanced data structures commonly occur in psychology where, for instance, raters (supervisors, military unit commanders, clinical diagnosticians) observe subsets of ratees that only partially overlap. Although fully crossed designs lead to efficient statistical estimation, it is rarely an efficient method for achieving distributed task outcomes in the real world.

To achieve the balanced designs needed for EMS estimation of the variance components, a common recommendation is that data be randomly discarded (Shavelson & Webb, 1991). However, information is a precious commodity in G-theory, and the negative effects of this practice on the precision of the variance component estimates cannot be overstated. Even with balanced data, the standard errors of the variance component estimates can be so large that the variance components are uninformative (Smith, 1978, 1982). Randomly discarding data to achieve balanced designs can be very costly, particularly because alternative estimation methods exist that do not require balanced designs.

The best general-purpose estimation technique available in modern computer packages is restricted maximum-likelihood estimation (REML; Patterson & Thompson, 1971). The REML estimates have qualities that make them attractive to researchers using G-theory. For random designs with no missing data, the generalizability coefficient calculated using the REML or EMS variance component estimates will be identical whenever the EMS estimates are nonnegative. For fully random designs with missing data, the REML estimates of the variance components are most appropriate because they do not require discarding data to achieve a balanced design. REML variance component estimates are available in virtually all major statistical packages, including SAS (proc mixed), SPSS, and STATA. The most powerful and flexible estimation method currently available is the mixed procedure in SAS.

G-Theory Coefficients

The focus of G-theory is on estimating the variance components associated with the sources of variance that can affect the generalizability of inferences. However, how does one determine if a source of variance is large, or how confident one should be when making inferences? To answer these questions, generalizability coefficients are computed.

The computation of generalizability coefficients is straightforward and results from the application of the intraclass correlation. The general form of the intraclass correlation is

$$\rho^2 = \frac{\sigma_t^2}{\sigma_t^2 + \sigma_e^2},$$ (7.2)

where σ_t^2 is the variance of the target (facet of differentiation) and σ_e^2 is the error variance. In the scenario above, the target variance is the variance associated with employees. The composition of the error variance is only slightly more complex.

In G-theory, there is a distinction between relative and absolute definitions of error depending on the type of decisions to which the researcher wishes to generalize. If the researcher is interested only in whether the relative ranking of persons stays the same across conditions (time, raters, tasks, contexts, or something else), then a relative definition of error is used in equation 7.2. This would be the relevant error term if top-down selection were used to fill positions in an organization. The ranking of applicants, not the magnitude of the score, determines selection. When the researcher is most concerned with the stability of the relative rankings across conditions, the relative error definition is used. In this case, only the sources of variance that contain interactions with the target are included in the error term, so the generalizability coefficient for relative decisions would be

$$\rho^2 = \frac{\sigma_a^2}{\sigma_a^2 + \left[\sigma_{a\beta}^2 + \sigma_{a\gamma}^2 + \sigma_{a\beta\gamma,e}^2\right]} \cdot \tag{7.3}$$

If it is important to the researcher that the differences between individuals stay constant across conditions, then an absolute definition of error is used. Absolute error terms are used when the magnitude of the score is important, such as in a pass-fail cutoff situation. The error term corresponding to the absolute decisions consists of all sources of variance other than the target variance. In the scenario presented above, the generalizability coefficient for absolute decisions would be

$$\rho^2 = \frac{\sigma_a^2}{\sigma_a^2 + \left[\sigma_\beta^2 + \sigma_\gamma^2 + \sigma_{a\beta}^2 + \sigma_{a\gamma}^2 + \sigma_{\beta\gamma}^2 + \sigma_{a\beta\gamma,e}^2\right]} \cdot \tag{7.4}$$

Generalizability coefficients will clearly be larger when based on the relative definition of error than when based on the absolute error definition. In most I/O psychology applications, the relative error is most relevant to the needed decisions.

Ideally, one would put confidence intervals around the resulting G-theory coefficient. Confidence intervals exist for specific forms of the intraclass correlation (Donner & Wells, 1986). However, there is no general form for the confidence interval that would encompass the multitude of intraclass correlations that could be computed. This is an issue very much in need of further research.

Only one more complication in the computation of generalizability coefficients needs to be considered before providing an example of how to implement the method. The generalizability coefficients presented in equations 7.3 and 7.4 represent the generalizability of ratings to a single randomly sampled level of either raters or tasks. In other words, how confident could I be that the decisions or inferences based on a single rater or a single task would generalize to the larger population of raters or tasks? Suppose, however, that decisions will be based on more than one rater or more than one task, and the resulting average of the ratings across raters or tasks is what the researcher intends to generalize? In this case, we need to consider generalizing the ratings from a set of conditions to a different, but equally large, set of conditions in the population (for example, raters).

Assume that we intend to make a top-down selection decision in an applied context (an inference about the best person for the job) based on the average rating of three raters observing performance on a single task. How confident should we be that this decision would generalize to other tasks and other sets (of three) raters? In this case, the generalizability coefficient, based on the absolute error, would be computed as

$$\rho^2 = \frac{\sigma_a^2}{\sigma_a^2 + \left[\sigma_\beta^2 + \dfrac{\sigma_\gamma^2}{3} + \sigma_{a\beta}^2 + \dfrac{\sigma_{a\gamma}^2}{3} + \dfrac{\sigma_{\beta\gamma}^2}{3} + \dfrac{\sigma_{a\beta\gamma,e}^2}{3}\right]} \cdot \tag{7.5}$$

In words, the variance components that contain a component associated with raters γ are divided by the number of raters on which the decision will be based. What if we were also interested in the average performance across a set of tasks? Assume that we intend to make a top-down selection decision in an applied context (an inference about the best person for the job) based on the average rating of four raters across the average performance on two tasks. The corresponding generalizability coefficient, based on the absolute error, would be computed as

$$\rho^2 = \frac{\sigma_a^2}{\sigma_a^2 + \left[\dfrac{\sigma_\beta^2}{2} + \dfrac{\sigma_\gamma^2}{4} + \dfrac{\sigma_{a\beta}^2}{2} + \dfrac{\sigma_{a\gamma}^2}{4} + \dfrac{\sigma_{\beta\gamma}^2}{2\cdot4} + \dfrac{\sigma_{a\beta\gamma,e}^2}{2\cdot4}\right]} \cdot \tag{7.6}$$

Any variance component containing a term for raters is divided by the number of raters. Similarly, any variance component containing a term for tasks is divided by the number of tasks. When both raters and tasks are represented in the same variance component, the number of raters and tasks is multiplied. Clearly, the error terms based on generalizing to sets of raters or sets of tasks will be smaller than those based on generalizing to a single rater or task. As a result, the generalizability coefficient will be greater.

The use of this technique can be prospective or retrospective. In other words, once you have estimated the variance components, you can answer questions about how much confidence you should have in generalizing the results of a particular study that has already been conducted. By experimenting with the numbers used to divide the variance components, you can also answer questions about how many raters or tasks need to be averaged to achieve desired levels of generalizability for future decisions. This is referred to as a decision study in G-theory.

Example

Day and Silverman (1989, 1992) examined performance ratings for forty-eight accountants on six job dimensions made by seven partners of a medium-sized accounting firm. As is typical in most field settings, every partner did not interact with all forty-eight accountants, and complete ratings were available for only eighteen accountants. To avoid discarding over 60 percent of the data to achieve a balanced design, REML estimation may be used under the assumption that the data are missing at random. Table 7.1 presents the SAS and SPSS syntax needed to obtain REML variance component estimates for this G-theory design. Table 7.2 presents the REML variance component estimates and standard errors for a reanalysis of their data, using all available information.

The largest variance component that contributes to error is associated with the highest-order interaction, which is a residual term

Table 7.1. SAS and SPSS Syntax for Obtaining REML Variance Component Estimates.

SAS Syntax for the Rating Example	SPSS Syntax for the Rating Example

PROC MIXED;
    CLASS task observer team;
    MODEL rating =;
    RANDOM employee | rater | task;
	VARCOMP
	    rating BY employee task rater
	    /RANDOM = employee task rater
	    /METHOD = REML
	    /CRITERIA = ITERATE(50)
	    /CRITERIA = CONVERGE(1.0E-8)
	    /DESIGN
	    /INTERCEPT = INCLUDE .

Table 7.2. REML Variance Component
Estimates from Day and Silverman.

Source	df	Variance Component	Standard Error
Employees (E)	47	0.82	0.20
Tasks (T)	5	0.32	0.22
Raters (R)	6	0.17	0.11
E × T	235	0.37	0.04
E × R	282	0.28	0.04
R × T	30	0.10	0.03
E × R × T, e	1410	0.56	0.02

accounting for variance unexplained by the main effects and two-way interactions. The high variance due to employees is promising because it indicates that there are differences between the performance ratings received by employees and that they are differentiable. The large variance components due to dimensions and the interaction of employees with dimensions indicate that there are differences in performance ratings across the dimensions and that certain employees are rated as performing better than others on particular dimensions. The employee by rater interaction suggests that raters have idiosyncratic ideas about which employees are the best performers.

How much confidence should a researcher have in inferences or decisions based on this error structure? If the researcher wished to generalize absolute inferences based on performance ratings obtained from a single rater observing performance on a single task across the larger population of possible raters and tasks, the generalizability coefficient would be

$$\rho^2 = \frac{.82}{.82 + \left[.17 + .32 + .28 + .37 + .10 + .56\right]} = .313. \qquad (7.7)$$

Generalizability coefficients are analogous to reliability coefficients and interpreted in the same manner. There are no hard-and-fast rules when interpreting these coefficients, but clearly a generalizability coefficient of .313 does not inspire great confidence in the results. If a researcher were interested in relative decisions, then the generalizability coefficient would be

$$\rho^2 = \frac{.82}{.82 + \left[.28 + .37 + .56\right]} = .404. \tag{7.8}$$

This is an improvement, but hardly impressive.

What would happen to the relative error generalizability coefficient if we used the average of the ratings provided by the seven raters? In this case, the generalizability coefficient would be

$$\rho^2 = \frac{.82}{.82 + \left[\frac{.28}{7} + .37 + \frac{.56}{7}\right]} = .626. \tag{7.9}$$

This is clearly much better than ratings provided by a single rater but still not acceptable. This coefficient assumes that future decisions would be based on the average rating provided by a randomly selected set of seven raters.

What if we used the average of the seven raters and the average of the six tasks? In other words, we wished to generalize our results to the average rating of seven raters based on six tasks. In this case, the relative-error generalizability coefficient would be

$$\rho^2 = \frac{.82}{.82 + \left[\frac{.28}{7} + \frac{.37}{7} + \frac{.56}{6 \cdot 7}\right]} = .91. \tag{7.10}$$

Finally, we have arrived at a level of generalizability that most researchers would be comfortable basing decisions on. However, having seven raters observe applicants perform six different tasks is not a very practical method for making decisions in most applied settings!

What if we used fewer raters and had them observe performance on more tasks? Assume that in future studies, we would use three raters and have them observe individuals performing ten separate tasks. In this case, the generalizability coefficient would be

$$\rho^2 = \frac{.82}{.82 + \left[\dfrac{.28}{3} + \dfrac{.37}{10} + \dfrac{.56}{10 \cdot 3}\right]} = .926, \tag{7.11}$$

which is also quite acceptable. By using this method, the optimal number of conditions that should be included when collecting data for a particular type of decision can be determined, depending on the constraints in the situation. That is all there is to it. By estimating variance components associated with the various sources of error, it is possible to identify the largest contributors to error and focus attention on reducing the error associated with the measurement condition. Also, by examining generalizability coefficients based on the mean of observations across a measurement condition (such as raters), it can be determined how large the set of conditions (such as an average rating based on how many raters) must be to achieve adequate levels of generalizability.

G-Theory for Mixed-Effect Models

The prior discussion and example addressed the computation of variance components and generalizability coefficients for the case when all factors are considered to be random samples from larger populations. However, it is often the case that a researcher has no intention of generalizing beyond the levels of a particular measurement condition that might affect the measurement process. If the G-theory study were conducted again, the same levels of the measurement condition would be used again. For instance, the seven partners who provided ratings in the example happen to be the entire population of partners in the accounting firm. Therefore, it may be reasonable to treat the raters in this data set as a fixed effect. In so doing, we restrict the inference space and should have more confidence in our ability to differentiate among employees.

The estimation of variance components is more complex when some of the factors included in the G-theory analysis are considered to be fixed effects. A heated debate on the estimation of variance components for models containing both random and fixed effects (mixed-effects models) is occurring in the statistical literature. Nelder and Lane (1995) refer to this problem as the "mixed-model muddle" (p. 382). The recent variance component estimation methods implemented in statistical software result in different definitions of the variance components than the methods based on the original methods developed by Sheffé (1959) and Cornfield and Tukey (1956). The controversy revolves around the treatment of interactions between fixed and random effects. The recently developed methods treat the interactions as random effects. The original methods treat them as quasi–random effects because they are subject to summation restrictions similar to those found in the definition of fixed effects. The complexities of this debate are beyond the scope of this presentation. Interested readers should consult Searle et al. (1992). I first present the traditional method for estimating variance components and computing G-theory coefficients when some of the factors are treated as fixed effects. I then discuss the implications of an alternative method for estimating variance components.

Conceptually, G-theory estimates variance components by averaging over the levels of the fixed effects. In the previous example, the facet of differentiation (the target) is employees, and the conditions of measurement being studied are raters and job tasks. The resulting design is a three-factor ANOVA (Employees × Tasks × Raters) with one observation in each cell. If the rater factor is considered to be fixed, the resulting variance components could be estimated by computing a two-way random-effects ANOVA (Employees × Tasks) for each of the raters. The resulting variance component estimates for each of the seven raters could then be averaged across the raters.

Computationally, G-theory estimates variance components by using functions of the variance components from the completely random design. A reduced G-theory design is formed by eliminating the fixed-effect factor (for example, raters) from the design. In the example, this would yield an Employees × Tasks design. The variance components for the reduced design are formed by starting with the corresponding variance components from the full design and adding the variance corresponding to the interaction between that source of variance and the fixed factor, divided by the number of levels in the fixed factor. In the example, the three remaining variance components in the reduced design are $\sigma_a^2, \sigma_\beta^2,$ and $\sigma_{a\beta,e}^2$. These variance components represent the random main effects for employees and tasks along with their interaction, which is confounded with the error term. The following equations are used to compute the variance components for the reduced design:

$$\sigma_{a*}^2 = \sigma_a^2 + \frac{\sigma_{a\gamma}^2}{n_r}$$

$$\sigma_{\beta*}^2 = \sigma_\beta^2 + \frac{\sigma_{\beta\gamma}^2}{n_r} \qquad (7.12)$$

$$\sigma_{a\beta,e*}^2 = \sigma_{a\beta,e}^2 + \frac{\sigma_{a\beta\gamma,e}^2}{n_r}$$

where the asterisk represents the variance components for the reduced design. Using the values in Table 7.2, the resulting variance components are

$$\sigma_{a*}^2 = .82 + \frac{.28}{7} = .86,$$

$$\sigma_{\beta*}^2 = .32 + \frac{.10}{7} = .33, \qquad (7.13)$$

$$\sigma_{a\beta,e*}^2 = .37 + \frac{.56}{7} = .45.$$

The generalizability coefficient for ratings of employees using a fixed set of raters for a single task, based on the absolute error, is

$$\rho^2 = \frac{\sigma_{a*}^2}{\sigma_{a*}^2 + \left[\sigma_{\beta*}^2 + \sigma_{a\beta,e*}^2\right]} = \frac{.86}{.86 + [.33 + .45]} = .524. \qquad (7.14)$$

The equivalent generalizability coefficient when raters were considered random was .313. Clearly, treating raters as a fixed effect yields a large improvement in the generalizability coefficient. Even so, the resulting generalizability coefficient is too low for confident decisions. If the decision is to be based on the average of the six tasks, then the generalizability coefficient is

$$\rho^2 = \frac{\sigma_{a*}^2}{\sigma_{a*}^2 + \left[\dfrac{\sigma_{\beta*}^2}{n_t} + \dfrac{\sigma_{a\beta,e*}^2}{n_t}\right]} = \frac{.86}{.86 + \left[\dfrac{.33}{6} + \dfrac{.45}{6}\right]} = .87, \qquad (7.15)$$

which is acceptable.

The newer methods for estimating variance components, based on maximum likelihood techniques, do not average over the levels of the fixed effect. Searle et al. (1992) provide an excellent discussion of the advantages and disadvantages of the two approaches to estimating variance components for mixed-effect models. For now, I provide a brief overview of the new methods and highlight potential problems with the current procedure for estimating variance components in G-theory. In the new parameterizations of the mixed-effect model, when a factor is treated as a fixed effect, the variance associated with the factor is simply removed from the random portion of the model. The variance component estimates for the remaining terms remain unchanged. If raters are considered to be a fixed effect, the variance associated with raters is removed from the error term (in a generalizability coefficient), but the interaction of raters with other random effects stays in the model as random effects. For instance, the generalizability coefficient for the absolute error term when raters are treated as a fixed factor would be

$$\rho^2 = \frac{\sigma_a^2}{\sigma_a^2 + \left[\sigma_\beta^2 + \sigma_{a\beta}^2 + \sigma_{a\gamma}^2 + \sigma_{\beta\gamma}^2 + \sigma_{a\beta\gamma,e}^2\right]}. \qquad (7.16)$$

A number of questions can be raised concerning the treatment of fixed effects in the current methods used in G-theory. For instance, consider the first transformation in equation 7.12. When raters are treated as a fixed factor, the variance associated with the interaction between employees and raters is added back into the variance component for employees. Now consider the implication of this transformation for the measurement theory on which G-theory is based. Recall that G-theory is an extension of Spearman's classic partition of observed variance into true and error variance, $\sigma_o^2 + \sigma_t^2 = \sigma_e^2$. G-theory decomposes the error variance into its constituent sources and, when not explicitly measured, fixed facets are included in the error term (Cronbach et al., 1972). Fixing a measured factor that contributes to the error variance must necessarily reduce the error variance. However, there is no measurement theory justification for why fixing a source of error variance should increase true score variance. This is exactly the point that Cardinet and Allal (1983, p. 18) were making when they stated that one of the reasons that G-theory has not affected science more is that "there is some confusion in the presentation of the roles of analysis of variance and of generalizability theory. . . . In designs that involve fixed conditions along a facet of observation, the interaction between persons and this facet is treated as a component of true (universe score) variance. Strictly speaking, such interaction does not affect the variance of the observed scores; that is, the sum of the interaction effects is zero for each person."

In addition, interesting information concerning the interactions between the fixed and random effects is lost by averaging over the levels of the fixed effects. The interactions between fixed and random effects are random effects that have associated variance components (Searle et al., 1992). However, conditioning the variance components on the mean of the fixed effects or, equivalently, averaging over the levels of the fixed factor before performing a generalizability analysis makes it impossible to examine these interesting variance components. The transformation in equation 7.12 highlights that these interactions are collapsed into the remaining three variance components and, as a result, cannot be interpreted as unique sources of variance.

Samuels, Casella, and McCabe (1991) provided a complementary perspective on the interactions between the random and fixed effects that helps clarify the choice between the two approaches to estimating variance components. According to these authors, the choice between the two model parameterizations should be consistent with the researcher's conceptualization of the interactions between random and fixed effects. If the researcher believes that the interactions between random and fixed effects represent an interesting and meaningful source of variance, which they termed *independent contributions,* then the new methods are most appropriate. For instance, in the previous example, the variance components would be considered independent contributions if the researcher believes that the interactions between raters and tasks or raters and employees represent interesting and unique sources of variance. The traditional methods for estimating variance components are most consistent with the analysis of randomized block designs, where the interaction is simply included to account for nonadditivity of the row and column effects and no substantive interpretation is attached to these variance sources.

In addition, it is quite possible that the mean of the variance components over the levels of the fixed effects is substantively uninteresting. No distributional assumptions are required for the fixed effects, and the levels of the fixed factor need not represent values along a continuum. In these cases, the mean of the variance components across levels of the fixed effects may be uninteresting or misleading. Shavelson, Webb, and Rowley (1989) and Shavelson and Webb (1991) recognized that the mean of the fixed effects is often uninteresting and presented an example of mathematics and reading instruction to illustrate their point. They considered averaging over the levels of the fixed effect (instructional content) to be comparing apples and oranges due to large differences in the instruction types. To avoid nonsensical interpretations of the conditional variance components, they recommended that the analysis be conducted within each level of the fixed factor. However, this strategy also makes it impossible to examine the potentially interesting variance components that represent the interactions between the fixed and random effects.

These issues simply raise questions about the manner in which variance components are treated in the mixed-effect model within G-theory. I am not yet proposing that the methods used in G-theory should be abandoned for the newer methods. In fact, I believe that further work is needed to determine whether the new methods for estimating variance components when some of the factors are fixed yield variance components that are consistent with the measurement theory behind G-theory. Brennan, Jarjoura, and Deaton (1980) strongly argue that the newer methods are inconsistent with the fundamental assumptions of G-theory. For now, I think it is important that researchers be aware that the treatment of fixed effects in modern computer packages, such as SAS and SPSS, is inconsistent with the original formulation of G-theory.

Finally, there is an important point that must be made before moving away from these examples. The design above included only raters and tasks. What if a researcher wanted to generalize the decisions across time? In other words, is the best performer at the current time also the best performer at a future point (an important issue for selection research)? Because the design did not include time as a condition, it is impossible to estimate the generalizability of inferences or decisions across time. If there is an important condition a researcher would like to generalize the results across, then it must be included in a research design, or no information is provided to aid the decision (DeShon, 1998).

A Lesson from History on the Importance and Complexity of Measurement

At the start of this chapter, I argued that the current treatment of error in I/O psychology has impeded scientific progress. I further argued that by carefully considering the error structure of our measurement procedures (through G-theory or other related methods), it is possible to improve the rate of scientific progress. However, to this point, I have demonstrated only how to perform a G-theory analysis. To provide some perspective on the importance of carefully thinking about the error structure of psychological measurements and the problems encountered when attempting to measure psychological constructs, I conclude this chapter with an example from the physical sciences.

Consider the measurement of temperature from the perspective of an early scientist who does not possess knowledge of thermodynamic laws. Take a moment before reading further, and consider how you would define the concept of temperature. The sensations of hot and cold are easily understood; even a child could communicate this fact. You know that when it is hot outside, you perspire, and when you touch something hot, you experience the sensation of heat. You know that when it is cold outside, you may get gooseflesh, and your lips may tingle. You know you can tell which of two objects is colder than the other by comparing the perception of heat or coldness experienced by touching the objects. Or can you? As it happens, the rate of heat transfer from a substance substantially affects the perception of heat or cold. For instance, imagine comparing by touch the outside of a wooden door and the metal doorknob on a cold winter day. The metal feels much colder than the wood, although both are exposed to the same temperature. Unless you understand the principles of heat transfer, using the sense of touch to determine relative temperature is an exercise in futility. But how can you begin to understand the principles of heat transfer unless you have an accurate and reliable measure of temperature?

If you were an early scientist, how would you go about measuring temperature? For all practical purposes, temperature is a construct. Unlike length or weight, temperature is unobservable; we can only infer its existence through its effects on other observable phenomena (for example, the effects of temperature on the state of water). In fact, along with a few other physical properties, such as atmospheric pressure, the problems encountered when attempting to measure temperature are highly similar to the problems encountered when attempting to measure most psychological constructs.

As it happens, early scientists noticed that perceived differences in temperature covaried with the volume of substances (air, water, spirits, mercury) in a container (Middleton, 1966). As a result, volume became the indicator of temperature. The history of the measurement of temperature represents a systematic exploration of the error structure that occurs when using volume as a measure of temperature. In fact, the field of meteorology and much of the study of gases resulted from investigations into the causes for error when assessing temperature.

The history of the thermometer represents, for the most part, a search for the sources of error in a measurement instrument. It also demonstrates the dynamic interplay of measurement and theory development. The earliest thermometers, developed in the 1600s, relied on the expansion and contraction of air when heated or cooled. There was no theory of temperature (or heat transfer) driving the development of the thermometer. Early instrument builders were simply developing a method to assess the natural occurrence of changes in temperature. Their early thermometers were not sealed and therefore were subject to barometric changes in the atmosphere. As a result, the open-air thermometers gave different readings when the temperature should have been fixed (such as the boiling point of water or the freezing point of ice). By recognizing this source of error, it became possible to develop more reliable thermometers by sealing the thermometer, thereby eliminating the effects of external air pressure. More important, theoretical information on the effects of air pressure (and more generally the properties of gases) was obtained. In fact, the development of the barometer occurred soon after the effects of air pressure were discovered (Middleton, 1964).

Once the thermometer was sealed off from the effects of the atmosphere, the fundamental questions addressed by the early thermometer makers dealt with the substance that should be used in the thermometer, the consistency of the instrument manufacture, and the scale used to assign numbers to the level of liquid in the thermometer. Water was not an acceptable liquid because it froze at low temperatures. Therefore, early thermometers typically used spirits (wine or other alcoholic substances) or oils. However, it was soon recognized that the proportion of alcohol in the spirit affected the magnitude of change in the substance and that results from different thermometers were not comparable due to differences in liquid. In addition, most liquids used in early thermometers did not have constant coefficients of expansion, and so the magnitude of change would differ depending on the temperature (unequal intervals of change). Many other substances were attempted before mercury (quicksilver) was settled on as the most useful substance. However, questions about the differences in the rate of expansion for different substances and for a particular substance at different temperatures led to theorizing about vapor pressure and further work on gases and the definition of an ideal gas. Furthermore, once standardized and reliable instruments were available for assessing temperature, it became possible to maintain and compare records of temperature in different areas of the world. This simple outcome led to the rise of the entire field of meteorology (Middleton, 1966).

Questions asked about the properties of gases and the rates of expansion of substances when exposed to different temperatures were intimately connected with some of the most important discoveries in science, such as the concept of atomic motion. Focusing on reducing the error involved in the early measurement of temperature led to remarkable scientific discoveries. In addition, once a reliable and standardized measure of temperature existed, it became possible to develop theory that led to the actual definition of temperature (McGee, 1988). Kelvin's definition of temperature was based on the fact that gas pressure increases as temperature increases. The opposite effect also occurs: gas pressure drops as temperature drops. Kelvin reasoned that this effect was due to thermal energy. Thermal energy decreased as temperature decreased, and as a result, the pressure exerted by a gas decreased. This led to an internally rigorous definition of temperature in terms of thermal energy.

Consider now what might have happened to the measurement of temperature if modern statistical procedures were available at the time. First, the reliability of the thermometer across a single condition of measurement (for example, alternate thermometers under the same set of conditions) would have been estimated and reported (this is the equivalent of using Cronbach's alpha to assess item consistency). The reliability of the measurement procedure across other conditions (atmospheric conditions, time, liquids, instrument makers, and others) would have been largely ignored. Second, when studying the relationship of temperature with other important variables, say, gas pressure, the relationship would have been corrected for unreliability in the measurement of temperature. This correction often addresses the question, "What would my data look like if they did not look like they do?" In other words, what would the relationship be if open-air thermometers were not affected by atmospheric pressure? What a silly question. Open-air thermometers will always be affected by atmospheric pressure. Similarly, what about correcting for the fact that a liquid does not have a constant coefficient of expansion. Again, it is better to identify the problem and find measurement techniques that are not affected by the problem than to act as if the world does not function the way it does. A different situation arises, however, when we discuss the problem of inconsistencies in the manufacture of the vessel containing the liquid. If we know that the thermometer does not have a constant inside diameter, then it makes some sense to correct for this fact given the hope that it is not the "state of the world" but rather a problem that can be fixed through improved instrument manufacturing techniques.

Using modern statistical methods, the relation between temperature and pressure would likely have been corrected for measurement error due to different forms (thermometers) but would not have been corrected for the many other factors affecting the measurement of temperature (nonlinear coefficients of liquid expansion, atmospheric pressure, vapor pressure, and so on). The result would have yielded a very messy scatterplot relating the various temperatures to the corresponding pressures. Under these conditions, it is quite likely that the ideal gas law and the law relating the pressure of a gas to the temperature would never have been discovered. Moreover, if the functional relationship between temperature and pressure remained amorphous, then Kelvin's rigorous definition of temperature, based on the relationship between temperature and pressure and atomic motion, would not have been possible. Finally, the lack of a search for the causes of error in the measurement of temperature would likely have made the discovery of the laws of thermodynamics impossible. Only with the development of reliable thermometers was it possible to distinguish between temperature and heat transfer effects (McGee, 1988).

Rather than correcting relationships for the unknown factors that affected the assessment of temperature, early researchers explored the causes of the errors. As thermometers improved, the theory of temperature improved. As a result of improvements in the theory of temperature, the assessment of temperature improved. Furthermore, the discoveries made in the process of measuring and understanding temperature resulted in fundamental insights that have shaped modern thought about the physical world. Why can't the same process occur in psychology? What might be discovered if we attempted to understand the causes of error in our domain of study and attempted to eliminate their influence on the assessment of our constructs?

Conclusion

G-theory is based on the analysis of variance and is just as flexible and powerful as that method. Due to space restrictions, only a single G-theory design was used in the examples. However, the methods of G-theory may be applied to any crossed or nested design. Shavelson and Webb (1991) and Brennan (1992) provide comprehensive coverage of the most frequently encountered designs for

G-theory studies, and these monographs should be consulted for further random- and mixed-effect designs. For more complex random-effects designs, such as random incomplete-blocks designs, standard research design texts can be used.

When and how should G-theory studies be conducted? Whenever a researcher develops a measurement instrument, the error structure of the instrument should be thoroughly explored. The factors that affect measurement error in the particular domain (such as time, raters, contexts, alternate forms, items, and method of measure administration) should be incorporated into the G-theory study. Variance components should be computed and reported along with generalizability coefficients. The number of measurement conditions needed to obtain acceptable levels of generalizability should also be explored and reported. In other words, if three raters are required to obtain an average rating with acceptable generalizability, then this information should be provided by the instrument developer. As the theory in a research area develops, it is necessary to revisit the G-theory results occasionally so that new developments and additional sources of error may be incorporated into the understanding of the error structure.

Have the stars finally aligned? Will the promise of G-theory finally be realized? Only time will tell. In this chapter, I have attempted to provide a jargon-free introduction to the methods of G-theory. I have also tried to provide a motive for critically thinking about the error structures present in our research instead of using statistical techniques to correct for the effects of measurement error. I worry that unless we focus our research attention on the factors that affect the measurement of our key constructs, the pace of scientific progress will not improve and may even slow. The current laissez-faire attitude toward measurement error is detrimental to our science. It is critical that the sources of error in our measurements be identified and that effort be expended to expunge the sources of error whenever possible. The integration of ideas in G-theory concerning the thoughtful treatment of error, coupled with the powerful modeling capabilities of structural equation modeling, provides a powerful vehicle for successful inference.

References

Brennan, R. L. (1992). *Elements of generalizability theory* (2nd ed.). Iowa City: ACT Publications.

Brennan, R. L., Jarjoura, D., & Deaton, E. L. (1980). *Some issues concerning the estimation and interpretation of variance components in generalizability theory* (ACT Tech. Bull. No. 36). Iowa City: American College Testing Program.

Cardinet, J., & Allal, L. (1983). Estimation of generalizability parameters. In L. J. Fyans Jr. (Ed.), *Generalizability theory: Inferences and practical applications*. New Directions for Testing and Measurement, no. 18. San Francisco: Jossey-Bass.

Cohen, J. (1994). The earth is round ($p < .05$). *American Psychologist, 49,* 997–1003.

Cornfield, J., & Tukey, J. W. (1956). Average values of mean squares in factorials. *Annals of Mathematical Statistics, 27,* 907–949.

Cortina, J. M., & Dunlap, W. P. (1997). On the logic and purpose of significance testing. *Psychological Methods, 2,* 161–172.

Cronbach, L. J., Gleser, G. C., Nanda, H., & Rajaratnam, N. (1972). *The dependability of behavioral measurements: Theory of generalizability for scores and profiles.* New York: Wiley.

Day, D. V., & Silverman, S. B. (1989). Personality and job performance: Evidence of incremental validity. *Personnel Psychology, 42,* 25–36.

Day, D. V., & Silverman, S. B. (1992, Aug.). *Examining the generalizability of field performance ratings.* Paper presented at the 100th Annual Convention of the American Psychological Association, Washington, DC.

DeShon, R. P. (1998). A cautionary note on measurement error corrections in structural equation models. *Psychological Methods, 3,* 412–423.

DeShon, R. P., & Morris, S. B. (in press). Modeling complex data structures: The general linear model and beyond. In S. G. Rogelberg (Ed.), *Handbook of research methods in industrial and organizational psychology.* Cambridge, MA: Blackwell.

Donner, A., & Wells, G. (1986). A comparison of confidence interval methods for the intraclass correlation coefficient. *Biometrics, 42,* 401–412.

Feldt, L. S., & Brennan, R. L. (1988). Reliability. In R. L. Linn (Ed.), *Educational measurement* (3rd ed., pp. 105–146). Old Tappan, NJ: Macmillan.

Frick, R. W. (1996). The appropriate use of null hypothesis testing. *Psychological Methods, 1,* 379–390.

Goldstein, H., & McDonald, R. P. (1988). A general model for the analysis of multilevel data. *Psychometrika, 53,* 455–467.

Hoyt, C. (1941). Test reliability estimated by analysis of variance. *Psychomerika, 6,* 153–160.

Hoyt, W. T. (2000). Rater bias in psychological research: When is it a problem and what can we do about it? *Psychological Methods, 5,* 64–86.

Loftus, G. R. (1994, Aug.). *Why psychology will never be a real science until we change the way we analyze our data.* Paper presented at the 102nd annual convention of the American Psychological Association, Los Angeles.

McGee, T. D. (1988). *Principles and methods of temperature measurement.* New York: Wiley-Interscience.

Middleton, W.E.K. (1964). *The history of the barometer.* Baltimore, MD: Johns Hopkins University Press.

Middleton, W.E.K. (1966). *The history of the thermometer and its uses in meteorology.* Baltimore, MD: Johns Hopkins University Press.

Murphy, K., & DeShon, R. P.(2000a). Inter-rater correlations do not estimate the reliability of job performance ratings. *Personnel Psychology, 53,* 873–900.

Murphy, K., & DeShon, R. P. (2000b). Progress in psychometrics: Can personnel psychology catch up? *Personnel Psychology, 53,* 913–924.

Nelder, J. A., & Lane, P. W. (1995). The computer analysis of factorial experiments: In memoriam–Frank Yates. *American Statistician, 49,* 382–385.

Patterson, H. D., & Thompson, R. (1971). Recovery of inter-block information when block sizes are unequal. *Biometrika, 58,* 545–554.

Rubin, D. B. (1974). Book review of the dependability of behavioral measurements: Theory of generalizability for scores and profiles. *Journal of the American Statistical Association, 69,* 1050.

Samuels, M. L., Casella, G., & McCabe, G. P. (1991). Interpreting blocks and random factors. *Journal of the American Statistical Association, 86,* 798–821.

Scheffé, H. (1959). *The analysis of variance.* New York: Wiley.

Schmidt, F. L. (1996). Statistical significance testing and cumulative knowledge in psychology: Implications for training researchers. *Psychological Methods, 1,* 115–129.

Searle, S. R., Casella, G., & McCulloch, C. E. (1992). *Variance components.* New York: Wiley.

Shavelson, R. J., & Webb, N. M. (1991). *Generalizability theory: A primer.* Thousand Oaks, CA: Sage

Shavelson, R. J., Webb, N. M., & Rowley, G. L. (1989). Generalizability theory. *American Psychologist, 44,* 922–932.

Smith, P. (1978). Sampling errors of variance components in small sample multifacet generalizability studies. *Journal of Educational Statistics, 3,* 319–346.

Smith, P. (1982). A confidence interval approach for variance component estimates in the context of generalizability theory. *Educational and Psychological Measurement, 42,* 459–466.

Spearman, C. (1907). Demonstration of formulae for true measurement of correlation. *American Journal of Psychology, 18,* 161–169.

Viswesvaran, C., Ones, D. S., & Schmidt, F. L. (1996). Comparative analysis of the reliability of job performance ratings. *Journal of Applied Psychology, 81,* 557–574.

CHAPTER 8

Confirmatory Factor Analysis

Charles E. Lance
Robert J. Vandenberg

Mulaik (1972) defined factor analysis (FA) as "a formal model about hypothetical component variables which account for the linear relationships that exist between observed variables" (p. 96). Similarly, we define FA generically as a family of mathematical-statistical approaches to summarizing interrelationships among some J observed (or manifest) variables in terms of some smaller number of K underlying factors (or latent variables). In a broad sense, FA encompasses the principal components (PC) model, in which the PCs are defined as weighted linear combinations of the observed variables, and the common FA model in which the observed variables are viewed as reflecting the common causal influences of underlying factors (hence, common factor analysis), and influences of other factors that are unique to each observed variable. In this chapter, we restrict our attention to the common factor model (for comparisons between the PC and common FA

This work was supported in part by grant AG15321–02 from the National Institutes of Health (G. M. Williamson, principal investigator) and the Centers for Disease Control and Prevention (CDC) and the National Institute for Occupational Safety and Health (NIOSH) (grant 1R010H03737–01A1; D. M. DeJoy, principal investigator). Its contents are solely the responsibility of the authors and do not necessarily represent the official views of the CDC or NIOSH.

models, see Snook & Gorsuch, 1989; Velicer & Jackson, 1990; Widaman, 1993).

The history of FA dates back nearly one hundred years to Spearman's (1904) initial development of the PC model. Mulaik (1972, 1986, 1987) provides histories of the philosophical issues and technical developments in the voluminous FA literature that has accumulated since Spearman's work. The earlier FA literature (especially up through the 1970s) relates to what is now referred to as exploratory FA (EFA), and there are a large number of reviews, across various substantive literatures, of the issues and decision points involved in conducting EFAs (Comrey, 1978; Fabrigar, Wegener, MacCallum, & Strahan, 1999; Ferguson & Cox, 1993; Ford, MacCallum, & Tait, 1986; Glass & Taylor, 1966). In recent years, however, there has been much more interest in what is now referred to as confirmatory factor analysis (CFA; Bentler, 1986, credits Tucker, 1955, for conceiving the distinction between EFA and CFA). CFA arose out of developments in EFA procedures, particularly multiple group FA and procrustean factor rotation (see Mulaik, 1972), and, most important, the theoretical and technical developments of Karl Jöreskog in the late 1960s and early 1970s (see Bentler, 1986). We acknowledge (as have others) that EFA *can* be applied in rigorous, quasi-confirmatory, hypothesis-testing modes, and in practice, CFA is applied sometimes in quite an exploratory fashion. Nevertheless, there are several issues that connect, and distinguish, prototypical applications of EFA and CFA (see Table 8.1).

Mathematical model. The fundamental theoretical-mathematical model is identical for the common FA model under EFA and under CFA. In both cases, the J observed variables (Xs) are presumed to reflect the influences of some $K < J$ underlying common factors (or latent variables—ξs) and additional factors that are unique to each measured variable (δs).[1] In Figure 8.1a, for example, each measured variable (X_j) reflects the (common) causal influences of one or more of the underlying factors (ξ_k), and the influence of its own unique factor (δ_j; also variously referred to as an error or disturbance term), or

$$\underline{X}_j = \lambda_{j1}\xi_1 + \dots \lambda_{jK}\xi_K + \delta_j \tag{8.1}$$

**Table. 8.1. Major Differences Between Typical
Applications of Exploratory and Confirmatory Factor Analysis.**

Issue	EFA	CFA
Mathematical model	Common factor or principal components model	Common factor model
Selection of measures	Varies widely	In relation to hypothesized latent variables (factors)
Number of factors	Determined from data	Specified a priori
Interpretation of factors	Inferred from factor loadings	Defined a priori from theory
Factor pattern matrix	Unconstrained (fully free)	Constrained (fixed and free elements)
Factor correlations	Estimated from rotation	Estimated directly
Goodness of fit	Not a big issue	Key, controversial issue

Figure 8.1b shows that the equations for all six observed variables shown in Figure 8.1a can be represented in the single matrix equation $x = \Lambda_x \xi + \delta$. We invoke the usual assumptions that factors and disturbances have zero means (i.e., $E[\xi_k] = E[\delta_j] = 0$) and that the unique factors are unrelated to the common factors (i.e., $E[\delta_j, \xi_k] = 0$) and to each other (i.e., $E[\delta_j \delta_{j'}] = 0$). As such, the common FA model (under EFA or CFA) seeks to partition variance in the observed variables into common variance (variance explained by the ξs) and unique variance (attributable to the δ_js; Mulaik, 1972). What differs, however, is how this is accomplished in practice, differences in research goals, and the inductive versus deductive approaches of EFA and CFA, respectively.

Selection of measures. Observed variables may be selected quite haphazardly for EFA (see Armstrong, 1967) or with some strong or weak conceptual expectations regarding the nature of the latent factors (Fabrigar et al., 1999). The emphasis in EFA is usually

Figure 8.1. Foundations of Factor Analysis.

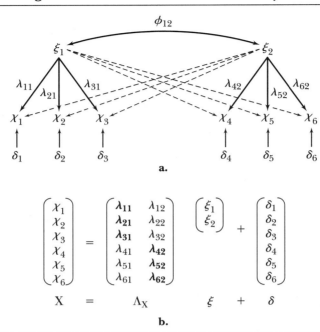

on discovering the common factors that drive interrelationships among the observed variables. By contrast, the emphasis in CFA is usually deductive, with the selection of observed measures being driven by a priori theoretical definitions of the latent factors. That is, observed measures are chosen specifically as they are presumed to reflect the content domain defined by latent factors.

Number of factors. The number of significant factors in EFA is usually determined empirically from the data being analyzed using procedures such as Kaiser's rule, the scree test, or parallel analysis (Fabrigar et al., 1999; Zwick & Velicer, 1986), or on the basis of the interpretability of the factor solution. In either case, the decision is inductive and usually quite subjective. This decision is a deductive one in CFA, with the number of factors and the a priori definitions of the respective latent factors determined in advance on the basis of theory.

Interpretation of factors. This also is typically an inductive task in EFA in which commonalities among observed measures that have relatively large loadings on respective factors are used to infer the nature of the underlying factors. For example, the solid arrows in Figure 8.1a are intended to represent the scenario in which X_1 to X_3 have strong connections to (large loadings on) ξ_1 and the broken arrows indicate that they have relatively weaker loadings on ξ_2. On the other hand, X_4 to X_6 have large loadings on ξ_2 and weaker loadings on ξ_1.[2] Then if, for example, X_1 to X_3 all refer to Job Satisfaction and X_4 to X_6 all refer to Job Tension, it might be (appropriately) induced that $\xi_1 (\xi_2)$ represents a latent Job Satisfaction (Job Tension) factor. In CFA, by contrast, ξ_1 and ξ_2 would be specified a priori as representing theoretical Job Satisfaction and Job Tension latent variables, respectively. Subsequently, these a priori theoretical definitions of ξ_1 and ξ_2 would guide the selection of appropriate observed variables (*X*s) to represent them.

Factor pattern matrix (Λ_X). In EFA it is typical to estimate all connections (factor loadings) between observed variables and the common factors. This is shown in Figure 8.1a as the collection of all solid and broken arrows from the ξs to the *X*s and in Figure 8.1b as the collection of all boldfaced and regular typed λ_{jk}s. It is the pattern of the relative magnitudes of the estimated factor loadings that normally gives rise to the interpretation of the nature of the factors in EFA. In CFA, however, the factor pattern matrix is constrained in the sense that only the a priori specified connections between the theoretically defined latent factors and the observed variables that are chosen to represent them are free to be estimated (the solid arrows and boldfaced λ_{jk}s in Figure 8.1). The remaining connections (the broken arrows and regular typed λ_{jk}s) are typically fixed equal to zero under the hypothesis that, for example, X_1 to X_3 represent ξ_1 and *not* ξ_2.

Factor correlations. Initially, the factors that are estimated in EFA are uncorrelated with one another, or orthogonal. Following the initial factor extraction, factors are usually rotated (transformed) so as to provide a more interpretable simple structure solution—one in which factor loadings are generally either very high or very low. Factor rotation procedures either preserve the orthogonality of the solution or allow correlations among the factors to be estimated in an oblique rotated solution. It is under oblique factor rotation procedures that factor correlations are estimated in EFA. In contrast, factor correlations (that is, correlations among the latent variables) are estimated directly in CFA in conjunction with the pattern of fixed and free factor loadings that are specified in the factor pattern matrix (Λ_X).

Goodness of fit. This issue concerns the extent to which the FA solution accounts for the variances and covariances among the observed variables, and although it has certainly not been ignored, it is generally not a critical issue in typical EFA applications. Rather, the concern in EFA is usually one of the ease with which the FA solution is interpretable. In contrast, and as we will see, model goodness of fit is a continuously researched and changing issue in CFA. This is because unlike EFA, CFA involves tests of the usefulness of an a priori theoretical model in terms of its ability to account for interrelationships among observed variables that the model is designed to explain.

We present these comparisons between EFA and CFA to highlight the facts that although both are supported by the same fundamental mathematical model, their applications in practice typically differ considerably in terms of analytic details and research goals. While EFA is generally used as an inductive tool for discovering factors that drive covariances among observed variables, CFA is generally used as a deductive approach to testing whether some a priori formulated theoretical model adequately explains covariances among observed variables. We now turn to a more detailed discussion of the CFA model.

Application of the CFA Model

In typical applications, CFA is used to test whether one or more theoretical models of relationships between conceptually defined latent variables (that is, common factors) and the corresponding observed variables (manifest indicators) chosen to represent them is viable when evaluated against sample data. Thus, the general question is whether the matrix of covariances among the observed measures implied by the theoretical model, $\hat{\Sigma}(\Theta)$, is consistent with the sample covariance matrix **S** (Bollen, 1989). If $\hat{\Sigma}(\Theta)$, is consistent with **S,** the theoretical model is said to fit the data well and its usefulness is confirmed (James, Mulaik, & Brett, 1982).[3] If $\hat{\Sigma}(\Theta)$ is not consistent with **S**, the theoretical model does not fit the data well and is rejected as a useful model. Table 8.2 summarizes the general steps in conducting CFAs. In the following sections, we discuss issues pertaining to each of these steps as they relate to an empirical example published previously by Mallard and Lance (1998; hereafter "ML98").

Define Theoretical Latent Variables

The general goal of the Mallard and Lance (1998) study was to develop and evaluate a measure of three specific forms of conflict between employees' work roles and their nonwork roles. Specifically, with the increasing presence of child-rearing women in the workforce over the past two decades and the increasing number of dual-earner families with children, the nonwork role of parent has become much more salient within the work environment than it was just two or three decades ago. In brief, based on their review of the literature, Mallard and Lance identified Parenting Interfering with Work (PIW $- \xi_1$), and Work Interfering with Parenting (WIP $- \xi_2$) as two forms of directional conflict between individuals' roles as employees and parents. They also defined a third form of General (G $- \xi_3$) parent-employee (P-E) conflict in terms of

Table 8.2. General Steps in Conducting Confirmatory Factor Analysis.

1. Define theoretical latent variables (factors) to be represented in the CFA.
2. Determine observed variables (manifest indicators) to represent each latent variable.
3. Collect data from a representative sample.
4. Specify a priori patterns of factor loadings, factor variances and covariances, and unique variances and covariances; formulate alternative, competing theoretical models.
5. Estimate model parameters and assess model goodness of fit.
6. Interpret the CFA solution.

"general perception[s] of conflict experienced from the inability to fulfill both employee and parent roles adequately" (p. 349). Note that Mallard and Lance were defining new theoretical constructs thought to be distinct from other, previously researched work-related conflict constructs. Hence, CFA was applied in the context of new scale development. It is more often the case, however, that researchers employ well-developed theoretical definitions of previously researched constructs (such as organizational commitment), which already exist, and CFA is therefore applied to ensure that the theoretical factor model defining the measures holds in this new sample.

Manifest Indicators of Latent Variables

Because Mallard and Lance (1998) was a scale development effort, the authors undertook extensive item generation and refinement procedures to develop observed measures (that is, items) for PIW, WIP, and G, including (1) examining existing, related scales (such as general work-family conflict) to cull out relevant items, (2) generating additional items using the three constructs' theoretical definitions as a basis, (3) subject matter expert review for item redundancy and clarity, and (4) internal consistency analyses (Cortina, 1993). In the end, they retained forty self-report survey items to represent PIW (fifteen items, such as, "Child care responsibilities take time I wish I could have for work"), WIP (seventeen items, such as, "I am required to be at work when I am needed at home with my children"), and G (eight items, such as, "I feel I am working two full time jobs, one at work and one as a parent"). Similar steps are required to develop (or, in many cases, redevelop) measures for unresearched or underresearched constructs (see Vandenberg, Self, & Seo, 1994, for an evaluation of O'Reilly & Chatman, 1986, on their Identification, Internalization, and Compliance commitment dimensions).

An important issue when discussing manifest indicators is the level of aggregation. Most often, researchers use individual items as manifest indicators of latent variables (Vandenberg & Lance, 2000). This strategy corresponds to Bagozzi and Heatherton's (1994) total disaggregation model for representing constructs (see also Bagozzi & Edwards, 1998). At the other extreme, a total aggregation model employs a single composite measure consisting of a simple sum of constituent scale items, in which corrections for unreliability could be invoked (see Bollen, 1989). Mallard and Lance (1998) used an intermediate partial disaggregation strategy in which they formed three composite manifest indicator "testlets" for each of the three P-E Conflict variables by randomly assigning scale items to composites (see Landis, Beal, & Tesluk, 2000, for a thorough review).

Data Collection

Mallard and Lance (1998) obtained data from 143 parent employees of two federal government agencies located in the southeastern United States. An important sampling issue is how large a sample should be obtained. This is a difficult question to address. On the one hand, CFA estimation procedures are based on asymptotic (large-sample) theory. Thus, large samples would appear to be necessary. However, as is well understood now, almost all models based on large samples appear to exhibit poor model fit when evaluated statistically (using the chi-square test). In addition, practical concerns can limit data collection, as in the Mallard and Lance (1998) study. Among the research on the topic of sample size, the findings of MacCallum, Widaman, Zhang, and Hong (1999) suggest that a sample size of around two hundred is generally adequate to achieve stable factor solutions, but these authors also show that adequacy is dependent on model characteristics (see also McCallum, Browne, & Sugawara, 1996). In general, though, the larger the sample size, the better.

Specify CFA Model and (Perhaps) Alternative Competing Models

The CFA model may be written in matrix form as

$$\mathbf{x} = \Lambda_x \xi + \delta, \tag{8.2}$$

where $\mathbf{x}$ ($\mathbf{x'} = [X_1, X_2, \ldots, X_J]$) is the column vector of the J observed variables, ξ ($\xi' = [\xi_1, \xi_2, \ldots, \xi_K]$) is the column vector of the K latent variables, δ ($\delta' = \delta_1, \delta_2, \ldots, \delta_J]$) is the column vector of

unique factors, and Λ_X is the $J \times K$ matrix of fixed and freely estimated loadings (λ_{jk}) of the jth manifest indicator on the kth latent
variable. Figure 8.2a shows the literal representation of equation
8.2 as it applies to our current example, where the λ_{jk}s in the λ_X
matrix are freely estimated loadings (regression coefficients) of
the Xs on the ξs, and 0s are (erstwhile) factor loadings whose values are fixed equal to zero (for example, PIW_1 presumably reflects,
or loads on ξ_1 [PIW], but not ξ_2 [WIP] or ξ_3 [G]). It is generally
assumed that δ_j and ξ_k are random variables with zero means, the
Xs are deviated from their means and are distributed multivariate
normal, and that the δ_j are uncorrelated with the ξ_k and each
other. Under these assumptions, the implied covariance matrix for
the Xs is

$$\Sigma_{xx'} = \Lambda_x \Phi \Lambda'_x + \Theta_\delta, \tag{8.3}$$

where Λ_X is as defined previously, Φ and Θ_δ are the covariance matrices for the ξ_ks and the δ_js, respectively. It is the pattern of fixed
and free elements in the Λ_X, Φ, and Θ_δ matrices that must be specified prior to testing the CFA model. The pattern for the Λ_X matrix
was discussed earlier (shown in Figure 8.2a). The patterns specified
for the Φ and Θ_δ matrices for our example are shown in Figures
8.2b and 8.2c, respectively. By convention, we assumed that the
unique factors (δ_js) for the P-E Conflict manifest indicators were
mutually uncorrelated, so that only the diagonal of the Θ_δ was estimated (see Figure 8.2c). On the other hand, it was hypothesized
that PIW, WIP, and G were distinct but related constructs. Consequently, covariances among the three factors were permitted to be
estimated freely in the off-diagonal portion of the Φ matrix (see Figure 8.2b). The diagonal of the Φ matrix (containing the variances
of the PIW, WIP, and G factors) deserves further comment. The
variances of the latent variables are not otherwise known or es-
timable (because the variables are latent, not directly measured),
and so must be determined in some manner. There are two options
to do so. One is to fix one otherwise freely estimated factor loading
in each column of Λ_X to some constant (for example, 1.0, in which
case the variance of the latent variable is fixed equal to that of the
MI whose factor loading is fixed equal to 1.0). The more conventional option in CFA, and the one that Mallard and Lance (1998)

Figure 8.2. CFA Specifications for the Hypothesized Three-Factor Conflict Model.

$$
\begin{bmatrix} PIW_1 \\ PIW_2 \\ PIW_3 \\ WIP_1 \\ WIP_2 \\ WIP_3 \\ G_1 \\ G_2 \\ G_3 \end{bmatrix}
=
\begin{bmatrix} \lambda_{11} & 0 & 0 \\ \lambda_{21} & 0 & 0 \\ \lambda_{31} & 0 & 0 \\ 0 & \lambda_{42} & 0 \\ 0 & \lambda_{52} & 0 \\ 0 & \lambda_{62} & 0 \\ 0 & 0 & \lambda_{73} \\ 0 & 0 & \lambda_{83} \\ 0 & 0 & \lambda_{91} \end{bmatrix}
\begin{bmatrix} \xi_1 \ (PIW) \\[4pt] \xi_2 \ (WIP) \\[4pt] \xi_3 \ (G) \end{bmatrix}
+
\begin{bmatrix} \delta_1 \\ \delta_2 \\ \delta_3 \\ \delta_4 \\ \delta_5 \\ \delta_6 \\ \delta_7 \\ \delta_8 \\ \delta_9 \end{bmatrix}
$$

(a)   x   = Λ_x ξ + δ

(b)

	ξ_1 (PIW)	ξ_2 (WIP)	ξ_3 (G)
ξ_1 (PIW)	ϕ_{11} (1.0)		
ξ_2 (WIP)	ϕ_{21}	ϕ_{22} (1.0)	
ξ_3 (G)	ϕ_{31}	ϕ_{32}	ϕ_{33} (1.0)

Φ (standardized)

(c)

	δ_1	δ_2	δ_3	.	.	.	.	δ_9
δ_1	θ_{11}							
δ_2	0	θ_{22}						
δ_3	0	0	θ_{33}					
.	.	.	.	.				
.	.	.	.	.	.			
.	.	.	.	.	.	.		
.	.	.	.	.	.	.	.	
δ_9	0	0	0	.	.	.	.	$\theta_{9.9}$

Θ_δ (diagonal)

invoked, is to fix the diagonal of Φ directly. That is, they standard-ized the latent variables by fixing each of their variances equal to 1.0 (as is shown in Figure 8.2b). As such, the off-diagonal elements of the Φ matrix are properly interpreted as containing the corre-lations among the latent variables (that is, interfactor correlations).

Alternative Models

PIW, WIP, and G are conceptually distinct latent variables, and al-though Mallard and Lance (1998) hypothesized that they would be related (target model), these latent variables may be empirically distinct as well. This implies an alternative model in which PIW, WIP, and G were uncorrelated with (orthogonal to) each other. On the other hand, Mallard and Lance (1998) argued that PIW, WIP, and G in fact might not be empirically distinguishable. For exam-ple, parent employees may not discriminate at all between the three proposed subcomponents of P-E Conflict, implying that, per-ceptually at least, WIP, PIW, and G all represent a single P-E Con-flict latent variable; that is, conflict may just be conflict when you have kids! This implies an alternative single-latent variable model as a plausible rival model to the three-factor target model. It may also be possible that parent employees may not discriminate the alternative directional conflicts implied by WIP versus PIW or that either WIP or PIW individually is not practically discriminable from General P-E Conflict (G). These possibilities pointed to three final alternative two-factor models in which (1) WIP and PIW, (2) WIP and G, and (3) PIW and G actually compose a single latent vari-able. All of these alternative models were evaluated in reference to a baseline (null) model (this model is defined below) and the tar-get three-factor model in reanalyses of the data in Mallard and Lance (1998).

Estimation

Technical developments in the estimation of CFA model parame-ters are reviewed extensively by Bentler (1986) and Bollen (1989). In one way or another, however, estimation procedures seek to min-imize the discrepancies (or, alternately, maximize the fit) between $\mathbf{S}$, the sample covariance matrix, and $\hat{\Sigma}(\Theta)$, the covariance matrix that is implied or "reproduced" on the basis of CFA model parameter estimates. We mention only the two most widely used fit functions. One of these is the least-squares fit function, defined as

$$F_{LS} = \mathbf{tr}[(\mathbf{S} - \hat{\Sigma}(\Theta)^2], \qquad (8.4)$$

where **tr** is the trace of a matrix. As such, F_{LS} minimizes the sum of squared discrepancies between the sample (**S**) and reproduced $\hat{\Sigma}(\Theta)$ covariance matrices. The more widely adopted maximum likelihood fit function is defined as

$$F_{ML} = \ln|\hat{\Sigma}(\Theta)| + \mathrm{tr}[(\mathbf{S}\hat{\Sigma}(\Theta)^{-1}] - \ln|\mathbf{S}| - \mathrm{p}, \qquad (8.5)$$

where **ln|A|** is the natural logarithm of the determinant of matrix **A**, and p refers to the total number of manifest indicators in the CFA. Thus, F_{ML} minimizes discrepancies in variances (that is, $\mathbf{tr}[\mathbf{S}\hat{\Sigma}(\Theta)^{-1}]$-p) and covariances (that is, $\mathbf{ln}|\hat{\Sigma}(\Theta)| - \mathbf{ln}|\mathbf{S}|$)) between **S** and $\hat{\Sigma}(\Theta)$. Both the least-squares and maximum-likelihood approaches seek an iterative solution for model parameter estimates such that when the value of the fit function differs by less than some (arbitrarily small) criterion value on the ith iteration as compared to the ith -1 iteration, the solution is said to have converged.

Overall Model Fit

Once a solution has converged, how well does $\hat{\Sigma}(\Theta)$ approximate **S**? Although there are many aspects to the topic of model fit, this question is one of the least settled issues. The question can be evaluated statistically since, asymptotically, N^*F_{ML} is distributed as the chi-squared statistic. With a given type I error rate (alpha), a statistically significant chi-square indicates that $\hat{\Sigma}(\Theta)$ differs from **S** beyond that which would be expected solely on the basis of sampling error. In this sense, the chi-square statistic represents a test of badness of fit, and herein lies a long-acknowledged dilemma. On the one hand, N^*F_{ML} is distributed as chi-square only asymptotically, that is, in large samples. But with large samples, most any model is likely to be statistically rejected, even if $\hat{\Sigma}(\Theta)$ differs only trivially from **S**. This is due to the direct dependency of the chi-square statistic on sample size (N). This dilemma is at the root of the voluminous literature on the assessment of model fit using alternative, overall goodness-of-fit indices (GFIs; Hu & Bentler, 1998, 1999; Marsh, Balla, & Hau, 1996; Marsh, Balla, & McDonald, 1988; Mulaik, James, VanAlstine, Bennett, Lind, & Stilwell, 1989). We review only a select few here.

One historically relevant alternative GFI is Bentler and Bonett's (1980) normed fit index (NFI),

$$NFI = \frac{F_B - F_M}{F_B} \qquad (8.6)$$

where F_B and F_M refer to GFIs for some baseline and some substantive model, respectively. Typically, the baseline model chosen is a null (or independence) model in which $\hat{\Sigma}(\Theta) = I$, and GFI is indexed in terms of chi-square so that, as usually assessed, NFI = $(\chi^2_{Null} - \chi^2_{Model})/\chi^2_{Null}$. As such, the NFI can be interpreted as the reduction in badness of fit realized by some substantive model as compared to the worst-possible fitting model (the null model). This is analogous to the R^2 estimated in multiple regression. Historically, NFIs greater than or equal to .90 have been interpreted as indicating acceptable model fit.

A second historically relevant overall GFI is the Tucker-Lewis Index (TLI):

$$TLI = \frac{\chi^2_B/df_B - \chi^2_M/df_M}{\chi^2_B/df_B - 1.0} \qquad (8.7)$$

Note that $E(\chi^2) = df$ and that $E(\chi^2/df = 1.0)$ under the central chi-square distribution. As such, the TLI can be interpreted as an index of the reduction in badness of fit provided by some substantive model as referenced to a baseline (usually the null) model as compared to the reduction in badness of fit referenced to the baseline model if the substantive model were true (Marsh et al., 1988). Historically, TLIs greater than or equal to .90 have been interpreted as indicating acceptable model fit.[4] However, Hu and Bentler (1999) argued recently to use .95 as the minimal criterion to infer good fit.

Marsh et al. (1988) recommended against the use of the NFI (and the class of type I incremental GFIs of which the NFI is a member) and in favor of the TLI (and other type II incremental

GFIs). This is because NFI, but not the TLI, is sensitive to sample size.[5] Recent reviews by Hu and Bentler (1998, 1999) of these and dozens of other overall GFIs also support the continued use of the TLI because it (1) is relatively insensitive to sample size, (2) is sensitive to model misspecifications (that is, it indicates appropriately when a model is inconsistent with the data), (3) is relatively insensitive to violations of assumptions of multivariate normality, and (4) is relatively insensitive to estimation method (that is, maximum likelihood versus alternative methods). On these bases, Hu and Bentler also recommended (along with revised critical values for indicating a well-fitting model) other commonly used GFIs, including Bentler's (1990) comparative fit index (CFI, $\geq .95$), McDonald and Marsh's (1990) relative noncentrality index (RNI, $\geq .95$), the standardized root mean residual (SRMSR, $\leq .08$), and Browne and Cudeck's (1993) root mean squared error of approximation (RMSEA, $\leq .06$). Briefly, these additional GFIs are as follows. Bentler's (1990) CFI may be written as

$$CFI = 1 - \frac{\max[(\chi_M^2 - df_M), 0]}{\max[(\chi_B^2 - df_B), (\chi_M^2 - df_M), 0]} \tag{8.8}$$

As such, the CFI uses information from the expected values of the chi-squares for some target model (χ_M^2) and some baseline (usually the null) model (χ_B^2) under the relevant noncentral chi-square distribution. Under the noncentral chi-square distribution $E(\chi^2) = df + NCP$, where NCP is the noncentrality parameter. Ordinarily, the estimated NCP for the target model ($\chi_M^2 - df_M$) will be considerably smaller than the NCP estimated for the baseline model ($\chi_B^2 - df_B$) so that CFI tends toward 1.00 for well-fitting models. Also, the estimated NCP for the target model will ordinarily be positive but can be negative in unusual cases that $\chi_M^2 < df_M$. In these cases, the numerator of the CFI is constrained to 0 by the requirement that it contains the maximum value of either the estimated NCP or 0.

Like the CFI, McDonald and Marsh's (1990) RNI is also what Hu and Bentler (1998) refer to as a type 3 noncentrality index:

$$RNI = \frac{(\chi_B^2 - df_B) - (\chi_M^2 - df_M)}{(\chi_B^2 - df_B)} \tag{8.9}$$

Thus, the RNI is similar in form to the NFI (see equation 8.6) but is constructed on the basis of the estimated noncentrality parameters for the baseline ($\chi_B^2 - df_B$) and target ($\chi_M^2 - df_M$) models and tends toward 1.00 for well-fitting models (those whose estimated noncentrality parameters are small relative to that of the baseline model).

The SRMSR is the square root of the average squared difference between corresponding elements in the sample correlation matrix and the one reproduced on the basis of model parameter estimates. Naturally, SRMSR tends toward 0.0 as the target model fits the data (that is, reproduces the observed correlations) well. Finally, the RMSEA can be written as

$$RMSEA = \left[\frac{\max[(\chi_M^2 - df_M)/(N-1),0]}{df_M} \right]^{1/2} \qquad (8.10)$$

so that it too is based on the estimated noncentrality parameter for the target model and tends toward 0.0 as the target model fits the sample data well. (See Hu & Bentler, 1998, 1999, for fuller discussions of these and several other overall GFIs.)

Other Fit Issues

Three other important issues regarding model fit are the admissibility of parameter estimates, parsimony, and comparisons among alternative models. Regarding the first of these, a CFA solution is proper if all parameter estimates are within admissible ranges. Inadmissible estimates include negative variances (negative unique variances are referred to as *Heywood cases*), and standardized factor loadings and factor intercorrelations greater than 1.00 in absolute value. Gerbing and Anderson (1987) discuss some causes of such "improper solutions" (including sampling error and model misspecification), and possible resolutions for them (such as alternative starting values, alternative model parameterizations, and constraining improper estimates to boundary values). Marsh (1994) warns, however, that improper solutions may well signal that the model being fit is simply inappropriate to the data, and thus one should eliminate that possibility before incorporating any "fixes" on what otherwise just might be a poor model.

A second issue concerns model parsimony. Perfect CFA model fit can always be achieved by fitting a model with 0 df. Degrees of freedom (df) refers to $[(p * p + 1)/2 - t]$, where p is the number of manifest indicators, $(p * p + 1)/2$ is the number of unique elements in a matrix of covariances among p manifest variables, and t is the number of free parameters estimated in the CFA. But interpreting a model with 0 df is just as much a tautology as is achieving an $r^2 = 1.00$ from a bivariate regression analysis including only two data points! The point is that well-fitting models can nearly always be achieved by freeing more and more parameters, but doing so sacrifices model parsimony by overparameterization (Mulaik et al., 1989; Williams & Holahan, 1994). As one approach to this problem, Mulaik et al. (1989) proposed a family of parsimony-adjusted GFIs (PGFI), the simplest of which is

$$PGFI = GFI \frac{df_M}{df_B} \qquad (8.11)$$

where GFI is some overall GFI such as the NFI, and df_M and df_B refer to model degrees of freedom for some substantive model and some baseline model (usually the null), respectively. This adjustment penalizes more highly parameterized models (which have fewer model df) than it does more parsimonious models (which have larger model df). Mulaik et al. (1989) argued that, all else equal, more parsimonious models (models that have larger PGFIs) are to be preferred. Unfortunately, little guidance as to what constitutes acceptable PGFIs is available.

Finally, it is often of interest to compare the relative fits of alternative, theoretically plausible models. This is especially useful if one model is nested within another. Model B is said to be nested within model A if it is a special case of model A, that is, if model B can be generated by imposing one or more additional restrictions on model A. For example, an orthogonal two-factor model is nested within an oblique two-factor model because the correlation between the two factors is restricted equal to zero in the orthogonal case. As a second example, a one-factor model is nested within a two-factor model in the sense that the one-factor model restricts the correlation between the two factors equal to 1.0. In either case, the difference between the two nested models' chi-square statistics is itself distributed as chi squared and can be evaluated at the difference between the models' dfs (Δdf):

$$\Delta\chi^2 = \chi_B^2 - \chi_A^2,$$
$$\Delta df = df_B - df_A. \qquad (8.12)$$

for models B nested within A. A nonsignificant chi-square indicates that the more parsimonious model B provides an equivalently good fit to the data, as does the less parsimonious model A and that the more parsimonious model B should be preferred. A significant chi-square indicates that model B fits significantly worse than does model A so that model A would be preferred.

The Example Continued

We reanalyzed data reported by Mallard and Lance (1998) using (1) the intercorrelations among the nine P-E Conflict testlets as input to the LISREL-8 (Jöreskog & Sörbom, 1993) program, (2) specifications for fixed and free model parameters as shown in Figure 8.2, and (3) the maximum likelihood estimation method. The annotated LISREL program (both traditional LISREL and SIMPLIS commands) for the target three-factor model is shown in Table 8.3. Overall GFIs for each model are shown in the top portion of Table 8.4, and as seen there, the Target model exhibited good fit to the data with respect to all GFIs. The nonsignificant chi-square statistic indicated that the matrix reproduced on the basis of the CFA model parameter estimates did not differ significantly from the sample matrix that was input for analysis, and values of all other GFIs surpassed criteria suggested by Hu and Bentler (1998, 1999; TLI, CFI, and RNI were greater than .95; SRMSR was less than .08; and RMSEA was less than .06). The alternative models generally failed to meet these criteria. The one exception was model 4 (a two-factor model consisting of PIW and WIP collapsed with G onto a single factor). Although this model was rejected statistically (chi-square test) and its RMSEA was above .06, its TLI, CFI, RNI, and SRMSR values indicated acceptable model fit. However, specific comparisons (see the lower portion of Table 8.4) between the Target model and each alternative model bring differences among them into clearer focus.

A comparison between the Target and the Orthogonal three-factor model (models 1 versus 5) represents an omnibus test of whether PIW, WIP, and G are significantly correlated. As Table 8.4 shows, the Δ chi-square comparison indicates that model 5 fits the data significantly worse than does model 1, indicating that the latent variables are significantly related to one another. The comparison between the Target and the one-factor models (models 1 versus 6) can be regarded as an omnibus test of discriminant validity as the Target model hypothesizes three distinct (but correlated) factors while the one-factor model hypothesizes only a single, undifferentiated factor. As shown, the Δ chi-square indicates that the one-factor model fits the data significantly worse than the target model, supporting the discriminant validity among PIW, WIP, and G. But are these three latent variables discriminable from one another individually? The remaining Δ chi-square comparisons address this. As seen in Table 8.4, the Target model fits the data significantly better than do any of the two-factor models. Importantly, the comparison between models 1 and 4 indicates that although model 4 appeared to fit the data well on the basis of its own overall GFIs, its fit was still inferior to that of model 1. Collectively, then, the evidence supports the Target model as the preferred CFA model.

Interpretation of the CFA Solution

Table 8.5 shows estimated factor loadings and unique variances (top portion) and factor intercorrelations (bottom portion) for the Target Three-Factor P-E Conflict model. As noted previously, the 0s in the factor pattern matrix represent factor loadings that were fixed equal to zero, and the variances of the latent variables were fixed equal to 1.0. Each freely estimated factor loading in Table 8.5 was statistically significant (each obtained T-value was greater than 3.00; minimum T-values should be 1.64 to be significant at $p < .05$), and the standardized factor loading for each observed variable on its intended factor (LV) was strong. This is additional evidence to that of the GFIs supporting the a priori theoretical assignment of the manifest indicators to their respective latent variables. Finally, note that the latent variables themselves are significantly intercorrelated. Given the conceptual nature of

Table 8.3. Annotated LISREL Program for TARGET P-E Conflict Model.

Traditional LISREL Commands

TARGET PARENT—EMPLOYEE CONFLICT SCALE DEVELOPMENT RUNS	**Title**
DA NI=9 MA=KM NO=143	**Specifies the number of Input Variables, the Korrelation matrix for analysis, and the Number of Observations
KM FI = A:\RMAT.PEC	**Specifies the location of the input data
LA	**LAbels for observed variables
*	
WIP1 WIP2 WIP3 PIW1 PIW2 PIW3 G1 G2 G3	
SELECT	**SElects all nine variables for analysis
*	
1 2 3 4 5 6 7 8 9 /	
MO NX=9 NK=3 TD=DI,FR PH=SY,FR	**MOdel statement that specifies 9 X variables, and **3 KSI variables for analysis, and the forms of the **Θ_δ (diagonal and free) and Φ (symmetric and free) ** matrices as shown in Figure 8.2
LK	**LAbels for the latent KSI variables
*	
WIP PIW GPEC	
PA LX	**PAttern matrix that specifies the a priori pattern of fixed (equal **to zero – 0) and freely estimated (denoted by 1s) factor loadings **in the λ_X matrix as shown in Figure 8.2
*	
1 0 0	
1 0 0	
1 0 0	
0 1 0	

```
0 1 0
0 1 0
0 0 1
0 0 1
0 0 1
FI PH(1,1) PH(2,2) PH(3,3)              **FIxes the diagonal of the Φ matrix and subsequently
VA 1.0 PH(1,1) PH(2,2) PH(3,3)          **sets their VAlues equal to 1.0 to standardize the KSIs
OU SE TV MI SS                          **Requests Standard Errors, T-Values, Modification
                                        **Indices, and the Standardized Solution as OUtput
```

SIMPLIS Command Statements

```
OBSERVED VARIABLES: WIP1 WIP2 WIP3 PIW1 PIW2 PIW3 G1 G2 G3
LATENT VARIABLES: WIP PIW GPEC
CORRELATION MATRIX: FI = A:\RMAT.PEC
SAMPLE SIZE = 143
WIP1 = WIP
WIP2 = WIP
WIP3 = WIP
PIW1 = PIW
PIW2 = PIW
PIW3 = PIW
G1 = GPEC
G2 = GPEC
G3 = GPEC
LISREL OUTPUT: RS MI TV SC
PATH DIAGRAM
END OF PROBLEM
```

Note: ** indicates coments that are not part of the program per se.

Table 8.4. Goodness-of-Fit Indices for P-E Conflict DEA Models.

Model	df	χ^2	TLI	CFI	RNI	SRMSR	RMSEA
1. Target three-factor	24	33.17	.99	.99	.99	.027	.052
2. Two-factor: PIW = WIP	25	141.06*	.85	.90	.90	.067	.180
3. Two-factor: PIW = G	25	137.38*	.88	.90	.90	.088	.180
4. Two-factor: WIP = G	25	62.56*	.95	.97	.97	.036	.100
5. Three orthogonal factors	27	296.93*	.68	.76	.76	.470	.270
6. One-factor	27	208.84*	.78	.84	.84	.080	.220

Model Comparison	Δdf	$\Delta\chi^2$
Model 1 versus model 5	3	263.76*
Model 1 versus model 6	3	175.67*
Model 1 versus model 2	1	107.89*
Model 1 versus model 3	1	104.21*
Model 1 versus model 4	1	29.39*

Note: df: model degrees of freedom; TLI: Tucker-Lewis index; CFI: comparative fit index; RNI: relative noncentrality index; SRMSR: standardized root mean squared residual; RMSEA: root mean squared error of approximation; PIW: Parenting Interfering with Work; WIP: Work Interfering with Parenting; G: General Parent-Employee Conflict.

*$p < .01$.

Table 8.5. Parameter Estimates for P-E Conflict Target Models.

Measures	Factors			
	WIP	PIW	G	$\theta_{\delta j}$
WIP-1	.90*	0	0	.19*
WIP-2	.89*	0	0	.21*
WIP-3	.87*	0	0	.25*
PIW-1	0	.89*	0	.20*
PIW-2	0	.92*	0	.14*
PIW-3	0	.90*	0	.19*
G-1	0	0	.74*	.46*
G-2	0	0	.78*	.39*
G-3	0	0	.94*	.12*
Factor Correlations	**WIP**	**PIW**	**G**	
WIP	1.00			
PIW	.79*	1.00		
G	.89*	.70*	1.00	

Note: PIW: Parenting Interfering with Work; WIP: Work Interfering with Parenting; G: General Parent-Employee Conflict.

$*p < .01.$

the P-E Conflict latent variables, this is not unexpected. Note, however, that the correlation between G and WIP is particularly high (.89). This explains why model 4 in Table 8.4 fit the data nearly as well as did the Target three-factor model: G and WIP are strongly related. Nevertheless, the Δ chi-square comparison between models 1 and 4 reported in Table 8.4 indicated that although the correlation between G and WIP is high, the two latent variables are not redundant.

Additional Issues in Conducting CFAs

Up to this point, we have considered differences between applications of EFA and CFA and fundamental issues and decision points in conducting CFAs, and have presented a continuing example application of CFA for scale development as illustrative of the steps involved in conducting CFA. In the section that follows, we discuss some other applications of CFA and alternative parameterizations of the CFA model discussed so far.

Uses of CFA

The example we presented illustrated the use of CFA as part of a scale development study to establish (1) that scale items (treated as testlets) reflect their intended underlying constructs (the latent variables), (2) interrelationships among the latent constructs intended to be represented, and (3) the discriminant validity of three distinct aspects of P-E Conflict. These are common purposes of CFA (Bagozzi & Phillips, 1991; Hinkin, 1995, 1998). But there are many other uses of CFA, a few of which we mention here.

Of particular importance, CFA is used as a preliminary step to establish a measurement model prior to estimating structural relationships among latent variables. Recall in the example that we estimated correlations among the latent variables but estimated no directional relationships. We might hypothesize, however, that PIW and WIP, as specific forms of P-E Conflict, give rise to, or cause, G, but it is important to evaluate the measurement properties of the PIW, WIP, and G as latent variables before directional, structural relationships are estimated. (Chapter Nine, this volume, goes into much greater detail on this subject.)

Another important application of CFA has been the analysis of multitrait-multimethod (MTMM) matrices (Campbell & Fiske, 1959). In this, CFA is used to relate observed measures (trait-method units) to latent Trait and Method factors. Widaman (1985, 1992) shows how comparisons among models contained within a taxonomy of CFA models for MTMM data can be used to establish convergent and discriminant validity and proportions of trait and method variance in observed measures. As such, CFA of MTMM data has become one of the major approaches to establishing the construct validity of measures. Becker and Cote (1994) and Conway (1996) present detailed reviews of the traditional linear CFA model and alternative CFA models for MTMM data, including Marsh's (1989) correlated uniqueness model and Browne's (1984) direct product model.

A third application of CFA is in tests for equivalent measurement operations across groups or over time (Vandenberg & Lance, 2000). The issue here is that, nominally, some measure may be identical for different groups (for example, a measure of organizational commitment). But, for example, because of cultural differences, economic conditions, or organizational interventions, one group (for example, in a collectivistic society) may interpret the measure and the meaning of its scale points differently from another group (say, in an individualistic society). In this case, CFA can be used to test for measurement equivalence, that is, test whether some measure actually represents the same latent variable and is scaled equivalently across groups (for reviews, see Horn & McArdle, 1992; Vandenberg & Lance, 2000).

A fourth application of CFA has been in the measurement of longitudinal change using latent growth modeling (LGM). As presented by McArdle (1988) and Willett and Sayer (1994), LGM uses measures of variables collected longitudinally as manifest indicators of Initial Status and Change latent variables. In this sense, LGM seeks to estimate true Initial Status and True Change on variables measured longitudinally. Willett and Sayer (1994), Duncan and Duncan (1995), Lance, Meade, and Williamson (2000), and Chapter Ten in this volume provide introductions to LGM, and Chan (1998) and Lance, Vandenberg, and Self (2000) present example applications of LGM in applied psychology.

Alternative Parameterizations of the CFA Model

The history of CFA has seen voluminous technical developments and alternative parameterizations of the CFA model (see Bentler, 1986). We mention only two alternative (LISREL-based) parameterizations here: the all-Y model and Rindskopf's (1983) parameterization. Implicitly, we have assumed so far that observed variables were manifest indicators for latent exogenous (predictor or antecedent) variables. Alternately, we could have assumed that they were manifest indicators for latent endogenous (criterion or consequent) variables. In this case, the CFA model equation is written, using LISREL-based notation as

$$y = \Lambda_Y \eta + \varepsilon \qquad (8.13)$$

and the covariance equation as

$$\Sigma_{YY'} = \Lambda_Y \Psi \Lambda'_Y + \Theta_\varepsilon \qquad (8.14)$$

This is referred to as an *all-Y model* because all measures are treated as if they are manifest indicators of latent endogenous variables, regardless of whether the latent variables are actually exogenous or endogenous. All-Y models are advantageous when, for example, one evaluates a measurement model containing both exogenous and endogenous latent variables (Bollen, 1989), or if one is constructing a basic LGM as a prerequisite to introducing predictors of latent Initial Status and Change variables (Willett & Sayer, 1994).

Rindskopf's (1983) parameterization has a different goal: that of avoiding so-called Heywood cases (negative estimates for unique variances). This model may be represented as

$$x = [\Lambda_X | \Lambda_\delta] \frac{[\xi]}{[\xi_\delta]} \qquad (8.15)$$

with covariance equation:

$$\Sigma_{XX'} = [\Lambda_X | \Lambda_\delta] \left[\begin{array}{c|c} \Phi & 0 \\ \hline 0 & I \end{array} \right] \left[\begin{array}{c} \Lambda'_X \\ \Lambda'_\delta \end{array} \right] \qquad (8.16)$$

for correlational data, where Λ_X and Φ are as defined previously in equation 8.3, Λ_δ is a $J \times J$ diagonal matrix of freely estimated loadings of the J Xs on J ξ_δ latent variables representing the Xs' disturbance terms, and **I** is a $J \times J$ identity matrix. In effect, the ξ_δs in equation 8.15 replace the δs in equation 8.2 and the $\Lambda_\delta \mathbf{I} \Lambda_\delta$ portion of equation 8.16 corresponds to Θ_δ in equation 8.3 but with one important difference: it is the squares of the elements in Λ_δ in equation 8.16 that are interpreted as the corresponding $\Theta_{\delta(j)}$ in equation 8.3. As such, regardless of whether the elements in Λ_δ for equation 8.16 are positive or negative, their squares must be positive, thus avoiding negative unique variance estimates that might otherwise occur in Θ_δ in equation 8.3.

Table 8.6 shows results from this reparameterization of the three-factor Target P-E Conflict model presented in Table 8.5. Note

Table 8.6. Parameter Estimates for P-E Conflict Target Model: Rindskopf Parameterization.

Measures	Factors			Disturbance Terms								
	ξ_1-WIP	ξ_2-PIW	ξ_3-G	ξ_4	ξ_5	ξ_6	ξ_7	ξ_8	ξ_9	ξ_{10}	ξ_{11}	ξ_{12}
WIP-1	.90*	0	0	.44*	0	0	0	0	0	0	0	0
WIP-2	.89*	0	0	0	.45*	0	0	0	0	0	0	0
WIP-3	.87*	0	0	0	0	.50*	0	0	0	0	0	0
PIW-1	0	.89*	0	0	0	0	.45*	0	0	0	0	0
PIW-2	0	.92*	0	0	0	0	0	.38*	0	0	0	0
PIW-3	0	.90*	0	0	0	0	0	0	.43*	0	0	0
G-1	0	0	.74*	0	0	0	0	0	0	.68*	0	0
G-2	0	0	.78*	0	0	0	0	0	0	0	.63*	0
G-3	0	0	.94*	0	0	0	0	0	0	0	0	.35*

Factor Correlations

	ξ_1-WIP	ξ_2-PIW	ξ_3-G	ξ_4	ξ_5	ξ_6	ξ_7	ξ_8	ξ_9	ξ_{10}	ξ_{11}	ξ_{12}
ξ_1-WIP	1.00											
ξ_2-PIW	.79*	1.00										
ξ_3-G	.89*	.70*	1.00									
ξ_4	0	0	0	1.00								
ξ_5	0	0	0	0	1.00							
ξ_6	0	0	0	0	0	1.00						
ξ_7	0	0	0	0	0	0	1.00					
ξ_8	0	0	0	0	0	0	0	1.00				
ξ_9	0	0	0	0	0	0	0	0	1.00			
ξ_{10}	0	0	0	0	0	0	0	0	0	1.00		
ξ_{11}	0	0	0	0	0	0	0	0	0	0	1.00	
ξ_{12}	0	0	0	0	0	0	0	0	0	0	0	1.00

that the first three columns in the upper portion of Table 8.6 correspond exactly to the factor loadings shown earlier in Table 8.5. These are, once again, the P-E Conflict testlets' loadings on their respective P-E Conflict latent variables. The remaining nine columns in the upper portion of Table 8.6 correspond to Λ_δ in equations 8.15 and 8.16 and represent the square roots of the P-E Conflict testlets' disturbance variances. For example, WIP-1's squared loading on ξ_4 ($.44^2 = .1936$) is equal to (within rounding error) the estimated disturbance variance for WIP-1 reported in Table 8.5 (.19). The lower portion of Table 8.6 shows the matrix of correlations among the latent variables. Note that the upper portion of this matrix corresponds exactly to the estimated factor correlations reported in Table 8.5, that is, the correlations among the latent P-E Conflict variables. Rows 4 though 12 and columns 1 through 3 of this matrix correspond to the **0** submatrix in equation 8.16, indicating that the unique factors (ξ_4 through ξ_{12}) are uncorrelated with the three P-E Conflict latent variables. Finally, the lower-right portion of this matrix consisting of the last nine rows and columns corresponds to the **I** submatrix in equation 8.16. Under the Rindskopf (1983) parameterization, this submatrix preserves the orthogonality of the disturbance terms (by virtue of the zero correlations specified amongst them) and guarantees that their variances are positive (the diagonal of this matrix consists entirely of 1.00s).

Conclusion

Because we have been using LISREL since its earliest mainframe days, it was our comfort level with it more than anything else that determined its use in this chapter. It is certainly not the only alternative available for structural equation modeling applications such as CFA. CFA may be conducted today using a variety of programs such as Amos (Arbuckle, 1996), CALIS (SAS/STAT, 1996), EQS (Bentler, 1995), and Mplus (Muthén & Muthén, 1999; note that Mplus now replaces LISCOMP). Each program offers many overlapping features, yet there are unique components to each, and they vary in ease of use. Nevertheless, the basic mathematical FA model underlying each is the same as that presented in this chapter.

Also, as a point of clarification, researchers are often confused as to the general hypothesis being tested in prototypical CFA applications. Many believe that the hypothesis supported through strong model fit is that the items load on their respective a priori factors. However, what is really being tested is the reasonableness of restricting parameters to zero (for example, setting item loadings to zero on theoretically irrelevant factors). Technically, therefore, strong model fit is indicating that the restrictions are reasonable, and any lack of fit means that the a priori pattern of fixed elements is overly restrictive. Whether that "overrestriction" is due to bad theory, bad measures, or something else can be determined only by closely examining the findings.

The literature on CFA is voluminous. This is due in large part to the fact that it is still evolving as a procedure as evidenced by the methodological research devoted to it alone. Hence, we encourage close monitoring of this literature as new recommendations come forth frequently as well as demonstrations as to limitations to or new areas of application. Research articles on CFA procedures are published frequently in many journals, including *Organizational Research Methods, Structural Equation Modeling, Applied Psychological Measurement, Psychological Methods,* and *Multivariate Behavioral Research.* Furthermore, RMNET (Research Methods Network) and SEMNET (Structural Equation Modeling Network) are monitored closely by leading experts, who willingly field questions on CFA. In addition, there are some excellent Web resources devoted to it. A central location for such resources is the Web page for the Research Methods Division of the Academy of Management (www.aom.pace.edu/rmd), which provides links to numerous other Web sites, the journals listed above, and information on how one joins both RMNET and SEMNET.

CFA represents a powerful tool for evaluating one's measures. The power, though, is not in the basic mathematical FA model underlying it, for it is essentially the same as that for EFA. Rather, the power comes from the theory used to define the measures in the first place. Because it is theory driven, researchers must think carefully through what the measures mean, and particularly relative to one another (model specification depends on it). Hence, the power of CFA lies in its ability to help us more closely evaluate the quality of our measures (their nomological network) as rooted in classical test theory (CTT) of true and error scores (Crocker & Algina, 1986, Lord & Novick, 1968; Nunnally & Bernstein, 1994) than could be achieved otherwise. Again, this is not a function of the computational algorithm but rather the fact that researchers must know what that nomological network is that describes their set of measures.

Notes

1. Each observed variable's unique factor (δ_j) is assumed to represent an amalgam of nonsystematic influences (e_j, including nonsystematic measurement error and random shocks) and systematic effects that are unique to the particular observed variable (s_j), that is, $\delta_j = s_j + e_j$.
2. This pattern of high and low loadings is also shown in the bold and regular typeface λ coefficients (the factor loadings) in the Λ_X matrix in Figure 8.1b.
3. This is not to say that a model that is determined to be useful provides a unique explanation of the data; theoretically, an infinite number of models might fit a given covariance matrix equally well. As a practical matter, several theoretically plausible models may fit a given sample covariance matrix (nearly) equally well, making the choice among them a very difficult one.
4. This is despite Bentler and Bonett's (1980) original admonition that "models with overall fit indices less than .9 *can usually be improved upon substantially*" (p. 600, emphasis added).
5. The undesirable sample size dependency of the chi-square statistic was the primary motivating factor underlying the development of the myriad alternative overall GFIs that exist today.

References

Arbuckle, J. L. (1996). *Amos users' guide, Version 3.6* Chicago: SPSS.

Armstrong, J. S. (1967). Derivation of theory by means of factor analysis or Tom Swift and his electric factor analysis machine. *American Statistician, 21,* 17–21.

Bagozzi, R. P., & Edwards, J. R. (1998). A general approach for representing constructs in organizational research. *Organizational Research Methods, 1,* 45–87.

Bagozzi, R. P., & Heatherton, T. F. (1994). A general approach to representing multifaceted constructs: Application to state self-esteem. *Structural Equation Modeling, 1,* 35–67.

Bagozzi, R. P., Yi, Y., & Phillips, L. W. (1991). Assessing construct validity in organizational research. *Administrative Science Quarterly, 36,* 421–458.

Becker, T. E., & Cote, J. A. (1994). Additive and multiplicative method effects in applied psychological research: An empirical assessment of three models. *Journal of Management, 20,* 625–641.

Bentler, P. M. (1986). Structural modeling and *Psychometrika:* An historical perspective on growth and achievements. *Psychometrika, 51,* 35–51.

Bentler, P. M. (1990). Comparative fit indices in structural models. *Psychological Bulletin, 107,* 238–246.

Bentler, P. M. (1995). *EQS structural equations program manual.* Encino, CA: Multivariate Software.

Bentler, P. M., & Bonett, D. G. (1980). Significance tests and goodness of fit in the analysis of covariance structures. *Psychological Bulletin, 88,* 588–606.

Bollen, K. A. (1989). *Structural equations with latent variables.* New York: Wiley.

Browne, M. W. (1984). The decomposition of multitrait-multimethod matrices. *British Journal of Mathematical and Statistical Psychology, 37,* 1–21.

Browne, M. W., & Cudeck, R. (1993). Alternative ways of assessing fit. In K. A. Bollen & J. S. Long (Eds.), *Testing structural equation models* (pp. 136–162). Thousand Oaks, CA: Sage.

Campbell, D. T., & Fiske, D. W. (1959). Convergent and discriminant validation by the multitrait-multimethod matrix. *Psychological Bulletin, 56,* 81–105.

Chan, D. (1998). The conceptualization of change over time: An integrative approach incorporating longitudinal means and covariance structures analysis (LMACS) and multiple indicator latent growth modeling (MLGM). *Organizational Research Methods, 1,* 421–483.

Comrey, A. L. (1978). Common methodological problems in factor analytic studies. *Journal of Consulting and Clinical Psychology, 46,* 648–659.

Conway, J. M. (1996). Analysis and design of multitrait-multirater performance appraisal studies. *Journal of Management, 22,* 139–162.

Cortina, J. M. (1993). What is coefficient alpha? An examination of theory and application. *Journal of Applied Psychology, 78,* 98–104.

Crocker, L., & Algina, J. (1986). *Introduction to classical and modern test theory.* Fort Worth, TX: Harcourt, Brace.

Duncan, T. E., & Duncan, S. C. (1995). Modeling the processes of development via latent variable growth curve methodology. *Structural Equation Modeling, 2,* 178–213.

Fabrigar, L. R., Wegener, D. T., MacCallum, R. C., & Strahan, E. J. (1999). Evaluating the use of exploratory factor analysis in psychological research. *Psychological Methods, 4,* 272–299.

Ferguson, E., & Cox, T. (1993). Exploratory factor analysis: A user's guide. *International Journal of Selection and Assessment, 1,* 84–94.

Ford, J. K., MacCallum, R. C., & Tait, M. (1986). The application of exploratory factor analysis in applied psychology: A critical review and analysis. *Personnel Psychology, 39,* 291–314.

Gerbing, D. W., & Anderson, J. C. (1987). Improper solutions in the analysis of covariance structures: Their interpretability and a comparison of alternative specifications. *Psychometrika, 52,* 99–111.

Glass, G., & Taylor, P. A. (1966). Factor analytic methodology. *Review of Educational Research, 36,* 566–587.

Hinkin, T. R. (1995). A review of scale development practices in the study of organizations. *Journal of Management, 21,* 967–988.

Hinkin, T. R. (1998). A brief tutorial on the development of measures for use in survey questionnaires. *Organizational Research Methods, 1,* 104–121.

Horn, J. L., & McArdle, J. J. (1992). A practical and theoretical guide to measurement invariance in aging research. *Experimental Aging Research, 18,* 117–144.

Hu, L., & Bentler, P. M. (1998). Fit indices in covariance structure modeling: Sensitivity to underparameterized model misspecification. *Psychological Methods, 3,* 424–453.

Hu, L., & Bentler, P. M. (1999). Cutoff criteria for fit indexes in covariance structure analysis: Conventional criteria versus new alternatives. *Structural Equation Modeling, 6,* 1–55.

James, L. R., Mulaik, S. A., & Brett, J. M. (1982). *Causal analysis: Assumptions, models, and data.* Thousand Oaks, CA: Sage

Jöreskog, K. G., & Sörbom, D. (1993). *LISREL-8 user's guide.* Chicago: Scientific Software International.

Lance, C. E., Meade, A. W., & Williamson, G. M. (2000). We *should* measure change—And here's how. In G. M. Williamson & D. R. Shaffer (Eds.), *Physical illness and depression in older adults: A handbook of theory, research and practice* (pp. 201–235). New York: Plenum.

Lance, C. E., Vandenberg, R. J., & Self, R. M. (2000). Latent growth models of individual change: The case of newcomer adjustment. *Organizational Behavior and Human Decision Processes, 83,* 107–140.

Landis, R. S., Beal, D. J., & Tesluk, P. E. (2000). A comparison of approaches to forming composite measures in structural equation modeling. *Organizational Research Methods, 3,* 186–207.

Lord, F. M., & Novick, M. R. (1968). *Statistical theories of mental test scores.* Reading, MA: Addison-Wesley.

MacCallum, R. C., Browne, M. W., & Sugawara, H. M. (1996). Power analysis and determination of sample size for covariance structure modeling. *Psychological Methods, 2,* 130–149.

MacCallum, R. C., Widaman, K. F., Zhang, S., & Hong, S. (1999). Sample size in factor analysis. *Psychological Methods, 4,* 84–99.

Mallard, A.G.C., & Lance, C. E. (1998). Development and evaluation of a parent-employee interrole conflict scale. *Social Indicators Research, 45,* 343–370.

Marsh, H. W. (1989). Confirmatory factor analysis of multitrait-multimethod data: Many problems and a few solutions. *Applied Psychological Measurement, 13,* 335–361.

Marsh, H. W. (1994). Confirmatory factor analysis of factorial invariance: A multifaceted approach. *Structural Equation Modeling, 1,* 5–34.

Marsh, H. W., Balla, J. R., & Hau, K. (1996). An evaluation of incremental fit indices: A clarification of mathematical and empirical properties. In G. A. Marcoulides & R. E. Schumacker (Eds.), *Advanced structural equation modeling: Issues and techniques* (pp. 315–353). Mahwah, NJ: Erlbaum.

Marsh, H. W., Balla, J. R., & McDonald, R. P. (1988). Goodness-of-fit indexes in confirmatory factor analysis: The effect of sample size. *Psychological Bulletin, 103,* 391–410.

McArdle, J. J. (1988). Dynamic but structural equation modeling of repeated measures data. In J. R. Nesselroade & R. B. Catell (Eds.), *Handbook of multivariate experimental psychology* (2nd ed.) (pp. 561–614). New York: Plenum.

McDonald, R. P., & Marsh, H. W. (1990). Choosing a multivariate model: Noncentrality and goodness of fit. *Psychological Bulletin, 107,* 247–255.

Mulaik, S. A. (1972). *The foundations of factor analysis.* New York: McGraw-Hill.

Mulaik, S. A. (1986). Factor analysis and *Psychometrika:* Major developments. *Psychometrika, 51,* 23–33.

Mulaik, S. A. (1987). A brief history of the philosophical foundations of exploratory factor analysis. *Multivariate Behavioral Research, 22,* 267–305.

Mulaik, S. A., James, L. R., Van Alstine, J., Bennett, N., Lind, S., & Stilwell, C. D. (1989). Evaluation of goodness-of-fit indices for structural equation models. *Psychological Bulletin, 105,* 430–445.

Muthén, B., & Muthén, L. (1999). *Mplus users' guide.* Los Angeles: Statmodel.

Nunnally, J. C., & Bernstein, I. H. (1994). *Psychometric theory* (3rd ed.). New York: McGraw-Hill.

O'Reilly, C. III., & Chatman, J. (1986). Organizational commitment and psychological attachment: The effects of compliance, identification and internalization on prosocial behavior. *Journal of Applied Psychology, 71,* 492–499.

Rindskopf, D. (1983). Parameterizing inequality constraints on unique variances in linear structural models. *Psychometrika, 48,* 73–83.

SAS/STAT (1996). *SAS/STAT users' guide, Version 6* (4th ed.). Cary, NC: SAS Press.

Snook, S. C., & Gorsuch, R. L. (1989). Component analysis versus common factor analysis: A Monte Carlo study. *Psychological Bulletin, 106,* 148–154.

Spearman, C. (1904). General intelligence, objectively determined and measured. *American Journal of Psychology, 15,* 201–293.

Tucker, L. R (1955). The objective definition of simple structure in linear factor analysis. *Psychometrika, 20,* 209–225.

Vandenberg, R. J., & Lance, C. E. (2000). A review and synthesis of the measurement invariance literature: Suggestions, practices, and recommendations for organizational research. *Organizational Research Methods, 3,* 4–69.

Vandenberg, R. J., Self, R. M., & Seo, J. H. (1994). A critical examination of the internalization, identification, and compliance commitment measures. *Journal of Management, 20,* 123–140.

Velicer, W. F., & Jackson, D. N. (1990). Component analysis versus common factor analysis: Some issues in selecting an appropriate procedure. *Multivariate Behavioral Research, 25,* 1–28.

Widaman, K. F. (1985). Hierarchically nested covariance structure models for multitrait-multimethod data. *Applied Psychological Measurement, 9,* 1–26.

Widaman, K. F. (1992). Multitrait-multimethod models in aging research. *Experimental Aging Research, 18,* 185–201.

Widaman, K. F. (1993). Common factor analysis versus principal component analysis: Differential bias in representing model parameters? *Multivariate Behavioral Research, 28,* 263–311.

Willett, J. B., & Sayer, A. G. (1994). Using covariance structure analysis to detect correlates and predictors of individual change over time. *Psychological Bulletin, 116,* 363–381.

Williams, L. J., & Holahan, P. J. (1994). Parsimony-based fit indices for multiple-indicator models: Do they work? *Structural Equation Modeling, 1,* 161–189.

Zwick, W. R., & Velicer, W. F. (1986). Comparisons of five rules for determining the number of components to retain. *Psychological Bulletin, 17,* 253–269.

Examining the Interrelationships Among Variables and Testing Substantive Hypotheses

CHAPTER 9

Structural Equation Modeling
A User's Guide
Roger E. Millsap

A structural equation model (SEM) represents a network of hypothesized linear relations among a set of variables. Commonly, the hypothesized relations are causal, and the model represents a causal theory. The use of SEMs in psychological research has steadily grown since the first accessible SEM software packages appeared in the late 1970s. Researchers in psychology now must have some familiarity with SEM methods in order to understand the research literature. This chapter offers a concise introduction to SEM for readers who have little previous exposure to the topic but may be familiar with the related techniques of regression and factor analysis. The chapter is organized around a series of questions that a novice user of structural equation methods might ask. An example of an actual application is used throughout the chapter to illustrate some of the difficulties often encountered when fitting complex path models in real data. The chapter seeks to present the essential flavor of SEM with a minimum of mathematical detail. Readers who seek a more formal treatment of SEM can consult the sources at the end of the chapter.

I thank Robert MacCallum and Chuck Hulin for permission to use the data presented in this chapter and Oi-Man Kwok for the figures.

What Is Structural Equation Modeling?

Structural equation modeling blends several familiar statistical methods to create a hybrid system that has wider scope than any of the individual methods considered in isolation. First, path analysis traditionally represents causal relations among a set of measured variables using linear equations. The equations formally resemble regression equations, with each equation expressing the modeled value of a criterion or endogenous variable as a linear function of one or more predictor variables, plus a residual or disturbance term. Unlike ordinary regression equations however, path model equations are conceived as explicitly causal, with the "regression" or path coefficients representing the direct causal influence of the predictor variable on the endogenous variable. In path analysis, predictor variables may themselves be endogenous in relation to other predictors or may serve purely as predictors. Variables of the latter type are denoted as exogenous variables in path analysis, and all other variables are regarded as endogenous. The path model represents a causal theory for the endogenous variables. Causal influences on the exogenous variables are not directly modeled.

A second statistical modeling tradition that is included in SEM is factor analysis. The factor analysis model represents each measured variable as a linear function of one or more common factors, plus a single unique factor. The common factors include influences on the measured variables that are shared among two or more such variables. For example, a set of items designed to measure skill in algebra might be hypothesized to share a single common factor of "knowledge of algebra." The unique factors include influences that are unique to each measured variable, such as random measurement error, or systematic components, such as method influences. Both the common and unique factors are denoted as *latent variables* in SEM, but interest focuses mainly on the common factors, and so references to latent variables often are meant to apply to the common factors. The factor model partitions the variance in each measured variable into two portions: one due to the collective influence of the common factors and the other to the unique factor for that variable. The portion due to the common factors is known as the *communality* in exploratory factor analysis.

Structural equation modeling combines the path-analytic and factor-analytic traditions into a single, unified representation. Each measured variable in an SEM is expressed as a linear function of one or more common factors and a single unique factor. Relations among the common factors are in turn represented by a set of path equations that capture the hypothesized causal paths among these latent variables. The common factors are intended to represent the constructs of interest to the researcher. The challenge facing the researcher is to specify an SEM model that faithfully expresses the researcher's causal theory for the constructs under study. The researcher must also carefully choose which measured variables are to serve as indicators of each hypothesized construct.

Structural equation modeling is a confirmatory method. It is designed for situations in which the researcher has one or more specific theories about relations among the variables under study. The researcher may have several contrasting hypotheses about these variables and may formulate contrasting SEMs for the same variables. Structural equation modeling is not a tool for exploratory data analysis, however, or for constructing theories to fit data. Researchers who wish to explore the factor structure that might underlie their measured variables should turn to exploratory factor analysis. For exploratory searches for causal structure, methods available in software such as TETRAD (Scheines, Spirtes, Glymour, & Meek, 1994; Scheines, Spirtes, Glymour, Meek, & Richardson, 1998) are useful.

An Empirical Example

Before proceeding, the data that will provide an example application will be introduced. MacCallum, Roznowski, and Necowitz (1992) first analyzed these data in their sampling study of model re-specification in SEM. The data were obtained using self-report questionnaires from 3,694 employees in two large midwestern hospitals in the United States. The two hospitals were similar in size, demographic characteristics, unionization, and other features. The data from the two hospitals are pooled for the purposes of this chapter.

The model to be tested in these data was inspired by the integrative model for employee withdrawal presented by Hulin, Roznowski, and Hachiya (1985). This integrative model depicts the antecedents of psychological withdrawal, turnover, and behaviors to enact change within an organization and is based on a review of the literature on attitudinal and situational influences on employee turnover. The data do not include measures of actual turnover but do include measures of withdrawal intentions and change behaviors. Also, only a portion of the antecedents for these two variables are measured in the data. These antecedent variables include work satisfaction, pay satisfaction, perceived work conditions, organizational citizenship behavior, and withdrawal behaviors. Each of the seven constructs or latent variables of interest was measured by multiple indicators in the form of questionnaire items. An item-level analysis will not be attempted here. Instead, item parcels were formed as sums of subsets of items that are hypothesized as measures of a given construct. Three parcels per construct were used as indicators for all but one of the seven constructs. The parcels have the advantage of generally higher intercorrelations and better approximations to continuity in comparison to the individual items. On the other hand, the use of parcels may mask measurement problems at the item level that would otherwise be detected using an item-level analysis.

The parcels for the work satisfaction and pay satisfaction latent variables were formed from items belonging to the Job Descriptive Index (JDI; Smith, Kendall, & Hulin, 1969), with several substitutions of items from Roznowski (1989). Each of the three work satisfaction parcels was based on five items, and each of the three pay satisfaction parcels was formed from three items. The perceived work condition latent variable was measured by two parcels, with one parcel formed from four items and the other from eight items. These twelve items were not part of the JDI and were apparently created specifically for the hospital questionnaire.

The parcels for the remaining four latent variables were formed from items that span different job behaviors and intentions. Withdrawal behaviors were measured using items that refer to passive withdrawal behaviors in the workplace. MacCallum et al. (1992) give examples of such items as "doing poor quality work," "arguing with coworkers," and "refusing to do assigned work." Eighteen items of this type were used to create three parcels for withdrawal behaviors. Organizational citizenship behavior (OCB) was measured by items reflecting positive or pro-organizational acts within the workplace, including volunteering for extra work and encouraging new employees. Twelve items were used to form three parcels for OCB. The change-behavior latent variable reflects behaviors whose goal is to improve work conditions in the workplace or in the larger job context. Items include "filing a grievance" or "making suggestions for needed change." Three parcels were formed from such items, with three items per parcel. The withdrawal cognitions latent variable refers to intentions and cognitions related to future withdrawal from the organization. MacCallum et al. (1992) included four parcels as indicators for this latent variable, but only three of these will be used here. The three parcels include items that refer to intentions for quitting, being late, or transferring out of the workplace. Across the seven latent variables of interest, twenty measured variables are used. The model to be fit to these data is discussed below.

How Do I Conduct a Structural Equation Modeling Analysis?

A SEM analysis has three broad stages: model specification, parameter estimation, and fit evaluation. *Model specification* requires the researcher to translate the theory to be tested into a particular model that is testable. Here the researcher must build the SEM to reflect both what is known about the phenomenon under study and what is theorized. The resulting model should be testable, or capable of being refuted by the data. *Parameter estimation* will use the data to obtain estimates of the model parameters that are optimal according to any one of several estimation methods. The choice of estimation method will depend on the model being tested and the distributional assumptions that are appropriate for the data. *Model fit evaluation* will use the parameter estimates to examine whether the hypothesized model can reproduce the structure found in the data. Fit evaluation will combine the use of large-sample formal tests of fit with a variety of goodness-of-fit indices. The fit indices assess global fit but also provide information on local fit within specific portions of the model. Fit evaluation precedes interpretation of the solution, because models that do not fit adequately will also generally fail to provide useful parameter estimates.

Model Specification

Model specification begins with the researcher's theory about the relationships among the variables under study. For convenience, a distinction is commonly made between the measurement portion of the model and the structural portion. The measurement model describes the relations between the measured variables and any latent variables that are hypothesized to underlie these measured variables. Specification of the measurement model will include the choice of the number of common factors and of which measured variables are directly related to each common factor. The structural portion of the model specifies the directional relations among the latent variables or, if no latent variables are included, among the measured variables. The choice of which latent variables are directly linked by paths, and which variables are only indirectly related, should be based on theory.

In addition to the specification of the measurement and structural portions of the model, the researcher should consider the nature of the measurement scales used, the distributional characteristics of the data, and the processes leading to any missing data. A tacit assumption in path analysis is that any variable that is endogenous is measured on a continuous scale, with an established unit of measurement. Purely exogenous variables may be discrete or even categorical, as can predictors in ordinary regression analysis. If an endogenous variable is dichotomous (such as turnover) or is measured in a few ordered categories, specialized procedures are needed to obtain correct standard errors and tests of fit (Muthén, 1984; Bartholomew, 1987). For any continuous endogenous variable, the most widely used estimation methods assume that the data are multivariate normal, with independent observations made on the persons under study. Multivariate normality can be checked using standard procedures (D'Agostino, 1986). In large samples, parameter estimates can still be accurate even if the normality assumptions are violated, although standard errors and fit statistics can be adversely affected (West, Finch, & Curran, 1995). Violations of independence assumptions can have more serious consequences. Study participants may have been sampled in clusters (for example, teams) or dyads (for example, supervisor-subordinate pairs). Independence assumptions are violated if the dependence among observations within these groups is ignored. Recent innovations in SEM procedures can provide the correct analysis in such cases if the dependence problems are recognized (Muthén & Satorra, 1995). If a substantial portion of the sample is missing values for some variables, the researcher should consider the best approach for handling this problem. Methods for handling missing data have evolved rapidly in the past two decades, and some of the advances are now incorporated in SEM software. (See Schafer, 1997, and Little & Rubin, 1987, for information on the general theory underlying modern methods for handling missing data.)

The specification of both the measurement and structural models must consider whether the model parameters are identified in each case. A parameter is identified if in theory, changes in the value of that parameter lead to changes in what we would expect to see in the data, given the model. If a parameter is not identified, different values for that parameter may all be consistent with the same data, and hence no unique solution for the parameter is possible. In many cases, the identification status of any model parameter can be checked by applying a few simple rules (Bollen, 1989; Pearl, 2000). Complex cases occasionally arise that require deep study. SEM software programs provide numerical checks for identification that will detect many identification problems.

Example. The measurement portion of the model to be evaluated in the example is specified by deciding how many latent variables are of interest and which measured variables are directly related to each latent variable. These questions are answered based on the researcher's understanding of the measured variables. In most cases, the measured variables are in fact selected to fulfill a particular measurement model. The twenty measured variables in the example data are intended to represent seven latent variables. Figure 9.1 depicts the hypothesized measurement model. Boxes represent measured variables, which are item parcels. Circles represent the common factors or latent variables hypothesized to underlie the twenty measured variables. The directed arrows linking the latent and measured variables indicate which measured variables are hypothesized as measures of each latent variable. In this model, each measured variable is linked to one and only one latent variable. These restrictions illustrate the difference between a confirmatory factor model as represented here and an exploratory factor model that does not restrict the loadings in this way (Lance & Vandenberg, 2001). The latent variables are all permitted to correlate in this model, but these correlations will be restricted by the structural model. These correlations are ordinarily represented by double-headed arrows in the measurement model diagram but are omitted in Figure 9.1 to simplify the figure. Finally, each measured variable is linked to its unique factor, with the unique factors denoted either with δ for exogenous variables or ε for endogenous variables. No correlations are permitted among the unique factors in Figure 9.1.

The pattern of linkages between measured and latent variables in Figure 9.1 is entirely determined by our understanding of the

Figure 9.1. Initial Measurement Model.

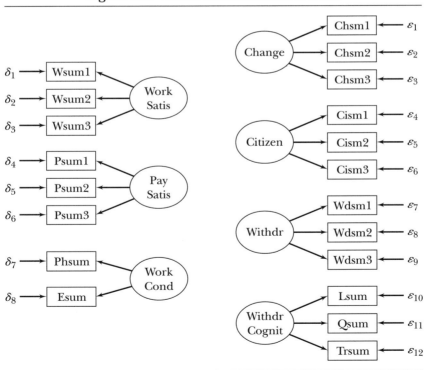

twenty measured variables and what they measure. For example, previous research using the JDI has identified the two latent variables of work satisfaction and pay satisfaction as being interpretable factors that underlie the six parcels linked to these factors in Figure 9.1. The remaining fourteen parcels include items that had either been used in previous research or were written for this study. The latter items were created following suggestions in Hulin et al. (1985). The specification of the measurement model for the new measures entails some risk because the intended factor structure for these items may fail to represent all of the important shared influences among them. We will return to this point.

The hypothesized structural model is shown in Figure 9.2. The first consideration in defining the structural model is the choice of which latent variables are to be exogenous. The exogenous latent variables are causally prior to all other variables, and relationships among the exogenous latent variables are unconstrained in the model. The integrative model of Hulin et al. (1985) asserts that the satisfaction and perceived work condition variables are causally prior to the other four latent variables, which concern behaviors or intentions. Hence the work satisfaction, pay satisfaction,

Figure 9.2. Initial Structural Model.

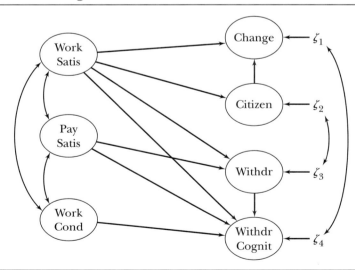

and perceived work condition latent variables are chosen as exogenous in Figure 9.2. Next, we must decide which paths linking exogenous and endogenous variables should be included. Each path to be included should be justifiable in terms of theory or previous research. In Figure 9.2, work satisfaction is directly linked to each of the four endogenous variables. Previous research has substantiated these linkages (Hulin et al., 1985). Pay satisfaction is hypothesized to influence only withdrawal and withdrawal cognitions. The theory here is that while pay dissatisfaction may influence withdrawal, pay satisfaction need not lead to citizenship behaviors or actions to change. Perceived work condition is linked only to withdrawal cognitions, or intentions to leave the organization. If the employee has negative perceptions of the physical environment and working conditions, intentions to leave the organization are strengthened without intermediate passive withdrawal behaviors.

The four endogenous latent variables are split into two parallel sets of two variables. First, OCB is hypothesized as an influence on change behaviors. The pro-organizational behaviors in OCB are seen as precursors to behaviors directed toward change in the workplace. Second, passive withdrawal behaviors are hypothesized as causally prior to intentions to leave the organization altogether. Note that no paths between these two pairs of variables are included.

In Figure 9.2, each endogenous variable is linked to a disturbance variable, symbolized with ζ. The disturbance variable accounts for causal influences on the endogenous latent variable that are unrelated to any other latent variable that has a direct path to the endogenous variable. Model specification must include decisions about whether to permit nonzero associations among the disturbance variables. Although identification problems can arise when disturbance variables covary, the assumption that all such disturbance variables are mutually uncorrelated is often too strong. If all disturbance variables are mutually uncorrelated, we have explained all of the covariances among the endogenous latent variables through the structural model. In many applications, it is improbable that all covariances among the endogenous variables can be explained through the structural path model. In this example, nonzero covariances will be permitted for disturbances within two pairs of endogenous variables: (citizenship, withdrawal behaviors) and (change, withdrawal cognitions). These specific pairs were chosen because covariances between these disturbances make theoretical sense and do not change the identification status of the model. The nonzero covariances are represented in Figure 9.2 by the curved double-headed arrows between disturbances within each pair of endogenous variables.

Once the full model is specified, we should evaluate the identification status of the model and its parameters. The model in the combined measurement and structural model can be shown to be identified. Bollen (1989) describes a two-step evaluation process for identification in path models with latent variables. The process first evaluates identification within the measurement model, followed by evaluation of the structural model. The measurement model in Figure 9.1 is identified given that (1) each measured variable loads on only one factor, (2) no covariances are permitted between the unique factors, (3) no correlations among the common factors are fixed to zero, (4) each factor is defined by at least two measured variables, and (5) one measured variable per factor has a fixed nonzero loading (fixed to one). These five conditions are sufficient to identify the measurement model but are not all necessary for identification. The structural portion of the model is also identified because it has a block-recursive structure (Bollen, 1989). Briefly, a block-recursive structure holds when the only nonzero correlations permitted among the disturbance variables are found for endogenous variables that are not connected by direct paths. Given that both the measurement and structural portions of the model are identified, the whole model is identified.

Turning to the distributional characteristics of the data, all of the measured variables are here regarded as being adequately approximated by continuous, interval-level scales of measurement. In reality, all of the measures have discrete values, but a sufficient number of scale points are present to provide some continuity. Multivariate normality will be assumed for the measured variables. This assumption is unlikely to be fully met in the example. The sample data can be used to evaluate whether multivariate normality is a reasonable assumption. Both data transformations and outlier trimming are potential ways of better approximating normality. Alternatively, one can pursue estimation methods that do not require multivariate normality. Here we will retain the normality assumptions and use maximum likelihood (ML) estimation.

Parameter Estimation

A variety of estimation methods are available in SEM, depending on the nature of the model and the characteristics of the data. When samples are large and the hypothesized model fits adequately, the different methods tend to yield similar estimates, and the choice of method is less important. In small samples, different estimation methods may yield varying results. The definition of *small* is contingent on the number of variables and the nature of the model. Samples under two hundred can be regarded as small in most applications. Large models with many observed variables will require large samples, but one should also consider the strength of the relations between the observed and latent variables (MacCallum, Widaman, Zhang, & Hong, 1999). If these relations are strong, good results are possible with smaller samples. In short, it is nearly impossible to give blanket recommendations for sample size requirements in SEM.

With few exceptions, estimation in SEM requires iterative, numerical algorithms. Each estimation method corresponds to a specific fitting function that is iteratively optimized during the estimation process. This process begins with start values for all parameters that are to be estimated. Software packages now generate start values automatically, but the researcher may need to supply start values for unusual models. The estimation algorithm iteratively improves the estimates, beginning with the start values, until a convergence criterion is fulfilled. Convergence is not guaranteed; ill-fitting models may fail to produce convergence, or poor start values may lead to convergence failures. Once convergence is achieved, the set of parameter estimates is taken as the final set of estimates.

When multivariate normality is tenable as a distributional assumption for the variables under study, ML estimation is a common choice. In this method, the fitting function to be optimized is equivalent to the normal likelihood function for the data. ML estimates are known to have useful properties in large samples when the normality assumptions are fulfilled. Alternatively, generalized least squares (GLS) estimation can be used in the normal case. This method should produce estimates that are close to the ML estimates in the normal case, but GLS can be used under weaker assumptions as well. Both ML and GLS estimation provide large-sample standard errors and fit statistics for the model. When normality assumptions are violated, ML and GLS can still give accurate point estimates of the parameters, but the standard errors and fit statistics may be inaccurate (West et al., 1995).

Given that the normality assumptions often do not strictly hold, estimation methods that perform well under minimal distributional assumptions have been actively sought. These methods resemble normal-theory GLS and are sometimes denoted weighted least squares (WLS) methods. The distinction between the two methods lies in the choice of weights in the fitting function in each case. Generally, the weights used in either method are functions of the estimated sampling variances for the elements of the covariance matrix being modeled. The sampling variances are estimated in different ways depending on which distributional assumptions are appropriate for the data. In nonnormal data, WLS methods may require large samples to be accurate due to the need to estimate the required weights along with the model parameters. Improvements in these methods are likely in the near future.

Researchers should be aware that any of the noted estimation methods may converge on a solution that includes impossible values for some estimates (for example, negative variance estimates). Software packages vary widely in how these events are handled. Problems of this type often indicate that the proposed model is inappropriate for the data at hand, although poor estimates can also be due to small samples in conjunction with parameters whose true values are near their boundary (for example, variances near zero). Wothke (1993) provides a useful discussion of some of these problems.

As in ordinary regression analysis, the values of the parameter estimates depend on the scaling chosen for the measured variables. One can estimate path coefficients in raw metric, using whatever scaling that is typically adopted for the measures being used, or one can obtain a standardized solution for the path coefficients by transforming the measured variables to have unit variance. Most SEM software programs will provide both solutions if requested. If the hypothesized model includes latent variables, some scaling must be created for these as well. Typically, one either scales each latent variable in the metric of one of its indicators (raw metric) or standardizes the latent variables by fixing their variances to unit values. In reporting the SEM parameter estimates, path coefficients based on standardized measured and latent variables are usually more easily interpreted. One exception to this rule arises in multiple-group studies in which the within-group standardizations can interfere with between-group comparisons.

Fit Evaluation

Once the parameter estimates under the proposed model are available, the model is evaluated for fit. One can distinguish between global fit indices, which evaluate the fit of the model as a whole using a single index, and local fit indices, which evaluate specific parts of the model for fit. Both types of indices are ordinarily of interest. In theory, one can treat the question of fit as a statistical hypothesis test in which the proposed model is the null hypothesis. This hypothesis is then rejected in favor of a general unconstrained alternative hypothesis if the chosen global fit index exceeds a critical value corresponding to the chosen alpha level. Most SEM researchers do not adopt this viewpoint (for a contrasting view, see Hayduk, 1996). The rationale for rejecting the strict hypothesis-testing viewpoint is that rejection of the null hypothesis of perfect fit is uninteresting in most applications. Rejection of the null hypothesis is compelled under trivial departures from perfect fit if the sample is large enough. Of greater interest is the question of whether the model is a good approximation. A difficulty with this notion of approximate fit is that there is no unique way of measuring the adequacy of approximation. As a consequence, no single index is exclusively relied on in assessing fit. The best practice is to report a variety of fit indices and to consider both these indices and any relevant background information in judging the adequacy of the model.

The oldest global fit index is the chi-square index, which is associated with the ML method of estimation. This chi-square statistic is appropriate as a test of perfect fit in large samples under multivariate normality. It is also produced under GLS estimation in the normal case and under WLS estimation with general distributional assumptions in very large samples. The literal interpretation of the chi-square statistic as a test statistic for hypothesis testing is no longer widely held in SEM. The chi-square value is usually reported along with its degrees of freedom however, and it is used in the calculation of other fit indices.

Another global fit index that has been used widely is the root mean square residual (RMSR), which essentially measures the typical unsigned difference between an element of the sample covariance matrix and the sample fitted covariance matrix. The fitted covariance matrix is created by substituting in the estimates for all model parameters in the equations that express the variances and covariances among the measured variables as a function of the model parameters. To illustrate, suppose that X is exogenous and Y is endogenous, with a direct path to Y from X. If the path equation is

$$Y = \gamma X + \zeta,$$

with γ the path coefficient and ζ the disturbance random variable with variance ψ, we can express the variance of Y and the covariance between Y and X under the path model as

$$\sigma_Y^2 = \gamma^2 \sigma_X^2 + \psi, \qquad \sigma_{YX} = \gamma \sigma_X^2.$$

The fitted variance of Y, and the fitted covariance between Y and X, could both be calculated by substituting estimates of γ, σ_X^2 ψ, into the above equations and solving. Note that with only X and Y in the model, the fitted variance and covariance will exactly match the sample variance and covariance. Once additional measured variables are included in the data, however, the above model may be unable to reproduce the variance of Y and the covariance between X and Y exactly because the model does not include these additional variables.

If the model fits perfectly in the sample, RMSR = 0. Sampling fluctuations are likely to render this index to be positive even if the model fits well in the population. Given variations in measurement scale metrics among the measured variables, the RMSR is more easily interpreted in its standardized form (SRMSR). A common rule of thumb for the SRMSR is that values less than .05 are consistent with a good fit for the model. Researchers must recognize, however, that this .05 cut point is relatively arbitrary and may not be especially useful under extreme conditions of small samples or large sets of measured variables.

A third global index that is similar in spirit to the RMSR is the root mean square error of approximation (RMSEA; Steiger & Lind, 1980). This index estimates the typical unsigned difference between an element of the population covariance matrix and the fitted population covariance matrix that would be generated from the model, adjusting for model degrees of freedom. The latter adjustment penalizes the investigator for including many parameters that reduce the degrees of freedom without materially adding to the fit of the model. RMSEA values less than .05 are typically regarded as indicating a good fit, with values between .05 and .08 indicating a fair fit (Browne & Cudeck, 1993). The comments already given concerning the SRMSR cut point apply equally here: the .05 and .08 cut points are based on limited practical experience rather than any theoretical criteria. Confidence intervals and hypothesis tests for the RMSEA are available. For example, one might evaluate a null hypothesis of close fit (for example, RMSEA below .05) against the alternative that the fit is not close (RMSEA above .05). Alternatively, one can create a confidence interval for the RMSEA at the desired confidence level and then check whether the value .05 lies within the interval. The assumptions required for the use of the RMSEA and its associated confidence intervals are essentially those required for ML estimation under normality, together with the requirement that the proposed model is not highly ill fitting.

A final set of global fit indices attempts to evaluate the fit of the proposed model in comparison to a highly restricted baseline model (Bentler, 1990; Bentler & Bonett, 1980; McDonald & Marsh, 1990). This baseline model can be selected in various ways, but researchers often select the null model, which stipulates that the measured variables are mutually uncorrelated. In the context of factor analysis, for example, this null model implies that no common factors underlie the measured variables. The fit index then measures the improvement in fit under the proposed model in relation to the null model, possibly with an adjustment for degrees of freedom. Several of these indices are available, and they generally range between 0 and 1.0, with values near 1.0 indicating a good fit. One widely used index of this type is the comparative fit index (CFI; Bentler, 1990). Values above .95 are considered good for this index (Hu & Bentler, 1999). The CFI and other such indices are radically different from the first three global indices because their frame of reference is the worst-case null model.

Local fit indices provide information about the impact of individual model restrictions on fit, or on the fit of the model to individual measured variables. Lagrange multiplier statistics (or modification indices) estimate the improvement in the global chi-square index if a given model restriction is relaxed. The potential number of such statistics is equal to the number of restrictions entailed by the model. Under the hypothesis of perfect fit for the proposed model, these statistics can be regarded as chi-square variates with df = 1 (assuming that only single restrictions are tested). These statistics have the same vulnerability to trivial misfits in large samples that was described for the global chi-square index. In large samples, one can also consider the expected parameter change statistics, which estimate the expected change in the value of a restricted parameter once the restriction is relaxed. If the expected change is negligible, the large Lagrange multiplier statistic might be ignored. Another set of local indices that are often useful are the elements of the sample residual covariance matrix. This matrix is the difference between the sample covariance matrix and the sample fitted covariance matrix under the model. The global RMSR is computed from these residuals. Covariance matrix elements with large residuals can suggest portions of the model that do not adequately reproduce the associations found in the data. The residuals are often standardized to aid in interpretation, but the definition of *standardized* will vary depending on the software package. In LISREL 8.30 (Jöreskog & Sörbom, 1996a), the standardization uses large-sample estimates of the standard errors of the residuals. These standard error estimates are inversely related to sample size, however, and so large, standardized residuals may be present in large samples even when the fit of the model is fairly good. A final point to remember with regard to the local indices is that in moderate to large models, many local index values will be produced due to the substantial number of model restrictions and variables. As a result, a few large local indices may arise for reasons of sampling error in modest samples. Investigators should search for interpretable patterns in these indices rather than place emphasis on a few isolated values.

Assuming that the hypothesized model does not fit, what is the next step? We generally wish to locate the source of the lack of fit at this stage. Careful examination of the local fit indices can sometimes shed light on this question, depending on the complexity of the model and the degree of misfit. If the fit is quite poor, there may be no obvious local source for the lack of fit because many different model constraints contribute to the poor fit. In less ill-fitting models, the lack of fit may appear to be localized in a few constraints, as indicated by the modification indices for example. The researcher may wish to remove these constraints to create a new model, one that is weaker than the original model in imposing fewer constraints. The process of altering the model in this manner is denoted *respecification.*

Respecification that is guided primarily by local fit information is likely to be misleading. In changing the model in this way, one is no longer conducting a confirmatory test of a model. Subsequent model fit evaluation is better characterized as exploratory data analysis. The chances of finding the right model through exploratory modifications are not good in general. Simulations have found that in data in which the true model is known, local fit indices produced by the wrong model often lead to respecifications that do not recover the true model (MacCallum, 1986; MacCallum et al., 1992). This problem is especially serious when the sample size is small, the model is large, and a substantial number of changes are needed in the ill-fitting model.

A more useful alternative to data-based modifications lies in the development of a set of competing models that represent contrasting hypotheses. These models are specified a priori rather than in response to sample fit information. The models are each separately evaluated for fit. The ideal outcome here is that one model emerges as fitting well, with competing models being rejected. Millsap and Meredith (1994) illustrate this use of competing models. Alternatively, the different models might be logically nested, with some models being special cases of other general alternative models. For example, model A might represent a special case of model B in which certain paths in B are omitted, with the omissions motivated by a theory that would suggest A is preferred to B. Nested sequences of models can be tested using chi-square difference statistics, but these statistics have the same weaknesses found in the standard chi-square test statistic. In other examples, the set of competing models will not include any nested models. The different models might represent different path configurations for the same measured variables, for example. Fit comparisons for nonnested models can use global fit indices appropriate for such comparisons, such as the Akaike information criterion (AIC) and related indices (see Burnham and Anderson, 1998, for a description of AIC theory).

Example: Parameter estimation and fit evaluation. The sample covariance matrix based on 3,694 survey participants was analyzed using LISREL 8.30 (Jöreskog & Sörbom, 1996a). The sample correlations and standard deviations are given in Table 9.1. The first model to be examined combines the measurement model in Figure 9.1 with the structural model in Figure 9.2. We will denote this combined model as the initial path model in what follows. The chapter appendix contains the LISREL program for this model and for other models fit to these data.

For the initial path model, the default start values provided by LISREL enable the program to converge to a solution. Once the parameter estimates are obtained, these estimates should be checked to see that all estimates are reasonable. Negative estimates for unique factor variances or disturbance variances are problematic, for example. Program messages stating that a parameter matrix is not positive definite or that a parameter may not be identified should be noted. Any identification problems should be thoroughly investigated before continuing. No such problems arise in this case.

The global fit statistics for the initial path model, and for all other models fit to these data, are given in Table 9.2. The global fit indices are not particularly good for the initial path model. The RMSEA value of .069 is not indicative of a close fit. The 90 percent confidence interval for the RMSEA is entirely above the threshold of .05. The SRMSR value of .065 exceeds the common threshold of .05 for this index. The CFI value of .91 is below the recommended threshold of .95. On the other hand, none of these indices suggests that the overall fit is poor. Instead, the fit occupies the middle ground between fit that is good enough to retain the model as specified and fit that is poor enough to dismiss the model altogether. How one proceeds in this case depends on the purpose of the

Table 9.1. Correlation Matrix and Standard Deviations for Example Data ($n = 3,694$).

	chsm1	chsm2	chsm3	cism1	cism2	cism3	wdsm1	wdsm2	wdsm3	lsum	qsum	trsum
chsm1	1.000											
chsm2	.366	1.000										
chsm3	.351	.320	1.000									
cism1	.383	.384	.395	1.000								
cism2	.318	.382	.356	.522	1.000							
cism3	.335	.364	.361	.586	.609	1.000						
wdsm1	-.059	-.089	-.175	-.062	-.062	-.026	1.000					
wdsm2	-.040	-.054	-.104	-.018	.034	.120	.611	1.000				
wdsm3	.102	.076	.004	.296	.182	.298	.488	.588	1.000			
lsum	.058	.028	.245	.041	.023	.016	-.158	-.089	-.114	1.000		
qsum	-.013	-.045	.125	-.065	-.056	-.103	-.381	-.330	-.371	.323	1.000	
trsum	.045	.035	.185	-.006	.034	.011	-.216	-.158	-.171	.470	.411	1.000
wsum1	.153	.140	.002	.187	.252	.313	.122	.229	.312	-.314	-.293	-.313
wsum2	.142	.143	-.009	.170	.231	.279	.150	.219	.307	-.311	-.303	-.316
wsum3	.086	.077	-.087	.118	.154	.200	.208	.232	.302	-.355	-.362	-.403
psum1	-.025	-.069	-.095	.009	-.026	-.012	.119	.037	.034	-.158	-.161	-.150
psum2	.030	-.011	-.051	.067	.063	.079	.061	.052	.078	-.143	-.142	-.111
psum3	.004	-.036	-.085	.011	.013	.012	.089	.036	.047	-.136	-.142	-.138
phsum	.018	.015	-.025	.037	.024	.055	.116	.084	.106	-.112	-.120	-.129
esum	-.031	-.011	-.112	-.028	-.008	.004	.151	.075	.092	-.154	-.189	-.178

	wsum1	wsum2	wsum3	psum1	psum2	psum3	phsum	esum
wsum1	1.000							
wsum2	.714	1.000						
wsum3	.692	.685	1.000					
psum1	.087	.113	.190	1.000				
psum2	.184	.206	.217	.667	1.000			
psum3	.141	.171	.225	.693	.679	1.000		
phsum	.197	.206	.283	.161	.159	.150	1.000	
esum	.177	.215	.319	.255	.226	.244	.455	1.000

chsm1	chsm2	chsm3	cism1	cism2	cism3	wdsm1	wdsm2	wdsm3	lsum	qsum	trsum
2.155	2.410	2.987	3.331	3.483	4.076	3.911	3.399	3.114	4.538	2.588	4.265

wsum1	wsum2	wsum3	psum1	psum2	psum3	phsum	esum
4.515	3.559	3.835	3.001	3.087	2.880	3.015	5.041

Table 9.2. Fit Statistics for Models in the Example Data (*n* = 3,694).

Model	Chi-Square	df	SRMSR	RMSEA (90 percent interval)	CFI
Initial path model	2,735.56	156	.065	.069 (.067–.072)	.91
Congeneric factor model	2,489.74	149	.057	.067 (.064–.069)	.92
MC factor model	381.20	71	.0099	.034 (.031–.038)	.99

research. If competing models are available, these would be evaluated in hopes of finding a model that is superior to the initial path model. We will pursue an alternative approach that examines two plausible explanations for the misfit in the initial path model.

Before proceeding with additional models, it is useful to examine some of the parameter estimates for the initial path model, along with some local fit indices that are suggestive of potential problems with this model. Table 9.3 presents the estimated factor loadings for the measurement model in Figure 9.1. Table 9.4 presents the estimated path coefficients for the structural model in Figure 9.2. All parameter estimates in Tables 9.3 and 9.4 are standardized with respect to both latent and measured variables. In Table 9.3, all factor loading estimates are substantial in magnitude and are statistically significant (significance is not surprising, given the large sample). In Table 9.4, it is clear that the contributions of pay satisfaction and work conditions to determining withdrawal cognitions are negligible. The same conclusion applies to the contribution of pay satisfaction to withdrawal behaviors. The remaining coefficient estimates are modest in size, with the exception of the path from citizenship to change behaviors. In the standardized metric, each coefficient gives the expected change in the endogenous variable in standard deviation units, given a change of one standard deviation in the predictor variable, and adjusting for any other predictor variables having direct paths to the endogenous variable.

Table 9.3. Completely Standardized Factor Loading Estimates from the Initial Path Model.

			Factors				
	Worksat	Paysat	Work C.	Change	Citizenship	Withdraw B.	Withdraw C.
wsum1	.84*						
wsum2	.83						
wsum3	.84						
psum1		.83*					
psum2		.81					
psum3		.84					
phsum			.60*				
esum			.76				
chsm1				.56*			
chsm2				.57			
chsm3				.61			
cism1					.73*		
cism2					.74		
cism3					.80		
wdsm1						.72*	
wdsm2						.83	
wdsm3						.71	
lsum							.60*
qsum							.62
trsum							.69

*Fixed to 1.0 for identification in raw metric solution. All loadings not shown are fixed to zero.

Table 9.4. Completely Standardized Path Coefficient Estimates from the Initial Path Model.

	Exogenous-Endogenous						
	Worksat	Paysat	Work C.	Change	Citizenship	Withdraw B.	Withdraw C.
Endogenous							
Change	−.16				.85		
Citizenship	.33						
Withdraw B.	.36	.00					
Withdraw C.	−.48	−.09	−.08			−.22	

Note: All estimates reach statistical significance at alpha = .05 except the Paysat to Withdraw B. path. All coefficients not shown are fixed to zero.

The local fit indices show a pattern of misfit that centers on a subset of the variables. The largest standardized residuals involve the set of withdrawal behavior variables (wdsm1, wdsm2, wdsm3) and their relations to other variables. In the factor loading matrix for the endogenous variables, large modification indices appear for the withdrawal behavior variables' fixed zero loadings on the change behavior and citizenship behavior factors (for example, index = 519.18 for wdsm3 on citizenship factor). Similarly, large modification indices for the withdrawal behavior variables appear in the off-diagonal elements of the unique factor covariance matrix. This pattern suggests a misspecification in the measurement portion of the model: the specified factor structure does not appear to be consistent with the data. We return to this possibility below.

The first explanation for the misfit found in the initial path model is that although the measurement portion of the model is correct, the structural portion of the model is wrong. In this scenario, there exists some alternative structural model that would fit well in comparison to the structure in the initial path model. Given the measurement model in Figure 9.1, the best-fitting structural model is one that is saturated, permitting perfect reproduction of the covariances among the seven latent variables. This saturated model places no structural constraints on the covariances among the latent variables. We can specify this saturated structural model as a confirmatory factor model that permits the common factors to correlate freely, while imposing the loading pattern in Figure 9.1 (Lance & Vandenberg, 2001). Each measured variable is permitted to load on one and only one factor. We will refer to this model as the *congeneric factor model,* with the term *congeneric* denoting the independent cluster loading pattern in Figure 9.1. The fixed loading constraints present in the initial path model are retained in this congeneric factor model.

The global fit statistics for the congeneric factor model are given in Table 9.2. The statistics show a relatively small improvement in fit in comparison to the full structural model. The RMSEA drops to .067, yet its confidence interval still lies wholly above the .05 threshold. The SRMSR drops to .057. The CFI improves only marginally. The implication of these results is that given the measurement model in Figure 9.1, none of the potential alternative structural models will show a substantial improvement in fit in comparison to the initial path model. The explanation for the misfit of the initial path model does not appear to lie in omitted or misspecified structural paths, given the measurement model.

Our search for a plausible explanation for the misfit of the initial path model leads to a second possibility. The congeneric factor model may itself be misspecified if some measured variables are influenced by more than one factor. This possible explanation is supported by the local fit index results already noted. Once we permit the measured variables to load on more than one factor, the potential number of factor models becomes enormous given seven factors and twenty measured variables. Among the class of factor models that permit such loading patterns, the model that will most closely reproduce the sample covariances is one that places only minimal constraints on the loadings. These minimal constraints render the model to be rotationally unique while permitting the measured variables to load freely wherever possible (Jöreskog, 1979). We will refer to this model as the minimally constrained (MC) factor model. Like the congeneric factor model, the MC factor model permits the seven factors to covary freely. The congeneric factor model is logically nested within the MC factor model, assuming that the constraints for identification are chosen to be the same in the two models. Several potential sets of minimal constraints could be specified for the MC model, all of which typically yield identical global fit indices (but see Millsap, 2001, for exceptions). In this case, the chosen constraints force one measured variable for each factor to load only on that factor, with the nonzero loadings fixed to one in all cases. These constraints were also used in both the congeneric factor model and the initial path model.

The global fit indices for the MC model are given in Table 9.2. A substantial improvement in fit is evident in comparison to both the congeneric and initial path models. The RMSEA estimate indicates a close fit, with the confidence interval now lying wholly below the .05 threshold. Both the CFI and the SRMSR estimates are excellent. The results suggest several conclusions. First, the loading constraints included in both the congeneric and initial path models were responsible for much of the misfit in those models. This conclusion follows from the fact that the removal of these constraints led to a substantial improvement in fit. Second, we have no evidence that more than seven common factors are needed to represent the twenty measured variables adequately. Note that we have not proven that seven common factors underlie the measured variables. We simply do not have evidence that a model that includes more than seven common factors would do substantially better than the MC model. Most important, we have no theory that would justify more than seven factors, and so we have no basis for building such a model as an SEM.

We have established that the pattern of relationships between the measured and latent variables in the full structural model is misspecified. What, then, is the correct pattern? It is tempting to use the MC results to answer this question, but we should recognize that in doing so, we shift our perspective from that of testing a model generated from substantive theory to one of data-based respecification. Respecifications of this sort are likely to mislead us because the fit of the resulting respecified model will generally be as good or better, at least in the sample that suggested the respecifications. A better use of the information provided by the MC model lies in suggesting changes that could be made in the model in a new study.

Proceeding in this spirit, the pattern of loading estimates provided by the MC model suggests that the congeneric constraints are adequate for the three exogenous factors but that some of the measured variables for the citizenship, withdrawal behavior, and withdrawal cognition factors will load on multiple factors. Specifically, cism2 and cism3 load substantially on both their factor (citizenship) and the change factor. In the withdrawal behavior factor, wdsm2 loads on the change factor also, and wdsm3 loads on the citizenship factor. Finally, qsum in the withdrawal cognition factor also loads on withdrawal behavior. Recall that the parcels for these four endogenous factors contain a mixture of newly written items and items used in previous research. The MC results suggest that the intended factor structure for these parcels does not fit the data. These problems undercut the interpretation of the structural model because we can no longer have confidence in our interpretation of the endogenous latent variables. We should alter the content of the twelve parcels by adding or deleting items to represent the four factors in a future study better.

What Can I Conclude from the Fit of a Model?

Once a decision is made about the fit of the proposed models, the researcher must interpret the results in relation to the questions that motivated the research. This interpretation is influenced by considerations that are unique to the situation, but some general interpretive themes can be identified that cut across many research contexts. We will set aside the possibility for now that we have failed to reject the model due to inadequate statistical power, and we will assume that larger samples would have led to the same conclusion. The fit of a proposed model says something not only about this model but also about the set of alternative models that are equivalent to this model. By *equivalent models,* we mean a set of models that yield identical global fit indices but differ from the proposed model in their specifications. The differences could involve reversals in the directions of certain paths or the addition of new paths along with the exclusion of others. The differences could also lie in the measurement portion of the model, as in permitting correlations among the unique factors to replace common factors. Given any proposed model, it is generally possible to find one or more equivalent models that are indistinguishable from the proposed model on the basis of global fit. Hence, the fit of any member of this set of models implies that any other member would fit also. The careful researcher will consider whether the alternative equivalent models are plausible for the data at hand. Some alternative models can be ruled out on the basis of research design considerations. In longitudinal data, alternative models that reverse causal paths to operate backward in time can be dismissed, for example. (For more information on the topic of equivalent models, see Lee & Hershberger, 1990; MacCallum, Wegener, Uchino, & Fabrigar, 1993; Stelzl, 1986; and Williams, Bozdogan, & Aiman-Smith, 1996.)

Most SEM applications incorporate some notion of causal influence in the model. To what extent does the fit of a proposed model have implications for the causal theory that led to the model? This question is important because many researchers conduct SEM analyses in hopes of testing such theories. Although the causal implications of SEM analyses are still widely debated (Cliff, 1983; Dempster, 1990; Freedman, 1987; Holland, 1988; McDonald, 1997;

Pearl, 2000; Shafer, 1996; Sobel, 1995), most theorists would agree on two points. First, causal inferences from SEM analyses rely on assumptions that cannot be directly tested using the SEM analysis. For example, all causally important variables are typically assumed to have been included in the model. The results of an SEM analysis cannot tell if some of these variables have been omitted from the model, however. It is up to the researcher to identify the important variables and to take steps to include them in the model. Second, the basis for any causal interpretation of the results lies largely in the nature of the research design rather than in the use of an SEM analysis. When an SEM is specified for data generated from a randomized experiment, the causal inferences drawn from the SEM analysis have force largely because of the origin of the data. Randomization eliminates many rival alternative models. When the same SEM is specified for data generated from an observational study, the use of SEM cannot generally recoup the loss of inferential power that results from the weaker research design. SEM analyses confer no special causal status on the data being analyzed. The influence goes in the opposite direction: good data provide the basis for the causal interpretation of an SEM.

To return to the issue of power, failure to reject a model raises the question of whether a larger sample would have led to rejection. Power considerations are relevant primarily in three SEM domains: the global chi-square test of fit, the tests involving the RMSEA index, and tests for the significance of individual parameter estimates. Fortunately, power calculation methods are now available for each of these domains. MacCallum, Browne, and Sugawara (1996) describe power calculation procedures used for tests of hypotheses on the RMSEA index. Given that tests of the null hypothesis that RMSEA = 0 are equivalent to the global chi-square test, their procedures also apply to questions of power for the chi-square test. The advantage of using the RMSEA index in this context is that power for tests of close fit as defined by the RMSEA can be determined. All of the procedures involving the RMSEA have two features: they apply only to global questions of fit, and they are not tied to any specific alternative model. In some applications, we may be interested in the value of a specific parameter or set of parameters in the model. The parameter of interest may be an individual path coefficient that represents a causal effect of interest, for example. For this situation, the power estimation procedure of Satorra and Saris (1985; Saris & Satorra, 1993) is especially useful. The procedure requires the researcher first to decide the magnitudes of the parameters of interest that he or she wishes to be able to detect. This decision is essentially the same as deciding the magnitude of the effect size one wants to detect in simpler power analyses, such as in ANOVA. One then uses these specified parameter values, along with full specification of all other parameter values in the model, to generate a covariance matrix. This covariance matrix is then used to calculate the power by fitting a restricted model that sets the parameters of interest to their values under the null hypothesis (for example, usually zero). The resulting chi-square value can be referred to the noncentral chi-square distribution to calculate power. This approach is highly flexible in that just about any hypothesis involving individual parameters can be evaluated for power.

Collectively, the available power calculation procedures can help the researcher decide whether the failure to reject the model can be considered a type II error. The procedures are also useful in planning for a sample size that will provide adequate power. Researchers often want to know how large the sample size should be to support an SEM analysis. One answer to this question is based on having a sample size that will permit rejection of the model with high probability if the model does not fit or fits below a desired threshold of approximation. The RMSEA-based procedures of MacCallum et al. (1996) can easily be done in advance of data collection. The power procedures of Satorra and Saris (1985) can also be done in advance, but it is necessary to specify values for the model parameters. These values could be based on previous research.

Example: Conclusions. We rejected two of the three models tested but can still ask whether our power was adequate to reject the fit of the third model, the MC factor model, using the RMSEA fit index. This model has 71 degrees of freedom, and our sample size is 3,694. Tables provided by MacCallum et al. (1996) reveal that our power is essentially 1.00 for tests of exact fit using the chi-square statistic or for tests of close fit using the RMSEA statistic. We can have confidence that if the MC model (or models equivalent to this model) did not provide an adequate approximation as defined by RMSEA less than .05, we would have detected this fact with a high probability.

Unfortunately, we do not have support for our initial path model. We have no strong evidence against the structural portion of the path model, and we could use this structural specification again once the measurement portion of the model has been modified. The results found in this example are not unusual. SEM can place strong demands on measurement, especially on the construct interpretations of measures. With twenty measured variables allocated to seven common factors under strict congeneric pattern constraints, the number of restrictions on the covariance structure among the measured variables is quite large, as revealed by the large drop in degrees of freedom in moving from the congeneric to MC factor models. The measured variables in the example could not meet the demands made by these restrictions. Our next research task will be the modification of these measures or their replacement with a new set of measures that conform to our target measurement model.

What Are Some Interesting Applications of SEM?

Some novel applications of SEM have become feasible recently with new developments in estimation algorithms and software. Other potential applications have been known for some time yet are underused. We briefly describe a number of available extensions to standard SEM analyses.

Multilevel SEM

We may wish to gather data in which the units under study are organized hierarchically within larger aggregates. Individual employees may be nested within local organizational branches of a company, for example, or employees may be nested within teams. In such data, we may measure variables at both the individual and the larger aggregate levels. We then may want to formulate models that operate at both the individual and aggregate levels. The analysis of this type of data should incorporate the known statistical dependencies among individuals who are nested within a common unit. For example, we might expect that employees within a given branch of a company share characteristics that are relevant to the variables under study. Data structures of this type are known as multilevel or hierarchical data structures. Methods for the analysis of such data have developed rapidly in recent years. The extension of SEM methods to encompass multilevel data is relatively recent (Longford & Muthén, 1992; McDonald & Goldstein, 1989; Muthén, 1989, 1994; Muthén & Satorra, 1995). This extension should be useful for organizational researchers who wish to study processes at both the individual and organizational levels.

Latent Growth Models

Models for longitudinal data have a long history in SEM, but latent growth models have appeared more recently (McArdle & Epstein, 1987; Meredith & Tisak, 1990; Tisak & Meredith, 1990). Latent growth models permit individual differences in growth trajectories over time to be modeled as a function of other variables measured on the individuals. The form of the growth curves can range from straight-line growth functions to higher-order polynomial growth functions. Latent growth models differ from traditional autoregressive models in permitting individuals to vary in the shapes of their growth curves, while modeling these individual differences. If individuals are assigned to different treatment conditions with multiple pretests and posttests, latent growth models can be used to evaluate treatment effects while including covariate information (Muthén & Curran, 1997). (For a recent text on latent growth curve models, see Duncan, Duncan, Strycker, Li, & Alpert, 1999. Chan, 2001, presents a more recent treatment.)

Mean Structures

Traditionally, path models have been specified without attention to the means of the measured variables. Some research designs necessarily require the consideration of mean structures however, such as multigroup ANCOVA designs. Sörbom (1978, 1982) was the first to show how means could be analyzed for this purpose within SEM. Sörbom (1978) described an ANCOVA procedure in latent variables in an SEM context that permits adjustments for measurement error in the covariates and outcome variables in the ANCOVA. Another application of SEM that should include means is the study of factorial invariance in multiple populations (Meredith, 1964; Reise, Widaman, & Pugh, 1993; Millsap & Everson, 1991). The purpose of these studies is to evaluate whether the factor structure of a set of measured variables differs across groups, with groups often defined by demographic variables such as sex, age, or ethnicity. While one can study factorial invariance without including mean structures, the omission of the mean structure may lead the investigator to conclude falsely that the measured variables have an invariant factor structure when in fact group differences exist (Meredith, 1993). Once multiple groups are considered, it also becomes possible to study group differences in means on the latent variables. Most SEM software packages now permit mean structures to be included in the model.

Discrete Data

The development of SEM procedures has been almost wholly devoted to the analysis of continuous measures, at least with respect to the endogenous portion of the model. Real data are often discrete in nature, however. Questionnaire items usually have discrete response scales with only a few scale points. SEM analyses performed at the item level should be done using methods that account for the discrete scales (Muthén, 1984; Bartholomew, 1987). In some applications, we wish to predict a discrete outcome, such as the presence or absence of some condition, such as employee turnover. Ordinary linear path models for such variables are misspecified in general, and standard logistic regression procedures do not model the measurement error in the predictors. SEM procedures for discrete measures permit one to model the measurement error while recognizing the discrete nature of the endogenous variables (Muthén, 1984). Until recently, methods for the analysis of discrete data in the SEM context have not been fully incorporated in the available SEM software. This situation is changing, with some major software packages now including options for analyzing discretely measured variables.

What Software Programs Are Available for SEM?

Researchers now have many choices with regard to SEM software. The available software programs all have varying strengths and weaknesses, but for standard SEM applications, any of the following programs will perform efficiently and accurately. The list that follows is not exhaustive, and the comments on each program are quite general. Interested researchers should consult the individual Web sites for more information.

LISREL 8.30

The LISREL program is one of the oldest SEM software programs (Jöreskog & Sörbom, 1996a). The latest version of the program gives users a range of estimation options, permits both linear and nonlinear parameter constraints, sets interval restrictions on parameters, and analyzes models for multilevel data. LISREL will fit models to discrete or ordered-categorical data through the use of the PRELIS (Jöreskog & Sörbom, 1996b) program, which handles a variety of tasks involving raw data, including calculation of descriptive statistics, missing data handling, and calculation of polychoric correlations. The SIMPLIS (Jöreskog & Sörbom, 1993) command language is a simplified version of the LISREL command syntax that is easier for new users. A free student version of LISREL may be downloaded from the Web. Complete information about the LISREL program is available at www.ssicentral.com/lisrel/mainlis.htm.

EQS 5.4

The latest version of this program (Bentler, 1995) offers a comprehensive package for SEM analysis that includes data entry and data exploration tools, graphically interactive model building, data simulation capabilities, missing data imputation, and a large array of fit statistic and model diagnostic information. A strong feature of this program is the availability of robust fit statistics that work well under departures from normality. Complete information about EQS is available at www.mvsoft.com.

AMOS

This program (Arbuckle, 1997) has built a strong reputation for ease of use, especially for novice users. The program is graphically interactive, permitting users to specify and test models by drawing the path diagram. The program also offers full information ML methods for handling missing data. A bootstrap feature permits users to obtain bootstrap estimates of standard errors. The program does not offer methods for analyzing ordered-categorical data. Complete information about AMOS is available at www.smallwaters.com.

Mplus 1.04

The Mplus program (Muthén & Muthén, 1998), the newest program among those listed here, offers great flexibility in model specification, permitting users to analyze multilevel or complex sample data and both continuous and discrete data. One can test latent variable mixture models, conduct simulations, test latent class models, and handle data that are missing by design. In ordered-categorical data, the program offers new estimation methods that function properly in modest samples. Robust estimation methods are available also. Complete information about the Mplus program is available at www.StatModel.com.

Mx

The Mx program (Neale, Boker, Xie, & Maes, 1999) differs from all of the other programs listed here in being free: both the program and its manual can be downloaded from the Web. Mx is one of the most flexible SEM programs available. A graphical user interface allows users to specify and test models by drawing a path diagram, but users may also use the script syntax. Users can create new fitting functions for estimation. A variety of linear and nonlinear parameter constraints may be used. A knowledgeable user can specify and fit just about any model using Mx. Complete information about the Mx program is available at www.griffin.vcu.edu/mx.

Where Can I Learn More About SEM?

At one time, nearly all of the resource material on SEM was to be found in technical journals, and very little of this material was written for beginners. This situation has changed considerably. A number of books on SEM now are written at a level that readers with some background in statistics can follow. Books in this category that have been published since 1990 include Hoyle (1995), Kline (1998), Loehlin (1992), Maruyama (1998), Mueller (1996), Raykov and Marcoulides (2000), and Schumacker and Lomax (1996). Hayduk (1987) is older but is still useful. At a more advanced level are texts such as Bollen (1989), Bollen and Long (1993), Hayduk (1996), and Marcoulides and Schumacker (1996). Byrne has written several texts designed to familiarize readers with specific SEM software programs. Byrne (1994) explains EQS, and Byrne (1998) describes the LISREL/PRELIS/SIMPLIS system. A few texts now address individual topics within the broader field of SEM, such as interaction effects in SEM (Jaccard & Wan, 1996; Schumacker & Marcoulides, 1998) and latent growth modeling (Duncan et al., 1999).

In addition to books, a number of journals regularly publish articles on SEM. These articles vary widely in difficulty, depending on the journal and author. *Structural Equation Modeling* is devoted exclusively to SEM. This journal includes a regular feature known as the "Teacher's Corner," which presents didactic articles on special topics in SEM. Other journals that often publish articles on SEM, both theoretical and applied, include *Multivariate Behavioral Research, Psychological Methods, Applied Psychological Measurement, Sociological Methodology, British Journal of Mathematical and Statistical Psychology, Psychometrika,* and *Educational and Psychological Measurement.*

Individuals who are new to SEM and enjoy interactions within a listserv environment should subscribe to the SEMNET listserv, a forum for questions and answers, and occasional heated debates, about all aspects of SEM methods. Questions range from the most basic to the highly technical. A surprising number of major figures in the SEM field contribute to the discussions. Software developers for many of the major SEM software programs are also contributors. To find out more about SEMNET, go to www.gsu.edu/~mkteer/semfaq.html, a site maintained by Ed Rigdon, who is a major contributor.

Appendix: Sample LISREL Programs

LISREL programs for the three models fit to the example data are given below. Text within brackets is added explanation; it is not LISREL syntax.

Initial path model: three exogenous factors, four endogenous factors

DA ni = 21 no = 3694 ma = cm
cm
*
4.644
1.900 5.808
2.259 2.300 8.920
2.752 3.081 3.930 11.098
2.389 3.208 3.701 6.051 12.128
2.947 3.577 4.394 7.959 8.645 16.616
−0.499 −0.839 −2.039 −0.804 −0.841 −0.420 15.295
−0.292 −0.443 −1.056 −0.203 0.404 1.665 8.115 11.551
0.685 0.571 0.040 3.073 1.969 3.780 5.944 6.226 9.695
0.566 0.306 3.315 0.616 0.357 0.305 −2.798 −1.366 −1.611 20.597
−0.032 0.114 0.113 −0.185 −0.241 −1.310 −2.814 −2.662
−2.175 0.700 5.579
−0.074 −0.283 0.963 −0.559 −0.501 −1.089 −3.855 −2.902
−2.988 3.796 1.792
6.699
0.418 0.357 2.359 -0.083 0.509 0.183 −3.606 −2.286 −2.269
9.088 1.568 4.542
18.190
1.487 1.522 0.031 2.819 3.962 5.759 2.157 3.515 4.380 −6.431
−1.364 −3.422
−6.029 20.384
1.087 1.226——0.093 2.018 2.869 4.044 2.084 2.647 3.406 −5.027
−1.113 −2.791
−4.797 11.471 12.669
0.710 0.710 −1.00 1.514 2.055 3.122 3.127 3.027 3.608 −6.176
−1.306 −3.591
−6.586 11.985 9.351 14.710

-0.161 -0.498 -0.851 0.090 -0.271 -0.146 1.398 0.374 0.317
-2.151 -0.570 -1.250
-1.917 1.174 1.208 2.189 9.005
0.202 - 0.084 -0.466 0.685 0.677 0.990 0.732 0.545 0.752
-2.010 -0.590 -1.134
-1.468 2.567 2.268 2.565 6.180 9.531
0.027 -0.250 -0.727 0.108 0.127 0.140 1.005 0.351 0.419 -1.774
-0.523 -1.058
-1.690 1.828 1.749 2.479 5.990 6.038 8.286
0.114 0.112 -0.224 0.367 0.254 0.670 1.368 0.858 0.991 -1.539
-0.606 -0.934
-1.661 2.677 2.208 3.278 1.459 1.482 1.303 9.090
-0.340 -0.132 -1.688 -0.475 -0.143 0.078 2.984 1.280 1.437
-3.515 -0.590
-2.472 -3.837 4.032 3.851 6.168 3.855 3.519 3.542 6.914 25.415
la
chsm1 chsm2 chsm3 cism1 cism2 cism3 wdsm1 wdsm2 wdsm3
lsum absum
qsum trsum wsum1 wsum2 wsum3 psum1 psum2 psum3 phsum
esum
se
1 2 3 4 5 6 7 8 9 10 12 13 14 15 16 17 18 19 20 21 /
[The above line selects out one variable to be excluded from the
analysis.]
mo ny = 12 ne = 4 nx = 8 nk = 3 lx = fi,fu ly = fi,fu ga = fr,fu be =
fi,fu te = fi,sy c
td = fi,sy ps = fi,sy
lk
work pay jobperc
le
change citiz withdr cognit
fr lx 2 1 lx 3 1 lx 5 2 lx 6 2 lx 8 3
fr ly 2 1 ly 3 1 ly 5 2 ly 6 2 ly 8 3 ly 9 3 ly 11 4 ly 12 4
fi ga 1 2 ga 2 2 ga 1 3 ga 2 3 ga 3 3
fr be 4 3 be 1 2
fr td 1 1 td 2 2 td 3 3 td 4 4 td 5 5 td 6 6 td 7 7 td 8 8
fr te 1 1 te 2 2 te 3 3 te 4 4 te 5 5 te 6 6 te 7 7 te 8 8
fr te 9 9 te 10 10 te 11 11 te 12 12
fr ps 1 1 ps 2 2 ps 3 3 ps 4 4 ps 4 1 ps 3 2

va 1.0 ly 1 1 ly 4 2 ly 7 3 ly 10 4
va 1.0 lx 1 1 lx 4 2 lx 7 3
ou rs mi sc

Congeneric factor model with seven factors

DA ni = 21 no = 3694 ma = cm
cm
*
[Covariance matrix goes here.]
la
chsm1 chsm2 chsm3 cism1 cism2 cism3 wdsm1 wdsm2 wdsm3
lsum absum
qsum trsum wsum1 wsum2 wsum3 psum1 psum2 psum3 phsum
esum
se
1 2 3 4 5 6 7 8 9 10 12 13 14 15 16 17 18 19 20 21 /
mo nx = 20 nk = 7 lx = fi,fu td = fi,sy
lk
change citiz withdr cognit work pay jobperc
fr lx 2 1 lx 3 1 lx 5 2 lx 6 2
fr lx 8 3 lx 9 3 lx 11 4 lx 12 4 lx 14 5
fr lx 15 5 lx 17 6 lx 18 6 lx 20 7
fr td 1 1 td 2 2 td 3 3 td 4 4 td 5 5 td 6 6 td 7 7 td 8 8
fr td 9 9 td 10 10 td 11 11 td 12 12 td 13 13 td 14 14
fr td 15 15 td 16 16 td 17 17 td 18 18 td 19 19 td 20 20
va 1.0 lx 1 1 lx 4 2 lx 7 3 lx 10 4 lx 13 5 lx 16 6 lx 19 7
ou rs mi sc

Minimally constrained factor model with seven factors

DA ni = 21 no = 3694 ma = cm
cm
*
[Covariance matrix goes here.]
la
chsm1 chsm2 chsm3 cism1 cism2 cism3 wdsm1 wdsm2 wdsm3
lsum absum
qsum trsum wsum1 wsum2 wsum3 psum1 psum2 psum3 phsum

esum
se
1 2 3 4 5 6 7 8 9 10 12 13 14 15 16 17 18 19 20 21 /
mo nx = 20 nk = 7 lx = fr,fu td = fi,sy
lk
change citiz withdr cognit work pay jobperc
[The following *fi* lines impose constraints on seven rows of the factor loading matrix. These constraints serve to identify the factor model. In each of the selected rows, all but one element is fixed to zero, with the nonzero element fixed to one. See Millsap (2001) for a full explanation of these constraints.]
fi lx 1 1 lx 1 2 lx 1 3 lx 1 4 lx 1 5 lx 1 6 lx 1 7
fi lx 4 1 lx 4 2 lx 4 3 lx 4 4 lx 4 5 lx 4 6 lx 4 7
fi lx 7 1 lx 7 2 lx 7 3 lx 7 4 lx 7 5 lx 7 6 lx 7 7
fi lx 10 1 lx 10 2 lx 10 3 lx 10 4 lx 10 5 lx 10 6 lx 10 7
fi lx 13 1 lx 13 2 lx 13 3 lx 13 4 lx 13 5 lx 13 6 lx 13 7
fi lx 16 1 lx 16 2 lx 16 3 lx 16 4 lx 16 5 lx 16 6 lx 16 7
fi lx 19 1 lx 19 2 lx 19 3 lx 19 4 lx 19 5 lx 19 6 lx 19 7
fr td 1 1 td 2 2 td 3 3 td 4 4 td 5 5 td 6 6 td 7 7 td 8 8
fr td 9 9 td 10 10 td 11 11 td 12 12 td 13 13 td 14 14
fr td 15 15 td 16 16 td 17 17 td 18 18 td 19 19 td 20 20
va 1.0 lx 1 1 lx 4 2 lx 7 3 lx 10 4 lx 13 5 lx 16 6 lx 19 7
ou rs mi sc

References

Arbuckle, J. L. (1997). *AMOS user's guide.* Chicago: Smallwaters.

Bartholomew, D. J. (1987). *Latent variable models and factor analysis.* London: Charles Griffin.

Bentler, P. M. (1990). Comparative fit indexes in structural models. *Psychological Bulletin, 107,* 238–246.

Bentler, P. M. (1995). *EQS structural equations program manual.* Encino, CA: Multivariate Software.

Bentler, P. M., & Bonett, D. G. (1980). Significance tests and goodness of fit in the analysis of covariance structures. *Psychological Bulletin, 88,* 588–600.

Bollen, K. A. (1989). *Structural equations with latent variables.* New York: Wiley.

Bollen, K. A., & Long, J. S. (Eds.). (1993). *Testing structural equation models.* Thousand Oaks, CA: Sage.

Browne, M. W., & Cudeck, R. (1993). Alternative ways of assessing model fit. In K. A. Bollen & J. S. Long (Eds.), *Testing structural equation models* (pp. 136–162). Thousand Oaks, CA: Sage.

Burnham, K. P., & Anderson, D. R. (1998). *Model selection and inference: A practical information-theoretic approach.* New York: Springer-Verlag.

Byrne, B. M. (1994). *Structural equation modeling with EQS and EQS/Windows.* Thousand Oaks, CA: Sage.

Byrne, B. M. (1998). *Structural equation modeling with LISREL, PRELIS, and SIMPLIS.* Hillsdale, N.J.: Erlbaum.

Chan, D. (2001). Latent growth modeling. In F. Drasgow & N. Schmitt (Eds.), *Measuring and analyzing behavior in organizations.* San Francisco: Jossey-Bass.

Cliff, N. (1983). Some cautions concerning the application of causal modeling methods. *Multivariate Behavioral Research, 18,* 115–126.

D'Agostino, R. B. (1986). Tests for the normal distribution. In R. B. D'Agostino & M. A. Stephens (Eds.), *Goodness-of-fit techniques* (pp. 367–390). New York: Dekker.

Dempster, A. P. (1990). Causality and statistics. *Journal of Statistics Planning and Inference, 25,* 261–278.

Duncan, T. E., Duncan, S. C., Strycker, L. A., Li, F., & Alpert, A. (1999). *An introduction to latent variable growth curve modeling.* Hillsdale, NJ: Erlbaum.

Freedman, D. A. (1987). As others see us: A case study in path analysis. *Journal of Educational Statistics, 12,* 101–128.

Hayduk, L. A. (1987). *Structural equation modeling with LISREL.* Baltimore, MD: Johns Hopkins University Press.

Hayduk, L. A. (1996). *LISREL issues, debates, and strategies.* Baltimore, MD: Johns Hopkins University Press.

Holland, P. W. (1988). Causal inference, path analysis, and recursive structural equations models. In C. Clogg (Ed.), *Sociological methodology* (pp. 449–484). Washington, DC: American Sociological Association.

Hoyle, R. H. (Ed.). (1995). *Structural equation modeling: Concepts, issues, and applications.* Thousand Oaks, CA: Sage.

Hu, L., & Bentler, P. M. (1999). Cutoff criteria for fit indexes in covariance structure analysis: Conventional criteria versus new alternatives. *Structural Equation Modeling, 6,* 1–55.

Hulin, C. L., Roznowski, M., & Hachiya, D. (1985). Alternative opportunities and withdrawal decisions: Empirical and theoretical discrepancies and an integration. *Psychological Bulletin, 97,* 233–250.

Jaccard, J., & Wan, C. H. (1996). *LISREL approaches to interaction effects in multiple regression.* Thousand Oaks, CA: Sage.

Jöreskog, K. G. (1979). A general approach to confirmatory factor analysis with addendum. In K. G. Jöreskog, D. Sörbom, & J. Magidson (Eds.), *Advances in factor analysis and structural equation models* (pp. 21–43). New York: Abt Associates.

Jöreskog, K. G., & Sörbom, D. (1993). *LISREL 8: Structural equation modeling with the SIMPLIS command language.* Chicago,: Scientific Software International.

Jöreskog, K. G., & Sörbom, D. (1996a). *LISREL 8 User's reference guide.* Chicago: Scientific Software International.

Jöreskog, K. G., & Sörbom, D. (1996b). *PRELIS 2 user's reference guide.* Chicago: Scientific Software International.

Kline, R. B. (1998). *Principles and practice of structural equation modeling.* New York: Guilford Press.

Lance, C., & Vandenberg, R. (2001). Confirmatory factor analysis. In F. Drasgow & N. Schmitt (Eds.), *Measuring and analyzing behavior in organizations.* San Francisco: Jossey-Bass.

Lee, S., & Hershberger, S. (1990). A simple rule for generating equivalent models in covariance structure modeling. *Multivariate Behavioral Research, 25,* 313–334.

Little, R.J.A., & Rubin, D. B. (1987). *Statistical analysis with missing data.* New York: Wiley.

Loehlin, J. C. (1992). *Latent variable models.* Hillsdale, NJ: Erlbaum.

Longford, N. T., & Muthén, B. (1992). Factor analysis for clustered observations. *Psychometrika, 57,* 581–597.

MacCallum, R. C. (1986). Specification searches in covariance structure modeling. *Psychological Bulletin, 100,* 107–120.

MacCallum, R. C., Browne, M. W., & Sugawara, H. M. (1996). Power analysis and determination of sample sizes for covariance structure modeling. *Psychological Methods, 1,* 130–149.

MacCallum, R. C., Roznowski, M., & Necowitz, L. B. (1992). Model modifications in covariance structure analysis: The problem of capitalization on chance. *Psychological Bulletin, 111,* 490–504.

MacCallum, R. C., Wegener, D. T., Uchino, N., & Fabrigar, L. R. (1993). The problem of equivalent models in applications of covariance structure analysis. *Psychological Bulletin, 114,* 185–199.

MacCallum, R. C., Widaman, K. F., Zhang, S., & Hong, S. (1999). Sample size in factor analysis. *Psychological Methods, 4,* 84–99.

Marcoulides, G. A., & Schumacker, R. E. (1996). *Advanced structural equation modeling: Issues and techniques.* Hillsdale, NJ: Erlbaum.

Maruyama, G. M. (1998). *Basics of structural equation modeling.* Thousand Oaks, CA: Sage.

McArdle, J. J., & Epstein, D. (1987). Latent growth curves within developmental structural equation models. *Child Development, 58,* 110–133.

McDonald, R. P. (1997). Haldane's lungs: A case study in path analysis. *Multivariate Behavioral Research, 32,* 1–38.

McDonald, R. P., & Goldstein, H. (1989). Balanced versus unbalanced designs for linear structural relations in two-level data. *British Journal of Mathematical and Statistical Psychology, 42,* 215–232.

McDonald, R. P., & Marsh, H. W. (1990). Choosing a multivariate model: Noncentrality and goodness of fit. *Psychological Bulletin, 107,* 247–255.

Meredith, W. (1964). Notes on factorial invariance. *Psychometrika, 29,* 177–185.

Meredith, W. (1993). Measurement invariance, factor analysis, and factorial invariance. *Psychometrika, 58,* 525–543.

Meredith, W., & Tisak, J. (1990). Latent curve analysis. *Psychometrika, 55,* 107–122.

Millsap, R. E. (2001). When trivial constraints are not trivial: The choice of uniqueness constraints in confirmatory factor analysis. *Structural Equation Modeling, 8,* 1–17.

Millsap, R. E., & Everson, H. (1991). Confirmatory measurement model comparisons using latent means. *Multivariate Behavioral Research, 26,* 479–497.

Millsap, R. E., & Meredith, W. (1994). Statistical evidence in salary discrimination studies: Nonparametric inferential conditions. *Multivariate Behavioral Research, 29,* 339–364.

Mueller, R. O. (1996). *Basic principles of structural equation modeling.* New York: Springer.

Muthén, B. (1984). A general structural equation model with dichotomous, ordered categorical, and continuous latent variable indicators. *Psychometrika, 49,* 115–132.

Muthén, B. (1989). Latent variable modeling in heterogeneous populations. *Psychometrika, 54,* 557–585.

Muthén, B. (1994). Multilevel covariance structure analysis. In J. Hox & I. Kreft (Eds.), Multilevel modeling [Special issue]. *Sociological Methods and Research, 22,* 376–398.

Muthén, B., & Curran, P. (1997). General longitudinal modeling of individual differences in experimental designs: A latent variable framework for analysis and power estimation. *Psychological Methods, 2,* 371–402.

Muthén, L. K., & Muthén, B. (1998). *Mplus user's guide.* Los Angeles: Muthén & Muthén.

Muthén, B., & Satorra, A. (1995). Complex sample data in structural equation modeling. In P. V. Marsden (Ed.), *Sociological methodology* (pp. 267–316). Washington, DC: American Sociological Association.

Neale, M. C., Boker, S. M., Xie, G., & Maes, H. H. (1999). *Mx: Statistical modeling* (5th ed.). Richmond, VA: Medical College of Virginia.

Pearl, J. (2000). *Causality: Models, reasoning and inference.* Cambridge: Cambridge University Press.

Raykov, T., & Marcoulides, G. A. (2000). *A first course in structural equation modeling.* Hillsdale, NJ: Erlbaum.

Reise, S. P., Widaman, K. F., & Pugh, R. H. (1993). Confirmatory factor analysis and item response theory: Two approaches for exploring measurement invariance. *Psychological Bulletin, 114,* 552–566.

Roznowski, M. (1989). Examination of the measurement properties of the Job Descriptive Index with experimental items. *Journal of Applied Psychology, 74,* 805–814.

Saris, W. E., & Satorra, A. (1993). Power evaluations in structural equation models. In K. A. Bollen & J. S. Long (Eds.), *Testing structural equation models* (pp. 181–204). Thousand Oaks, CA: Sage.

Satorra, A., & Saris, W. E. (1985). The power of the likelihood ratio test in covariance structure analysis. *Psychometrika, 50,* 83–90.

Schafer, J. L. (1997). *Analysis of incomplete multivariate data.* New York: Chapman & Hall.

Scheines, R., Spirtes, P., Glymour, C., & Meek, C. (1994). *TETRAD II: User's manual.* Hillsdale, NJ: Erlbaum.

Scheines, R., Spirtes, P., Glymour, C., Meek, C., & Richardson, T. (1998). The TETRAD Project: Constraint based aids to causal model specification. *Multivariate Behavioral Research, 33,* 65–117.

Schumacker, R. E., & Lomax, R. G. (1996). *A beginner's guide to structural equation modeling.* Hillsdale, NJ: Erlbaum.

Schumacker, R. E., & Marcoulides, G. A. (Eds.). (1998). *Interaction and nonlinear effects in structural equation modeling.* Hillsdale, NJ: Erlbaum.

Shafer, G. (1996). *The art of causal conjecture.* Cambridge, MA: MIT Press.

Smith, P. C., Kendall, L. M., & Hulin, C. L. (1969). *The measurement of satisfaction in work and retirement.* Skokie, IL: Rand-McNally.

Sobel, M. E. (1995). Causal inference in the social and behavioral sciences. In G. Arminger, C. C. Clogg, & M. E. Sobel (Eds.), *Handbook of statistical modeling for the social and behavioral sciences* (pp. 1–38). New York: Plenum.

Sörbom, D. (1978). An alternative to the methodology for analysis of covariance. *Psychometrika, 43,* 381–396.

Sörbom, D. (1982). Structural equation models with structured means. In K. G. Jöreskog & H. Wald (Eds.), *Systems under indirect observation: Causality, structure, predictions.* Amsterdam: North-Holland.

Steiger, J. H., & Lind, A. (1980). *Statistically based tests for the number of common factors.* Paper presented at the annual meeting of the Psychometric Society, Iowa City.

Stetzl, I. (1986). Changing the causal hypothesis without changing the fit: Some rules for generating equivalent path models. *Multivariate Behavioral Research, 21,* 309–331.

Tisak, J., & Meredith, W. (1990). Descriptive and associative developmental models. In A. von Eye (Ed.), *Statistical methods in longitudinal research* (pp. 387–406). Orlando, FL: Academic Press.

West, S. G., Finch, J. F., & Curran, P. J. (1995). Structural equation models with non-normal variables: Problems and remedies. In R. H. Hoyle (Ed.), *Structural equation modeling* (pp. 56–75). Thousand Oaks, CA: Sage.

Williams, L. J., Bozdogan, H., & Aiman-Smith, L. (1996). Inference problems with equivalent models. In G. A. Marcoulides & R. E. Schumacker (Eds.), *Advanced structural equation modeling: Issues and techniques* (pp. 279–314). Hillsdale, NJ: Erlbaum.

Wothke, W. (1993). Nonpositive definite matrics in structural modeling. In K. A. Bollen & J. S. Long (Eds.), *Testing structural equation models* (pp. 256–293). Thousand Oaks, CA: Sage.

CHAPTER 10

Latent Growth Modeling

David Chan

Many research areas in industri al/organizational (I/O) psychol-ogy such as learning and skill acquisition (Kanfer & Ackerman, 1989), newcomer adaptation (Vandenberg & Self, 1993), and per-formance modeling (Hofmann, Jacobs, & Gerras, 1992) are con-cerned with the study of continuity, change, and processes that unfold in various ways over time. Although the research questions asked differ across these areas, a focus common across the investi-gations is the central issue of interindividual differences in patterns of intraindividual change over time. It is well established that many important questions concerning intraindividual change over time can be adequately addressed only by using longitudinal data col-lected from multiwave (three or more) study designs (for details, see Chan, 1998a). Unfortunately, many I/O researchers are often puzzled by the different ways to analyze longitudinal data. Without adequate analytical tools to turn data into empirical evidence and valid inferences, important research questions on change over time either remain questions or receive misleading answers.

Significant methodological advances in the past decade allow researchers to draw direct inferences from longitudinal data re-garding the various aspects of change over time, including their causes and correlates. In particular, a flexible data analysis method known as latent growth modeling (LGM) has been gaining atten-tion in the methodological literature. This technique, which is based on structural equation modeling, has been successfully ap-plied to address important substantive research questions in a variety of fields, including substance use (Duncan & Duncan, 1994), antisocial behavior (Stoolmiller, 1994), and development of social skills (Chan, Ramey, Ramey, & Schmitt, 2000), although application in substantive I/O research is only starting to emerge (Chan, 1998a, Chan & Schmitt, 2000).

This chapter provides a relatively nontechnical introduction of LGM as a unified data analysis method for modeling different aspects of change over time corresponding to various facets of the change phenomenon under investigation. (A more comprehensive treatment of the method, which includes integrating longitudinal mean and covariance structures analysis and multiple indicator latent growth modeling, is available in Chan, 1998a.)

The chapter is organized as follows. First, the LGM method is described and explained in detail. Next, a set of hypothetical data on newcomer adaptation is used to illustrate the application of the method. The value of the method in addressing different types of substantive research questions is then explicated using nine fundamental questions on change over time as the conceptual bases and organizing principles. Advantages, limitations, and advanced extensions of LGM are discussed.

The Method

Measurement Invariance
Across Time as Prerequisite for LGM

To assess patterns of intraindividual change over time, we require a longitudinal design in which data on the construct of interest are collected from the same sample of individuals at the same time repeatedly over a few time waves with either equal or unequal time intervals. Like many other longitudinal data analysis procedures, the application of LGM assumes that the same construct is being measured and that it is being measured with the same precision across time in the period under investigation. When this important assumption of measurement invariance (equivalence) across time is violated, interpretation of LGM results becomes problematic (Chan, 1998a). At best, it is difficult to make direct comparisons of measurements across time. At worst, it produces meaningless or misleading results on change trajectories when apples at one time point are being compared with oranges at another. Unfortunately, measurement invariance concerns have been neglected by prior work on LGM, and insofar as one can tell from the published reports of substantive studies, many researchers have failed to establish measurement invariance prior to application of LGM. Chan (1998a) provides technical details and a step-by-step description on how to perform measurement invariance assessments prior to LGM analyses. Because this chapter focuses on the LGM method, it will suffice here to state that measurement invariance over time should be established prior to fitting latent growth models because evidence of invariance allows meaningful direct interpretations of the change trajectories produced in LGM analyses. (For more details on issues of measurement invariance, see Chapter Six, this volume, and Vandenberg & Lance, 2000.)

The Technique of Latent Growth Modeling

After measurement invariance across time has been established, we can proceed to apply LGM analyses to the longitudinal data. This section describes the LGM method. To be consistent with the descriptions and notations that I have presented elsewhere, this section follows closely the description of LGM provided in Chan (1998a) and Chan and Schmitt (2000). More technical details of LGM are available in Chan (1998a), Meredith and Tisak (1990), Muthén (1991), Stoolmiller (1994), and Willett and Sayer (1994).

LGM provides a unified framework for modeling interindividual differences in the attributes (that is, parameters) of individual change trajectories (in other words, individual growth curves). For example, in a simple straight-line growth model, the two important attributes of the variable's change trajectory are the intercept and the slope. In a study of new incumbents on a job (perhaps one exploring newcomer adaptation), the intercept would correspond to the initial status of the variable: the value of the variable at the point of job entry. The slope corresponds to the rate of change in the variable: the rate of increase or decrease over the period under study (for example, from time 1 to time 4). The task in the LGM analysis is to identify an appropriate growth curve form that accurately and parsimoniously describes intraindividual change over time (at the aggregate level of analysis) and allows the examination of interindividual differences in the parameters (intercept and slope) that describe the pattern of intraindividual change over time (at the individual level of analysis). The LGM analysis can be used to estimate the means and variances of the two parameters and examine if the two parameters are correlated with each other. The LGM analysis can also be used to examine associations between the growth parameters and individual difference predictor variables. Different univariate latent growth models can also be combined to form a multivariate latent growth model. In a multivariate growth model, parameters from different change trajectories can be correlated to examine cross-domain associations. Hence, hypotheses concerning initial status and rate of change of different variables can be tested.

The model depicted in Figure 10.1 represents the basic form of a univariate latent growth model in which the two parameters, intercept and slope, describe a systematic pattern of individual differences in intraindividual change over time. The figure shows the model for a focal variable (such as feedback seeking) measured at four points in time (Y1, Y2, Y3, Y4) equally spaced at, say, one-month

Figure 10.1. Representation of a Basic Latent Growth Model.

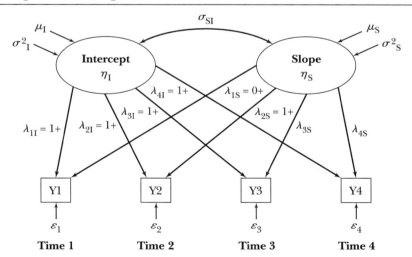

intervals. Using LISREL notation, the first growth factor, labeled Intercept, η_I, is a constant for any given individual across time; hence, the fixed values of 1.0 for factor loadings (λ_{1I} to λ_{4I}) on the repeated measures. The intercept factor (sometimes called the Initial Status factor) represents information about the mean, μ_I, and variance, σ^2_I, of the collection of individual intercepts of each individual's growth curve. The second growth factor, labeled Slope (sometimes called the Change factor), η_S, represents information about the mean, μ_S, and variance, σ^2_S, of the collection of individual slopes of each individual's growth curve. Both growth factors, which are estimated from the data, are allowed to covary (estimated as σ_{SI}) as indicated by the double-headed curved arrow between the factors. This allows the researcher to model any intercept-slope covariance that may occur due to statistical artifacts (such as ceiling or floor effects) or some substantive reason. The ε's represent error variances in the repeated measures. Provided the model is identified, the error variances can be either freely estimated or fixed at certain values. They can also be constrained to be equal across repeated measurements. Similarly, any of the six error covariances can be either freely estimated or fixed at certain values including zero, thus allowing a variety of a priori error covariance structures to be modeled, including heteroscedasticity and different forms of correlated errors.

The scaling of the slope can be controlled by the choice of the slope factor loadings, λ_{1S} to λ_{4S} (these loadings are basis coefficients, see Chan, 1998a). Changing the slope factor loadings simply rescales the slope factor mean and variance by constants; it does not change the fundamental meaning or affect the significance tests of the slope parameters. However, the intercept factor is inextricably bound to the timescale. Changing the slope factor loadings alters the timescale and in turn affects the meaning and interpretation of the intercept factor mean and variance. Because we want the intercept factor to represent initial status assessed at time 1, the intercept should be located at Y1. Meredith and Tisak (1990) have shown that at least two slope factor loadings must be fixed to two different values to identify the model. By fixing the slope factor loading of Y1 and Y2 to 0 and 1, respectively, the intercept will be located at Y1. The remaining two (if there are four time points, three if there are five time points, and so on) slope factor loadings can either be freely estimated or fixed to specific values. Freely estimating the remaining two loadings amounts to modeling unspecified trajectories where the shape of the trajectory is allowed to be determined by data (such a model is referred to as the *unspecified two-factor model;* in such a model, the slope factor is better interpreted as a general shape factor). If the model fits well, the fitted means plotted against the observed time metric give a visual representation of the nature or shape of the change trajectory. Model fit is assessed using the various fit indexes in structural equation modeling. Note that freely estimating factor loadings beyond those required for model identification results in a form of growth function with maximal fit to the data. But more parsimonious functional forms may also provide a good model fit. For example, a trajectory in the form of a linear change can be hypothesized by fitting a model that specified the slope factor loadings to be 0, 1, 2, and 3, for Y1, Y2, Y3, and Y4, respectively. Because this linear factor model is nested within the unspecified two-factor model, the two models can be compared for incremental fit using the chi-square difference test for nested model comparisons in structural equation modeling.

In the unspecified two-factor model, the slope factor is more accurately a slope-shape factor in which information about the slope (the general linear trend) and the shape of the growth curve are confounded. This is because the model represents the data using a curve that is a linear spline (Meredith & Tisak, 1990), which is a piecewise curve consisting of successive straight-line pieces that do not necessarily fall on the same overall straight line (Stoolmiller, 1995). To disconfound slope and shape, more than two factors need to be specified in the model, with each factor representing a specific growth parameter. For example, in a quadratic trajectory model, one can specify a model with three factors representing the intercept, linear, and quadratic terms, respectively (Willett & Sayer, 1994).

Although the maximally fitting unspecified two-factor model could serve as a starting point from which more specific form of trajectories are tested, the model is exploratory and atheoretical with respect to functional form. Theories of change would imply fitting specified trajectory forms to the data. A specified trajectory model corresponding to the hypothesized pattern of change is obtained by fixing the slope factor loadings accordingly. For example,

if the time intervals are equal, then to fit a trajectory corresponding to a linear change, we simply fit a model that specified the
slope factor loadings to be 0, 1, 2, 3. If the time intervals are unequal, then a linear trajectory can be obtained by respecifying the
slope factor loadings accordingly. For example, if the last time interval is twice the length of each of the preceding intervals, the
slope loadings will be fixed at 0, 1, 2, 4 to represent a linear trajectory. Curvilinear trajectories can be specified in an LGM by
adding factors corresponding to the higher-order nonlinear terms,
thus disconfounding slope and shape of the trajectory. For example, a quadratic trajectory model can be specified by adding to the
linear trajectory model a third factor corresponding to the quadratic term. The factor loadings on this third factor are obtained
by squaring the loadings (0, 1, 2, 3) for the linear (that is, slope)
factor, fixing the quadratic factor loadings to (0, 1, 4, 9). Figure
10.2 presents such a quadratic trajectory model. Note that adding

**Figure 10.2. Representation of a Basic
Quadratic Trajectory Latent Growth Model.**

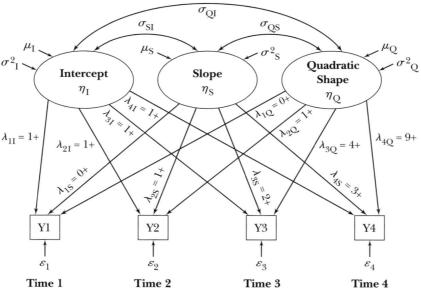

a quadratic factor to a linear trajectory model increases the number of estimated parameters by four (quadratic factor mean, μ_Q; quadratic factor variance, σ^2_Q; intercept-quadratic factor covariance, σ_{QI}; and slope-quadratic factor covariance, σ_{QS}).

The basic latent growth model in Figure 10.1 can be respecified to include time-invariant individual predictors of change. The respecified model is similar to the basic model except that it also estimates the effects of individual predictors on the intercept and slope (and shape in the case of curvilinear models) factors. The individual predictor can be specified as a manifest variable, a latent factor assessed by multiple indicators, or a latent factor assessed by a single indicator with error variance fixed using the reliability estimate of the indicator, using the following formula: error variance = (1 minus reliability) times observed variance). Figure 10.3 depicts an example of a respecification of the basic model in Figure 10.1. In this respecified model, the time-invariant individual predictor is represented as an exogenous factor, ξ_P (for example, Neuroticism, ξ_P), assessed by three indicators (say, P1, P2, P3). The intercept and slope factors are now represented as endogenous factors. The structural effects (γ's) from the latent predictor to the latent growth factors (intercept and slope) are freely estimated. Thus, the respecified model allows tests of hypotheses about associations between individual predictors (note that more than one predictor can be included in the model) and individual differences in initial status (intercept) and rate of change (slope).

The models depicted in Figures 10.1 to 10.3 are univariate latent growth models. Multivariate latent growth models can be fitted by simply combining two or more univariate models, thereby allowing the estimation of covariances between intercept, slope, or shape factors from different focal variables and structural effects from the same individual predictors to these factors. Hence, hypotheses about cross-domain (that is, multivariate) relationships between attributes of change trajectories and differential predictions of these attributes across domains can be tested. For example, in a newcomer adaptation study by Chan and Schmitt (2000), the cross-domain relationship specifying a positive association between rate of increase in task mastery and rate of decrease in information seeking was evaluated by assessing the latent correlation between the slope factor for task mastery and the slope factor for

Figure 10.3. Representation of a Linear Trajectory Latent Growth Model with Latent Individual Predictor.

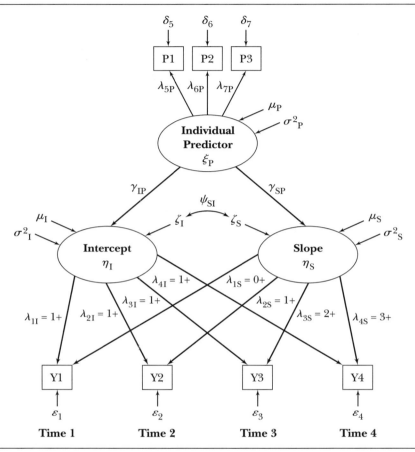

Note: σ^2_I and σ^2_S are unconditional variances that are not an explicit part of the LGM model that includes predictors but they are output by LISREL 8 as part of the default covariance matrix of eta and ksi. The predictor may also be represented as a manifest variable or a single-indicator latent variable with indicator error variance fixed using the formula: (1 minus indicator reliability) times indicator variance.

information seeking. Finally, latent growth models (univariate or multivariate) can be fitted simultaneously to different groups of individuals; hence, multiple-group LGM analyses can be performed to test between-groups invariance or difference of one or more of the specified relationships in the latent growth model.

Latent growth models can be run using most popular structural equation modeling programs such as AMOS 3.6 (Arbuckle, 1997), EQS 5 (Bentler, 1995), and LISREL 8 (Jöreskog & Sörbom, 1993). These programs provide fit indexes to assess model fit to the data. Popular indexes include Jöreskog and Sörbom's (1989) adjusted-goodness-of-fit index (AGFI), Bentler and Bonett's (1980) non-normed fit index (NNFI), Bentler's (1990) comparative fit index (CFI), Jöreskog and Sörbom's (1986) standardized root mean square residual (SRMR), and Steiger's (1990) root mean square error of approximation (RMSEA). For values of AGFI, NNFI, and CFI, the convention of close to or above .90 is typically adopted as an indication of good fit, although Hu and Bentler (1998) recommended .95 as the cutoff. SRMR values above .10 and RMSEA values above .08 are typically taken to indicate poor fit (see Browne & Cudeck, 1993). Following the current widely accepted practice in structural equation modeling, multiple fit indexes should be used in evaluating each model to provide convergent validity evidence in model fit assessment. The chi-square difference test can be used to assess statistical significance of incremental fit in nested model comparisons.

Instructive Example

LGM provides a flexible and unified analytical framework for assessing distinct aspects of intraindividual change over time. This section provides an instructive example to illustrate the application of LGM to obtain empirical answers to substantive research questions on change over time. The example is adapted from the illustrative longitudinal study and hypothetical data set that I presented in Chan (1998a).

Consider a study in which the researcher is interested in the growth trajectories (change patterns over time) of newcomers' feedback seeking and job involvement during the first few months on the job. The researcher hypothesizes (on the basis of some theory of behavior or just an educated guess) that intraindividual changes in both feedback seeking and job involvement would follow a linear trajectory, with levels on each variable increasing at a constant rate (that is, a positive slope). The researcher believes that there are systematic interindividual differences in initial status (intercept at time 1) and in the rate of change (slope) that can be partly accounted for by newcomers' levels of Neuroticism. Specifically, it is hypothesized that Neuroticism positively predicts initial status of feedback seeking, as well as job involvement. Accordingly, individuals high on Neuroticism who are starting a new job worry more and hence seek more feedback and involve themselves more in the job. In addition, the researcher believes that Neuroticism would predict rate of change in feedback seeking in a negative direction. The argument here is that individuals high on Neuroticism worry constantly and therefore maintain relatively constant levels (that is, a more gradual slope) of feedback seeking over time, whereas individuals low on Neuroticism seek more feedback over time (a steeper slope) as they focus more attention on the job. Because Neuroticism positively predicts initial status but negatively predicts rate of change in feedback seeking, initial status is expected to be negatively associated with rate of change, but the researcher wonders whether this negative association may also be due to variables other than Neuroticism.

No formal hypothesis concerning the prediction of rate of change in job involvement is formulated. The researcher wants to examine if the hypothesized relationships hold for both male and female newcomers. Finally, the researcher wants to explore cross-domain (feedback seeking–job involvement) relationships between growth factors and whether Neuroticism would account for some of these relationships.

To test these hypotheses, the researcher conducted a longitudinal panel study in which six hundred newcomers (three hundred males, three hundred females) on a job were repeatedly assessed on feedback seeking and job involvement on four measurement occasions equally spaced at one-month intervals beginning from the end of the first month on the job (Time 1). At Time 1, a personality measure was administered to assess the time-invariant construct of Neuroticism.

Tables 10.1 and 10.2 present the hypothetical means, standard deviations, and correlations of the study variables for males and females, respectively. For simplicity, we will assume that the Neuroticism measure has a reliability of .80, which was used to fix the value of the error variance of the single-indicator measure of the Neuroticism construct. Assuming that measurement invariance across time and gender groups has been established,[1] I will use the data in Table 10.1 to demonstrate single-group LGM analyses (feedback seeking to demonstrate univariate models; feedback seeking and job involvement to demonstrate multivariate models) and the data presented in both Tables 10.1 and 10.2 to demonstrate multiple-group (between-gender groups) LGM analyses. The means, standard deviations, and correlations of the measures analyzed serve as data input to the LISREL 8 program, which was used to run all LGM analyses reported here. LISREL program specifications for the relevant models are presented in the chapter appendix.

Single-Group Univariate LGM Analyses

The first step in the LGM analysis was to obtain a basic growth model that adequately and parsimoniously describes the form of intraindividual change over time and individual differences in the intraindividual change. Next, the growth model was respecified to include the time-invariant Neuroticism variable to examine predictions of these individual differences in growth parameters. For all models, error variances for measures were freely estimated, and error covariances were fixed at zero; that is, all models specified heteroscedasticity and independence of errors in the repeated measures.[2] The intercept factor loadings on the repeated measures were always fixed at 1, indicating that the intercept factor is a constant for any given individual across time.

Table 10.3 summarizes the univariate growth models fitted to the male feedback seeking data in Table 10.1. The first three models (Models G1, G2, G3) in the table were fitted to establish an adequate and parsimonious basic growth model. The first model is nested under the second, and both are nested under the third. Hence, difference in model fit can be directly assessed using the chi-square difference test. Model G1 is a "strict stability" (Stoolmiller, 1994) or "no-growth" model, which specified only a single factor

Table 10.1. Hypothetical Data Set for Males: Means, Standard Deviations, and Correlations for Feedback Seeking, Job Involvement, and Neuroticism ($n = 300$).

| | Feedback Seeking | | | | Job Involvement | | | | Neuroticism |
| | Time 1 | Time 2 | Time 3 | Time 4 | Time 1 | Time 2 | Time 3 | Time 4 | Time Invariant |
	FY1	FY2	FY3	FY4	JY1	JY2	JY3	JY4	P1
FY1	1.00								
FY2	.63	1.00							
FY3	.55	.60	1.00						
FY4	.40	.50	.62	1.00					
JY1	.51	.25	.26	.19	1.00				
JY2	.22	.24	.22	.20	.42	1.00			
JY3	.19	.23	.20	.25	.35	.38	1.00		
JY4	.19	.20	.23	.18	.19	.32	.41	1.00	
P1	.40	.40	.33	.20	.50	.45	.40	.42	1.00
M	15.00	16.50	18.20	19.70	17.00	19.05	20.80	23.00	13.02
SD	.91	.96	1.02	1.04	2.05	2.50	2.90	3.50	2.12

Table 10.2. Hypothetical Data Set for Females: Means, Standard Deviations, and Correlations for Feedback Seeking, Job Involvement, and Neuroticism ($n = 300$).

	Feedback Seeking				Job Involvement				Neuroticism Time Invariant
	Time 1	Time 2	Time 3	Time 4	Time 1	Time 2	Time 3	Time 4	Time Invariant
	FY1	FY2	FY3	FY4	JY1	JY2	JY3	JY4	P1
FY1	1.00								
FY2	.61	1.00							
FY3	.56	.61	1.00						
FY4	.41	.51	.61	1.00					
JY1	.50	.23	.25	.19	1.00				
JY2	.23	.25	.22	.21	.41	1.00			
JY3	.19	.22	.21	.26	.36	.37	1.00		
JY4	.18	.21	.22	.19	.20	.32	.40	1.00	
P1	.40	.41	.31	.21	.51	.44	.40	.41	1.00
M	16.03	17.50	19.10	20.70	17.20	19.10	20.90	23.10	13.10
SD	.90	.95	1.01	1.05	2.07	2.60	3.00	3.50	2.10

Table 10.3. Model Fit Indices and Nested Model Comparisons in LGM Analyses of Male Feedback Seeking ($n = 300$).

Model Specification	χ^2	df	Model Comparison	$\Delta\chi^2$	Δdf	NNFI	CFI	RMSEA
Model G1 (no growth)	1,913.80*	8				.70	.61	.89
Model G2 (positive linear growth)	9.42	5	G1 vs. G2	−1,904.38*	3	.99	.99	.05
Model G3 (positively accelerated quadratic growth)	6.71	1	G2 vs. G3	−2.71	4	.93	.99	.14
Model G4 (positive linear growth with Neuroticism as predictor)	12.95*	7				.98	.99	.05

*$p < .05$.

representing the intercept with no slope or growth factors. This model was rejected, NNFI = .70, CFI = .61, RMSEA = .89, indicating that some form of growth models may be appropriate. Next, a linear growth trajectory model, Model G2, was fitted to the data. To specify a linear growth trajectory, the slope factor loadings were fixed at 0, 1, 2, and 3 for the feedback seeking measures at Times 1, 2, 3, and 4, respectively. Model G2, which is consistent with our imaginary researcher's hypothesis, provided a good fit to the data and a clearly significant increase in fit over the no-growth model (Model G1), $\Delta \chi^2 = 1,904.38$, $\Delta df = 3$, $p < .05$. Inspection of the LISREL estimates associated with Model G2 revealed that all estimates were significantly different from zero, $p < .05$. The intercept mean showed that on average, males began feedback seeking at Time 1 with an initial status on the latent factor of 14.99. The positive slope mean showed that on average, males increased feedback seeking at a constant rate of 1.57 latent unit per month over the four-month period of study. The significant intercept variance (.64) and slope variance (.07) indicated true individual differences in the initial status of and rate of increase in feedback seeking, respectively. The significant and negative intercept-slope covariance (unstandardized = $-.08$; standardized (that is, correlation) = $-.38$) confirmed the researcher's expectation that initial status of feedback seeking is negatively associated with its rate of increase.

Before proceeding to respecify Model G2 to include the individual predictor (Neuroticism), growth models specifying more complex trajectory forms can be evaluated to determine if they provide significant incremental fit over a linear growth trajectory model. Of course, in practice, most researchers might not proceed to test more complex models if the (simpler) hypothesized model fit the data. But for the purpose of illustration, a quadratic trajectory model specifying a quadratic shape growth parameter in addition to the intercept and slope growth parameters was fitted to the data. The quadratic shape growth parameter was represented by a factor with associated loadings fixed at 0, 1, 4, and 9 for the feedback-seeking measures at Times 1, 2, 3, and 4, respectively. The linear trajectory model is nested under the quadratic trajectory model because the former can be obtained by fixing four specific parameters in the latter to zero: quadratic factor mean and variance, quadratic-intercept factor covariance, and quadratic-slope factor covariance. As shown in Table 10.3, this quadratic trajectory model, Model G3, did not provide a significant increase in fit over the linear trajectory model, $\Delta_\chi = 2.71$, $\Delta df = 4$, $p > .05$. Hence, the more parsimonious linear trajectory model was preferred over the quadratic trajectory model. Note that for any pair of nested models, the more complex (less constrained) model will always fit better than the less complex model (according to the two-model chi-square values). Therefore, it is important that selection of the most adequate growth model be determined on the basis of both theoretical and statistical grounds.

To evaluate the researcher's hypothesis that Neuroticism could help account for individual differences in intraindividual change, the linear trajectory model was respecified to include as a predictor a Neuroticism factor assessed by a single indicator (assuming an indicator reliability of .80 and fixing the indicator error variance using the formula: error variance = (1 minus reliability) times observed variance). Neuroticism was specified as an exogenous latent variable with direct effects on the intercept and slope factors now specified as endogenous latent variables. (The complete LISREL specifications for estimating this model are presented in the chapter appendix.) As shown in Table 10.3, this respecified linear trajectory model (Model G4) provided a good fit to the data. Figure 10.4 presents the associated unstandardized and standardized LISREL estimates. As shown in the figure, Neuroticism has significant direct effects on the intercept and slope factors, and the directions are consistent with the researcher's hypotheses. Neuroticism is positively associated with feedback seeking at initial status, as indicated by the direct effect (unstandardized $\gamma_{IP} = .23$; standardized $\gamma_{IP} = .55$, $p < .05$), but negatively associated with rate of change in feedback seeking (unstandardized $\gamma_{SP} = -.03$; standardized $\gamma_{SP} = -.21$, $p < .05$). That is, Neuroticism predicted interindividual differences in intraindividual changes in feedback seeking in a pattern consistent with the hypothesized relationships as described earlier in the hypothetical study. A pseudo-R^2 statistic can be computed to provide an estimate of the proportion of variance of a growth factor accounted for by the predictor (Willett & Sayer, 1994). This statistic is obtained by comparing the residual variances, ζ_I, ζ_S, which are partial variances controlling for the linear effects of the predictor, with the corresponding unconditional

Figure 10.4. LGM Model (Model G4 in Table 10.3) for Male Feedback Seeking (with Neuroticism as Predictor) with Associated Unstandardized LISREL Estimates.

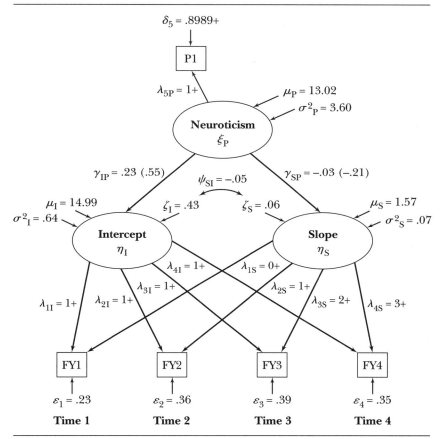

Note: All parameter estimates are significant at $p = .05$. A parameter value with a plus sign indicates that the parameter is fixed at that value. Values in parentheses are completely standardized direct structural effects. σ^2_I and σ^2_S are unconditional variances that are not an explicit part of this LGM model (because the model includes a predictor) but they are output by LISREL 8 as part of the default covariance matrix of eta and ksi.

variances, σ^2_I, σ^2_S, using the formula $R^2 = (\sigma^2 - \zeta)/\sigma^2$. The comparisons showed that the inclusion of the Neuroticism in the growth model reduced the unexplained variance in the intercept and slope by 33 percent $(.64 - .43)/.64)$ and 14 percent $(.07 - .06)/.07)$, respectively. This may be interpreted as Neuroticism having moderate and small importance in the prediction of interindividual differences in feedback-seeking initial status and rate of change, respectively. There remained a significant negative association between feedback-seeking initial status and rate of change, unstandardized ψ_{SI} (factor error covariance) $= -.05$, standardized ψ_{SI} (factor error correlation) $= -.24$, $p < .05$, even after their respective associations with Neuroticism were taken into account. Perhaps the researcher could account for this negative association between initial status and rate of change by including additional individual predictors in the growth model. Using the formula: $R^2 = (\sigma_{SI} - \psi_{SI})/\sigma_{SI}$, Neuroticism was found to account for 37 percent of the intercept-slope covariance (there remained 63 percent of the intercept-slope covariance to be accounted for). In other words, after including Neuroticism as the common cause to account for the correlation between feedback-seeking initial status and rate of change, the correlation dropped by a magnitude of .14, from $-.38$ to $-.24$. The researcher might consider including additional individual predictors in the growth model to explain the remaining correlation $(-.24)$.

Multiple-Group Univariate LGM Analyses

Recall that the researcher wanted to know whether the various hypothesized relationships hold for both gender groups. Multiple-group LGM analyses were performed to assess between-gender group similarities and differences in intraindividual change. I will use the male and female feedback-seeking data (see Tables 10.1 and 10.2) to illustrate multiple-group univariate LGM analyses, although the procedure can be directly extended to assess multiple-group multivariate (gender similarities and differences in feedback seeking-job involvement relationships) LGM analyses.

To assess if the change patterns in feedback seeking specified in the LGM model depicted in Figure 10.4 apply equally to males and females, a multiple-group univariate LGM analysis was performed in which multiple-group growth models were fitted simultaneously to the male and female feedback-seeking and Neuroticism data presented in Tables 10.1 and 10.2. The basic logic of the analysis is identical to the multiple-group structural equation modeling assessment (presumably familiar to many readers of this chapter; for introduction, see Jöreskog & Sörbom, 1993, or Kline, 1998), in that a hierarchy of nested models with increasing restrictive between-group constraints on model parameters is specified and fitted to the data to test for invariance of relationships corresponding to relevant parameters.

Because the example assumed that measurement invariance has been established across gender groups, the error variances for the measures within each gender group were freely estimated but constrained to be equal across groups. All error covariances were fixed at zero. That is, all multiple-group growth models fitted here specified heteroscedasticity and independence of errors in the repeated measures within gender groups and homoscedasticity of errors across groups.[3]

Prior to fitting any multiple-group LGMs, single-group LGM analyses similar to those already described for males were performed for females. In the interest of space, the detailed results for the female data are not reported here. It suffices to state that the final growth model obtained for females was also a model specifying a linear growth trajectory with interindividual differences in the growth parameters representing initial status (intercept) and rate of change (slope) in feedback seeking that are systematically associated with Neuroticism. Hence, linear growth trajectories were specified for both males and females in all multiple-group growth models reported.

For all multiple-group growth models, the intercept, slope, and Neuroticism factor means in the male group were fixed using the associated parameter values obtained from the earlier single-group growth model that adequately described males (Model G4 in Table 10.3). Fixing these factor means in the male group was necessary for model identification purposes. The female means for the intercept and slope factors were either freely estimated or fixed to be equal to the corresponding male values depending on the specific multiple-group growth model. The male-female difference in factor (latent) means directly represented the magnitude of gender difference in mean for each of the two growth factors. The intercept and slope factor variances and the direct structural effects from Neuroticism to intercept and slope were freely estimated or constrained to be equal and estimated across gender groups depending on the specific multiple-group growth model. For all models, the error covariance between the intercept and slope factors was freely estimated for each gender group. This was to allow between-gender group comparison of the magnitude of association between initial status of and rate of change in feedback seeking that remained after their respective associations with Neuroticism were taken into account.

Table 10.4 summarizes the multiple-group growth model fitted to the male and female observed mean vectors and covariance matrices on feedback seeking and Neuroticism.[4] The purpose of fitting the first three models reported in the table was to examine gender differences in intraindividual change at the group level. First, an unconstrained model, Model M1, which freely estimated the intercept and slope factor means in the female group and freely estimated across gender groups the intercept and slope factor variances, intercept-slope factor covariance, and direct structural effects from Neuroticism to intercept and slope was fitted to the data. Model M1 provided a good fit (NNFI = .99, CFI = .99, RMSEA = .02), indicating that intraindividual change in both gender groups was well represented by the same basic functional form (linear) of growth trajectory with the individual predictor (Neuroticism). Next, a second and more constrained model, Model M2, which had the same model specifications as the first model except that the female intercept mean was fixed as equal to the male intercept mean, was fitted to the data. This more constrained model is nested under the first model, and the difference in model fit was significant, $\Delta_\chi^2 = 7.16$, $df = 1$, $p < .05$. The significant reduction in fit from Model M1 to Model M2 is taken as evidence of gender difference in feedback seeking at initial status (i.e., intercept mean). Hence, subsequent models reported in Table 10.4 freely estimated the female intercept mean. The third model shown in the table, Model M3, had the same model specifications as Model M1 except that the female slope mean was fixed as equal to the male slope mean. This model did not result in a significant decrease in model fit from Model M1, $\Delta_\chi^2 = .04$, $\Delta df = 1$, $p > .05$, providing evidence of equality of rate of change in feedback seeking across gender groups. On the basis of parsimony, Model M3 was preferred over Model M1.

The remaining three models reported in Table 10.4 were fitted to the data for the purpose of examining gender differences in interindividual differences in intraindividual change. Model M4 was identical to Model M3, except that the intercept variance was constrained to be equal and estimated across gender groups. This model did not result in a significant decrease in model fit from Model M3, $\Delta_\chi^2 = .12$, $\Delta df = 1$, $p > .05$, providing evidence of equality of individual differences in feedback seeking at initial status across gender groups. Next, Model M5, which was identical to Model M4 except that the slope variance was constrained to be equal and estimated across gender groups, was fit to the data. Model M5 did not result in a significant decrease in model fit from Model M4, $\Delta_\chi^2 = .05$, $\Delta df = 1$, $p > .05$, providing evidence of equality of individual differences in rate of change in feedback seeking across gender groups. Finally, Model M6, which was identical to Model M5 except that the structural effects from Neuroticism to the intercept and slope factors were constrained to be equal and estimated across gender groups, was fitted to the data. Model M6 did not result in a significant decrease in model fit from Model M5, $\Delta_\chi^2 = .43$, $\Delta df = 2$, $p > .05$, providing evidence that the validity of predicting individual differences in initial status of and rate of change in feedback seeking on the basis of individual differences in Neuroticism is invariant across gender groups.

On the basis of parsimony and model fit, Model M6 was selected as the most adequate model for describing intraindividual change in the two gender groups. Results of the series of nested model comparisons reported in Table 10.4 and inspection of the LISREL estimates in Model M6 (all parameter estimates in each gender group were significantly different from zero, $p < .05$) showed that the researcher's hypothesized patterns of intraindividual change were invariant across gender groups. Although females, at initial status, reported significantly higher feedback seeking (intercept mean = 15.98) than males (intercept mean = 14.99), both gender groups shared the same basic form of intraindividual change over time (a positive linear trajectory) with the same rate of increase in feedback seeking (slope mean = 1.57) over the period of study. In addition, patterns of interindividual

Table 10.4. Model Fit Indices and Nested Model Comparisons in Multiple-Group LGM Analyses of Feedback Seeking (300 Males, 300 Females).

Model Specification	χ^2	df	Model Comparison	$\Delta\chi^2$	Δdf	NNFI	CFI	RMSEA
Model M1 Free intercept mean and slope mean in female group Free intercept variance, slope variance, and structural effects across groups	24.54	20				.99	.99	.02
Model M2 Free slope mean in female group Equal intercept mean across groups Free intercept variance, slope variance, and structural effects across groups	31.70	21	M1 vs. M2	7.16*	1	.99	.99	.03
Model M3 Free intercept mean in female group Equal slope mean across groups Free intercept variance, slope variance, and structural effects across groups	24.58	21	M1 vs. M3	.04	1	.99	.99	.02

Model	Description	χ^2	df	Comparison	p	Δdf			
Model M4	Free intercept mean in female group	24.70	22	M3 vs. M4	.12	1	.99	.99	.01
	Equal slope mean and intercept variance across groups								
	Free slope variance and structural effects across groups								
Model M5	Free intercept mean in female group	24.75	23	M4 vs. M5	.05	1	.99	.99	.01
	Equal slope mean, intercept variance, and slope variance across groups								
	Free structural effects across groups								
Model M6	Free intercept mean in female group	25.18	25	M5 vs. M6	.43	2	.99	.99	.01
	Equal slope mean, intercept variance, slope variance, and structural effects across groups								

Note: Model M6 was selected as the most adequate multiple-group LGM model.

*$p < .05$.

differences in intraindividual change were invariant across gender groups. The extent of interindividual differences in initial status of and rate of change in feedback seeking were equal across gender groups (see Model M3 versus Model M4 and Model M4 versus Model M5 in Table 10.4). Consistent with the researcher's hypotheses, Model M6 showed that for both gender groups, Neuroticism was positively associated with initial status of feedback seeking but negatively associated with rate of change. Neuroticism predicted initial status and rate of change with equal validity across groups (see Model M5 versus Model M6 in Table 10.4). The intercept-slope error covariance was negative and virtually identical across gender groups (male = $-.0381$, SE = $.0173$; female = $-.0354$, SE = $.0174$), indicating that the negative association between initial status of and rate of change in feedback seeking that remained after their respective associations with Neuroticism were taken into account was equal in magnitude across gender groups. In sum, the multiple-group LGM analyses provided evidence that the researcher's hypothesized patterns of intraindividual change were invariant across gender groups.

Single-Group Multivariate (Cross-Domain) LGM Analyses

I will use the complete data from the male group reported in Table 10.1 to demonstrate the assessment of cross-domain relationships using multivariate LGM analyses. Many questions of substantive interest concern cross-domain relationships. For example, the question on whether one can predict newcomers' rate of change in feedback seeking from their rate of change in job involvement is a cross-domain relationship question that requires multivariate LGM analyses.

Cross-domain relationships in intraindividual changes are represented and evaluated using multivariate growth models, which are essentially straightforward combinations of univariate growth models. Prior to fitting multivariate LGMs, univariate LGM analyses should be performed to ensure that intraindividual changes are adequately captured within each domain. Although the nature of the functional form of a univariate trajectory can be tested within a multivariate LGM, it is almost always advisable to perform univariate LGM analyses first to determine the basic functional form of the growth trajectories and then perform multivariate LGM analyses only to assess relationships between trajectories from different variables. This is because the validity of the parameters obtained in a multivariate model is strongly dependent on the adequate specification of growth in the associated univariate models (Stoolmiller, 1994). Hence, univariate LGM analyses similar to those already reported for male feedback seeking were performed for male job involvement. In the interest of space, it suffices to state that results from the series of nested model comparisons and the final LGM model selected based on parsimony and model fit, NNFI = .99, CFI = .99, RMSEA = .01, showed that intraindividual changes in male job involvement too were adequately represented by a positive linear growth trajectory model with systematic individual differences in initial status and rate of change that were predictable from individual differences in Neuroticism.

The entire observed mean vector and covariance matrix of the relevant variables for the male data (the complete data reported in Table 10.1) served as the input for the multivariate LGM fitting procedure. Note that the input included the observed covariances between feedback-seeking and job involvement variables so that cross-domain relationships could be estimated. Two multivariate LGM models were formed by combining the two univariate linear trajectory growth models (feedback seeking and job involvement, respectively). In the first multivariate growth model fitted, the Neuroticism predictor was excluded from the model (hence, variable information on Neuroticism reported in Table 10.1 was not used) because the primary cross-domain relationships of interest were the associations between growth parameters (the intercepts and slopes) from different domains. In this model, the six factor covariances between the growth factors (the intercept and slope factors) were freely estimated. The model fit the data well: NNFI = .96, CFI = .97, RMSEA = .06. For ease of interpretation, we will examine the cross-domain factor correlations, which were decomposed from the estimated factor covariances (dividing the factor covariance by the square root of the product of the two corresponding factor variances). Table 10.5 presents the factor correlations among the growth parameters. As shown in the table, all cross-domain factor correlations are significant, and their values

Table 10.5. Completely Standardized Latent Correlations Among Growth Factors in Multivariate LGM Model (Without Neuroticism as Predictor) of Feedback Seeking and Job Involvement, from Male Data in Table 10.1; $n = 300$).

Growth Factor	1	2	3	4
Feedback-seeking intercept	—			
Feedback-seeking slope	−.43	—		
Job involvement intercept	.60	−.35	—	
Job involvement slope	−.21	.44	−.39	—

Note: All correlations are significant at $p = .05$.

range from moderate to high. The intercept-intercept factor correlation (.60) indicates that at initial status (Time 1), feedback seeking and job involvement are highly and positively correlated. In addition, the slope-slope factor correlation (.44) indicates that individuals who increased their feedback seeking at higher rates also tended to be those who increased involvement in their jobs at higher rates. Although the positive and substantial intercept-intercept and slope-slope correlations indicate that change patterns in feedback seeking and job involvement are interrelated, the cross-domain intercept-slope correlations provide some evidence that feedback seeking and job involvement are distinct. Whereas initial status of job involvement is associated with its own rate of change (−.39) and with the rate of change in feedback seeking (−.35) to the same extent, initial status of feedback seeking is more highly associated with its own rate of change (−.43) than with the rate of change in job involvement (−.21).

To examine if Neuroticism could account for the cross-domain relationships, the multivariate LGM model was respecified to include Neuroticism as the single individual predictor for the four growth factors (two intercepts and two slopes). This was accomplished by specifying a direct structural effect from Neuroticism to each of the four growth factors. All six pairwise residual covariances between growth factors were freely estimated to represent the amount of covariation between two growth factors that remained even after taking into account their associations with the predictor (Neuroticism). This respecified model fit the data well: NNFI = .95, CFI = .96, RMSEA = .07. Note that this model (with Neuroticism) and the previous model (without Neuroticism) are not nested, and no direct comparison of overall model fit using the chi-square difference test is possible.

Table 10.6 presents the estimates of the direct structural effects from this respecified model. Neuroticism is significantly associated with each of the four growth factors, $p < .05$. For ease of interpretation, we will examine the completely standardized structural effects, γ's, from Neuroticism to the four growth factors. As shown in the table, at initial status (Time 1), Neuroticism predicts both feedback seeking ($\gamma_{I(F),P} = .53$) and job involvement ($\gamma_{I(J),P} = .66$) in the same direction and to a large extent. Hence, a substantial portion of the high association between feedback seeking and job involvement at initial status (see Table 10.5) is attributable to the fact that at initial status, individuals high in Neuroticism are likely to seek more feedback and be more involved in their job, a fact that is consistent with the researcher's hypotheses. A comparison between the intercept-intercept residual factor covariance, $\Psi_{I(J),I(F)} = .3598$, (partial intercept-intercept covariance controlling for the linear effects of Neuroticism) and the unconditional intercept-intercept factor covariance, $\Sigma_{I(J),I(F)} = .8580$, estimated by LISREL yields a pseudo-R^2 of .58 ($[.8580 - .3598]/.8580$). That is, the inclusion of Neuroticism reduced the unexplained covariance between the

Table 10.6. Completely Standardized Structural Effects from Neuroticism to Growth Factors in Multivariate LGM Model of Feedback Seeking and Job Involvement (from Male Data in Table 10.1; $n = 300$).

Growth Factor	Structural Effect γ from Neuroticism to Growth Factor
Feedback-seeking intercept, $\eta_{I(F)}$	.53
Feedback-seeking slope, $\eta_{S(F)}$	$-.19$
Job involvement intercept, $\eta_{I(J)}$	.66
Job involvement slope, $\eta_{S(J)}$	.17

Note: All parameter estimates are significant at $p = .05$.

two true intercepts by 58 percent, suggesting that Neuroticism is important in accounting for the cross-domain association in true interindividual differences at initial status.

As shown in Table 10.6, Neuroticism predicts rate of change in feedback seeking negatively ($-.19$) but rate of change in job involvement positively ($.17$). In addition, the magnitude of the predictive validity is relatively small. Therefore, individual differences in Neuroticism cannot be used to explain the positive association between the two rates of change. The slope-slope residual factor covariance, $\Psi_{S(J),S(F)} = .1012$ (SE = $.0232$), is essentially identical to the unconditional slope-slope factor covariance, $\sigma_{S(J),S(F)} = .0973$ (SE = $.0235$), estimated by LISREL, indicating that the inclusion of Neuroticism does not account for the unexplained covariance between the two true slopes. That is, Neuroticism is not an explanation for the cross-domain association in true interindividual differences in rate of change.

Because Neuroticism predicts both feedback seeking intercept and job involvement slope positively (Table 10.6), it cannot be used to account for the negative association between initial status of feedback seeking and rate of change in job involvement (see Table 10.5). On the other hand, because Neuroticism predicts job involvement intercept positively but predicts feedback-seeking slope negatively (Table 10.6), it may account for some portion of the negative association between initial status in job involvement and rate of change in feedback seeking (Table 10.5). A comparison between the residual factor covariance between job involvement intercept and feedback seeking slope, $\Psi_{I(J),S(F)} = -.1041$, and the corresponding unconditional factor covariance, $\sigma_{I(J),S(F)} = -.1659$, yields a pseudo-$R^2$ of .37. That is, the inclusion of Neuroticism reduced the unexplained covariance between true job involvement intercept and true feedback-seeking slope by 37 percent, suggesting that Neuroticism is important in accounting for the cross-domain association in true interindividual differences between initial status of job involvement and rate of change in feedback seeking.

As demonstrated in this instructive example, an adequate multivariate LGM model can be used to examine cross-domain relationships between different facets of intraindividual change by modeling the associations between growth factors from the different domains. The multivariate LGM model can also be respecified to include one or more individual predictors. By examining the structural effects from predictors to growth factors and comparing the relevant cross-domain residual factor covariances, which are partial covariances controlling for linear effects of predictors, to the corresponding cross-domain unconditional factor covariances, we may gain some understanding of these cross-domain relationships by assessing the extent to which they are attributable to the individual predictors.

Nested multivariate LGM model comparisons can be performed to test for equality of parameters across domains, although one should be careful that the comparison makes conceptual sense. For example, it is usually not meaningful to make direct comparisons between the mean levels of two conceptually different variables such as initial status of feedback seeking versus initial status of job involvement.

Multiple-Group Multivariate (Cross-Domain) LGM Analyses

Multiple-group multivariate growth models can also be fitted simultaneously to two or more groups. Different cross-domain parameter estimates representing different group-level (factor means) or individual-level (factor variance and covariance, structural effects) attributes or relationships can be either freely estimated or fixed equal (or to some a priori value) across groups. The procedures for multiple-group analysis of multivariate growth models are straightforward extensions of those in the multiple-group analysis of univariate LGMs already discussed.

LGM and Fundamental Questions on Change over Time

Chan (1998a) enumerated nine fundamental questions on change over time as the conceptual bases and organizing principles for describing the types of substantive questions that can be addressed by LGM and its various extensions.

Q1. *Is an observed change over time (and observed between-group differences in change over time) due to meaningful systematic differences or random fluctuations resulting from measurement error?* A major limitation shared by many traditional longitudinal or repeated measures analytic models (among them, repeated measures ANOVA, repeated measures regression, and time series) is that measurement error is not adequately taken into account when specifying the model and estimating the parameters. Results of the analyses from these traditional models can be severely affected by measurement error (Arvey & Cole, 1989; Rogosa, Brandt, & Zimowski, 1982). In addition, many of the models make the classic independence of errors assumption, which may be violated in repeated measurement in multiwave designs. This independence assumption is likely to be violated in longitudinal data collected on measurement occasions closely spaced together using identical measures.

Similar to standard structural equation modeling, LGM addresses the possible distortion of findings on true intraindividual change due to measurement error by explicitly incorporating them in the model specification. Error variances are explicitly modeled. Specific relationships between the error terms (specific error covariance structures such as different patterns of autocorrelated errors) can also be modeled and estimated. Hence, the LGM analysis allows the estimation of structural parameters at the same time, accounting for both random and nonrandom (correlated) measurement errors (James, Mulaik, & Brett, 1982; Williams & Podsakoff, 1989).

Chan (1998a) demonstrated how the standard LGM analysis can be extended to a multiple-indicator latent growth model (MLGM) analysis. In MLGM, the focal variable, such as job involvement, is represented as a latent construct measured by multiple indicators at each time point. An advantage of MLGM models over standard LGM models is that the use of multiple indicators in MLGM models allows reliable variance in the focal variable at each time point to be partitioned into true construct (common) variance and nonrandom (unique) error variance, thereby mitigating the distorting effects on estimates of true change in the focal construct over time.

Q2. *Is the change over time reversible?* The question on the reversibility of change over time can be construed in terms of the functional form of the intraindividual growth trajectory. For example, monotonically increasing or decreasing (for example, linear) functional forms represent irreversible (within the time period studied) change in the sense that there is no returning or restoring to previous levels on the focal variable. On the other hand, a nonmonotonic functional form (such as an inverted U) would represent reversible change over time. The LGM procedure allows exploratory assessments and confirmatory tests of reversibility by identifying possible functional forms of the true growth trajectory (by fitting the two-factor unspecified growth model) and explicitly modeling and testing different specific functional forms, respectively. The nested comparison between a linear trajectory model and a quadratic trajectory model described in the numerical illustration provides an example of testing different specific functional forms.

Q3. *Is the change over time proceeding in one single pathway or through multiple different pathways?* A researcher could examine if two or more groups of individuals follow the same or different trajectories as they proceed from one time point to another (through intervening time points measured in the study) using either exploratory or confirmatory multiple-group LGM analyses. These groups can be either natural occurring groups such as gender and ethnic groups or manipulated groups such as experimental versus control groups, in which different growth trajectories are hypothesized or assessed. For example, in a four-time-point study, two groups may have the same value on the focal variable at initial status (Time 1) and at end point (Time 4), but one group follows a positive linear trajectory and the other a positively accelerated monotonically increasing trajectory. That is, change from one value of the focal variable at Time 1 to another value at Time 4 could proceed through multiple different pathways.

Q4. *Is the change on the quantitative variable proceeding in a gradual manner, or is it characterized as large-magnitude shifts at each time interval?* This question is addressed in the LGM procedure by the nature of the growth trajectory, specifically, the slope and shape growth factors in the LGM model selected to represent the data. For example, if change is characterized by a linear trajectory, then a low slope factor mean indicates gradual change, whereas a high slope factor mean indicates large-magnitude change. As noted in the discussion on measurement equivalence, if change over time is a progression through a series of qualitatively distinct stages, then representing and interpreting the change over time in terms of the growth parameters (slope and shape) of a trajectory is misleading and not meaningful because the same single construct is not being assessed across the different time points. Hence, it is important to precede application of LGM with measurement-invariance assessments. Chan (1998a) addresses invariance concerns by proposing a two-phase unified procedure that detects qualitative changes (using measurement invariance assessments) in phase 1 prior to modeling quantitative changes using growth modeling in phase 2.

Q5. *Is the change over time (or across groups) to be considered as alpha, beta, or gamma change?* Golembiewski, Billingsley, and Yeager (1976) distinguished three types of change: alpha, beta, and gamma. Alpha change refers to changes in absolute levels given a constant conceptual domain and a constant measuring instrument. Assessment of change over time is often directly based on absolute differences in responses on some measuring instrument; that is, true change is assumed to be alpha change. However, the reliance on absolute differences as a direct indicator of change over time assumes measurement invariance (equivalence) of responses across repeated measurements. We can meaningfully speak of alpha change only when there is measurement invariance of responses across time. Measurement invariance could be construed as absence of beta and gamma changes.

Beta change refers to changes in absolute level complicated by changes in the measuring instrument given a constant conceptual domain. Beta change occurs when there is a recalibration of the measurement scale. That is, in beta change, the observed change results from an alteration in the respondent's subjective metric or evaluative scale rather than an actual change in the construct of interest. When beta change occurs, there is a stretching or shrinking in the measurement scale, rendering direct comparisons between absolute levels observed before and after the change problematic.

Gamma change refers to changes in the conceptual domain. Gamma change (that is, change in the meaning or conceptualization of the constructs of interest) can take a variety of forms. For example, in the language of factor analysis, the number of factors (a factor representing a construct) assessed by a given set of measures may change from one time point to another. Alternatively, the number of factors may remain constant across time, but a differentiation process occurs so that the factor intercorrelations decrease over time, or an integration process may occur so that the factor intercorrelations increase over time (see the discussion on process composition models in Chan, 1998b, for a substantive example in organizational research).

When there is gamma or beta change over time, it is not meaningful to represent and interpret the change pattern over time using a growth trajectory. Hence, it is important to link the concept of measurement invariance and type of change (alpha, beta, and gamma) to the change assessment and inference.

The issue of measurement invariance of responses is fundamental to virtually all change assessment techniques. Unfortunately, invariance is merely assumed and seldom tested even in situations where lack of invariance is likely. A major limitation in many traditional analytic models (such as repeated measures ANOVA) is that the analysis proceeds as if beta and gamma changes never existed or assuming, by faith, that they are not present in any nontrivial manner substantial enough to affect the meaningfulness and accuracy of the analysis. At best, the researcher is aware of the potential distortions in the results due to beta and gamma changes but has no means of estimating the extent of the problem.

Standard applications of latent growth models have assumed, without testing, the absence of beta and gamma changes over time and in the case of multiple-group models, across groups. In the presence of beta or gamma change, the growth parameters, and indeed the growth trajectory itself, cannot be meaningfully interpreted. Chan (1998a) addresses this fundamental problem in his two-phase modeling procedure that ensures meaningful interpretations of growth trajectories and parameters by first testing the assumption of no beta and gamma changes and establishing measurement invariance in phase 1 prior to fitting latent growth models in phase 2. (For more detailed discussions of the concepts and assessments of alpha, beta, and gamma changes, see Chan, 1998a, 2000; Meyer, Allen, & Gelatly, 1990; Millsap & Hartog, 1988; Schaubroeck & Green, 1989; Schmitt, 1982; Thompson & Hunt, 1996; Vandenberg & Self, 1993; and Chapter Eight, this volume.)

Q6. *Is the change over time occurring at the individual, group, or both levels of conceptualization?* Any analytic technique that is restricted to only one level of conceptualization and analysis is limited in an important way because the assumption of no or "irrelevant" change at the other level is not tested. The LGM procedure conceptualizes and analyzes change over time at both levels. At the group level, the nature of intraindividual change over time is represented (conceptualized) by a single well-fitting growth trajectory that may take on a variety of functional forms (linear or quadratic, for example). At the individual level, intraindividual change is explicitly modeled, and interindividual differences in intraindividual change are represented by the individual's values on the relevant growth factors (intercept, slope) defining the individual growth trajectory. The presence of systematic interindividual differences is indicated by a statistically significant factor variance value (different from zero) associated with the relevant growth parameter. Examples of these and other growth parameters and their interpretations were provided in the numerical illustration.

Q7. *In addition to detecting interindividual differences in intraindividual change, can we predict (and, hence, increase our understanding of) these differences?* For example, can individual differences at initial status predict individual differences in the rate of change? Are there individual difference variables, such as cognitive ability, that can predict individual differences on these two or other growth parameters? Do these individual difference variables account for the associations between growth parameters? As demonstrated in the numerical example, the LGM procedure addresses these questions by estimating covariances between growth factors in a basic growth model and respecifying the basic model to include relevant individual predictor variables. Structural effects from predictor variables to growth factors represent the extent to which interindividual differences in the growth factors are associated with the predictors. In addition to examining these structural effects, residual factor covariances, which are partial covariances controlling for linear effects of predictors, can be compared to the corresponding unconditional factor covariances to assess the extent to which associations between growth factors are attributable to the predictor variables.

Q8. *Are there cross-domain relationships in change over time?* This question is addressed explicitly by multivariate latent growth models. Recall that after establishing adequate growth models in each domain, these different univariate growth models can be combined to form multivariate growth models in which growth parameters of trajectories from different domains can be correlated to examine cross-domain relationships in the change phenomenon under investigation. For example, hypotheses concerning the relationship between initial status in one domain and rate of change in another domain can be tested. In addition, predictor variables can be included in a multivariate LGM to assess the extent to which they can account for the cross-domain relationships by comparing residual and unconditional factor covariances in the same manner described in Q7.

Q9. *Do the various relationships with respect to specific facets of change over time vary or remain invariant across groups?* As described in the instructive example, specific between-group equality or differences in various specific facets of intraindividual changes can be explicitly modeled and tested using multiple-group LGM analyses. Note that the first eight questions can be construed and addressed in terms of either a single group or multiple groups.

LGM Versus HLM

Prior to discussing its limitations and extensions, it is relevant to compare LGM with a closely parallel class of techniques that can be used to analyze change over time. These techniques are generally referred to as *random coefficients models* in the biostatistics (Laird & Ware, 1982) and educational (Bryk & Raudenbush, 1987, 1992) traditions. To provide a more concrete comparison, I focus on hierarchical linear modeling (HLM), a specific random coefficients modeling technique that has received much attention in organizational research recently. (Excellent introductions to HLM, including its technical detail, are provided in Bryk & Raudenbush, 1987, 1992, and Hofmann, 1997. Organizational examples of substantive applications of the HLM procedure to analyze change over time can be found in Deadrick, Bennett, & Russell, 1997; Hofmann, Jacobs, & Baratta, 1993; and Hofmann et al., 1992.)

While HLM is a developed to analyze multilevel data, the technique can be used to analyze intraindividual change over time for a group of individuals. Conceptually, it accomplishes the analysis using a two-step procedure. First, an individual-level model is constructed. This model is essentially a regression for each individual on time. The regression models the individual's growth trajectory including residual variance. Each trajectory is determined by a set of parameters at the individual level. This level 1 model is a within-subjects model and can be used to assess if and how individuals change on the focal variable over time. Next, a higher-level model (level 2) is constructed to explain the variance in the individual-level regressions. This model is constructed by regressing the individual-level parameters on one or more predictor variables selected by the researcher. This level 2 model is a between-subjects model that can be used to examine if and how individual difference or other predictor variables (such as a grouping variable) are associated with individual growth trajectories. Like the LGM procedure, HLM is able to address several fundamental questions on change. Because it models the nature of intraindividual changes over time, interindividual differences in these changes, and associations between these differences and individual predictors, HLM addresses questions concerning reversibility (Q2), unitary versus multipath (Q3), group versus individual level (Q6), systematic individual differences (Q7) and, to an extent, multiple-group invariance (Q9) of intraindividual change.

However, HLM is limited in its ability to address the other four of the nine fundamental questions on change. A limitation acknowledged by many users of HLM is the inflexibility of the procedure when dealing with measurement error or residuals (Q1). For example, with respect to modeling intraindividual change over time, HLM makes the strict statistical assumption that the level 1 errors are independent and homoscedastic (Bryk & Raudenbush, 1987, 1992).[5] The independent errors assumption is likely to be unrealistic in many actual longitudinal panel data sets, especially those in which repeated measurements occurred at short time intervals, thereby increasing the likelihood of autocorrelated measurement errors. The LGM procedure does not have to accept unchecked the independent measurement errors assumption or the homoscedasticity assumption. Because LGM models are implemented in a structural equation modeling framework, they can specify any a priori error covariance structure (provided the model is identified) without restricting the structure to any shape or pattern. The researcher can also perform nested model comparisons to select among alternative theoretically reasonable error structures. For example, the researcher can specify a model assuming a pairwise autocorrelated and heteroscedastic error structure and compare it with a (nested) model assuming an independent and heteroscedastic error structure to assess the difference in fit between the two models. Another advantage of the LGM procedure over HLM and other random coefficient models that employ observed but not latent variables is that LGM can be readily elaborated to represent the focal change variable and individual predictors of change as latent variables assessed by multiple indicators, thereby providing maximum likelihood correction for measurement errors in these variables (Chan, 1998a).

The LGM procedure can also be readily extended into a two-phase procedure so that it precedes growth trajectory modeling with measurement-invariance analyses to detect possible qualitative changes (Q4) or beta and gamma changes (Q5) over time and across groups. Neither of these change questions can be addressed within HLM or random coefficient models without latent variables. In the presence of these changes, the parameter estimates in HLM become uninterpretable. Of course, one can always establish measurement invariance using structural equation modeling techniques prior to performing HLM. Finally, HLM does not have the flexibility of modeling cross-domain relationships relating different focal change variables (Q8) in the manner possible using the LGM procedure.

Limitations and Extensions of the LGM Method

The LGM procedure is not intended to handle categorical variables, although it may be possible to adapt it to accommodate categorical and other nonnormal variables because it is implemented within a latent variable framework (see Muthén, 1984, 1996). When the change variable is categorical and the interest is in modeling qualitative changes or shifts over time from one categorical state to another, analytic models such as survival analysis, events history analysis, and latent class analysis for stage-sequential dynamic variables are well suited. (Excellent examples of substantive applications of these three analytic models are available in Chapter Thirteen, this volume; Harrison & Hulin, 1989; and Collins, 1991, respectively.)

Because LGM is implemented within a structural equation modeling framework, the procedure shares many of the strengths and weaknesses of structural equation modeling. Examples of strengths include the ability to account explicitly for the biasing effects of random measurement error and model different a priori error covariance structures, test a variety of complex theoretical interrelationships among variables, make more direct inferences from and enhance the explanatory power of nonexperimental data by testing and ruling out alternative models, assess the effects of imposing restrictive assumptions on a set of relationships, and assess a variety of specific measurement and structural relationships across multiple groups. The LGM procedure can also be easily extended to incorporate mediational effects linking predictors to focal change variables using intervening variables. Li, Duncan, and Acock (2000) showed how interaction effects can be incorporated in the LGM procedure.

Longitudinal panel studies face the typical problem of attrition. Because LGM assumes a longitudinal panel design and structural equation modeling requires large sample sizes, the issue of insufficient sample sizes is likely to be relevant in actual applications of the procedure. This limitation is not an inherent weakness of LGM over and above the large sample size requirement in structural equation modeling and the limited information problem in longitudinal designs due to subject attrition independent of the choice of analytic model. When subjects are lost at different repeated measurement occasions, we have incomplete data at the individual level across the selected number of time waves. With respect to modeling growth trajectories, recent extensions of standard LGMs have been developed to deal with this incomplete data problem. These extensions essentially apply the logic of convergence analysis to "recover" missing longitudinal information. Accounts and empirical examples of these extensions are available in Duncan and Duncan (1994), Duncan, Duncan, and Hops (1996), and McArdle and Hamagami (1991). Note, however, that although these extensions may be able to deal adequately with random missing data situations, they are likely to lead to model misspecifications and misleading interpretations due to biased parameter estimates when there are nonrandom patterns of missing data.

No amount of sophistication in an analytic model can turn invalid inferences resulting from inadequate design, measurement, or data into valid inferences. Like any other analytic model, the LGM procedure has no magical solutions if the study design and instrument development are poor or if the researcher selected measurements, time intervals, and duration of study that fail to capture the true causal intervals underlying the change process over time. For example, an important but often neglected issue in the interpretation of results from a longitudinal design concerns the length of the time interval (the interval between $Time_t$ and $Time_{t+1}$) in the time-ordered period of study. A change that is in fact continuous and gradual can appear in the results as large in magnitude if the time interval is too large. The converse of the problem can also occur when there is a mismatch between the length of the entire time period in the study and the actual causal interval. A change that is in fact large in magnitude would not be revealed in the results if the time period selected for study is smaller than the true causal interval. There is some evidence that the time interval for repeated measurements can have dramatic effects on the results of the analysis performed, including substantial changes in the magnitude of the effect sizes (Cohen, 1991; Collins & Graham, 1991; Gollob & Reichardt, 1991). The bad news is that we almost never have a good approximation of what the true causal interval is. Researchers have to make some judgments when selecting time intervals and the time period in the study based on some educated guess from theory and previous research findings.

Problems of design (and data) and problems of analytic models should be distinguished. When useful data from adequately performed longitudinal research are available, the LGM procedure provides a powerful and flexible approach to structure the data for substantive interpretation by conceptualizing and analyzing different specific facets of change over time corresponding to the fundamental questions on the nature of change. Theories of the change phenomenon can be evaluated by systematically testing different specific growth models representing competing ways of describing and explaining the data.

The substantive application of LGM (or any analytic model for that matter) has to be based on adequate theoretical foundations.

For example, it is almost always possible to get an empirically good-fitting growth model simply by sequentially increasing the fit of the model through a series of atheoretical nested models differing in the number of freely estimated parameters in the error variance-covariance matrix. The resulting atheoretical model would probably have little substantive meaning and would probably not cross-validate in a different sample. With respect to error structures, the researcher should ideally have a theory of error (for example, specifying a particular form of method variance), model and test the hypothesized and alternative error structures, and provide convergent validity for the theory by further modeling and testing relevant error structures using additional measures (for example, including an additional measure of the hypothesized method variance construct).[6] Without adequate theory and conceptualization, the power and flexibility of LGM is easily abused, leading to inaccurate assessments and invalid inferences regarding the true nature of change. Conversely, with adequate theory, design, and measurement, LGM provides a unified approach for conceptualizing and analyzing different facets of change over time.

Appendix: LISREL 8 Program Specifications

Following are the LISREL 8 program specifications for estimating Model G2, Model G3, and Model G4 reported in this chapter. Comments that are not part of the specification file, are in brackets.

Model G2

Model G2, male feedback seeking, positive linear growth [optional]
DA NG=1 NO=300 NI=5
LA
'F1' 'F2' 'F3' 'F4' 'P1'
KM=MFEED.COR [MFEED.COR is an external file containing intercorrelations of F1, F2, F3, F4, P1, as in Table 10.1.]
SD=MFEED.SD [MFEED.SD is an external file containing standard deviations of F1, F2, F3, F4, P1, as in Table 10.1.]
ME=MFEED.MS [MFEED.MS is an external file containing means of F1, F2, F3, F4, P1, as in Table 10.1.]

SE
1 2 3 4/
MO NY=4 NE=2 TY=ZE TE=SY,FI PS=SY,FI AL=FI BE=FU,FI
LE
'FINT' 'FSLO'
MA LY
1 0
1 1
1 2
1 3
FR TE 1 1 TE 2 2 TE 3 3 TE 4 4
FR PS 1 1 PS 2 2 PS 2 1
FR AL 1 AL 2
OU SE SC MI RS TV ND=4 AD=OFF IT=1000

Model G3

Model G3, male feedback seeking, positive accelerated quadratic
growth [optional]
DA NG=1 NO=300 NI=5
LA
'F1' 'F2' 'F3' 'F4' 'P1'
KM=MFEED.COR
SD=MFEED.SD
ME=MFEED.MS
SE
1 2 3 4/
MO NY=4 NE=3 TY=ZE TE=SY,FI PS=SY,FI AL=FI BE=FU,FI
LE
'FINT' 'FSLO' 'FQUA'
MA LY
1 0 0
1 1 1
1 2 4
1 3 9
FR TE 1 1 TE 2 2 TE 3 3 TE 4 4
FR PS 1 1 PS 2 2 PS 3 3 PS 2 1 PS 3 1 PS 3 2
FR AL 1 AL 2 AL 3
OU SE SC MI RS TV ND=4 AD=OFF IT=1000

Model G4

Model G4, male feedback seeking, positive linear growth with Neuroticism as predictor [optional]

```
DA NG=1 NO=300 NI=5
LA
'F1' 'F2' 'F3' 'F4' 'P1'
KM=MFEED.COR
SD=MFEED.SD
ME=MFEED.MS
SE
1 2 3 4 5/
MO NY=4 NE=2 TY=ZE TE=SY,FI PS=SY,FI AL=FI BE=FU,FI c
NX=1 NK=1 TX=ZE TD=SY,FI KA=FR PH=SY,FR GA=FU,FI
LE
'FINT' 'FSLO'
MA LY
1 0
1 1
1 2
1 3
FR TE 1 1 TE 2 2 TE 3 3 TE 4 4
FR PS 1 1 PS 2 2 PS 2 1
FR AL 1
FR AL 2
LK
'NEU'
MA LX
1
VA .8989 TD 1 1 [this line fixed the error variance of P1, assum-
ing a reliability of .80 for P1]
FR KA 1
FR GA 1 1 GA 2 1
OU SE SC MI RS TV ND=4 AD=OFF IT=1000
```

Notes

1. Because most readers of this chapter are probably familiar with the use of nested structural equation model comparisons to assess measurement invariance, assessments of measurement invariance across time and gender groups are not reported here. To conduct such as-

sessments, multiple indicators of the focal construct are required at each time point, and the same set of indicators is required across time and groups. For readers unfamiliar with invariance assessment procedures, see Chan (1998a).

2. Models specifying different error covariance structures can be easily fitted to the data, provided the models are identified. For example, if there are reasons to expect that the same systematic error of measurement occurred at T1 and T3, an error covariance structure that freely estimates the T1-T3 error covariance can be fitted to the data.

3. Similar to standard multiple-group structural equation models, multiple-group growth models specifying different error covariance structures across groups can easily be fitted to the data, provided the models are identified.

4. Other nested hierarchies different from that presented in Table 10.4 may be formulated, provided they make theoretical sense.

5. In the organizational literature, *HLM* is often used to refer interchangeably to the statistical technique as described by Bryk and Raudenbush (1992) and the popular HLM software program they developed. As a specific statistical technique in the form described by Bryk and Raudenbush, HLM makes a key assumption that level 1 errors are independent and homoscedastic. The HLM software program does not have the capability to model error covariance structures and heteroscedasticity. As noted in Chapter Twelve (this volume), the lack of this capability is unique to the HLM software and not an inherent weakness of the general class of random coefficient modeling statistical techniques. Random coefficient modeling techniques can be implemented in other software programs (for example, S-PLUS) to model error covariance structures and heteroscedasticity. For more details, see Chapter Twelve, this volume.

6. Williams and Anderson (1994) have proposed a powerful and flexible latent variable approach to modeling method variance that allows the researcher to assess the impact of different method factors that might be hypothesized to affect relationships between substantive constructs. Organizational applications of this method are available in Chan (2001) and Schmitt, Pulakos, Nason, and Whitney (1996).

References

Arbuckle, J. L. (1997). *Amos user's guide*. Chicago: Smallwaters.

Arvey, R. D., & Cole, D. A. (1989). Evaluating change due to training. In I. Goldstein (Ed.), *Training and development in organizations* (pp. 89–117). San Francisco: Jossey-Bass.

Bentler, P. M. (1990). Comparative fit indexes in structural models. *Psychological Bulletin, 107,* 238–246.

Bentler, P. M. (1995). *EQS structural equations program manual.* Encino, CA: Multivariate Software.

Bentler, P. M., & Bonett, D. G. (1980). Significance tests and goodness of fit in the analysis of covariance structures. *Psychological Bulletin, 88,* 588–606.

Browne, M. W., & Cudeck, R. (1993). Alternative ways of assessing model fit. In K. A. Bollen & J. S. Long (Eds.), *Testing structural equation models* (pp. 136–162). Thousand Oaks, CA: Sage.

Bryk, A. S., & Raudenbush, S. W. (1987). Application of hierarchical linear models to assessing change. *Psychological Bulletin, 101,* 147–158.

Bryk, A. S., & Raudenbush, S. W. (1992). *Hierarchical linear models.* Thousand Oaks, CA: Sage.

Chan, D. (1998a). The conceptualization and analysis of change over time: An integrative approach incorporating longitudinal means and covariance structures analysis (LMACS) and multiple indicator latent growth modeling (MLGM). *Organizational Research Methods, 1,* 421–483.

Chan, D. (1998b). Functional relations among constructs in the same content domain at different levels of analysis: A typology of composition models. *Journal of Applied Psychology, 83,* 234–246.

Chan, D. (2000). Detection of differential item functioning on the Kirton Adaption-Innovation Inventory using multiple-group mean and covariance structures analysis. *Multivariate Behavioral Research, 35,* 169–199.

Chan, D. (2001). Modeling method effects of positive affectivity, negative affectivity, and impression management in self reports of work attitudes. *Human Performance, 14,* 77–96.

Chan, D., Ramey, S., Ramey, C., & Schmitt, N. (2000). Modeling intraindividual changes in children's social skills at home and at school: A multivariate latent growth approach to understanding between-settings differences in children's social skills development. *Multivariate Behavioral Research, 35,* 365–396.

Chan, D., & Schmitt, N. (2000). Interindividual differences in intraindividual changes in proactivity during organizational entry: A latent growth modeling approach to understanding newcomer adaptation. *Journal of Applied Psychology, 85,* 190–210.

Cohen, P. (1991). A source of bias in longitudinal investigations of change. In L. M. Collins & J. L. Horn (Eds.), *Best methods for the analysis of change* (pp. 18–25). Washington, DC: American Psychological Association.

Collins, L. M. (1991). Measurement in longitudinal research. In L. M. Collins & J. L. Horn (Eds.), *Best methods for the analysis of change* (pp. 137–148). Washington, DC: American Psychological Association.

Collins, L. M., & Graham, J. W. (1991). Comments on "A source of bias in longitudinal investigations of change." In L. M. Collins & J. L. Horn (Eds.), *Best methods for the analysis of change* (pp. 26–30). Washington, D.C.: American Psychological Association.

Deadrick, D., Bennett, N., & Russell, C. (1997). Using hierarchical linear modeling to examine dynamic performance criteria over time. *Journal of Management, 23,* 745–757.

Duncan, S. C., & Duncan, T. E. (1994). Modeling incomplete longitudinal substance use data using latent variable growth curve methodology. *Multivariate Behavioral Research, 29,* 313–338.

Duncan, T. E., Duncan, S. C., & Hops, H. (1994). The effects of family cohesiveness and peer encouragement on the development of adolescent alcohol use: A cohort-sequential approach to the analysis of longitudinal data. *Journal of Studies on Alcohol, 55,* 588–599.

Golembiewski, R. T., Billingsley, K., & Yeager, S. (1976). Measuring change and persistence in human affairs: Types of change generated by OD designs. *Journal of Applied Behavioral Science, 12,* 133–157.

Gollob, H. F., & Reichardt, C. S. (1991). Interpreting and estimating indirect effects assuming time lags really matter. In L. M. Collins & J. L. Horn (Eds.), *Best methods for the analysis of change* (pp. 243–259). Washington, DC: American Psychological Association.

Harrison, D., & Hulin, C. (1989). Investigation of absenteeism: Using event history models to study the absence-taking process. *Journal of Applied Psychology, 74,* 300–316.

Hofmann, D. A. (1997). An overview of the logic and rationale of hierarchical linear models. *Journal of Management, 23,* 723–744.

Hofmann, D. A., Jacobs, R., & Baratta, J. (1993). Dynamic criteria and the measurement of change. *Journal of Applied Psychology, 78,* 194–204.

Hofmann, D. A., Jacobs, R., & Gerras, S. J. (1992). Mapping individual performance over time. *Journal of Applied Psychology, 77,* 185–195.

Hu, L., & Bentler, p. M. (1998). Fit indices in covariance structure modeling: Sensitivity to underparameterization model misspecification. *Psychological Methods, 3,* 424–453.

James, L. R., Mulaik, S. A., & Brett, J. M. (1982). *Causal analysis: Assumptions, models, and data.* Thousand Oaks, CA: Sage.

Jöreskog, K., & Sörbom, D. (1986). *LISREL 6: Analysis of linear structural relationships by maximum likelihood and least square methods.* Chicago: Scientific Software International.

Jöreskog, K., & Sörbom, D. (1989). *LISREL 7: A guide to the program and applications* (2nd ed.). Chicago: SPSS.

Jöreskog, K., & Sörbom, D. (1993). *LISREL 8 user's reference guide.* Chicago: Scientific Software International.

Kanfer, R., & Ackerman, P. L. (1989). Motivational and cognitive abilities: An integrative/aptitude-treatment interaction approach to skill acquisition. *Journal of Applied Psychology, 74,* 657–690.

Kline, R. B. (1998). *Principles and practice of structural equation modeling.* New York: Guilford Press.

Laird, N. M., & Ware, J. H. (1982). Random-effects models for longitudinal data. *Biometrics, 38,* 963–974.

Li, F., Duncan, T. E., & Acock, A. (2000). Modeling interaction effects in latent growth models. *Structural Equation Modeling, 7,* 497–533.

McArdle, J. J., & Hamagami, F. (1991). Modeling incomplete longitudinal and cross-sectional data using latent growth structural models. In L. M. Collins & J. L. Horn (Eds.), *Best methods for the analysis of change* (pp. 276–304). Washington, DC: American Psychological Association.

Meredith, W., & Tisak, J. (1990). Latent curve analysis. *Psychometrika, 55,* 107–122.

Meyer, J. P., Allen, N. J., & Gelatly, I. R. (1990). Affective and continuance commitment to the organization: Evaluation of measures and analysis of concurrent and time-lagged relations. *Journal of Applied Psychology, 75,* 710–720.

Millsap, R. E., & Hartog, S. B. (1988). Alpha, beta, and gamma change in evaluation research: A structural equation approach. *Journal of Applied Psychology, 73,* 574–584.

Muthén, B. O. (1984). A general structural equation model with dichotomous, ordered categorical, and continuous latent variable indicators. *Psychometrika, 49,* 115–132.

Muthén, B. O. (1991). Analysis of longitudinal data using latent variable models with varying parameters. In L. M. Collins & J. L. Horn (Eds.), *Best methods for the analysis of change* (pp. 1–17). Washington, DC: American Psychological Association.

Muthén, B. O. (1996). Growth modeling with binary responses. In A. V. Eye & C. Clogg (Eds.), *Categorical variables in developmental research: Methods of analysis* (pp. 37–54). Orlando, FL: Academic Press.

Rogosa, D. R., Brandt, D., & Zimowski, M. (1982). A growth curve approach to the measurement of change. *Psychological Bulletin, 92,* 726–748.

Schaubroeck, J., & Green, S. G. (1989). Confirmatory factor analytic procedures for assessing change during organizational entry. *Journal of Applied Psychology, 74,* 892–900.

Schmitt, N. (1982). The use of analysis of covariance structures to assess beta and gamma change. *Multivariate Behavioral Research, 17,* 343–358.

Schmitt, N., Pulakos, E. D., Nason, E., & Whitney, D. J. (1996). Likability and similarity as potential sources of predictor-related criterion bias in validation research. *Organizational Behavior and Human Decision Processes, 68,* 272–286.

Steiger, J. H. (1990). Structural model evaluation and modification: An interval estimation approach. *Multivariate Behavioral Research, 25,* 173–180.

Stoolmiller, M. (1994). Antisocial behavior, delinquent peer association and unsupervised wandering for boys: Growth and change from childhood to early adolescence. *Multivariate Behavioral Research, 29,* 263–288.

Stoolmiller, M. (1995). Using latent growth curve models to study developmental processes. In J. M. Gottman (Ed.), *The analysis of change* (pp. 103–138). Hillsdale, NJ: Erlbaum.

Thompson, R. C., & Hunt, J. G. (1996). Inside the black box of alpha, beta, and gamma change: Using a cognitive-processing model to assess attitude structure. *Academy of Management Review, 21,* 655–690.

Vandenberg, R. J., & Lance, C. E. (2000). A review and synthesis of the measurement invariance literature: Suggestions, practices, and recommendations for organizational research. *Organizational Research Methods, 3,* 4–69.

Vandenberg, R. J., & Self, R. M. (1993). Assessing newcomers' changing commitments to the organization during the first 6 months of work. *Journal of Applied Psychology, 75,* 557–568.

Willett, J. B., & Sayer, A. G. (1994). Using covariance structure analysis to detect correlates and predictors of individual change over time. *Psychological Bulletin, 116,* 363–381.

Williams, L. J., & Anderson, S. E. (1994). An alternative approach to method effects by using latent-variable models: Applications in organizational behavior research. *Journal of Applied Psychology, 79,* 323–331.

Williams, L. J., & Podsakoff, P. M. (1989). Longitudinal field methods for studying reciprocal relationships in organizational behavior: Toward improved causal analysis. In B. M. Staw & L. L. Cummings (Eds.), *Research in organizational behavior* (Vol. 11, pp. 247–292). Greenwich, CT: JAI Press.

CHAPTER 11

Alternatives to Difference Scores

Polynomial Regression Analysis and Response Surface Methodology

Jeffrey R. Edwards

For decades, difference scores have been widely used in industrial/organizational (I/O) psychology research. Difference scores typically consist of the algebraic, absolute, or squared difference between two measures or the sum of squared or absolute differences between profiles of measures. Difference scores are widely used in research on the congruence (that is, fit, similarity, or agreement) between two constructs as a predictor of outcomes. Examples of such research include person-environment fit as a predictor of attitudes, behavior, and well-being (Chatman, 1989; Edwards, 1991; French, Caplan, & Harrison, 1982; Kristof, 1996), value fulfillment as a predictor of satisfaction (Dawis & Lofquist, 1984; Locke, 1976; Rice, McFarlin, Hunt, & Near, 1985), met expectations as a predictor of absenteeism, turnover, and organizational commitment (Porter & Steers, 1973; Wanous, Poland, Premack, & Davis, 1992),

The author thanks Daniel M. Cable and Ian O. Williamson for their help in collecting the data used in the empirical example.

and self-other agreement as a predictor of managerial effectiveness (Atwater & Yammarino, 1997; Fleenor, McCauley, & Brutus, 1996).

Despite their widespread use, difference scores are prone to numerous methodological problems (Cronbach, 1958; Edwards, 1994; Johns, 1981). For instance, difference scores are often less reliable than either of their component measures. Difference scores are also inherently ambiguous, given that they combine measures of conceptually distinct constructs into a single score. Furthermore, they confound the effects of their component measures on outcomes and impose constraints on these effects that are rarely tested empirically. Finally, they reduce an inherently three-dimensional relationship between their component measures and the outcome to two dimensions.

Problems with difference scores can be avoided by using polynomial regression analysis (Edwards, 1994; Edwards & Parry, 1993). In essence, polynomial regression replaces difference scores with the component measures that constitute the difference and higher-order terms such as the squares and product of these measures. This approach provides comprehensive tests of relationships that motivate the use of difference scores, as well as relationships that are more complex than difference scores can represent. The polynomial regression approach also creates new opportunities for theory development by encouraging researchers to conceptualize the joint effects of the components on an outcome not as a two-dimensional function, but instead as a three-dimensional surface. Studies using this approach have shown that difference scores often severely distort the joint effects of their components on various outcomes (Atwater, Ostroff, Yammarino, & Fleenor, 1998; Edwards, 1996; Edwards & Harrison, 1993; Edwards & Rothbard, 1999; Elsass & Veiga, 1997; Finegan, 2000; Hesketh & Gardner, 1993; Hom, Griffeth, Palich, & Bracker, 1999; Irving & Meyer, 1994, 1995; Johnson & Ferstl, 1999; Kalliath, Bluedorn, & Strube, 1999; Livingstone, Nelson, & Barr, 1997; Slocombe & Bluedorn, 1999; Van Vianen, 2000; Westman & Eden, 1996). Moreover, the three-dimensional surfaces examined in these studies often reveal complexities that were anticipated in theories of congruence (French et al., 1982; Kulka, 1979; Naylor, Pritchard, & Ilgen, 1980; Rice et al., 1985) but have eluded empirical investigation due to the use of difference scores.

This chapter provides an overview of polynomial regression analysis as an alternative to difference scores. The chapter begins with a review of major problems with difference scores. The polynomial regression procedure is then discussed, followed by an empirical example that compares this procedure to the use of difference scores. Next, response surface methodology is presented, which provides a comprehensive framework for analyzing features of surfaces relating two components to an outcome. The chapter concludes with a discussion of the strengths and limitations of the polynomial regression approach and directions for future methodological developments in congruence research.

Problems with Difference Scores

Difference scores are prone to numerous methodological problems. This section summarizes these problems, focusing on situations in which a difference score is used as a predictor of an outcome. Many of these problems also pertain to difference scores as dependent variables (Edwards, 1995) and as measures of change (Cronbach & Furby, 1970; Werts & Linn, 1970), although methods that avoid these problems differ from those that apply when difference scores are used as predictors. Alternatives to difference scores as dependent variables and measures of change are summarized later in this chapter.

Reduced Reliability

Perhaps the most widely known problem with difference scores is low reliability. Although difference scores are not necessarily unreliable (Rogosa & Willett, 1983; Zimmerman & Williams, 1982), they are often less reliable than their component measures (Johns, 1981). The source of this problem is evidenced by the formula for the reliability of an algebraic difference between two measures (Johns, 1981; Nunnally, 1978),

$$a_{(X-Y)} = \frac{\sigma_X^2 a_X + \sigma_Y^2 a_Y - 2\sigma_{XY}}{\sigma_X^2 + \sigma_Y^2 - 2\sigma_{XY}} \tag{11.1}$$

where X and Y are the two measures constituting the difference, a_X and a_Y are the reliabilities of the measures, σ_X^2 and σ_Y^2 are the variances of the measures, and σ_{XY} is the covariance between the measures. When X and Y are positively correlated (as is usually the case in congruence research), the reliability of the algebraic difference between X and Y is often less than the reliability of either X or Y. For example, if X and Y have unit variances, reliabilities of .75, and are correlated .40, the reliability of their difference is .58. Reliabilities of other difference scores can be derived using principles for the reliabilities of squares, products, and weighted linear combinations of measures (Bohrnstedt & Marwell, 1978; Nunnally, 1978). For example, a squared difference between two normally distributed measures with zero means, unit variances, reliabilities of .75, and a correlation of .40 has a reliability of .09. Reliabilities of profile similarity indices tend to be higher due to the large number of dimensions on which differences are calculated (O'Reilly, Chatman, & Caldwell, 1991). However, these dimensions are often conceptually heterogeneous, which creates interpretational problems regarding the meaning of the "true score" to which the reliability estimate refers (Hattie, 1985).

Ambiguous Interpretation

Difference scores collapse measures of conceptually distinct constructs into a single score that is inherently ambiguous. It may be tempting to interpret difference scores based on the weights implicitly assigned to the component measures when the difference is calculated. For example, an algebraic difference may seem to represent equal but opposite contributions of its component measures. However, the variance of a difference score depends not only on the weights assigned to the component measures, but also on the variances and covariance of these measures. This can be seen by the following formula for the variance of an algebraic difference:

$$\sigma_{(X-Y)}^2 = \sigma_X^2 + \sigma_Y^2 - 2\sigma_{XY}. \tag{11.2}$$

As equation 11.2 shows, X and Y account for equal amounts of the variance in their difference only when σ_X^2 and σ_Y^2 are equal. In practice, component measure variances are likely to differ, as when person-organization fit is assessed for different people within the same organization (Chatman, 1991; O'Reilly et al., 1991) or supervisor-subordinate agreement is assessed for different subordinates who share the same supervisor (Meglino, Ravlin, & Adkins, 1989). In extreme cases, one component is a constant and therefore has no variance, as when multiple employees are compared to a single job profile (Caldwell & O'Reilly, 1990). In such cases, a difference score is simply a rescaled version of the component measure with nonzero variance.

Additional ambiguities pertain to the interpretation of absolute and squared difference scores. As with algebraic differences, the variances of absolute and squared differences give greater weight to the component measure with larger variance, as can be seen by applying formulas for the variances and covariances of squares and products (Bohrnstedt & Goldberger, 1969; Goodman, 1960). However, the interpretation of absolute and squared difference scores also depends on the joint distribution of the component measures. Typically, absolute and squared differences are interpreted as symmetric measures of congruence, given that they treat positive and negative differences the same. However, this interpretation implies that both positive and negative scores contributed to the difference. If scores are predominantly positive or negative, then an absolute or squared difference effectively reduces to a unidirectional measure of congruence, analogous to an algebraic difference. For example, studies of need fulfillment show that people often receive less than they want of various intrinsic and extrinsic rewards (Wanous & Lawler, 1972). Therefore, need fulfillment scores calculated by subtracting wanted amount from received amount are predominantly negative, and absolute or squared differences based on these scores should not be interpreted as symmetric indices of need fulfillment.

Confounded Effects

The coefficient relating a difference score to an outcome is typically viewed as the effect of congruence, not the effects of the difference score components. However, because a difference score is calculated from its component measures, it captures nothing more than the combined effects of its components, and these effects are confounded when they are reduced to a single coefficient. In many cases, this coefficient conceals substantial differences in the effects of the components. For example, studies of the relationship between job satisfaction and the difference between actual and wanted job attributes have found that this relationship is markedly reduced when actual job attributes are statistically controlled (Sweeney, McFarlin, & Inderrieden, 1990; Wall & Payne, 1973). Because controlling for actual job attributes transforms the algebraic difference score into a partialed measure of wanted job attributes (Wall & Payne, 1973; Werts & Linn, 1970), these findings indicate that the relationship between the algebraic difference score and satisfaction primarily represents the influence of actual job attributes.

Some researchers have attempted to disentangle absolute and squared difference scores from their components by statistically controlling both component measures (French et al., 1982; O'Brien & Dowling, 1980; Rice, McFarlin, & Bennett, 1989; Tsui & O'Reilly, 1989). However, when the component measures are controlled, the coefficient on the difference score cannot be interpreted separately from the coefficients on the component measures. For example, a positive coefficient on an absolute difference is typically interpreted as a V-shaped relationship between congruence and an outcome. Controlling for the component measures can substantially alter the shape of this relationship, depending on the coefficients obtained for the component measures. For example, if the coefficient on $|X - Y|$ is positive, the coefficient on X equals the coefficient on $|X - Y|$, and the coefficient on Y is the opposite of the coefficient on $|X - Y|$, then the left side of the V-shaped relationship implied by the positive coefficient on $|X - Y|$ is flat, meaning that only positive differences are related to the outcome. Similarly, controlling for the components of a squared difference shifts the turning point of the implied U-shaped relationship to the left or right, such that the coefficient on the squared difference no longer represents the effects of deviations from perfect congruence.

Untested Constraints

Difference scores impose constraints on the relationship between the component measures and the outcome. These constraints can be identified by writing an equation using a difference score as a predictor, distributing the coefficient on the difference score through the equation, and comparing the resulting expression to an equation that uses the components of the difference as separate predictors. For example, an equation using an algebraic difference score as a predictor is as follows:

$$Z = b_0 + b_1(X - Y) + e \qquad (11.3)$$

where X and Y are component measures and Z is the outcome. Distributing b_1 through the difference score yields

$$Z = b_0 + b_1 X - b_1 Y + e. \qquad (11.4)$$

Now consider an equation that uses X and Y as separate predictors of Z:

$$Z = b_0 + b_1 X + b_2 Y + e. \qquad (11.5)$$

Comparing equation 11.5 to equation 11.4 shows that using an algebraic difference score as a predictor is equivalent to constraining the coefficients on X and Y in equation 11.5 to be equal in magnitude but opposite in sign ($b_1 = -b_2$).

The constraints imposed by a squared difference score can be identified in a similar manner. The following equation uses a squared difference score as a predictor:

$$Z = b_0 + b_1(X - Y)^2 + e. \qquad (11.6)$$

Expanding this equation yields the following:

$$Z = b_0 + b_1 X^2 - 2b_1 XY + b_1 Y^2 + e. \qquad (11.7)$$

Thus, a squared difference score effectively uses X^2, XY, and Y^2 as predictors. The corresponding unconstrained equation uses these three terms supplemented by X and Y, given that unbiased estimation of coefficients on squared and product terms requires the inclusion of their constituent terms (Aiken & West, 1991; Cohen, 1978):

$$Z = b_0 + b_1 X + b_2 Y + b_3 X^2 + b_4 XY + b_5 Y^2 + e. \qquad (11.8)$$

Comparing equation 11.7 to equation 11.8 shows that using a squared difference score as a predictor imposes the following constraints on equation 11.8: (1) $b_1 = 0$; (2) $b_2 = 0$; (3) $b_3 = b_5$; and (4) $b_3 + b_4 + b_5 = 0$.[1]

The constraints imposed by an absolute difference score are somewhat more difficult to identify, given that an absolute difference is a logical rather than a mathematical transformation. However, this transformation can be expressed in equation form by introducing a dummy variable (here labeled W) that equals 0 when $X \geq Y$ and equals 1 when $X < Y$, as follows:

$$Z = b_0 + b_1(1 - 2W)(X - Y) + e. \tag{11.9}$$

The term $(1 - 2W)$ reduces to 1 when X is greater than or equal to Y and -1 when X is less than Y. Therefore, when $(X - Y)$ is positive or zero, its sign is unaltered, whereas when $(X - Y)$ is negative, its sign is reversed. Thus, equation 11.9 is equivalent to using an absolute difference score as a predictor. Expanding equation 11.9 yields

$$Z = b_0 + b_1 X - b_1 Y - 2b_1 WX + 2b_1 WY + e. \tag{11.10}$$

Now consider an unconstrained piecewise linear equation containing the same terms as those in equation 11.10:

$$Z = b_0 + b_1 X + b_2 Y + b_3 W + b_4 WX + b_5 WY + e. \tag{11.11}$$

Equation 11.11 includes W as a separate predictor to obtain unbiased estimates of the coefficients on the product terms WX and WY (Aiken & West, 1991; Cohen, 1978). Comparing equation 11.10 to equation 11.11 reveals that using an absolute difference score as a predictor imposes the following constraints on equation 11.11: (a) $b_1 = -b_2$; (b) $b_4 = -b_5$; (c) $b_3 = 0$; and (d) $b_4 = -2b_1$.[2]

Dimensional Reduction

Finally, difference scores reduce an inherently three-dimensional relationship between the component measures and the outcome to two dimensions. This phenomenon is illustrated by Figures 11.1

and 11.2, which depict two-dimensional functions for algebraic, absolute, and squared difference scores and their three-dimensional counterparts. A comparison of these figures shows that the two-dimensional straight line implied by an algebraic difference score corresponds to a three-dimensional plane with equal but opposite slopes with respect to the X- and Y- axes. Similarly, the two-dimensional V-shaped function associated with an absolute difference score corresponds to a three-dimensional V-shaped surface

Figure 11.1. Two-Dimensional Difference Score Functions.

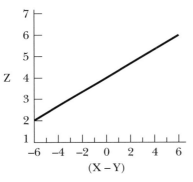

a. Two-Dimensional Algebraic
Difference Function

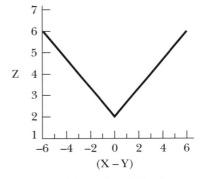

b. Two-Dimensional Absolute
Difference Function

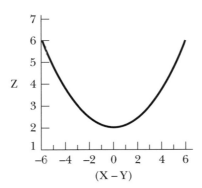

c. Two-Dimensional Squared
Difference Function

with its minimum along the $Y = X$ line. Finally, the two-dimensional U-shaped function for a squared difference score corresponds to a three-dimensional U-shaped surface with its minimum along the $Y = X$ line. By reducing these inherently three-dimensional surface to two-dimensional functions, difference scores discard information and oversimplify the relationship of the components with the outcome.

Figure 11.2. Three-Dimensional Difference Score Surfaces.

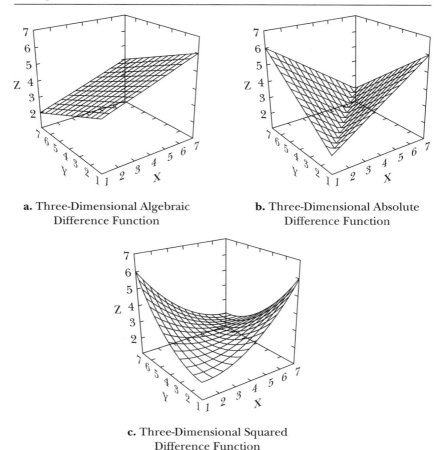

a. Three-Dimensional Algebraic
Difference Function

b. Three-Dimensional Absolute
Difference Function

c. Three-Dimensional Squared
Difference Function

Polynomial Regression as an Alternative to Difference Scores

Problems with difference scores may be addressed by using polynomial regression analysis. This section outlines the fundamental principles of polynomial regression, followed by a discussion of the mechanics of the approach and an empirical example that compares polynomial regression to the use of difference scores.

Basic Principles and Assumptions

The polynomial regression approach is based on three principles. First, congruence should be viewed not as a single score, but instead as the correspondence between the component measures in a two-dimensional space. From this perspective, perfect congruence is not a point, but instead is a line along which the component measures are equal. Incongruence is represented by the perpendicular distance of the component scores from the line of congruence. Viewing congruence in this manner captures the magnitude and direction of incongruence between the components as well as the absolute levels of the components. Difference scores embody the assumption that the absolute levels of the components can be disregarded, and this assumption carries a burden of proof that is readily evaluated by viewing congruence in a two-dimensional space. More fundamentally, component measures used to calculate difference scores invariably represent conceptually distinct constructs (such as expected and actual work experiences) or the same construct from different perspectives (say, supervisor and subordinate values), and these distinctions should be maintained in data analysis and interpretation.

Second, the effect of congruence on an outcome should be treated not as a two-dimensional function, but instead as a three-dimensional surface relating the two components to the outcome. These surfaces may be used to test simple congruence hypotheses associated with difference scores (see Figure 11.2) as well as complex congruence hypotheses that difference scores cannot represent. These surfaces invite researchers to develop and test hypotheses regarding the effects of congruence that take into account the full range of both component measures. For example, person-environment fit theory suggests that outcomes may differ depending on whether perfect fit refers to low versus high levels of person and environment constructs (Edwards, Caplan, & Harrison, 1998). Hypotheses such as these are necessarily overlooked when the three-dimensional relationship between congruence and an outcome is reduced to two dimensions.

Third, the constraints associated with difference scores should not be imposed on the data, but instead should be treated as hypotheses to be tested empirically. For example, the constraint imposed by an algebraic difference score ($b_1 = -b_2$ in equation 11.5) represents a hypothesis that the components have equal but opposite effects on the outcome. Similarly, the constraints imposed by absolute and squared difference scores constitute compound hypotheses regarding the joint effects of the components on the outcome. Testing these constraints generates evidence to evaluate the conceptual model on which the difference score is based. Without testing these constraints, the conceptual model underlying a difference score evades empirical scrutiny and therefore cannot be falsified. Different sets of constraints may be tested to compare alternative models, thereby obtaining strong inference tests of congruence effects (Platt, 1964).

The polynomial regression approach is based on the following assumptions. First, the component measures should be commensurate, meaning that they express the components in terms of the same content dimension (Caplan, 1987; Graham, 1976). Examples of commensurate measures are actual and desired challenge, expected and received pay, and supervisor and subordinate reports of performance. Commensurate measurement is required to ensure the conceptual relevance of the component measures to one another and is necessary to meaningfully interpret results in terms of congruence. Second, it is assumed that the component measures use the same numeric scale. Scale equivalence is required to determine the degree of correspondence between the component measures and compare coefficient estimates. Third, like any application of regression analysis, it is assumed that all measures are at the interval or ratio level and that the component measures contain no measurement error (Kennedy, 1992; Pedhazur, 1997). This latter assumption is rarely satisfied, given that most measures in the social sciences contain some degree of error.

The implications of violating this assumption are considered later in this chapter.

Application of Polynomial Regression Analysis

As with most methods of analysis, polynomial regression may be applied in either a confirmatory or exploratory manner. Some researchers have mistaken polynomial regression as inherently exploratory (Tinsley, 2000), which is clearly at odds with how it has been presented and applied (Edwards, 1994; Edwards & Harrison, 1993; Edwards & Rothbard, 1999). Given that it frames difference score constraints as hypotheses to be tested, the polynomial regression procedure is first and foremost confirmatory. Polynomial regression analyses should be exploratory only if theory is not sufficiently developed to derive hypotheses for the joint effects of the components on the outcome. Moreover, results from exploratory analyses are subject to cross-validation and conceptual scrutiny. As forcefully stated elsewhere, "It is folly to construct elaborate post hoc interpretations of complex surfaces that are not both generalizable and conceptually meaningful" (Edwards, 1994, p. 74).

Confirmatory Approach

The confirmatory procedure begins by selecting a conceptual model of congruence and identifying the corresponding regression equation. The asymmetric congruence model implied by an algebraic difference score requires a linear equation that uses both component measures as predictors (equation 11.5). The symmetric congruence model implied by a squared difference requires a quadratic equation (equation 11.8), and the symmetric model corresponding to an absolute difference requires a piece linear equation (equation 11.11). These two models are similar, in that both predict symmetric effects of incongruence and no slope along the line of perfect congruence. However, the quadratic equation can capture curvilinearity, whereas the piecewise linear equation can depict abrupt changes in slope. Moreover, the quadratic equation allows a test of the hypothesis that the surface changes shape along the line of perfect congruence, whereas the piecewise linear equation incorporates this hypothesis as an assumption through the coding of W and provides no means to verify this assumption. A conservative approach is to use both equations to test symmetric congruence hypotheses and determine whether their results yield the same substantive conclusions.

After the appropriate equation is identified and estimated, analyses should be conducted to evaluate the model of interest. Support for the model rests on four conditions: (1) the variance explained by the equation differs from zero; (2) the coefficients follow the appropriate pattern, meaning that coefficients expected to have nonzero values differ from zero and have the correct sign; (3) the constraints corresponding to the model are satisfied; and (4) the variance explained by the set of terms one order higher than those in the equation does not differ from zero. The first condition is a simple omnibus test to establish that the equation explains variance in the outcome. The second condition verifies the general form of the model (for example, satisfaction is maximized rather than minimized along the line of perfect congruence) and rules out situations in which constraints are satisfied because all coefficients are near zero. The third condition determines whether the relative magnitudes of the coefficients correspond to the model of interest. Finally, the fourth condition ensures that the model does not underestimate the complexity of the joint effects of the components on the outcome. The third and fourth conditions provide support for the model when their associated tests are not statistically significant. Therefore, it is important to establish that these tests have adequate statistical power (Cohen, 1988).

Exploratory Approach

If no model is hypothesized a priori, polynomial regression may be applied in an exploratory manner. This approach involves estimating equations of progressively higher order (linear, quadratic, cubic, and so on) by adding the required terms in sets until the increment in variance explained does not differ from zero. These analyses should be supplemented by diagnostic procedures to detect outliers and influential cases (Belsley, Kuh, & Welsch, 1980), which can dramatically affect the variance explained by higher-order terms. Moreover, results from the exploratory approach should be cross-validated to ensure that the obtained results do not merely reflect sampling variability. If the results are replicated across samples and are conceptually meaningful, they may be used to develop hypotheses to test in subsequent confirmatory studies (Runkel & McGrath, 1972).

Empirical Illustration

The polynomial regression procedure is illustrated using data from 366 M.B.A. students engaged in the job search process. All respondents completed commensurate scale-equivalent measures of actual and desired levels of various attributes of a job they were actively pursuing and their anticipated satisfaction with the job. Actual and desired job attribute measures contained three items and used seven -point scales with anchors ranging from "none at all" to "a very great amount." To avoid ceiling effects, measures of desires asked respondents to indicate job attribute levels that were adequate, not ideal (Locke, 1969). Measures were created by averaging the relevant items and subtracting the scale mid-point (4), producing scores that could range from -3 to $+3$. Scale centering reduces multicollinearity between the component measures and their associated higher-order terms (Cronbach, 1987) and facilitates the interpretation of coefficients on first-order terms when higher-order terms are in the equation (for a quadratic equation, the coefficients on X and Y represent the slope of the surface at the midpoint of X and Y scales, and for the piecewise linear equation, the coefficient on W represents the vertical shift in the surface at the midpoint of the X and Y scales). This illustration uses measures of actual and desired autonomy, prestige, span of control, and travel. Reliabilities were estimated using coefficient alpha and produced values ranging from .826 to .945 for measures of actual and desired job attributes and a value of .930 for the satisfaction measure. For all analyses, X represents actual amount, Y represents desired amount, and Z represents satisfaction.

Prior to analysis, data were screened for outliers and influential cases, using leverage, Cook's D statistic, and standardized residuals from quadratic regression equations (Belsley et al., 1980; Fox, 1991) as criteria. Cases that exceeded the minimum cutoff on all three criteria (Bollen & Jackman, 1990) and were clearly discrepant from other cases on plots that combined these criteria were dropped. This procedure was conservative, affecting no more than five cases per job attribute. Removing outliers, influential cases, and cases with missing data yielded sample sizes ranging from 358 to 360. With alpha at .05 and power at .80, these sample sizes were able to detect a reduction in R^2 of about .02 for tests of the algebraic difference constraint and .03 for tests of the absolute and squared difference constraints. Previous research indicates that the reduction in R^2 produced by difference score constraints is often much larger than these values (Edwards, 1994; Edwards & Harrison, 1993). Therefore, the statistical power available to test difference score constraints was deemed adequate. In addition, using the same alpha and power criteria, these sample sizes were able to detect increases in R^2 about .03 for the sets of terms one order higher than those in the unconstrained algebraic, absolute, and squared difference equations. This increase in R^2 represents a small effect size (Cohen, 1988), and therefore the statistical power for tests of higher-order terms was also considered adequate.

Confirmatory Approach

Results from confirmatory analyses of the algebraic difference model are shown in Table 11.1, and surfaces corresponding to the constrained and unconstrained equations are displayed in Figures 11.3 and 11.4. For all four job attributes, the constrained equations indicate that satisfaction increased as actual amount approached desired amount and continued to increase as actual amount exceeded desired amount. The unconstrained equations yielded significant R^2 values and coefficients on X and Y that were significant and in the appropriate direction. The constraint imposed by the algebraic difference score ($b_1 = -b_2$; see equation 11.4) was rejected for autonomy, prestige, and travel but was not rejected for span of control, as indicated by F-ratios reported in the column labeled F_C in Table 11.1. However, the higher-order terms were significant for all four job attributes, as shown by F-ratios in the column labeled F_H in Table 11.1. Thus, the first two conditions of the confirmatory approach were satisfied for all four job attributes, but the third condition was satisfied only for span of control, and the fourth condition was not satisfied for any job attribute.

Table 11.1. Algebraic Difference Model.

Job Attribute	Constrained Equation		Unconstrained Equation				
	(X−Y)	R^2	X	Y	R^2	F_C	F_H
Autonomy	0.393**	.115**	0.445**	−0.301**	.127**	4.782*	5.933**
Prestige	0.342**	.097**	0.503**	−0.249**	.149**	21.697**	8.616**
Span of Control	0.157**	.026**	0.169**	−0.143*	.027**	0.281	6.230**
Travel	0.118**	.020**	0.144**	−0.048	.032**	4.587*	12.247**

Note: Sample sizes for autonomy, prestige, span of control, and travel were 360, 358, 358, and 359, respectively. For columns labeled (X−Y), X, and Y, table entries are unstandardized regression coefficients from equations in which X is the actual amount, Y is the desired amount, and the dependent variable (Z) is satisfaction. The column labeled F_C contains F-ratios for the test of constraints imposed by the algebraic difference score, which is equivalent to the test of difference in R^2 values for the constrained and unconstrained equations (degrees of freedom for these F-ratios are 1 and N−3). The column labeled F_H contains F-ratios for the test of higher-order terms, which for the linear equation include the three quadratic terms X^2, XY, and Y^2 (degrees of freedom for these F-ratios are 3 and N−6).

*$p < .05$. **$p < .01$.

Figure 11.3. Constrained Linear Surfaces.

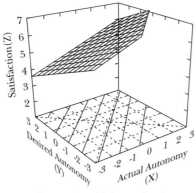

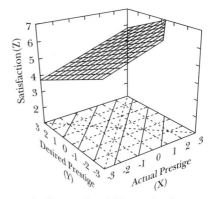

a. Constrained Linear Surface
for Autonomy

b. Constrained Linear Surface
for Prestige

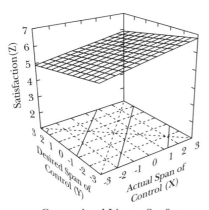

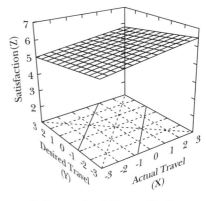

c. Constrained Linear Surface
for Span of Control

d. Constrained Linear Surface
for Travel

Figure 11.4. Unconstrained Linear Surfaces.

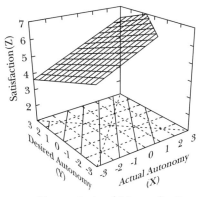

a. Unconstrained Linear Surface
for Autonomy

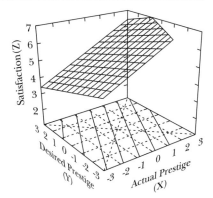

b. Unconstrained Linear Surface
for Prestige

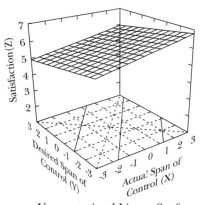

c. Unconstrained Linear Surface
for Span of Control

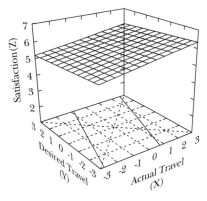

d. Unconstrained Linear Surface
for Travel

Results for the absolute difference model are shown in Table 11.2 and Figures 11.5 and 11.6. For autonomy, prestige, and travel, the constrained equations indicated that satisfaction was greatest when actual and desired amounts were equal and decreased as actual amount deviated from desired amount in either direction. Although similar results were obtained for span of control, the coefficient on the absolute difference score was not significant. The unconstrained equations yielded significant R^2 values for all four job attributes. Coefficients were consistent with the expected pattern (positive coefficients on X and WY, negative coefficients on Y and WX, a coefficient of zero on W) for autonomy, prestige, and travel but not for span of control, which yielded a single negative coefficient on desired amount. The constraints imposed by the absolute difference score were rejected for all four job attributes, as indicated by the F-ratios in the F_C column in Table 11.2. In addition, significant higher-order terms were found for prestige, span of control, and travel, as evidenced by F-ratios in the F_H column of Table 11.2. Thus, the first two conditions of the confirmatory approach were satisfied for autonomy, prestige, and travel, but the third condition was not satisfied for any job attribute, and the fourth condition was satisfied only for autonomy.

Results for the squared difference model are provided in Table 11.3 and Figures 11.7 and 11.8. For all four job attributes, the constrained equations indicated that satisfaction was maximized when actual and desired amounts were equal and decreased as actual amount deviated from desired amount in either direction. The unconstrained equations yielded significant R^2 values for all four job attributes, but the expected pattern of coefficients (coefficients of zero on X and Y, positive coefficients on X^2 and Y^2, and a negative coefficient on XY) was not supported for any job attribute. The constraint imposed by the squared difference score was rejected for all four job attributes, but significant higher-order terms were not found for any job attribute, as shown by the F-ratios reported in the F_C and F_H columns of Table 11.3, respectively. Hence, for all four job attributes, the first and fourth conditions of the confirmatory approach were satisfied, but the second and third conditions were not satisfied.

Table 11.2. Absolute Difference Model.

Job Attribute	Constrained Equation		Unconstrained Equation							
	$|X-Y|$	R^2	X	Y	W	WX	WY	R^2	F_C	F_H
Autonomy	−0.531**	.105**	0.643**	−0.449**	0.094	−0.663**	0.541*	.152**	5.008**	1.944
Prestige	−0.372**	.050**	0.847**	−0.436**	0.227	−0.753**	0.472**	.200**	16.458**	2.245*
Span of Control	−0.136	.009	0.178	−0.217*	0.164	−0.119	0.248	.036*	2.444*	3.064**
Travel	−0.231**	.038**	0.667**	−0.570**	−0.288	−0.709**	0.734**	.112**	7.401**	2.228*

Note: Sample sizes for autonomy, prestige, span of control, and travel were 360, 358, 358, and 359, respectively. For columns labeled $|X-Y|$, X, Y, W, WX, and WY, table entries are unstandardized regression coefficients from equations in which X is actual amount, Y is desired amount, W is a dummy variable that equals 0 when $X \geq Y$ and equals 1 when $X < Y$, and the dependent variable (Z) is satisfaction. The column labeled F_C contains F-ratios for the test of constraints imposed by the absolute difference score, which is equivalent to the test of difference in R^2 values for the constrained and unconstrained equations (degrees of freedom for these F-ratios are 4 and $N - 6$). The column labeled F_H contains F-ratios for the test of higher-order terms, which for the piecewise linear equation include the six quadratic terms X^2, XY, Y^2, WX^2, WXY, and WY^2 (degrees of freedom for these F-ratios are 6 and $N-12$).

*$p < .05$. **$p < .01$.

Figure 11.5. Constrained Piecewise Linear Surfaces.

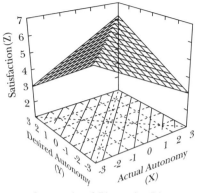

a. Constrained Piecewise Linear
Surface for Autonomy

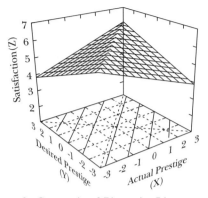

b. Constrained Piecewise Linear
Surface for Prestige

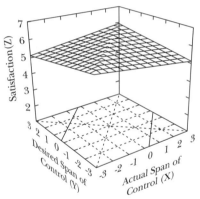

c. Constrained Piecewise Linear
Surface for Span of Control

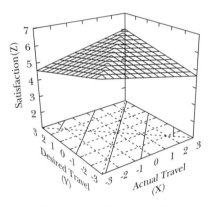

d. Constrained Piecewise Linear
Surface for Travel

Figure 11.6. Unconstrained Piecewise Linear Surfaces.

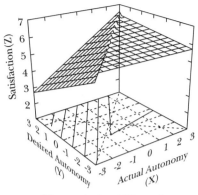

a. Unconstrained Piecewise
Linear Surface for Autonomy

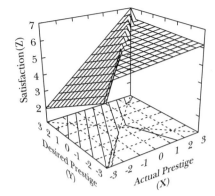

b. Unconstrained Piecewise
Linear Surface for Prestige

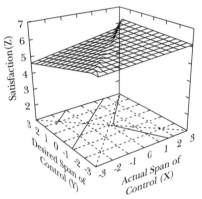

c. Unconstrained Piecewise Linear
Surface for Span of Control

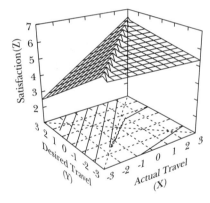

d. Unconstrained Piecewise
Linear Surface for Travel

Table 11.3. Squared Difference Model.

Job Attribute	Constrained Equation		Unconstrained Equation							
	$(X-Y)^2$	R^2	X	Y	X^2	XY	Y^2	R^2	FC	FH
Autonomy	−0.183**	.096**	0.197*	−0.293**	−0.056	0.276**	−0.035	.169**	7.744**	2.344
Prestige	−0.140**	.040**	0.525***	−0.308**	−0.184**	0.287**	−0.034	.207**	18.523***	1.574
Span of Control	−0.067**	.015**	0.267**	−0.097	0.037	0.146*	−0.069	.076**	5.812**	0.773
Travel	−0.083**	.051**	0.247**	−0.131*	−0.130**	0.231**	−0.104**	.124**	7.340**	1.791

Note: Sample sizes for autonomy, prestige, span of control, and travel were 360, 358, 358, and 359, respectively. For columns labeled $(X-Y)^2$, X, Y, X^2, XY, and Y^2, table entries are unstandardized regression coefficients from equations in which X is the actual amount, Y is the desired amount, and the dependent variable (Z) is satisfaction. The column labeled F_C contains F-ratios for the test of constraints imposed by the squared difference score, which is equivalent to the test of difference in R^2 values for the constrained and unconstrained equations (degrees of freedom for these F-ratios are 4 and $N-6$). The column labeled F_H contains F-ratios for the test of higher-order terms, which for the quadratic equation include the four cubic terms X^3, X^2Y, XY^2, Y^3 (degrees of freedom for these F-ratios are 4 and $N-10$).

*$p < .05$. **$p < .01$.

Figure 11.7. Constrained Quadratic Surfaces.

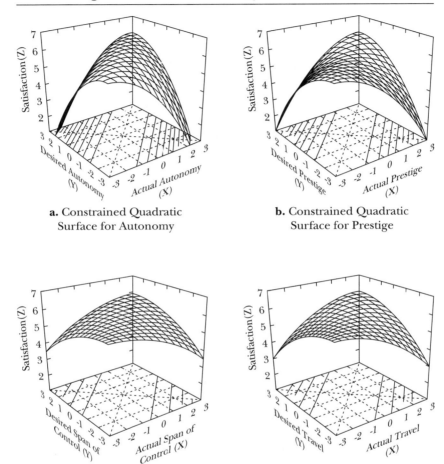

a. Constrained Quadratic
Surface for Autonomy

b. Constrained Quadratic
Surface for Prestige

c. Constrained Quadratic
Surface for Span of Control

d. Constrained Quadratic
Surface for Travel

Figure 11.8. Unconstrained Quadratic Surfaces.

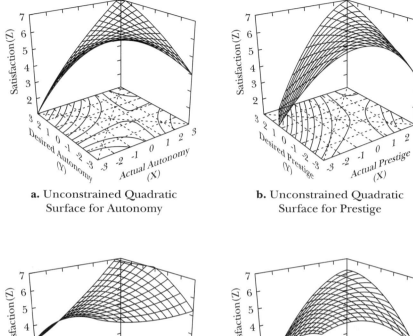

a. Unconstrained Quadratic
Surface for Autonomy

b. Unconstrained Quadratic
Surface for Prestige

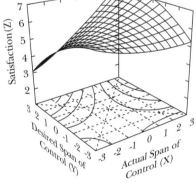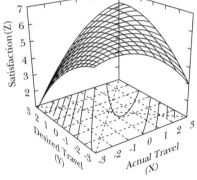

c. Unconstrained Quadratic
Surface for Span of Control

d. Unconstrained Quadratic
Surface for Travel

Exploratory Approach

Application of the exploratory approach indicated that for all four job attributes, sets of linear and quadratic terms were significant, whereas the set of cubic terms was not significant. Results from these analyses can be extracted from Tables 11.1 and 11.3, as follows: (1) tests of the two linear terms as a set correspond to tests of the R^2 values for the linear equations in Table 11.1; (2) tests of the three quadratic terms as a set are provided by the F-ratios in the F_H column of Table 11.1; and (3) tests of the four cubic terms as a set are provided by the F-ratios in the F_H column of Table 11.3. Thus, the final exploratory equations correspond to the quadratic equations shown in Table 11.3. These equations indicate an interaction between actual and desired amounts for autonomy and span of control, an interaction and curvilinearity with regard to actual amount for prestige, and an interaction and curvilinearity for both actual and desired amount for travel. It should be noted that with the outliers and influential cases retained in the data, exploratory analyses yielded cubic equations for autonomy, prestige, and travel and a sextic (sixth-order) equation for span of control. Comparing surfaces for these equations to those for the quadratic equations showed that the additional higher-order terms added minor curvatures to capture a few discrepant cases but did not alter the overall shapes of the surfaces.

Response Surface Methodology as a General Analytic Framework

The preceding analyses indicate that the effects of congruence between actual and desired job attributes on satisfaction are captured by quadratic regression equations. To formally analyze and interpret the surfaces implied by these equations, it is useful to apply response surface methodology (Box & Draper, 1987; Khuri & Cornell, 1987; Myers, 1971). Response surface methodology comprises a collection of procedures for estimating and interpreting three-dimensional surfaces relating two variables to an outcome. Response surface methodology is relevant to the study of congruence for two reasons. First, empirical applications of polynomial regression analysis show that difference scores rarely survive confirmatory analyses (Edwards, 1991, 1994; Edwards & Harrison,

1993; Edwards & Parry, 1993). Consequently, substantive interpretation is usually based on three-dimensional surfaces such as those shown in Figures 11.4, 11.6, and 11.8. When the surfaces are planar (as in Figure 11.4), interpretation is relatively straightforward, whereas when surfaces are curvilinear (as in Figure 11.8), interpretation can be more difficult. Response surface methodology provides a formal means to analyze and interpret these surfaces. Second, a central premise of polynomial regression is that the effects of components on the outcome should be conceptualized in three dimensions. Accordingly, theory building and hypothesis testing should focus on surfaces as whole entities, which requires the use of response surface methodology. This section discusses the fundamentals of response surface methodology for quadratic regression equations and applies this methodology to data from the preceding empirical example.

Key Features of Response Surfaces

Response surface methodology involves the analysis of various features of surfaces corresponding to polynomial regression equations. For a quadratic equation, the surface can be one of three types: (1) concave, meaning the surface is dome shaped; (2) convex, meaning the surface is bowl shaped; and (3) saddle, which combines upward and downward curvature to produce a saddle-shaped surface. For each of these surfaces, response surface methodology involves the analysis of three key features.

   The first feature is the stationary point of the surface, which is the point at which the slope of the surface is zero in all directions. For a concave surface, the stationary point is at the overall maximum of the surface. For a convex surface, the stationary point represents the overall minimum of the surface. Finally, for a saddle surface, the stationary point lies at the intersection of the lines along which the upward and downward curvatures of the surface are greatest. The location of the stationary point can be calculated using the coefficients from a quadratic regression equation (equation 11.8) using the following formulas,

$$X_0 = \frac{b_2 b_4 - 2 b_1 b_5}{4 b_3 b_5 - b_4^2} \qquad (11.12)$$

$$Y_0 = \frac{b_1 b_4 - 2b_2 b_3}{4b_3 b_5 - b_4^2} \qquad (11.13)$$

where X_0 and Y_0 represent the coordinates of the stationary point with respect to the X- and Y-axes. For example, using coefficients from the quadratic equation for autonomy (see Table 11.3) yields the following values for X_0 and Y_0:

$$X_0 = \frac{(-0.293)(0.276) - 2(0.197)(-0.035)}{4(-0.056)(-0.035) - 0.276^2} = 0.982$$

$$Y_0 = \frac{(0.197)(0.276) - 2(-0.293)(-0.056)}{4(-0.056)(-0.035) - 0.276^2} = 0.315.$$

The second key feature is the principal axes of the surface, which are perpendicular to one another and intersect at the stationary point. The principal axes describe the overall orientation of the surface with respect to the X, Y plane. For a concave surface, the first principal axis is the line along which the downward curvature of the surface is minimized, and the second principal axis is the line along which the downward curvature of the surface is maximized. For a convex surface, the first principal axis is the line along which the upward curvature of the surface is maximized, and the second principal axis is the line along which the upward curvature of the surface is minimized. Finally, for a saddle surface, the first principal axis is the line along which the upward curvature of the surface is maximized, and the second principal axis is the line along which the downward curvature of the surface is maximized.

The principal axes can be expressed using equations that describe a line in the X,Y plane. An equation for the first principal axis is as follows:

$$Y = p_{10} + p_{11}X. \qquad (11.14)$$

The equation for the slope of the first principal axis (p_{11}) is as follows:

$$p_{11} = \frac{b_5 - b_3 + \sqrt{(b_3 - b_5)^2 + b_4^2}}{b_4}. \qquad (11.15)$$

Two properties of equation 11.15 should be noted. First, if b_3 and b_5 are equal (corresponding to the constraints imposed by a squared difference score), equation 11.15 reduces to $|b_4|/b_4$. Consequently, the slope of the first principal axis is either -1 or $+1$, depending on whether b_4 is negative or positive, respectively. Second, if b_4 equals 0, both the numerator and denominator of equation 11.15 become 0, rendering it undefined. In this case, one of three conclusions may be drawn regarding the first principal axis, depending on the relative magnitudes of b_3 and b_5: (1) if b_3 is greater than b_5, the first principal axis has a slope of 0, meaning it runs parallel to the X-axis; (b) if b_3 is less than b_5, the first principal axis has a slope of infinity, meaning it runs parallel to the Y-axis; (3) if b_3 and b_5 are equal, the surface is a symmetric dome or bowl (depending on whether b_3 and b_5 are negative or positive, respectively) and therefore has no unique set of principal axes.

Once X_0, Y_0, and p_{11} have been obtained, p_{10} can be calculated as follows:

$$p_{10} = Y_0 - p_{11} X_0. \tag{11.16}$$

Coefficients from the quadratic equation for autonomy yield the following values for p_{11} and p_{10}:

$$p_{11} = \frac{-0.035 - (-0.056) + \sqrt{[-0.056 - (-0.035)]^2 + 0.276^2}}{.276} = 1.079$$

$$p_{10} = -0.315 - (1.079)(0.982) = -1.375.$$

An equation for the second principal axis can be written as

$$Y = p_{20} + p_{21} X. \tag{11.17}$$

The equation for the slope of the second principal axis, p_{21}, is as follows:

$$p_{21} = \frac{b_5 - b_3 - \sqrt{(b_3 - b_5)^2 + b_4^2}}{b_4}. \tag{11.18}$$

Note that equation 11.18 is identical to equation 11.15, except that the sign preceding the expression $\sqrt{(b_3-b_5)^2+b_4^2}$ is reversed. Thus, if b_3 and b_5 are equal, equation 11.18 reduces to $-|b_4|/b_4$, and the slope of the second principal axis is either -1 or $+1$, depending on whether b_4 is positive or negative, respectively. Analogously, if b_4 equals 0, equation 11.18 is undefined, and one of three conclusions may be drawn regarding the second principal axis: (1) if b_3 is greater than b_5, the second principal axis has a slope of infinity, running parallel to the Y-axis; (2) if b_3 is less than b_5, the second principal axis has a slope of 0, running parallel to the X-axis; (3) if b_3 and b_5 are equal, the surface is a symmetric dome or bowl, depending on whether b_3 and b_5 are negative or positive, respectively, and no unique set of principal axes exists.

Using X_0, Y_0, and p_{21}, the following equation may be used to calculate p_{20}:

$$p_{20}=Y_0-p_{21}X_0. \tag{11.19}$$

Again using coefficients from the quadratic equation for autonomy, the following values for p_{21} and p_{20} are obtained:

$$p_{21}=\frac{-0.035-(-0.056)-\sqrt{[-0.056-(-0.035)]^2+0.276^2}}{.276}=-0.927$$

$$p_{20}=-0.315-(-0.927)(0.982)=0.594.$$

In congruence research, it is often useful to locate the principal axes relative to lines other than the X- and Y-axes. For instance, studies of congruence often hypothesize that an outcome is maximized along the line of perfect congruence. This hypothesis implies a first principal axis that runs along the $Y = X$ line, such that $p_{10} = 0$ and $p_{11} = 1$. Rotation of the first principal axis off the $Y = X$ line is indicated by deviation of p_{11} from 1. The lateral shift of the axis from the $Y = X$ line can be gauged by the point at which the axis crosses the $Y = -X$ line. This point is obtained by substituting $-X$ for Y in the equation for the first principal axis and solving for X, which yields $-p_{10}/(p_{11} + 1)$. Analogously, if a hypothesis predicts that an outcome is minimized along the line of perfect congruence, the second principal axis should run along the $Y = X$ line, meaning that $p_{20} = 0$ and $p_{21} = 1$. The rotation of the axis from the $Y = X$ line is indicated by the deviation of p_{21} from 1, and the lateral shift of the axis along the $Y = -X$ line is given by $-p_{20}/(p_{21} + 1)$.

The third response surface feature involves the shape of the surface along lines in the X, Y plane. The shape of the surface along any line can be calculated by substituting the expression for the line into equation 11.8. For example, studies of congruence often hypothesize that an outcome is minimized or maximized along the line of perfect fit. This hypothesis implies that the surface is flat along the $Y = X$ line. The shape of the surface along the $Y = X$ line can be analyzed by substituting X for Y in equation 11.8, which yields the following:

$$Z = b_0 + b_1 X + b_2 X + b_3 X^2 + b_4 X^2 + b_5 X^2 + e.$$

$$= b_0 + (b_1 + b_2) X + (b_3 + b_4 + b_5) X^2 + e. \tag{11.20}$$

Equation 11.20 shows that along the $Y = X$ line, the slope of the surface at the point $X = 0$ (and, by construction, $Y = 0$) equals $(b_1 + b_2)$, and the curvature of the surface equals $(b_3 + b_4 + b_5)$.[3] If these sums differ from zero, the hypothesis that the surface is flat along the $Y = X$ line is rejected. For autonomy, the shape of the surface along the $Y = X$ line is

$$Z = 5.825 + [0.197 + (-0.293)] X + [-0.056 + 0.276 + (-0.035)] X^2 + e.$$

$$= 5.825 - 0.096 X + 0.185 X^2 + e.$$

Studies of congruence are also concerned with the slope of the surface along the $Y = -X$ line, which runs perpendicular to the $Y = X$ line. In particular, if a hypothesis states that an outcome is maximized along the line of perfect congruence, then the surface should be curved downward along the $Y = -X$ line and flat at the point $X = 0$, $Y = 0$ (where the $Y = -X$ line intersects the $Y = X$ line). The shape of the surface along the $Y = -X$ line can be obtained by substituting $-X$ for Y in equation 11.8, which produces the following:

$$Z = b_0 + b_1 X - b_2 X + b_3 X^2 - b_4 X^2 + b_5 X^2 + e.$$

$$= b_0 + (b_1 - b_2) X + (b_3 - b_4 + b_5) X^2 + e. \tag{11.21}$$

The quantity $(b_3 - b_4 + b_5)$ may be used to analyze the curvature of the surface along the $Y = -X$ line. If this quantity is negative, the surface is curved downward along the $Y = -X$ line, whereas if this quantity is positive, the surface is curved upward along the $Y = -X$ line. If the quantity $(b_1 - b_2)$ equals zero, the surface is flat along the line of perfect congruence at the point $X = 0$, $Y = 0$. In conjunction, these quantities may be used to test the hypothesis that the outcome is maximized or minimized along the line of perfect congruence. The shape of the surface for autonomy along the $Y = -X$ line is:

$$Z = 5.825 + [0.197 - (-0.293)] X + [-0.056 - 0.276 + (-0.035)] X^2 + e.$$

$$= 5.825 + 0.490 X - 0.367 X^2 + e.$$

The shape of a surface along its principal axes can be analyzed in a similar manner. For example, the shape of the surface along the first principal axis can be derived by substituting the expression for the axis $Y = p_{10} + p_{11} X$) into equation 11.8:

$$
\begin{aligned}
Z = {} & b_0 + b_1 X + b_2 (p_{10} + p_{11} X) + b_3 X^2 + b_4 X (p_{10} + p_{11} X) \\
& + b_5 (p_{10} + p_{11} X)^2 + e \\
= {} & b_0 + b_2 p_{10} + b_5 p_{10}^2 + (b_1 + b_2 p_{11} + b_4 p_{10} + 2 b_5 p_{10} p_{11}) X \\
& + (b_3 + b_4 p_{11} + b_5 p_{11}^2) X^2 + e.
\end{aligned}
\tag{11.22}
$$

As equation 11.22 shows, the slope of the surface along the first principal axis at the point $X = 0$ (where the first principal axis crosses the Y-axis) is given by $(b_1 + b_2 p_{11} + b_4 p_{10} + 2 b_5 p_{10} p_{11})$, and the curvature of the surface is $(b_3 + b_4 p_{11} + b_5 p_{11}^2)$. For autonomy, the shape of the surface along the first principal axis is

$$
\begin{aligned}
Z = {} & 5.825 + (-0.293)(-1.375) + (-0.035)(-1.375^2) \\
& + [0.197 + (-0.293)(1.079) + (0.276)(-1.375) \\
& + 2(-0.035)(-1.375)(1.079)] X \\
& + [-0.056 + (0.276)(1.079) + (-0.035)(1.079^2)] X^2 + e. \\
= {} & 6.162 - 0.395 X + 0.201 X^2.
\end{aligned}
$$

Analogously, the shape of the surface along the second principal axis is obtained by substituting the expression for this axis ($Y = p_{20} + p_{21}X$) into equation 11.8:

$$
\begin{aligned}
Z &= b_0 + b_1 X + b_2(p_{20} + p_{21}X) + b_3 X^2 + b_4 X(p_{20} + p_{11}X) \\
&\quad + b_5(p_{10} + p_{11}X)^2 + e \\
&= b_0 + b_2 p_{20} + b_5 p_{20}^2 + (b_1 + b_2 p_{21} + b_4 p_{20} + 2b_5 p_{20} p_{21}) X \\
&\quad + (b_3 + b_4 p_{21} + b_5 p_{21}^2) X^2 + e.
\end{aligned}
\tag{11.23}
$$

For autonomy, the shape of the surface along the second principal axis is

$$
\begin{aligned}
Z &= 5.825 + (-0.293)(0.594) + (-0.035)(0.594^2) \\
&\quad + [0.197 + (-0.293)(-0.927) + (0.276)(0.594) \\
&\quad + 2(-0.035)(0.594)(-0.927)]X \\
&\quad + [-0.056 + (0.276)(-0.927) + (-0.035)(-0.927^2)]X^2 + e \\
&= 5.639 + 0.671X - 0.342X^2.
\end{aligned}
$$

Confidence Intervals and Tests of Significance

The expressions for response surface features introduce complications for significance testing and the construction of confidence intervals. For expressions involving linear combinations of regression coefficients, such as those preceding X and X^2 in equations 11.20 and 11.21, standard errors can be calculated using ordinary rules for variances of linear combinations of random variables (DeGroot, 1975). However, these rules do not apply to expressions that contain nonlinear combinations of regression coefficients, such as the formulas for the stationary point and principal axes and the shape of the surface along the principal axes. For these expressions, sampling distributions can be derived empirically using the jackknife or bootstrap (Efron & Tibshirani, 1993; Mooney & Duval, 1993). In general, the bootstrap is superior to the jackknife in terms of bias and efficiency (Efron & Tibshirani, 1993) and is therefore preferred for response surface analysis. Bootstrap sampling distributions of stationary points and principal axes are often nonnormal due to extreme values produced when the denominators for the equations used to calculate these quantities are near zero. Therefore, confidence intervals and critical values should be derived using the percentile method, which involves rank-ordering the obtained bootstrap quantities and identifying values that represent the percentiles of interest (for example, 2.5 percent and 97.5 percent for a 95 percent confidence interval; Efron & Tibshirani, 1993). To provide sufficient values in both tails of the sampling distribution, a large number of bootstrap samples should be used. Efron and Tibshiari (1993) recommend at least one thousand samples, and formulas provided by Booth and Sarkar (1998) indicate that at least five thousand samples are needed to maintain a small proportion of resampling error (such as 5 percent) for the five regression coefficients used to calculate response surface features. Given that these figures are lower bounds, it is advisable to use a larger number of bootstrap samples (say, ten thousand) for response surface analysis. The bootstrap can be implemented using algorithms in statistical packages such as SYSTAT (1999).

Empirical Example

Response surface analysis is illustrated using results from the quadratic regression equations estimated for the sample of M.B.A. students described earlier (see Table 11.3). Stationary points and principal axes for the surfaces corresponding to these equations are reported in Table 11.4, and shapes of these surfaces along lines of interest are reported in Table 11.5. The surfaces represented by these results are shown in Figure 11.9. For each surface, the X, Y plane displays information useful for interpreting the surface. Specifically, the $Y = X$ line runs from the near corner to the far corner of the plane, and the $Y = -X$ line runs from the left corner to the right corner of the plane. The shape of the surface along the $Y = X$ line indicates whether the outcome varies when the two components are congruent, whereas the shape of the surface along the $Y = -X$ line represents the effects of incongruence on the outcome. The first principal axis is represented by a solid line, the second principal axis is plotted as a heavy dashed line, and the principal axes intersect at the stationary point. Finally, the data

Table 11.4. Stationary Points and Principal Axes.

Job Attribute	Stationary Point		First Principal Axis		Second Principal Axis	
	X_0	Y_0	p_{10}	p_{11}	p_{20}	p_{21}
Autonomy	0.982*	−0.315	−1.375*	1.079**	0.594	−0.927**
Prestige	0.919	−0.651	−2.168**	1.651**a	−0.094	−0.606**b
Span of Control	−0.719	−1.464	−1.097	0.510*a	−2.876*	−1.962*b
Travel	29.367	31.985	−0.873**	1.119**	58.232	−0.894**

Note: Sample sizes for autonomy, prestige, span of control, and travel were 360, 358, 358, and 359, respectively. Columns labeled X_0 and Y_0 contain stationary point coordinates in the X,Y plane. Columns labeled p_{10} and p_{11} contain intercepts and slopes, respectively, of the first principal axis. Columns labeled p_{20} and p_{21} contain intercepts and slopes, respectively, of the second principal axis. Significance levels are based on confidence intervals constructed from coefficients from ten thousand bootstrap samples, using the percentile method to determine critical values.

[a]The 95 percent confidence interval for the slope of the first principal axis excluded 1.00.

[b]The 95 percent confidence interval for the slope of the second principal axis excluded − 1.00.

* $p < .05.$ ** $p < .01.$

Table 11.5. Slopes Along Lines of Interest.

Job Attribute	Y = X		Y = −X		First Principal Axis		Second Principal Axis	
	a_X	a_{X^2}	a_X	a_{X^2}	a_X	a_{X^2}	a_X	a_{X^2}
Autonomy	−0.096	0.185**	0.490**	−0.367*	−0.395*	0.201**	0.671*	−0.342*
Prestige	0.217**	0.069	0.833**	−0.505**	−0.362	0.197**	0.681	−0.370**
Span of Control	0.170**	0.114**	0.364*	−0.178	0.135	0.093**	−0.741	−0.515
Travel	0.116*	−0.003	0.378**	−0.465**	0.102	−0.002	24.641	−0.420**

Note: Sample sizes for autonomy, prestige, span of control, and travel were 360, 358, 358, and 359, respectively. For each line ($Y = X$, $Y = −X$, first principal axis, second principal axis), a_{X^2} represents the curvature of the surface along the line, and a_X represents the slope of the surface along the line at $X = 0$. For slopes along the $Y = X$, $Y = −X$ lines, significance levels are based on confidence intervals for linear combinations of regression coefficients. For slopes along the first and second principal axes, significance levels are based on confidence intervals constructed from coefficients from ten thousand bootstrap samples, using the percentile method to determine critical values.

*$p < .05.$ **$p < .01.$

Figure 11.9. Response Surface Analyses.

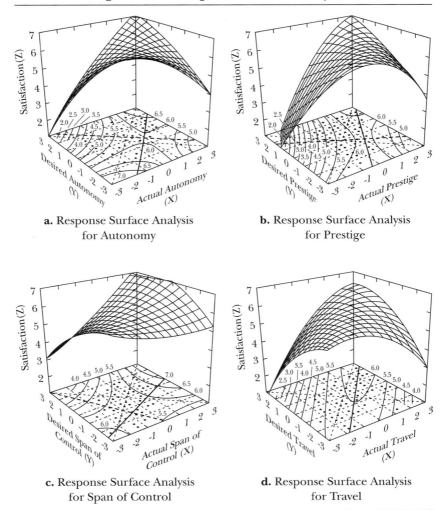

a. Response Surface Analysis
for Autonomy

b. Response Surface Analysis
for Prestige

c. Response Surface Analysis
for Span of Control

d. Response Surface Analysis
for Travel

used to estimate the surface are plotted in the X, Y plane to indicate the region of the surface on which interpretation should be focused (portions of the surface that extend beyond the data are extrapolations that should be disregarded).

The power of response surface methodology invites more thorough development of hypotheses regarding the effects of components on outcomes. For the data presented here, theories of job satisfaction (Locke, 1976, Rice et al., 1985) and person-environment fit (Edwards et al., 1998; French et al., 1982) indicate that for most job attributes, satisfaction should decrease as actual amount falls short of desired amount. When actual amount exceeds desired amount, satisfaction may increase, decrease, or remain constant, depending on how excess amounts influence fulfillment regarding other job attributes (Edwards, 1996; Edwards & Rothbard, 1999; Harrison, 1978). For autonomy, excess amounts may provide the person with influence to achieve fulfillment on other job attributes. However, at high levels, excess autonomy can bring a burden of responsibility, which may reduce satisfaction. Therefore, satisfaction should increase as actual autonomy exceeds desired autonomy, perhaps tapering off when excess autonomy is substantial. Similar arguments apply to prestige, in that excess prestige may provide influence and, at the same time, signify increased responsibility. Excess span of control may imply higher status and therefore increase satisfaction, although these benefits are probably outweighed by the increased workload of managing others. Therefore, satisfaction is likely to decrease for excess span of control. Similarly, excess travel may convey the status of representing an organization externally, but these benefits are probably overwhelmed by feelings of disruption and fatigue. In summary, for all four job attributes, satisfaction should increase as actual amount increases toward desired amount. For autonomy and prestige, satisfaction should continue to increase as actual amount exceeds desired amount, tapering off when excess amounts are large. For span of control and travel, satisfaction should decrease as actual amount exceeds desired amount.

Theories of person-environment fit (Edwards et al. 1998; French et al., 1982) also suggest that satisfaction may be higher when actual and desired amounts are both high than when both are low. Achieving high desired levels of job attributes conveys a sense of competence and self-efficacy, given that high aspirations have been successfully achieved (White, 1959). In contrast, achieving low desired levels merely signifies that a modest goal has been met. Therefore, for all four job attributes, satisfaction should be higher when actual and desired job attributes are both high than when both are low.

These predictions regarding the effects of actual and desired job attributes on satisfaction can be comprehensively assessed using response surface methodology, as illustrated below. For autonomy, the surface was saddle-shaped, with its stationary point just to the right of the $Y = X$ line. The first principal axis was nearly parallel to the $Y = X$ line, as indicated by a p_{11} value that did not differ from 1.00. The quantity $-p_{10}/(1 + p_{11})$ was 0.661, and its 95 percent confidence interval excluded zero, indicating that the first principal axis was shifted to the right of the $Y = X$ line. In contrast, the second principal axis did not differ from the $Y = -X$ line, as evidenced by a slope and intercept that did not differ from -1.00 and 0.00, respectively. The surface was curved upward along the $Y = X$ line, and its slope at the point $X = 0$, $Y = 0$ did not differ from zero. The surface was also curved upward along the first principal axis but was negatively sloped where the surface crossed the Y-axis ($Y = -1.375$). Because few respondents reported low levels of actual and desired autonomy (only six respondents had scores below the line running parallel to the $Y = -X$ line and intersecting the $Y = X$ line at $X = -1$, $Y = -1$), these results indicate that along the $Y = X$ line and first principal axis, satisfaction increased at an increasing rate. Along the $Y = -X$ line and second principal axis, the surface was curved downward and positively sloped where either line crossed the Y-axis. Substantively, these results indicate that satisfaction was maximized not along the line of perfect congruence, but instead along a line indicating that actual amount slightly exceeded desired amount. Thus, satisfaction was higher when respondents had slightly more autonomy than they considered adequate. Satisfaction was also higher when actual and desired amounts of autonomy were both high than when both were moderate, indicating that wanting and attaining a great deal of autonomy may itself lead to satisfaction.

The surface for prestige was also saddle-shaped, with its stationary point about one unit to the right of the point $X = 0$, $Y = 0$

along the $Y = -X$ line. The first principal axis was rotated counterclockwise from the $Y = X$ line, as evidenced by a p_{11} value that was significantly greater than 1.00. The quantity $-p_{10}/(1 + p_{11})$ was 0.818, and its 95 percent confidence interval excluded zero, indicating that the axis was shifted to the right of the $Y = X$ line. Correspondingly, the second principal axis was rotated counterclockwise from the $Y = -X$ line, as shown by a p_{21} value that was significantly greater than -1.00. The surface had a positive linear shape along the $Y = X$ line, as indicated by a positive slope at the point $X = 0$, $Y = 0$ and curvature that did not differ from zero. Along the $Y = -X$ line, the surface had a downward curvature and a positive slope at the point $X = 0$, $Y = 0$. The surface displayed significant upward curvature along the first principal axis and downward curvature along the second principal axis, and the slope of the surface along either axis at the point $X = 0$ did not differ from zero. In conjunction, these results indicate that satisfaction increased as actual prestige approached desired prestige and continued to increase as actual prestige exceeded desired prestige, although at a decreasing rate. In addition, satisfaction was higher when actual and desired prestige were both high than when both were low. Finally, the rotation of the surface indicated that when actual prestige was moderate (near the midpoint of the scale), satisfaction was greatest when actual amount exceed desired amount by about two units, whereas when actual prestige was high, satisfaction was greatest when actual amount and desired amount were approximately equal.

The surface for span of control was also saddle-shaped, with its stationary point to the right of the $Y = X$ line where X and Y were both negative. The first principal axis was rotated clockwise from the $Y = X$ line, as shown by a p_{11} value that was significantly less than 1.00. The quantity $-p_{10}/(1 + p_{11})$ was 0.727, but its 95 percent confidence interval included zero, thereby failing to reject the null hypothesis of no lateral shift along the $Y = -X$ line. As would be expected, the second principal axis also indicated a clockwise rotation, as evidenced by a p_{21} value that was significantly less than -1.00. Along the $Y = X$ line, the surface was curved upward and had a positive slope at the point $X = 0$, $Y = 0$, whereas along the $Y = -X$ line, the surface had a positive linear slope. In contrast, the surface had an upward curvature along the first principal axis and was essentially flat along the second principal axis. Substantively, these results indicated that satisfaction increased as actual span of control increased toward desired span of control and continued to increase as actual span of control exceeded desired span of control, although at a decreasing rate. Moreover, when actual span of control was high, satisfaction was highest when actual span of control was greater than desired span of control, perhaps due to the increased rewards brought by managing large numbers of subordinates.

Finally, the surface for travel was concave with its stationary point near the $Y = X$ line but well beyond the range of the data. The first principal axis was nearly parallel to the $Y = X$ line, as indicated by a p_{11} value that did not differ from 1.00. The quantity $-p_{10} / (1 + p_{11})$ was 0.412, and its 95 percent confidence interval excluded zero, meaning that the first principal axis was shifted to the right of the $Y = X$ line. As would be expected, the second principal axis was essentially parallel to the $Y = -X$ line, as shown by a p_{21} value that did not differ from -1.00. However, because the second principal axis was far outside the range of the data, it should be disregarded when interpreting the surface. The surface had a positive linear slope along the $Y = X$ line and had a downward curvature along the $Y = -X$ line with a positive slope at $X = 0$, $Y = 0$. The shape of the surface along the first principal axis was similar to the shape along the $Y = X$ line, although the positive linear slope along the axis produced a 95 percent confidence interval that included zero. Overall, these results indicate that satisfaction was maximized along a line where actual travel slightly exceeded desired travel. In addition, satisfaction was slightly higher when actual and desired travel were both high than when both were low, suggesting that wanting and attaining a great deal of travel may produce a marginal increase in satisfaction.

Discussion

Advantages of Polynomial Regression Analysis

The polynomial regression procedure offers several advantages over the use of difference scores. First, polynomial regression circumvents problems of reduced reliability created when component measures are subtracted from one another. Second, by using component measures in their original form, polynomial regression avoids ambiguities that result when the component measures are reduced to a single score. Third, whereas difference scores confound the effects of their components, polynomial regression allows comprehensive assessment of the separate and joint effects of the components. Fourth, polynomial regression offers tests of constraints imposed by difference scores, treating these constraints as hypotheses regarding the combined effects of the components on the outcome. Finally, polynomial regression preserves the inherently three-dimensional relationship between the components and the outcome, thereby enabling researchers to develop and test congruence hypotheses that are more comprehensive and complex than the simplified models implied by difference scores.

The empirical illustration of the polynomial regression procedure demonstrated its advantages over difference scores. For all four job attributes, algebraic difference scores indicated that satisfaction increased as actual amount increased toward desired amount and continued to increase as actual amount exceeded desired amount. In contrast, absolute and squared difference scores suggested that satisfaction was maximized when actual and desired amounts were equal and decreased as actual amount deviated from desired amount in either direction. Although these results are conceptually plausible when taken individually, they are logically inconsistent when considered jointly, given that they indicate opposite effects on satisfaction when actual amounts exceeded desired amounts. In contrast, polynomial regression analysis rejected the models implied by the algebraic, absolute, and squared difference scores for each job attribute. Response surface analyses produced results that were largely consistent with hypotheses that considered asymmetric effects of incongruence and variation in satisfaction along the line of congruence. These results add to a growing body of research that consistently rejects constraints imposed by difference scores and yields conceptually meaningful surfaces relating components to outcomes.

Limitations and Areas for Further Development

Despite its advantages, polynomial regression analysis has several limitations that provide avenues for further methodological development. First, it adopts the standard regression assumption that independent variables are measured without error. As component measure reliability decreases, coefficient estimates may be biased upward or downward. This problem can be particularly pronounced for higher-order terms used in quadratic equations. For example, if two component measures have zero means and unit variances and are uncorrelated, the reliability of their product equals the product of their reliabilities (Bohrnstedt & Marwell, 1978). Measurement error was not severe for the empirical example presented earlier, for which reliabilities of all squared and product terms exceeded .823. Nonetheless, even modest amounts of measurement error can affect tests of constraints and response surface features. Problems created by measurement error may be addressed using structural equation modeling with latent variables (Bollen, 1989; Jöreskog & Sörbom, 1996). Structural equation modeling is straightforward for linear equations such as equation 11.5, and multiple groups structural equation models can be applied to piecewise linear equations such as equation 11.11. Methods for estimating quadratic equations may be derived from procedures for testing interactions between latent variables (Jaccard & Wan, 1996; Jöreskog & Yang, 1996). Chi-square difference tests may be used to test constraints imposed by difference scores, and structural equation parameters may be used to calculate and test response surface features.

Second, to examine the effects of congruence on multiple dimensions simultaneously, polynomial regression equations require a large number of terms. For instance, if the effects of congruence on the four job attributes from the empirical example were analyzed simultaneously, a regression equation with twenty independent variables would be required. With this approach, the effects of congruence on each job attribute are analyzed using the five quadratic terms for that attribute, and the quadratic terms for the remaining job attributes would be treated as covariates. This approach provides estimates of the effects of congruence on each job attribute, taking into account congruence on all other job attributes. Alternately, separate equations can be used to examine the effects of congruence for each dimension, and type I error rate can be controlled using the Bonferroni correction. Although using separate equations is relatively simple, it may introduce bias due to omitted variables (James, 1980). This potential bias may be taken into account by recognizing that the effects of congruence for a particular dimension also reflect the effects of congruence for other dimensions excluded from the equation.

Third, polynomial regression analysis applies only to congruence as a predictor. When congruence is an outcome, different analytical procedures are required. Edwards (1995) presents multivariate regression procedures that provide alternatives to algebraic and absolute difference scores as dependent variables. Alternatives to squared difference scores as dependent variables are more difficult to derive, but hypotheses that motivate the use of squared difference scores can usually be tested using procedures that apply to absolute difference scores. However, these procedures incorporate the assumption that the effects on the components change in slope where the two components are equal, which may not be the case. This assumption can be tested using alternatives to squared difference scores as dependent variables, although these procedures await further development.

Finally, although polynomial regression can be applied to change scores as independent variables, it does not apply to change scores as dependent variables. Although some researchers advocate using change scores as dependent variables (Allison, 1990; Liker, Augustyniak, & Duncan, 1985), doing so is tantamount to using the initial value of the dependent variable as a covariate and constraining its coefficient to unity (Cronbach & Furby, 1970). This constraint may be tested by estimating the coefficient and determining whether its confidence interval includes unity. When change involves multiple waves, growth curve modeling may be applied (Rogosa, Brandt, & Zimowski, 1982). Although this procedure has advantages over change scores, it transforms successive values of the dependent variable into intercept and slope coefficients, thereby discarding information regarding deviations of the dependent variable from the growth curve. Research has yet to explore fully the comparative advantages of growth curve modeling, change scores, and using lagged values of dependent variables as covariates.

Conclusion

For decades, researchers have recognized that difference scores present numerous methodological problems. These problems can be avoided with polynomial regression analysis, which provides comprehensive tests of hypotheses that difference scores are intended to capture. Moreover, polynomial regression allows researchers to pursue research questions that cannot be addressed using difference scores. These questions involve fundamental issues in congruence research, such as asymmetries in the effects of incongruence and differences in congruence effects depending on the absolute levels of the components. Questions such as these have been raised in theories of congruence (French et al., 1982; Kulka, 1979; Naylor et al., 1980; Rice et al., 1985), but research into these questions has languished due to the limitations of difference scores. Polynomial regression matches the inherent complexity of congruence theories and allows researchers to comprehensively test predictions from these theories and pursue new theoretical questions that previously could not be addressed.

Notes

1. Given the constraint $b_3 = b_5$, the constraint $b_3 + b_4 + b_5 = 0$ is equivalent to $b_4 = -2b_3$ or $b_4 = -2b_5$ (Edwards, 1994).
2. Given the constraints $b_1 = -b_2$ and $b_4 = -b_5$, the constraint $b_4 = -2b_1$ is equivalent to $b_4 = 2b_2$, $b_5 = 2b_1$, or $b_5 = -2b_2$.
3. To allow meaningful interpretation of the slope of the surface at the point $X = 0$, $Y = 0$, it is assumed that the component measures are scale centered, as in the empirical example used here.

References

Aiken, L. A., & West, S. G. (1991). *Multiple regression: Testing and interpreting interactions.* Thousand Oaks, CA: Sage.

Allison, P. D. (1990). Change scores as dependent variables in regression analysis. In C. C. Clogg (Ed.), *Sociological methodology 1990* (pp. 93–114). Washington, DC: American Sociological Association.

Atwater, L. E., Ostroff, C., Yammarino, F. J., & Fleenor, J. W. (1998). Self-other agreement: Does it really matter? *Personnel Psychology, 51,* 577–598.

Atwater, L., & Yammarino, F. (1997). Self-other rating agreement: A review and model. *Research in Personnel and Human Resource Management, 15,* 121–174.

Belsley, D. A., Kuh, E., & Welsch, R. E. (1980). *Regression diagnostics: Identifying influential data and sources of collinearity.* New York: Wiley.

Bohrnstedt, G. W., & Goldberger, A. S. (1969). On the exact covariance of products of random variables. *American Statistical Association Journal, 64,* 1439–1442.

Bohrnstedt, G. W., & Marwell, G. (1978). The reliability of products of two random variables. In K. F. Schuessler (Ed.), *Sociological methodology 1978* (pp. 254–273). San Francisco: Jossey-Bass.

Bollen, K. A. (1989). *Structural equations with latent variables.* New York: Wiley.

Bollen, K. A., & Jackman, R. W. (1990). Regression diagnostics: An expository treatment of outliers and influential cases. In J. Fox & J. S. Long (Eds.), *Modern methods of data analysis* (pp. 257–291). Thousand Oaks, CA: Sage.

Booth, J. G., & Sarker, S. (1998). Monte Carlo approximation of bootstrap variances. *American Statistician, 52,* 354–357.

Box, G.E.P., & Draper, N. R. (1987). *Empirical model-building and response surfaces.* New York: Wiley.

Caldwell, D. F., & O'Reilly, C. A. (1990). Measuring person-job fit with a profile comparison process. *Journal of Applied Psychology, 75,* 648–657.

Caplan, R. D. (1987). Person-environment fit theory and organizations: Commensurate dimensions, time perspectives, and mechanisms. *Journal of Vocational Behavior, 31,* 248–267.

Chatman, J. A. (1989). Improving interactional organizational research: A model of person-organization fit. *Academy of Management Review, 14,* 333–349.

Cohen, J. (1978). Partialed products *are* interactions: Partialed powers *are* curve components. *Psychological Bulletin, 85,* 858–866.

Cohen, J. (1988). *Statistical power analysis for the behavioral sciences* (2nd ed.). Orlando, FL: Academic Press.

Cronbach, L. J. (1958). Proposals leading to analytic treatment of social perception scores. In R. Tagiuri & L. Petrullo (Eds.), *Person perception and interpersonal behavior* (pp. 353–379). Stanford, CA: Stanford University Press.

Cronbach, L. J. (1987). Statistical tests for moderator variables: Flaws in analyses recently proposed. *Psychological Bulletin, 102,* 414–417.

Cronbach, L. J., & Furby, L. (1970). How we should measure "change"— or should we? *Psychological Bulletin, 74,* 68–80 (erratum, *Psychological Bulletin, 74,* 218).

Dawis, R. V., & Lofquist, L. H. (1984). *A psychological theory of work adjustment.* Minneapolis: University of Minnesota Press.

DeGroot, M. H. (1975). *Probability and statistics.* Reading, MA: Addison-Wesley.

Edwards, J. R. (1991). Person-job fit: A conceptual integration, literature review, and methodological critique. In C. L. Cooper & I. T. Robertson (Eds.), *International review of industrial and organizational psychology* (Vol. 6, pp. 283–357). New York: Wiley.

Edwards, J. R. (1994). The study of congruence in organizational behavior research: Critique and a proposed alternative. *Organizational Behavior and Human Decision Processes, 58,* 51–100 (erratum, *58,* 323–325).

Edwards, J. R. (1995). Alternatives to difference scores as dependent variables in the study of congruence in organizational research. *Organizational Behavior and Human Decision Processes, 64,* 307–324.

Edwards, J. R. (1996). An examination of competing versions of the person-environment fit approach to stress. *Academy of Management Journal, 39,* 292–339.

Edwards, J. R., Caplan, R. D., & Harrison, R. V. (1998). Person-environment fit theory: Conceptual foundations, empirical evidence, and directions for future research. In C. L. Cooper (Ed.), *Theories of organizational stress* (pp. 28–67). Oxford: Oxford University Press.

Edwards, J. R., & Harrison, R. V. (1993). Job demands and worker health: Three-dimensional reexamination of the relationship between person-environment fit and strain. *Journal of Applied Psychology, 78,* 628–648.

Edwards, J. R., & Parry, M. E. (1993). On the use of polynomial regression equations as an alternative to difference scores in organizational research. *Academy of Management Journal, 36,* 1577–1613.

Edwards, J. R., & Rothbard, N. P. (1999). Work and family stress and well-being: An examination of person-environment fit in the work and family domains. *Organizational Behavior and Human Decision Processes, 77,* 85–129.

Efron, B., & Tibshirani, R. (1993). *An introduction to the bootstrap.* New York: Chapman & Hall.

Elsass, P. M., & Veiga, J. F. (1997). Job control and job strain: A test of three models. *Journal of Occupational Health Psychology, 2,* 195–211.

Finegan, J. E. (2000). The impact of person and organizational values on organizational commitment. *Journal of Occupational and Organizational Psychology, 73,* 149–169.

Fleenor, J. W., McCauley, C. D., & Brutus, S. (1996). Self-other rating agreement and leader effectiveness. *Leadership Quarterly, 7,* 487–506.

Fox, J. (1991). *Regression diagnostics: An introduction.* Thousand Oaks, CA: Sage.

French, J.R.P., Jr., Caplan, R. D., & Harrison, R. V. (1982). *The mechanisms of job stress and strain.* New York: Wiley.

Goodman, L. A. (1960). On the exact variance of products. *American Statistical Association Journal, 55,* 708–713.

Graham, W. K. (1976). Commensurate characteristics of persons, groups, and organizations: Development of the Trait Ascription Questionnaire (TAQ). *Human Relations, 29,* 607–622.

Hattie, J. (1985). Methodology review: Assessing unidimensionality of tests and items. *Applied Psychological Measurement, 9,* 139–164.

Harrison, R. V. (1978). Person-environment fit and job stress. In C. L. Cooper & R. Payne (Ed.), *Stress at work* (pp. 175–205). New York: Wiley.

Hesketh, B., & Gardner, D. (1993). Person-environment fit models: A reconceptualization and empirical test. *Journal of Vocational Behavior, 42,* 315–332.

Hom, P. W., Griffeth, R. W., Palich, L. E., & Bracker, J. S. (1999). Revisiting met expectations as a reason why realistic job previews work. *Personnel Psychology, 52,* 97–112.

Irving, P. G., & Meyer, J. P. (1994). Reexamination of the met-expectations hypothesis: A longitudinal analysis. *Journal of Applied Psychology, 79,* 937–949.

Irving, P. G., & Meyer, J. P. (1995). On using direct measures of met expectations: A methodological note. *Journal of Management, 21,* 1159–1175.

Jaccard, J., & Wan, C. K. (1996). *LISREL approaches to interaction effects in multiple regression.* Thousand Oaks, CA: Sage.

James, L. R. (1980). The unmeasured variable problem in path analysis. *Journal of Applied Psychology, 65,* 415–421.

Johns, G. (1981). Difference score measures of organizational behavior variables: A critique. *Organizational Behavior and Human Performance, 27,* 443–463.

Johnson, J. W., & Ferstl, K. L. (1999). The effects of interrater and self-other agreement on performance improvement following upward feedback. *Personnel Psychology, 52,* 271–304.

Jöreskog, K. G., & Sörbom, D. (1996). *LISREL 8 user's reference guide.* Chicago: Scientific Software International.

Jöreskog, K. G., & Yang, F. (1996). Nonlinear structural equation models: The Kenny-Judd model with interaction effects. In G. A. Marcoulides & R. E. Schumacker (Eds.), *Advances in structural equation modeling* (pp. 57–88). Hillsdale, NJ: Erlbaum.

Kalliath, T. J., Bluedorn, A. C., & Strube, M. J. (1999). A test of value congruence effects. *Journal of Organizational Behavior, 20,* 1175–1198.

Kennedy, P. (1992). *A guide to econometrics.* Cambridge, MA: MIT Press.

Khuri, A. I., & Cornell, J. A. (1987). *Response surfaces: Designs and analyses.* New York: Marcel Dekker.

Kristof, A. L. (1996). Person-organization fit: An integrative review of its conceptualization, measurement, and implications. *Personnel Psychology, 49,* 1–49.

Kulka, R. A. (1979). Interaction as person-environment fit. In L. R. Kahle (Ed.), *New directions for methodology of behavioral science* (pp. 55–71). San Francisco: Jossey-Bass.

Liker, J. K., Augustyniak, S., & Duncan, G. J. (1985). Panel data and models of change: A comparison of first difference and conventional two-wave models. *Social Science Research, 14,* 80–101.

Livingstone, L. P., Nelson, D. L., & Barr, S. H. (1997). Person-environment fit and creativity: An examination of supply-value and demand-ability versions of fit. *Journal of Management, 23,* 119–146.

Locke, E. A. (1969). What is job satisfaction? *Organizational Behavior and Human Performance, 4,* 309–336.

Locke, E. A. (1976). The nature and causes of job satisfaction. In M. Dunnette (Ed.), *Handbook of industrial and organizational psychology* (pp. 1297–1350). Skokie, IL: Rand McNally.

Meglino, B. M., Ravlin, E. C., & Adkins, C. L. (1989). A work values approach to corporate culture: A field test of the value congruence process and its relationship to individual outcomes. *Journal of Applied Psychology, 74,* 424–434.

Mooney, C. Z., & Duval, R. D. (1993). *Bootstrapping: A nonparametric approach to statistical inference.* Thousand Oaks, CA: Sage.

Myers, R. H. (1971). *Response surface methodology.* Needham Heights, MA: Allyn & Bacon.

Naylor, J. C., Pritchard, R. D., & Ilgen, D. R. (1980). *A theory of behavior in organizations.* Orlando, FL: Academic Press.

Nunnally, J. C. (1978). *Psychometric theory* (2nd ed.). New York: McGraw-Hill.

O'Brien, G. E., & Dowling, P. (1980). The effects of congruency between perceived and desired job attributes upon job satisfaction. *Journal of Occupational Psychology, 53,* 121–130.

O'Reilly, C. A., Chatman, J. A., & Caldwell, D. F. (1991). People and organizational culture: A Q-sort approach to assessing person-organization fit. *Academy of Management Journal, 34,* 487–516.

Pedhazur, E. J. (1997). *Multiple regression in behavioral research* (3rd ed.). New York: Holt.

Platt, J. R. (1964). Strong inference. *Science, 146,* 347–353.

Porter, L. W., & Steers, R. M. (1973). Organizational work and personal factors in employee turnover and absenteeism. *Psychological Bulletin, 80,* 151–176.

Rice, R. W., McFarlin, D. B., & Bennett, D. E. (1989). Standards of comparison and job satisfaction. *Journal of Applied Psychology, 74,* 591–598.

Rice, R. W., McFarlin, D. B., Hunt, R. G., & Near, J. P. (1985). Organizational work and the perceived quality of life: Toward a conceptual model. *Academy of Management Review, 10,* 296–310.

Rogosa, D., Brandt, D., & Zimowski, M. (1982). A growth curve approach to the measurement of change. *Psychological Bulletin, 92,* 726–748.

Rogosa, D., & Willett, J. (1983). Demonstrating the reliability of the difference score in the measurement of change. *Journal of Educational Measurement, 20,* 335–343.

Runkel, P. J., & McGrath, J. E. (1972). *Research on human behavior: A systematic guide to method.* New York: Holt.

Slocombe, T. E., & Bluedorn, A. C. (1999). Organizational behavior implications of the congruence between preferred polychronicity and experienced work-unit polychronicity. *Journal of Organizational Behavior, 20,* 75–99.

Sweeney, P. D., McFarlin, D. B., & Inderrieden, E. J. (1990). Using relative deprivation theory to explain satisfaction with income and pay level: A multistudy examination. *Academy of Management Journal, 33,* 423–436.

SYSTAT 9.0 [Computer software]. (1999). Chicago: SPSS.

Tinsley, H.E.A. (2000). The congruence myth: An analysis of the efficacy of the person-environment fit model. *Journal of Vocational Behavior, 56,* 147–179.

Tsui, A. S., & O'Reilly, C. A. III. (1989). Beyond simple demographic effects: The importance of relational demography in superior-subordinate dyads. *Academy of Management Journal, 32,* 402–423.

Van Vianen, A.E.M. (2000). Person-organization fit: The match between newcomers' and recruiters' preferences for organizational cultures. *Personnel Psychology, 53,* 113–149.

Wall, T. D., & Payne, R. (1973). Are deficiency scores deficient? *Journal of Applied Psychology, 58,* 322–326.

Wanous, J. P., & Lawler, E. E. III. (1972). Measurement and meaning of job satisfaction. *Journal of Applied Psychology, 56,* 95–105.

Wanous, J. P., Poland, T. D., Premack, S. L., & Davis, K. S. (1992). The effects of met expectations on newcomer attitudes and behaviors: A review and meta-analysis. *Journal of Applied Psychology, 77,* 288–297.

Werts, C. E., & Linn, R. L. (1970). A general linear model for studying growth. *Psychological Bulletin, 73,* 17–22.

Westman, M., & Eden, D. (1996). The inverted-U relationship between stress and performance: A field study. *Work and Stress, 10,* 165–173.

White, R. W. (1959). Motivation reconsidered: The concept of competence. *Psychological Review, 66,* 297–333.

Zimmerman, D. W., & Williams, R. H. (1982). Gain scores in research can be highly reliable. *Journal of Educational Measurement, 19,* 149–154.

CHAPTER 12

Multilevel Random Coefficient Modeling in Organizational Research
Examples Using SAS and S-PLUS
Paul D. Bliese

Data collected from organizations are often hierarchical in nature. Individual-level data are nested within work groups, work group data are nested within departments, and so on. The hierarchical nature of the data poses several interesting challenges. First, it can bias standard error estimates if the nested nature of the data is ignored. When standard error estimates are biased, one runs the risk of drawing incorrect inferences from statistical models. Second, nested data provide an opportunity to incorporate several different levels of analysis into a single statistical model simultaneously, thereby examining the influence of contextual effects. This potentially allows one to explain phenomena more richly than if one relied on only single-level models.

Recently, multilevel random coefficient (MRC) models have become popular in the analysis of nested data. MRC models have been used to study a wide range of organizational phenomena, including citizenship behavior (Kidwell, Mossholder, & Bennett, 1997), collective efficacy (Jex & Bliese, 1999), coping (Jex, Bliese, Buzzell, & Primeau, 2001), leadership consensus (Bliese & Britt, 2001), procedural justice (Mossholder, Bennett, & Martin, 1998), safety (Hofmann & Stetzer, 1998, 1996), satisfaction with health services (Jimmieson & Griffin, 1998), and social support (Bliese & Castro, 2000). In these studies, the authors explicitly considered the hierarchical nature of their data and used MRC analyses to conduct the analyses.

MRC models are conceptually similar to familiar regression models, except that MRC models include additional variance terms to account for hierarchical structure. In this chapter, I discuss the logic behind and the assumptions underlying the estimation of MRC models. I also provide several illustrative examples. Multilevel random coefficient models can be estimated using a number of statistical programs, including HLM (Bryk & Raudenbush, 1992; Byrk, Raudenbush, & Congdon, 1994), MLn (see Kreft & de Leeuw, 1998), PROC MIXED for SAS (see Littell, Milliken, Stroup, & Wolfinger, 1996; Singer, 1998), VARCL (Longford, 1990), and the NLME library for R and S-PLUS (Pinheiro & Bates, 2000). In this chapter, I use the notation from Bryk and Raudenbush's *Hierarchical Linear Models* (1992) because this notation is likely to be most familiar to organizational researchers. I do not, however, use the associated HLM program to illustrate MRC models in the examples for two reasons. First, detailed examples based on HLM are readily available elsewhere (Hofmann, 1997; Heck & Thomas, 2000); second, I want to demonstrate that MRC models can be estimated using software packages that are readily available to many researchers. Consequently, I provide examples of model estimation in SAS (which is licensed at many universities) and with the NLME library for R and S-PLUS. Note that R is available as free software under the terms of the Free Software Foundation's GNU General Public License and can be obtained from www.r-project.org. Despite the fact that these programs are widely available, there are few illustrations of MRC model estimation using these programs in the organizational literature.

Error in Regression Models

To lay the framework for understanding MRC models, let us begin by exploring potential sources of error in familiar ordinary least squares (OLS) models. Consider a simple OLS regression model with one independent variable:

$$Y_i = \beta_0 + \beta_1 x_i + r_i \qquad (12.1)$$

In this model, β_1 is the slope or the parameter estimate for x, and β_0 is the intercept. The error term (or residual) in this model is r_i. The regression model provides a means of predicting individual i's value on Y as a function of his or her response to x. If an individual's predicted Y value matches the actual value, then there is no error, and the residual for that individual is zero. In most cases, of course, the predicted value for Y differs from the actual value for Y, so r_i values for individuals in the sample are typically nonzero.

In this regression model, the variability of the residuals (defined as σ^2) plays an important role in statistical inference. This is because σ^2 is used to identify significant predictors. Almost any predictor (even a bad one) is likely to explain some variance in the dependent variable. That is, it is likely to reduce the variance of the residuals to some degree. Sigma-squared allows one to determine whether this explained variance is trivial or significant. If sigma-squared is relatively unchanged with the addition of an independent variable, then we conclude that the independent variable has no incremental predictive value. In contrast, if it is significantly reduced, then we conclude that the independent variable is predictive of the dependent variable.

The regression model presented in equation 12.1 makes some important assumptions about the nature of the residuals. For one thing, it assumes that the residuals will be normally distributed with a mean of zero: in half the cases, the predicted Y values should be overpredictions, and in half the cases, the predicted Y values should be underpredictions, and this should result in a mean value of 0. Furthermore, a histogram of the residuals should result in a normal or gaussian distribution with most of the residual values close to zero.

Another assumption of OLS models is that the residuals should be constant across the levels of the independent variables (they should have homoescadiscity). That is, we try to avoid models that have little or no error when x is small but that have increasingly large error as x increases, or vice versa. When the variance of the residuals changes as a function of x , we say that heteroscedasticity is present. The third assumption that the OLS model makes about residuals is that they are independent. That is, the residual from individual 1 should not be related (that is correlated) with any of the other residuals in the sample. In statistical notation, we can summarize these assumptions by stating that $r_i \sim$ i.i.d. $N(0, \sigma^2)$, where i.i.d. means "independent, identically distributed."

Violations of the assumption of nonindependence are what interest us most in this chapter. This is because it appears that OLS models are relatively robust to violations of normality and to homoscedasticity (see Glass, Peckham, & Sanders, 1972; although see Bradley, 1980a, 1980b, for an alternative view). OLS models, however, are *not* robust to violations of nonindependence (Kenny & Judd, 1986; Puvar & Nath, 1984). As I will show, violations of nonindependence turn out to be quite problematic.

Nonindependence

One of the reasons why violations of nonindependence are important to organizational researchers is that nonindependence is ubiquitous. Kenny and Judd (1996) note that "observations may be dependent, for instance, because they share some common feature, come from some common source, are affected by social interaction, or are arranged spatially or sequentially in time" (p. 138). Nonindependence due to membership in groups is common because group membership and social interaction help shape individuals' interpretations of and reactions to their environments. I have reviewed literature elsewhere that has shown that organizational researchers are likely to encounter nonindependence in their dependent variables when studying factors as diverse as individual well-being, job satisfaction, and personality (see Bliese, 2000b). Thus, even organizational researchers who have no substantive interest in multilevel modeling do, as a matter of good science, need to have a substantive interest in nonindependence.

Consider a simple case of nonindependence plotted in Figure 12.1. These could be data from two work groups. One group (the circles) might be composed of experienced employees who have mastered their training (X) and whose performance (Y) reflects this mastery. The other group might be novices (the blocks). Notice that the group plotted using circles has higher values on Y than does the group plotted using boxes. Also notice that the slopes for the two groups differ. The slope for the circle group is represented using a dotted line; the slope for the blocks is represented using a solid line, and the common slope (ignoring group membership) is represented using the dashed line.

In Figure 12.1, nonindependence is present because the values of Y are related to or dependent on group membership; if the

Figure 12.1. OLS Regression Parameters for Two Groups and the Pooled Estimate.

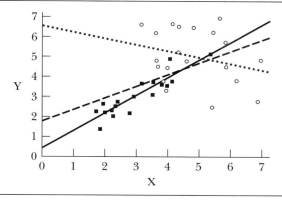

Note: The slope and intercept for the group of circles is the dotted line. For the group of blocks, it is the solid line, and for the pooled estimate, it is the dotted line.

data were independent, we would expect the squares and circles to be evenly distributed in the plotted figure. Instead, they cluster. Notice that in this example, they cluster by both X and Y, but in practice we are most concerned with nonindependence on Y. When nonindependence due to groups is present, it means that the residuals (r_i) for members of group J are more similar to each other than would be expected by chance. That is, the residuals are correlated. This is clearly illustrated in the figure. Observe the dashed regression line—the line that ignores group membership. The observations for the blocks are almost all negative; they fall below the dashed line. In contrast, the observations for the circles are primarily above the dashed line. Because the observations tend to cluster either above or below the line, the residuals tend to be either positive (the circle group) or negative (the block group) depending on the grouping condition. In other words, the residuals tend to be correlated with group membership.

In the situation depicted by the dashed line in Figure 12.1 (where one fails to model group membership), two key sources of variation are ignored. First, the dashed line ignores the fact that there are between-group differences in average Y values: the circles have higher Y ratings than do the blocks. Second, the dashed line ignores the fact that the X-Y relationship for one group is different from the X-Y relationship in the other group. For the blocks, there is a positive relationship between X and Y, but for the circles the relationship between X and Y is negative. It is clear that ignoring these differences is likely to lead to problems in statistical inference.

MRC modeling builds on the simple idea that whenever groups are present, one is likely to have several new sources of random variation that are not captured in simple regression models. The power of MRC models comes from the fact that one can directly model these other sources of variance and thereby develop a better understanding of the data.

Visualizing Multilevel Variance

Understanding the logic behind MRC models requires understanding how the hierarchical structure of data can be mathematically represented in separate variance terms. In this section, we go into detail about the multilevel variance terms in a two-level MRC model. In so doing, let us return to regression equation 12.1, but this time let us add an additional index, j, to keep track of group membership. In this case, j will vary from 1 to the number of groups in the sample:

$$Y_{ij} = \beta_{0j} + \beta_{1j} x_{ij} + r_{ij} \tag{12.2}$$

Just to review, in equation 12.2, Y_{ij} represents the response from the ith individual in group j. Once we have indexed group membership, several possibilities emerge. For instance, we might consider the possibility that the intercept, β_{0j}, and the slope, β_{1j}, will differ across groups (as they apparently do in Figure 12.1). As a researcher, one must now decide how to treat these potential group differences.

One option is to decide that slopes and intercepts across groups should not be allowed to vary. This has the effect of forcing all intercepts, β_{0j}, to be the same value across all groups, and it forces all slopes, β_1, to be the same value across all groups. We could designate this model in equation form using Bryk and Raudenbush's (1992) notation as follows:

$$Y_{ij} = \beta_{0j} + \beta_{1j} x_{ij} + r_{ij} \tag{12.3a}$$

$$\beta_{0j} = \gamma_{00} \tag{12.3b}$$

$$\beta_{1j} = \gamma_{10} \tag{12.3c}$$

Here, γ_{00} represents the common intercept across groups, and γ_{10} represents the common slope across groups. In this model, we are simply saying that a specific value of x will consistently be related to a value of Y, regardless of group membership. This is equivalent to estimating a model that ignores group membership as we did with the dashed line in Figure 12.1.

Model 12.3 is not really a random coefficient model, because there are no multilevel variance terms. That is, neither the intercept nor the slope is permitted to vary randomly as a function of group membership. If we estimated this model using the MRC programs listed earlier, we would for all intents and purposes be estimating a simple regression equation such as that presented in equation 12.1.

In order for the model to be a random coefficient model, either the intercept or the slope must be allowed to vary as a function of group membership. The most common random coefficient model is one where the intercept is allowed to vary randomly. This model is designated as

$$Y_{ij} = \beta_{0j} + \beta_{1j} x_{ij} + r_{ij} \tag{12.4a}$$

$$\beta_{0j} = \gamma_{00} + u_{0j} \tag{12.4b}$$

$$\beta_{1j} = \gamma_{10} \tag{12.4c}$$

Notice that we have now included the error term, (u_{0j}), for the intercept γ_{00}. If we return to the simple example involving two groups and estimate model 12.4, we can predict parameter estimates for both groups from the resulting MRC model. If we examine these predicted parameter estimates, we see that both groups have a common slope (specifically 0.23) but a different intercept. Specifically, the circles have an intercept of 3.85, and the boxes have an intercept of 2.40. Figure 12.2 plots these slopes and intercepts.

While allowing intercepts to vary randomly appears to improve the model, we still have the option of including a random term for the slope. A model that includes this term is designated as

$$Y_{ij} = \beta_{0j} + \beta_{1j} x_{ij} + r_{ij} \tag{12.5a}$$

$$\beta_{0j} = \gamma_{00} + u_{0j} \tag{12.5b}$$

$$\beta_{1j} = \gamma_{10} + u_{1j} \tag{12.5c}$$

Figure 12.2. MRC Models with Random Intercepts.

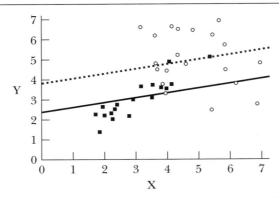

Notice the inclusion of u_{1j}, the error term for the slope. Estimating this model using the running example and the resulting MRC model to predict parameter estimates for each group yields Figure 12.3. The figure looks very much like Figure 12.1, where we estimated a separate regression equation for each group. That is, in both figures, the two groups differ in terms of intercepts and slopes.

It is important to recognize that when we estimated model 12.5, we allowed the slopes and the intercepts to vary randomly, and we used this information to predict slope and intercept values for the two groups. In the example, the MRC approach and the separate-regression-equation-for-each-group approach yield similar (but not identical) intercept and slope estimates. Specifically, the MRC estimates of the intercept for group 1 were 6.36 versus 6.52 in the OLS model, and the MRC estimate of the intercept for group 2 was 0.47 versus 0.42 in the OLS model. These small changes in the intercept estimates in the MRC models serve to move each group closer to the pooled intercept estimate of 4.23. The effect on slopes was similar in that the MRC estimates moved each group slightly closer to the pooled slope estimate.

Although the separate regression equation and MRC analysis results were very similar in this example, the slope and intercept estimates from the two approaches will be different in many other cases. This is because the estimates based on the MRC model predictions take more information into consideration than do the sep-

**Figure 12.3. MRC Model with Random Intercept
and Slope Terms Yielding the Predicted Intercept and
Slope Values for the Group of Circles and Group of Blocks.**

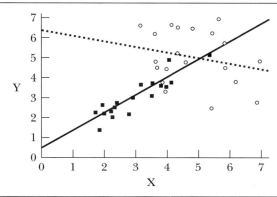

arate regression equations. Specifically, when one estimates slopes and intercepts separately, the slope and intercept estimates are based on only one piece of information: the X and Y values for each group. In contrast, when one uses an MRC model to produce estimates of slopes and intercepts, the estimates are based on three pieces of information: the X and Y values for each group, the pooled intercept and slope values across groups, and the precision of the group estimate (based largely on group size). Because the random coefficient model bases its estimates on three pieces of information, the intercept and slope estimates from a specific group are adjusted or "shrunken" to resemble slopes and intercepts from other groups, with more shrinkage occurring for small groups than for large groups (see Bryk & Raudenbush, 1992).

Note that when MRC models are used in organizational research, one will generally *not* be interested in predicting intercepts and slopes for specific groups. Values for specific groups are primarily of interest to practitioners. In theoretical work, researchers will be generally interested in knowing simply whether the intercepts and slopes randomly vary. Nonetheless, the preceding examples with the two groups give a sense of how freeing and fixing various multilevel variance components translate into assumptions about the group-level properties of the data.

To round out the discussion of sources of variance in nested models, we need to return to u_{0j} and u_{1j}, the terms associated with the intercept and slope, respectively. Recall that in the simple regression equation, the residual, r_i, refers to the difference between the observed and predicted Y value for individual i. The total error in the model is estimated using the variance of r_i, which is designated as σ^2. Sigma-squared is important because significance in the regression model is based on the degree to which we can explain σ^2. This means that in terms of statistical inference, we are more interested in the variance of the residual, σ^2, than in the residuals themselves.

The same is also true in MRC models. In these models, we are more interested in the variance of u_{0j} and u_{1j} than in u_{0j} and u_{1j} themselves. This is because when the variance of u_{0j} is large, it indicates that the intercepts among groups differ. When the variance of u_{1j} is large, it indicates that the slopes across groups differ (see Kreft & de Leeuw, 1998). In MRC models, the variance of the intercept, u_{0j}, is designated as τ_{00}. The variance of the slope, u_{1j}, is designated as τ_{11}. In cases where there are multiple random slope estimates (for example, u_{1j}, u_{2j}, u_{3j}), the variance of the slope estimates are designated as τ_{11}, τ_{12}, τ_{13}, and so on.

Finally, MRC models also routinely provide estimates of the covariance between u_{0j} and u_{1j}. That is, they estimate the degree to which the intercept errors are related to slope errors. This covariance term is designated as τ_{01} for the covariance between the intercept and the first slope, τ_{02}, for the covariance between the intercept and the second random slope, and so on.

Now that we have covered the sources of variation in a MRC model, let us return to equation 12.5 and substitute equations 12.5b and 12.5c into 12.5a to derive a single equation. To clarify the process, I do so in two steps:

$$Y_{ij} = (\gamma_{00} + u_{0j}) + (\gamma_{10} + u_{1j})x_{ij} + r_{ij} \qquad (12.6a)$$

$$Y_{ij} = \gamma_{00} + \gamma_{10}x_{ij} + (u_{0j} + u_{1j}x_{ij} + r_{ij}) \qquad (12.6b)$$

The single equation in 12.6b is a multilevel random coefficient model equation containing both a random intercept and a random slope. The equation is comprised of two components. The fixed-effect part of the equation, γ_{00} and $\gamma_{10}x_{ij}$, contains the estimates of the overall intercept and slope, respectively. The random-effects part, $(u_{0j} + u_{1j}x_{ij} + r_{ij})$, defines the error structure of the model and represents the error due to between-group intercept differences, between-group slope differences, and within-group residuals, respectively. When there is no between-group variation in intercepts or slopes, equation 12.6b simplifies into the simple regression equation that was first presented (equation 12.1).

Before concluding the discussion of sources of variation, let me provide a visual representation of all sources of variation in a single figure. In Figure 12.4, I have plotted the number of hours that students spend on homework (X) and their Math Achievement score (Y) for two schools. This data are a subset of the data used by Kreft and de Leeuw (1998). Consider the left panel and the error associated with r_{ij}. Individual number 1 in group number 1 has a Math Achievement score of about 58. Based on the within-group regression line (the solid line), one would expect him or her to have a score of about 44. The difference between the estimated and actual value is represented by r_{11}, and the variance of all r_{ij} values is σ^2. Next consider the error term, u_{0j}. The bar on the far left labeled γ_{00} represents the common intercept for all groups. The value of this intercept term is a score of about 45. This value indicates that, overall, schools are expected to have average Math Achievement scores of 45 if students did no homework. Group 1, however, has an intercept of 51. This means that school 1 would be expected to have an average score of 51 even if students did no homework. The difference between the predicted intercept and the actual intercept is represented by the error term, u_{01}. The variance of this error term across all groups is τ_{00}.

Finally, consider the error term $u_{1j}x_{ij}$. This error term for the slope is more complex than are the other two error terms and is visually represented in the right panel. The dotted line in the right panel indicates the common slope, γ_{10}. The solid line represents the slope for school 2. The difference between the two slopes is captured by the error term u_{12} whose variance across all groups is τ_{11}. Interestingly, however, if we want to predict how much error is associated with the slope for an individual within a specific group, we need to know both the individual's x value and the magnitude of the error term u_{1j}. For example, consider individual 1, who has an

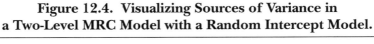

Figure 12.4. Visualizing Sources of Variance in a Two-Level MRC Model with a Random Intercept Model.

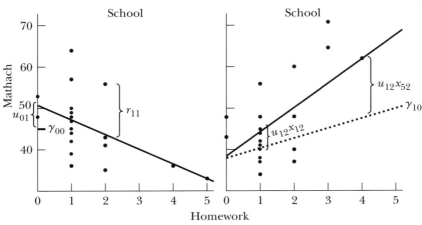

x value of 1 and a Y value equal to the group's expected Y value (the solid line). The error for the difference between Y_{10} and the within-group slope for individual 1 in group 2 is relatively small ($u_{12}x_{12}$). That is, there is relatively little error associated with slope differences for this individual. In contrast, consider individual 5 in group 2, who has an x value of 4 and whose Y value matches the predicted Y value for the group. In individual 5's case, the error for the difference between Y_{10} and the within-group slope is relatively large ($u_{52}x_{52}$). Thus, the total amount of error associated with u_{12} varies as a function of individual x values.

At this point, we have identified the three key sources of variance in a simple two-level MRC model: σ^2, τ_{00}, and τ_{11}. As we will discuss in detail, the essence of estimating substantive MRC models boils down to the act of determining which of these sources of variance is significant and trying to identify variables that are predictive of each source of variance. That is, in MRC models, one attempts to predict within-group variation (σ^2), between-group variation in intercepts (τ_{00}), and between-group variation in slopes (τ_{11}). By clearly defining sources of variance in this way, two benefits are accrued. First, it helps ensure that standard errors for parameter estimates are properly specified and estimated. Second, specifying separate sources of variance allows one to build statistical models that simultaneously incorporate higher- and lower-level influences. I address each of these issues below, beginning with the implications for standard error estimation.

Standard Error Estimation

In discussing how nonindependence affects standard error estimation, let us use an example and reanalyze data presented in Bliese and Halverson (1996). These data will serve as the illustrative example throughout the remainder of the chapter. Briefly, the data consist of survey responses from 7,382 soldiers who are members of ninety-nine U.S. Army companies. The dependent variable in all of the analyses is General Well-Being, which was assessed by a self-report rating of physical and mental health. These data are available as part of the multilevel package for R (see Bliese, 2000a).

There are several independent variables that Bliese and Halverson discuss, but in this section we focus on the variable Cohesion: soldiers' self-reports of the kinship and bonding within the company. We consider two forms of cohesion: Personal Cohesion and Group Cohesion. Personal Cohesion represents individuals' self-ratings of the kinship and bonding within the company. Personal Cohesion scores vary across individuals within the same group. Group Cohesion, in contrast, is the companies' average Personal Cohesion score assigned back to the individual. Group Cohesion varies across companies but is constant within companies.

In multilevel terminology, Personal Cohesion is a level 1 variable: it varies among members of the same group. The second independent variable, Group Cohesion, is a level 2 variable: the same score is assigned to each group member, so all variation is between-group variation. We can think of Group Cohesion as being a cross-level operator (James & Williams, 2000).

We need to make two assumptions about these data. One is that the slope between Personal Cohesion and General Well-Being is constant across groups. By making this assumption, we need only consider two variance terms (σ^2 and τ_{00}). The second assumption is that the dependent variable, General Well-Being, significantly varies as a function of group membership; in other words, General

Well-Being needs to display nonindependence due to groups. As I demonstrate, this assumption is supported. For demonstrative purposes, however, I randomly increased the degree to which General Well-Being varies as a function of group membership by adding a random term to each individual's General Well-Being value. This random term is identical for all members in the same group but differs across groups. This is analogous to a situation where a group-level factor affects General Well-Being among group members in some groups but not in others. Importantly, however, this group-level factor does not simultaneously affect Personal Cohesion.

After the manipulation, the estimate of nonindependence for General Well-Being is 0.29. In other words, the variance associated with τ_{00} represented 29 percent of the total variance. This can also be interpreted as meaning that 29 percent of the variability in Individual Well-Being scores can be "explained" by group membership (see Bryk & Raudenbush, 1992). Later I discuss the estimation of nonindependence in more detail. At this point, however, it is important just to note that the nonindependence or clustering associated with the dependent variable is 0.29.

Although it would be ill advised, we could ignore group differences and estimate an OLS regression model with the data just described. This model would provide parameter estimates for Personal Cohesion and Group Cohesion. These parameter estimates would tell us how much well-being changes as a function of Personal and Group Cohesion. The model would also provide standard error estimates that would tell us whether the parameter estimates for Personal Cohesion and Group Cohesion were significant. Recall that standard error estimates are based on variance estimates and that standard errors are used to calculate t-values that form the basis for statistical significance (p-values).

The issue we are facing here is this: Because we ignored group membership in an OLS regression model, should we believe the reported t-values from our statistical package output? The answer is no.

Interestingly, ignoring group membership in nested data causes us to be *more* likely to conclude that Group Cohesion (a level 2 variable) is significant even if it is not (increasing the probability of making a type I error). In contrast, ignoring nonindependence makes us *less* likely to conclude that Personal Cohesion (a level 1 variable) is significant even if it is significant (increase the probability of making a type II error). The reasons for this are detailed in Bliese and Hanges (2001) using random coefficient modeling notation. Kenny and Judd (1986) discuss this issue in detail from an experimental ANOVA perspective involving nested versus crossed designs.

To understand why standard errors are affected differently for level 1 versus level 2 variables, we must go back to the sources of variance discussed in the preceding section. Since slopes do not vary across groups, we have to contend with only two sources of variance: within-group variation (σ^2) and between-group variation in intercepts (τ_{00}). In the example above, τ_{00} is greater than zero. We know this because General Well-Being varies significantly across groups. (Recall that group membership "explained" 29 percent of the variance in well-being.)

To test whether Personal Cohesion (the level 1 variable) is significant, we need to know the within-group variance, σ^2. This variance estimate is important because it is used to estimate the standard error of the level 1 variable. The OLS regression model, however, does not partition the variance into the separate between-group and within-group components. Consequently, the OLS regression model bases the standard error estimate for the level 1 variable on the total variance ($\tau_{00} + \sigma^2$). In our example where the between-group variance is nonzero (and positive), $\tau_{00} + \sigma^2$ will, of course, be larger than σ^2. Large variances relative to parameter estimates result in reduced power, thereby leading to too many type II errors. So in the example, we would be more likely to conclude that Personal Cohesion was nonsignificant if we calculated an OLS regression model ignoring group membership.

In the specific example, we can show the effects of ignoring nonindependence by contrasting two models: an OLS model ignoring group membership and a multilevel random coefficient model with a random intercept term. Notice in Table 12.1 that the standard error for the random coefficient model is smaller than the standard error for the OLS model. These standard error differences result in higher t-values for the random coefficient model. (The slope estimates also differ slightly from each other, but the differences are minor and have little impact on the differences between t-values.)

Table 12.1. OLS Versus Random Coefficient Models, Level 1 Variable Example

	Value	Standard Error	t-value
Personal Cohesion: OLS	0.254	0.014	18.121
Personal Cohesion: MRC	0.249	0.012	20.780

It is clear that ignoring nonindependence in this case makes one less likely to conclude that the level 1 variable is significant. Ironically, however, the opposite effect occurs for level 2 variables such as Group Cohesion. Recall that a level 2 variable is one that varies only across groups: all individuals in the same group receive the same score. In the case of level 2 variables, one is too likely to conclude that the level 2 variable is significant (commit a type I error). This effect is well documented (Bryk & Raudenbush, 1992; Klein et al., 2000), but it is worth reviewing why this occurs.

The appropriate variance term for the null model on which to base estimates of standard errors for a level 2 variable is $\tau_{00} + \sigma^2/n$, where n represents the number of individuals within the group. As Bliese and Hanges (2001) note, this is an interesting term, and it is useful to consider both parts of the term separately. The first component, τ_{00}, is straightforward. It is simply the estimate of the between-group variation in intercepts (means). The second component, σ^2/n, reflects the fact that when τ_{00} is zero, the variance of the group mean is a direct function of individual-level variance and group size. Bliese and Hanges (2001) provide a simple example. Consider creating 10,000 normally distributed random numbers with a mean of 0 and a variance of 1. If one arbitrarily creates 100 groups from these 10,000 numbers, this will ensure that τ_{00} is zero. If groups are arbitrarily created to have a size of 100, and group means are calculated based on the 100 group members, then the variance of the group means will be .01 (1.00/100). If one arbitrarily creates 1,000 groups of size 10, the variance of the 1,000 group means will be .10 (1.00/10). Thus, level 1 variance and group size are a key component of the expected group-level variance.

Consequently, the appropriate variance term on which to base standard errors for a level 2 variable is composed of true group-level variance in the dependent variable (τ_{00}) and some residual level 1 variance that varies as a function of group size (σ^2/n). Recall, however, that in our OLS model, which ignores group membership, τ_{00} and σ^2 are not separately calculated. Thus, in the OLS model, the significance of the level 2 variable, Group Cohesion, is based on $(\tau_{00} + \sigma^2)/n$, or total variance divided by n (where n represents group size).

If τ_{00} equals zero, both OLS and MRC use the same variance term, and both analytic approaches will return the same estimate for the standard error. If τ_{00} is larger than zero, however, then ($\tau_{00} + \sigma^2)/n$ from the OLS model will be smaller than $\tau_{00} + \sigma^2/n$ from the MRC model. In this case, the standard error for our level 2 variables will be too small. This will increase the probability of committing type I errors.

For an example, consider the standard error differences between an OLS model and a random coefficient model when we predict general well-being from Group Cohesion (a level 2 variable that is constant for all members of the same group). Notice in Table 12.2 that the standard error estimate for the OLS model is about half the magnitude of the standard error estimate for the MRC model. This results in a t-value for the OLS model that is substantially higher than the t-value in the MRC model. (The parameter estimates also vary, but most of the difference in the t-value is due to standard error differences.)

In summary, it should be apparent that ignoring the nested nature of data is a poor idea. As a matter of good science, one should test for possible nonindependence in one's data (see also Bliese, 2000b; Bliese & Hanges, 2001; Kenny & Judd, 1986). If nonindependence is present, it needs to be appropriately handled. Failing to account for nonindependence can cause one to miss significant

Table 12.2. OLS Versus Random Coefficient Models, Level 2 Variable Example.

	Value	**Standard Error**	t-value
Group Cohesion: OLS	0.281	0.051	5.505
Group Cohesion: MRC	0.314	0.097	3.233

findings in level 1 variables or conclude that level 2 variables are significant when, in fact, they are not.

Note that nonindependence can be controlled for in models other than MRC and that there is extensive literature on controlling for nonindependence in ANOVA models. Kenny (1996) points out, however, that the application of ANOVA models "is limited in that generally the designs must be perfectly balanced (equal group sizes), with no missing data, and the fixed variables must be categorical. Determining expected mean squares with unbalanced designs can be difficult and time consuming. Moreover, the solution may refer only to the study at hand and may be of little use for future work. Because of these difficulties, multilevel models . . . are gaining favor" (pp. 73–74).

Thus, it is clear that MRC models have considerable utility as a way of controlling for nonindependence in organizational settings where designs are commonly unbalanced, missing data are frequently present, and one often has both continuous and categorical predictors.

MRC models, however, do more than control for nonindependence in messy data situations (despite the obvious value of this contribution). They can also be used to test substantive relationships in ways that cannot be done using ANOVA models. Using MRC models to test multilevel hypotheses is the topic of the next section.

Multilevel Modeling

Recall that in a typical two-level MRC model, one potentially has three important sources of variation: within-group variation (σ^2), between-group variation in intercepts (τ_{00}), and between-group variation in slopes (τ_{11}). When one uses MRC to control for nonindependence (as discussed in the previous section), one is primarily interested in determining whether τ_{00} is significant—that is, knowing whether the dependent variable clusters as a function of group membership. If clustering occurs, one includes the variance term τ_{00} in the model and thereby avoids potential biases in standard error estimates. Note that in doing so, one does not necessarily care why τ_{00} is significant; one is simply controlling for the fact that τ_{00} is significant.

In multilevel modeling, one moves beyond controlling for additional sources of variance to trying to identify factors that are related to these sources of variability. Specifically, one wants to know (1) what level 1 factors are related to the within-group variance σ^2; (2) what group-level factors are related to the between-group variation in intercepts τ_{00}; and (3) what group-level factors are related to within-group slope differences, τ_{11}. In the next sections, I reanalyze portions of the Bliese and Halverson data set to illustrate a typical sequence of steps that one might use in multilevel modeling. In the example, I provide illustrative code for how to estimate these models in SAS and with the NLME package (Pinheiro & Bates, 2000) in S-PLUS. (Note that the NLME package is also available for R, so the code for S-PLUS is identical to the code for R; see also Bliese, 2000a.)

Because multilevel modeling involves predicting variance at different levels, one typically begins a multilevel analysis by determining the levels at which significant variation exists. In the case of the two-level model (the only models that I consider here), one generally assumes that there is significant variation in σ^2—that is, that lower-level variation is present (this is commonly assumed in OLS models as well). One does not necessarily assume, however, that there will be significant between-group intercept variation or between-group slope variation.

Step 1: Testing for Intercept Variability

One commonly begins testing MRC models by determining whether there is significant variability in the intercepts across groups (see Bryk & Raudenbush, 1992; Hofmann, 1997). If τ_{00} does not significantly vary, there may be little reason to use random coefficient modeling since simpler OLS modeling will be adequate.

Tests for differences in the intercepts are conducted by estimating an unconditional means model. An unconditional means model does not contain any predictors but includes a random intercept variance term allowing group intercepts to differ. This model essentially looks at how much variability there is in group mean Y values (that is, how much variability there is in the intercept). In the two-stage HLM notation, the model is:

$$Y_{ij} = \beta_{0j} + r_{ij}$$
$$\beta_{0j} = \gamma_{00} + u_{0j}$$

In combined form, the model is $Y_{ij} = \gamma_{00} + u_{0j} + r_{ij}$. This model states that the dependent variable is a function of a common intercept γ_{00} and two error terms: the between-group error term, u_{0j}, and the within-group error term, r_{ij}. This model provides two estimates of variance: τ_{00}, for how much each group's intercept varies from the overall intercept, and σ^2, for how much each individual's score differs from the group mean. The fixed component of this model is γ_{00}, and the random component is $u_{0j} + r_{ij}$. Bryk and Raudenbush (1992) note that this model is directly equivalent to a one-way random-effects ANOVA—an ANOVA model where one predicts the dependent variable as a function of group membership.

The unconditional means model provides between-group and within-group variance estimates in the form of τ_{00} and σ^2, respectively. As with the ANOVA model, it is often valuable to determine how much of the total variance is between-group variance. This can be accomplished by calculating the Intraclass Correlation Coefficient (ICC) using the formula: $\text{ICC} = \tau_{00} / (\tau_{00} + \sigma^2)$ (see Bryk & Raudenbush, 1992; Kreft & de Leeuw, 1998). The ICC is equivalent to Bartko's (1976) ICC(1) formula and to Shrout and Fleiss's ICC(1,1) formula (see Bliese, 2000b). Both of these latter two ICC measures are estimated from one-way random-effects ANOVA models. Note that the estimates of within-group and between-group variance from the random coefficient model will be nearly identical to those from the ANOVA model as long as restricted maximum likelihood estimation (REML) is used in the random coefficient modeling (this is the default in most programs). If full maximum likelihood is used, the variance estimates may differ somewhat from the ANOVA estimates, particularly if sample sizes are small. All programs allow a choice between the two options.

There are two ways of determining whether the between-group variation in the intercepts is significant. HLM provides standard error estimates for τ_{00}, and these standard error estimates can be used to determine whether τ_{00} significantly differs from 0. In HLM, these estimates are found under the heading "Final Estimate of Variance Components." In both SAS and S-PLUS, these estimates must be specifically requested. Singer (1998) notes that there are concerns about the accuracy of the standard error estimates. Specifically, Singer states that the standard error estimates are based on large sample approximations and may not be useful with small sample sizes. In addition, Singer notes that the variance components are known to have skewed sampling distributions, but the significance tests are based on normal approximations.

To avoid these problems, an alternative method is to compare -2 log-likelihood values between a model containing a random intercept and a model without a random intercept. The -2 log-likelihood values are standard output in HLM ("Deviances"); SAS ("-2 Log Likelihood"), and S-PLUS ("logLik"; one must multiply these values by -2). If the -2 log-likelihood value for the model with the random intercept is significantly larger than the model without the random intercept (based on a chi-square distribution), then one concludes that the model with the random intercept is significantly "better" than the model without the random intercept. A significant chi-square indicates significant intercept variation.

As an illustration of the first step in an MRC analysis, let us re-analyze portions of the data presented in Bliese and Halverson (1996). In the following examples, we will be interested in three variables: soldiers' ratings of their own general well-being (WBEING), soldiers' ratings of unit leadership (LEAD), and soldiers' ratings of work hours (HRS). Group membership in the ninety-nine army companies is designated as GRP.

We start the analysis of this data set by determining how much of the variation in the dependent variable (well-being) is a function of group membership. That is, we begin by estimating the model $WBEING_{ij} = \gamma_{00} + u_{0j} + r_{ij}$. In this model, we are stating that individual well-being is a function of the overall mean well-being (the intercept γ_{00}) plus some between-group variation (u_{0j}) and some within group variation (r_{ij}).

In S-PLUS, we define the model using the following notation where > is the S-PLUS command prompt:

```
>NULL.MODEL<-lme(WBEING~1,
random=~1|GRP,data=bh1996)
```

The routine is "lme," which stands for "linear mixed effect" model. The fixed part of the equation is WBEING ~ 1, which specifies that well-being is being predicted by an intercept, and the random part of the equation is random = ~ 1|GRP which specifies that there is a random intercept that varies across groups.

In SAS, the notation is:

```
PROC MIXED COVTEST;
    CLASS GRP;
    MODEL WBEING = /SOLUTION;
    RANDOM INTERCEPT/SUB = GRP;
```

The COVTEST option in PROC MIXED instructs the program to estimate the standard errors associated with the variance estimates. The CLASS GRP line specifies that group membership is a categorical or classification variable. The fixed part of the equation is MODEL WBEING = /SOLUTION; note that the lack of predictors between the equals sign and the slash indicates an intercept-only model. The random component is RANDOM INTERCEPT/SUB = GRP. This specifies that there is a random intercept that varies among groups.

For brevity, I will focus on S-PLUS output in this chapter. For additional help with PROC MIXED models and SAS output, see Singer (1998) or Littell et al. (1996).

In the NLME package for S-PLUS, the variance components for the null model are extracted using the VarCorr function.

```
>VarCorr(NULL.MODEL)
GRP = pdSymm(~ 1)
                Variance Std      Dev
(Intercept)   0.03580077   0.1892109
   Residual   0.78949727   0.8885366
```

The variance of the intercepts across the ninety-nine groups, τ_{00}, is 0.036. The variance of the within-group residuals, σ^2, is 0.789. Recall that ICC is defined as $\tau_{00}/(\tau_{00} + \sigma^2)$, which translates into $0.036/(0.036 + 0.789)$, or 0.044. This indicates that 4 percent of the variance in General Well-Being is due to or related to group membership.

As the next part of our examination of the random intercept, we might want to know whether the variance estimate of 0.036 is significantly larger than zero. The COVTEST option in PROC MIXED provides standard error estimates for the variance components (see Singer, 1998, for details). In HLM, the estimates are given in the table labeled "Final Estimation of Variance Components." In the NLME package for S-PLUS, we use the intervals command and examine the output related to the random effects:

```
>intervals(NULL.MODEL)
Approximate 95 percent confidence intervals
. . . .
Random Effects:
  Level: GRP
                    lower          est.         upper
sd((Intercept))   0.1568524    0.1892109    0.228245
```

The intervals command returns standard deviations estimates instead of variance estimates. Squaring the standard deviation estimate of 0.189 returns the variance estimate of 0.0358 that we have already encountered. The results from the intervals command indicate that the standard deviation estimate of the lower confidence interval is 0.156 (its variance is 0.024), while the standard deviation estimate of the upper confidence interval is 0.228 (variance of 0.052). These 95 percent confidence intervals do not include 0, so we conclude that τ_{00} is significantly larger than zero.

The alternative method is to test the -2 log-likelihood ratios between a model with and a model without a random intercept. To specify a model without a random slope in S-PLUS we estimate a generalized least square (GLS) model predicting general well-being from a common intercept. This is done using the gls command in the NLME package:

```
>NULL.MODEL.2<-gls(WBEING~1,data=bh1996)
```

In SAS we estimate the model:

```
PROC MIXED COVTEST;
      CLASS GRP;
      MODEL WBEING = /SOLUTION;
```

Note that in SAS, we no longer have the line "RANDOM INTERCEPT/SUB = GRP;". By removing this line, we no longer estimate a model where the intercept randomly varies across groups.

In S-PLUS, the log-likelihood value for the gls model without the random intercept is $-9,768.5$, so the "-2 REML Log-Likelihood" value is 19,537.0 (it is 19,536.20 in SAS). The log-likelihood value for the model with the random intercept is $-9,674.1$, yielding a "-2 REML Log-Likelihood" value of 19,348.2 (19,347.3 in SAS). In S-PLUS, the difference of 188.8 is significant on a chi-squared distribution with one degree of freedom (one model estimated a random intercept, the other did not, and this results in the one df difference). These results suggest significant intercept variation. Note that one can compare log-likelihood values between models in S-PLUS simply by using the anova command with the two models:

```
> anova(NULL.MODEL, NULL.MODEL.2)
```

In summary, we would conclude that there is significant intercept variation in terms of General Well-Being scores across the ninety-nine army companies in the sample. We also estimate that 4 percent of the variation in individuals' well-being score is a function of the group to which he or she belongs.

Step 2: Predicting Intercept Variance

At this point in the example, we have two sources of variation that we can attempt to explain in subsequent modeling: within-group variation (σ^2) and between-group intercept (that is, mean) variation (τ_{00}). In many cases, these may be the only two sources of variation that we are interested in explaining, so let us begin by building a model that predicts these two sources of variation.

To make things interesting, let us assume that individual General Well-Being is related to individual reports of work hours. We expect that individuals who report high work hours will report low general well-being. At the same time, let us also assume that average work hours in an army company are related to the average general well-being of the company *over and above* the effect due to the individual-level work-hours and well-being relationship. Using Hofmann and Gavin's (1998) terminology, this means that we are testing an incremental model where the level 2 variable predicts unique variance after controlling for level 1 variables.

The incremental model that we are proposing can also be considered a contextual model. Contextual models clearly illustrate that "an aggregate variable often measures a different construct than its namesake at the individual level" (Firebaugh, 1978, p. 560). Elsewhere, I have defined the relationships between aggregate and lower-level variables as being a "fuzzy composition" process (Bliese, 2000b). In a fuzzy composition process, one recognizes that the aggregate variable is a fuzzy representation of the lower-level construct; the aggregate variable is simultaneously similar to yet different from the lower-level variable.

In this specific case, one can argue that aggregate work hours provide a better measure of externally mandated work requirements than do individual reports of work hours (Bliese & Halverson, 1996). Individuals may work long hours for any number of reasons (for example, to avoid family responsibilities, to try to get ahead, or because they have a Type A personality); however, an entire army company is likely to work long hours only if there are externally imposed reasons. Thus, individual work hours and group mean work hours both measure some aspect of work time, but both must be considered fuzzy representations of each other, particularly if work hours cluster by group, as they do here.

The first choice to make in testing the contextual model is how to center the variables. That is, we have to decide whether any transformations of the variables are necessary. Three options are available: (1) to perform no transformation and use the raw variables, (2) to grand-mean center the variables by subtracting the variable's overall mean from each variable, and (3) to group-mean center the variables by subtracting the variables' group mean from each variable.

Hofmann and Gavin (1998) provide an excellent discussion of centering choices and show that choice must be driven by one's theoretical model. They argue that the best choice when testing an incremental model is either no transformation or grand-mean centering. The two centering choices are equivalent, although grand-mean centering can facilitate model estimation (see Bryk & Raudenbush, 1992; Hofmann & Gavin, 1998). For simplicity, we will use raw variables in the test of our incremental work hour model.

The form of the model using Bryk and Raudenbush's (1992) notation is:

$$WBEING_{ij} = \beta_{0j} + \beta_{1j}(HRS_{ij}) + r_{ij}$$
$$\beta_{0j} = \gamma_{00} + \gamma_{01}(G.HRS_{j}) + u_{0j}$$
$$\beta_{1j} = \gamma_{10}$$

Consider each row of the notation. The first row states that individual general well-being is a function of the groups' intercept, plus a component that reflects the linear effect of individual reports of work hours plus some random error. In other words, individual well-being is being predicted from individual reports of work hours. The second line states that each group's intercept is a function of some common intercept (γ_{00}) plus a component that reflects the linear effect of average group work hours (G.HRS) plus some random between-group error. In other words, intercept differences in well-being among groups (which are equivalent to mean differences in well-being) are being predicted by the average number of work hours reported by the group. The third line states that the slope between individual work hours and well-being is fixed; it is not allowed to vary randomly across groups.

When we combine the three rows, we get an equation that looks like a common regression equation with an extra error term (u_{0j}). This error term indicates that WBEING intercepts (that is, means) can randomly differ among groups. The combined model is:

$$WBEING_{ij} = \gamma_{00} + \gamma_{10}(HRS_{ij}) + \gamma_{01}(G.HRS_{j}) + u_{0j} + r_{ij}$$

The code to estimate this model in the NLME package for S-PLUS is:

```
>MODEL.1>-lme(WBEING ~HRS+G.HRS,
random =~1|GRP,data=bh1996)
```

where G.HRS represents average group hours in the Bliese and Halverson (1996) data set. (In SAS, the period is replaced with an underline because variable names containing periods are not accepted in SAS: G_HRS). In PROC MIXED, the code is:

```
PROC MIXED;
    CLASS GRP;
    MODEL WBEING=HRS G_HRS /SOLUTION
    DDFM=BW NOTEST;
    RANDOM INTERCEPT /SUB=GRP TYPE=UN;
```

For our purposes, what is important to note about the code for both programs is that there is a fixed component and a random component. The fixed component (WBEING~HRS+G.HRS and MODEL WBEING=HRS G_HRS) corresponds to $WBEING_{ij} = \gamma_{00} + \gamma_{10}(HRS_{ij}) + \gamma_{01}(G.HRS_j)$ in our equation above. The random component (random=~1|GRP in S-PLUS and RANDOM INTERCEPT /SUB=GRP in PROC MIXED) corresponds to $u_{0j} + r_{ij}$ in our equation above.

Both SAS and S-PLUS assume that r_{ij} will always be included as a random component, so this is never explicitly specified in the code. That is, both programs assume that there will be random error within a group for the difference between an individual's predicted value and observed value. Similarly, both programs assume that there will be an intercept associated with the fixed part, so this does not have to be explicitly provided either. For instance, one could define the fixed part in S-PLUS as WBEING~1+HRS+G.HRS if one wanted to show explicitly that there was an intercept associated with the fixed components, but to do so would be unnecessary.

To analyze this model, both S-PLUS and SAS require that the group-level variable be reassigned back to the individual. In contrast, in HLM, one begins with two data sets (an individual data set and a group data set), and HLM links these together into an SSM file (see Bryk et al., 1994). Thus, in SAS and S-PLUS one needs a data set such as that presented in Table 12.3. (The rows were arbitrarily selected and do not represent all group members, so the group means of the shown HRS variable do not match the mean as reported in the G.HRS variables.)

With a data set with these characteristics, one can test the model, $WBEING_{ij} = \gamma_{00} + \gamma_{10}(HRS_{ij}) + \gamma_{01}(G.HRS_j) + u_{0j} + r_{ij}$. The results from this model (using lme) are presented in Table 12.4.

Notice that individual work hours are significantly negatively related to individual well-being. Furthermore after controlling the

Table 12.3. Example of the Data Structure for SAS and S-PLUS.

Row Number	GRP	WBEING	HRS	G.HRS
1	1	2.11	12	10.97
2	1	3.33	11	10.97
3	1	2.11	12	10.97
1551	25	3.72	12	10.41
1552	25	1.56	10	10.41
1553	25	4.72	10	10.41
1554	25	2.33	13	10.41
1555	25	1.5	11	10.41
5000	80	3	18	11.36
5001	80	1.83	12	11.36
5002	80	0.94	10	11.36
5003	80	2.22	11	11.36
5004	80	3.83	11	11.36

Table 12.4. Model Results (No Centering).

	Value	Standard Error	df	t-value	p-value
(Intercept)	4.742	0.214	7,282	22.178	0.000
HRS	−0.046	0.005	7,282	−9.501	0.000
G.HRS	−0.127	0.019	97	−6.544	0.000

individual-level relationship, the average work hours reported by a group (G.HRS) are related to the group's well-being intercept. That is, average work hours in a group are related to the average well-being of the group. These results provide evidence of contextual effects associated with average work hours (see Bliese & Halverson, 1996, for a covariance theorem–based analysis that also identifies a group work hour contextual effect).

At this point one can also estimate how much of the variance was explained by these two predictors. Because individual work hours were significantly related to well-being, we expect that it will have "explained" some of the within-group residual variance σ^2. Similarly, because average work hours were related to the group well-being intercept, we expect that it will have "explained" some of intercept variance, τ_{00}. Recall that in the null model, the variance estimate for the within-group residuals, σ^2, was 0.789, and the variance estimate for the intercepts, τ_{00}, was 0.036. In contrast, the variance estimates from the model with the two predictors are 0.780 and 0.014. That is, the variance of the within-group residuals decreased from 0.789 to 0.780, and the variance of the between-group intercepts decreased from 0.036 to 0.014. We can calculate the percentage of variance explained by using the following formula:

$$\text{Variance Explained} = 1 - \frac{\text{Variance with Predictor}}{\text{Variance without Predictor}}$$

To follow through with our example, work hours explained $1 - (0.780/0.789)$ or 0.011 (1 percent) of the within-group variance in σ^2, and group-mean work hours explained $1 - (0.014/0.036)$ or 0.611 (61 percent) of the between-group intercept variance τ_{00}. Although the logic behind variance estimates appears straightforward (at least in models without random slopes), the variance estimates should be treated with some caution because they are partially dependent on how one specifies the models. (See Snijders & Bosker, 1994, 1999, for an in-depth discussion of variance explained calculations.)

Returning to the interpretation of the results presented in Table 12.4, I cannot emphasize enough that the centering choice affects the model results. Consider the case if work hours had been group mean centered; that is, the group-mean score had been subtracted from each individual score (I designate this as W.HRS for within-group centered). In this case, a significant G.HRS value does not indicate a contextual effect. That is, it does not indicate that the group's average work hours have a relationship with well-being over and above the individual work hours effect. When the level 1 variable is group-mean centered, the level 2 variable contains both level 1 and level 2 effects, so if the level 1 variable is significant, the level 2 variable will also be significant (Bliese, 2000b; Firebaugh, 1978; Hofmann & Gavin, 1998). To illustrate this, note the results from an analysis with a group-mean-centered work hours variable presented in Table 12.5. Observe that the coefficient estimate for W.HRS is identical to the previously reported value for HRS (-0.046); however, the coefficient for G.HRS is now -0.174. With rounding error, the value of -0.174 is equal to -0.127 (G.HRS effect) plus -0.046 (W.HRS effect).

One way to understand the effect of group-mean centering is to note that group-level relationships always mimic individual-level relationships. This will occur even if there are no group effects, as would be the case if individuals were randomly assigned to groups (see Bliese, 2000b). Consequently, if there were no group effects associated with G.HRS, we would expect the relationship between G.HRS and the average group well-being to be -0.046 because the individual-level relationship between HRS and WBEING is -0.046.

When we group-mean center a variable, however, we take out any group effect from the level 1 variable. This forces the group-mean variable (G.HRS) to be independent from the group-mean-centered variable (W.HRS) (see Dansereau, Alutto, & Yammarino, 1984). Although G.HRS and W.HRS are independent, it is still the case that part of the relationship between G.HRS and average group well-being is a reflection of the individual-level HRS and WBEING relationship. This combination of events essentially causes the raw relationship to be reflected in both the W.HRS and WBEING relationship and in the G.HRS and WBEING intercept relationship. That is, we essentially count the individual-level relationship twice: once at level 1 and once at level 2. Parenthetically, this is partially why multilevel structural equation modeling is so complex; multilevel structural equation modeling uses two covariance matrices: one based on group-mean-centered variables and the other on group-mean variables. Although these two covariance matrices are independent, the group-mean matrix still reflects

Table 12.5. Model Results (Group-Mean Centering).

	Value	Standard Error	df	t-value	p-value
(Intercept)	4.742	0.214	7,282	22.178	0.000
HRS	-0.046	0.005	7,282	-9.501	0.000
G.HRS	-0.174	0.019	97	-9.234	0.000

individual-level relationships that must be properly accounted for in the model specification (see Heck & Thomas, 2000).

To test whether a contextual effect is present when group-mean centering is used, we must test whether the level 2 coefficient ($-.174$) is significantly different from the level 1 coefficient ($-.046$) (see Bryk & Raudenbush, 1992; Hofmann & Gavin, 1998). In the example, the two slopes are significantly different.

Step 3: Testing for and Explaining Slope Variance

Let us continue our analysis by trying to explain the third source of variation: variation in our slopes (τ_{11}, τ_{12}, and so on). To do this, let us examine another variable in our modeling: army company members' ratings of leadership consideration. Analyses of survey data from army personnel often reveal that soldiers' perceptions of leadership consideration are positively related to their general well-being, but it is possible that the strength of this relationship varies among army companies. Consider a plot of the relationship between leadership consideration and general well-being for the first twenty-four army companies in the Bliese and Halverson (1996) data set in Figure 12.5. Notice that the relationship between leadership consideration and well-being is generally positive. At the same time, however, the relationship is stronger in some groups than in others.

Presumably, the relationship between leadership consideration and well-being is partially dependent on characteristics of the groups. In this running example, we might hypothesize that when groups are under a lot of strain from work requirements, the relationship between leadership consideration and well-being will be relatively strong. In contrast, when groups are under little strain, we expect a relatively weak relationship between leadership consideration and well-being. We expect these relationships because we believe that leadership is relatively unimportant in terms of individual well-being when groups are under little stress, but that the importance of leadership consideration increases when groups are under high stress. We are, in essence, proposing a contextual effect in an occupational stress model (Bliese & Jex, 1999).

This proposition represents a cross-level interaction. Specifically, it proposes that the slope between leadership consideration

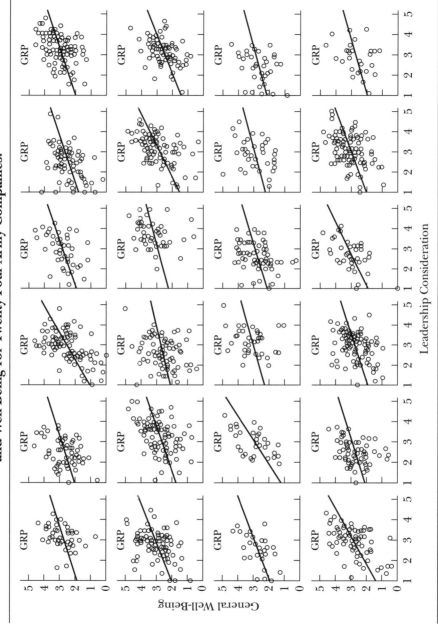

Figure 12.5. Individual Reports of Leadership Consideration and Well-Being for Twenty-Four Army Companies.

and well-being within groups varies as a function of a level 2 variable: group work demands. In random coefficient modeling, we test this hypothesis by examining whether a level 2 variable explains a significant amount of the level 1 slope variation among groups. In our example, we will specifically be testing whether average work hours in the group "explains" group-by-group variation in the relationship between leadership consideration and well-being.

We begin the analysis of slope variability by adding leadership consideration to the model and testing whether there is significant variation in the leadership consideration and well-being slopes across groups. Once again, we must consider centering issues. When testing a cross-level interaction model as we are doing here, Hofmann and Gavin (1998) contend that the best centering choice for the level 1 variable is group-mean centering because it provides the "purest" estimate of the within-group slope. In contrast, slope estimates based on raw variables and grand-mean-centered variables may be partially influenced by between-group factors. This can result in spurious cross-level interactions that are actually due to group-mean interactions (Hofmann & Gavin, 1998). Group-mean-centered variables have between-group effects removed, so cross-level interactions cannot be the spurious by-product of group-mean interactions.

In practice, spurious cross-level interactions are rare, so one can generally use raw or grand-mean-centered variables to test for cross-level interactions as long as one runs an additional model with group-mean-centered variables to check for spurious interaction effects (D. Hofmann, personal communication, October 2000). To reduce the number of models illustrated in this chapter, however, I will simply use group-mean centering on the leadership consideration variable throughout. Note, nonetheless, that the models that I estimate with the group-mean-centered variable are very similar to the raw score or grand-mean-centered models.

In the example, we group-mean center the leadership consideration measure, labeling it W.LEAD (within leadership). Also, since we ultimately intend to use average work hours in a group as a level 2 variable in a cross-level interaction, we will grand-mean center group average work hours (we subtract the overall work hour mean from the group mean). Grand-mean centering does not affect model interpretation, but it does facilitate model estimation in random coefficient models just as it does in multiple regression models (Bryk & Raudenbush, 1992). We will specify the grand-mean-centered average work hour variable as GG.HRS. To illustrate the calculation of GG.HRS, we add GG.HRS to the Bliese and Halverson (1996) data set using the following S-PLUS command:

```
>bh1996$GG.HRS<-bh1996$G.HRS-mean(bh1996$HRS)
```

This command creates a new variable (GG.HRS) by subtracting the work hour grand mean from each group's average work hour value.

The MRC model that we test using these data is:

$$WBEING_{ij} = \beta_{0j} + \beta_{1j}(HRS_{ij}) + \beta_{2j}(W.LEAD_{ij}) + r_{ij}$$

$$\beta_{0j} = \gamma_{00} + \gamma_{01}(GG.HRS_j) + u_{0j}$$

$$\beta_{1j} = \gamma_{10}$$

$$\beta_{2j} = \gamma_{20} + u_{2j}$$

The last line of the model includes the error term u_{2j}. This term indicates that the leadership consideration and well-being slope is permitted to vary randomly across groups. The variance term associated with u_{2j} is τ_{12}. It is this variance term that interests us in the cross-level interaction hypothesis. Note that we have not permitted the slope between individual work hours and individual well-being to vary randomly across groups.

In combined form, the model is:

$$WBEING_{ij} = \gamma_{00} + \gamma_{10}(HRS_{ij}) + \gamma_{20}(W.LEAD_{ij}) + \gamma_{01}(GG.HRS_j) + u_{0j} + u_{2j}*W.LEAD_{ij} + r_{ij}.$$

In S-PLUS, this model is designated as:

```
>lme(WBEING~HRS+W.LEAD+GG.HRS,
random=~W.LEAD|GRP,data=bh1996)
```

In PROC MIXED the model is specified:

```
PROC MIXED;
      CLASS GRP;
      MODEL WBEING=HRS W_LEAD GG_HRS /SOLUTION
      DDFM=BW NOTEST;
      RANDOM INTERCEPT W_LEAD /SUB=GRP TYPE=UN;
```

Note that in both models, we have added the level 1 group-mean-centered leadership consideration variable (W.LEAD) to both the fixed part of the model and to the random part of the model. Adding the W.LEAD term to the random part of the model specifies that the individual-level leadership consideration and well-being slope is allowed to vary randomly among groups.

What we are interested in from this model is whether τ_{12}, the slope between leadership consideration and well-being, significantly varies from one group to the next. We have two options in testing for significant slope variation, as we did when we tested for significant intercept variation. The first option is to examine the standard error estimates associated with the variance term. Recall that these are standard output in HLM and can be obtained using the COVTEST option in PROC MIXED and the intervals option in the NLME package for S-PLUS. The intervals option in S-PLUS indicates that the variance estimate for τ_{12} is .011, and lower- and upper-slope variation estimates are .004 and .029, respectively. Because these estimates do not include zero, it suggests that there is significant slope variation in the leadership consideration and well-being slopes among groups.

The other option is to test the -2 log-likelihood ratios between a model with and a model without a random slope for leadership consideration and well-being. We have already estimated a model with a random slope; to estimate a model without a random slope, we simply change the random statements in SAS and S-PLUS. In both programs, the random statement drops the WLEAD term. Specifically, in PROC MIXED, the random statement is now "RANDOM INTERCEPT /SUB=GRP TYPE=UN; in S-PLUS it is random=~1|GRP.

The log-likelihood value for the model with the random slope is $-8{,}919.336$, resulting in a -2 log-likelihood of 17,838.67. The log-likelihood value for the model without the random slope is $-8{,}928.691$, resulting in a -2 log-likelihood of $17{,}857.38$. The difference of 18.71 is significant on two degrees of freedom. Note that there are two degrees of freedom because the model with the random slope also estimates a covariance term for the slope-intercept relationship. The log-likelihood results indicate that the model with the random effect for the leadership consideration and well-being slope is significantly better than the model without this random effect. This indicates significant slope variation.

The final model that we examine is one where we try to explain the variation in the leadership consideration and well-being slope. Recall that we proposed that this variation might be related to the groups' work demands, and we suggested that we could assess work demands using the average number of work hours that group members reported working. In Bryk and Raudenbush's (1992) notation, the model that we are testing is:

$$WBEING_{ij} = \beta_{0j} + \beta_{1j}(HRS_{ij}) + \beta_{2j}(W.LEAD_{ij}) + r_{ij}$$

$$\beta_{0j} = \gamma_{00} + \gamma_{01}(GG.HRS_j) + u_{0j}$$

$$\beta_{1j} = \gamma_{10}$$

$$\beta_{2j} = \gamma_{20} + \gamma_{21}(GG.HRS_j) + u_{2j}$$

Notice that we have simply added average work hours as a predictor of the vertical cohesion and well-being slope. In combined form, the model is:

$$WBEING_{ij} = \gamma_{00} + \gamma_{10}(HRS_{ij}) + \gamma_{20}(W.LEAD_{ij}) + \gamma_{01}(GG.HRS_j) + \gamma_{21}(W.LEAD_{ij} * GG.HRS_j) + u_{0j} + u_{2j} * W.LEAD_{ij} + r_{ij}.$$

In S-PLUS we specify this model as:

```
>lme(WBEING~HRS+W.LEAD+GG.HRS+W.LEAD:GG.HRS,
random=~W.LEAD|GRP,data=bh1996)
```

In PROC MIXED we specify the model as:

```
PROC MIXED;
    CLASS GRP;
    MODEL WBEING=HRS W_LEAD GG_HRS
    W_LEAD*GG_HRS /SOLUTION
    DDFM=BW NOTEST;
    RANDOM INTERCEPT W_LEAD /SUB=GRP TYPE=UN;
```

The results from the S-PLUS lme model, presented in Table 12.6, indicate that individual reports of leadership consideration were significantly related to well-being: individuals who reported positive perceptions of leadership consideration tended to report that they had high well-being. Notice, however, that there is also a significant cross-level interaction (the last row). This result indicates that average work hours explained a significant portion of the variation in τ_{12}: the vertical cohesion and well-being slope.

The form of the interaction supports our proposition (see Figure 12.6). Soldiers' perceptions of leadership consideration are positively related to their well-being regardless of the number of hours that the group, on average, works; however, the relationship between leadership consideration and well-being is stronger (steeper slope) in groups with high work hours than in groups with low work hours. Another way to think about the interaction is to note that well-being really drops (in relative terms) when one perceives that leadership is low in consideration *and* one is a member of a group with high work hours. This supports our proposition

Table 12.6. Model Results (Cross-Level Interactions).

	Value	**Standard Error**	*df*	*t*-value	*p*-value
(Intercept)	3.099	0.053	7,280	58.405	0.000
HRS	−0.028	0.004	7,280	−6.268	0.000
W.LEAD	0.506	0.017	7,280	29.925	0.000
GG.HRS	−0.145	0.019	97	−7.468	0.000
W.LEAD:GG.HRS	0.040	0.020	7280	2.030	0.042

that considerate leadership is relatively more important in a high-work-demand context.

This model can also be used to estimate how much of the variation in the slopes is "explained" by the group work hours. Recall that the estimate of the between-group slope variance, τ_{12}, in the model with no slope predictors is 0.011. The estimate of the variance once average work hours has "explained" the slope variance is 0.009. Thus, average group work hours account for $1 - (0.009/0.011)$, or 18 percent of the slope variance. Once again, I emphasize that this is a rough estimate, and I direct readers to Snijders and Bosker (1994, 1999) for additional information on estimating effect sizes.

In organizational psychology, cross-level interactions of this nature have been investigated by a number of researchers (Bliese & Britt, 2001; Hofmann & Stetzer, 1998; Jex & Bliese, 1999; Kidwell et al., 1997). In an interesting variation of the cross-level test for interactions, a colleague and I modified the common two-way cross-level interaction design to test a three-way cross-level interactive effect. Specifically, we tested whether an expected interaction term between two level 1 variables (role conflict and work overload) varied significantly across groups and whether we could explain the between-group variation in the interactive term with a

Figure 12.6. Cross-Level Interaction of Group Work Hours (Level 2 Contextual Effect) on Leadership and Well-Being Relationship.

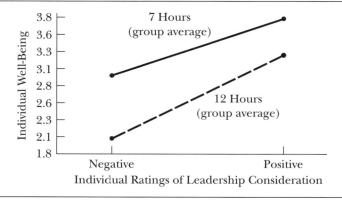

level 2 variable (group supervisory support). In the analyses, we found evidence of variation in the interaction term among groups, and we "explained" this variation by differences in group-level supervisory support (see Bliese & Castro, 2000). I mention this simply to illustrate that the basic two-level hierarchical model can be extended to test more complex three-way interactive effects without necessarily adding hierarchical levels to the analyses.

Multilevel Modeling Conclusion

In summary, I have illustrated in a series of steps how one might go about modeling intercept and slope variance in multilevel random coefficient models. I believe that the ability to identify and model these additional sources of variance will greatly enrich our understanding of organizational phenomena.

Extending Models and Key Variations

Here I briefly discuss variations of the multilevel modeling theme in terms of analyzing individual change over time and the statistical assumptions underlying random coefficient models.

Individual Growth Modeling

Although it may not be immediately apparent, multilevel random coefficient models can be remarkably useful for modeling individual change over time (Bryk & Raudenbush, 1987, 1992; Little, Schnabel, & Baumert, 2000; Pinheiro & Bates, 2000). When modeling changes over time, repeated observations are nested within individuals (thus resulting in a hierarchical structure).

The basic idea in this type of modeling is that individuals presumably differ on the dependent variable in terms of intercepts and slopes over time. For instance, at the onset of the measurement trials, some individuals might have high ability and others might have low ability. Using multilevel modeling similar to that described in the previous section, one can identify individual characteristics (level 2 variables in this case) that are related to these initial (intercept) differences. In addition to initial differences, it is likely that the slope of change over time will vary across individuals. For instance, some individuals might improve over time (steep slope), and others might remain unchanged or decline over time. One can potentially investigate the individual (level 2) factors that are related to these slope changes. (See Hofmann, Jacobs, & Baratta, 1993, or Deadrick, Bennett, & Russell, 1997, for examples modeling individual changes in performance over time.)

Using random coefficient modeling to assess individual changes over time has many similarities to using latent growth curve methodology (see Chapter Ten, this volume; Chan, 1998; Chan, Ramey, Ramey, & Schmitt, 2000; Chan & Schmitt, 2000; Ployhart & Hakel, 1998). Willett and Sayer (1994) do an excellent job of clearly identifying the parallels between random coefficient modeling and latent growth curve methodology. It is important to note, however, that Willett and Sayer focus on an older version of the HLM program, and so two of the limitations that they identify (the inability to model autocorrelation and the inability to model heteroscedasticity) are unique to this version of HLM. PROC MIXED and the NLME package in S-PLUS are capable of modeling level 1 autocorrelation and heteroscedasticity.

Autocorrelation and heteroscedasticity arise when modeling change over time, because when one models time as a factor, it is likely that observations temporally close will be more correlated than will observations far apart in time (autocorrelation). It is also possible that responses may become more (or less) variable over time, so heteroscedasticity can be present. Neither of these issues is likely to arise when modeling individuals nested within groups.

With the ability to model autocorrelation and heteroscedasticity, MRC models estimated in SAS and using the NLME library in R and S-PLUS provide powerful tools for modeling change over time. One particular strength of growth models estimated in these packages (in contrast to latent growth models) is that MRC models do not require time-structured data (Willett & Sayer, 1994). Willett and Sayer note that in MRC models, "each individual in the data set can possess an empirical growth record containing different numbers of waves of data with randomly assigned temporal spacing" (p. 379). In certain situations, this may make MRC models more flexible than latent growth models.

Key Statistical Assumptions

Multilevel random coefficient modeling, like any other statistical modeling approach, has several key assumptions. Bryk and Raudenbush (1992) list five assumptions associated with multilevel random coefficient models:

1. The level 1 errors (r_{ij}) should be independent and normally distributed, and have a mean of zero. Furthermore, the variance of the errors should be the same across groups. Formally we can define this as $r_{ij} \sim N(0, \sigma^2)$. In growth modeling, we can relax this assumption when we estimate the models with SAS and S-PLUS, but we must then carefully specify the form of the nonindependence in r_{ij} (for example, autocorrelation).
2. The level 1 predictors are assumed to be independent of r_{ij}. Formally we can define this as: $\text{Cov}(X_{qij}, r_{ij}) = 0$ for all q.
3. Errors at level 2 are multivariate normal with a mean of 0, a variance τ_{qq}, and a covariance τ_{qq}'. Furthermore, the level 2 errors are assumed to be independent among level 2 units.
4. The level 2 predictors are independent of the level 2 errors.
5. The errors at level 1 are independent of the errors at level 2. Formally, $\text{Cov}(r_{ij}, u_{qj}) = 0$ for all q.

Researchers should be cognizant of these assumptions because violations of these assumptions may make one's results suspect. To my knowledge, little is known about how robust multilevel random coefficient models are to violations of these assumptions.

Conclusion

As Littell et al. (1996) note, random coefficient modeling has become computationally feasible only in recent years. It is clear, however, that this modeling technique has had, and will continue to have, a profound impact on organizational research. In this chapter, I have shown that multilevel random coefficient models are important to a wide variety of researchers. Clearly for researchers who are interested in multilevel theory, random coefficient modeling provides a formidable tool with which to conduct analyses; however, even researchers who are not directly interested in multilevel theory need to understand how the hierarchical nature of organizational data affects their analyses. This implies, of course, that researchers need to collect group membership information routinely. By collecting group membership data, they can reconstruct the hierarchical nature of the organization and determine whether the hierarchy affects one's data in terms of either a nuisance variable or substantive, contextual factors.

References

Bartko, J. J. (1976). On various intraclass correlation reliability coefficients. *Psychological Bulletin, 83,* 762–765.

Bliese, P. D. (2000a). *Multilevel Modeling in R: A brief introduction to R and the multilevel and NLME packages.* Washington, DC: Walter Reed Army Institute of Research.

Bliese, P. D. (2000b). Within-group agreement, nonindependence, and reliability: Implications for data aggregation and Analysis. In K. J. Klein & S. W. Kozlowski (Eds.), *Multilevel theory, research, and methods in organizations* (pp. 349–381). San Francisco: Jossey-Bass.

Bliese, P. D., & Britt, T. W. (2001). Social support, group consensus and stressor-strain relationships: Social context matters. *Journal of Organizational Behavior, 22,* 425–436.

Bliese, P. D., & Castro, C. A. (2000). Role clarity, work overload and organizational support: Multilevel evidence of the importance of support. *Work and Stress, 14,* 65–73.

Bliese, P. D., & Hanges, P. (2001, August). *Non-independence in random-coefficient models: It is not only about too much Type I error.* Paper presented at the Sixty-First Academy of Management meetings, Washington, DC.

Bliese, P. D., & Halverson, R. R. (1996). Individual and nomothetic models of job stress: An examination of work hours, cohesion, and well-being. *Journal of Applied Social Psychology, 26,* 1171–1189.

Bliese, P. D., & Jex S. M. (1999). Incorporating multiple levels of analysis into occupational stress research. *Work and Stress, 13,* 1–6.

Bradley, J. V. (1980a). Nonrobustness in classical tests on means and variances: A large-scale sampling study. *Bulletin of the Psychonomic Society, 15,* 275–278.

Bradley, J. V. (1980b). Nonrobustness in Z, t, and F tests at large sample sizes. *Bulletin of the Psychonomic Society, 16,* 333–336.

Bryk, A. S., & Raudenbush, S. W. (1987). Application of hierarchical linear models to assessing change. *Psychological Bulletin, 101,* 147–158.

Bryk, A. S., & Raudenbush, S. W. (1992). *Hierarchical linear models.* Thousand Oaks, CA: Sage.

Bryk, A. S., Raudenbush, S. W., & Congdon, R. T. (1994). *Hierarchical linear modeling with the HLM/2L and HLM/3L programs.* Chicago: Scientific Software International.

Chan, D. (1998). The conceptualization and analysis of change over time: An integrative approach incorporating longitudinal means and covariance structures analysis (LMACS) and multiple indicator latent growth modeling (MLGM). *Organizational Research Methods, 1,* 421–483.

Chan, D., Ramey, S., & Ramey, C., Schmitt, N. (2000). Modeling intraindividual changes in children's social skills at home and at school: A multivariate latent growth approach to understanding between-settings differences in children's social skills development. *Multivariate Behavioral Research, 35,* 365–396.

Chan, D., & Schmitt, N. (2000). Interindividual differences in intraindividual changes in proactivty during organizational entry: A latent growth modeling approach to understanding newcomer adaptation. *Journal of Applied Psychology, 85,* 190–210.

Dansereau, F., Alutto, J. A., & Yammarino, F. J. (1984). *Theory testing in organizational behavior: The variant approach.* Upper Saddle River, NJ: Prentice Hall.

Deadrick, D. L., Bennett, N., & Russell, C. J. (1997). Using hierarchical linear modeling to examine dynamic performance criteria over time. *Journal of Management, 23,* 745–757.

Firebaugh, G. (1978). A rule for inferring individual-level relationships from aggregate data. *American Sociological Review, 43,* 557–572.

Glass, G. V., Peckham, P. D., & Sanders, J. R. (1972). Consequences of failure to meet assumptions underlying the fixed effects analyses of variance and covariance. *Review of Educational Research, 42,* 237–288.

Heck, R. H., & Thomas, S. L. (2000). *An introduction to multilevel modeling techniques.* Hillsdale, NJ: Erlbaum.

Hofmann, D. A. (1997). An overview of the logic and rationale of hierarchical linear models. *Journal of Management, 23,* 723–744.

Hofmann, D. A., & Gavin, M. (1998). Centering decisions in hierarchical linear models: Theoretical and methodological implications for research in organizations. *Journal of Management, 24,* 623–641.

Hofmann, D. A., Jacobs, R., & Baratta, J. (1993). Dynamic criteria and the measurement of change. *Journal of Applied Psychology, 78,* 194–204.

Hofmann, D. A., & Stetzer, A. (1996). A cross-level investigation of factors influencing unsafe behaviors and accidents. *Personnel Psychology, 49,* 307–339.

Hofmann, D. A., & Stetzer, A. (1998). The role of safety climate and communication in accident interpretation: Implications for learning from negative events. *Academy of Management Journal, 41,* 644–657.

James, L. R., & Williams, L. J. (2000). The cross-level operator in regression, ANCOVA, and contextual analysis. In K. J. Klein & S. W. Kozlowski (Eds.), *Multilevel theory, research, and methods in organizations* (pp. 382–424). San Francisco: Jossey-Bass.

Jex, S. M., & Bliese, P. D. (1999). Efficacy beliefs as a moderator of the impact of work-related stressors: A multi-level study. *Journal of Applied Psychology, 84,* 349–361.

Jex, S. M., Bliese, P. D., Buzzell, S., & Primeau, J. (2001). The impact of self-efficacy on stressor-strain relations: Coping style as an explanatory mechanism. *Journal of Applied Psychology, 86,* 401–409.

Jimmieson, N., & Griffin, M. A. (1998). Linking staff and client perceptions of the organization: A field study of client satisfaction with health services. *Journal of Occupational and Organizational Psychology, 71,* 81–96.

Kenny, D. A. (1996). The design and analysis of social-interaction research. *Annual Review of Psychology, 47,* 59–86.

Kenny, D. A., & Judd, C. M. (1986). Consequences of violating the independence assumption in analysis of variance. *Psychological Bulletin, 99,* 422–431.

Kenny, D. A., & Judd, C. M. (1996). A general procedure for the estimation of interdependence. *Psychological Bulletin, 119,* 138–148.

Kidwell, R. E., Mossholder, K. M & Bennett, N. (1997). Cohesiveness and organizational citizenship behavior: A multilevel analysis using groups and individuals. *Journal of Management, 23,* 775–793.

Klein, K. J., Bliese, P. D., Kozlowski, S.W.J., Dansereau, F., Gavin, M. B., Griffin, M. A., Hofmann, D. A., James, L. R., Yammarino, F. J., & Bligh, M. C. (2000). Multilevel analytical techniques: Commonalities, differences, and continuing questions. In K. J. Klein & S. W. Kozlowski (Eds.), *Multilevel theory, research, and methods in organizations* (pp. 512–553). San Francisco: Jossey-Bass.

Kreft, I., & de Leeuw, J. (1998). *Introducing multilevel modeling.* Thousand Oaks, CA: Sage.

Littell, R. C., Milliken, G. A., Stroup W. W. & Wolfinger, R. D. (1996). *SAS system for mixed models.* Cary, NC: SAS Institute.

Little, T. D., Schnabel, K. U., & Baumert, J. (2000). *Modeling longitudinal and multilevel data: Practical issues, applied approaches and specific examples.* Hillsdale, NJ: Erlbaum.

Longford, N. T. (1990). *VARCL: Software for variance component analysis of data with nested random effects (maximum likelihood).* Princeton, NJ: Educational Testing Service.

Mossholder, K. W., Bennett, N., & Martin, C. L. (1998). A multilevel analysis of procedural justice context. *Journal of Organizational Behavior, 19,* 131–141.

Pinheiro, J. C., & Bates, D. M. (2000). *Mixed-effects models in S and S-PLUS.* New York: Springer.

Ployhart, R. E., & Hakel, M. D. (1998). The substantive nature of performance variability: Predicting interindividual differences in intraindividual performance. *Personnel Psychology, 51,* 859–901.

Puvar, R., & Nath, R. (1984). Exact F-tests in an ANOVA procedure for dependent observations. *Multivariate Behavioral Research, 19,* 408–420.

Shrout, P. E., & Fleiss, J. L. (1979). Intraclass correlations: Uses in assessing rater reliability. *Psychological Bulletin, 86,* 420–428.

Singer, J. D. (1998). Using SAS PROC MIXED to fit multilevel models, hierarchical models, and individual growth models. *Journal of Educational and Behavioral Statistics, 24,* 323–355.

Snijders, T.A.B., & Bosker, R. J. (1994). Modeled variance in two-level models. *Sociological Methods and Research, 22,* 342–363.

Snijders, T.A.B., & Bosker, R. J. (1999). *Multilevel analysis: An introduction to basic and advanced multilevel modeling.* Thousand Oaks, CA: Sage.

Willett, J. B., & Sayer, A. G. (1994). Using covariance structure analysis to detect correlates and predictors of individual change over time. *Psychological Bulletin, 116,* 363–381.

CHAPTER 13

Structure and Timing in Limited Range Dependent Variables

Regression Models for Predicting If and When

David A. Harrison

In industrial/organizational (I/O) psychology, linearity rules. Our knowledge base is built on a foundation of linear methods: classical test theory, product-moment correlations, multiple regression, and psychometric meta-analysis. There are clear advantages to this emphasis on what is straight. Linear forms are simple to understand, easy to program, straightforward to estimate, and robust to mistakes—even fairly big ones (Dawes & Corrigan, 1974). Just as important, most I/O professionals are trained in linear techniques, which are designed to model smooth, symmetric, and well-behaved dependent variables. Nevertheless, in the past two decades, there has been steady growth in the specification and application of nonlinear approaches to measurement, modeling, and data analysis. In this chapter, I describe one such set of nonlinear techniques: regression models for infrequent or otherwise limited range dependent variables (LRDVs).

When Do LRDV Approaches Make Sense?

Before moving to the nuts and bolts of LRDV methods, it is important to note their limitations. The models I describe in this chapter are not multivariate; they predict only a single, observable criterion. They are susceptible to unknown consequences of measurement error. They generally do not make assumptions about latent distributions of the propensity for the behavior or event to occur, although LRDV models can be fit in those circumstances if one is willing to propose latent thresholds (Harrison & Hulin, 1989).

All LRDV techniques do involve observable outcomes that are either discrete or bounded in some way. Most involve criteria that take a small number of finite values: low base rate behaviors, performance attainments, or other events that are sparsely distributed over time or units of study. Some of the clearest differences between linear and LRDV models occur when the LRDV is a change in state (if or when), rather than a change in degree (how much). This difference also marks the well-known distinction of ordinal, interval, and ratio types of measurement from nominal measurement, which is assumed in many LRDV techniques. The idea of a transition rate indexing a nominal change from one state (say, working) to another (say, unemployed) is central to the LRDV models (predicting when) covered at the end of this chapter.

When Criteria Have Ugly Distributions

Despite I/O psychology's emphasis on linearity, there are many meaningful criteria that can be regarded as LRDVs. For most individual employees or work groups, generally dysfunctional events such as turnover, grievances, transfers, absenteeism, accidents, injuries, medical claims, incidents of violence or harassment, dismissal, suspensions, and other disciplinary actions happen infrequently during natural organizational time periods such as a month or year. Their distributions are either dichotomous, or discrete and highly skewed. During the same time periods, generally favorable LRDVs might include promotions, commendations, publications, pay raises, reenlistment, enrollment in training or development, certification, goal attainment, project completion, mentoring, client acquisition, and even retirement. Indeed, any discrete choice, including one that marks the beginning, end, or clear change in a work relationship, can have the characteristics of an LRDV.

When Linear Functions Do Not Fit

Ugly distributions can create problems for linear techniques. To understand why and how, I will review the assumptions of linear models.

Model

Multiple linear regression (MLR) is the hammer that I/O psychologists use to pound out predictions and test structural hypotheses in applied psychology (Stone-Romero, Weaver, & Glenar, 1995). It is built for a particular box of nails, and those nails are not LRDVs. To be more specific, the population MLR model with $j = 1, 2, \ldots, p$ predictors is familiar:

$$E(Y|X) = \beta_0 + \beta_1 X_1 + \beta_2 X_2 + \ldots \beta_p X_p \qquad (13.1)$$

where $E(Y|X)$ refers to the expected value of Y given a vector of values on the predictors, X. Errors in the model, ε_i, are normally distributed deviations of Y_i from $E(Y_i|X)$. When comparing MLR with LRDV models, it is helpful to think of all types of regression as really involving two models: one that specifies how the expected value of Y depends on a combination of predictors and the other that specifies how the distribution of errors is supposed to behave. In the case of MLR, the expected value of Y is specified to follow a linear, additive function of the X_j's. Errors are specified to follow a normal distribution with a mean of 0.

In terms of how a regression equation is specified, a helpful concept for contrasting MLR with LRDV models is the *link function,* $g[E(Y|X)]$, which indicates what has to be done to $E(Y|X)$ so that it is connected to the Xs in a linear, additive way. In keeping with the idea that there are really two models embedded in every regression model, the link function does not necessarily determine the distribution of errors. For MLR, the link function is so simple that it is usually not even mentioned; g equals I, the identity function, which means nothing gets done to transform $E(Y|X)$. It retains its original identity: $g[E(Y|X)] = E(Y|X)$. This is not the case for LRDV models. Their link functions are nonlinear and more complex.

Linearity

The regression coefficients in the MLR model, β_j, are partial slopes. Their magnitude depends on which other X_j variables are in the model but not the particular values that those variables take. As an example, suppose a law firm uses law school grade point average (GPA) as an index of cognitive ability to help select candidates for its junior-level positions. Using MLR, two applicants with GPAs of 3.00 and 3.20 would be predicted to have the same differential in their job performance as two applicants with GPAs of 3.75 and 3.95.

This constancy of slopes is widely understood and does not cause a lot of hand wringing with most dependent variables. However, if Y is dichotomous, reflecting whether (1) or not (0) a junior-level lawyer gets promoted to a partner position, then $E(Y|X) = E(Y{=}1|X)$. That is, the dependent variable is now the probability of such a promotion. Regression equation 13.1 becomes the linear probability model (Aldrich & Nelson, 1984).

At this point, the simplicity of constant slopes in MLR starts to cause trouble. An applicant with a perfect GPA and high values on other predictors might have a predicted probability of promotion that was greater than 1. And if the law firm is highly selective in its promotion of junior lawyers to partners, cognitive ability might be more diagnostic (have a stronger impact) in the upper portions of the continuum than in the lower and middle portions. All junior lawyers without exceptional cognitive ability would be highly unlikely to be promoted. Although the sign of the GPA predictor would still be positive, and the signs of main effect coefficients are the same in the MLR model as in the LRDV models discussed in this chapter, their coefficient *sizes* might differ greatly. Those differences in coefficients might lead to different conclusions about the proper weighting of law school GPA in the selection of junior lawyers.

A more familiar context for a dichotomous criterion is the turnover area, where arguments have raged for years about the appropriate treatment of the dependent variable (Williams & Peters, 1998). Consider, as a running example, a data set involving 298 employees who filled out an attitude survey while they worked in the bakery-deli department of a regional supermarket chain in the southwestern United States. The supermarket chain was interested in understanding, predicting, and eventually controlling turnover among this set of employees. Therefore, the LRDV in the data set was an archival record of who left (1) or who stayed (0) within a six-month postsurvey period. Included in the survey was the strongest predictor of turnover identified in past research, withdrawal cognitions, that is, private ruminations about leaving one's job (Hom & Griffeth, 1995).

Contrasting with the law firm example, a .5 standard deviation increase in the low range of the withdrawal cognitions continuum might have a strong effect on the probability that someone will quit, as that change might constitute crossing a psychological threshold of turnover plans. In the mid- to upper range, however, the impact of a .5 standard deviation increase might be somewhat muted. Once the threshold is crossed, the effect flattens out. In other words, behavioral consequences might be stronger in the lower than in the upper ranges of withdrawal cognitions. Other variables in the turnover data set are listed in Table 13.1. They include sex, age, tenure, job status, and perceived cohesiveness of the group in which the employee was working.

The nonlinearity of LRDV models makes them better suited to each of these two types of situations. Linearity (constancy of slope) cannot hold for continuous predictors and binary dependent variables. Trying a series of power transformations in MLR for either GPA or withdrawal cognitions in the examples above would be a scattershot modeling approach. For LRDV models, the slope of Y on X_j implicitly and automatically changes over the range of X_j.

Estimation

The MLR model is often called ordinary least squares, or OLS, regression. The name is accurate on its face but misleading in its implication. The same calculations that produce least-squares estimates also produce maximum likelihood estimates. So OLS regression might as well be called maximum likelihood regression.

Despite giving the same parameter estimates for multiple regression, however, there is no general equivalence for least squares and maximum likelihood estimation in other statistical situations. Rather than relying on unique (closed-form) solutions, maximum likelihood estimates in more complex models are obtained from iterative algorithms. Such estimates also have superior large-sample properties: consistency (unbiasedness), efficiency (smallest standard errors of all consistent estimators), and normality (distributed around the parameter in a way that makes confidence intervals and statistical tests straightforward). Furthermore, statistical tests based

Table 13.1. Linear, Logistic, and Probit Prediction of Bakery-Deli Employee Turnover (n = 298), by Demographic and Psychological Variables.

	Linear Regression			Logistic Regression			Probit Regression		
	Coefficient	Effect	Test	Coefficient	Effect	Test	Coefficient	Effect	Test
	b	$r(y,x_j:x_{j\neq k})$	t	b	Odds(b)	χ^2	b	Odds(b)	χ^2
Main effect terms									
Intercept	−.155		1.14	−5.849**		10.69**	−3.298**		11.41**
Sex (female = 0, male = 1)	−.033	−.042	.83	−.150	.860	.11	−.068	.898	.07
Age	−.001	−.008	.17	−.010	.990	.02	−.009	.984	.08
Tenure	−.001	−.045	.90	−.025**	.975	6.01**	−.013**	.980	5.93**
Job Status (part-time = 0, full-time = 1)	−.037	−.048	.96	−.288	.750	.37	−.118	.828	.21
Withdrawal Cognitions (WTDCOGS)	.043**	.376	7.17**	.441**	1.554	43.68**	.236**	1.459	43.36**
Group Cohesiveness (GRPCOH)	.289**	.149	2.95**	.094**	1.099	8.28**	.052**	1.086	8.32**
Interactions or higher-order terms									
WTDCOGS × GRPCOH ("snowball")	.002**	.597	2.77**	−.001	.999	.01	.000	1.000	.01
Logistic WTDCOGS	−.143**	−.200	4.04**	−.509	.601	.98	−.245	.678	.94
Box-Tidwell WTDCOGS	.089**	.226	4.60**	.381	1.465	2.08	.191	1.357	2.01
Overall statistics for main effects model									
Null model deviance (D_0)				223.58			219.03		
Model deviance (D_m)				144.82			146.23		
Likelihood ratio (G^2) or Overall F	16.14**			78.76***			72.80**		
(Pseudo) R^2 for main effects model	.25			.23			.22		

*$p < .05$. **$p < .01$.

on ratios of the functions used in maximum likelihood estimation are the most powerful tests that can be constructed. Given the option in LRDV analyses, it is almost always preferable to base coefficient estimates and hypothesis tests on maximum likelihood algorithms.

When Other MLR Assumptions Are Not Met

The MLR model carries several other well-known assumptions. Some of them are necessary for getting good point estimates of the β parameters. All of them are necessary for getting accurate standard errors for the β estimates, and therefore accurate statistical tests. Fleshing out and comparing these assumptions gives an idea of the possible utility of LRDV models.

Dimensionality of the Predictor Space

As with most other statistical models, one must assume that the number of predictors in an MLR model, p, is correct. There should be no missing or extra X_j's, although the former is a cardinal sin and the latter is a menial one. Another way to state this assumption is to say that error variance in a regression model is assumed to be random. If it has a systematic component because of missing predictors but those predictors are uncorrelated with X_j's already in the model, regression coefficients in MLR will not be affected. However, if the same is true for LRDVs, it is equivalent to a condition referred to as *unobserved heterogeneity* or *overdispersion* (more systematic variance) in Y relative to what the LRDV model predicts. This condition can bias LRDV parameter estimates and skew statistical tests.

Independence and Homoscedasticity of ε_i

The MLR model holds that the ε_i are uncorrelated with one another and uncorrelated with the x_{ij}. Errors have a constant variance across the range of each X_j. The former assumption is also made in LRDV models, but not the latter. A simple plot of residuals, e_i, versus predictor values, x_{ij}, can check the veracity of the homoscedasticity assumption in MLR. When MLR is misapplied to LRDVs, the residuals tend to have noticeable patterns. In an MLR equation used to predict the promotion of junior-level lawyers or the turnover of bakery-deli employees, predictors with strong positive coefficients (such as GPA or withdrawal cognitions) will likely show a clear majority of negative residuals at the upper end of their range. Predicted probabilities (the $\hat{y}$'s) will tend to be too high, and observed errors, $y_i - \hat{y}_i = e_i$, will tend to be negative. A mirror image of this imbalance (that is, positive residuals) will show up at the lower end of the predictor's range. For predictors with strong negative coefficients, the pattern would be reversed. Finally, for both lower and upper ranges of such predictors, the e_i would have markedly different variance than in the middle.

Distribution Shape for ε

Much of the power in any statistical model comes from what it stipulates about the shape of the error distribution. A final assumption in MLR is that all of the ε_i are drawn from a normal distribution. The most critical feature of this assumption for MLR is that it forces the distribution of any Y to be continuous (and therefore measured on at least an interval-level scale) and unbounded in the population. Neither assumption is true for LRDVs. Although discreteness in Y reduces the power of MLR, especially in detecting important interaction effects (Russell & Bobko, 1982), it is the latter condition that creates the most problems for MLR when it is applied to LRDVs (Hosmer & Lemeshow, 1989; Menard, 1995).

As implied in the law firm example, the boundedness of LRDVs can create nonsensical predictions in MLR. It can also create biased parameter estimates (King, 1988). Standard errors for MLR tend to be too small when misapplied to LRDVs, leading to a higher chance of type I errors (Garner, Mulvey, & Shaw, 1995; Long, 1997). Nonlinear transformations of the X_j's or the use of weighted least-squares estimation only partially alleviate these problems. It can exacerbate others, such as creating higher correlations between the predictors and the residuals (Aldrich & Nelson, 1984). In sum, misapplication of MLR to LRDVs can lead to incorrect conclusions about the phenomenon being studied (see Huselid & Day, 1991, for an empirical demonstration). Hence, there is a clear need for application of LRDV models in I/O psychology. One set of those models is best suited to predicting the distributional *structure* of an LRDV: if or how much it occurs. Another set of models adds a *timing* dimension to that structure, predicting when the LRDV occurs as well.

General Issues in LRDV Modeling

As a group, LRDV models are not yet part of the orthodoxy in applied research, and they are not put into practice in the same ways by major statistical packages. Use of default programming options may be dangerous, because the default options usually exist to provide faster computations or to conform to modeling situations that might be atypical for I/O psychology. Consequently, I note caveats in analytic steps and statistical programs, especially in SAS and SPSS. Packages that deal with these issues more adroitly are Greene's (1999) LIMDEP and STATA (2000). The former was developed specifically for LRDVs in econometrics, and the latter includes the widest range of statistical choices among available software.

Another feature that ties together the LRDV models described in this chapter is that their expectation portion, $E(Y|X)$, follows the same general function. That is, each one contains some extension of the following equation:

$$E(Y|X) = \exp(\beta_0 + \beta_1 X_1 + \beta_2 X_2 + \ldots \beta_p X_p). \qquad (13.2)$$

The *exp* portion of equation 13.2 refers to the base of the natural logarithm, a handy number in many statistical applications. After taking logs of both sides, equation 13.2 becomes

$$\log[E(Y|X)] = \beta_0 + \beta_1 X_1 + \beta_2 X_2 + \ldots \beta_p X_p. \qquad (13.3)$$

Now the link function, g, is no longer trivial. It is the natural logarithm of $E(Y|X)$. This property makes the LRDV techniques part of a larger family of log-linear models: nonlinear and distinct from MLR in the link function, but linear and familiar in terms of the string of regression parameters. In other words, LRDVs share a good deal of the structure of MLR but not all of it. The dependent variable follows a complex transformation of the original criterion, Y. These log-linear equations are part of a burgeoning area of applied statistics referred to as generalized linear models (Liang & Zeger, 1986; McCullagh & Nelder, 1989). This broad class of models includes LRDVs as well as techniques for analyzing multiway contingency tables, which have sometimes been misidentified as the sole type of "log-linear" analysis.

Predicting If: Logistic and Probit Regression for Binary LRDVs

Dichotomous criteria are the most limited of the LRDVs. Many possible models can relate a dichotomous criterion to a set of predictors (Cox, 1970), but two choices stand out: logistic (logit) or cumulative normal (probit) regression. These two are preferred over other LRDV models because of their flexibility in incorporating a variety of predictors and their availability in recent software tools. They are seeing increasing application in I/O-related journals, although logistic regression is used much more often (Ganzach, Saporta, & Weber, 2000). Textbooks with a slant toward behavioral science applications are available for both of these types of regression (DeMaris, 1992; Hosmer & Lemeshow, 1989; Menard, 1995). Because different LRDV models share many mathematical and procedural underpinnings (Long, 1997; Maddala, 1983), learning the fundamentals of logit and probit regression makes other LRDV regression models much easier to understand.

The words *logit* and *probit* have become nicknames for the respective link functions of each of these forms of regression. A logit is the log odds of any binary variable that occurs with some probability *P*. Applied to a dependent variable, *Y*, *logit modeling* and *logistic regression* mean the same thing. Because the term *logit* (short for "logistic probability unit") is used in a number of other statistical contexts, I use *logistic regression* exclusively in this chapter.

Formal Model for Logistic Regression

One could inappropriately fit MLR to a binary outcome, for which $\text{Prob}(Y=1)$ would be the likelihood of some event occurring for everyone with an identical set of x_{ij} scores. However, the lower and upper bounds of $\text{Prob}(Y=1)$ at 0.0 and 1.0 mean that the true relationship of *Y* with almost any X_j is likely to be nonlinear, generating biased statistical tests in MLR and impossible predicted values. The way to get around this boundedness problem in an LRDV model is to create a link function for *Y* that removes its upper (1) and lower (0) limits. For logistic regression, the first step is to create an *odds ratio,* or $\text{Prob}(Y=1)/\text{Prob}(Y=0)$. The odds ratio is commonly used in epidemiology, biology, and medicine, where it is just as ubiquitous as the correlation coefficient is in I/O psychology. Still, an odds ratio is bounded at its lower end by zero. To get a link function g that allows $g[E(Y|X)]$ to range from negative to positive infinity, the odds ratio is transformed by taking its natural logarithm (log). That transformation yields all of the following equivalencies:

$$g[E(Y|X)] = \log[\text{Prob}(Y=1|X)/\text{Prob}(Y=0|X)]$$
$$= \text{logit}(Y|X) = \log \text{ odds of } (Y|X) \quad (13.4)$$

Each of the terms in the equations above are just different words or expressions used to describe the same transformation of the dependent variable. These expressions set up the following logistic regression model for the expected values of Y in the population:

$$\text{logit}(Y|X) = \beta_0 + \beta_1 X_1 + \beta_2 X_2 + \dots \beta_p X_p \quad (13.5)$$

Although the logit (log-odds) itself might be a new concept, the right-hand side of this model is identical to the right-hand side of MLR. After parameters are estimated, however, equation 13.5 is often reexpressed to make it easier to understand how the coefficients indicate effects on Y:

$$\text{Odds}(Y|X) = \text{Prob}(Y=1|X)/\text{Prob}(Y=0|X)$$
$$= \exp^{(\beta_0 + \beta_1 X_1 + \beta_2 X_2 + \dots \beta_p X_p)} \quad (13.6)$$

That is, equation 13.6 shows how a change in X_j affects the odds that Y will happen, which is easier to think about than an effect of X_j on the log odds of Y. If one is more comfortable thinking about effects on probabilities rather than odds, equation 13.5 would become:

$$\text{Prob}(Y=1|X)$$
$$= (\exp^{\beta_0 + \beta_1 X_1 + \beta_2 X_2 + \dots \beta_p X_p}) / (1 + \exp^{\beta_0 + \beta_1 X_1 + \beta_2 X_2 + \dots \beta_p X_p}) \quad (13.7)$$

Now the left-hand side of the model is equivalent to MLR (when it is used to predict a dichotomous criterion), but the right-hand side is much more complex. Equation 13.7 also makes the nonlinear nature of logistic regression easier to see.

Equations 13.5, 13.6, and 13.7 are all mathematically equivalent. Each expresses the logistic regression model, and each tells the same underlying story about the data. However, each does so in a slightly different style. Readers who are familiar with item response theory (IRT; see Chapter Four, this volume) should note that if equation 13.7 had only one X_j and it were renamed *theta*, it would be identical to the two-parameter logistic model (if a rescaling constant of 1.7 was multiplied by the exponentiated terms). Indeed, if the person parameters (thetas) in the two-parameter IRT model were already known, item parameters could be estimated with logistic regression.

Formal Model for Probit Regression

Another type of binary regression relies on the cumulative normal distribution function, which is the ogive or S-shaped curve that one sees, for instance, when plotting percentiles of individual test scores. This probit link function indexes how much area there is under the normal curve to the left of a particular value. When someone looks up tabled probabilities for a standard normal distribution at the back of a statistics book, he or she is using a type of probit function. For example, the well-known critical value of 1.96 is associated with a probit of .975 (.025 of the area of a standard normal distribution falls to the right of 1.96). To simplify some notation, let Z be the sum of X_j predictors multiplied by their β_j coefficients in a regression model, $Z = \beta_0 + \beta_1 X_1 + \ldots \beta_p X_p$. The expression for a probability unit (the basis of the *probit* nickname) is:

$$\mathrm{Prob}(Y=1|X) = \Phi(Z) = \int_{-\infty}^{Z} (1/\sqrt{2\pi}) \exp(-u^2/2)\, du. \quad (13.8)$$

Equation 13.8 has some impressive-looking math, but it is simply a formal way to write out what the cumulative normal distribution looks like. The expression under the integral sign is just the formula for a standard normal curve, with du attached so that it can be integrated (so an area underneath it can be computed). The integral ranges from negative infinity, which is the lower bound of a standard normal distribution, to the value of Z described earlier. The Greek letter Φ is a conventional and short-handed way to express "cumulative normal" without having to write out the long equation 13.8 expression each time. Expressing the probit model so that it has the same elements on the right side of the equation as other LRDV models, equation 13.8 becomes

$$[\Phi^{-1}]\text{Prob}(Y=1|X) = \text{probit}(Y|X) = \beta_0 + \beta_1 X_1 + \ldots \beta_p X_p \quad (13.9)$$

The probit link function, g, is the inverse of the cumulative normal: $[\Phi^{-1}]$.

Just as with logistic regression, there are other ways to rewrite equation 13.9 so that the β coefficients are easier to interpret. Equation 13.8 already expresses the probit model in terms of probabilities. The following expression is for those who are more comfortable thinking in terms of odds:

$$\text{Odds}(Y=1|X) = \Phi(Z)/[1-\Phi(Z)] \quad (13.10)$$

Comparison of Models

A visual comparison of the functions specified by linear, logistic, and probit regression can underscore how they are distinct. Each one is presented in Figure 13.1, relating $\text{Prob}(Y=1)$ to a single predictor, X. In Figure 13.1, the over- and underprediction of probabilities for high and low levels of X in MLR is shown fairly clearly. Moving to the LRDV models, the discrepancies between the logistic and probit regression predictions are very small after the logistic model is rescaled with the 1.7 constant mentioned earlier. One would need huge samples (more than one thousand observations), or lots of extreme values for X, to have a decent chance at teasing the logistic and probit models apart. Even then, predicted probabilities would never differ by more than .02 (Aldrich & Nelson, 1984). Hence, in most situations, there is no strong empirical advantage or general justification for recommending one of these two LRDV models over the other.

There may be a normative justification. Logistic regression is preferred in biological, public health, medical, and insurance literatures because of the quick transformation it allows of coefficients into odds ratios. Odds are a ratio of probabilities $\text{Prob}(Y=1)/[1-\text{Prob}(Y=1)]$. Therefore, probability (often referred to as

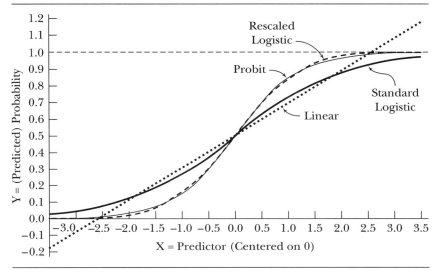

Figure 13.1. Comparison of Logistic, Probit, and Linear Regression Functions for Predicting the Probability of a Dichotomous Criterion.

risk) can also be computed quickly as odds/(odds + 1). Probit is used more often in economics, transportation, production operations, and logistics (as if the statistical terminology were not confusing enough). Sociology uses both. A brief look at applied psychology and related journals over the past five years shows that logistic regression dominates. It may be a more familiar choice for presenting results to an I/O audience.

Assumptions and Robustness to Violations

Logistic and probit regression models make several assumptions, some of which parallel the assumptions of MLR. First, they rely on random sampling from a population of independent Y_i observations. As with MLR, violations of this assumption do not bias coefficient estimates. However, they do produce standard error estimates that are too small and type I errors that are too big (Robinson, 1982). There are also no standard "fix-ups" for autocorrelation in any of the LRDV models, including logistic and probit regression. Instead, researchers have to use longitudinal LRDV models (Liang & Zeger, 1986).

Second, although logistic and probit regression models allow correlations among the X_j variables, there can be no complete dependencies between them. High, but not complete, multicollinearity causes the same problems in LRDV models as it does in MLR: numerical imprecision, less stable coefficient estimates, and higher standard errors (which means less powerful statistical tests). Multicollinearity problems are also exacerbated by low ratios of sample size to the number of predictors, even more so in LRDV models than in MLR.

Third, as is true of all statistical models, logistic and probit regression assume that the stipulated form of the relationship between the X_j's and Y is correct. This includes specifying the right set and number of predictors, p, as well as the appropriate shape for the LRDV function. As long as the true relationships between each X_j and Y are monotonic (that is, always increasing or always decreasing), then violations of the exact S-shaped logistic or probit functional forms in equations 13.5 and 13.9 have minor consequences for model fit, coefficient estimation, and testing.

In a clever extension to testing for nonlinear predictors in MLR, one can enter the Box-Tidwell (1962) transformation of continuous X_j's in logistic regression. Entering this term, $X_j \ln[X_j]$, provides a general assumption test of linearity in the logit, much like its application in MLR, where it provides an estimate of β in the (nonlinear) term $X^{\beta x}$. Note that the X_j must be scored to take positive values before the Box-Tidwell transformation is possible. The estimated coefficient for this term in logistic regression also turns out to be a good guess at the power transformation that X_j might need if one wants to improve model fit. A significant negative weight for this Box-Tidwell term means that the logistic model is predicting probabilities that are too extreme and need to be tempered. A positive weight signifies the opposite pattern (Hosmer & Lemeshow, 1989; see Menard, 1995, for an empirical example).

The fourth and final assumption deals with the second "model" of errors embedded within logistic and probit regression. Both models specify a particular distribution of $\varepsilon_i = Y_i - E(Y_i = 1 | X)$, which are simply the observed values of Y_i minus the predicted or expected probabilities. To simplify notation again, predicted or expected probabilities are often referred to as $\pi_i(x)$ rather than the more cumbersome $E(Y_i=1|X)$. In MLR, the ε_i's are mandated to be normally distributed. In contrast, both the logistic and probit regression models mandate binomial ε_i's. In addition, the ε_i's must be heteroscedastic, because the variance of a binomial distribution depends on its mean. That is, for each expected value or predicted probability, $\pi(x)$, the variance of the errors is $\pi_i(x)[1 - \pi_i(x)]$. This variance is largest when the predicted probability for Y_i is $\pi_i(x) = .5$. It gets smaller as the $\pi_i(x)$'s approach 0 or 1. Because of this distributional property and the nonlinear nature of the regression function in equations 13.7 and 13.8, the raw ε_i's are not squared and summed to help evaluate the fit of the model as in MLR. Still, there are some reasonable LRDV analogues to the MLR idea of a sum of squared errors, and I turn to them below.

Residuals and Fit

The foremost consideration in an assessment of LRDV model fit is not a single test or index such as R^2. Instead, it is a set of checks for violations of statistical assumptions. Fortunately, most of the assumptions already listed are straightforward to verify. A logical analysis of one's sampling design or data collection strategy should answer questions about nonindependence. A correlation matrix of the independent variables provides evidence about multicollinearity or linear dependence. Tolerance indices or variance inflation factors for those variables can be obtained from any MLR routine. Functional forms can be assessed by plotting the means of Y_i against successive discrete segments of each predictor X_j. For data sets with only a few observations falling in the outer ranges of X_j and thus only a few high or low predicted values of $\text{Prob}(Y_i=1)$, a linear probability model might work just as well as a nonlinear one.

As with MLR, residuals in logistic and probit regression harbor a wealth of diagnostic information about model fit. Recall that each of the LRDV regression models contains p predictors. Consider that all combinations of values on those p predictors can form $k = 1, 2, \ldots, K$ vectors or patterns: X_k. As p goes up or if the predictors are continuous rather than discrete, it becomes increasingly unlikely that several observations (persons) will share identical values on *all* the predictors. This is fairly typical for I/O applications, and in those circumstances, K approaches n, which is the sample size. The more that n exceeds K, the better the statistical properties of the residuals are. For this reason, authors sometimes suggest segmenting or "discretizing" continuous predictors when doing diagnostic tests (McCullagh & Nelder, 1989).

The residual for each person with the same predictor pattern k is obtained by subtracting the mean or predicted probability from the observed value of the criterion: $e_i = y_i - \hat{\pi}(x_k)$. Because each y_i has to be 0 or 1, and each $\hat{\pi}(x_k)$ has to range from 0 to 1, then the e_i can range from only -1 to $+1$. It is instructive to talk about these residuals in terms of the example of bakery-deli employees. Suppose that for each nineteen-year-old female with six months' tenure, working part time, who has withdrawal cognitions = 8 (on a two-item summated scale ranging from 2 to 14) and group cohesiveness = 9 (on the same scale), the predicted probability of turnover is $\hat{\pi}(x_k) = .62$. Each person who has that predicted probability will be observed as having quit (1) or not (0). Therefore, her residual will have an e_i value of either .38 or .62, respectively. The variance of these residuals will be $\hat{\pi}(x_k)[1 - \hat{\pi}(x_k)]$: $.38 \times .62 = .24$ in this example. For some other employee with a predicted value of $\hat{\pi}(x_k) = .89$, the two residual values would be .11 and .89, and the residual variance for them would be .10. This binary LRDV situation is substantially different from MLR, because the assumption in MLR is that there is a normal distribution of e_i's, with a constant variance, surrounding predicted values at each level of the predictor.

To get more familiar-looking residuals with roughly the same variance across the range of the predictors, the e_i's are often standardized by dividing them by a factor that includes the square root of their variance estimate: $e_i/\mathrm{sqrt}\{\hat{\pi}(x_k)[1 - \hat{\pi}(x_k)]\}$. These *Pearson residuals*, or r_i, can be constructed for any LRDV model. They are referred to as *standardized* residuals in SPSS and *chi-square* residuals in SAS, because they have a zero mean and approximately unit variance. If they are divided further by $\mathrm{sqrt}\{1 - h_k\}$, where h_k is a value indexing the regression "leverage" or influence of a particular covariate pattern k (see Hosmer & Lemeshow, 1989, who pioneered much of the work on logistic regression diagnostics), the resulting distribution of standardized Pearson residuals, r_{si}, will have exactly unit variance. However, all of the r_{si} will not necessarily form a normal distribution, even when all modeling assumptions have been met (Menard, 1995). Once these residuals are obtained, they can be examined to find observations for whom the model fits poorly, by using univariate or bivariate plots.

If the Pearson residuals are summed and squared, they can be used to construct a badness-of-fit index, the Pearson chi-square. This index is suggested to have a chi-square distribution with degrees of freedom equal to $n - p - 1$. High values of this chi-square with significant p-values can indicate serious assumption violations. However, low values with insignificant p-values are not a sign that all modeling assumptions are met. As noted above, there is also a problem when the spread of data across all K possible combinations of values in the predictor space is sparse: the chi-square statistic will have an unknown distribution. For this case, Hosmer and Lemeshow (1989) developed their own version of chi-square that groups data into eight to twelve sets of predictor values, but these chi-square values can depend heavily on the grouping thresholds. Although this residual test is given as part of statistical output, the information it provides does not necessarily help in demonstrating conformity to assumptions, especially if sample size is small and the predictors are continuous (Long, 1997).

Other diagnostic indices are available for each observation. Influence statistics such as DFBETA (the effect of removing an observation on each coefficient estimate) and C (Cook's distance, the effect of removing an observation on the entire vector of coefficient estimates) are as informative in LRDV regression as they are in MLR. In addition, most programs allow users to print the iteration history of the maximum likelihood parameter estimates. When the estimation algorithm does not converge or parameter estimates are abnormally large (for example, larger than one hundred), this iteration record can help to pinpoint problems.

One of those kinds of problems includes *complete separation* and *quasi–complete separation,* both of which nullify the maximum likelihood estimates of logistic or probit regression parameters. Complete separation is equivalent to perfect prediction in a two-group discriminant analysis, the finding of a set of weights for the X_j that completely separates (creates no overlap in) the predicted values for persons in one group (for whom $Y_i = 1$) from those in another group (for whom $Y_i = 0$). Another way to think about complete separation is to note that it occurs when there is a perfect (1.0) point-biserial correlation between y_i and $\hat{y}_i$. Quasi-complete separation occurs when such a point-biserial correlation is nearly 1.0 (for instance, when it is .98 or .99). This situation should be rare for I/O psychologists, but it does become more likely with a large number of predictors relative to sample size. In that sense, these problems are similar to severe overfitting in MLR models. The problems are indicated in logistic and probit regression by very large coefficients and standard error estimates, with those estimates increasing substantially during each iteration of the maximum likelihood algorithm. When complete separation occurs, the number of predictors needs to be reduced, or some of the predictors need to be recoded to provide more overlap between observations.

Estimation and Overall Tests

The iterations in maximum likelihood estimation lead to a final set of values that constitute (-2 times) the log-likelihood for the logistic or probit regression model in question. This number will show up in the "intercept and covariates" column of an SAS printout or the "chi-square" column of SPSS. It is generally called the *deviance,* or D_m, for the fitted model. It is critical to have a solid understanding of what D_m represents, because it is the source of almost all of the important statistical tests in an LRDV regression.

Due to the desirable properties of maximum likelihood estimation, D_m is distributed as a χ^2 with $n - p - 1$ (residual) degrees of freedom. Just as with structural equations modeling (see Chapter Three, this volume), this D_m chi-square is really a "badness"-of-fit statistic. Bigger values indicate worse fit. When constructing models or adding terms to a LRDV equation, such as in the testing of moderators or incremental prediction, one wants to see a reduction in D_m. In this way, D_m is directly analogous to the sum of squared errors (SSE) in linear regression. The contribution of each observation i to D_m is an additional type of standardized residual, or "deviance residual" in LRDV models. It is often labeled as d_i. The distribution of these d_i residuals also has a mean of zero and a unit variance in large samples.

Another critical deviance statistic is D_0. It is (-2 times) the log-likelihood of a model that has no predictors, hence the 0 subscript.

It can be thought of as the deviance for a null model, and it is directly analogous to the total sum of squares (SST) in linear regression. In fact, if one uses a maximum likelihood algorithm to estimate a conventional linear regression, both D_0 and D_m would be exactly equal to SST and SSE, respectively. The null model deviance, D_0, is also distributed as a χ^2, but with $n - 1$ degrees of freedom. In SAS, D_0 shows up in the "intercept only" column of the output; in SPSS, it is called the "initial log likelihood."

The model deviance, D_m, also has an important diagnostic purpose. It can be used to reflect lack of fit in the model that might be due to overdispersion. When D_m is evaluated against its degrees of freedom, as with the chi-square statistic, it provides information about the average deviation that each Y_i has from $E[Y_i|X]$. When those deviations are within specifications, then $D_m/(n - p - 1)$ will not be significantly higher than chance levels. If this test statistic is significant, the residuals have some unmodeled structure that spreads observed values more widely or in some more patterned way around the predicted values than the model assumes. That is, the ε_i's have some real but unaccounted for extra heterogeneity around the regression curve than would be expected by chance. Additional predictors or an overdispersed version of logistic or probit regression would then be needed (Long, 1997).

One of the other handy properties of the deviance statistics is that D_0 is nested within D_m. That is, the null model reflected by D_0 is merely a reduced (with no X_j's) version of the target model. Therefore, as with other chi-square statistics, the difference between D_0 and D_m is also distributed as a chi-square, with degrees of freedom equal to the number of predictors, p. This chi-square difference, $D_0 - D_m = G^2$, is also called the *likelihood ratio statistic*. It is referred to as the "chi-square for covariates" in SAS and the "model chi-square" in SPSS. If the predictors are of substantive interest, I/O psychologists will want large and statistically significant values of G^2. Given the earlier connections of D_0 with SST and D_m with SSE, it is perhaps not surprising that G^2 is directly analogous to the regression sum of squares (SSR). The significance of the G^2 statistic is comparable to the significance of the F-test for the overall MLR model, a test that at least one of the predictors has a nonzero coefficient.

The bottom of Table 13.1 lists the D_m, D_0, and G^2 indices for logistic and probit regression models used to predict turnover among the bakery-deli employees described earlier. The D_m values of 144.82 (logistic) and 146.03 (probit) for the two types of LRDV models would be evaluated against a chi-square distribution with $298 - 6 - 1 = 291$ degrees of freedom, to gauge badness of fit. Both of these indices are well below the critical values of that test (high p-values), which is the desired result. To test the predictiveness of the overall model—the omnibus effect of the six predictors—one would evaluate the G^2 values (78.76 for logistic regression, 72.80 for probit regression) against chi-square distributions with six degrees of freedom. Both of these values have p-values well below .001, indicating a clear improvement in the prediction of turnover by including the six predictors.

Perhaps because of these strong parallels, and definitely because of the strong emphasis on variance explained in MLR equations, much effort has been spent developing a single index akin to R^2 that would reflect the overall goodness of fit of a logistic or probit regression model (or any LRDV for that matter). From the current crop of suggestions, the one that is nearest to the R^2 from MLR, in terms of both its absolute value and its interpretive similarity, is attributed to Maddala (1983). It is a transformation of the likelihood ratio chi-square:

$$\text{pseudo } R^2 = 1 - [\exp - (G^2/N)]. \tag{13.11}$$

In fact, if equation 13.11 were applied to MLR results, it would give an identical value to conventional R^2 (Long, 1997). Although it cannot quite reach 1.0 (because the LRDV model would be "saturated" by using up all of its degrees of freedom), it can be adjusted for the number of predictors in the same way as various shrinkage formulas are used in MLR. Pseudo-R^2 values for the LRDV models estimated in the turnover example are shown at the bottom of Table 13.1.

Specific Tests

One of the greatest sources of confusion regarding logistic and probit regression stems from statistical tests of the β's for each of the j predictors. There are three types of such tests: Wald, Score, and likelihood ratio. All rely on constrained or unconstrained versions of the log-likelihood function but in different ways. All three are asymptotically equivalent, which means that in very large samples, they will produce almost identical test statistics and p-values. All of the tests are formulated as a squared ratio of each parameter estimate to its standard error. This ratio is evaluated against a chi-square with one degree of freedom. All use maximum likelihood estimates for the β_j's.

However, the tests differ in how standard errors are computed. Most important, the Wald test has standard errors that are too large when regression coefficients are themselves large (Hauck & Donner, 1977; Jennings, 1986). The Score test is based on Lagrange multipliers and is not as efficient as the likelihood ratio test, meaning that it is similar to the Wald test in having reduced power (heightened rates of type II error). The likelihood ratio test relies on the same logic as the overall G^2 test of fit. To compute it, the deviance statistic, D_m, is estimated for the target or "full" model (with *full model* meaning the same here as it does in MLR tests). Then another deviance statistic, D_{rm}, is estimated for a reduced model that does not contain the predictor of interest. The difference between D_{rm} and D_m is the likelihood ratio test, which has a chi-square distribution with one degree of freedom.

Unfortunately, the former, less desirable tests are usually found in statistical output from packages such as SAS and SPSS, and the latter, best test, is usually not. To estimate it, one needs to perform logistic or probit regression analyses on a model that contains all p predictors, and then on each of the $j = 1, \ldots, p$ separate models that do not include predictor j. The chi-square differences and likelihood ratio tests can be obtained by subtraction.

Another alternative in SAS is to supplement PROC LOGISTIC and PROC PROBIT with PROC GENMOD, using the latter procedure to fit each LRDV model with an option (TYPE 3) giving likelihood ratio estimates for all parameters. If one does so for the same data set, there will be a surprise lurking in the results. PROC LOGISTIC gives coefficient estimates that have the opposite sign as all the other methods, in SAS and elsewhere. Unless one overrides the default options in this procedure, it fits models to $\text{Prob}(Y_i = 0)$ rather than $\text{Prob}(Y_i 1)$. Of course, one can simply reverse the signs of the confusing PROC LOGISTIC coefficients instead.

Interpretation

Once coefficients have been estimated and some judgment has been made about which X_j's are contributing to the prediction of Y, the effect sizes associated with each of those contributions need to be interpreted. Here, there are fundamental differences between LRDV models and MLR. To help illustrate how to interpret effects, I refer to the logistic and probit regression results in the second and third columns of Table 13.1. The test statistics for each predictor are based on the likelihood ratio procedure described previously. For comparison purposes, results from an MLR analysis of the same data are shown in the first column. Each type of analysis has its own coefficients, effect sizes, and statistical tests. The effect size estimates for MLR are partial correlations. The effect sizes for probit and logistic models are partial odds ratios, which are discussed in detail a little further on.

Demographic characteristics of the bakery-deli employees were included in the model to test the prediction that their effects on turnover are fully mediated by psychological variables. The sequential logic of mediation and moderation tests is identical in MLR and LRDV models. If distal variables have significant coefficients when proposed mediators are already included in the logistic regression equation, those distal variables have some unique (unmediated) effect (James & Brett, 1984). Two psychological mediators were of special interest in Table 13.1: withdrawal cognitions and group cohesiveness. The former variable is one of the immediate precursors of turnover behavior (Hom & Griffeth, 1995). The latter has seen relatively little investigation as a turnover antecedent. Although it is commonly believed that more cohesive work groups tend to inhibit turnover, there are situations in which it might facilitate a sort of collective exit from the firm (Krackhardt & Porter, 1989).

As with MLR, the signs of main effect coefficients in logistic and probit regression convey whether changes in a predictor are associated with increases (positive) or decreases (negative) in the probability of the criterion. In addition, they are partial coefficients in that they depend on the inclusion of other variables in the regression model. The size of a coefficient estimate also reflects the observed scale of its predictor. For predictors that have relatively large numerical scales, the coefficients will be small—even if they are statistically reliable. Table 13.1 shows this to be the case with tenure. It has a significant, unique effect on the probability of turnover, but because it was measured in months, the coefficient estimate is only $b = -.025$ in the logistic regression model ($-.013$ in probit regression). The significance of this coefficient rejects the psychological mediation hypothesis described above. Tenure has a unique effect on turnover even when withdrawal cognitions and group cohesiveness are accounted for. Its unique (unmediated) effect also *was not detected in the MLR model.* The negative sign of the tenure coefficient indicates that bakery-deli employees who had invested more time with their employer before the survey was conducted were less likely to leave the store afterward.

Standardizing the predictors before analysis can reduce apparent disparities in the sizes of b values. And as with MLR, standardization can help one compare the relative impacts of different X_j. That approach will not only alleviate the problem of different types of (singly or doubly) "standardized estimates" being reported by different statistical packages; it will also help to keep the numerical algorithms from failing to converge, which is more likely when the independent variables have widely different scales of magnitude (Long, 1997). Alternatively, one can simply multiply the b by the standard deviation of the predictor. Tenure had a standard deviation of 30.51 months; therefore, the coefficient for a standardized version of tenure would have been $30.51 \times -.025 = -.761$.

Unlike in MLR, the β's in logistic and probit regression do not carry the assumption of a constant slope of relationship with $\text{Prob}[Y=1|X]$. A unit difference along any predictor might bring about a different effect on the probability of turnover if that difference were a change from $x_{ij} = 2$ to 3 versus a change of $x_{ij} = 3$ to 4. To get to a scaleless continuum of effect size, coefficient estimates are converted to odds ratios. For logistic regression, getting an odds ratio is simply a matter of computing $\exp(b)$ for each estimate (see equation 13.6 and note that $\exp^{(\beta_0 + \beta_1 X_1 + \beta_2 X_2 + \ldots \beta_p X_p)} = \exp^{(\beta_0)} \exp^{(\beta_1 X_1)} \exp^{(\beta_2 X_2)} \ldots \exp^{(\beta_p X_p)}$). The odds ratio for a unit change in withdrawal cognitions was 1.55, meaning that the odds of quitting was 55 percent higher than the previous level for every one-point increase on the original withdrawal cognitions scale. If the standardization technique described above were applied (multiplying the b in Table 13.1 by 3.03, which is the standard deviation for withdrawal cognitions), it would show that a one-standard deviation increase in withdrawal cognitions was associated with a whopping odds ratio of 3.81.

Getting odds ratios from probit regression coefficients requires access to an inverse normal function or to a printed table with values listed for areas under the normal curve. To convert each b, it must be treated as a standard normal deviate (a z-score), and the ratio of areas below versus above the z-score will then form the odds ratio (see equation 13.10). Although the coefficients will be smaller by an average of $\approx 1/1.7$ in probit versus logistic regression, predicted probabilities and odds ratios from these two LRDV models will be highly similar for statistically significant predictors. Results in Table 13.1 bear this out. For instance, the odds ratio associated with a one-unit change in group cohesiveness was 1.099 for logistic regression and 1.086 for probit regression.

Other Distinctions from MLR

In addition to central issues of model structure, assumptions, estimation, testing, and interpretation, there are a few other unique (from MLR) features worth noting.

Confidence Intervals

With the standard errors given by most statistical programs for the b's, one can construct confidence intervals using the conventional (symmetric) technique of adding and subtracting a product of the standard error and some critical value from the normal distribution to b (for example, $1.96 \times \mathrm{SE}(b)$ for a 95 percent confidence interval). However, confidence intervals around odds ratios are asymmetric, because odds cannot be negative. To create an appropriate confidence interval around an odds ratio, one must first find the upper and lower limits of the confidence interval around b using the conventional procedure and then plug the upper and lower limits into the odds ratio formulas described in the preceding section.

For example, the b for withdrawal cognitions in the logistic regression was .441. Therefore, the odds ratio is $\exp(.441)=1.554$, which is shown in the middle column of Table 13.1. To construct a confidence interval around this ratio, one would go back to the coefficient estimate, $b = .441$, and subtract or add $1.96 \times \text{SE}(b)$ to this to get its 95 percent lower and upper limits. In this instance, the standard error is .067, and the end points of the b confidence interval are .310 and .572. Exponentiating each of these limits, $\exp(.310) = 1.363$, and $\exp(.572) = 1.772$, gives lower and upper limits for a 95 percent confidence interval around the odds ratio. It is asymmetric: thinner on the lower than the upper side of 1.554.

Discriminant Analysis

Another area of confusion, and sometimes even debate, revolves around the use of LRDV models to help discriminate group centroids in a multidimensional space of independent variables—to answer questions about *who* rather than *if*. The different substantive questions, however, generate the same statistical need. For a two-group case, there are no apparent advantages to using discriminant analysis instead of logistic or probit regression to construct a prediction equation for group membership. In moderate sample sizes (more than one hundred), LRDV regression models have equivalent or better power than discriminant analyses (Efron, 1975). Their statistical architecture also allows significance tests for each individual variable in the logistic or probit model, with the further advantage of allowing any type of numerical predictor, including interactions. Discriminant analysis, on the other hand, assumes a multivariate normal distribution for the predictors. Violations of multivariate normality lead to biased estimates of both coefficients and discriminant functions (Hosmer & Lemeshow, 1989). Also, discriminant analysis cannot easily accommodate different within-group covariance matrices (interactions preclude its use).

Interactions

The treatment of interactions also signals a final, tricky distinction between applications of MLR and logistic or probit regression. Recall that in all forms of LRDV regression, the link function is nonlinear. Each X_j already has a changing strength of effect on Y, *interacting with itself* in predicting Y (DeMaris, 1992). Although signs of main effects terms are consistent between the two approaches, when higher-order terms such as interactions and power-transformed predictors (such as X_j^2) are included, all bets are off.

There is a demonstration of this in Table 13.1. To test the idea of a "snowball effect"—that the closeness of one's work group tends to accentuate the effect of tendencies to leave or stay with an organization—I entered a multiplicative interaction of group cohesiveness and withdrawal cognitions into each of the regression models. This had virtually no impact on the LRDV models, but it significantly improved prediction in the (improper) linear model. Similar circumstances were noted by Huselid and Day (1991) in their tests of the interactive effects of job involvement and organizational commitment on turnover, and by Ganzach et al. (2000), in their tests of the joint effect of motivation and ability on performance. The reason for this divergence is that in the MLR model, interaction tests gauge differences in *absolute* risk for X_j across moderator levels because of the constancy of slopes within those levels. In logistic and probit regression, the interaction tests gauge differences in *relative* risk for X_j across levels of the moderator, in this case relative to the risk at one unit less on the X_j (Kessler, 1983).

Tests of other nonlinear effects also show serious discrepancies between MLR and LRDV models. For example, I entered the Box-Tidwell transformation of withdrawal cognitions into probit and logistic regression to assess how well they fit their own log-linear specification. In both cases, the inclusion of the $X_j \ln(X_j)$ term had no detectable effect. However, when the same term was included in the MLR model, it explained unique variance in Y. An incorrect conclusion might have been reached if an incorrect linear (MLR) model was used.

To come full circle in the tests of model fit, I also created a logistic transformation of withdrawal cognitions: $\exp(X_j)/[1+\exp(X_j)]$. If LRDV models provide better predictions of turnover in the bakery-deli employee population, this ratio from equation 13.7 (which could be used for any predictor) should explain unique variance in the MLR model but not in the logistic or probit regression models. Furthermore, because the latter two models flatten the regression slopes in the tails of X_j, where Prob(Y) is bounded at 0 and 1, this ratio term should have a significant, negative coefficient when it is included in a linear probability model. Tests in Table 13.1 show that this is indeed the case.

Extensions to Logistic and Probit Regression

Many other LRDV models exist, each with a log-linear form or link function.

Polytomous and Ordered Dependent Variables

There are often situations, such as in studies of any discrete choice (choose 1 of m options), when the dependent variable is polytomous or multicategory rather than dichotomous or binary. Application of MLR would be completely meaningless under these conditions, but multinomial logit or multinomial probit LRDV models would be appropriate. The former LRDV model is the most tractable. It involves a simple extension to the logic and estimation of logistic regression, and it does not involve any new assumptions (Long, 1997). If the multiple response categories are ordered rather than nominal, then ordinal logit and ordinal probit would be useful LRDV models (Agresti, 1990). These latter models were developed for dependent variables that have a finite number of discrete but ordered response levels that cannot be treated as equal-sized intervals, such as when someone assigns ranks to the elements of a set of behavioral alternatives.

Predicting How Often: LRDV Regression for Counts

A final extension or, more appropriately, an entire class of LRDV models, applies to situations in which the criterion is observed over a long enough time period to generate frequencies or counts beyond 0 and 1 (for example, publications for a first-year faculty member or number of grievances filed). Distributions of these data will have a clear, positive skew and will appear truncated at the left, with a mode equal to 0 or 1. Because the variance of a count increases with its mean, both the limited range and the strong heteroscedasticity in count data mandate the use of analytic techniques other than MLR.

Poisson and negative binomial regression models have been developed to deal with such circumstances. Poisson regression assumes that each observation (person, group, firm) has its own rate parameter that governs how often the criterion occurs. It also involves an assumption that the mean of the criterion count equals its variance. However, variances in count data are typically higher than their means (a kind of overdispersion). Negative binomial regression allows this overdispersion but accounts for it by estimating more parameters (Garner et al., 1995). Both types of models can underestimate the proportion of zero counts in real data, necessitating some modifications (Long, 1997).

Predicting When: Regression Models for Event History LRDVs

Each of the models introduced in this chapter rests on the same basic log-linear specification and LRDV assumptions. However, all of the models described so far are built to predict the overall structure of a criterion distribution, answering questions about *if* or *how much*. They assume a stationary or constant process of the X_j's generating Y. The models described next are designed to predict the *when* of the dependent variable. In doing so, these event history analyses move even further beyond the limits of MLR. They are robust to censoring (a type of truncation of observations), and they can incorporate conventional (X_j) and time-varying ($X_j(t)$) predictors in explaining any dynamic but dichotomous criterion. As such, they are one of the few methodological tools that allow a close examination of causal lags.

Occurrence and Time

In logistic and probit regression, the criterion is the (non-)occurrence of some variable ($Y = 0$ or 1). In event history analyses, the criterion is the rate of Y's occurrence over time. That Y variable can be observed behavior, a performance attainment, or any event marking a discontinuous change in state for the persons being studied. The key additional datum is T, the time until that change in state occurs. That is, for each person i in one's sample, fitting event history models requires a binary Y_i, and a discrete or continuous T_i, both of which are combined to estimate a time-dependent rate. In I/O psychology, event history models have been applied most often to turnover, because firms typically keep records of if (Y_i) and when (T_i) employees leave and because the models simultaneously solve base-rate and time-insensitivity problems of other approaches (Dickter, Roznowski, & Harrison, 1996; Harrison, Virick, & William, 1996; Somers & Birnbaum, 1999).

To apply event history analysis to the bakery-deli employee data, I would need employee quit dates to calculate T_i (if an employee did quit). Unfortunately, these data were not available. So to illustrate some of the features of these time-based LRDV models, I will use separate data from a set of day care centers, where the organization was interested in the consequences of employee turnover. That is, they were concerned that employee (caregiver) turnover stimulated customer turnover in the caregivers' classrooms. The example I analyze includes data on the turnover (Y_i) and length of stay (T_i) of 326 customers (children), predicted by demographics (age, sex, siblings enrolled), season of enrollment, and employee (caregiver) turnover rate.

Nature, Scale, and Boundaries of Time

Time is part of the dependent variable in event history models. Therefore, well-reasoned choices regarding the nature, scale, origin, and end point for time are critical for proper modeling. First, one must decide whether the nature of T_i observation is continuous or discrete. This decision determines the statistical form of the event history model to be estimated. If one has analog records of when the criterion events occur, then continuous-time models are preferred. If the criterion is measured at spacings or regular intervals along the timescale, as in a panel design, then discrete-time models are more appropriate. In the customer turnover example, there was a record for the exact day that each child started and stopped attending the day care center. Hence, I can treat time as continuous. If time had been measured less precisely, say, with only the month of enrollment or month of turnover recorded, I would have treated time as discrete.

This first choice should be made in consideration of a second issue: the presumed scale of time for the process studied (Kelly & McGrath, 1986). If there is an immediate impact of caregiver turnover on parental decisions to take their children out of a day care center, then monthly data would give only a coarse, discrete approximation to what is likely a more finely grained process. On the other hand, if I were studying how personality or work values affected retirement decisions, monthly or even yearly data might be regarded as a continuous-time record.

A related issue of timescale is the likely number of "ties" in the observation of T (two or more people for whom the observed T_i are equal). Wider, more discrete time intervals generate more ties. Estimation of continuous-time models can be complicated and biased by having many tied observations (Yamaguchi, 1989). Under these circumstances, discrete-time models are preferred. Still, discrete-time versions of event history models are quite powerful. When sample sizes are large and measurement spacings are not too wide, statistical results from discrete-time models are quite similar to those from continuous-time models (Efron, 1988).

The third and fourth choices about time deal with the ending (t_E) and starting points (t_S) of one's observation window. The best advice regarding t_E is to choose it so that $t_E - t_S$ is as long as possible yet still relevant for the process under study. This will capture the largest number of complete or uncensored observations of T_i (see below for a description of censoring).

The choice of time's origin, the point at which $T = 0$ for everyone, is more critical and more difficult. The overarching rule is to choose t_S so that it marks either onset of exposure to any "risk" or any nonzero probability that $Y = 1$ could occur, or onset of exposure to risks stemming from the independent variables one is investigating (Allison, 1995). To maintain the logic of prediction, as well as to ensure that causes precede effects, the observation window for Y_i and T_i should *follow* the timing of measured values of the X_{ij}. If an I/O researcher was studying promotion to law firm partner as predicted by law school GPA, then t_S would be the starting date of each lawyer's tenure with the firm. If a researcher was studying turnover as a function of withdrawal cognitions and perceived group cohesiveness, such as in the bakery-deli example, then t_S would be the date of questionnaire administration.

In my example of customer turnover, the choice of t_S is more difficult. Some independent variables, such as age, gender, season, and the presence of attending siblings, exist at the point of day care enrollment. However, data on the turnover of the children's caregivers were not available until August 1, 1998. For children who were enrolled earlier, their known exposure to caregiver turnover could not be assessed until August 1, 1998. That date was assigned as their time origin (t_S). For those who enrolled after August 1, their time origin was their enrollment date, because that was the point at which I could assess their exposure to caregiver turnover. Observations stopped fifteen months later, on November 14, 1999.

Censoring

As might be apparent from the description so far, time-based LRDV models work best when the dichotomous criterion has occurred for as many observations in the sample as possible. Indeed, a base rate of 100 percent for $Y = 1$, would prohibit the use of logistic or probit regression because the binary criterion would be a constant. Yet it would be ideal for event history analyses because the full value of T_i would be known for every person. If Y_i is 0 when the observations are stopped (the event has not occurred yet for person i), then T_i is said to be *censored*. However, rather than throw out this information and study only quitting customers rather than all customers, censored observations are retained and used to help estimate parameters in event history models. They show that the time until the criterion lasted *at least* as long as $t_E - t_S$.

Several types of censoring are shown in Figure 13.2. Person (customer) 5, who (hypothetically) did not leave the day care center until May 1999, has a *right-censored* observation of T_i. Person 3, who (hypothetically) started at the day care center before observations began, has a *left-censored* observation. When both types of censoring occur, an observation is *doubly censored*. In each case, I know that the true "survival" time is something greater than the observed T_i. (Event history models terminology originated in medical research, for which the criterion was literally time to death; in many texts and articles, these LRDV models are termed *survival analyses*.) Inclusion of left-censored and doubly censored observations is possible in event history data, but it does make estimation more difficult for the effect of time-based predictors, such as season of enrollment.

Right-censored observations of T_i are not a serious problem for event history models if the right-censoring process is independent of the process that generates the event of interest and if there are enough uncensored observations per estimated parameter (for

Figure 13.2. Left-Censored, Right-Censored, and Uncensored Observations in Event History Data.

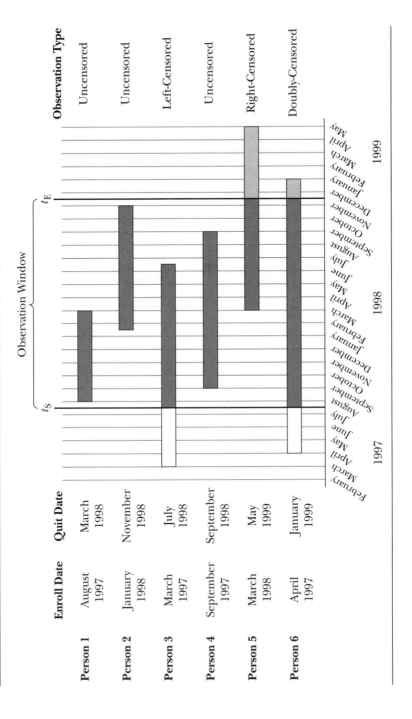

example, more than ten). If the censoring process is related to the behavioral process under study, then biased parameter estimates are likely. In the example of predicting promotion to partner in a law firm, a right-censored observation would occur if a junior lawyer left before he or she was promoted. If those who left the firm were poorer performers (Harrison, Virick, & William, 1996), then it is also likely they would have taken longer to get promoted. This systematic type of right censoring in event history data would lead to underestimates of the impact of GPA on promotion attainment. Still, it is important to note that either random or systematic censoring would bias MLR parameter estimates, if one tried to predict the T_i or even $\log(T_i)$ using conventional linear regression. In this way, event history models account for how the T_i are limited (by censoring) range criteria, but MLR does not.

Hazard Rates

Data on the occurrence (Y_i) and timing (T_i) of the criterion jointly define the dependent variable in event history models: an individual's hazard rate or $\lambda_i(t)$. In fact, these LRDV analyses are often called *hazard rate models*. If time is measured continuously, then the hazard rate for some criterion event Y is defined mathematically as

$$\lambda_i(t) = \lim_{\Delta t \to 0} \text{Prob}(Y_i = 1 | t + \Delta t, \ T_i \geq t)/\Delta t. \qquad (13.12)$$

Another, and mathematically identical, way to define the hazard rate is

$$\lambda_i(t) = \lim_{\Delta t \to 0} \text{Prob}(t \geq T_i \geq t + \Delta t | T_i \geq t)/\Delta t. \qquad (13.13)$$

These equations specify a substantially different criterion from what is used in MLR or other linear analyses. The mathematical complexity of the equations might cloud their central idea. The Δt term refers to an infinitesimally small $(\Delta t \to 0)$ interval after some point in time, t. A hazard rate is the "unobserved rate at which events occur" (Allison, 1984, p. x), or the instantaneous risk that the timing of $Y_i = 1$ will fall in that small interval between t and $t + \Delta t$, given that the $Y_i = 1$ event has not yet occurred. This latter idea makes it clear that a hazard rate is conditional on person i lasting *at least* until time *t*. In the customer turnover example, this would mean that the time-dependent hazard is based on customers who have not left yet—those who are still "at risk" at time *t*. Those who have already quit are no longer part of the "risk set." That is, customers who quit in their first ninety days are not used to estimate $\lambda(t = 91)$ and beyond.

If time is measured in discrete units, then the hazard rate is somewhat easier to define and understand, because $\Delta t = 1$ (or some whole number). Substituting this into equation 13.13 gives

$$\lambda_i(t) = \text{Prob}(t \geq T_i \geq t+1 | T_i \geq t). \tag{13.14}$$

That is, in discrete time, the criterion is defined as a simple probability rather than as a rate. It is the likelihood that the timing of $Y_i = 1$ will fall in the interval between t and $t + 1$, given that it has not yet occurred for person *i*. If time were measured in discrete months in the customer turnover example, the hazard rate would be the probability of a customer quitting in each month of the observation period. Discrete-time hazard rate models are therefore very similar to logistic and probit regression. They extend those earlier LRDV models in that a repeated observation of the binary *Y* is made for each individual across successive time intervals, until $Y_i = 1$ occurs. In this time-based extension, $\text{Prob}(t=1|X)$ becomes $\text{Prob}(Y=1|X \text{ and } t)$.

Comparison of Hazard Rate Models

The notion of a hazard rate is fundamental to any event history model. It is important to explore and clarify some of its features. First, the hazard rate is defined in terms of an unobserved probability—hence, my use of the Greek notation, $\lambda_i(t)$, instead of what is often noted as $h_i(t)$ (Allison, 1984). One estimates the $\lambda_i(t)$ at the same time those estimates are regressed on a set of predictors (see below). Second, although there is a baseline or mean hazard that can change over time for everyone, $\lambda_0(t)$, each individual *i* is assumed to have his or her own hazard rate, $\lambda_i(t)$. It is this variation in the $\lambda_i(t)$ that is modeled in event history analyses, by regressing the $\lambda_i(t)$ estimates on a set of predictors, X_{ij}. Combining these two features of hazard rates leads to the equivalence, $E(Y_i=1|t,X) = \lambda_i(t)$.

To accommodate the fact that hazard rates are always positive, predictors are exponentiated in event history models:

$$E(Y_i = 1 | t, X) = \lambda_i(t) = f[\lambda_0(t)] \exp(\beta_1 X_1 + \beta_2 X_2 + \ldots \beta_p X_p). \quad (13.15)$$

The only difference between this general form for event history models and the general form for all LRDV models (see equation 13.2) is the f term. It contains what would have been β_0, in logistic, probit, or linear regression, but in event history models, this intercept or baseline hazard rate is allowed to fluctuate over time. As I describe below, the specification of f identifies how hazard rates change over time and therefore which particular event history model is used. Taking logs of each side of equation 13.15 reveals a familiar regression form (see equation 13.3):

$$\log[\lambda_i(t)] = \log(f[\lambda_0(t)]) + \beta_1 X_1 + \beta_2 X_2 + \ldots \beta_p X_p. \quad (13.16)$$

Again, the difference between this and other types of LRDV models is the use of a time-varying intercept term, $\log(f[\lambda_0(t)])$, instead of β_0. There are a variety of ways that this term, and therefore $\log[\lambda_i(t)]$, might depend on time. This is a third critical feature of hazard rates and the event history models they are embedded in. Specification of f (often called the *hazard function*) always creates a one-to-one relationship between the individual hazard rates, $\lambda_i(t)$ and the observed distribution times of T_i (often called the *survivor function*).

Exponential Model

The simplest event history model is one for which $\lambda_0(t)$ is flat over time. With a constant baseline hazard, (1) $\lambda_0(t)$ becomes λ, which would have the normal interpretation of an intercept, (2) $1/\lambda$ is the expected length of time until the criterion event occurs, such as turnover, which is sometimes called the *median survival time*, and (3) the distribution of T_i follows a simple exponential curve. For I/O researchers studying events in which fluctuations over time are random but differences across persons are systematic, an exponential model would be appropriate. For example, if there were no seasonal changes in the likelihood that children would be taken from their day care centers, one might fit an exponential hazard rate model. In fact, if there were no censored data, one could fit this model by log-transforming the observations of times T_i and doing a conventional MLR to predict them.

Monotonic Models

Unfortunately, an exponential model is highly unlikely to fit data of interest to I/O psychologists because risks of events are seldom constant over time (Singer & Willett, 1991). For the more likely case of time-varying risks, two popular specifications for f are the Weibull and Gompertz models. The main difference between the two is that the Weibull model can be undefined when $t = 0$ (that is, at the time origin t_S). Both models assume that the baseline hazard rate, $\lambda_0(t)$, is always increasing or always decreasing over time (Yamaguchi, 1989). If there is theory or evidence that the rate of the criterion shows a steady decline or rise over t, then either of these models can be useful. For example, theories contending that stress or negative outcomes accumulate on the job might predict a monotonically increasing hazard rate (also called *positive duration dependence*) for employee turnover. Theories contending that day care customers become more attached to a center as they invest more time and effort in repeated transactions might predict a monotonically decreasing hazard rate (also called *negative duration dependence*) for customer turnover.

All of the three preceding models share two basic characteristics. They are *proportional hazards models* in that at any point in time, the ratio of the hazard rates for any two individuals is a constant proportion—a consistent shift upward or downward from the baseline hazard, $\lambda_0(t)$. That is, they assume parallel risk curves over time for any two persons in the population. This proportionality can be seen by creating a ratio of hazard functions for persons i and j from equation 13.15. Because the baseline, $\lambda_0(t)$, is same for both persons, it drops out of the ratio:

$$\lambda_i(t)/\lambda_j(t) = \exp[\beta_1(x_{i1}-x_{j1})+\beta_2(x_{i2}-x_{j2})+\ldots\beta_p(x_{iP}-x_{jP})]. \quad (13.17)$$

Equation 13.17 is useful for interpreting coefficients in event history models. If X_1 was a dummy variable indicating group membership, then $\exp(\beta_1)$ would reflect how much higher or lower the risk of the criterion was for persons with $x_1 = 1$ versus $x_1 = 0$. This difference in risk would be consistent over time.

The second characteristic these models share is that they are parametric. They involve full specification and estimation of the β coefficients and f, but estimation of the latter term is made possible by restrictive assumptions about f's time-dependent shape. Only a handful of processes in the behavioral sciences have been shown to have monotonically increasing or decreasing hazard rates for a binary criterion (for example, mastering a particular task; Singer & Willett, 1991). Generally, a researcher does not have a strong a priori basis for requiring a particular (constant or monotonic) pattern of risk over time. Evidence about the shape of $\lambda_0(t)$ is needed. To get such evidence, the time continuum can be broken into discrete segments. Using nonparametric methods for estimating f but not the βs (PROC LIFETEST in SAS, SURVIVAL in SPSS), one can get a sense of whether the parametric assumptions hold. I applied the nonparametric analyses to the day care customer data set (see Figure 13.3), using monthly time segments. The analyses revealed a complex hazard for customer turnover that fell from the first through the sixth month, then rose to the eleventh month, then

Figure 13.3. Empirical Hazard Rate for Customer Turnover from the Start of the Study's Observation Window.

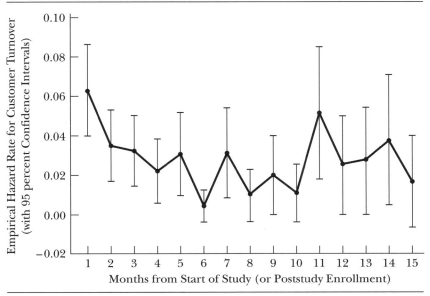

fell again. Application of the parametric models would have created a serious misspecification of f and therefore seriously biased (and invalidated) tests of β coefficients.

Formal Model for Cox Regression

Fortunately, there is another widely available model that has the simplicity of proportional hazards but does not force any particular shape on the baseline hazard rate. It allows the risk of the event of interest to vary freely over time. This flexible and very well-known type of event history analysis was developed by Cox (1972), and it is often referred to as the *Cox model* or *Cox regression*. In fact, the original article by Cox is one of the top one hundred most cited papers in the history of science (Garfield, 1990). As with all other LRDV models, predictors can still be incorporated into a regression-type equation, and their effects can be estimated:

$$\log[\lambda_i(t)] = \log[\lambda_0(t)] + \beta_1 X_1 + \beta_2 X_2 + \ldots \beta_p X_p. \qquad (13.18)$$

To simplify notation, $\log[\lambda_0(t)]$ can be referred to as $\beta_0(t)$:

$$\log[\lambda_i(t)] = \beta_0(t) + \beta_1 X_1 + \beta_2 X_2 + \ldots \beta_p X_p. \qquad (13.19)$$

In addition to the interpretations of $\beta_0(t)$ given above, this time-varying intercept term could be thought of as the hazard rate for someone with 0 values on all of the predictors. If the X_j were all standardized, $\beta_0(t)$ would be the underlying hazard rate for the average (on all predictors) person. Through this time-varying intercept, Cox regression contains all of the models described above as special cases. If $\beta_0(t)$ were a constant β_0 over time, equation 13.19 would simplify to the exponential event history model. If $\beta_0(t)$ were $\beta_0 \times t$, equation 13.19 would become the Gompertz model. If $\beta_0(t)$ were $\beta_0 \times \log(t)$, equation 13.19 would become the Weibull model.

If an I/O researcher is primarily interested in estimating the effects of predictors on the time-dependent rate or likelihood of some criterion, there is no better tool than Cox regression. It is perhaps the best default model for those interested in what contributes to the prediction of *when* something will happen. Most of the major statistical packages offer Cox regression. In

SAS, the routine is PROC PHREG; in SPSS, it is COXREG. Between the two, SAS gives more diagnostic information about residuals and model fit, as well as allowing greater control over model specification.

As with all other LRDV models, the Cox model does make several simplifying assumptions. More important, researchers primarily interested in describing the course of the common, underlying hazard over time should use the parametric models. Cox regression is a semiparametric model, because the β's are estimated, but the $\beta_0(t)$ is not (that is, f is unknown). I deal with these assumptions and estimation issues in the next two sections.

Assumptions

All of the hazard rate models described here, including Cox regression, were developed to analyze one pair of Y_i and T_i values per case. That is, they assume independent observations. If one modeled the hazard rate of repeated events, such as a series of promotions or repeated instances of turnover (Judge & Watanabe, 1995), statistical tests would show inflated rates of type I error. As in linear, logistic, and probit regression, the estimated β's from Cox regression would be unbiased, but their standard errors would be underestimated.

Another assumption, consistent with the LRDV models already described in this chapter, is that there is no unobserved heterogeneity in hazard rates. That is, all individual sources of variance in hazard rates are captured by the X_j predictors. This is similar to the assumption of no (correlated) missing variables in a linear regression. If the unobserved heterogeneity is uncorrelated with the existing predictors, violation of this assumption does not bias tests of coefficient estimates for the X_j. However, it can bias, and even change, the sign of the coefficient estimate for $\lambda_0(t)$ under some conditions. Specifically, if high-risk persons are experiencing the criterion more quickly than low-risk persons, and this difference in risk is not captured by the predictors, such unobserved heterogeneity can create the mistaken impression that the baseline risk is declining over time (a false "liability of newness" effect; Long, 1997). If the baseline hazard increases or is nonmonotonic, unobserved heterogeneity is not an issue.

An assumption unique to the event history models described in this chapter is that of proportional risks or hazards over time for any two individuals, i and j. Essentially, this means there are no time-by-predictor interaction effects on the hazard rate. Tests of the proportionality assumption involve adding time × predictor (X_j^*t or $X_j^*\log(t)$) interaction terms to an equation that already contains main effects of the X_j. If these terms are significant, they obviate the use of the Weibull, Gompertz, and exponential models. However, unbiasedness of coefficients and standard errors hold in the Cox model as long as these nonproportional interaction terms are included in the regression equation (Allison, 1984). In addition to this statistical test, one can overlay plots of the time-dependent hazard rates for persons with different levels of a specific predictor—for example, children with (1) versus without (0) siblings attending the day care center. If the plots are parallel, the proportional hazards assumption holds for that predictor.

Residuals and Fit

None of the formal expressions of these event history models contains an ε term. This does not mean that the models assume errorless prediction or that they are deterministic. Instead, there is randomness in the relationship between the predicted and observed hazard rates. Those who have exactly the same values on all the predictors will not necessarily have exactly the same observed value for times, T_i, or events, Y_i, *although they would be predicted to do so.* As with other regression models, differences between the predicted and observed values are residuals.

Shapes of these residual distributions are fairly esoteric. For example, residuals from exponential and Weibull models follow one- and two-parameter "extreme value" distributions; both are unimodal but not necessarily symmetric. Because the Cox model is semiparametric (it does not estimate a baseline hazard), the specific shape of distribution of residuals is unknown. The residuals themselves are complex to calculate. A form of "martingale residuals" can be obtained and standardized to have an approximately symmetric distribution, with a mean of zero and standard deviation of one (in SAS, through the RESDEV option). Univariate plots of these residuals should be inspected for large outliers. Bivariate plots of residuals from uncensored observations of T_i against each of the X_j should be inspected for nonrandom patterns. Statistics such as DFBETA and the likelihood displacement index, LD (the event history analogue of Cook's distance), are also available for diagnosing highly influential observations.

Moving to fit indices, one disadvantage that event history analyses share with other LRDV models is that there is no well-accepted single statistic, such as an R^2 in MLR, that reflects how well hazard rates are being modeled. On the other hand, one of the advantages of event history analyses is their similarity to logistic and probit regression—in fit assessment, estimation, testing, and interpretation of coefficients. Cox regression models are estimated through a kind of maximum likelihood procedure that is similar to the previous LRDV models. It generates a null model badness-of-fit chi-square, D_0, and a full model badness-of-fit chi-square, D_m. As with the earlier LRDV models, the difference between these two, $D_0 - D_m$, is equal to G^2, which is once again distributed as a chi-square with p degrees of freedom. The G^2 test is akin to the F test for an overall model in MLR. That G^2 can also be plugged into equation 13.11 to get a pseudo-R^2.

In the data described previously, I obtained values for all these omnibus fit indices from a Cox regression predicting the hazard rate of day care customer turnover. The indices are shown in the third column of Table 13.2. The second column contains similar indices from a logistic regression, where the dependent variable is (log odds of) Y_i (with no use of the corresponding T_i). The first column contains standard fit indices from a linear regression, where the dependent variable is T_i (with no use of the corresponding Y_i). Note that longer times are associated with lower hazard rates, so MLR will generate coefficients with opposite signs from the two LRDV analyses. For Cox regression of the customer turnover data, $G^2 = 69.71$ ($p < .01$), using thirteen demographic (for example, gender and customer age) and human resource (caregiver turnover rate) variables. The pseudo-R^2 was .26.

In terms of what one would see in major statistical packages, the null model chi-square, D_0, is labeled "-2 Log Likelihood" for "Block 0" (the null state of the Cox regression equation) in SPSS output. It is labeled "-2 Log L, Without Covariates" in SAS output. The full model chi-square, D_m, is labeled "-2 Log Likelihood" for "Block 1" in SPSS and "-2 Log L, With Covariates" in SAS. Finally, G^2 is listed as "Change from Previous Step, Chi-Square" under "Block 1" in SPSS

Table 13.2. Linear, Logistic, and Cox Prediction of Customer Turnover (n = 236), by Demographic and Human Resource Variables.

Main Effect Terms	Linear Regression[a]			Logistic Regression[b]			Cox Regression[c]		
	Coefficient	Effect	Test	Coefficient	Effect	Test	Coefficient	Effect	Test
	b	$r(y_b \cdot x_j \cdot x_{j \neq k})$	t	b	Odds(b)	χ^2	b	Hazard Ratio(b)	χ^2
Intercept	25.771**		4.95**	.886		2.36			
Sex (female = 0, male = 1)	2.097	.002	.78	-.262	.860	.11	-.208	.812	1.07
Classroom									
Infants	9.583	.008	1.68	-2.340**	.096	12.42**	-2.037**	.130	13.32**
One year olds	-3.026	-.001	-.58	-.465	.628	.67	-.504	.604	1.67
Two year olds	7.909	.006	1.44	-1.400*	.247	5.25*	-1.183**	.306	7.53**
Four year olds	-7.610	-.004	-1.14	-.549	.577	.55	-.059	.943	.01
Five year olds	-.277	-.000	-.05	-.504	.604	.62	-.420	.657	.98
Six year olds and older	-5.612	-.004	-1.19	.132	1.141	.06	.091	1.095	.08
Previous Customer Tenure	.216**	.170	7.85**	-.002	.998	.30	-.007*	.993	7.13**
Sibling Enrolled (no = 0, yes = 1)	.617	.000	.26	-.288**	.750	10.48**	-.613**	.542	6.65**
Enrollment term									
Fall	-.623	-.001	-.18	-.814*	.443	4.56*	-.277	.758	1.29
Winter	13.488**	.025	2.99**	-.860	.423	2.84	-.865*	.421	6.38*
Spring	5.496	-.005	1.34	.039	1.040	.01	-.074	.929	.07
Caregiver turnover rate	-1.522*	-.015	-2.33*	.218**	1.244	8.37**	.213**	1.237	15.35**
Overall statistics									
Null model deviance (D_0)				326.08			933.06		
Model deviance (D_m)				275.85			863.25		
Likelihood ratio (G^2) or overall F	10.80**			50.23**			69.71**		
(Pseudo)R^2 for full model	.35			.19			.26		

[a] Dependent variable is Retention Time.
[b] Dependent variable is Quitting.
[c] Dependent variable is Hazard Rate.

*$p < .05$; **$p < .01$.

and "Likelihood Ratio Chi-Square" in SAS. From the "Block" language, it is clear that SPSS is geared more toward a stepwise or model-building approach. Caveats against using such a data-driven testing strategy are just as strong in LRDV as they are in MLR.

Estimation and Tests

There are a few subtle differences in how parameters are estimated and tested in Cox regression versus other LRDV models.

Partial Likelihood

One of the main reasons Cox regression is so well known and so widely used is that Cox (1972) developed a clever estimation procedure at the same time he developed the LRDV model. This procedure, called *partial likelihood estimation,* drops intractable information about the baseline hazard, $\beta_0(t)$, from the likelihood function and instead provides only estimates of the regression parameters for each predictor. Relative to maximum likelihood estimation of the parametric models already described, partial likelihood estimation of Cox regression parameters is therefore slightly less efficient and has somewhat larger standard errors. Still, it provides normal and unbiased estimates in large samples (Efron, 1977). It is obviously much more robust to the shape of the baseline hazard, because it allows that baseline to change over time in *any* way, without affecting the β_j.

Perhaps even more remarkable, the partial likelihood estimates also rely only on the rank order of observed times. Any monotonic transformation of the T_i yields identical regression coefficients. Hence, time scale is less of an issue in Cox regression than it is in the exponential, Weibull, and Gompertz models. Sample size is more of an issue, because of the lower efficiency of partial likelihood estimation. In that regard, it is the number of uncensored observations (not the percentage of such observations) per parameter that is important for getting estimates that have the desirable properties I noted.

Ties

As might be expected from a technique depending on only the rank order of observed times (*the T_i*), ties in those observed times create estimation problems for Cox models. Supplemental procedures have to be used when 10 to 20 percent of the people who experience the event do so at times that are not unique (Yamaguchi, 1991). This is not an issue with other event history models. For example, if I were studying turnover in the military, a large number of personnel would quit at the same two-, four-, or six-year point following their enlistment. Only SAS provides multiple options for handling ties in Cox regression in major statistical packages. Among the approximation procedures in SAS, the TIES = EFRON (Efron, 1977) method gives the best estimates (Hosmer & Lemeshow, 1999). Among the likelihood-based procedures, the TIES = EXACT procedure is preferred even though it is computationally intensive. It assumes ties are a result of imprecise measurement and posits a latent but unique ordering for the T_i's.

Tests for Individual Predictors

Construction of tests for the unique contribution of each predictor to the hazard rate happens in the same way for Cox regression as it does for logistic and probit regression. An estimate of β_j for each predictor is divided by its standard error and then squared. Under the null hypothesis, the resulting ratio is distributed as a chi-square with one degree of freedom. Depending on the way the standard errors are calculated, however, one can get Wald, score, or likelihood ratio chi-squares. Unfortunately, as with the earlier LRDV models, the Wald (and sometimes the score) tests are reported by program defaults. The likelihood ratio tests have better properties, but to get them, it is again necessary to perform regression analyses on a model that contains all p predictors, and then on each of the $j = 1, \ldots, p$ separate models that do not include predictor j. The chi-square differences and therefore the likelihood ratio test for each of the b_j are obtained by subtraction.

Interpretation of Coefficients

Estimates of Cox regression parameters share some of the same interpretation as estimates of linear (MLR) and logistic regression parameters. They reflect the unique contribution of each variable to the predictive power of the model, given that all other predictors are included. The sign of a parameter estimate reflects the overall direction of effect. Independent variables with negative coefficients are associated with decreases in the risk of the criterion *throughout the range of time covered by the investigation*. In my data, the larger the value of an X_j having a negative coefficient, the lower the time-dependent rate of customer turnover. Independent variables with positive coefficients are associated with increased risk.

Likelihood ratio tests for each of the independent variables in the customer turnover data set are shown in Table 13.2. Sex, age of the child, and whether the child had a sibling enrolled at the day care center constituted seven of the eight demographic predictors. Instead of assuming a linear effect for age, I created dummy variables that corresponded to the classroom the child was enrolled in at the start of the observation period (infant, one year old, and so on, with the three-year-old classroom as the omitted group). Although age might have an overall positive effect on turnover risk, this day care center charged higher rates and spent a great deal of resources on their accredited kindergarten program for five-year-old children, which is one of the highest ages in the sample.

As Allison (1995) suggested, I also used the length of a customer's stay before the study began as an eighth demographic variable, to account for the effects of alternative time origins (different definitions of start time). That is, I created another predictor measuring prestudy "tenure" at the day care center, much as a medical researcher might use the time elapsed between diagnosis and entry into a study as a covariate in predicting the posttreatment survival times of patients undergoing an experimental treatment. The theoretical basis for including all these predictors flows from a social exchange premise. Parents who have invested more in their relationship with the day care center, through enrolling younger children, more children (siblings), or longer prestudy enrollment periods, should have lower hazard rates of turnover.

Two other sets of independent variables included the season of a child's initial enrollment and the rate of caregiver turnover he or she was exposed to while attending the day care center. The former predictors were treated as dummy variables, with summer serving as the omitted season. Relative to fall enrollees, spring enrollees might have less a priori commitment to staying. Theoretically, caregiver (employee) turnover represents a diminution of social exchange. Whatever depth of relationship or attachment a child has developed with his or her caregiver has to be rebuilt from scratch when a caregiver quits and is replaced by someone else, nearly zeroing out the level of the customer's social attachment to that day care center.

For each of these predictors, it is instructive to compare Cox regression results in the third column of Table 13.2 to the linear and logistic regression results in the first and second columns. As Table 13.2 shows, there is no intercept estimate in Cox regression. However, Cox modeling identified six of thirteen predictors as important (statistically significant) contributors to the hazard rate for customer turnover. Logistic regression tagged five of thirteen predictors as significant. Linear regression (MLR) identified only three. The MLR results in the first column seem to reflect the time-sensitive predictors (significant coefficients for prestudy customer tenure, season of enrollment) more strongly than the other predictors, which is reasonable given the dependent variable in MLR is time (more accurately, $\log(T_i)$). On the other hand, the logistic regression results in the second column seem to reflect more of the time-insensitive predictors (significant coefficients for two of the classroom dummy variables, as well as the indicator of whether or not a sibling was enrolled). This might also be expected, given that the dependent variable is a transformation of the binary Y_i and does not incorporate time. The Cox regression results are a combination of both of these kinds of predictors, illustrating the greater power and utility it holds for such data.

The magnitude of an individual coefficient estimate has nearly the same meaning in Cox regression as it does in logistic regression. To interpret a coefficient estimate, b_j, it is helpful to exponentiate it: $\exp(b_j)$. In logistic regression, this exponentiated coefficient is the odds ratio associated with predictor j. In Cox regression and many other event history models, the exponentiated coefficient is the *hazard ratio*. It indicates a shift of the entire baseline hazard rate (see Figure 13.3) upward or downward for every one-unit increase in the predictor. For example, the estimated coefficient for caregiver turnover was $b = .213$ ($p < .01$), which supports the social exchange perspective. Exponentiating this yields a hazard ratio of $\exp(b) = 1.237$, meaning that for every instance of caregiver turnover per year that a child is exposed to, there is a 23.7 percent higher risk that the child will be removed from the day care center by his or her parents (controlling for the other variables in the model).

The predictor indicating whether a child was in the infant classroom (for children below age one) has an estimated coefficient of $b = -2.037$ ($p < .01$). Because it is a dummy variable, it has a fairly simple interpretation. In a group coded as 1, the event (turnover) happens at $\exp(\beta)$ times the rate that it happens in the group coded as 0, throughout the length of the study. The hazard ratio for being in the infant classroom is $\exp(b) = .130$. Relative to all other children, children who are enrolled as infants are estimated to have an 87 percent lower risk of being withdrawn by their parents, at any time.

Extensions and Alternatives in Event History Models

Since the original development and widespread appreciation of Cox regression, there have been a number of variations proposed.

Time-Dependent Predictors

A final advantage of Cox regression over other event history models is that it can easily be extended to incorporate time-dependent covariates:

$$\log[\lambda_i(t)] = \beta_0(t) + \beta_1 X_1 + \beta_2 X_2 + \ldots \beta_p X_p + \beta_p X_p(f). \quad (13.20)$$

For instance, if I had data on the exact date that each caregiver quit in each classroom, I could enter a "counter" (that goes up by 1 on the day that each additional caregiver quits) as a time-varying covariate in the model. In terms of the proportion hazards assumption, this means that for each point in time that the $X_p(t)$ variable increases, the hazard function takes a step upward by $\beta_p \times X_p(t)$ (see Harrison et al., 1996, for an example involving turnover and a change in pay). Although estimation of this model is more computationally intensive, it is still done using partial likelihood. Both SPSS and SAS offer options for including time-dependent predictors.

Repeated Events

Sometimes the criterion of interest to an I/O researcher cannot be equated with survival, because it can happen repeatedly over time. For example, one might want to study several instances of turnover over successive jobs (Judge & Watanabe, 1995) or several "spells" of absenteeism (Harrison & Hulin, 1989). In these circumstances, observations of Y_i or T_i are not independent. Conventional event history models such as Cox regression will have biased standard errors, and in some cases biased parameter estimates. Tuma and Hannan (1984) offer several alternatives for analyzing repeated events that are quite different from Cox modeling. Wei, Lin, and Weissfeld (1989) proposed repeated event techniques that can be incorporated into the Cox regression procedures of SAS (Allison, 1995).

Other Parametric Models

When hazard rates for different sets of individuals are not proportional, there are a number of other event history models available. Two of these have the added benefit of allowing a nonmonotonic hazard function. A log-normal model assumes that the risk of the criterion rises once and then falls back with increasing time. Researchers often use a log-logistic model for the opposite pattern: the hazard rate falls initially and then levels off or rises later (although it can be used for the former pattern as well). Both of these models are limited to a single peak or a single valley in the hazard function over time. Therefore, they would not properly fit situations such as the hazard rate of customer turnover seen in Figure 13.3.

Discrete-Time Models

One of the happiest surprises of event history analysis is that models which chop up the time continuum into discrete intervals can be nearly as powerful and sometimes more readily interpretable than the continuous-time models I have described here (Efron, 1988). For example, there is a simple, discrete-time version of Cox regression referred to as the proportional odds model (Harrison et al., 1996; Singer & Willett, 1993):

$$\text{logit}(Y|X,t) = \beta_{0(t=1)} + \beta_{0(t=2)} + \dots \qquad (13.21)$$
$$+ \beta_{0(t=k-1)} + \beta_1 X_1 + \beta_2 X_2 + \dots \beta_p X_p$$

In this model, the log-odds (logit) of the event in any time period t is a linear function of the usual string of predictors, as well as time itself, weighted by intercepts (β_0) for each of $t = 1, 2, \dots, k - 1$ successive time periods. This set of estimated intercepts provides a piecewise view of the baseline hazard rate that is not available in standard Cox regression. By treating each discrete time period for each person as a separate observation, the proportional odds model can be estimated and fit using conventional logistic regression software.

Conclusion

Many important criteria to I/O psychologists are dichotomous, censored, or otherwise limited in range. Rather than analyzing these criteria using inappropriate linear models and perhaps reaching incorrect substantive conclusions, a variety of log-linear models are both flexible and readily available. Although they involve slightly different assumptions and extra care in their application, logistic and probit regression are the preeminent forms of analysis in predicting *if* for binary dependent variables. For some binary dependent variables, *when* is a more important question. Cox regression, as one of several forms of event history analysis, is the preeminent technique for modeling the time-dependent rate that a criterion occurs.

References

Agresti, A. (1990). *Categorical data analysis*. New York: Wiley.

Aldrich, J. H., & Nelson, F. D. (1984). *Linear probability, logit, and probit models*. Thousand Oaks, CA: Sage.

Allison, P. D. (1984). *Event history analysis: Regression for longitudinal event data*. Thousand Oaks, CA: Sage.

Allison, P. D. (1995). *Survival analysis using the SAS system: A practical guide*. Cary, NC: SAS Institute.

Box, G.E.P., & Tidwell, P. W. (1962). Transformation of the independent variables. *Technometrics, 4,* 531–550.

Cox, D. R. (1970). *The analysis of binary data*. New York: Chapman & Hall.

Cox, D. R. (1972). Regression models and life tables. *Journal of the Royal Statistical Society, B34,* 187–220.

Dawes, R. M., & Corrigan, B. (1974). Linear models in decision making. *Psychological Bulletin, 81*(2), 95–106.

DeMaris, A. (1992). *Logit modeling: Practical applications*. Thousand Oaks, CA: Sage.

Dickter, D., Roznowski, M., & Harrison, D. A. (1996). Temporal tempering: An event history analysis of the process of voluntary turnover. *Journal of Applied Psychology, 81,* 705–716.

Efron, B. (1975). The efficiency of logistic regression compared to normal discriminant function analysis. *Journal of the American Statistical Association, 70,* 892–898.

Efron, B. (1977). The efficiency of Cox's likelihood function for censored data. *Journal of the American Statistical Association, 76,* 312–319.

Efron, B. (1988). Logistic regression, survival analysis, and the Kaplan-Meier curve. *Journal of the American Statistical Association, 83,* 414–425.

Ganzach, Y., Saporta, I., & Weber, Y. (2000). Interaction in linear versus logistic models: A substantive illustration using the relationship between motivation, ability, and performance.

Garfield, E. (1990, Feb. 12). One hundred most cited papers of all time. *Current Contents.*

Garner, W., Mulvey, E. P., & Shaw, E. C. (1995). Regression analysis of counts and rates: Poisson, overdispersed Poisson, and negative binomial models. *Psychological Bulletin, 118,* 392–404.

Greene, W. H. (1999). *LIMDEP: User's manual and reference guide, Version 7.0.* Plainview, NY: Econometric Software.

Harrison, D. A., & Hulin, C. L. (1989). Investigations of absenteeism: Using event history models to study the absence-taking process. *Journal of Applied Psychology, 74,* 300–316.

Harrison, D. A., Virick, M., & William, S. (1996). "Working without a net:" Time, performance, and turnover under maximally contingent rewards. *Journal of Applied Psychology, 81,* 331–345.

Hauck, W. W., & Donner, A. (1977). Wald's test as applied to hypotheses in logit analysis. *Journal of the American Statistical Association, 72,* 851–853.

Hom, P. W., & Griffeth, R. W. (1995). *Employee turnover.* Cincinnati: South-Western.

Hosmer, D. W., & Lemeshow, S. (1989). *Applied logistic regression.* New York: Wiley.

Hosmer, D. W., & Lemeshow, S. (1999). *Applied survival analysis: Regression modeling of time to event data.* New York: Wiley.

Huselid, M. A., & Day, N. E. (1991). Organizational commitment, job involvement, and turnover: A substantive and methodological analysis. *Journal of Applied Psychology, 76,* 380–391.

James, L. R., & Brett, J. M. (1984). Mediators, moderators, and tests for mediation. *Journal of Applied Psychology, 69,* 307–321.

Jennings, D. E. (1986). Judging inference adequacy in logistic regression. *Journal of the American Statistical Association, 81,* 471–476.

Judge, T. A., & Watanabe, S. (1995). Is the past prologue? A test of Ghiselli's hobo syndrome. *Journal of Management, 21,* 211–229.

Kessler, R. C. (1983). Methodological issues in the study of psychosocial stress. In H. B. Kaplan (Ed.), *Psychosocial stress: Trends in theory and research.* Orlando, FL: Academic Press.

Kelly, J. R., & McGrath, J. E. (1988). *On time and method.* Thousand Oaks, CA: Sage.

King, G. (1988). Statistical models for political science event counts: Bias in conventional procedures and evidence for the exponential Poisson regression model. *American Journal of Political Science, 32,* 838–863.

Krackhardt, D., & Porter, L. W. (1986). The snowball effect: Turnover embedded in communication networks. *Journal of Applied Psychology, 71,* 50–55.

Liang, K.-Y., & Zeger, S. L. (1986). Longitudinal data analysis using generalized linear models. *Biometrika, 73,* 13–22.

Long, J. S. (1997). *Regression models for categorical and limited dependent variables.* Thousand Oaks, CA: Sage.

Maddala, G. S. (1983). *Limited dependent and qualitative variables in econometrics.* Cambridge: Cambridge University Press.

McCullagh, P., & Nelder, J. A. (1989). *Generalized linear models* (2nd ed.). New York: Chapman & Hall.

Menard, S. (1995). *Applied logistic regression.* Thousand Oaks, CA: Sage.

Robinson, P. M. (1982). On the asymptotic properties of estimators with limited dependent variables. *Econometrica, 50,* 27–42.

Russell, C. J., & Bobko, P. (1992). Moderated regression analysis and Likert scales: Too coarse for comfort. *Journal of Applied Psychology, 77,* 336–342.

Singer, J. D., & Willett, J. B. (1991). Modeling the days of our lives: Using survival analysis when designing and analyzing studies of the duration and the timing of events. *Psychological Bulletin, 110,* 268–290.

Singer, J. D., & Willett, J. B. (1993). It's about time: Using discrete-time survival analysis to study duration and the timing of events. *Journal of Educational Statistics, 18,* 155–195.

Somers, M. J., & Birnbaum, D. (1999). Survival versus traditional methodologies for studying employee turnover: Differences, divergences and directions for future research. *Journal of Organizational Behavior, 20,* 273–284.

Stone-Romero, E. F., Weaver, A. E., & Glenar, J. L. (1995). Trends in research design and data analytic strategies in organizational research. *Journal of Management, 21,* 141–157.

Tuma, N. B., & Hannan, M. T. (1983). *Social dynamics: Models and methods.* Orlando, FL: Academic Press.

Wei, L. J., Lin, D. Y., & Weissfeld, L. (1989). Regression analysis of multivariate incomplete failure time data by modeling marginal distributions. *Journal of the American Statistical Association, 84,* 1065–1073.

Williams, C. R., & Peters, L. H. (1998). Correcting turnover correlations: A critique. *Organizational Research Methods, 1,* 88–103.

Yamaguchi, K. (1991). *Event history analysis.* Thousand Oaks, CA: Sage.

CHAPTER 14

Computational Modeling in Organizational Sciences
Contributions of a Third Research Discipline

Charles Hulin
Andrew G. Miner
Steven T. Seitz

Computational modeling is well suited to exploring issues of stability, change, and effects of structural metamorphosis where patterns of continuities and discontinuities have changed. It is well suited to studying organizational behavior patterns rather than isolated behaviors. Questions of hierarchical influences on individuals in groups embedded in organizations embedded in environments, all of which dynamically and differentially influence our dependent variables, yield to modeling efforts. Computational modeling allows us to escape, at least partially, the tyranny of Heisenberg's uncertainty principal as manifested in behavioral sciences. We can model systems in action without influencing them through the observational process. In this chapter, this research discipline is described.

Examples of Computational Models

Expressways, structural elements of urban transportation systems, are generated and expanded as a result of occasionally (mis)informed decisions that reflect intersections of political agendas, public policies, and everyday needs of thousands of individuals. The

Pigou-Knight-Downs paradox identifies conditions under which adding more lanes of traffic in a restricted access area, such as an expressway or a bridge, will lead to no change in capacity or travel speeds (Arnott & Small, 1994). Nevertheless, the construction effort may raise expectations and increase traffic. When traffic volume and commuting time *increase* after what were thought to be improvements, as they are predicted to by the Pigou-Knight-Downs paradox, no one would be surprised (Rebuilt Kennedy hasn't been a moving experience, 1994). Decisions about expressways could—and should—be informed by computational modeling.

On a less cosmic level, in the realm of postwork and postcommuting activities, modeling has confirmed that the perception of bubbles in a glass of Guinness stout as sometimes *descending* rather than *rising* is not an artifact of the drinking process. Under certain conditions of temperature, bubbles near the middle of a glass of the stout rise, as we would expect them to, but small bubbles near the sides of a glass may descend because of the viscosity of the stout and laws of fluid dynamics (Fountain, 2000).[1] Knowledge of such modeling results could reduce the number of arguments about the phenomenon or inform wagers by those willing to bet on a known outcome.

Public policymakers and organizational researchers, no less than those who commute to work or observe bubbles in glasses of stout, frequently overlook the value of computer models. Computational models are largely ignored by those studying or managing behaviors of people in organizations in spite of the value of computational modeling for understanding cognition (Posner, 1989; Lewandowski, 1993), behaviors of individuals in organizations (Hanisch, Hulin, & Seitz, 1996; Seitz, Hulin, & Hanisch, 2000), behaviors of individuals in groups (Stasser, 2000a), management science (Williams et al., 1994), and organizational theory (Carley & Prietula, 1994).

Overview

Changing behavior patterns may tell us more about organizations and behaviors in organizations than cross-sectional snapshots of frozen processes. Neither of our traditional research disciplines, experimentation or correlational studies, is well suited to answer questions about changes in behavior patterns or about the effects of change on individuals in organizations. These often require experimental and control groups in organizations and lengthy observation periods to detect periods of changing behaviors (following organizational or technological change), followed by quasi-stationary new patterns. Long-term databases describing stability and normal, stochastic variation around expected patterns are a necessary part of studies of change.

We often use methods of inquiry ill suited to address new issues in behavioral sciences. There is some agreement that cross-sectional, limited-duration longitudinal panel designs will not answer many emerging questions; they limit inferences about dynamic models of patterns of behaviors and other manifestations of underlying constructs. However, we continue to use inappropriate designs that create "methodological stalemates" (Larson & Csikszentmihalyi, 1983). Causal modeling of static relations among estimates of constructs is not adapted to studies of dynamic, reciprocal, or recursive relationships (Glomb, Munson, Hulin, Bergman, & Drasgow, 1999). Meta-analysis will not help us when we meta-analyze statistics describing static relations of individual, isolated behaviors obtained in cross-sectional studies.

Computational modeling spans the conceptual complexity of individuals in all their differences responding to job events and features within the context of complex, dynamic organizations that are located in still more macro-environments. Computational modeling can represent multiple forces acting on individuals and simulate likely responses and emergent processes that contribute to general theories.

Some models begin with configurations of conditions and ask what future states are likely to exist if certain theories accurately account for relevant processes—for example:

- Given current levels of satisfaction in an organization and current sanctions on specific withdrawal behaviors, what patterns of withdrawal behaviors are likely to emerge across time under the assumptions of different models of withdrawal and stable levels of unemployment (Munson & Hulin, 2000)?
- If interpersonal contacts in organizations are almost all within work groups, what patterns of opinion change, consolidation, and clustering are likely to be observed (Latané, 2000)?

Other computational models ask about conditions that may not exist in today's mundane environments. The usefulness of assuming counterfactual conditions and asking about results of known processes in such situations may be a function of the age and development of a field of study. Information about parameters defining processes and distributions of events is likely to be greatest at the margins of a field early in its scientific development. Empirical research in organizations is easiest to do, and is most often done, in the centers rather than the margins of our fields. But we need to ask:

- What will happen to the flow of gases in conditions of zero gravity and (approximate) absolute zero temperature?
  Black holes will be created (Smarr, 1985).
- What patterns of change, consolidation, and clustering of opinions are likely to be observed if command and control forms of organization are replaced by matrix organizations that largely replace within-group interpersonal contact with contacts with members of other functional groups?
  We do not know.

In modeling, we can create virtual organizations with theoretically important parameter values defining situations within which psychological and organizational processes unfold. When information is needed about the margins of conceptual space, modeling may be the only effective research discipline available. Asking about extremely rare organizational environments or situations may tell us much about organizational forms and behaviors within organizations that may soon exist, as well as within organizations that function at the margins of today's environments.

Modeling addresses limitations of our two standard research paradigms when testing implications of causal, dynamic theories. The passage of time, real or simulated, is necessary before we can assign directions to links among constructs in our models. Paradoxically, modeling research allows a level of realism not possible in experimentation and a temporal-serial perspective not possible even in panel-based studies. Computer simulations can be thought of as complex, multifactor, sequential experiments conducted "in silica"; the output of one iteration in a simulation, modified by stochastic shocks and dynamic feedacross, becomes the input for the next iteration. Iterated simulations of dynamic systems allow us to tease apart dynamic forces whose effects emerge as we examine empirical and virtual traces of these forces interacting over time—computational or real—in complex settings—virtual or mundane.

Cadences and periodicities in behavior processes, controlled or treated as noise in experiments or cross-sectional snapshots of individual differences, are preserved in modeling studies. Different cadences and trajectories unfolding across behavioral episodes become signals rather than noise in computational modeling. We can distinguish among multiple dynamic trajectories of individuals if observed across iterations; within one cross-sectional snapshot, these are treated as error. Visual time compression in aviation radar allows us to distinguish between low and slow private aircraft and anomalous propagation; virtual time allows us to distinguish signals about dynamic behavioral trajectories from a welter of background noise. Dynamic processes are rarely captured, even in panel designs. Our selection of time intervals on the basis of rules of thumb or convenience rather than empirical data or theoretical propositions may be the culprit. Munson, Hulin, and Drasgow (2000) and Glomb et al. (1999) provide examples of the difficulties and benefits of longitudinal empirical studies of dynamic behavioral processes.

Modeling allows us to simulate behavioral processes without intrusive measurement; we can study the simulated world without contaminating it. We can place forces on a process that push it in one direction or another, input stochastic events into an ongoing process, or manipulate characteristics of an organization without exposing organizational members to the "illumination" and instrumentation required to assess the state, location, and trajectory of each member (Olsen, 2000).

Computational Modeling

Modeling normally begins with a propositional inventory or propositional calculus, a series of if-then statements derived from one or more theories or conceptual models of behavior or cognitive processes or derived by integrating many related empirical studies (Seitz et al., 2000). A propositional inventory is a set of symbolic statements that link antecedent conditions of behaviors (or other responses relevant to the theory) and possibly co-occurring antecedent conditions, effects of other stochastically co-occurring responses, and exogenous variables that define limiting conditions of the scope of the theory and the processes described by the theory.

In social and behavioral sciences, developing a propositional inventory for a theory or model that is sufficiently precise to generate unambiguously testable links among variables and sufficiently encompassing to comprise the entire theory or model may be the most intellectually challenging step in the process of computational modeling. Writing computer code may be more time-consuming for some projects, but given a sound propositional inventory, the code can be generated. It is not at all clear that a sound propositional inventory can be developed as the basis for a computational model given the state of many theories and conceptual models in social and behavioral sciences. Verbal theories are often too vague to yield unambiguous relational statements linking the constructs and variables of theory. Some theories contain internal contradictions or present hypotheses about the responses of individuals in cells that should be empty. Hackman and Oldham's (1976) job characteristics theory (JCT), for example, described relationships among constructs in which job characteristics, *JC,* are predicted to affect psychological states, *PS,* and psychological states are hypothesized to affect some job outcomes, *O,* including satisfaction, performance, and attendance. Thus, *JC* → *PS* and *PS* → *O.* These simple, bivariate hypotheses could be expressed in a propositional inventory. Problems with this theory occur because an individual difference variable, grown need strength, *GNS,* is hypothesized to moderate both of the above relationships. But given the specific form of moderating influence hypothesized by JCT, when we attempt to moderate the *PS* → *O* link with *GNS,* we find that the low *GNS,* high *PS* cell must be empty. Regardless of the state of job characteristics, low *GNS* individuals cannot develop high psychological states from even the most motivating job characteristics (Ilgen, Hollenbeck, Tower, & Waldschmidt, 1995). Empirical research on JCT was conducted for several years without this logical inconsistency being noted. A propositional inventory of JCT would have revealed the internal inconsistency and may have led to the revision of the theory without fifteen years of inconclusive empirical research.

Translating literary theories into an internally consistent propositional inventory is illustrated below in relation to computational models of organizational withdrawal.

Modeling Organizational Withdrawal

Decisions by individuals to withdraw from a work organization are manifested in many ways. Employees can enact one or several behaviors that may bear little obvious relation to each other. Exogenous factors in the form of labor market conditions and organizational sanctions on certain forms of organizational withdrawal may blur lines differentiating already fuzzy sets of withdrawal behaviors.

Job satisfaction appears to be a predictor of most organizational withdrawal behaviors (Hanisch & Hulin, 1990, 1991), although Weiss and Cropanzano (1996) have offered an amendment to these findings. They argue that job affect, an emotional component of job attitudes, is more likely to be related to spontaneous work withdrawal; cognitive evaluations of a job, a cognitive component of job attitudes and the component most often assessed under the label of job satisfaction, are more likely to be related to longer-term, more reasoned job withdrawal behaviors.

Several theoretical models have been proposed to account for relations among individual withdrawal behaviors:

Independent forms of withdrawal model (March & Simon, 1958) assumes two forms of withdrawal, quitting and absenteeism, that are unrelated because they have different psychological functions and consequences.

Compensatory behaviors model (Hill & Trist, 1955) hypothesizes that enacting a single withdrawal behavior in varying amounts in response to negative job attitudes will reduce dissatisfaction and stress to the point where other withdrawal behaviors need not be enacted. One behavior is assumed to compensate for the need to enact any other withdrawal behavior.

Spillover model of withdrawal (Beehr & Gupta, 1978) argues that there is a nucleus of withdrawal behaviors that occur together; aversive job situations and negative job attitudes generate nonspecific avoidance tendencies that spill over from a behavior, once enacted, to others in the nucleus of behaviors without being mediated by precipitating attitudes. The influence is from aversive job situations to negative attitudes to withdrawal behaviors directly to other withdrawal behaviors.

Progression of withdrawal model (Baruch, 1944; Melbin, 1961; Lyons, 1972; Rosse, 1988) describes a process in which employees progress through mild withdrawal behaviors, to increasingly stronger ones, and finally to quitting. Absenteeism and quitting should be addressed as a single problem because "the small decision which is taken when the worker absents himself is a miniature version of the important decision he makes when he quits his job" (Herzberg, Mausner, Peterson, & Capwell, 1957, p. 103). This model hypothesizes a stochastically ordered set of behaviors, ranging from trips to the water cooler to major withdrawal behaviors of absenteeism and quitting, in response to negative job attitudes that are enacted progressively until a behavior is reached that reduces job stress or negative job attitudes to a tolerable level.

These models are described verbally in the literature and have been used to explain different patterns of empirical findings. Unfortunately, the verbal descriptions of the models do not generate unambiguous statements about expected relations among different behaviors. A number of assumptions must be made to develop a propositional inventory from each model. There are no guarantees that the assumptions we have made would have been made by the developers of the models had they confronted the issues. However, every reader of a modeling study can correct assumptions made by the modelers and redo the modeling with a modified set of assumptions. Effects of changed assumptions can be evaluated. The philosophy that every reader is a source of corrections can be carried too far, but writing a propositional inventory as an explicit part of the research has a self-correcting aspect.

Hanisch, Hulin, and Seitz (1996; in press) and Seitz et al. (2000) have developed a software package that simulates withdrawal behaviors under a variety of environmental conditions (for example, unemployment levels), organizational variables (for example, sanctions on different withdrawal behaviors), and individual differences.

WORKER is a C++ program based on fuzzy set theory; neither the language nor the mathematical basis of the program is dictated by the models or the behaviors being modeled. A propositional inventory has been written for each model of withdrawal already described. Each propositional inventory appears in the library of theoretical models in the program. (A description of the program, its internal logic, and descriptive results addressing the logic of its modules is presented in Hanisch et al., 1996.)

Propositional inventories for withdrawal models are described below. Steps common to all the models are described first. These propositional inventories are taken from Seitz and Miner (2001). The WORKER software goes beyond these propositional inventories, but the inventories here capture the differences among the models and can be implemented using relatively simple programming languages, including spreadsheets.

The core of the program is a series of modules that relate job attitudes sampled in time i to job behaviors enacted in time i and, using feedback and feedacross loops, to attitudes in time $i + 1$. In several models, there are direct influences from behaviors in time i to probabilities of behaviors in time $i + 1$ that represent the increasingly negative sanctions for repeated occurrences of certain withdrawal behaviors, such as absence or tardiness. Each individual can be represented as a vector of job attitudes, with each element in the vector representing an attitude or behavioral propensity toward one of the behaviors. Characteristics such as age, tenure, gender, department, and blue-, white-, or pink-collar job category, which may be useful in certain analyses, can be added to the vector. Job attitudes, organizational sanctions, or environmental characteristics can be distributed across groups of individuals defined by these characteristics as desired by researchers. These are ignored in this discussion. The attitudes can be sampled from a variety of distributions with specifiable properties; the distribution from which the attitudes are sampled makes a difference, but for discussion purposes, we will assume normal distributions with unit variance and means of zero.

Correlations among the attitudes toward withdrawal behaviors can be established by the researcher. After an initial job attitude, I, is sampled from the desired distribution, the second and subsequent attitudes can be constructed according to the formula: $Att_J = Att_I * r_{IJ} + \sigma$ where r_{IJ} is the desired correlation between attitude I and attitude J and σ is a random variable with a mean of 0 and a variance of $1 - r_{IJ}^2$. Equivalently, the loadings of each attitude variable on a common factor can used to determine the correlations among all attitudes according to the formula $r_{IJ} = F_I F_J$, where F_I and F_J are the loadings of attitudes I and J on the common factor; $R = FF'$ in matrix notation, where R is the intercorrelation of attitudes and F is the vector of loadings of attitude variables on the common factor.

For this discussion, attitude variables are treated as behavioral propensities. This is statistically reasonable (Hulin, 1992; Hanisch & Hulin, 1990, 1991). Continuously distributed behavioral propensities can be converted to binary scores reflecting enacted withdrawal behaviors by establishing a threshold λ_i for each behavior along the attitude scale to achieve the distribution of binary behaviors the modeler desires. The threshold for each behavior can be chosen to correspond to empirical data; tardiness would be more frequent and have a lower threshold than absences that would be more frequent and have a lower threshold than turnover. Stochastic shocks can be added to the translation from behavioral propensities to enacted behaviors by randomly converting a large percentage, but less than 100 percent, of those above the threshold, λ_i, into scores of 1, indicating that the behavior was enacted while randomly converting a small percentage, greater than 0 percent, of propensity scores below λ_i into scores of 1.

This process for converting attitudes (behavioral propensities) into binary representations of enacted behaviors treats all propensities above λ_i equally in terms of the probability of enacting the behavior and all propensities below λ_i equally in terms of the probability of not enacting the behavior. A more sophisticated procedure would establish a monotonically increasing function relating behavioral propensity to the probability of enacting the behavior. A monotonic function with a steeply rising curve near λ_i would control the frequency of behavior I and would translate values below the threshold into low probabilities and values above the threshold into higher values. This can be accomplished by converting normally distributed propensity scores truncated on the -3 to $+3$ interval into probabilities using a z to p transformation. Such a transformation converts the continuously distributed propensity scores into continuously distributed probabilities and preserves differences among individuals throughout the distribution of propensity scores. The nonlinear transformation of z to p has the familiar normal ogive form, with a steeply rising function in the region of zero on the z-score distribution, corresponding to a p value of .5, and flatter portions transformed scores between 0 and .2 and between .8 and 1.0 on the probability scale. Alternatively, z scores can be transformed into p values with the point of inflection on the transformation function rescaled to λ_i by rescaling the z scores to have a mean of λ_i and expressing all propensity scores on the new scale with a mean of λ_i and a variance of 1. Scores equal to λ_i would correspond to p values of .5; the function transforming the rescaled z scores to p values would still have an ogive form, but the inflection point would correspond to λ_i; the transformation function would rise steeply in the region of λ_i and would again be flatter near the extremes. All continuously distributed, transformed propensity scores can be translated into a binary score of 0 or 1, reflecting whether the individual enacted the behavior by a random process by drawing a random number for each simulee and each behavior from a uniform distribution on the interval 0 to 1. If the number drawn is less than the value representing the probability of enacting the behavior, the behavior is scored as enacted. If it is greater than the probability of enacting the behavior, the behavior is scored as not enacted. Other transformations of propensities into probabilities are possible. Behaviors for which there may logically be more than one occurrence may be handled by establishing more than one cutting score. The cutting scores divide the propensity continuum into regions of zero occurrences, one occurrence, two, three, or more depending on the length of the time period, the behavior being simulated, and the organizational reality of many absences or several late arrivals in one time period.

In each time period of the simulation, an individual's attitude scores, treated as behavioral propensities, are translated into one or more withdrawal behaviors as described. Initial correlations among the attitudes and between the attitudes and behaviors are controlled by the modeler's input parameters as described. Frequencies of behaviors and correlations among enacted behaviors across time periods are often the output of interest. These are influenced by correlations among the attitudes, correlations between each attitude and its related behavior, stochastic feedback and feedacross from the enacted behaviors, and structural relations of the model being simulated.

Stochastic feedback and feedacross from the enacted behaviors are important forces on the process and often significantly influence the emergent properties of the output in unexpected ways. For each behavior enacted in a time period, there is a feedback function from the behavior to the precipitating attitude. If the behavior is enacted, the attitude is changed, or, equivalently, the behavioral propensity is reduced by a random amount varying around a parameter value set by the modeler. This assumption is part of the propositional inventory because withdrawal behaviors are assumed to be functional. They are often costly to enact and are enacted by employees to reduce the amount of dissatisfaction. The statistical relationships between job attitudes and a number of withdrawal behaviors (Hanisch & Hulin, 1990, 1991; Hulin, 1992) and rationality on the part of the employees makes the functionality assumption psychologically reasonable. However, this assumption and the derived feedback and feedacross functions go beyond the original statements of the models of the withdrawal behaviors described. It was added because of the empirically established relationships between job attitudes and job or work withdrawal behaviors and because most withdrawal behaviors are enacted at some cost to individuals and, assuming rationality, individuals are unlikely to enact costly behaviors if they are not functional.

Reductions in behavioral propensities or increases in job satisfaction because of feedback from enacted behaviors are controlled by the researcher and reflect assumptions about the effects of functional behaviors on their precipitating attitudes. A mean value for the feedback onto the attitude in the metric of the standard deviation of the attitude scores places the feedback function on the appropriate scale. For enacted behaviors, values of the mean feedback effect ranging from .1 to .25 standard deviation units of the attitude distribution have been explored in WORKER. Variance around these means may also be established in the metric of the variance of the original attitude scores. This behavior functionality assumption can be effectively turned off by setting the mean amount of the feedback onto the precipitating attitude to zero.

A small percentage of the simulees in the sample, randomly chosen, may have their attitudes changed by an amount, σ, to simulate the effects of stochastic shocks that impinge on individuals. σ may be selected from a distribution with a mean of zero and a variance of $(1 - r_{xx}^2)$, where r_{xx} represents the assumed or simulated reliability of attitude measurements. The square root of the variance of σ, $\sqrt{(1 - r_{xx}^2)}$, represents the standard error of measurement of the scale. Reliabilities of attitude scores can be set to the same value or can differ from attitude to attitude; the values of reliabilities can be based on results of empirical studies in the literature. Reliabilities ranging from .70 to .90 are commonly found. Larger values of r_{xx} generate smaller standard errors of measurement and larger correlations between the same attitude across two time periods absent random shocks and feedback from enacted behaviors.

Three withdrawal behaviors will be assumed for the development of propositional inventories of the four models described. WORKER allows up to ten behaviors to be modeled; for simplicity, this discussion is limited to three. Depending on the model being simulated, different feedback and feedacross functions from the behaviors enacted in each time period are used to update the job attitudes in the current and subsequent time periods.

Independent Forms of Withdrawal

Behaviors are hypothesized to occur independent of each other. We assume a behavioral family of three withdrawal behaviors, I, J, and K, that are mutually exclusive and exhaustive of the withdrawal behaviors that can be enacted. This gives a behavioral repertoire $\{I, J, K\}$.[2] For purposes of this discussion, behavior J represents absenteeism, and behavior K represents quitting; behavior I is a generic withdrawal behavior, such as taking long breaks or tardiness. The propositional calculus has the following components:

- If behavior J is enacted in the current time period, directly decrease the probability by a specified amount that it will be enacted in the subsequent time period.[3]
- If behavior K is enacted, remove the individual from the sample of employees. Replace with another individual.[4]

- If behavior I is enacted, do nothing to the likelihood of I in the next time period.
- Evaluate all behaviors to see if they should be enacted. If yes, enact those that should be enacted.
- Implement any model-required feedback or feedacross effects from enacted behavior to precipitating job attitude. Update job attitudes by relevant stochastic quantities plus feedback and feedacross functions, and carry updated job attitudes forward to next time period.
- Move to the next time period.

The independent forms model, as described by the propositional inventory, will not necessarily generate uncorrelated behaviors in any one time period. The precipitating attitudes and behavioral propensities may be correlated depending on the parameter settings used by the modeler. Furthermore, if there were environmental features or organizational sanctions in place that suppress the frequency of some, but not all, behaviors, this would increase the correlations among the behaviors. The label of the model describes a lack of a direct functional relationship among any of the behaviors. For example, there is no direct influence on behavior J from the occurrence of behavior I of K.

Compensatory Behaviors

The compensatory behaviors model hypothesizes that different withdrawal behaviors are functionally equivalent. If one behavior is blocked by environmental or individual factors, any other behavior in the withdrawal repertoire can be enacted and will compensate for the one blocked. Here,

- Stochastically block one of the three possible withdrawal behaviors by raising the threshold for enacting it to an arbitrarily high level.
- Evaluate all behaviors to see if they should be enacted. If yes, enact those that should be enacted. If no behaviors should be enacted, then enact none.
- If behavior J is enacted in the current time period, directly decrease the probability by a specified amount that it will be enacted in the subsequent time period.

- If any behavior is enacted, decrease the probability by a variable amount that either of the others will be enacted. Reevaluate all behaviors to see if they should be enacted.
- If behavior K is enacted, remove the individual from the sample of employees. Replace with another individual.
- Implement any model-required feedback or feedacross effects from enacted behavior to precipitating job attitude. Update job attitudes by any relevant stochastic quantity plus feedback and feedacross functions, and carry updated job attitudes forward to the next time period.
- Move to the next time period.

Spillover of Behaviors Model

Beehr and Gupta (1978) argued that withdrawal behaviors should be positively correlated because there is a nucleus of withdrawal behaviors that occur together. Relations among this nucleus of behaviors can be expressed as correlations among binary variables or as conditional probabilities that, for example, behavior J will occur given that behavior I has occurred. The spillover effects referred to in the label of this model are direct effects from one behavior directly onto other behaviors in the repertoire. These direct spillover effects are not mediated through any of the job attitudes or related behavioral propensities. There can be some debate if these spillover effects are simultaneous effects that increase the probability of one withdrawal behavior given that another has occurred in the same time period or if the spillover effects should be from time period i to time period $i + 1$. Our reading of the model suggests that the effects should be simultaneous, but we have programmed both a simultaneous and a forward spillover version in WORKER:

- Evaluate all behaviors to see if they should be enacted. Enact those that should be enacted. If any behavior is enacted, increase the likelihood that each of the other two behaviors will be enacted by 25 percent. Reevaluate remaining behaviors for whether they should be enacted.
- If behavior J is enacted in the current time period, directly decrease the probability by a specified amount that it will be enacted in the subsequent time period.

- If behavior *K* is enacted, remove the individual from the sample of employees. Replace with another individual.
- Implement any model-required feedback or feedacross effects from enacted behavior to precipitating job attitude.
- Move to the next time period.

Progression of Withdrawal

The progression of withdrawal model hypothesizes that withdrawal behaviors are enacted in a partially ordered (stochastic) sequence from most to least severe. The concept of severity of withdrawal behaviors was originally proposed by Baruch (1944) and used by Melbin (1961), Lyons (1972), and Rosse (1988) in their research and discussions on the progression of withdrawal model. Those (stochastically) most likely to be enacted within the repertoire of withdrawal behaviors are less severe; those more severe would occur later, if at all, in the sequence. Severity of withdrawal and cost to the individual for enacting the behavior are likely to be somewhat correlated. When behaviors are ordered for severity of withdrawal, they are also partially ordered according to the cost to the individual, with those least costly (emotionally, financially) being more likely to be enacted. Researchers who use fuzzy set theory to describe behavioral sets (Hanisch et al., 1996) might use the belongingness of the behavior to the set of withdrawal behaviors to order the behaviors. Quitting one's job might have the highest degree of belongingness of the behaviors to this set. Retirement would also have a high degree of belongingness, but not as high as quitting, because this behavior can be partially undone by the retiree and the organization and because retiring has many social norm components for some employees. Different orderings, based on different constructs, are likely to be empirically related. A procedure that capitalizes on the information in different ways of ordering the behaviors would offer advantages over reliance on only one.

Whatever construct is used to order the behaviors—severity, personal cost to employee, degree of belongingness—we would expect to see tardiness enacted before absences and absences before quitting, for example. Behaviors are enacted according to this partially ordered sequence until one is reached and enacted that succeeds in reducing an employee's negative job attitudes below a threshold or reducing the propensity for that behavior below a threshold. The propositional inventory for this model of organizational withdrawal would have the following entries:

- Order the behaviors from the least to most severe form of withdrawal, *I* being least and *K* being most severe.
- Evaluate all behaviors for action.
- If behavior *I* was enacted in previous time period, increase the likelihood that behavior *J* will happen by 25 percent.
- If behavior *J* was enacted in the previous time period, increase the likelihood that behavior *K* will happen by 25 percent.
- Enact those behaviors that were identified for action.
- If behavior *K* is enacted, remove the individual from the sample of employees. Replace with another individual.
- Implement any model-required feedback or feedacross effects from enacted behavior to precipitating job attitude.
- Move on to the next time period.

Results of Modeling Studies

Hanisch et al.'s (1996, in press; Seitz, Hulin, & Hanisch, 2000) WORKER implements the models. Hanisch (2000) and Munson and Hulin (2000) have used this software to explore a number of theoretical and applied questions about organizational withdrawal, questions that are difficult or impossible to ask using correlational or experimental research disciplines.

Hanisch (2000) simulated the effects of organizational interventions targeted toward reducing absenteeism and early retirement in different simulation runs under the assumptions of the spillover, compensatory, and progression of withdrawal models. The interventions were modeled by imposing sanctions on absenteeism and early retirement partway through runs simulating behavioral propensities, attitudes, and frequencies of tardiness, absenteeism, turnover, and early retirement. The organizational sanctions that Hanisch stimulated had the expected effects on the targeted behaviors and on their associated behavioral propensities and attitudes toward the behavior: behavioral propensities increase, attitudes toward the behaviors increase, and the frequency of the behavior decreases following the interventions (because of the sanctions that targeted the behaviors but not the attitudes or propensities). These changes are the equivalent of method checks in experimental studies. The important and informative emergent properties of the different models in Hanisch's simulated interventions are the effects on the nontargeted behaviors. These effects are often nonintuitive and varied as a function of which model of withdrawal behavior was being simulated. The differences in effects on nontargeted behaviors demonstrate the importance of modeling research on different withdrawal models in understanding how individuals attitudinally and behaviorally withdraw from a work organization.

Hanisch (2000) found, under the assumptions of the spillover model of organizational withdrawal, that simulating an absenteeism intervention by imposing sanctions on absenteeism resulted in the expected decrease in absenteeism, a slight increase in tardiness, and decreases in turnover and early retirement that mirrored the changes in absenteeism. Following an organizational intervention that made turnover and early retirement less attractive than it was in the baseline condition, Hanisch found that all withdrawal behaviors decreased. These effects probably are due in part to the replacement of departed employees by drawing their replacements from a distribution of job attitudes similar to the distribution that existed at the beginning of the simulation runs. With fewer employees quitting or retiring, the effect of introducing new employees was reduced. These results indirectly document the complexity of variables and processes that influence the withdrawal process and whose operation influence the structure among withdrawal behaviors. Turnover influences the structure of withdrawal behaviors among the sample of employees through the mechanism of the incoming replacement workers and their attitudes. Studies based on computational modeling can easily investigate these influences by removing those who quit from the sample but not replacing them, or removing and replacing them, or recording them as quitting but leaving them in the sample. This latter counterfactual sample would be impossible to study empirically, but such a manipulation may offer insights into the withdrawal process that are impossible to gain in more traditional ways.

Hanisch's simulations of interventions on absenteeism in the progression of withdrawal model were nonintuitive and complex. Under baseline conditions, with no differential sanctions imposed on any behavior, the proportions of those enacting all behaviors (absenteeism, tardiness, turnover, early retirement) show sinusoidal waves that cycle across time with the behaviors showing similar periodicities, with peaks and troughs occurring at similar points in time. Following the imposition of sanctions on absenteeism, the cycles were flattened for all behaviors; absenteeism continued to cycle slightly with a gradual rather than an abrupt decrease in the proportion of those enacting the behavior following the intervention. Following organizational interventions that decreased the attractiveness of turnover and early retirements, the proportion of simulees enacting these behaviors decreased to very low values with little cycling, and the proportion of those enacting absenteeism and tardiness showed gradual increases across time with little cycling.

If the progression of withdrawal model provides an accurate account of the withdrawal process, the effects of organizational interventions will depend on the extremity of the behavior sanctioned or the belongingness of the behavior to the fuzzy set of withdrawal behaviors. The information contained in the patterns of behaviors simulated by the progression of withdrawal model is also greater than in the other models. Seitz and Miner (2001) argue that so little information is contained in the independent forms of withdrawal model that its apparent fit to empirical data may be artifactual. This latter point is illustrated by the following study.

Munson and Hulin (2000) evaluated model and data fit properties using WORKER to simulate withdrawal behaviors and empirical data from self-reports of 127 faculty members at a university. Based on the self-report data, Munson and Hulin argued that the intercorrelations of the simulated behaviors should be generally positive and of low to moderate strength, with correlations of approximately .20. Among the most extreme behaviors simulated (tampering with equipment so they could avoid doing their job, drinking and taking drugs after work because of things that happened at work), correlations should be approximately zero because of their low base rates. On the basis of these criteria, Munson and Hulin concluded that in this sample of organizational employees, the independent forms of withdrawal model provided the best approximation to the empirical, self-report data. This may have been because the reported withdrawal behaviors in this (very satisfied) sample had low base rates and, hence, low intercorrelations with each other and relative low correlations with their antecedent attitudes.

Additional evidence in the form of stability of attitudes toward specific withdrawal behaviors and the incidence of those behaviors was offered by Munson and Hulin in support of the independent forms of withdrawal model. These stability matrices showed the expected superdiagonal form in which correlations of either attitudes or behaviors from adjacent time periods were moderately large, with progressively smaller correlations between behaviors or attitudes as the time periods being simulated become more remote. This superdiagonal (in)stability matrix has been obtained in many other abilities and behaviors that have been studied in organizational settings (Henry & Hulin 1987, 1989; Hulin, Henry, & Noon, 1990). Seitz and Miner's information-theoretic argument does, however, raise questions about the conclusions that Munson and Hulin reached.

Work groups in organizations provide an illustration of dynamic modeling in organizations. Moving from individuals to groups in organizations provides an excellent example of the reach and scope of modeling in organizational studies.

Individuals in Groups in Organizations

Organizations consist of collections of (usually) hierarchically arranged individuals linked in an overall structure characterized by task specialization and horizontal differentiations among individuals to accomplish a series of interconnected tasks. In this conceptualization, individuals are fundamental building blocks of organizations. Study of organizations should begin with individuals as the basic data; we develop a knowledge of organizations from an accumulated knowledge of individuals.

Groups, as either building blocks of organizations or sources of variables that control variance in the behaviors of individuals, seem to be permanent in organizations. Unfortunately, research on intact, task-oriented groups in work organizations is difficult to do and infrequently done. Securing organizational cooperation for research on groups, where the number of work groups must be reasonably large, is problematical. Applications of hierarchical linear modeling (Chapter Twelve, this volume; Byrk & Raudenbush, 1992; Hoffman, Griffin, & Gavin, 2000) that nest individuals within groups and estimate both within-group and between-group effects have partially solved the statistical estimation problems in this area.

The logistics of studying intact groups remain problematical, so we have borrowed much from laboratory-based, experimental studies of groups and have assumed these findings will generalize to intact groups in organizations (Moreland & Levine, 1988; Goodman, 1986). The role of groups as fundamental elements of organizations may rest on an empirical basis with unknown external validity. Research on work groups may benefit from computational modeling as an alternative or in addition to continued experimental study of groups of college sophomores who interact once for forty minutes and the infrequent field study of intact work groups.

Conceptualizing organizations as collections of linked individuals and attempting to develop our knowledge of organizations by building from individuals to the level of the organization is analogous to arguing that individual choices of people, acting in their own self-interests, not control by hidden hands, create an economy (Smith, 1776/1994). This assumes that organizations emerge from choices of individuals; they are not dictated or commanded from above. This bottom-up approach challenges macro-theorists who characterize the search for psychological explanations for macro-phenomena as misguided reductionism. But to understand organizations and to study them efficiently, we should study and understand individuals and individual psychological processes, the building blocks for most things organizational: conflicts, conformity, consolidation, decisions, and behaviors. Understanding social cognition within the context of decision-making groups may involve understanding individual cognition; processes that are dependent solely on group mechanisms and procedures may be of minor importance. Misspecification of the level at which psychological processes operate can lead to erroneous hypotheses about mechanisms at the higher level.

Situations where lower-level interacting units combine outputs to produce higher-level phenomena are excellent targets for computational models. Interacting units can be modeled to behave according to only local rules governing individuals. Combined, the lower-level units can produce behavioral traces at a higher level that appear ordered according to some higher-level rule. Output from the modeling studies run with local rule assumptions can be compared with empirical results. If modeling results comport with empirical results, confidence in the specifications of the processes is increased.

One possible application of computational modeling is the interaction of individuals in small decision-making groups. Such groups are often convened in organizations under the assumption that decisions of groups are superior to the aggregated outputs of an equivalent number of individuals working alone. A group containing members from inventory control, engineering, human resources, and marketing is often assumed to make better decisions about methods to produce a new product than would any of the individuals working alone. In order for the group to make the best decision, the individual group members must share and weight information efficiently. That is, the member from engineering must share the information he or she has, and the marketing person must weight it appropriately. If group members fail to share and weight information appropriately, the group will make a suboptimal decision.

The situation described in the example has been studied using the hidden-profiles paradigm (Stasser & Titus, 1985). In such situations, information is distributed across members of the group in such a way that they must efficiently combine and weight their information to make the "correct" decision. Without such combination, the group will make an incorrect, or at least a nonoptimal, decision. Three similar but competing models of group decision making in these situations have been proposed and tested in laboratory settings (Chernyshenko, Miner, Baumann, & Sniezek, under review; Larson, Foster-Fishman, & Keys, 1994; Gigone & Hastie, 1993, 1996; Stasser, Taylor & Hanna, 1989; Stasser & Titus, 1985).

Results from laboratory experiments can be used to estimate parameters of models and provide tests of competing models. However, such a process is inefficient for testing models across the many different conditions in which groups function, across the useful range of group sizes, and with a sufficient number of groups in each condition to ensure that meaningful differences will be found if they exist. Computational modeling can aid group researchers if used appropriately in conjunction with laboratory research. Once a model is derived and its computational instantiation validated against empirical data, computational simulation can be used to explain empirical results, test a model's implications, and extend its reach.

Computational models have aided group researchers in two distinct ways: testing implications of models under conditions not easily replicable in the laboratory and guiding researchers in the design of empirical studies and aiding the interpretation of results.

Stasser (2000) argues that understanding what groups do may require understanding what individuals do and how several individuals' minds work together when involved in a group discussion precedent to a group decision. Stasser began a series of modeling studies of group decision making based on empirical observations of consensus decision making in small groups and models of individual decision making. Analogically constructed models of group decision making, heavily influenced by models of (cognitive) information processing by individuals, were the core of the development of his modeling program, DISCUSS. Constructs were added that are important in group decision making when group members hold preferences for alternatives prior to any group discussion; when their information sets overlap incompletely; and when they share part, but not all, of their information during a group decision-making session. Stasser generated a computational model of group decision making under these conditions that provided ways to test alternative explanations for phenomena he had observed in his earlier empirical work with decision-making groups; these alternative explanations would be nearly impossible to test in a laboratory situation.

Stasser (1988, 2000) and Stasser and Taylor (1991) used DISCUSS to simulate order of speaking; relative time spent speaking; information presented in each speaking turn; group decision or consensus, if any, after each speaking turn; and other aspects of group discussion based on individual decision making. The parameters of DISCUSS are based on empirical data from past studies. The output of DISCUSS can be compared to the output of actual four-person groups studied in laboratory settings. Variations of group decision-making procedures, as well as different ways of treating evaluations of alternatives, yielded different results. Perhaps of greatest importance for this discussion, collective information sampling, incomplete sharing as modeled by speaking turns, speaking frequency, and information exchange as represented in DISCUSS can account for groups' failures to discover hidden information and subsequent failures to make optimal decisions. Advocacy versus nonadvocacy of decision alternatives by speakers had no effect on distributions of postdiscussion preferences among the three alternatives.

A subsequent version of DISCUSS included refinements in the selection of speakers. These refinements, contained in SPEAK (Stasser & Taylor, 1991), were based on empirical observations of "megaturns" in speaking in which individuals spoke several times in a short temporal interval, with subsequent falloff in their contributions across time. Rules governing the order in which group members speak would be impossible to enforce in the laboratory to ensure that "megaturns" occurred appropriately and could be studied. Instead, Stasser (2000) used DISCUSS and SPEAK computational models of group decision making to simulate virtual groups. Based on the results of thousands of simulated group discussions, he concluded that speaking patterns did little to influence group decisions in the vast majority of situations, contrary to conventional wisdom. Because group research requires a very large number of experimental participants in each condition, it would have been difficult to test the influence of different patterns of speaking on group performance in a lab setting.

A second way that computational models have aided group researchers is illustrated by recent work on a conceptual model derived from DISCUSS. In this case, a computational model illustrated the limitations of output from an empirical study (Miner, Chernyshenko, & Stark, 2000).

The researchers began with the goal of testing the validity of their computational model. They found their model was useful; it predicted actual group decisions at a better-than-chance rate. However, it also revealed an interesting characteristic of group decisions that could not have been observed otherwise: the expected variance in group decisions was so large that it would be difficult for researchers to evaluate efficiently the validity of any model using laboratory data. The virtual groups made explicit decisions according to the rules of the model after approximately thirty speaking cycles, where one speaking cycle occurs when one person mentions an item of information and the others hear it and take it into account. Because of time constraints in laboratory settings, the average number of cycles completed by twenty-nine laboratory groups in a recent study was twenty-two; groups observed in the laboratory did not spend enough time in discussion to allow the signal provided by the model to emerge. At the point that most laboratory groups stopped their discussion, the virtual groups still had not definitively reached a final decision point. The computationally modeled groups illustrated that laboratory researchers need to entice or allow their laboratory groups to discuss for longer periods of time. The slow convergence from diverging opinions to group consensus that took place over the course of the speaking cycles would have been impossible to know or hypothesize without the output of the computational model.

Other work by Stasser also demonstrates this point. He found that expected effect sizes, derived from computational models, suggest that laboratory studies of small groups, usually six members or fewer, and numbers of groups in each experimental condition, usually between ten and fifteen, fall far short of providing an optimal range of group sizes or statistical power to detect differences in group decision making processes. The sparse data in many regions of the theoretical and experimental space available from experimental studies of groups contrast strongly with the power of computational modeling to generate data from a sufficient range of group sizes, up to and including twelve-person groups, and a sufficient number of groups per condition to have the power to detect differences where they exist. Available empirical observations fail to illuminate many important interfaces between theory and expected data.

Such a use of computational modeling, providing input into meta-method issues, may aid psychological researchers in making point or range predictions about effect sizes (Schmidt, 1992). Given a valid conceptual model of a real-world process, researchers interested in the performance of the process under new conditions can model those conditions before testing them using an experimental or correlational design. Output from computational models may allow researchers to design efficient studies with the power to detect expected effects and to move away from relatively meaningless null predictions. Similar to the way that Miner et al. (2000) generated expectations about the temporal effects of speaking cycles, other researchers might generate point predictions about expected effect sizes under different assumptions about the underlying model. These predictions can aid in the design of empirical studies and hypothesis testing. Complexity inherent in models of organizational behavior has surpassed the point where intuition can generate predictions about the emergent properties across speaking cycles or other behavioral episodes generated by interacting influences of myriad relevant variables.

Software

Although the number of organizational behavior researchers with significant experience or training in programming is growing, their absolute numbers are small. Without such experience, the tasks of translating complex verbal conceptual models of human behavior into propositional calculus and then into computer algorithms may be significant barriers to entry into computational modeling. Some methods, however, are easier to accomplish than others. We present one relatively easy way to progress from a conceptual model to a series of quasi-mathematical statements to code.

Miner et al.'s differential cue weighting (DCW) model, was programmed using Microsoft Excel and the programming language that comes bundled with it, Visual Basic for Applications (VBA). We discuss the Excel/VBA method because it is probably more easily accessible to organizational researchers than other languages.

The visual nature of Excel makes programming more accessible to users than traditional code, where data matrices are stored in memory. Because Excel stores data in worksheet cells, matrices can be manipulated and observed easily. Excel simplifies the programming because it has modules that perform graphing functions and simple statistical analysis that allow output to be combined and presented on the fly with little programming by the user. Excel and VBA are also easily accessible because of their widespread sales. Many researchers probably have Excel and VBA on their computers. Finally, even users with minimal familiarity with coding in VBA can program using Excel's macro-feature. This feature was used in the development stages of the DCW model to generate a shell within which more complex operations were coded by hand.

A computational model written in Excel or VBA would likely consist of three kinds of objects: worksheets, forms, and modules. Worksheets store data and display results. One worksheet might summarize the output from the simulations, and other sheets might contain each individual's information and decisions at various points during the simulation. Forms are the user's interface with the code. On these objects, the user might enter model parameters, such as the method for "selecting" speakers (round-robin, random with repeats, random without repeats), and other parameters relevant to group discussion. Forms can be constructed within the VBA editor. Modules, which also reside in the VBA editor and operate on the values in the worksheets, house the code. Modules are invoked by user actions on forms, such as pressing buttons, or internally by procedures written into the code. Modules are the workhorses of a VBA program; they respond to user actions and conduct computations and worksheet manipulations.

For example, in the DCW model, each individual group member's knowledge is represented by a series of columns on a worksheet. Each column represents an individual's knowledge at one cycle of the discussion. Each entry in a column represents a numerical estimate of the virtual person's knowledge and weighting of a piece of information. At the beginning of the simulation, these columns represent the distinct set of information the person possesses: what he or she came into the discussion with and what he or she has heard from others. The computational simulation procedure updates these values as the group discussion proceeds according to the rules outlined in the model of information sampling and weighting. For example, if person A hears a new piece of information mentioned by another group member, person A's numerical weighting for this piece of information is updated from 0, indicating the person does not have the information, to some new value based on the current rules of the model. The weight may remain at zero if the module specifies that information discussed by others can be ignored or not heard.[5]

In their simulations, Miner at al. (2000) used parameters recovered from empirical results to generate rules by which individuals considered information. These numerical estimates, representing each person's weighted information at a given stage of the group discussion, were then combined according to a mathematical combination model to arrive at a group decision. A version of a lens model was used to combine information in a manner that reflects weighting of information and preferences for the alternatives. Preferences can be scaled to reflect the individual's certainty for the alternative. Possibilities for combining individual decisions into group decisions include majority rule, minority rule, and weighted combination models that take into account not only opinions but the strength of those opinions. In their tests of the DCW model, Miner at al. (2000) used a weighted combination scheme.

Such a procedure is repeated many times until the modeler's stopping point is reached. In their simulations, Miner et al. (2000)

emulated actual laboratory groups and stopped at the point at which the laboratory group stopped discussion. Other groups were run with different rules for stopping, including a percentage of overall information being discussed or the groups' reaching a conclusion with a specified degree of certainty that was estimated by the algorithm combining the individuals' preferences.

To investigate the stability of a group's decision, hundreds of groups were run. Due to random factors built into the information sampling process (for example, different items of information may be discussed and in a different order), the group decision was not always the same even given identical starting points. The exact trajectory taken by the group on its course toward a final decision depends on many events that occur during the discussion. The discussion that occurred in the laboratory was one of the many that were possible. The crucial item of interest was whether the laboratory group outcome fits into the distribution of outcomes generated by the computational model.

Computational models written in this way rely heavily on Excel's visual nature to interpret output and throughput at all stages of computation. Because Excel is a visual program, it is relatively easy to track each step in the execution of the model in order to describe and understand more completely the effects of different manipulations. In the DCW model, numerical values were tracked using graphs that summarized individual and group-level output as the simulation proceeded. Worksheets from individual groups were also saved for combination with others to generate expected distributions of output.

Once programming is completed, simulated groups can be run in large batches; programs and computers are tireless. Because most models include stochastic processes to account for the operations of random events and variables not included in the model, a large number of groups are generally run to allow these effects to generate expected distributions of the output. Each random event becomes incorporated into the discussion of a group and can significantly alter the course of a single group's discussion. However, if a large number of groups is run, any single event has less influence over the overall picture that emerges.

Excel and the bundled VBA editor provide nontechnical users with a powerful development environment. The ubiquity of this application makes computational modeling accessible to any researcher with a dynamic theory and a little time to devote to developing programming skills. With minimal training, the powerful programming tool sitting on most researchers' desktop computers can be used to translate a set of statements about behavior into rules that operate on populations of virtual subjects numbering in the thousands.

Modeling and Groups

An important contribution of modeling is the complexity of the emergent properties at the system level that can be generated by repeated applications of local rules describing the operation of individual processes. Latané's (2000) research on conflict, clustering, conformity, and diversity in macro–social systems demonstrates the social system effects that are generated by bottom-up application of local rules. Computational modeling by Stasser (2000) and by Miner et al. (2000) similarly documents the lawful, regular complexity generated by individuals' sharing and weighing information precedent to group decision making. These efforts raise questions about top-down, hidden-hand, macro-influences on many organizational phenomena. Based on the modeling results discussed, an accurate statement about group processes might stress that individuals are the information-processing and behaving units. Groups and organizations do not "behave" without individuals' acting. Individuals behave in social—organizational—settings and are influenced by macro-level variables. But these variables should be conceptualized as influencing individuals rather than as acting directly on groups or organizations. Before invoking macro-level explanations, modeling studies could determine if the complexity and order often attributed to hidden hands or macro-level forces cannot be explained more parsimoniously by the repeated applications of individual, local processes and rules.

Decision making by groups in organizations is defended by arguing that each member brings unique information to the discussion; an airing of the unique and nonredundant information results in better decisions. However, empirical results suggest that information possessed by all group members is likely to be discussed; it has a statistical advantage in being sampled. Unique information is less likely to get discussed because of the same statistical advantage favoring shared information. Many unshared items of information are not mentioned during discussions and remain unshared after discussion; unshared information has little influence on group decisions. The output of information weighting models (Miner et al., 2000) suggests that organizational resources spent to inform individual decision makers or to hire smarter decision makers who will inform themselves may lead to better decisions than those generated by inefficient groups under conditions of distributed information.

Conclusion

The argument that nothing can be discovered using computational modeling no longer receives support from informed researchers. There are too many examples where applications of well-constructed computational models in a variety of scientific areas from astronomy (Smarr, 1985) to public health (Seitz & Mueller, 1994) to cognitive psychology (Lewandowski, 1993) have generated important information about fundamental processes. Examples of computational modeling discussed in this chapter contain evidence of emergent processes that contribute directly to our understanding of phenomena. The benefits of computational modeling go beyond the direct contributions to our knowledge of basic constructs in many fields of study. Computational modeling can make significant contributions to meta-method issues that will enable researchers to use standard research paradigms and empirical methods more efficiently.

One such area is the use of computational modeling to make point predictions for empirical studies based on findings from modeling runs. Researchers can produce output in which, if a model is correct, they can learn about the expected values of parameters and statistics reflecting underlying processes. Empirical confirmation of such point predictions goes well beyond testing relatively meaningless null hypotheses. Comparisons of expected findings across conditions and variances within conditions contribute not only to our understanding of the processes being simulated. Just as important are the contributions to efficient design of empirical studies and perhaps the knowledge that empirical study of some models and phenomena is impossible, or extremely difficult at best, because of logistics and other practical issues. The results generated by DISCUSS and SPEAK reported by Stasser may have changed the design or even execution of many laboratory studies whose range of group sizes and cell frequencies made detection of expected differences highly unlikely. These results also suggest that the range of group sizes required for some effects to emerge may not be realized in most experimental studies of group decision making.

Results of the DCW model reported by Miner et al. may also influence the design of experimental studies of group decision making; the number of speaking turns or episodes required to reveal meaningful differences in group decisions may extend beyond the possible range of captivity of experimental laboratory subjects.

Temporal effects revealed by computational modeling of organizational withdrawal by Hanisch (2000) also contain important meta-method information. The effects of organizational interventions designed to influence the frequencies of certain withdrawal behaviors were not apparent immediately following the intervention. Under the assumption of some models of organizational withdrawal, these effects became evident over the course of several time periods. This information should inform organizational researchers about the timing of their behavioral observations following organizational interventions.

Computational modeling requires a different repertoire of skills than many organizational researchers possess. But these skills are different only in kind from the research skills we already have; they are not arcane. Their acquisition and use, given the breakthroughs in programming language and the availability of fast, powerful, high-capacity computers, are by no means impossible. The benefits of well-designed computational modeling are significant and reach well beyond the information they generate about instant behavioral processes or organizational issues under investigation. These benefits extend to meta-method issues and questions about organizational forms and conditions that do not (yet) exist. Modeling is not a panacea for research problems. It is an alternative research discipline whose strengths complement those of our two standard disciplines. Its appropriate use will enable us to learn about fundamental processes and the usefulness of research designs for studying some of these processes.

Notes

1. Rising liquid, carried by the large bubbles that rise in the middle of the glass, flows to the sides of the glass and descends carrying small bubbles with it.
2. The original statement of the independent forms of withdrawal model described relations between only two withdrawal behaviors, absence and quitting. This example increases the repertoire to include more than two behaviors and expands the independent forms of withdrawal model described by the propositional inventory beyond the limits originally described by March and Simon. It seems justified by empirical findings (Hanisch & Hulin, 1990, 1991) describing two families of withdrawal behaviors and showing that such behaviors as retirement and tardiness could be considered elements of a job withdrawal repertoire.
3. This proposition is not part of any specific withdrawal model; it is intended to simulate an organizational reality that excessive absenteeism over a short period may lead to termination of employment. The reduction in the probability can be set by the modeler to a reasonable amount.
4. Quitting leads to an individual's being removed from the sample. If a researcher's focus is on the behaviors enacted by the surviving members of the original sample of employees, any individuals who quit are removed from the sample without replacement. Individuals who quit may be replaced by sampling another individual from the original distributions of job attitudes or by sampling from different distributions to reflect historical or organizational changes that have occurred since the original sample was drawn. Characteristics of the replacement simulee that are related to either job attitudes or propensities to engage in certain of the withdrawal behaviors influence the simulation.
5. In the DCW model, these weights were derived empirically in a manner similar to a policy-capturing study. Twenty-nine three-person groups participated in discussions where the information they possessed, discussed, and used in making their decisions was tracked and used to estimate how it was weighted (Chernyshenko et al., under review).

References

Arnott, R., & Small, K. (1994). The economics of traffic congestion. *American Scientist, 82,* 446–455.

Baruch, D. W. (1944). Why they terminate. *Journal of Consulting Psychology, 8,* 35–46.

Beehr, T. A., & Gupta, N. (1978). A note on the structure of employee withdrawal. *Organizational Behavior and Human Performance, 21,* 73–79.

Byrk, A. S., & Raudenbush, S. W. (1992). *Hierarchical linear models: Applications and data analysis methods.* Thousand Oaks, CA: Sage.

Carley, K. M., & Prietula, M. (1994). ACTS theory: Extending the model of bounded rationality. In K. Carley & M. Prietula (Eds.), *Computational organizational theory* (pp. 55–87). Hillsdale, NJ: Erlbaum.

Chernyshenko, O. S., Miner, A. G., Baumann, M. R., & Sniezek, J. A. (under review). *The impact of information distribution and group discussion on member judgment: The differential cue weighting model.*

Fountain, H. (2000, Jan. 11). Analyzing the tempest in a pint of stout. *New York Times on the Web.*

Gigone, D., & Hastie, R. (1993). The common knowledge effect: Information sharing and group judgment. *Journal of Personality and Social Psychology, 65,* 959–974.

Gigone, D., & Hastie, R. (1996). The impact of information on group judgment: A model and computer simulation. In E. White & J. H. Davis (Eds.), *Understanding group behavior: Vol. 1. Consensual action by small groups* (pp. 221–251). Hillsdale, NJ: Erlbaum.

Glomb, T. M., Munson, L. J., Hulin, C. L., Bergman, M. E., & Drasgow, F. (1999). Structural equation models of sexual harassment: Longitudinal explorations and cross-sectional generalizations. *Journal of Applied Psychology, 84,* 14–28.

Goodman, P. S., and associates (Eds). (1986). *Designing effective work groups.* San Francisco: Jossey-Bass.

Hackman, J. R., & Oldham, G. R. (1976). Motivation through the design of work: The test of a theory. *Organizational Behavior and Human Performance, 16,* 250–279.

Hanisch, K. (2000). The impact of organizational interventions on behaviors: An examination of models of withdrawal. In D. R. Ilgen & C. L. Hulin (Eds.), *Computational modeling of behavioral processes in organizations* (pp. 33–60). Washington, DC: American Psychological Association.

Hanisch, K. A., & Hulin, C .L. (1990). Retirement as a voluntary organizational withdrawal behavior. *Journal of Vocational Behavior, 37,* 60–78.

Hanisch, K. A., & Hulin, C. L. (1991). General attitudes and organizational withdrawal: An evaluation of a causal model. *Journal of Vocational Behavior, 39,* 110–128.

Hanisch, K. A., Hulin, C. L., & Seitz, S. T. (1996). Mathematical/computational modeling of organizational withdrawal processes: Benefits, methods, and results. In G. Ferris (Ed.), *Research in Personnel and Human Resources Management* (Vol. 14, pp. 91–142). Greenwich, CT: JAI Press.

Hanisch, K. A., Hulin, C. L., & Seitz, S. T. (in press). Temporal dynamics and emergent properties of organizational withdrawal behaviors and models. In M. Erez, U. Kleinbeck & W. Theirry (Eds.), *Work motivation in the context of globalizing economies*. Hillsdale, NJ: Erlbaum.

Henry, R. A., & Hulin, C. L. (1987). Stability of skilled performance across time: Some limitations on utilities. *Journal of Applied Psychology, 72,* 457–462.

Henry, R. A., & Hulin, C.L. (1989). Additional evidence on the decrement in the validities of predictions of skilled performance across time and performance sessions. *Journal of Applied Psychology, 74,* 365–367.

Herzberg, F., Mausner, B., Peterson, B., & Capwell, D. (1957). *Job attitudes: Review of research and opinion*. Pittsburgh, PA: Psychological Services of Pittsburgh.

Hill, J. M., & Trist, E. L. (1955). Changes in accidents and other absences with length of service: A further study of their incidence and relation to each other in an iron and steel works. *Human Relations, 8,* 121–152.

Hoffman, D. A., Griffin, M. A., & Gavin, M. B. (2000). The application of hierarchical linear modeling to organizational research. In K. Klein & S.W.J. Kozlowski (Eds.), *Multilevel theory, research, and methods in organizations* (pp. 467–511). San Francisco: Jossey-Bass.

Hulin, C. L. (1992). Adaptation, persistence, and commitment in organizations. In M. D. Dunnette (Ed.), *Handbook of industrial organizational psychology* (2nd ed., pp. 445–505). Palo Alto, CA: Consulting Psychologists Press.

Hulin, C. L., Henry, R. A., & Noon, S. L. (1990). Adding a dimension: Time as a factor in the generalizability of predictive relationships. *Psychological Bulletin, 107,* 328–340.

Ilgen, D. R., Hollenbeck, J. R., Tower, S. L., & Waldschmidt, D. M. (1995). *Computational models and theory building in industrial and organizational psychology*. Unpublished manuscript.

Larson, J. R., Jr., Foster-Fishman, P. G., & Keys, C. B. (1994). The discussion of common and unique information in decision-making groups. *Journal of Personality and Social Psychology, 67,* 446–461.

Larson, R. S., & Csikszentmihalyi, M. (1983). The experience sampling method. In H. R. Reis (Ed.), *New directions for methodology of social and behavioral science: Naturalistic approaches to studying social interactions* (Vol. 15, pp. 41–46). San Francisco: Jossey-Bass.

Latané, B. (2000). Pressures to uniformity and the evolution of cultural norms. In D. Ilgen & C. Hulin (Eds.), *Computational modeling of behavioral processes in organizations: The third scientific discipline in behavioral research* (pp. 189–215). Washington, DC: American Psychological Association.

Lewandowski, S. (1993). The rewards and hazards of computer simulations. *Psychological Science, 4,* 236–242.

Lyons, T. (1972). Turnover and absenteeism: A review of relationships and shared correlates. *Personnel Psychology, 25,* 271–281.

March, J. G., & Simon, H. A. (1958). *Organizations.* New York: Wiley.

Melbin, M. (1961). Organizational practice and individual behavior: Absenteeism among psychiatric aides. *American Sociological Review, 26,* 14–23.

Miner, A. G., Chernyshenko, O. S., & Stark, S. E. (2000). *A dynamic computational model of cue weighting during group discussion.* Paper presented at the Fifteenth Annual Conference of the Society for Industrial and Organizational Psychology, New Orleans, LA.

Moreland, R. L., & Levine, J. M. (1988). Group dynamics over time: Development and socialization in small groups. In J. E. McGrath (Ed.), *The social psychology of time: New perspectives.* Thousand Oaks, CA: Sage.

Munson, L. J., & Hulin, C. L. (2000). Applications of computational modeling to organizational behavior: Issues of model/data fit. In C. L. Hulin & D. R. Ilgen (Eds.), *Computational modeling of behavioral processes in organizations: The third scientific discipline in behavioral research* (pp. 69–84). Washington, DC: American Psychological Association.

Munson, L. J., Hulin, C. L., & Drasgow, F. (2000). Temporal dynamics and sexual harassment: Assessing the effects of sexual harassment over time. *Personnel Psychology, 53,* 21–46.

Olsen, F. (2000, June 28). Researchers turn to computer models to learn what experiments cannot teach. *Chronicle of Higher Education Daily News.* Available at: www.chronicle.com/infotech.

Posner, M. I. (Ed.) (1989). *Foundations of cognitive science.* Cambridge, MA: MIT Press.

Rebuilt Kennedy hasn't been a moving experience. (1994, Oct. 16). *Chicago Tribune,* pp. 1–2.

Rosse, J. G. (1988). Relations among lateness, absence, and turnover: Is there a progression of withdrawal? *Human Relations, 41,* 517–531.

Schmidt, F. L. (1992). What do data really mean? Research findings, meta-analysis, and cumulative knowledge in psychology. *American Psychologist, 47,* 1173–1181.

Seitz, S. T., & Hulin, C. L. (under review). Social-ecosystem risk, politics, and internal unrest. Manuscript submitted for publication.

Seitz, S. T. Hulin, C. L., & Hanisch, K. A. (2000). Simulating withdrawal behaviors in work organizations: An example of a virtual society. *Nonlinear Dynamics, Psychology, and Life Sciences, 4,* 33–66.

Seitz, S. T., & Miner, A. G. (2001). Integration of catastrophe theory with models of employee withdrawal: Computational models. In J. M. Brett & F. D. Drasgow (Eds.), *Psychology of work: Theoretically based empirical research.* Hillsdale, NJ: Erlbaum.

Seitz, S. T., & Mueller, G. E. (1994). Viral load and sexual risk: Epidemiologic and policy implications for HIV/AIDS. In E. H. Kaplan & M. L. Brandeau (Eds.), *Modeling the AIDS epidemic: Planning, policy, and prediction* (pp. 461–480). New York: Raven Press.

Smarr, L. L. (1985). An approach to complexity: Numerical computations. *Science, 228,* 403–408.

Smith, A. (1776/1994). *The wealth of nations: An inquiry into the nature and causes.* New York: Modern Library.

Stasser, G. (1988). Computer simulation as a research tool: The DISCUSS model of group decision making. *Journal of Experimental Social Psychology, 24,* 393–422.

Stasser, G. (2000a). Information distribution, participation, and group decisions: Exploration with the DISCUSS and SPEAK models. In C. L. Hulin & D. R. Ilgen (Eds.), *Computational modeling of behavioral processes in organizations: The third scientific discipline in behavioral research* (pp. 69–84). Washington, DC: American Psychological Association.

Stasser, G. (2000b). *Participation patterns in decision-making teams and minority influence.* Paper presented at the Fifteenth Annual Conference of the Society for Industrial and Organizational Psychology; New Orleans, LA.

Stasser, G., & Taylor, L. (1991). Speaking turns in face-to-face discussions. *Journal of Personality and Social Psychology, 60,* 675–684.

Stasser, G., Taylor, L. A., & Hanna, C. (1989). Information sampling in structured and unstructured discussions of three- and six- person groups. *Journal of Personality and Social Psychology, 57,* 67–78.

Stasser, G., & Titus, W. (1985). Pooling of unshared information in group decision making: Biased information sampling during discussion. *Journal of Personality and Social Psychology, 48,* 1467–1478.

Weiss, H. M., & Cropanzano, R. (1996). Affective events theory: A theoretical discussion of the structure, causes and consequences of affective experiences at work. In B. M. Staw & L. L. Cummings (Eds.), *Research in organizational behavior* (Vol. 19, pp. 1–74). Greenwich, CT: JAI Press.

Williams, T. J., Bernus, P., Brosvic, J., Chen, D., Doumeingts, G., Nemes, L., Nevins, J. L., Vallespire, B., Vlietstra, & Zoetekouw, D. (1994). Architectures for integrating manufacturing activities and enterprises. *Computers in Industries, 24,* 111–139.

CHAPTER 15

Meta-Analysis
A Review of Quantitative Cumulation Methods

Hannah R. Rothstein
Michael A. McDaniel
Michael Borenstein

Meta-analysis is the quantitative combination of information from multiple empirical studies to produce an estimate of the overall magnitude of a relationship or impact of an intervention. Meta-analysis is critically important for the development of cumulative knowledge because in most research areas, the sample size required to estimate precisely the magnitude of a relationship cannot be attained with a single study. The imprecise estimates from individual studies typically resulted in bodies of research literature showing highly variable results. This state of affairs often caused researchers to conclude that the results were mixed and the magnitude of the relationship was not known. Then, despite the often-large volume of accumulated data, suggestions were made that additional research was needed. Policymakers, viewing the large number of studies completed and the lack of consensus concerning what the data really showed, often concluded that empirical research could not generate knowledge and cast aspersions on the value of the social and behavioral sciences.

Because of the limited information value of a single study, the research community has long recognized that data from multiple studies must be combined to yield definitive results. Prior to meta-analysis, this synthesis typically took the form of narrative reviews, which were at best subjective and at times misleading. The results of narrative reviews rarely had substantial impact on either scientific thinking or public policy. With the advent and widespread acceptance of meta-analysis, this situation has changed dramatically. Research reviews based on meta-analysis are considered by many to be a cornerstone of scientific endeavor. The Science section of the *New York Times* reports the results of meta-analyses on a regular basis. The U.S. government relies on meta-analysis to establish the effectiveness of medical treatments. There are now ten federally funded centers for evidence-based medicine whose mission is to meta-analyze the medical literature and inform clinical practice. Various government agencies, including the National Institute of Mental Health, now require or encourage researchers to conduct a meta-analysis of existing research before they will fund a proposed study. In Great Britain, new health care policies and practices set by the National Health Service are based on meta-analytic findings. In short, meta-analysis has fundamentally changed the knowledge base in many sciences, as well as its perceived value.

This chapter provides a brief history of meta-analysis, outlines its goals, and explains its advantages over narrative reviews. It discusses the five major stages in conducting a meta-analysis and then provides substantial detail concerning the data analysis stage. It describes several topical issues concerning aspects of meta-analysis. It concludes with an overview of software and provides details of individual software resources in the chapter appendix.

A Brief History of Meta-Analysis

Modern techniques of meta-analysis have developed over the past fifteen or twenty years, but precursors of these methods go back about a hundred years (Cooper & Hedges, 1994; Olkin, 1990). The literature includes some isolated examples of meta-analysis dating to the first half of the twentieth century. Pearson in 1904 used techniques remarkably similar to current meta-analytic methods to determine whether a vaccine was effective in preventing typhoid (it was), Fisher (1932) discussed quantitative combination of the results of multiple studies in the 1920s, and Thorndike (1933) used combinatorial methods to integrate findings in intelligence research during the 1930s. During World War II, Stouffer, Suchman, DeVinney, Star, and Williams (1949) developed a combinatorial method to study American soldiers. From then on, meta-analysis was rarely used until the mid-1970s, when Glass (1976) coined the term *meta-analysis* (meaning "analysis of analyses") and used the method to assess the efficacy of psychotherapy (Glass, McGaw, & Smith, 1981). At about the same time that Glass and his colleagues were inventing their meta-analytic method, Schmidt and Hunter (1977) were independently devising similar procedures to solve the mystery of the apparent situational specificity of employment test validities in the field of industrial/organizational (I/O) psychology. Concurrently, Rosenthal (1978) was developing combinatorial methods to disentangle expectancy effects in social psychology. Hedges and Olkin (1980, 1983, 1984, 1985) began publishing their work in the early 1980s. A short time later, meta-analytic methodology was adopted by the medical community as the foundation for the emerging field of evidence-based health care (the forerunner of the Cochrane Collaboration published a groundbreaking review of obstetrics practices in 1989 and the first formally designated Cochrane Center was funded in 1992) (Chalmers, 1993).[1] Since the early 1980s, meta-analysis has become an increasingly important tool for both research and policy in a growing list of scientific disciplines. As of the date of this writing, there are 3,338 articles linked to the keyword *meta analysis* in the Psycinfo database. A recent search of the term *meta-analysis* using a popular Internet search engine yielded 34,179 hits.

The Goals of Meta-Analysis

All modern meta-analytic methods share two related goals: deriving the best estimate of the population effect size and determining the source or sources of variance, if any, around this best estimate of the population effect size. Meta-analysis allows the use of statistical procedures to determine the best estimate of the population effect size and whether an effect is uniform across an entire body of studies. In the event that the effect varies across studies, meta-analytic procedures assist the researcher in determining the sources of variation. All meta-analytic methods used in the social sciences subscribe to these goals and are best regarded as variations on a theme. Most of the differences among various meta-analytic approaches stem from differences concerning what constitutes the best estimate of the effect size, what sources of variance are considered when examining effect size variability, and what approaches are used in evaluating possible sources of effect size variance.

Advantages of Meta-Analysis over Narrative Reviews

More than twenty years ago, Cooper and Rosenthal (1980) provided empirical evidence that conclusions drawn after using statistical combining procedures were different from those resulting from the traditional methods on which narrative reviews were based. They showed that using statistical rather than traditional methods for reviewing studies increased both perceived support for and estimated magnitude of the effect being examined. Although this does not demonstrate that the statistical method produced more accurate results, we believe that on a priori grounds, meta-analytic research synthesis is more likely to produce accurate results than does the narrative method for reviewing research because it conforms more closely to the canons of good scientific practice; that is, it is more systematic and objective. A well-conducted meta-analytic review is carefully constructed around the same set of research and reporting procedures as the ones used in primary studies. There is some interdisciplinary variation in how strictly researchers adhere to a prescribed set of procedures. In medicine, for example, detailed and specific checklists and handbooks are available to guide researchers through each step of the meta-analysis (Oxman, 1995; Clarke & Oxman, 1999).

In a properly reported meta-analysis, the researcher publicly specifies his or her decision rules at each step of the review, and the resulting reviews are presented in a fairly standardized form, making it easier to follow and to evaluate critically a meta-analytic review than a typical narrative review. Such procedures enhance the replicability of a meta-analysis and reduce the likelihood that independent meta-analyses of the same domain will contradict each other compared to narrative reviews. In addition, if the results of two meta-analytic reviews disagree, it is easier to determine the source of the discrepancies. Explicitness and transparency of procedures are hallmarks of a properly conducted meta-analysis.

I/O psychologists have generally been quite thorough in their descriptions of decision rules. The decision rules often concern detailed specifications of what types of measures are acceptable for inclusion in the meta-analysis and which are not. For example, McDaniel, Whetzel, Schmidt, and Maurer (1994) listed a variety of interviews they excluded from their meta-analysis. Such interviews consisted of those conducted with psychiatric populations, interviews that lasted under one minute, and interviews in which the person who made the ratings was not present at the interview. McDaniel, Morgeson, Finnegan, Campion, and Braverman (2001) specified which measures they accepted as job performance measures and which measures they rejected. The rejected measures included years of school beyond high school, hierarchical level in the organization, number of subordinates, years of management experience, salary, rates of promotion, and tenure.

Five Steps of a Research Synthesis

Cooper (1982) developed a five-stage model of research synthesis that provides an overall strategy for conceptualizing and conducting meta-analysis. (In fields outside psychology, *research synthesis* is the term for what psychologists call meta-analysis; *meta-analysis* is reserved for the data-analytic stage of the synthesis.) The first three stages of Cooper's model are problem formulation, data collection, and data evaluation. During problem formulation, the purpose of the review is elucidated, and the question being asked is defined clearly enough so that only studies that address this question will be included in the research synthesis. In the data collection stage, a search strategy is identified, and the literature is searched for relevant studies (Dickerson, 1994; Reed & Baxter, 1994; White, 1994). Part of the strategy is devoted to locating so-called fugitive or unpublished studies (Rosenthal, 1994). In the data evaluation stage, the studies that have been retrieved are coded on critical features, such as whether they contain enough information for analysis (generally an effect size estimate, standard deviation or standard error, and sample size), operational definitions of the independent and dependent variables, the methods used in conducting the studies, and sample type. Whether a study feature is critical will depend on the objectives of the meta-analysis. Those studies (or effects within studies) that meet the criteria for inclusion in the meta-analysis are retained.

As an example, in the McDaniel et al. (1994) interview meta-analysis, several study features were judged critical. The interview literature had long drawn a distinction between structured and unstructured interviews, and thus the level of structure in the interview was coded. The authors also categorized the content of the interview as situational, nonsituational but job related, or psychological. Interviews were classified as board interviews or individual interviews. The performance measures were coded as job performance, training performance, or tenure.

The final two stages of Cooper's model address data analysis and interpretation and public presentation of results. The goals are to perform the statistical synthesis of study outcomes of included studies, draw appropriate inferences and conclusions, examine threats to the validity of conclusions, and present these in a format that will be easily understandable and useful to the audience of researchers or policymakers at whom the syntheses are aimed.

I/O psychologists have typically emphasized the statistical aspects of meta-analysis. After some initial debate about extrastatistical considerations (Bullock & Svyantek, 1985; Jackson, 1984; Rothstein & McDaniel, 1989; Schmidt, Hunter, Pearlman, & Hirsh 1985), discussion of issues other than data analysis largely disappeared from the published literature in I/O psychology. This situation is unfortunate, because in other disciplines, this is where many of the recent controversies have raged and subsequent advances in meta-analytic methodology have been made. In line with the expectations of many of our I/O colleagues, we will focus initially on the data-analytic aspects of meta-analysis. Later in the chapter, however, we raise other issues that deserve the renewed attention of our colleagues.

The Data Analysis Stage of Meta-Analysis

We begin the section by introducing various classes of effect sizes, which are commonly examined in a meta-analysis. Next, we discuss approaches to estimating the population effect size and offer a detailed review of how variability in effect sizes is addressed.

Specifically, we draw distinctions between fixed- and random-effect models, provide an overview of psychometric meta-analysis approaches to explaining variance, and conclude with a review of methods for evaluating potential moderators as sources of the effect size variance.

Effect Sizes

The class of statistics cumulated in a meta-analysis is called an *effect size*. An *effect* is any statistic that indicates the degree to which a given event is present in a sample (Cohen, 1988). Unlike statistical significance tests, effect sizes are independent of sample size. I/O psychologists are most familiar with correlation coefficients and standardized mean differences, and in fact, most meta-analyses that have been conducted in our field have used correlations (either directly, or transformed to Fisher's *z*) or standardized mean differences (Glass's delta, Hedges' *g*, Hedges' *d*, or Cohen's *d*). However, many effect size measures exist. Rosenthal (1994) offered a concise review of many effect size estimates, their interrelationships, and their relation to statistical tests of significance. Other effect sizes, particularly for studies using dichotomous measures (that is, differences in proportions), also exist. These include odds ratios, rate differences, and risk differences. Fleiss (1994) outlined the benefits of using the odds ratio rather than other approaches of group comparisons on dichotomous measures, and Haddock, Rindskopf, and Shadish (1998) provided a primer for meta-analyses of studies with dichotomous data using odds ratios as effect sizes.

Let us say that we wish to conduct a meta-analysis of studies examining the effect of behavior modification programs on attendance at work. Chances are that in a group of studies, this has been assessed in a variety of ways, including the difference in the proportion of trained versus untrained employees with good attendance records, the mean difference in attendance between trained and untrained employees, or the correlation between scores on a test administered at the end of training and the number of work days the employee was at work in the subsequent year. Each of these indicates the effect of behavior modification training on attendance; they are thus all measures of effect size. In a meta-analysis, the results of individual studies can and must all be transformed from their original metric into a common measure of effect size so that the study effects can be compared and an overall effect size calculated. Statistical tests such as *t*-tests, *F*-tests, and chi-square statistics are not effect sizes because for any given effect, their value increases as the sample size of the study increases. Thus, they cannot be input directly into a meta-analysis, but must first be transformed into pure effect size measures. Several books and computer software packages provide additional information about effect sizes and their transformations (Hedges & Olkin, 1985; Hunter & Schmidt, 1990; Rosenthal, 1994; Shadish, Robinson, & Lu, 1994). Kubeck, Delp, Haslett, and McDaniel (1996) provide details on several ways of transforming statistics reported in the studies to the needed effect sizes.

Estimating the Population Effect Size

A major goal of meta-analysis is to estimate the population effect size. However, unlike primary studies, where each individual's score has an identical impact on the average, a meta-analysis differentially weights the effect contributed by each study. This is necessary because each study has a different sample size, and effect sizes based on large samples will be better estimates of the population effect than will effect sizes based on studies with small samples. Thus, in order to obtain the best estimate of the population effect, studies with large samples need to be given greater weight than smaller studies. All modern meta-analytic methods weight the effect sizes from individual studies before combining them. Methods developed by Hedges and Olkin (1985, in press) and others weight studies by the inverse of the sampling error variance; the Hunter and Schmidt (1990) method weights directly by sample size. These two weighting schemes are actually quite similar and generally yield very similar results for correlational data.

In most meta-analysis approaches, the weighted mean effect size is argued to be the population effect size. In contrast, advocates of psychometric meta-analysis (Callendar & Osburn, 1980; Hunter & Schmidt, 1990; Raju & Burke, 1983; Schmidt & Hunter, 1977) argue that the weighted mean effect size is a biased estimate of the population effect size. The mean effect size, which is referred to as the observed mean effect size in this literature, is known to be downwardly biased. This bias always occurs due to less-than-perfect reliability in the measured variables. In some situations, the mean effect size is also downwardly biased due to range restriction in the measured variables. Hunter and Schmidt (1990) offered several approaches for correcting the mean observed effect size to estimate the population effect size more accurately.

The distinction between the definition of the population effect size for psychometric meta-analysis and that of other meta-analysis methods is related to the distinction between latent and indicator variables. Psychometric meta-analysis defines the population effect size as a latent, or construct-level, effect size. Other meta-analytic approaches define the population effect size as an indicator, or observed, effect size.

Finally, we note that there is nothing preventing adherents of other methods of meta-analysis from correcting the observed effect sizes in order to estimate the latent effect size. Hedges and Olkin (1985) briefly addressed the effects of measurement error on correlations. Aguinis and Pierce (1998) have demonstrated how to apply the psychometric meta-analysis corrections within the Hedges and Olkin (1985) meta-analytic approach.

Most applications of meta-analysis in I/O psychology have employed the psychometric meta-analysis approach. In these applications, typically information is presented on both the observed effect sizes and the population effect sizes. For example, in a study concerning age differences in job-related training performance, Kubeck et al. (1996) report both observed and population effect size information. Typically, the discussion of the results emphasizes the information on population effect size.

Variability in Effect Sizes

The second goal of a meta-analysis is to ascertain whether the effect sizes in the meta-analysis are homogeneous. All modern methods of meta-analysis recognize the role of sampling error in the observed variability of effect sizes. All modern methods remove the effects of sampling error variance before reaching a conclusion about the homogeneity or heterogeneity of effects. Current approaches to meta-analysis disagree, however, about how to treat the variability remaining after sampling error variance is accounted for.

In our discussion of variability in effect sizes, we first explain the difference between fixed- and random-effect size models in meta-analysis. We then review the psychometric meta-analytic approach for correcting statistical artifacts as sources of variance across studies in effect size. We conclude this section with a discussion of approaches to evaluating moderators as potential sources of effect size variance.

Fixed Versus Random Effects

Two different statistical models, fixed effects and random effects, have been developed within the general meta-analytic approach to examine and interpret the mean and variance of effect sizes. Usually the fixed-effects model is used if the researchers have reason to believe that all of the studies in the meta-analysis estimate a common population effect, that is, that the study effects are homogeneous. Random-effects models are appropriate whenever there is reason to suspect that the studies are truly heterogeneous, that is, they are not drawn from a single population.

In the fixed-effects model, the sole source of variability is assumed to be sampling error. When the set of effect sizes is actually heterogeneous, the fixed-effects model underestimates the degree of heterogeneity present and produces erroneously narrow confidence and credibility values. Random-effects models of meta-analysis do not assume homogeneity of effects. They treat the effect size from each study as drawn from a distribution of study effects. In this model, the study effects represent samples from a population. Although random-effects models estimate the average population effect, they also estimate between-study variability. Random-effects models correctly estimate confidence intervals when heterogeneity is present but also when it is absent.

According to Hedges and Vevea (1996), "Fixed effects-models treat the effect-size parameters as fixed but unknown constants to be estimated and usually (but not necessarily) are used in conjunction with assumptions about the homogeneity of effect parameters" (p. 486). They argue that it is sometimes appropriate to use fixed-effects models even when there is substantial heterogeneity of results.

Although almost all published studies employ fixed-effects models, we argue that this is bad practice. Hunter and Schmidt

(2000) advocated greater routine use of random-effects models. They demonstrated that fixed-effects models typically yield a type I bias in significance tests for mean-effect sizes and moderator analyses. Random-effects models do not have this bias. In addition, in the presence of variance in population parameters, the fixed-effects model yields confidence intervals that are too narrow and thus overstate the degree of precision in meta-analytic results. Most researchers would agree that there are always some moderators which create variability in population values (National Research Council, 1992). Even in the absence of substantive moderator variables, there are methodological variations across studies, such as differences across studies in reliability of variables, which will cause variation in study population parameters. We thus support the Hunter-Schmidt position that the random-effects model should be used in most cases.

Hunter and Schmidt are not alone in their advocacy of random-effects models. Hedges (1994), Raudenbush (1994), and Rosenthal (1995) have also noted that fixed-effects models can lead to inflated type I error rates and underestimation of confidence intervals. Finally, the National Research Council (1992) recommended the wider use of random-effects models. We note that most applications of meta-analysis in I/O psychology have employed the psychometric meta-analysis approach, which is a random-effects procedure (Hunter & Schmidt, 2000).

Statistical Artifacts

Although all modern approaches to meta-analysis recognize sampling error as a source of variance across studies in effect size, psychometric meta-analysis recognizes other statistical artifacts that cause effect size variance. The psychometric approach (Hunter & Schmidt, 1990) is concerned with the detection of and correction for all errors that derive from study imperfections, which Hunter and Schmidt call "artifacts." Hunter and Schmidt (1994) have stated unequivocally, "While it is important to control and estimate bias in isolated studies, it is even more important to reduce such errors in . . . meta-analysis" (p. 324). Their point of view is that unless such errors are eliminated, it will be virtually impossible to develop cumulative knowledge in the social sciences. With the exception of a few brief comments (see Rosenthal, 1994), advocates of meta-analysis outside the psychometric meta-analysis tradition are largely silent on the merits of the psychometric meta-analysis approach. For such individuals, the approach is not so much criticized as it is ignored.

Schmidt and Hunter's sources of error are familiar to any student of psychometrics. The artifacts fall into two categories: unsystematic and systematic. The unsystematic source of error in a meta-analysis is sampling error. Due to random factors that make samples unrepresentative of the population, sample estimates of effect sizes will vary from their population parameter. These are uncorrectable at the level of the individual study; however, meta-analysis greatly reduces sampling error by cumulating across studies. The systematic errors include error of measurement in both variables (for correlations), measurement error in the dependent variable for comparisons among groups, dichotomization of continuous variables, range restriction or range enhancement, deviation from perfect construct validity in variables, and reporting or transcriptional errors. For many of these, it is possible to quantify the influence of the artifact on effect size and to adjust or correct for it. Most of these artifacts attenuate the population correlation; thus, the observed correlation is lower than the population parameter by some amount. In addition, individual study correlations are affected by artifacts in different amounts, and thus some of the observed variation across the correlations in a meta-analysis is also spurious. Thus, artifacts also affect the researcher's ability to assess the true homogeneity or heterogeneity of the correlations. Fortunately, Schmidt and Hunter have also derived procedures to correct between-study variability for the influence of artifacts. Hunter and Schmidt (1990) have forcefully demonstrated the likelihood that the typical study in the behavioral sciences is prey to contamination by most of these sources of error, as well as the magnitude of the impact of these errors.

Moderator Analysis

To varying extents, all modern meta-analysis methods recognize that effect sizes vary across studies due to nonsubstantive factors such as sampling error and differences across studies in measurement reliability and other artifactual factors. Once these nonsubstantive factors have been considered, variance in effect sizes across studies that is due to substantive factors often remains. Specifically, effect sizes often vary systematically as a function of additional variables (moderators). The discovery and evaluation of interactions or moderating effects in individual studies are often problematic due to low power and the fact that a moderator variable may be acting but not measured in the study. Cooper (1982) argued that meta-analysts should routinely examine whether different outcomes, implementations, or types of subjects influence results. He noted that a strength of meta-analysis is that it can look at these moderators even when no individual study has done so, if studies can be appropriately categorized on the hypothesized moderator. He proposed that meta-analysts formally test the difference between average effect sizes in different subgroups to see if they are significantly different. Hedges and Olkin (1985) have developed the statistical means for performing heterogeneity analysis. Homogeneity analysis compares the observed variance to that expected from sampling error and tests the result by calculating how likely it is that the observed variance in effect sizes would result if sampling error alone was responsible. The homogeneity statistic, Q, is used to determine the probability of observing the variance. If the p-value of the statistic is .05 or less, the meta-analyst rejects the null hypothesis that sampling error alone explains the variance in effect sizes and proceeds to look for study characteristics that have produced the variation in effect size. Studies are subgrouped based on particular characteristics, and the average effect sizes for those groups are tested for homogeneity in the same way as if the overall average effect size had been tested. Subgrouping continues until the null hypothesis of no true variation cannot be rejected or until no further plausible moderators are available.

Hunter and Schmidt (1994) disagree with Cooper on two primary grounds. First, they argued that searching for moderators without compelling a priori evidence to do so is likely to lead to identification of spurious moderators, because of capitalization on chance. Second, they claim that the same reasons that make statistical significance testing inappropriate for individual studies (for example, problems with statistical power and confusing statistical with practical significance; see Cohen, 1994) make it an inappropriate choice in meta-analysis. Schmidt and Hunter reject any formal testing of the difference between observed and expected variances as a simplistic application of hypothesis testing. Their recommendation is for the researcher to focus on the magnitude of the remaining variance after the effects of sampling error and other artifacts have been accounted for. If, in the researcher's expert opinion, the remaining variance is substantial and there are sufficient theoretical or other grounds on which to predict that a moderator may exist, moderator analysis is appropriate. If so, the proposed moderator is used as the basis for subgrouping studies, and the meta-analyst compares the average effect sizes in each subgroup to the overall average effect. Yusuf, Wittes, Probstfield, and Tyroler (1991) had many of the same objections to subgroup analyses as do Schmidt and Hunter. Addressing the medical research community, they "encourage skepticism toward most reported subgroup effects" (p. 97) and "urge interpreting an observed subgroup effect in the context of other available information" (p. 98). Overton (1998) conducted a series of simulations on moderator detection that suggested that homogeneity testing prior to moderator analysis "is appropriate only when the search for moderator effects is exploratory and control is required to minimize the capitalization on chance" (pp. 364–365); theory-guided moderator analysis does not require this control. This is analogous to the difference in ANOVA between the stringency of requirements for post hoc analysis versus those for a priori contrasts.

Additional Issues

As in any other rapidly emerging science, a number of additional issues concerning meta-analysis deserve attention. In this section of the chapter, we address several of these issues: visual presentation of meta-analytic findings, study quality, publication bias, and robustness of meta-analysis to violations of assumptions.

Visual Presentation of Meta-Analytic Findings

Researchers employing meta-analysis invest substantial effort in their work. Few undertake such reviews "because of the time required to write them and because of the trauma sometimes experienced during the writing of an excellent critical review" (Bernier and Yerkey, 1979, pp. 48–49, cited in White, 1994). Despite the labor of producing a meta-analysis, authors typically place little effort into the communication of the results. Light, Singer, and Willet (1994) summarized the typical practice of presenting tabular results and then described a variety of simple visual approaches to communicate meta-analytic results better. Their primary message is that graphic displays of data impose structure and order on what otherwise would be a large mass of perplexing data points. Graphs can be used to communicate the overall message of the meta-analysis and highlight important subgroup differences. They particularly recommend graphic displays that incorporate confidence intervals, stem and leaf plots, and tabular displays organized in a meaningful fashion, such as by magnitude of effect size.

I/O psychologists have not taken full advantage of the information value of graphics and tabular displays. We illustrate the advantages of graphical displays by providing a revised presentation of the data in Kubeck et al. (1996). In their article, these authors followed the typical practice in industrial/organizational psychology by displaying data sorted by author. Exhibit 15.1 shows the Kubeck et al. data for correlations between age and training mastery sorted by magnitude of effect. The exhibit provides the study name, the name of the effect size, the sample size, the correlation coefficient, and the confidence interval for each correlation coefficient. The exhibit makes it readily apparent that most of the correlations between age and training mastery are negative. It also shows that several of the positive correlations are from samples with very small sizes. Restructuring the exhibit to sort the effect sizes by their sample size makes it clear that many of the most aberrant correlations, both high and low, are from studies with small samples. None of this is obvious in the original graphic.

The Role of Study Quality

There is substantial disagreement among meta-analytic approaches concerning the role that study quality should play in meta-analysis. The position of the members of the Cochrane Collaboration (Clarke & Oxman, 1999) is that only methodologically rigorous studies be included in a meta-analysis. They contend that a meta-analysis based on a small number of high-quality studies is more likely to be accurate (valid) than a larger meta-analysis that includes lower-quality studies. They argue that effect sizes in low-quality studies vary systematically from those extracted from better-quality studies. (It is worth noting that some have argued that the better studies will have larger effects, while others have suggested they will have smaller effects.) Hunter and Schmidt (1990) believe that a meta-analyst's assessment of study quality can introduce an unnecessary subjective element into the meta-analysis. They and Glass (1976) have argued that there is no justification for either a priori exclusion of studies based on quality or for assigning quality-based weight to included studies. Evidence for this position is provided by Moher and Olkin (1995), who have reported that different ways of incorporating quality scores can affect the inclusion of studies and alter the overall conclusions of the meta-analysis. Both Hunter and Schmidt and Glass suggest that the proper time to consider the impact of study quality on effect size is during the examination of sources of heterogeneity in meta-analytic results. The features of study quality that are thought to influence effect size can be coded and examined for moderating effects.

Publication Bias

Critics have argued that meta-analytic results are likely to be skewed in the direction of significant and positive results because studies with these results are more likely to be published, and therefore more likely to be retrieved during meta-analytic search procedures, a phenomenon known as *publication bias*. The usefulness of meta-analysis can be limited by the existence of publication bias, which can lead the meta-analysis to yield incorrect results. When the potential for severe bias exists in a given analysis, it is imperative that this fact be identified. On the other hand, when the potential for bias can be effectively ruled out, then this should also be reported, because it is a key factor in establishing the validity of the results. A wide array of methods is available to address the issue of publication bias, but these have been rarely used, and most are entirely unfamiliar to I/O psychologists. This section briefly reviews the research

Exhibit 15.1. Training Mastery Data.

Citation	EffectName	NTotal	Effect
Belbin (1958)	Cloth mending (activity)	19	.372
Belbin & Serjean (1963)	Tailor Women-s (bespoke)	8	.245
Barber (1965)	Maintenance	51	.171
Belbin & Serjean (1963)	Tailor Men-s (wholesale)	24	.136
Gomez et al. (1984)	Computer text editing	40	.100
Kluge (1988)	Computer MBT errors	35	.070
Tannenbaum et al. (1963)	Blueprint reading II	17	.065
Webster et al. (1993)	Computer (work)	32	.040
Kluge (1988)	Computer IBT errors	37	.010
Hughes & McNamara (1961)	Computer (PI)	70	-.025
Tannenbaum et al. (1963)	Intro to electronics	53	-.060
Tannenbaum et al. (1963)	Oil refinery production	30	-.062
Hughes & McNamara (1961)	Computer (classroom)	42	-.070
Tannenbaum et al. (1963)	Oil refinery instrument	15	-.075
Belbin (1969)	Electrical (Discovery)	47	-.087
Tannenbaum et al. (1963)	Telephone operator errors	369	-.092
Corbin (1986)	Computer training	216	-.109
Tannenbaum et al. (1963)	Basic electronics	38	-.114
Belbin (1964)	Postal (Activity)	105	-.150
Neale et al. (1968)	Map reading (medium)	17	-.155
Barber (1965)	Spray gun	31	-.178
Belbin (1964)	Postal (Traditional)	325	-.180
Giannetto (1993)	Welfare (standard)	254	-.203
Czaja et al. (1989)	Computer (instructor)	45	-.218
Downs (1968)	Carpenters	213	-.223

Citation	EffectName	NTotal	Effect	Forest Plot
Giannetto (1993)	Welfare (Self-efficacy)	25	–.230	
Smith (1938)	Manual labor	155	–.234	
Entwisle (1959)	Nonexperienced drivers	352	–.234	
Welford (1958)	Bus driver	694	–.240	
Belbin (1958)	Cloth mending (exposure)	14	–.245	
Belbin & Serjean (1963)	Tailor Men-s (bespoke)	40	–.248	
Barber (1965)	Scaffolding	37	–.249	
Belbin (1969)	Electrical (Standard)	36	–.274	
Morrow et al. (1993)	Flight simulation	28	–.298	
Czaja et al. (1989)	Computer (computer)	45	–.301	
Czaja (1978)	Visual inspec. (errors)	84	–.313	
Tannenbaum et al. (1963)	Electronic tech	18	–.335	
Gist et al. (1988)	Computer (tutorial)	75	–.389	
Tannenbaum et al. (1963)	Optical tooling	46	–.396	
Elias et al. (1987)	Computer	45	–.429	
Gist et al. (1988)	Computer (modeling)	72	–.441	
Downs (1968)	Welders	112	–.457	
Czaja et al. (1989)	Computer (manual)	45	–.469	
Tannenbaum et al. (1963)	Blueprint reading I	17	–.491	
Egan & Gomez (1985)	Computer text editing	33	–.500	
Webster et al. (1993)	Computer (play)	36	–.540	
Entwisle (1959)	Experienced drivers	283	–.546	
Neale et al. (1968)	Map reading (long)	18	–.552	
Dodd (1967)	Gasman	13	–.747	
Neale et al. (1968)	Map reading (short)	16	–.778	

Source: Adapted from Kubeck et al. (1996, pp. 105–107).

literature on publication bias and introduces I/O psychologists to a variety of methods for empirically assessing its existence.

The problem of publication bias is that studies that overestimate the magnitude of an effect are more likely to find their way into a meta-analysis than studies that underestimate the magnitude of the effect. This is because for any given sample size, the study that overestimates the treatment effect is more likely to have a significant p-value, and is thus more likely to be published. Evidence suggests that publication bias is an issue that meta-analytic researchers need to consider. Hedges and Olkin (in press) cite three studies that found that the relative rate of publication for nonsignificant versus significant findings to be 61 percent, 80 percent, and 96 percent. They noted that these surveys were based on medical journals and present evidence that bias is substantially higher in the social sciences (Cooper, DeNeve, & Charlton, 1997; Greenwald, 1975; Sterling, Rosenbaum, & Weinkam, 1995). Other researchers identified groups of studies as they were begun and followed them over a period of years to see which were published and which were not (Easterbrook, Berlin, Gopalan, & Matthews, 1991; Dickerson, Min, & Meinert, 1992). They too found publication bias that tended to exaggerate the size of effects.

It is important to distinguish between the possibility that publication bias exists and its practical impact on meta-analyses. To understand the practical impact, it helps to consider three levels of impact, based on the concordance between reported results and those that would have been reported if all relevant studies had been included. Impact could be called minimal when the two versions of the analysis yielded very similar estimates of the effect size and its variability, modest when the effect size changed somewhat but the key finding and conclusion (for example, that the effect is substantial and generalizable or it is not) did not, and severe when the basic conclusion of the analysis (for example, that the selection tool has a useful level of validity) is called into question. The two surveys that have addressed this question indicated that although publication bias exists, the conclusions in most cases are still valid. These studies (Egger et al., 1997; Sutton et al., 2000), both conducted on meta-analyses of medical research, found that the impact of bias was minimal in 50 percent of meta-analyses, modest in 45 percent and severe in only 5 percent. Hedges and Olkin (in press) suggested that in the social sciences, where studies are more likely to be small and isolated than large and programmatic, publication bias is likely to be a more serious problem. We know there is a large unpublished literature in I/O psychology but have little, if any, empirical data on bias. Likelihood of bias may vary by research area, particularly by whether research is theoretical or applied. In I/O psychology, publication bias may also be introduced by the fact that consulting firms and in-house researchers for organizations view their research results as proprietary.

Three kinds of techniques have been developed to help meta-analysts deal with publication bias. One set, designed to detect publication bias, is best exemplified by a graphical diagnostic called the *funnel plot* (Light & Pillemer, 1984), although it also includes explicit statistical tests. The second set of techniques, designed to assess the sensitivity of conclusions of an analysis to the possible presence of publication bias, includes Rosenthal's file drawer n and its variants. The third set of techniques, designed to adjust effect size estimates for the possible effects of publication bias under some explicit model of publication selection, includes estimation techniques involving weighted distributions. The first two sets of procedures are relatively simple and will be presented here. The complexity of the third set is beyond the scope of this chapter. Readers interested in the adjustment of effect sizes are referred to Duval and Tweedie (2000), Vevea and Hedges (1995), and Iyengar and Greenhouse (1988).

Detection of Publication Bias

The funnel plot is a plot of effect size estimates from each individual study on the x-axis versus some measure of each study's sample size (such as sample size, the standard error of the effect size, or the inverse of the standard error) on the y-axis. If there is no publication bias, the effect size estimates from the small studies will be broadly scattered across the bottom of the graph, with less scatter as the sample sizes increase. The plot will be symmetric about its central axis, with a width that decreases with the standard error, resembling an inverted funnel (see Figure 15.1a). If there is publication bias, the plot becomes asymmetric. If the bias is because smaller studies with nonsignificant results do not get published, the top two quadrants will remain symmetric around the central axis, but there will be a gap at one of the bottom corners of the plot (see Figure 15.1b). Of course, there are reasons other than publication bias for asymmetry, including other retrieval biases and true heterogeneity of studies; nevertheless, the funnel plot is useful as a means of alerting the researcher that there may be a problem that needs to be explored. There are also statistical tests to assess asymmetry (Begg, 1994; Egger, Smith, Schneider, & Minder, 1997).

Assessment of Sensitivity of Conclusions to Publication Bias

This set of techniques is usually referred to as *file drawer analyses*, because they typically involve imputing the number of effect sizes estimates with zero effects (corresponding to the unpublished studies left in researchers' file drawers) that would be necessary to reduce the observed meta-analytic result to zero or, alternatively, to an operationally meaningless level (Hunter & Schmidt, 1990; Orwin, 1983; Pearlman, Schmidt, & Hunter, 1980). These are based on Rosenthal's original (1979) suggestion of computing the number of "missing" studies with zero effect that would be necessary to reduce the meta-analytic result to statistical nonsignificance. Meta-analyses based on small numbers of studies are particularly vulnerable to the file drawer problem. When the required number of "missing" studies is implausibly large, the meta-analytic findings may be considered robust to the potential effects of publication bias. For example, McNatt (2000) recently used file drawer analysis to show that it would take 367 "missing" studies (on interper-

Figure 15.1. Funnel Plots.

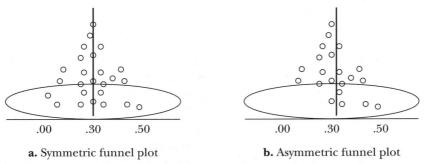

a. Symmetric funnel plot   b. Asymmetric funnel plot

sonal expectancy effects in management) that averaged a zero effect to reduce his observed effect size of $d = 1.13$ (a large effect) to $d = .05$ (a trivially small effect). Unfortunately, McNatt's study is the exception in contemporary I/O practice. Although several early studies included file drawer analyses and we recommended its routine use in 1989 (Rothstein & McDaniel), most I/O meta-analyses done in the past decade have ignored it. Rosenthal (1995) has developed the coefficient of robustness and the counternull statistic (Rosenthal & Rubin, 1994) as additional methods of assessing the robustness of meta-analytic findings.

Robustness to Violations of Assumptions

Overton (1998) recently demonstrated that accuracy of a meta-analytic model when its assumptions are met does not guarantee its robustness to violations of assumptions. After demonstrating the accuracy of several fixed- and random-effects models when the data conformed to the models' assumptions, Overton tested the vulnerability of fixed-effects and random-effects models to violations of the assumptions underlying each model. Using simulated correlation data, he assessed the ability of each type of model to detect moderator effects and found problems with both types of models. Specifically, when between-studies differences were random, fixed-effects models grossly underestimated sampling error variance, leading in some cases to extremely inflated type I error rates exceeding .50, or more than ten times the alpha level of .05, and confidence intervals that captured the true moderator effect only about half the time. Random-effects models were just as bad in cases where between-studies differences were fixed. Here, sampling error variance was greatly overestimated; the probability of detecting a true moderator effect was 5 percent, and confidence intervals were much too wide. Overton suggests that meta-analysts can avoid many of these errors by developing an adequate understanding of the inferences that can be made with each type of model and by selecting a model on the basis of the question and data at hand.

Oswald and Johnson (1998) examined the robustness, bias, and stability of meta-analysis statistics for correlation coefficients. Specifically, they used Monte Carlo simulations to examine the behavior of rho, the estimate of the population effect, and sigma squared, the estimate of the true population variance, when the assumptions of linearity and homoscedasticity were violated in specified ways. The meta-analysis method they tested was Hunter and Schmidt's (1990) random-effects method, in which correlations are individually corrected for the statistical artifacts of sampling error variance, measurement unreliability, and range restriction. They found that on average, the estimate of rho was accurate, but there was a small degree of bias in the variance estimate. In most cases, the bias in the estimate was negative, leading to increases in type II error. Their main conclusion, in agreement with arguments made earlier by Schmidt and Hunter, was that quantitative efforts to detect moderators must be supplemented by the judgment of the researcher. Based on their findings, they also caution against relying on the estimates of population parameters provided by meta-analyses of small number of studies, or those with a small total n (for example, $n \times K < 5,000$). It is clear that more work is needed before we can reach general conclusions about the robustness of meta-analysis to violations of assumptions and equally clear that it is important for this work to be undertaken soon.

Sensitivity analysis, another approach to robustness of results, is an attempt to answer the question of what would happen to the results and conclusions of a meta-analysis if different decisions had been made about what data to include or how to analyze them. A meta-analyst should be able to demonstrate that his or her results and conclusions are not dependent on the inclusion or exclusion of a particular study or on the use of a specific formula or model. As Greenhouse and Iyengar (1994) have suggested, a sensitivity analysis does not need to be quantitative. In fact, the most basic sensitivity analysis is for the researcher to think about the decisions that were made at each step of the meta-analysis and to ask, "What would have happened if I had made a different choice at this point?" I/O psychologists have spent too little time pondering the impact of decisions made prior to the data analysis stage on the results and conclusions of the meta-analysis.

A variety of tools are available to assist in sensitivity analysis. Several of these, including funnel plots, the calculation of fail-safe ns, and the comparison of results of fixed- and random-effects calculations, have been mentioned in this chapter. Other sensitivity analyses include examination of the data for atypical characteristics such as extreme skew of the distribution of studies or the presence of outliers. Where these are present, the researcher might compare the results of meta-analysis of a trimmed data set with those of the meta-analysis of the full complement of studies. The results of a meta-analysis may be considered robust if it can be shown that specific decisions do not affect the overall conclusions. As Greenhouse and Iyengar (1994) have concluded, a meta-analysis can be useful even if its conclusions are shown to be decision sensitive, because its problem features have been identified and can receive attention.

Software for Meta-Analysis

There is a variety of meta-analysis software available. In the chapter appendix, we summarize the software. Most of the software is written for DOS operating systems and can be relatively frustrating to use for those accustomed to graphical interfaces common to the Windows operating system or Macintosh machines. Given the diversity of approaches to meta-analysis, it should not be surprising that there is no single software package that runs all forms of meta-analysis. For those interested in running fixed- or random-effects meta-analysis in the Hedges and Olkin (1985) tradition, there are several options. Less software is available for analyses in the tradition of Hunter and Schmidt (1990). Much of the software is free; however, the more user-friendly software is not.

Conclusion

Meta-analysis has elevated the task of integrating research results to the level of scientific endeavor. It offers a means of overcoming many of the problems presented by single studies and by narrative literature reviews in the quest to develop cumulative knowledge. We believe that it has the potential to transform the face of behavioral science. As a methodological tool, meta-analysis is particularly needed at this point in our scientific history. There are so many studies being done that quantitative methods are required to integrate them. As many I/O research areas mature, the focus turns from large-magnitude effects (which for the most part have already been found) to new ones that are likely to be of small or moderate magnitude. These are exactly the type of effects that are likely to be missed by single studies with small samples. Without meta-analysis, correct identification of these effects is practically impossible.

The validity of a meta-analysis is dependent on careful attention to design, conduct, analysis, and reporting, as is the validity of any other scientific study. Furthermore, whereas meta-analysis is an observational method, it has all the strengths and weaknesses of this approach. Debate concerning the statistical aspects of meta-analysis has produced significant advances in meta-analysis compared to its status when it was introduced. These advances include awareness of the superiority in most situations of the random-effects method, refinements in formulas, and psychometric corrections. Unfortunately, the other steps of meta-analysis have barely developed, and at times they have moved backward. Meta-analytic researchers who want to ensure valid results must consider and attempt to control potential threats to validity that may arise at each step of the meta-analysis. Those who fail to do so will only provide fuel for those critics of meta-analysis who have declared the entire method invalid because of some poorly done meta-analyses.

Careful consideration and clear documentation of the research questions, procedures, assumptions, and methods, supplemented by sensitivity analysis, will help produce high-quality meta-analyses that are persuasive to even the most diehard critics. Even more important, the meta-analyses thus produced will have more to contribute to the advancement of knowledge in I/O psychology.

Appendix: Summaries of Software for Meta-Analysis

META (Meta-analysis, easy to answer).

Author	David Kenny, University of Connecticut.
Operating system	DOS.
Effect size measures	Works with effect sizes for standardized differences (Cohen's *d,* with the option of the Hedges correction), correlations (user specifies use of *r* directly, or Fisher

transformation), and difference between proportions (arcsine, logit, and probit transformations). Allows user to choose the effect size measure and provides transformations to that effect size measure.

Input data	The user can input data manually, or the program can retrieve data from an existing file.
Statistical models	The user can select either fixed-effects or random-effects analysis.
Computation and output	The program computes an effect size for each study, pools the effect sizes, and tests them for homogeneity. Effects can be weighted by sample size, inverse of study variance, or user-inputted values. The program tests whether the average effect size is different from zero and computes the combined probability. The test of heterogeneity is dependent on the effect size measure used. The program does not correct for artifacts. This program provides the following summary statistics: Number of studies, total n, average effect size, sigma of effect sizes, sampling error sigma, sigma of effect sizes with sampling error removed, binomial effect size display, test of homogeneity, combined p-values, and file drawer analysis. Results are stored in an output data file, which can be recalled for later analyses, or read into spreadsheet programs or statistical packages.
Cost and availability	META is available free of charge, although the author suggests that users make a donation of twenty-five dollars to their favorite charity. The program, documentation, and two sample data files can be downloaded from nw3.nai.net/~dakenny/meta.htm.
Remarks	Easy to download and use

True Epistat (Version 5.3)

Author	Tracy L. Gustafson.
Operating system	DOS.
Effect size measures	Standardized differences, correlation co-efficients, odds ratios, relative risks and risk differences.
Input data	Accepts data in the form of test statistics, such as t or F, and p values, and performs transformations to effect sizes.
Statistical models	Fixed and random effects
Computation and output	Tables and graphs showing overall effect and confidence intervals. Graphs also show effects and confidence intervals for each study. The program generates funnel plots to examine publication bias.
Cost and availability	$500. Available from Epistat Services, 2011 Cap Rock Circle, Richardson, TX 75080.
Remarks	The software is more user friendly than most others and includes a manual with nearly one hundred examples.

DSTAT (Version 1.1)

Author	Blair T. Johnson.
Operating system	DOS.
Effect size measures	Correlation coefficients, means and variance estimates, t-test statistics, F-test statistics, proportional data, chi-squares, and p-values. Performs transformations into Cohen's g, a standardized mean difference. Can adjust for small sample bias into Hedges' d.
Input data	Study label, effect size (g), sample sizes, study characteristics
Statistical models	Fixed effects only
Computation and output	Overall effect, confidence interval, and outlier analyses; categorical and continuous fixed-effects models; assists in analyz-

	ing output from standardized regression programs.
Cost and availability	\$125. Johnson, B. T. (1993). DSTAT 1.10: Software for the meta-analytic review of research literatures. Hillsdale, NJ: Erlbaum.
Remarks	DSTAT 1.10 is one of the more user-friendly programs. All options are menu driven. Users can customize many operating specifications.

Meta-Analyst

Author	Joseph Lau, New England Medical Center.
Operating system	DOS.
Effect size measures	Two by two tables only. Odds ratios, relative risks, and risk ratios.
Input data	The user creates ASCII text files with the following data: study name, year, experimental group events, experimental group total, control group events, control group total, covariate 1 (optional), covariate 2 (optional).
Statistical models	Fixed and random effects.
Computation and output	Tables and graphs showing overall effect and confidence intervals.
Cost and availability	Free. Available from Joseph Lau, at joseph.lau@cs.nemc.org.
Remarks	Limited use for most industrial/organizational applications but extremely accurate.

Hunter and Schmidt programs

Authors	John E. Hunter, Michigan State University. Frank L. Schmidt, University of Iowa.
Operating system	DOS.
Effect size measures	Correlation coefficients, standardized mean differences.
Input data	Correlation coefficients, standardized mean differences, sample size, reliability, and range restriction information.

Statistical models	Methods consistent with Hunter and Schmidt (1990). Bare bones, individual corrections for artifacts, and artifact distribution.
Computation and output	Source code is available to audit computations. Output may be printed.
Cost and availability	Free. Available in Hunter and Schmidt (1990) and from Frank L. Schmidt, University of Iowa.
Remarks	Many users find the software to be unfriendly.

Comprehensive Meta Analysis

Authors	Michael Borenstein and Hannah Rothstein, Biostatistical Programming Associates.[2]
Operating system	Windows 95/98/ME, NT4.0/2000.
Effect size measures	Mean differences, correlation coefficients, odds ratios, relative risks, and rate differences.
Input data	The database is arranged hierarchically. The user defines any number of studies and, for each study, any number of outcomes. Outcomes may be entered as means, proportions, correlations, t-values, p-values, or other statistics. The program performs all conversions automatically. Data may be entered directly into dialog boxes or imported from Excel. Citations, abstracts, and notes for each study can be stored.
Statistical models	A wide variety of computational algorithms for fixed-effects and random-effects models including Hedges and Olkin, Schmidt and Hunter, Mantel-Haenszel, DerSimonian and Laird, and Fleiss and Peto.

Computation and output	The program creates a schematic (forest plot) that represents each study as a point estimate with confidence intervals. User may add columns for statistics, moderator variables, and other information and may sort or group by any variable. Graphs may be exported to Word, PowerPoint, and other programs in a variety of formats, including PDF and WMF. Users may view the details of computations and export them to a spreadsheet.
Cost and availability	$995. There are substantial discounts for academic use and students and free evaluation copies. Contact Biostat, 14 North Dean Street, Englewood, NJ 07631, or at www.meta-analysis.com.
Remarks	Clear, intuitive interface. Study abstracts can be imported from other programs using drag and drop. The program includes an on–screen interactive guide, a Help system, and a manual with worked examples and documentation of algorithms. Development of this program was funded by the National Institutes of Health.

SAS Macros

Authors	Morgan C. Wang, University of Central Florida. Brad J. Bushman, Iowa State University.
Operating system	Any operating system that runs SAS.
Effect size measures	Probability values, standardized mean differences, and correlations coefficients.
Input data	Data are input into an SAS system file.
Statistical models	The software includes a variety of graphical methods, meta-analyses for the odds ratio, standardized mean differences, vote

	counting methods, methods to combine effect size estimates and vote counts (Bushman & Wang, 1995, 1996), fixed- and random-effects models, and analysis of correlated effect sizes (Kalaian & Raudenbush, 1996).
Computation and output	Source code for the macro is available to audit computations. Output can be printed or saved to a file.
Cost and availability	$45 from SAS Institute, Cary, NC. Wang, M. C., & Bushman, B. J. (1999). *Integrating results through meta-analytical review using SAS software* (software available with book). Cary, NC: SAS Institute.
Remarks	Requires some familiarity with SAS.

MetaWin 2.0

Authors	Michael Rosenberg, Dean Adams, and Jessica Gurevitch.
Operating system	Windows 95/98/NT.
Effect size measures	Mean differences, correlation coefficients (Fisher's z-transform), odds ratios, response ratios, relative risk, and risk difference.
Input data	Accepts three types of primary data: means, standard deviations, and sample size; 2×2 contingency tables; and correlation coefficients. Data can be entered directly into a MetaWin spreadsheet or read from a text file, Excel file, or Lotus File.
Statistical models	Fixed-effects and random-effects models.
Computation and output	Cumulative mean effects, confidence intervals and heterogeneity tests, and cumulative meta-analysis. Tests for publication bias, resampling tests, and fail-safe n. Graphical displays include histograms, scatter plots, and funnel plots.

Cost and availability	$150. Available from Sinauer Associates, 23 Plumtree Road, Sunderland, MA 01375
Remarks	The 128-page manual describes the statistical theory of meta-analysis and use of the program.

Notes

1. The Cochrane Collaboration is a worldwide group of thousands of medical researchers who conduct and publish meta-analyses of health care. A similar organization, the Campbell Collaboration, was started in 1999 to conduct and disseminate meta-analysis in education and social welfare.

2. Two of the three authors of this chapter are also authors of this software and have a commercial interest in its promotion.

References

Aguinis, H., & Pierce, C. A. (1998). Testing moderator variable hypotheses meta-analytically. *Journal of Management, 24,* 577–592.

Begg, C. (1994). Publication bias. In H. Cooper & L. V. Hedges (Eds.), *The handbook of research synthesis* (pp. 399–409). New York: Russell Sage Foundation.

Bernier, C. L., & Yerkey, A. N. (1979). *Cogent communication: Overcoming reading overload.* Westport, CT: Greenwood Press.

Bullock, R. J., & Svyantek, D. J. (1985). Analyzing meta-analysis: Potential problems, an unsuccessful replication, and evaluation criteria. *Journal of Applied Psychology, 70,* 108–115.

Bushman, B. J., & Wang, M. C. (1995). A procedure for combining sample correlation coefficients and vote counts to obtain an estimate and a confidence interval for the population correlation coefficient. *Psychological Bulletin, 117,* 530–546.

Bushman, B. J., & Wang, M. C. (1996). A procedure for combining sample standardized mean differences and vote counts to estimate the population standardized mean difference in fixed effects models. *Psychological Methods, 1,* 66–80.

Callender, J. C., & Osburn, H. G. (1980). Development and test of a new model for validity generalization. *Journal of Applied Psychology, 65,* 543–558.

Chalmers, I. (1993). Effective care in midwifery: Research, the professions and the public. *Midwivers' Chronicle and Nursing Notes, 106,* 3–13.

Clarke, M., & Oxman, A. D. (Eds.). (1999). *Cochrane reviewers' handbook 4.0.* Oxford: Cochrane Collaboration.

Cohen, J. (1988). *Statistical power analysis for the behavioral sciences* (2nd ed.). Hillsdale, NJ: Erlbaum.

Cohen, J. (1994). The earth is round (p < .05). *American Psychologist, 49,* 997–1003.

Cooper, H. (1982). Scientific guidelines for conducting integrative research reviews. *Review of Educational Research, 52,* 291–302.

Cooper, H., DeNeve, K., & Charlton, K. (1997). Finding the missing science: The fate of studies submitted for review by a human subjects committee. *Psychological Methods, 2,* 447–452.

Cooper, H., & Hedges, L. V. (1994). Research synthesis as a scientific enterprise. In H. Cooper & L. V. Hedges (Eds.), *The handbook of research synthesis* (pp. 3–14). New York: Russell Sage Foundation.

Cooper, H., & Rosenthal, R. (1980). Statistical versus traditional procedures for summarizing research findings. *Psychological Bulletin, 87,* 442–449.

Dickerson, K. (1994). Research registers. In H. Cooper & L. V. Hedges (Eds.), *The handbook of research synthesis* (pp. 71–84). New York: Russell Sage Foundation.

Dickerson, K., Min, Y., & Meinert, C. (1992). Factors influencing the publication of research results: Follow-up of applications submitted to two institutional review boards. *Journal of the American Medical Association, 267,* 374–378.

Duval, S., & Tweedie, R. (2000). Trim and fill: A simple funnel plot based method of testing and adjusting for publication bias in meta-analysis. *Biometrics, 56,* 276–284.

Easterbrook, P., Berlin, J., Gopalan R., & Matthews, D. (1991). Publication bias in clinical research. *Lancet, 337,* 867–882.

Egger, M., Smith, G., Schneider, M., & Minder C. (1997). Bias in meta-analysis detected by a simple, graphical test. *British Medical Journal, 315,* 629–634.

Fisher, R. (1932). *Statistical methods for research workers* (4th ed.). London: Oliver and Boyd.

Fleiss, J. L. (1994). Measures of effect size for categorical data. In H. Cooper & L. V. Hedges (Eds.), *The handbook of research synthesis* (pp. 245–260). New York: Russell Sage Foundation.

Glass, G. V. (1976). Primary, secondary and meta-analysis of research. *Educational Researcher, 5,* 3–8.

Glass, G. V., McGaw, B., & Smith, M. (1981). *Meta-analysis in social research.* Thousand Oaks, CA: Sage.

Greenhouse, J., & Iyengar, S. (1994). Sensitivity analysis and diagnostics. In H. Cooper & L. V. Hedges (Eds.), *The handbook of research synthesis* (pp. 383–398). New York: Russell Sage Foundation.

Greenwald, A. (1975). Significance, nonsignificance, and interpretation of an ESP experiment. *Journal of Experimental and Social Psychology, 11,* 180–191.

Haddock, C., Rindskopf, D., & Shadish, W. (1998). Using odds ratios as effect sizes for meta-analysis of dichotomous data: A primer on methods and issues. *Psychological Methods, 3,* 339–353.

Hedges, L. V. (1994). Statistical considerations. In H. Cooper & L. V. Hedges (Eds.), *The handbook of research synthesis* (pp. 29–38). New York: Russell Sage Foundation.

Hedges, L. V., & Olkin, I. (1980). Vote counting methods in research synthesis. *Psychological Bulletin, 88,* 359–369.

Hedges, L. V., & Olkin, I. (1983). Clustering estimates of effect magnitude from independent studies. *Psychological Bulletin, 93,* 563–573.

Hedges, L. V., & Olkin, I. (1984). Nonparametric estimators of effect size in meta-analysis. *Psychological Bulletin, 96,* 573–580.

Hedges L., & Olkin, I (1985). *Statistical methods for meta-analysis.* Orlando, FL: Academic Press.

Hedges, L., & Olkin, I. (in press). *Statistical methods for meta-analysis* (2nd ed.). Orlando, FL: Academic Press.

Hedges, L. V., & Vevea, J. L. (1996). Estimating effect size under publication bias: Small sample properties and robustness of a random effects selection model. *Journal of Educational and Behavioral Sciences, 21,* 299–332.

Hunter, J. E., & Schmidt, F. L. (1990). *Methods of meta-analysis: Correcting error and bias in research findings.* Thousand Oaks, CA: Sage.

Hunter, J. E., & Schmidt, F. L. (1994). Correcting for sources of artifactual variance across studies. In H. Cooper & L. V. Hedges (Eds.), *The handbook of research synthesis* (pp. 323–338). New York: Russell Sage Foundation.

Hunter, J. E., & Schmidt, F. L. (2000). Fixed effects vs. random effects meta-analysis models: Implications for cumulative knowledge in psychology. *International Journal of Selection and Assessment, 8,* 275–292.

Iyengar, S., & Greenhouse, J. (1988). Selection models and the file drawer problem. *Statistical Science, 3,* 109–135.

Jackson, S. E. (1984, Aug.). *Can meta-analysis be used for theory development in organizational psychology?* Paper presented at the meeting of the American Psychological Association, Toronto, Canada.

Kalaian, H. A., & Raudenbush, S. W. (1996). A multivariate mixed linear model for meta-analysis. *Psychological Methods, 1,* 227–235.

Kubeck, J. E., Delp, N. D., Haslett, T. K., & McDaniel, M. A. (1996). Does job-related training performance decline with age? *Psychology and Aging,* 11, 92–107.

Light, R., & Pillemer, D. (1984). *Summing up: The science of reviewing research.* Cambridge, MA: Harvard University Press.

Light, R. J., Singer, J. D., & Wilted, J. B. (1994). The visual presentation and interpretation of meta-analysis. In H. Cooper & L. V. Hedges (Eds.), *The handbook of research synthesis* (pp. 439–453). New York: Russell Sage Foundation.

McDaniel, M. A., Morgeson, F. P., Finnegan, E. B., Campion, M. A., & Braverman, E. P. (2001). Use of situational judgment tests to predict job performance: A clarification of the literature. *Journal of Applied Psychology, 86,* 730–740.

McDaniel, M. A., Whetzel, D., Schmidt, F. L., & Maurer, S. (1994). The validity of the employment interview: A comprehensive review and meta-analysis. *Journal of Applied Psychology, 79,* 599–616.

McNatt, D. (2000). Ancient Pygmalion joins contemporary management: A meta-analysis of the result. *Journal of Applied Psychology, 85,* 314–322.

Moher, D., & Olkin, I. (1995). Meta-analysis of randomized controlled trials: A concern for standards. *Journal of the American Medical Association, 274,* 1962–1963.

National Research Council. (1992). *Combining information: Statistical issues and opportunities for research.* Washington, DC: National Academy Press.

Olkin, I. (1990). History and goals. In K. W. Wachter & M. L. Straf (Eds.), *The future of meta-analysis* (pp. 3–10). New York: Russell Sage Foundation.

Orwin, R., (1983). A fail-safe *N* for effect size in meta-analysis. *Journal of Educational Statistics, 8,* 157–159.

Oswald, F., & Johnson, J. (1998). On the robustness, bias and stability of statistics from meta-analysis of correlation coefficients: Some initial Monte Carlo findings. *Journal of Applied Psychology, 83,* 164–178.

Overton, R. C. (1998). A comparison of fixed effects and mixed (random effects) models for meta-analysis tests of moderator variable effects. *Psychological Methods, 3,* 354–379.

Oxman, A. (1995). Checklists for review articles. In I. Chalmers & D. Altman (Eds.), *Systematic reviews.* London: BMJ Publishing Group.

Pearlman, K., Schmidt, F., & Hunter, J. (1980). Validity generalization results for clerical tests used to predict job proficiency and training success in clerical occupations. *Journal of Applied Psychology, 65,* 373–406.

Pearson. K. (1904). Report on certain enteric fever inoculation statistics. *British Medical Journal, 2,* 1243–1246.

Raju, N. S., & Burke, M. J. (1983). Two new procedures for studying validity generalization. *Journal of Applied Psychology, 68,* 382–395.

Raudenbush, S. W. (1994). Random effects models. In H. Cooper & L. V. Hedges (Eds.), *The handbook of research synthesis* (pp. 301–322). New York: Russell Sage Foundation.

Reed, J. C., & Baxter, P. M. (1994). Using reference databases. In H. Cooper & L. V. Hedges (Eds.), *The handbook of research synthesis* (pp. 57–70). New York: Russell Sage Foundation.

Rosenthal, M. C. (1994). The fugitive literature. In H. Cooper & L. V. Hedges (Eds.), *The handbook of research synthesis* (pp. 85–96). New York: Russell Sage Foundation.

Rosenthal, R. (1978). Combining results of independent studies. *Psychological Bulletin, 85,* 185–193.

Rosenthal, R. (1979). The "file drawer problem" and tolerance for null results. *Psychological Bulletin, 86,* 638–641.

Rosenthal, R. (1994). Parametric measures of effect size. In H. Cooper & L. V. Hedges (Eds.), *The handbook of research synthesis* (pp. 232–244). New York: Russell Sage Foundation.

Rosenthal, R. (1995). Writing meta-analytic reviews. *Psychological Bulletin, 118,* 183–192.

Rosenthal, R., & Rubin, D. (1994). The counternull value of an effect size: A new statistic. *Psychological Science, 5,* 329–334.

Rothstein, H. R., & McDaniel, M. A. (1989). Guidelines for conducting and reporting meta-analyses. *Psychological Reports, 65,* 759–770.

Schmidt, F. L., & Hunter, J. E. (1977). Development to a general solution to the problem of validity generalization. *Journal of Applied Psychology, 68,* 529–540.

Schmidt, F. L., Hunter, J. E., Pearlman, K., & Hirsh, H. R. (1985). Forty questions about validity generalization and meta-analysis. *Personnel Psychology, 38,* 697–798.

Shadish, W. R., Robinson, L., & Lu, C. (1999). *ES: A computer program and manual for effect size calculation.* St. Paul, MN: Assessment Systems Corporation.

Sterling, T., Rosenbaum, W., & Weinkam, J. (1995). Publication decisions revisited: The effect of the outcome of statistical tests on the decision to publish and vice versa. *American Statistician, 49,* 108–112.

Stouffer, S., Suchman, E., DeVinney, L., Star, S., & Williams, R. (1949). *The American soldier: Vol. 1, Adjustment during army life.* Princeton, NJ: Princeton University Press.

Sutton, A., Duval, S., Tweedie, R., Abrams, K., & Jones, D. (2000). Empirical assessment of effects of publication bias in meta-analysis. *British Medical Journal, 320,* 1574–1577.

Thorndike, E. L. (1933). The effect of the interval between test and retest on the consistency of the IQ. *Journal of Educational Psychology, 25,* 543–549.

Vevea, J., & Hedges L. (1995). A general linear model for estimating effect size in the presence of publication bias. *Psychometrika, 60,* 419–435.

White, H. D. (1994). Scientific communication and literature retrieval. In H. Cooper & L. V. Hedges (Eds.), *The handbook of research synthesis* (pp. 41–56). New York: Russell Sage Foundation.

Yusuf, S., Wittes, J., Probstfield, J., & Tyroler, H. (1991). Analysis and interpretation of treatment effects in subgroups of patients in randomized clinical trials. *Journal of the American Medical Association, 266,* 193–198.

Name Index

Gardner, D., 351, 398
Garfield, E., 484, 496
Garfinkle, H., 18, 41
Garner, W., 453, 474, 496
Gavin, M., 424, 425, 429, 433, 443, 444, 517, 531
Gaylord, R. H., 100, 122
Gelatly, I. R., 335, 348
Gerbing, D. W., 236, 252
Gerras, S. J., 302, 347
Geston, P. R., 165, 187
Gibbons, R., 100–101, 108, 117, 122
Gigone, D., 519, 530
Gilliland, S. W., 54, 86
Glaser, B. G., 17, 19, 22–24, 26, 28, 29, 36, 37–38, 41, 193
Glass, G. V., 222, 252, 404, 443, 536, 540, 549, 566
Glenar J. L., 448, 497
Gleser, G. C., 8, 13, 218
Glomb, T. M., 500, 502, 530
Glymour, C., 259, 300
Goldberg, L. R., 130, 145, 153
Goldberger, A. S., 354, 395
Golden-Biddle, K., 17, 24, 42
Goldstein, H., 194, 218, 288, 299
Golembiewski, R. T., 334, 347
Gollob, H. F., 341, 347
Goodman, P. S., 354, 397, 518, 530
Gopalan, R., 552, 566
Gordon, S. R., 82
Gorsuch, R. L, 222, 254
Graham, J. R., 118
Graham, J. W., 341, 347
Graham, W. K., 361, 397
Green, S. G., 335, 348
Greene, W. H., 454, 496
Greenhouse, J., 553, 556, 557, 567
Greenwald, A., 567
Griffeth, R. W., 351, 398, 450, 468, 496
Griffin, M. A., 402, 444, 517, 531
Guilford, J. P., 100, 118
Gulliksen, H., 157, 185
Gupta, N., 504, 512, 529

Gurevich, J., 564
Gustafson, T. L., 560

H

Haak, S. W., 57, 62, 84
Hachiya, D., 259, 297
Hackman, J. R., 503, 530
Haddock, C., 540, 567
Haenszel, W., 169, 170, 174, 177–179, 186, 562
Hakel, M. D., 440, 445
Halverson, R. R., 413, 419, 425, 428, 431, 442, 4221
Hamagami, F., 340, 348
Hambleton, R. K., 116, 118, 119, 156, 157, 159, 162, 185, 186
Hamdan, M. A., 118
Hammersley, M., 18, 41
Hanges, P., 415, 416, 417, 442
Hanisch, K. A., 131, 132, 153, 499, 504–507, 509, 514, 515, 528–530
Hanna, C., 533
Hannan, M. T., 494, 497
Hansche, D., 182, 185
Hanson, M. A., 44, 55, 56, 64, 71, 73, 76, 77–78, 81, 84
Harms, H. J., 48, 62, 86, 87
Harnisch, D. L., 111, 119
Harris, M., 79–80, 84
Harris, S. G., 20, 40, 41
Harrison, D., 10, 11–12, 339, 347
Harrison, D. A., 446, 447, 475, 479, 493–496
Harrison, R. V., 350, 351, 361, 362, 365, 376, 388, 397, 398
Hartog, S. B., 335, 348
Haslett, T. K., 541, 568
Hastie, R., 519, 530
Hattie, J., 106, 110, 119, 121, 353, 398
Hau, K., 234, 253
Hauck, W. W., 467, 496
Hawks, T. F., 41
Hayduk, L. A., 270, 292, 297
Heatherton, T. F., 228, 250

Subject Index